Sharp Cut

Sharp Cut

Harold Pinter's Screenplays and the Artistic Process

Steven H. Gale

THE UNIVERSITY PRESS OF KENTUCKY

Publication of this volume was made possible in part
by a grant from the National Endowment for the Humanities.

Scholarly publisher for the Commonwealth,
serving Bellarmine University, Berea College, Centre
College of Kentucky, Eastern Kentucky University,
The Filson Historical Society, Georgetown College,
Kentucky Historical Society, Kentucky State University,
Morehead State University, Murray State University,
Northern Kentucky University, Transylvania University,
University of Kentucky, University of Louisville,
and Western Kentucky University.

Editorial and Sales Offices: The University Press of Kentucky
663 South Limestone Street, Lexington, Kentucky 40508-4008

    07 06 05 04 03   5 4 3 2 1

Library of Congress Cataloging-in-Publication Data

Gale, Steven H.
Sharp cut : Harold ▓▓▓▓▓▓▓▓ plays and the artistic process / Steven H. Gale.
     p.   cm.
   Includes bibliographical references and index.
   ISBN 0-8131-2244-9 (cloth : alk. paper)
   1. Pinter, Harold, 1930– —Motion picture plays. 2. Motion picture plays
—History and criticism. 3. Pinter, Harold, 1930– I. Title.
PR6066.I53 Z6467 2002
791.43'6—dc21   2002152558

This book is printed on acid-free recycled paper meeting
the requirements of the American National Standard
for Permanence in Paper for Printed Library Materials.

Manufactured in the United States of America.

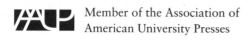 Member of the Association of
American University Presses

To Kathy, Shannon, Ashley, and Heather,
and to Linda Gale, the Wetzels, the Goodwins,
the Johnsons, and the Corums,
and in memory of my father, Norman A. Gale,
my mother, Mary Wilder Hasse,
and my brother Bill,
as always, with all my love and thanks

Contents

Preface

I HAVE BEEN INTERESTED in Harold Pinter's film scripts since my first viewing of *The Servant,* and I intended to include a full analysis of the screenplays in *Butter's Going Up: A Critical Analysis of Harold Pinter's Work.* I soon realized, however, that I could not do this, because the focus of that volume was on the stage plays, and the press felt that the book was already long enough. Thus, although I discussed the screenplays in that volume, the discussion was not in the depth that I wanted. So, when I finished *Butter,* I decided to do a full-length study of all of Pinter's film scripts; that was a natural outgrowth of my earlier study, especially since there had been almost nothing scholarly written about them at the time.

This situation changed, naturally, and the number of articles being written has increased considerably (see *The Pinter Review: Collected Essays,* edited by Francis X. Gillen and me, for example, and my edited collection *The Films of Harold Pinter*). Still, the average number of film-related essays in *The Pinter Review* tends to be about one per issue, and the only monograph dedicated to Pinter's screenplays is Joanne Klein's *Making Pictures: The Pinter Screenplays* (1985), which is devoted only to his early cinematic adaptations of other people's works. There has been no complete examination of his work in the cinema.

Furthermore, given that most early critical studies of Pinter's films were conducted by drama scholars, it is not surprising that almost none of them examined his films as films. Instead, critics such as Wilbur H. Reames Jr., in his 1978 dissertation, "Harold Pinter: An Introduction to the Literature of His Screenplays," and Klein in her *Making Pictures* examine only the published screenplays, the written versions of the works. Even Neil Sinyard in his examination of several of Pinter's films in *Filming Literature* only touches on the cinematic qualities and techniques involved. There can be no doubt that these evaluations of Pinter's screenwriting contain insights into the meaning of the films and that they are interesting and useful, yet there is seldom any discussion of how that meaning is dependent upon the form in which it is presented. There is little discussion of individual shots, for example, to demonstrate how a camera angle or movement within a shot affects the meaning. And, when the film version is compared with the original from which it was adapted, again the comparisons are of scripts, not the actual presentations.

Alfred Hitchcock labeled adaptations of stage plays "photographs of people talking."[1] When the scenarist and the director commence their task with the attitude that they are merely photographing a stage play, this assessment is likely to be accurate and is probably the rule rather than the exception. It is not true in Pinter's case. Perhaps due to his experience with radio and television drama prior to his work in the cinema, he is aware that each medium presents unique challenges and possibilities, that work in each medium must be approached differently. Because he is aware of some of the possibilities that can be exploited only in film, he sets about to write film scripts, not scripts to be filmed. The differences can be seen clearly when he translates his own stage plays to celluloid. What works on stage (given its intimacy and live action) may not work on film, so he avoids it. Conversely, film allows him to move about in space and time more freely and to use the camera's focusing operations in ways that are not possible on the stage. This means that sometimes when he is adapting his own plays, he must rewrite, even restructure, these works in order to accommodate changes that must be made or to take advantage of changes that can be made. It is interesting that the more extensive studies of Pinter's films heretofore have virtually ignored this component of his work.

This is surprising, for the intensity with which Pinter has concentrated on screenwriting is demonstrated by his creation of eight movie scripts in the six-year period 1968–1973 and the release of three films based on his scripts in a single year, 1990. Moreover, the writer's cinematic canon has continued to grow (he has written many more full-length film scripts than plays over the past two decades), so the number of manuscripts and films to be worked with has continued to increase. And, as noted above, the authors of most of the studies that have been published approach the material from a literary or theatrical point of view. My interest is in the cinematic side as well, and I am especially intrigued by the artistic process, a tracing of the changes made during the writing and then the shooting of the film that lead to the end product.

Moreover, to fully appreciate Pinter's achievement as a screenwriter, espe-cially for those with a drama background, it is necessary to have an under-standing of the historical and theoretical contexts, of the difference between film and drama, and of the nature of adaptation. In Roy Armes's words, "Any analysis of plays or films as drama must constantly take into account their inextricable dual identity as both drama text . . . and performance text" (46). Accordingly, I have included discussions of these subjects in the introduction.

As with any work of art, it is not only the pieces that are interesting; it is also how the artist puts them together. Thus, in my analyses I look for mean-ing (themes) and how that meaning is expressed. This involves a study of the structure, imagery, and similar components; the cinematic elements; and how Pinter transfers ideas from the original (pages) to a film script (film)—that is, what kinds of decisions he makes and why he makes them. This requires a consideration of whether alterations are demanded by differences in the media or whether they are made by the screenwriter intentionally for other reasons, such as thematic changes.

When I began to examine Pinter's films for *Butter's Going Up,* I looked at them much as I looked at the plays. That is to say, I was interested mostly in the finished product as a work of art. In studying the plays, I was aware that there is a difference between how people in the theatre and those in literature see the dramas. Theatrical people tend to be interested primarily in the production aspects and to minimize the literary elements; literary critics frequently have little understanding of performance and examine plays in terms of the manipulation of language on a printed page. I tried to strike a balance, on the assumption that a written play has somewhat the same rela-tionship to a stage performance as a blueprint has to a house. I believe that it is solely by considering both aspects of the work that one can reach a true understanding of what it means and how that meaning was achieved. Only then is the work whole.

A similar argument can be made in film studies. Cinema scholars often look at a film from a completely different perspective than do literary schol-ars. In the theatre, it is true that the director's and the actors' interpretations as well as the set designer's conception can have an effect on a stage produc-tion. Nevertheless, the script remains the same with each mounting, and there is an aesthetic theory in which it is posited that the characteristic struc-ture of the universe is chaos but that a drama is a means of imposing a temporary and replicable order on that chaos. Presumably, this is not true with film, for once the celluloid has been exposed, developed, and edited, the images remain the same no matter who shows it or how many times it is seen, so although the images may be repeated, there is no reordering of the chaotic material since the idea of chaos is not considered. This is not completely accurate, of course. For instance, I have included notations when there are apparent differences in running time as cited in various sources. These differences may be significant (as in the case of *The French Lieutenant's Woman*, the television version being thirty minutes shorter than the theatrical release) or they may simply reflect minimal differences in individual timers.

The films and the availability of Pinter's scripts in published form and the unpublished typescripts that the writer himself gave me provided plenty of material to work with, but the creation of the Pinter Archives at the British Museum proved to be manna from Heaven, for I could literally follow step-by-step the development of the individual scripts from the first page of handwritten notes or lines to the released film. In fact, the amount of material almost became overwhelming, especially when combined with the holdings at the British Film Institute and the Academy of Motion Picture Arts and Sciences. At the same time, the increased availability of VCR tapes also made my shot-by-shot analysis much easier; and as more people became interested in the films, there were more scholars with whom I could share information and discussions.

In this volume I have chosen to present the twenty-six film scripts in chronological order from 1963 to 2000 rather than in categories (screenplays filmed, unfilmed screenplays, adaptations of other writers' novels, adaptations of Pinter's stage plays), because I believe that this allows for a clearer tracking of Pinter's progress as a screenwriter. I include credit information (source, date of release, production company, director, cast, crew, running time, color/black-and-white) at the beginning of the discussion of screenplays that have been filmed. There are six exceptions to this structure: two scripts that have not been filmed, two scripts that were filmed for television, one script from which Pinter removed his name, and one film that he directed are examined in the chapter titled "Bits and Pieces."

As I did in my study of the stage plays, I look for the meaning of each film and how that meaning is expressed. This involves considering them as self-contained works of art, but material from the published scripts and papers from the Pinter Archives are consulted, too. In the case of the films, not only do I consider the structure, imagery, and so on, I also examine both the script and the finished film cinematically—which means individual shots, sequences, montages, and so forth. Complicating matters, however, is the question of authorship and the potential copy-text debate, which I discuss in relation to specific screenplays.

The intriguing thing about these scripts is how they developed, how the artistic process functioned. What alterations were made and when, why the changes were made, whether they had any effect on the meaning of the work, and whether they were required in order to better express that meaning— these are the operative questions. Also, in consideration of the differences between the media, I am interested in looking at whether the alterations were demanded by those differences or by Pinter's intent.

One of the difficulties in the scholarly examination of a film is that there are so many technical things happening at once that, even though they should all be relevant in expressing the film's meaning, often form predominates over context in a discussion of film. The dilemma is how to balance the two elements. Each of Pinter's films is examined in what is essentially a stand-alone chapter, but with interrelationships between the films clearly delineated. Nonetheless, my approach in discussing the various films differs, since there is no reason to repeat the same kind of information in relation to every film. For instance, in my analysis of *The Servant,* because I know that a goodly portion of my audience will be coming from a theatre background, I provide a fairly comprehensive scene-by-scene explication rather than approaching the work from either a purely thematic or a stylistic point of view and rather than dealing with blocks of meaning or examining individual techniques and cinematic devices. This is done for two reasons. First, because this is the screenwriter's first film, this approach establishes a standard against which his other works can be judged to determine how much he changed over time or whether he treats different themes in different ways. Second, it allows us to see how Pinter views the medium and how he creates his adaptations. Thus, this longest chapter in the volume is used to set up everything that will be done in the following chapters.

I examine the opening sequence in detail when discussing *The Caretaker,* and although opening sequences would be important in other analyses, my focus might be on Pinter's use of camera angles and other cinematic devices (*The Servant*), his use of objets d'art (*Accident*), or his innovative approaches to adaptation (*The French Lieutenant's Woman*). I examine each of his screenplays, but again the depth of the analysis varies from work to work, depending on my focus and whether the work has received the attention that it deserves (*The Pumpkin Eater, Reunion*).

Because I assume that most readers of this study will be more familiar with Pinter's dramas than with the novels that he adapts, I have given less space to the discussion of the stage versions of his plays than to the discussions of the novels (in addition, I have dealt with the meanings of and techniques in the plays in *Butter's Going Up*). In a couple of cases (*The Proust Screenplay, Lolita,* and *Victory*), I examine texts that have not been filmed. I spend time on *Lolita* because of the high quality of the film script, which has not yet been published, and on *Victory* because the screenplay itself reveals quite a bit about the screenwriter's artistic approach and cinematic vision, and, since the films were never made, it is only through the screenplays that certain information can be gleaned. In a couple of other cases (*The Handmaid's Tale* and *The Remains of the Day*), I devote very little space to analyzing the films because Pinter does not regard them as his work.

To some extent, the existence of the archives allows me to do what I have described above, because scholars now have access to both the released film and the author's manuscripts. Unfortunately, the archives are not always as helpful as they might be: the contents of the boxes are not inventoried, so as various examiners look at the material, it gets moved around chronologically. In addition, much of the material is undated; when I asked Pinter about the order of certain versions of the scripts, he admitted that he was not good at remembering dates. Actually, it should be no surprise that much is not dated; in fact, that so much of it does have a date, down to the month and day, is unexpected until one sees how careful Pinter is in researching historical details for his scripts.

Finally, some of the author's scripts were written for television (*Tea Party; Langrishe, Go Down; The Heat of the Day*), but because they were shown only in a limited theatrical setting, I have not analyzed them in depth in this volume. I conclude with both a bibliography containing a works-cited section and a selected bibliography because there were a number of sources that the reader might find valuable and important yet which I did not cite in my text.

Movies are illusionary, phantasmagoric. They are but light and shadow momentarily reflected from a silver screen, yet they seem solid and real, and they can be as enlightening and emotionally moving as anything that can be grasped in one's hand. In the history of the motion picture, Harold Pinter is one of the most successful creators of screenplays, the raw material from which movies are fashioned.

I hope that in *Sharp Cut: Harold Pinter's Screenplays and the Artistic Process* I have provided a text that will allow for a fuller understanding of

Pinter's artistic approaches to filmmaking and to his finished works. There is a tremendous amount still to be done on his writing for the cinema; each screenplay could be studied in as much detail as I have done in the case of *The Servant.* Indeed, when I began the volume, it was my intention to include analyses of all of the television scripts as well, since they are so clearly related to the film scripts that I have examined, but the length of this study became too great to accommodate that wish. I hope, then, that this study will serve as a starting point for some of the explorations to come.

Portions of the chapters on *The Servant, The Caretaker, The French Lieutenant's Woman,* and *The Pumpkin Eater* appeared in *The Pinter Review,* edited by Francis Gillen and Steven H. Gale, 1990, 1995–1996, 1999, 2000; *Pinter at Sixty,* edited by Katherine H. Burkman and John L. Kundert-Gibbs (Bloomington, Indiana Univ. Press, 1993); and *Harold Pinter: A Casebook,* edited by Lois Gordon. In addition, I have drawn on my work in *Butter's Going Up, The Films of Harold Pinter, Notes on Contemporary Literature,* and *Critical Essays on Harold Pinter.*

THIS LONG-TERM PROJECT began virtually with the publication of *Butter's Going Up* in 1977. I actually started putting my notes together for *Sharp Cut* in 1980. For many reasons beyond my control, including Harold Pinter's continuing work in screenwriting, I did not finish it until 2002. The massive amount of study required could not have been made nor this volume published if I had not had a great deal of support. Pinter's openness and willingness to talk with me and to answer questions that I posed in numerous letters and e-mails over the years was invaluable. I have always found him generous in providing me material in the form of unpublished scripts and other materials, and I thank him for this.

Kentucky State University, with the support of the Board of Regents and then Chairman Louie B. Nunn, provided me with a semester of reduced teaching assignments; a National Endowment for the Humanities Travel to Collections grant (a category of grant sadly no longer available) allowed me to visit the Margaret Herrick Library at the Academy of Motion Picture Arts and Sciences (AMPAS) Center for Motion Picture Study in Beverly Hills to examine their unique collection of materials related to Pinter's films; and a grant from the KSU Faculty Research Fund permitted me to examine the holdings in the Pinter Archives at the British Library in London.

Along the way I also had immense help in obtaining materials from Mary Lou Dove, the librarian at Missouri Southern State College; Susan Martin,

Linda UmBayemake Joachim, and Lori Muha at Kentucky State University's Blazer Library; the reference librarians at the state libraries and archives and at the Paul Sawyier Library in Frankfort, Kentucky (Beverly Kunkle, Mildred Polsgrove, Rita Douthitt, Glenn Lewis, Nancy Rice, Mark Kinnaird, and Mary Greathouse); Sally Brown, Director of Modern Collections at the British Library; and Faye Thompson, Director of Special Collections at the Herrick Library at AMPAS, her Research Archivist Barbara Hall, and their staffs. Their time-consuming efforts and often necessarily quite inventive approaches to collecting material for me went well beyond the call of duty; my job would have been a lot more difficult without their assistance. I appreciate, too, the help given me by the staff at the BBC offices in London, where I viewed *Langrishe, Go Down.*

Emil Roy at the University of Southern California introduced me to Pinter's drama, William Blackburn showed me how to analyze literature, and Leon Howard and Florence Ridley at the University of California at Los Angeles gave me support in the early years of my career. Among the scholars who freely gave of their time and resources for this current study were Chris Hudgins (with whom I spent a fine and illuminating week gathering information from the archives at the British Library), Tom Adler, Frank Gillen, and many others. Louis Marks, one of Pinter's producers; the screenwriter's agent, Judy Daish; and several of his secretaries (including Angela, Caroline, and Ros) made it easy for me to obtain some information that would not have been available otherwise. James D. Murphy kept my computer running, and my secretarial staff over the many years aided me by checking sources, helping with the correspondence, typing, and all of the other details that go into producing a manuscript. Thanks to Elaine Wesley, Lisa Gayle Brown, Laurel Chipman, Kim Bales, and Kim Bickers; Kim Bickers spent hours in the library helping to prepare the final manuscript. My wife, Kathy, offered useful suggestions and helped in the proofreading.

My father and Linda provided moral support; and, as always, I want to thank Kathy and my three daughters, Shannon, Ashley, and Heather, for their motivation, inspiration, and help, and especially for their patience.

Chronology of Pinter's Screenwriting

1960 *The Birthday Party* televised (Associated Rediffusion Television, March 22)

    A Night Out televised (BBC Third Programme, March 1; ABC Armchair Theatre, April 24)

    Night School televised (Associated Rediffusion Television, July 21)

1961 *The Collection* televised (Associated Rediffusion Television, May 11)

1963 *The Lover* televised (Associated Rediffusion Television, March 28)

    The Servant

    Film version of *The Caretaker* (*The Guest*)

1964 *The Pumpkin Eater*

1965 *Tea Party* televised (BBC-1, March 25)

1966 *The Quiller Memorandum*

1967 *The Basement* televised (BBC-TV, February 28)

    Accident

1968 Film version of *The Birthday Party*

1969 *Pinter People* televised (NBC Experiment in Television)

    The Go-Between

1972 *The Proust Screenplay* (BBC-TV, April 10)

    Film version of *The Homecoming*

1974 *Butley*

    The Rear Column (BBC-TV)

1976 *The Last Tycoon*

1978 *Langrishe, Go Down* televised (BBC-2 Television, September 20)

1981	*The French Lieutenant's Woman*
1982	Film version of *Betrayal*
	Victory written (published 1990)
	The Hothouse televised (BBC-TV)
1985	*One for the Road* televised (BBC-TV, July 25)
	The Dumb Waiter televised
1986	*Turtle Diary*
1987	*The Dumb Waiter* televised (ABC Television, May 12)
	The Room televised (ABC Television, December 26)
1989	*The Birthday Party* televised (BBC-2, June 1)
	The Heat of the Day televised (BBC)
	Reunion
1990	*The Handmaid's Tale*
	The Comfort of Strangers
	The Heat of the Day televised (PBS)
1991	*The Remains of the Day* (script written, but rewritten and Pinter not credited)
	Old Times televised (BBC-TV, London)
1992	*Party Time* televised (Channel 4, London, November 17)
1993	*The Trial*
1994	*Lolita* (script written)
	The Heat of the Day televised (in America on PBS's Masterpiece Theatre [WGBH, Boston, September 30])
1996	Film version of *Landscape*
	Pinter works on an adaptation of *The Diaries of Etty Hillesum.*
1997	Adaptation of "The Dreaming Child" completed
2000	Adaptation of *King Lear* completed
2002	*Langrishe, Go Down*

Introduction

SINCE VERY EARLY in cinematic history, stage plays have served as sources for motion pictures. One of the first instances of this practice occurred in 1908 when the French movie company Film d'Art produced its inaugural offering, *The Assassination of the Duke of Guise*. The most famous of these early films, and the first from Film d'Art to be screened in the United States, was the Sarah Bernhardt vehicle *Queen Elizabeth*. Featuring members of the Comédie Française and directed by Louis Mercanton, *Queen Elizabeth* was released in 1912. In France, Charles Pathe's 1909 film version of *Les Misérables* was the first "long" or feature film (a movie at least forty minutes in duration or four reels of 35 mm film), and his production company released a silent version of Charles Dickens's novel *Oliver Twist* the same year. The first feature film produced in the United States was another adaptation of *Oliver Twist,* also released in 1912, and the second feature-length American film was director James Keane's cinematic version of William Shakespeare's *The Life and Death of King Richard III*,[1] which appeared five months later, in October 1912. Obviously, then, the tradition of drawing upon literature, especially the theatre, for material was well established internationally almost as soon as the medium was viewed as an art form.

From early on, too, there has been critical discussion about the relationship between film and drama as well as the characteristics and nature of filmed plays. When Hitchcock called film adaptations of stage plays "photographs of people talking," he was referring to the danger inherent in synchsound cinema. The initial attempts to translate serious drama into a cinematic medium were unimaginative, noncinematic, wooden exhibitions. Although the declamatory nature of stage acting is clearly not suited to the exaggerating intimacy of the camera lens, even more disappointing is the fact that directors ignored the potentialities of their new medium to interpret material in innovative ways that would be effective because of the medium's very nature. They seldom employed any of the characteristics of the film art other than the simple utilization of a camera. Takes were long and static. Little movement of the camera occurred, and very few shots were included that underscored or amplified the dialogue of the original play text.[2] In many scenes the stationary camera was merely turned on to record what was taking place on an essentially theatrical stage, and the cuts seemingly came only at the end of the scene. Even today there are disheartening examples of this approach to filmed drama. At the same time, there is also some significant work being done in this area by Harold Pinter, one of the premier writers of the twentieth century.

Contemporary British dramatist Pinter is by consensus the most important and most influential English-language playwright alive.[3] His artistic achievements have been connected primarily with his work in the theatre,[4] but for years he also quietly built a reputation as a master screenwriter. In the 1980s and 1990s, his artistic attention was focused almost exclusively on his screenwriting. In the forty years since his first scripted film, *The Servant,* appeared in 1962, he has had numerous cinematic successes, in terms of both popular acceptance and critical acclaim, and he has won several prestigious awards for his work. Among his theatrical contemporaries, only Tom Stoppard, David Mamet, and possibly John Osborne have achieved equivalent critical and popular success with their screenwriting.

In his study *Sixties British Cinema,* Robert Murphy is highly complimentary about Pinter's films. Nevertheless, while Pinter's screenplays meet some of the four listed criteria for a national cinema ("economic terms, with the focus on the film industry rather than film texts"; "exhibition and consumption"; "attempts to privilege the cultural specificity"; "representation . . . [of a] common style or world view. . . . common themes, motifs, or preoccupations. . . . project the national character, [etc.]"),[5] he definitely is not considered a "British" screenwriter.

But as will be seen, there are connections between his work and the national cinema. First, Pinter's movement between media is not unique in British film history: Julian Petley and Geoff Brown have documented that the British cinema has continually looked to the legitimate stage in England for source material, actors, and directors. More significantly, Lindsay Anderson, in an article that he published in the university magazine *Sequence* while he was at Oxford University in the mid-1950s, coined the term *Free Cinema* to describe a short-lived episode of social realism in the British cinema. Those who belonged to this "movement" included Anderson, Karel Reisz, and Tony Richardson.[6] There had been a tradition of adaptation in the cinema from the very beginning, of course, but the climate was right for Pinter's adaptation of *The Servant,* which followed on the heels of a whole series of adaptations of contemporary plays and novels that focused on the working class: Osborne, *Look Back in Anger* (1958, directed by Richardson); John Braine, *Room at the Top* (1959, Jack Clayton, recipient of two Academy Awards); Allan Sillitoe, *Saturday Night* and *Sunday Morning* (1960, Reisz); Osborne, *The Entertainer* (1960, Richardson); Shelagh Delaney, *A Taste of Honey* (1961, Richardson); and Sillitoe, *The Loneliness of the Long Distance Runner* (1962, Richardson). The links between Pinter and these films and directors is obvious over the course of his career.

Besides being entered in major festivals, Pinter's films have been listed among the year's ten best consistently. Among the major awards that he has received are the Berlin Film Festival Silver Bear and an Edinburgh Festival Certificate of Merit for *The Caretaker* in 1963, the British Screenwriters Guild Award and the New York Film Critics Best Writing Award for *The Servant* in 1964, the British Film Academy Award for *The Pumpkin Eater* in 1965, the Cannes Film Festival Special Jury Prize and a National Board of Review Award for *Accident* in 1967, the Cannes Film Festival Golden Palm for Best Film and the British Film Academy Award for *The Go-Between* in 1971, and a National Board of Review Best English-Language Film Award for *The Last Tycoon* in 1975. His more recent films, *The French Lieutenant's Woman, Betrayal, Turtle Diary, The Handmaid's Tale,* and *The Trial* have also been praised. Indeed, critics claim that Pinter's distinctive style and unmistakable writing ability have been responsible for the best work done by several of his directors. The impressive list includes Joseph Losey, Michael Anderson, Jack Clayton, Reisz, Elia Kazan, Robert Altman, Paul Schrader, Jerry Schatzberg, David Jones, and John Irvin, and the consensus of opinion among film critics and scholars is that virtually all of these directors have done their best work from his screenplays. Films made from Pinter's film scripts, with his authorship being the common denominator, are considered so laudable that they are even used as examples in film studies textbooks.[7]

As is true with his stage plays, Pinter's films focus on human relationships. In the film industry this means that they are classified as "little films" rather than "big films," which are epic in nature. Early in his drama-writing career, Pinter was asked why he did not write about political or sociological issues. He answered that those issues are irrelevant until one understands human nature, that people neither can nor will communicate with one another because they are afraid of what they might find out about themselves, and, because people are always changing, they cannot predict what they are going to do next, let alone what others are going to do. It makes more sense, he concluded, to explore individual interpersonal relationships than to deal with political concerns.[8]

From his first play on, of course, some audience members have found Pinter's stage plays oblique. His dramas, especially the later works, depend almost entirely on words—and the dialogue may seem grammatically and logically disconnected, though this does not mean that his words alone are not powerful (the endings of *Old Times* and *Ashes to Ashes,* for instance, leave audiences sitting in stunned silence). A film script differs from a drama script in that it is the words that carry the primary meaning in a drama, whereas in a film the visual images are usually as important and frequently more important than the words. Given the financial element that drives filmmaking and requires relative simplicity, movie plots tend to be more linear and structurally clear; this makes his motion pictures more accessible to the less discerning. Equally important in his success is his effective use of montage, the defining element in film.[9]

The extent of Pinter's filmic accomplishments is implied by Andrew Sarris's conclusions in his *The American Cinema*: "*The Servant* and *Accident* have done more for Losey's general reputation than all his [at that time twenty] other pictures put together," and "Michael Anderson's career [thirteen previous films] is so undistinguished until *The Quiller Memorandum* that two conclusions are unavoidable, one that Harold Pinter was the true auteur of *The Quiller Memorandum,* and two Pinter found in Anderson an ideal metteur en scene for his (Pinter's) very visual conceits" (Sarris, *American Cinema*, 96, 252). According to film historian David Cook, the Pinter-Losey collaboration "produced some of the most significant British films" of the 1960s and 1970s (493). Parenthetically, Alexander Walker's explanation for this successful union is that "Pinter curbed Losey's tendencies to baroque romanticism" and Losey "amplified Pinter's economy by visual suggestiveness" (215). In reviewing *The Go-Between*, Hollis Alpert declares: "When Losey collaborates with Pinter, he is one of the world's finest directors. When he doesn't, he is hit-or-miss" ("The Losey Situation," 42).

Notwithstanding the praise that his screenplays garnered internationally, as late as the mid-1990s the author found it ironic that his contributions were largely unrecognized in his own country. While he was aware of film festivals and series in which his films were featured and discussed extensively in many countries, even in such exotic locales as Kentucky, in England there was no such distinction, and largely his work had been ignored. This was remedied in 1996 when a major retrospective of his cinematic work was presented at the National Film Theatre in London.[10] That Pinter has made such a mark in a field in which the director is the recognized superstar is a tribute to his talent as a writer.[11]

The author's diversity is demonstrated by his ability to draw on a variety of media for his sources. Of his twenty-five film scripts, five are adaptations of his own dramas: *Betrayal, The Birthday Party, The Caretaker* (released in the United States as *The Guest*), *The Homecoming,* and *Landscape*. At least fourteen of his other plays, *The Basement, The Collection, The Dumb Waiter, The Lover, No Man's Land, The Hothouse, Mountain Language, Night School, A Night Out, One for the Road, Old Times, Party Time, The Room,* and *Tea Party,* plus *Pinter People* (a cartoon compilation of some of his revue sketches that Losey called "quite a brilliant piece of work"),[12] have been televised, some of them in more than one version.[13] Sixteen of the remaining film scripts are cinematic translations of other writers' novels (several of them are based on books given him by director Losey): Nicholas Mosley, *Accident;* Adam Hall, *The Berlin Memorandum* (released as *The Quiller Memorandum*); Ian McEwan, *The Comfort of Strangers;* John Fowles, *The French Lieutenant's Woman;* L.P. Hartley, *The Go-Between;* Margaret Atwood, *The Handmaid's Tale;* Aidan Higgins, *Langrishe, Go Down;* F. Scott Fitzgerald, *The Last Tycoon;* Penelope Mortimer, *The Pumpkin Eater;* Marcel Proust, *À la recherche du temps perdu* (*Remembrance of Things Past;* the script was published as *The Proust Screenplay* but never filmed); Kazuo Ishiguro, *The Remains of the Day* (although the script was written in 1990 and the film was released in 1993, Pinter took his name off the project); Fred Uhlman, *Reunion;* Robin Maugham, *The Servant;* Franz Kafka, *The Trial;* Russell Hoban, *The Turtle Diary;* and Joseph Conrad, *Victory* (published but not yet filmed). He has also written a script based on Isak Dinesen's short story "The Dreaming Child" and an adaptation of William Shakespeare's *The Tragedy of King Lear,* and he has directed one film from another dramatist's play, Simon Gray's *Butley*.[14]

Pinter has authored several television adaptations as well, including a filmed version of Elizabeth Bowen's *The Heat of the Day,* and it is important to note that in answer to questions about the difference between his work in television and in film, he said that he makes "no distinction between working for television and feature film"[15] and in fact finds that they share "one identical discipline: economy,"[16] although there are some obvious differences, which partly may account for the fact that the writer has produced more screenplays than television scripts.

In 1961, the year before *The Servant* was released but the year after *Night School* was televised by Associated Rediffusion Television, the dramatist was interviewed for *The Twentieth Century* by Richard Findlater in the piece titled "Writing for Myself." The appeal of television was high:

> Writing for television? I don't make any distinction between kinds of writing, but when I write for the stage I always keep a continuity of action. Television lends itself to quick cutting from scene to scene, and nowadays I see it more and more in terms of pictures. When I think of someone knocking at a door, I see the door opening in close-up and a long shot of someone going up the stairs. Of course the words go with the pictures, but on television, ultimately, the words are of less importance than they are on the stage. A play I wrote called *A Night Out* did, I think, successfully integrate the picture and the words, although that may be because I wrote it first for radio. . . . I don't find television confining or restrictive, and it isn't limited to realism, necessarily. Its possibilities go well beyond that. (Pinter, "Writing for Myself," 11)

Pinter's attraction to media other than drama is even reflected in his stage works. He utilizes cinematic techniques in *Mountain Language* with the analog of a voice-over, in *Party Time* he uses lighting to create the correlative of cuts by lighting one group while keeping another in darkness and alternating between them, and in *Old Times* he makes the film *Odd Man Out* a central image in the action and has Deeley identify himself as Orson Welles (using the same words that Welles used in the voice-over credits for *The Magnificent Ambersons* [1942], a movie that Pinter mentions by name in an interview, and *Macbeth* [1948]).[17]

Among the obvious differences between film and television is the size of the screen; everything is enlarged on a movie screen. This difference means that, since things are so much larger on a theatrical screen, they stand out more than they do on a television screen, and the acting must be more subtle—the idea that less is more. Furthermore, movies seem more real on the big screen than they do on the television screen; more detail is visible and a better sense of proportion and perspective is achieved. It is important that those viewing videotaped motion pictures on a television screen be aware of this phenomenon, for it affects the viewer's reception of the film. Not only are there conspicuous disparities, such as that a movie seen on a theatrical screen appears larger than life, whereas one watched on television appears smaller than life, but there are also other, more subtle, differences.

Both physically and psychologically, a television presentation of a theatrical release reduces the image and diminishes the effect. The standard theatrical ratio of 1:85x1 is forced into a ratio of 1:33x1, so some significant cropping may be done to make a theatrical film fit a television screen (in the case of a wide-screen film, the differential is even greater, since the wide-screen ratio is 2.35:1). Moreover, unlike a movie screen, a standard television screen is still curved, not flat. Thus, the television image is comparatively elongated, which means that for the original theatrical image to fit top to bottom on the television screen, edges, particularly the sides, have to be cropped to fit.[18] This alters the perspective that the director and the photographer originally created on celluloid. It also means that the image is smaller and less clear, that certain things visible on the big screen do not show up or details that stand out in the original are made barely discernible.[19] It may be that these considerations are part of the reason that Pinter has concentrated on screenwriting instead of television.

In any case, his screenplay writing has been critically successful. John Russell Taylor concludes that *The Pumpkin Eater* and *The Quiller Memorandum* are "essays in writing technique" and that *The Servant* and *Accident* assume "the character of Pinter creations" (*Harold Pinter*, 20). Martin Esslin concurs, finding that while in general the artist's approach to the cinema has been in the role of a "conscientious and highly professional craftsman," nevertheless "much of his characteristic quality remains and enriches the films, most notably the ones which have been directed by Joseph Losey [at that time *The Servant* and *Accident*], a film-maker whose sensibility is beautifully attuned to Pinter's terse, elliptic style, his silences and pauses" (*Theatre of the Absurd*, 255).[20] As David Lodge has pointed out, "silence, a characteristic feature of Pinter's drama, is extraordinarily potent on the stage, because of the audiences' assumption that drama consists of speech or significant action" (66). A fine example of this is the three-minute silence at the end of *Old Times,* an extremely long time on stage, but also extraordinarily effective.

Actually, Losey's comments about his collaboration with Pinter on *The Servant* unwittingly provide further evidence of the screenwriter's genius.

The Servant, Losey told James Leahy, is about false values: "of the consequences of, the ultimate deterioration resulting from, living by false values—
turning the relationship upside down to expose the falsity of values on both
sides, a falsity leading, finally, to utter degradation and disaster for all concerned. . . . Every society has its false values . . . and the question . . . is the
degree to which people are free to explore them, combat them, change them."[21]
Exactly how Losey defined false values is not clear from his statements in the
interview, but even given the widest semantic latitude in his definition, Losey
is only minimally right about the meaning that the screenplay conveys.

Notwithstanding his manifest screenwriting ability, Pinter has occasionally had some trouble getting his screenplays filmed, in spite of the facts that
they tend to be artistically pleasing and, though they cannot compete with
the *Rambo, Star Wars,* or *Freddie* movies, they do fairly well at the box
office. Still, critical reactions have been mixed: some reviewers like virtually
everything that Pinter has written for the screen; others like almost nothing.
Most of the films are considered more artsy (read "European"?) than commercial, which means that much of middle America never sees them. *The
Comfort of Strangers,* for instance, played for only one week in a specialty
film house in Louisville, Kentucky, and was never screened in Lexington.
The Trial, which played for a week at an art house in Lexington, was never
screened in Tampa, Florida. Leonard Maltin, a popular American reviewer,
rated *Accident, The French Lieutenant's Woman, The Go-Between,* and *The
Servant* at three and a half stars out of a possible four. *Betrayal* and *The
Comfort of Strangers* were given one and a half stars, his lowest rating category except for "BOMB." *The Trial* is not even listed.

Obviously, part of the reason for the hesitancy of studios to produce
Pinter's work has to do with his themes. Movie studios tend to be run by
young people (mostly men) in their twenties and thirties who wield an amazing amount of power, given their ages. This phenomenon may explain the
repetitive dreck that is produced having to do with sex, violence, growing
up, and so forth. These arbiters of taste like to glorify juvenile subjects like
bathroom humor and sexual innuendo; their development seems to have
been arrested at somewhere between eight years of age and the eighth grade.
Jim Carrey (in his Ace Ventura role), Adam Sandler, *Dumb and Dumber*
(1994), and *There's Something about Mary* (1998) are their cultural icons.
In contrast, like his dramas, Pinter's film scripts are reputed to represent a
pessimistic view of life in his documenting the breakdowns in relationships
between individuals—the menace-verification-communication triad—and this

evaluation may be apropos for films such as *The Servant* and *The Comfort of Strangers*. Nevertheless, ultimately the majority of his screenplays lead to an understanding that promises improvement (*The Quiller Memorandum, Accident, The Go-Between, The Last Tycoon, The French Lieutenant's Woman, Betrayal, The Proust Screenplay, The Remains of the Day, Lolita,* and even *The Servant, The Comfort of Strangers, The Trial,* and *Victory*) or, frequently, end on a hopeful note. The connection between the brothers in *The Caretaker* is more firmly reestablished, as is the relationship in *The Pumpkin Eater,* a new order is delineated in *The Homecoming, Turtle Diary* is uplifting, and *The Handmaid's Tale* details the destruction of a repressive society, for example.

Because the majority of Pinter's screenplays are adaptations, a consideration of the difference between the media and of the art of adaptation is illuminating.[22] As a point of departure, the nature of stage plays can be compared and contrasted with that of films. The differences between prose and film as media are obvious. The differences between drama and film are less apparent, in part because the performance aspects of these two media are superficially similar and in part because the development of film as an art form, at least during the early years of cinema history, was often fairly closely allied with theatre. After all, both drama and film utilize visual images, sound, movement, actors, scenery, makeup, and so forth, and the audience sits in a darkened communal theatre to view the action.

When moving pictures were first being made commercially, many of the actors and directors were drawn from the stage, and that practice has continued. The plots, the kind of acting, and the sets frequently reflected this theatrical connection. It is no wonder that film was seen essentially as an extension of the theatre in the public mind, and that literary critics, who were slow to accept drama as a legitimate subject of scholarly study because they were not sure how to deal with an art form that kept moving and that was different from performance to performance, were very happy to reject even more strongly a critical study of film. It was a genre that, by virtue of the combination of its connection with theatre and its popular acceptance, was thereby demonstrably even less worthy of intellectual attention than was theatre.

Louis Giannetti has pointed out that in the live theatre the spectator remains in a stationary position and that space is three-dimensional, that the stage player interacts with the audience, and that drama is a medium of low visual saturation (i.e., the "audience must fill in certain meanings in the ab-

sence of visual detail" [227–29]). The opposite is true with film. Film viewers identify with the camera lens's point of view, space is two-dimensional
and thus less "real" to the viewer, and the actor's performance is fixed forever. In addition, while the audience is live in both cases, the stage actor may
be affected by the audience, whereas the screen actor obviously cannot be.
Stage performers are well aware of how vitally different performances of the
same material can be, depending upon the nature of individual audiences (a
dead spot can kill a comedy), even literally altering the actors' performances.
At a film screening, the nature of an audience may affect the members of that
audience and their reaction to the movie, but that effect applies only to the
audience, and the performance remains the same.

Demands on the audience are different as well. Not to belabor the obvious, but whereas the reader can exercise some control over the medium of
prose by reading slowly or quickly, stopping to contemplate, and creating
mental images stimulated by the words on the page, none of this is possible
with live drama or film. Indeed, though the observer's mind is free to manipulate information, to mentally juxtapose scenes, the sense of observation
is especially strong because the basic image has been presented in such a way
that drama and film are more intrinsically revelatory in nature than is prose,
which relies heavily on an actively contemplative audience. Like drama, film
has a social context not just because of its content, but also because it is
experienced in the company of other people. A novel is read alone. This
difference accounts for many of the disparate reactions between the audiences of the two media.

Prose, drama, and film may force or encourage the audience to reach
similar conclusions, but the means whereby this is accomplished vary significantly. Of the three genres, film functions the most reactively. That is, the
audience has the least amount of say in determining how to interpret the
material being presented. The ultimate result, therefore, may be that the conclusions reached in the various genres cannot be exactly the same: just as
language influences what can be thought, the variations in how thoughts can
be expressed in the genres impose limits on what can be thought.

Each genre necessarily operates most effectively in some instances and
less effectively in others. Because the stage is a medium of low visual saturation, language is stressed in plays, and the audience must be constantly aware
and proactive. Since film is highly visually saturated, the text is so densely
detailed with information that the audience can remain intellectually pas-
sive. This allows the filmmaker to do things not easily replicated on stage. In

The Servant, as Giannetti notes, theme and characterization are "communicated primarily through the use of camera angles" (234). A film adapter, then, must take a number of antithetical things into consideration, especially because unexpected differences may occur when transferring a stage play to the screen. For instance, Francis Gillen experimented with putting part of *The Dumb Waiter* on film at the University of Tampa in 1992 and found that the dominant character on screen was the one sitting rather than the one standing.

Generally speaking, there are three approaches used in translating a literary work to celluloid: a loose, a faithful, or a literal adaptation. With a loose adaptation, essentially the main idea, a character, or a situation is taken from the source and is used to structure the film script. As a result, the degree of fidelity to the original is minimal; Akira Kurosawa's *Throne of Blood,* which is derived from Shakespeare's *Tragedy of Macbeth,* is a prime example of this type of transformation. In a faithful adaptation, an attempt is made to create a cinematic translation that is as true to the spirit of the literary work as possible; Pinter's film version of Fowles's *The French Lieutenant's Woman* exemplifies this approach. The literal adaptation applies primarily to stage plays, and the intent is to produce as accurate a copy as possible. *The Caretaker* is an example of this genre.

Talking about the relationship between the source and a film adaptation, Dudley Andrew uses the term "the fidelity of transformation" (101) in discussing three kinds of adaptation: borrowing, intersecting, and transforming. For Otto Preminger, there is nothing to discuss. He claims that "People often come to me and ask if the film is going to be faithful to the book. 'Faithful to the book.' Once an author sells (and 'sells' is a very hard word) the film rights, he gives up any claim to have somebody do it 'faithfully.'"[23] Elsewhere Preminger has been equally explicit about his own approach to adaptations: "Some characters don't interest me so I drop them, others who are minor in the book appeal strongly to me and I develop them to become more attractive. I may create new characters altogether. I have no obligation, nor do I try, to be 'faithful' to the book" (Packard, 44).

Ray Bradbury accepts the challenge of cinematic adaptation from a different perspective: "When you adapt another person's book, it's got to get into your bloodstream so completely that it can come out on an emotional level and be recreated. It has to be recreated through your emotions and not rethought. Your emotions will do the rethinking for you."[24]

Nunnally Johnson "learned to look for the backbone, the skeleton of a novel, what this fellow was setting out to tell, so that actually he could have told it in a nightletter. Almost."[25] Johnson adds, "The screenwriter's duty, his loyalty, is not to the book. Whenever I work on adaptations, my eye is on the audience, not the author. If, afterwards, the author chooses not to like it, but the audience did, all I can say is, 'Well, there it is. That's my business. Pleasing an audience. Not pleasing an author.'"[26]

William Goldman's approach is more intellectual than Bradbury's, similar to Johnson's: "What one tries to do in an adaptation is, two things: First of all, ad nauseum you try to find what is the spine of the piece. Plus, you have to think what was it that thrilled you? What was the pleasure that the book gave you, or the play gave you, or the story or the article? What moved you? Who moved you? Now, you have to combine those two things somehow. You have to keep those elements that were moving . . . either to laughter or to tears. Plus keeping the story straight."[27] Pinter would not accept Preminger's premise in its strictest sense (that is, essentially to ignore the source), yet he is willing to alter the materials from his source. This is because he regards his source with an attitude that lies between those expounded by Bradbury and Goldman.

In summing up the differences between the media, Syd Field has said that novels usually are about someone's internal life within the mind-scape of dramatic action, a play is composed of the language of dramatic action, and a screenplay is "a story told with pictures, placed within the context of dramatic structure." The screenwriter is concerned with the details of externals.[28] He says that adaptations are original screenplays, that the source material is only a starting point, and that the screenwriter "is not obligated to remain faithful to the original material" so long as the integrity of the source material is maintained when that material is turned into a visual experience. He sums up the adaptation process as "NOT being true to the original. A book is a book, a play a play, an article an article, a screenplay a screenplay" (216).

Novels lend themselves to broad, multiple subjects because of the nature of prose, which is to be read leisurely, can easily engage the reader in mentally manipulating the material over long periods of time, and depends upon the elusive nature of words themselves so that the reader's use of his or her imagination is an integral part of the process. Films are more confined. There is a limit to the amount of time that they can take, and the images are controlled in ways that obviate the use of the audience's imagination far more strictly than words do.

William Packard declares, "There are a lot of great novels that simply would not translate well onto the screen. The novels of Franz Kafka are haunting in their remorseless sense of doom, and the novels of Marcel Proust are brilliant in their subtlety of perception, and the novels of James Joyce are overwhelming in their momentum of stream of consciousness. But the greatness of all these authors depends so much on their strong narrative genius for telling what they have to tell in a peculiar way, that it is not likely that any of these works could ever be successfully translated into screen terms without a profound loss" (38). It is interesting that Pinter has chosen to try his hand at adapting the work of two of these three authors; while the cinematic translations have not been complete successes, neither have they been the complete failures that Packard predicted. Pinter's mishaps are understandable and his successes all the more laudable when one comprehends some of the obstacles that an adapter must overcome.

In *Aspects of the Novel,* E.M. Forster complains that "the novel tells a story. . . . That is the highest factor common to all novels, and I wish that it was not so, that it could be something different—melody, or perception of the truth, not this low atavistic form" (45). This grievance is even more apropos in conventional filmmaking, where the simple, straightforward storytelling character of the medium is both an obvious rationale for the medium's existence and a natural development, given the linear, image-making nature of the medium itself. As Terrence Rafferty observes, "movies charge through their narratives more swiftly and more relentlessly than conventional novels do, and *allow even less latitude for reflection*" (74, emphasis mine). At the base, Pinter strives to do what thus may seem impossible, to transform to the screen something that (at this point in cinematic technology) cannot be fully transmitted. That something is the novelist's ability through the narrative process to transcend the story line, to go beyond the story.

Screenwriters who create *Terminator*-style movies have few problems in this area because they are dealing almost exclusively with story; Pinter chooses the labor of working with novels that contain this subtle, transcendent element for which there is no actual correspondence in cinematic language. As a screenwriter he tries to exploit this aspect of the original. He is not always triumphant, though sometimes he is extraordinarily so. In viewing *The French Lieutenant's Woman,* there is an immediate awareness that the film is a masterpiece. The photography, direction, sets, acting, and dialogue coalesce even in the opening sequence to impress this response upon the audience. As with most genres of art, in film the audience's appreciation of the artifact grows in proportion to the realization and understanding of the craftsmanship involved in the creation of the artifact. The elements cited above in *The French Lieutenant's Woman,* the carefully designed, intricate structure of *The Servant*—these are direct results of what is called for in Pinter's screenplays.

Certainly, given his decision to work with novelistic sources throughout his career, the challenge of this artistic act must be of some consequence to him. Complicating his decision is the fact that, as Andrew says, "Generally film is found to work from perception toward signification, from external facts to interior motivations and consequences, from the givenness of a world to the meaning of a story cut out of that world. Literary fiction works oppositely" (101). Thomas Elsaesser claims that, at least in part, "the primary need which the cinema promises to fulfill is to codify an experience of reality which is directly sensual: it offers the world as an emotional spectacle" (172). Indeed, Orson Welles claimed that "Film is the most emotional medium in the world."

Ingmar Bergman has addressed the complex and difficult problem of translating narrative voice into cinematic terms: "There are many reasons why we ought to avoid trying to film all of existing literature—but the most important reason is that the irrational dimension, which is the heart of a literary work, is often untranslatable and that in its turn kills the special dimension of the film. If despite this we wish to translate something literary into filmic terms, we are obliged to make an infinite number of complicated transformations which most often give limited or non-existent results in relation to the efforts expended" ("Each Film Is My Last," 97–98).

As Bergman implies, cinematic devices are often inadequate to accomplish this kind of transference. Commenting on the inadequacy of voice-overs, James Agee says, "to read from the text of a novel—not to mention interior monologues—when people are performing on the screen, while it may elevate the literary tone of the production, which I doubt, certainly and inescapably plays hell with it as a movie" ("Agee on Film").

On top of these problems that confront the adapter, Esslin is of the opinion that "movie writing is an exercise in skills," and thus Pinter is more conscious of technique and less under the influence of the muse of inspiration when he writes for the screen than when he writes for the stage.[29] Money is a concern for the author, too, according to Esslin, which is why Pinter did the screenplays for *The Pumpkin Eater* and *The Handmaid's Tale*. However, despite these elements that should lead to the contrary, Pinter's films are almost always superior to their sources, in part because he distills the essence of the original.

Artists frequently have proved incapable of verbally articulating the essence of the works of art that they have created (which is why they have chosen to express themselves in art as opposed to essays); they have sometimes refused to comment, letting the art stand for itself (e.g., T.S. Eliot); and on occasion they have even lied or joked about their work (e.g., Pinter's comment about "the weasel under the cocktail cabinet" that was widely dissected by critics). Nevertheless, if Losey really thought that Pinter's script for *The Servant* was about false values, he was only partly right, for, as is demonstrated below in the analysis of the film, the movie both has more depth of meaning and is broader in scope than a demonstration that false values lead to degradation. It may be true that Losey's interpretation fits the source novel, but if the director believes that the movie's theme is no more profound than the novel's, then Pinter's script forced him to make a better movie than he intended or realized. This is possibly the ultimate confirmation of Pinter's script-writing ability—that it overcomes, that the talents of those who are involved in translating the words on the page into cinematic images are forced to perform at their highest level.

Film is a relatively new art form, the only plastic art form to be developed in the twentieth century, and the field of film aesthetics is still emerging. Few hard and fast rules for analyzing a film have been developed. As is discussed throughout this study, observing the obvious differences between the media can lead to a unified approach to understanding film. Certain elements such as characterization, imagery, symbolism, plot, word choice, and structure occur in poetry, prose, drama, and film and can thus be examined in all four media, but there are additional ingredients such as sound and image included in a film that require attention—and all of these elements are delivered at a pace controlled by the artist, not the audience (who cannot ask the characters to repeat their dialogue). Although some of these cinematic elements occur in drama too, the fundamental difference between drama and film is the shot, the basic unit of film. It is this last component that distinguishes film from other art forms, because shots can be used to make discontinuous action continuous and to make continuous action discontinuous. Special effects (slow motion, fast motion, process shots), focus, camera angles (including elevation, distance—close-up, extreme long shot—and so forth), and shifts of point of view provide for new methods of expression.

For these reasons, even though I examine the traditional literary elements, I have chosen to concentrate on those devices that are peculiarly cinematic.

Until the 1990s, when Tipper Gore's music movement made an impact on the audio-recording field, film was the only artistic medium with a formal rating system used to inform and/or protect the public. Museums that are open to all people, regardless of the museum-goer's age, regularly feature paintings and statues of battle scenes and nudes. That similar representations on film are considered too dangerous for the public to decide whether or not to attend without some sort of forewarning speaks to the nature and consequent power of film.

What kind of metaphor is created when you see a statue or a painting as opposed to moving images on a screen? The statue or the painting is solid and is perceived as a work of art; the moving images cause the viewer to be immediately integrated into, to become a part of, the work of art. As a result of this incorporation, the events on the screen become part of the life of the observer living in a real world as opposed to living in an intellectual world. There is a transcendence that goes beyond the art to the *you*. The statue is real—you can touch it—yet you are aware that you are touching an *object*; there is no syzygy, no engulfed merging, with the objectified. Art can capture the essence of something symbolically or representationally. With a movie, you know that you are watching light and shadow, but emotionally you become caught up in and part of the action instead of observing it and taking things in vicariously, second hand. There is no question that Rembrandt's use of light in his series of paintings "The Passion of Christ" is artistry at its purest; there is also no question that no painter has ever imparted on canvas the emotional impact of the sequence in Nicolas Roeg's *Don't Look Now* (1973) when Donald Sutherland lifts his drowned daughter out of the stream. When looking at Brueghel's *Icarus,* it is possible to understand intellectually the artist's comment and to sympathize or to even empathize with the fallen youth, to be moved by his plight, to apply the lesson to one's own life. But, the action is stopped; the viewer does not feel the fall. With *The Comfort of Strangers* you want to intercede. You feel the razor. At the same time, of course, it is the image to which the audience reacts. In other words, there is still a separation between the art object and the observer.

Another obvious characteristic of film that sets it aside from other media is that it is the only medium in which all of the trades involved in creating the objet d'art are publicly recognized. When the credits roll, everyone who has had anything to do with the production is listed, from the director to the caterer to the auditor to the insurance carrier to the boom operator, to the best boys (electricians), the grips, the greensmen, the drivers, and the carpenters. The technological and collaborative aspects of the medium cannot be ignored.

In prose and poetry, the focus is on the words—they are either on the page or they are not. In critical analyses of these genres, the interest lies in *which* words are included and in what order they appear or in what structure they are embedded. In drama the dressed set provides an unarticulated background against which the words are spoken, giving the dialogue an added dimension, and the actors' actions during the utterance of the words are a metalanguage that enhances the meanings conveyed through the words. In film, the focus is on the visual images. In film, words are akin to the spoken language in opera—the emotional and even the intellectual content is conveyed through the visual or musical image, and the words serve as enhancers and help to fine-tune the meaning rather than carrying the mass of that meaning, just as the music from an aria in Giacomo Puccini's *Madam Butterfly* or Franz Schubert's "Ave Maria" certainly creates an overwhelming emotional response whether the words are attached or not.

Also involved is the concept of control. With poetry and prose, the reader's mind has the widest range for imaginative response. With drama the author's delineation is more obviously imparted, because of the set that is detailed; the stage is not an imaginary part of the audience's individual constructs—they see three-dimensionally with their eyes what the playwright wants them to see rather than creating it in their minds. With film the delineation is further made graphic because the audience's attention is completely directed by what the camera is focused upon. Furthermore, the principle of choice is vital—everything seen on the screen has been decided upon in advance (that is why there are storyboards and design conferences, and so forth). The type of shot (close-up, two-shot, or whatever) is chosen; the angle of the shot is chosen; the lighting is chosen; the character's placement and position are chosen; the items included in the set are chosen. One can assume that if something is there, it has been picked to create a specific effect or for a particular reason related to the movie's content.

Some contemporary critics give privileged status to the spoken word over the written word, and the deconstructionist perspective of some demands that a multitude of mutually exclusive readings may necessarily all be correct and that the critic (or reader or audience) is at least as important as the creative artist, because a work of art serves as nothing more than a con-struct from which the critic can create any meaning desired; they apparently feel no real need to justify the creation. Notwithstanding such views, those who write know the importance of choice, the care taken in producing just the right word or phrase or juxtaposition in order to convey the exact, precise meaning desired. The element of choice is especially important to artists, and over the years many artists have written about the writing process, have been interested in the imaginative process. William Wordsworth and Samuel Taylor Coleridge in the late eighteenth century and John Irving in the twentieth century, among many others, have explored these topics in their own creative and critical works. And, Pinter has demonstrated publicly an awareness and interest in these processes, as evidenced by his essays "Writing for Theatre" and "Writing for Myself" and comments in letters and interviews throughout his career.

Deny it he may, but Pinter has had a fairly well set theoretical idea about the nature of writing from early on in that career. In his novel *The Dwarfs,* which dates from the early 1950s, the character Pete says, "each idea must possess stringency and economy and the image, if you like, that expresses it must stand in exact correspondence and relation to the idea" (77). The author seems never to have felt confined to any one genre or to feel that there is a great gap between the genres. This attitude has allowed him to experiment with adaptations throughout his career. He converted "The Black and White," a short story written in 1954–1955, into a review sketch in 1959. Similarly, "Tea Party" was written as a prose piece in 1963 and converted into a television play in 1964.

Furthermore, possibly more than most of his contemporaries—and this may be one of the main reasons for his success—Pinter knows the power of words. When novelist Henry Miller wrote *Tropic of Cancer* and *Tropic of Capricorn,* he was trying to explain the nature of art and the artist and the role of the artist in society. To do this he felt that it was necessary to capture his audience's attention through the use of graphic sexual descriptions and four-letter words. Having gotten their attention, he could then proceed to state his case. Unfortunately for Miller, his audience was either shocked by the novels' content (resulting in the books being banned in the United States for many years) or they were not shocked. In either case, Miller failed to achieve his purpose of informing his audience because the first group of people were so shocked that they would not, or could not, read the volumes, and the second group found the overuse of expletives boring, so they did not read the novels either.

Pinter's understanding of the power of words was demonstrated in his 1966 interview with Lawrence M. Bensky when he said that he used four-letter words infrequently because he objected to "this scheme afoot on the part of many 'liberal-minded' persons to open up obscene language to general commerce. It should be the dark secret language of the underworld. There are very few words—you shouldn't kill them by overuse. . . . They're great, wonderful words, but must be used very sparingly."[30] Elsewhere he has commented that such words are too powerful—once you use them, you lose control of them.

Likewise, because he understands the effect that words can have, Pinter has been concerned about their misuse. His 1985 sketch "Precisely" is evidence of his awareness of how language can be used imprecisely. In the play two men, presumably governmental minions from the department that predicts such things, discuss the "exact" number of people who will die in a nuclear war:

A. . . . Twenty million. That's what we've said. Time and time again. It's a figure supported by facts. We've done our homework. Twenty million is a fact. When these people say thirty I'll tell you exactly what they're doing—they're distorting facts.

. . . .

B.   Give me another two, Stephen.

[A *stares at him.*]

A.   Another two?

B.   Another two million. And I'll buy you another drink. . . .

A.   [*Slowly*] No, no, Roger. It's twenty million. Dead.

B.   You mean precisely?

A.   I mean dead. Precisely.

. . . .

B.   Twenty million dead, precisely?

A.   Precisely. (Pinter, "Precisely," 37)

Pinter further comments on the importance of language in his political opinion piece "Oh, Superman," which was broadcast on BBC Channel 4 on May 31, 1990:

What all this adds up to is a disease at the very centre of language, so that language becomes a permanent masquerade, a tapestry of lies. The ruthless and cynical mutilation and degradation of human beings, both in spirit and body, the death of countless thousands—these actions are justified by rhetorical gambits, sterile terminology and concepts of power which stink. Are we ever going to look at the language we use, I wonder? Is it within our capabilities to do so?

Do the structures of language and the structures of reality (by which I mean what actually *happens*) move along parallel lines? Does reality essentially remain outside language, separate, obdurate, alien, not susceptible to description? Is an accurate and vital correspondence between what is and our perception of it impossible? Or is it that we are obliged to use language only in order to obscure and distort reality—to distort what is—to distort what happens—because we fear it?[31]

Given Pinter's appreciation of how significant the manipulation of something as tenuous as language can be, film must contain a tremendous appeal as a medium in which to work. Not only is the cinematic primal matter manipulable, but also, in no other medium is the product so holistic. Each element reenforces and expands upon what every other element is used to present.

From the beginning Pinter has been interested in the expressive possibilities inherent in film. "The cinema was tattooed into me from a very early age," he told Lee Langley (Langley, "From 'Caretaker' to 'Servant'"). In another interview years later, he asserted "The cinema was my life really" (Gussow, "Pinter on Pinter," 19). He remembers that he was especially taken with American gangster films, British war films, strong social films, and Russian masterpieces. Among the films that he has specifically cited are *L'age d'or* (1930), *Que viva Mexico* (1932), *The Glass Key* (1935), *Un carnet du bal* (1937), *The Grapes of Wrath* (1940), *The Ox-Box Incident* (1943), *The Way Ahead* (1944), *Boomerang!* (1947),[32] and John Ford movies such as *The Long Voyage Home* (1940).[33] As a fourteen-year-old, he joined a film club where he was introduced to the work of Luis Buñuel and Jean Cocteau, as well as Robert Wiene's *Cabinet of Dr. Caligari* (1919): "I ran right into Eisenstein and Pudovkin and [Alexander] Dozhenko . . . and Buñuel and Cocteau . . . [Marcel] Carné, [Julien] Duvivier . . . Jules Dassin . . . William Wellman" (Gussow, *Conversations,* 139). In 1947, as a schoolboy member of the Hackney Downs Literary and Debating Society, he debated the topic "Realism and Post-realism in the French Cinema," and the following year he took part in the debate on the subject "Film Is More Promising in Its Future as an Art Form than the Theatre." That this was more than simply an ephemeral academic interest is demonstrated by his taking one of his first lovers, Dilys Hamlett, to see Buñuel's extraordinarily inventive *Un Chien andalou* in 1951.[34]

As he did in the theatre, Pinter soon became involved with many aspects of filmmaking. Besides writing screenplays, he has acted in and directed films.[35] In fact, "I'd like to direct more films," he says. "It has been the hardest work I've ever known, but deeply enjoyable."[36] The importance of the two roles of director and author can be inferred from the fact that many great directors (Welles, John Huston, Bergman, Akira Kurosawa, Woody Allen, Altman, Michelangelo Antonioni, Vittorio DeSica, Billy Wilder, Federico Fellini, François Truffaut, Buñuel, Satyajit Ray) assume both positions. In 1983 Pinter became a director at United British Artists.

And, as his career progressed and he gained experience in the cinema, Pinter began utilizing cinematic techniques in his stage dramas more frequently; even though there is not as much carryover, he also employs dramatic methodology in his film scripts. Actually, in some ways his predisposition for things cinematic has been manifest subtly in several techniques that he uses in his plays. Describing Pinter's characteristic pause, director Peter Hall says, "A pause is really a bridge where the audience thinks that you're this side of the river, then when you speak again, you're the other side" (Raymond, "Letter," 39). This is similar to the definition of a jump cut. In *Old Times*, his best stage play, he uses the concept of a jump cut in the opening scene.[37]

A critic approaching Pinter's work in the cinema must keep in mind that the author's attention to these kinds of details is for only one reason: he is trying to communicate some meaning, and he constantly seeks the most effective manner to do so. The sophomore syndrome—the idea that everyone is entitled to an opinion and everyone's opinion is equally valid—has invaded literary criticism, and it is just as wrong in this field as it is in the classroom. *Moby-Dick* is not about grape-picking in the Sonoma Valley, no matter how much a critic may want it to be. True, there may well be universal realities and human insights contained in Herman Melville's novel that apply to grape-pickers or Wall Street brokers or street venders, but *Moby-Dick* is not about those people except insofar as certain universals are applicable. There may be differences of opinion about the exact meaning of Robert Frost's poem "Stopping by Woods on a Snowy Evening," but the meaning of the poem is limited to a category or box of meaning having to do with nature, death, and obligations. Anyone who reads the work as a treatise on whaling is wrong. Boynton caught the essence of this axiom in her cartoon showing a large teacher pig holding a book and sitting in a chair while surrounded by eight little student piglets. The caption reads: "There is is no such thing as a wrong answer. However, if there were such a thing, that certainly would have been it."

The primary reason that an artist creates, whether in sculpture, music, dance, laser light shows, or film scripts, is to communicate an idea or a feeling to an audience. The artist's success is determined by how well that communication works, although it need not be a complete communication. As long as the core of John Donne's "Valediction Forbidding Mourning" is understood, minor nuances may enrich the audience's experience with the poem without invalidating it; various people will incorporate different segments or images or metaphors from the poem into their beings, yet all of these elements will be drawn from a kernel of meaning that Donne intended to impart.

In the early 1980s, Stoppard spoke at Westminster College in Fulton, Missouri. After his talk he entertained questions from the audience. One question, typically freshmanish in nature, elicited a telling response. "Do you put all of those meanings into your works that the critics tell us are there?" a young man asked. Stoppard's answer was in the form of a parable. "Suppose I pop over to Switzerland one evening to conduct some business," he said. "Because I am only going to be gone overnight, I take a small bag into which I put a shaving kit, a clean shirt, and a change of underwear. When I return the next day, the customs inspector asks me if I have anything to declare. No, I say, I just spent the night on a quick business trip and I didn't purchase anything. That's fine, the customs inspector declares, but I need to take a peek just for the heck of it. The customs inspector then proceeds to pull chocolate bars, gold coins, Swiss watches, cheeses, and other such items out of the bag. And what do you make of this? the inspector demands. Well," Stoppard says, "I can't deny that they are there; I just don't remember having packed them."

Consciously or not, Stoppard did pack them. Moreover, they all related to Switzerland—for example, there were no boomerangs included. Equally important, Stoppard's reply contains an admission of some level of awareness of what he put into the bag. To an artist precision is important. When John Keats talks about a "still unravish'd bride of quietness" in his "Ode on a Grecian Urn," all three meanings of the word "still" are applicable—quiet, unmoving, as yet. His choice of words, then, is appropriate, even if he did not realize that all three meanings are compatible. In any case, Keats chose the word.

On a purely practical note, Christina Hamlett finds that whereas a novel is typically about four hundred pages long and comprised of approximately 65 percent narrative and 35 percent dialogue, the average screenplay is about 120 pages long and is composed of master shots and dialogue (6, 8), so the mere physical differences must be attended to in adaptation. Traditionally, because of their length and composition, novels tend to unfold in a comparatively leisurely fashion; with movies, the transitions may be minimal and more abrupt—and because of the visuals, less needs to be said in words. The audience is expected to make many of the connections based on its experience with montage. Granted that it may seem a contradiction, an adapter still must be a storyteller first and foremost, and Pinter has proved himself a master in his years of writing for the stage. His scripts for *The French Lieutenant's Woman* and *Lolita* prove that this talent has carried over to his screenwriting.

Film is storytelling with visual images instead of words. Film historian Kevin Brownlow defines a motion picture's "prime requirement" as "pace and speed" (272). American playwright-screenwriter Mamet says that the difference between screenwriting and playwriting is that "the purpose of a screenplay is to tell the story so the audience wants to know what happens next, and to tell it in pictures. Movies are basically about plot. They're about the structure of incidents, one incident causing the next to happen. A play doesn't have to be that. It has to have a *plot* as some sort of spine, but the spine can be very simple: two guys waiting for Godot to show up."[38] Ultimately, of course, it is impossible to capture the essence of a film as though it were words on a page—because a film's essence is not words but the juxtaposition of visual images. In talking about the difference between movies and prose fiction, Charlie Hamm declares that "film deals with events while the novel looks at the *consequences . . .* of events."

An artist chooses to work in a particular genre because that genre is the best one available to express a specific emotion or concept, because he or she feels comfortable with the genre, or because the genre represents a creative challenge—or perhaps for a combination of reasons. Part of the appeal of the sonnet for a poet, for example, is the need to put into a carefully prescribed format of meter, rhyme scheme, and length whatever it is that is being expressed and to do so in a way that is clear and at the same time artistically done. Amazingly, the fact that language is artificial and has no inherent meaning has come as a surprise to the members of some of our contemporary movements in literary criticism. Writers have understood this fact from the beginning of time, and part of the attraction of literature has been the challenge of molding words to extract whatever the author intends.

There are two approaches to raw materials, that of the craftsman and that of the artist. If the craftsman wants to form a vase out of a pile of clay, he or she does so by forcing the clay into a preconceived shape. Even though there are always small impurities or air bubbles in the clay, the draftsperson forces the material to conform to the prescribed form. Thus, depending on the level of the potter's ability, every vase that is produced is essentially the same, all of them of good quality and virtually interchangeable dimensions. Nathaniel Hawthorne's Dr. Aylmer in "The Birth-mark" is so obsessed with the perfection of beauty that ultimately he kills his wife when he tries surgically to remove her one blemish, a small birthmark. He tries to impose his will on the raw material, with tragic consequences.

In contrast, an artist is one who draws a work of art out of the material, as Michelangelo claimed to do in his sculpting. In working with clay, instead of forcing the clay to fit into a specified form as a craftsperson would, the artist makes a vase, but it is a vase that allows the nature of its constituent materials to have an effect on the end product. All of the artist's vases are vases, yet each one is slightly different, a difference determined by the degree of moistness or purity of the clay. The artist has still forced the clay to be a vase, but the vase is a work of art, not a vessel. The inherent beauty is thereby allowed to emerge during the creative process as opposed to being submerged to the clay worker's preconceived intent. Hawthorne's "Drowne's Wooden Image" reflects this attitude toward the material as Drowne, the carver who fashions ships' figureheads, seeks the features that are contained within the wood instead of working the wood to fit his design.

A corollary to this can be seen in Pinter's playwriting career. In an interview with Kathleen Halton, the dramatist mentions that, given a situation, he develops it within its own framework. "I've never started a play from any kind of abstract idea or theory," he repeats. "You arrange *and* you listen, following the clues you leave for yourself, through the characters" (Halton, 195). Elsewhere he says: "Finding the characters and letting them speak for themselves is the greatest excitement of writing. I would never distort the consistency of a character by a kind of hoarding in which I say, 'by the way, these characters are doing this because of such and such.' I find out what they are doing, allow them to do it, and keep out of it" (Hewes, 58). In his early, revealing interview with Bensky, Pinter further explains: "I don't know what kind of characters my plays will have until they . . . well, until they *are*. Until they indicate to me what they are, I don't conceptualize in any way. Once I've got the clues I follow them—that's my job, really, to follow the clues. . . . Sometimes I'm going along and I find myself writing 'C. comes in' when I didn't know that he was going to come in; he *had* to come in at that point, that's all" (358). Many who have no experience with the creative arts have not believed Pinter's profession of not knowing that C would "come in." They suggest that authors have better control of their materials, that writers work things out in advance. The reason that C could come in at that point without Pinter's foreknowledge, however, is simple. Having created a logical situation and unified characters, as Aristotle would say, the play-wright has also created a condition in which it is consistent with the situa-tion and the characters as they have been developed for C to come in. Pinter may, indeed, have been surprised by C's appearance; in retrospect, however, that appearance is predictable.

The results of a conscious manipulation of materials is more obvious in film than it is in other literary genres. George Bernard Shaw's differentiation between the stage and movies is simple: "The film lends itself admirably to the succession of events proper to narrative and epic, but physically imprac-ticable on the stage."[39] Pinter's decision to work in film is at least partially based on his realization that the medium affords him advantages lacking in his other options and that as a result he can better express his current inter-ests in film than he can in drama, poetry, or prose. He recognizes the possi-bilities and impossibilities in filmmaking, and he permits the material to come into play, but his imprint is obvious in what he fashions.

As a dramatist, Pinter carefully chooses the words that he uses to con-struct his stage plays. Moreover, he is aware of the process of writing. So, too, does Pinter the film writer carefully choose the words and visuals that become his movie scripts. Bertolt Brecht stated that drama "should be a demonstration," not a "presentation." This definition is even more appro-priate when applied to film, and Pinter has taken it to heart. He has always been intrigued by images, even as he has been captured by words. When he wrote his first two dramas, *The Room* and *The Birthday Party*, he began with pictures that he carried in his mind. When he began *Old Times*, it was a line of dialogue that stimulated him. With his motion picture scripts, it seems that the visual is forefronted. In discussing *The Go-Between,* Pinter explains his approach to writing a screenplay: "The only way I could actually write the script was to *see* it happening, *shot by shot.*"[40]

Related to the exercise of choice, the phenomenon of "opening out" comes into play in film to a degree not possible in drama. This element has been present in Pinter's films from the beginning, as evidenced in *The Servant* by the extraneous nonsynchronous noise of children playing outside Tony's apartment, which is heard several times, the din of airplanes passing overhead, cars in the streets, and other such sounds (the children, the planes, and the street traffic are never seen), and the introduction of the group of playful young girls at the telephone booth. All of this seems to be an effort to make the audience conscious of the fact that there is an external—and intrusive—real world beyond what is seen on the screen. Pinter has spoken specifically about this concept in connection with his adaptation of *The Caretaker* (see below).

Among the most important features—and the one that has the most impact—that distinguish film from prose, poetry, and drama is the ability of the artist to vary the audience's perceived distance from a given focal point, from an extreme close-up to an extreme long shot, and the rapid juxtaposition of shots to create linkages that would not otherwise be possible. In Sergei Eisenstein's theory of montage, a shot must be "uninflected"; it must not be evocative. That is to say, the meaning of the shot does not derive from narration but instead from its juxtaposition with other shots in a series, the effect of which is to transmit meaning visually based on information determined by the relationship of the shots within the series. Mamet summarizes nicely Eisenstein's theory that montage is "*a succession of images juxtaposed so that the contrast between these images moves the story forward in the mind of the audience*" (*On Directing,* 2).[41] A movie, then, should be a series of uninflected shots (i.e., no shot in itself contains a specific meaning, and the shots are unrelated individually) put together in such a way that they tell a story. It is the order of the shots that allows/forces the audience to create the drama in their own minds. Christian Metz contends that "The cinema begins where ordinary language ends; at the level of the 'sentence'—the film-maker's minimum unit and the highest properly linguistic unit of language," that a cinematic shot is "not comparable to the word in a lexicon; rather it resembles a complete statement (of one or more sentences)" (*Film Language,* 81, 100).

Film theorists have pointed out the capacity of the medium to convert space into time and time into space. A cinematic shot can be used to lengthen or shorten time (through the use of slow or fast motion). From his earliest screenplays, Pinter has demonstrated his understanding of these phenomena. Other theorists have spoken about the nature of time in a film and how time can be manipulated. Although a shot in a movie can last anywhere from a millisecond to minutes, the span of the average shot is between ten and fifteen seconds. Because of this, time can be expanded or contracted dramatically in a film. The use of slow motion or fast motion permits time to become subjective. Editing allows for the simultaneity of time as well. In *The Caretaker,* for instance, the camera moves back and forth between Mick waiting for his brother and Aston and Davies as they walk down the street toward the flat. Similarly, critics argue, time and space become interchangeable—time can be converted into space and space can be converted into time. In another example from *The Caretaker,* the length of the tracking shot that follows Mick's car as he drives around the traffic circle preserves the physical sense of the concrete distance traveled on a one-to-one basis.

Clearly, in the beginning, Pinter was attracted to film because of the technical possibilities involved. Some of these possibilities are rather simple. He expressed delight, for instance, in talking about filming *The Caretaker,* because the movie camera allowed him to move the action outside the single room of the stage play. The stage necessarily places physical limitations on the set; with the camera Pinter felt that he could "open out" the drama and show that there is a real world outside the room.[42] Another technical appeal lies in the pure mechanics of modern filmmaking. Interviewed by Langley in 1964, Pinter recalls, "the other day I went into the cutting room for the first time, and saw exactly how it's done, how it's all put together. I wanted to try and cut some dialogue, and I asked the director if we could cut a line in one place and make it a pause. He twiddled a few things, and the line was gone—had become a pause. You can delete dialogue, alter rhythm. This is marvelous" (Langley, "From 'Caretaker' to 'Servant'").

Determining a screenwriter's contribution to a finished film is difficult. Actually, of course, the question of who is responsible for what in a film is a perplexing and sometimes unanswerable, albeit intriguing, question. After the fact, S.J. Perelman and his cowriters were not sure about who wrote many of the gags that appeared in their Marx Brothers pictures *Horse Feathers* and *Monkey Business*—but the movies were funny. And, even published scripts are not always reliable. There can be tremendous differences even between a shooting script and a film, since changes are frequently made during the shooting itself.

In addition to the question of authorship and the potential copy-text debate inherent in the collaborative process of filmmaking, Pinter's screenwriting has led to several anomalies: the publication of unfilmed scripts (*The Proust Screenplay* and *Victory*), the complete on-the-set rewrite of a screenplay by the actors and the directors (*The Handmaid's Tale*), and the creation of a screenplay published in Pinter's original form (*The Remains of the Day*) that has been rewritten by another author and subsequently filmed. The existence of these film scripts is a potential bibliographic theoretician's nightmare.[43] However, for the literary/film critic, the interesting thing about the scripts is how they developed—what alterations were made and when, why were they made, did they have any effect on the meaning of the work, were they required in order to better express that meaning; these are the operative questions.

In a note by Pinter included at the beginning of the published version of the screenplay for *The French Lieutenant's Woman,* the writer points out that "This is the final version with which we began shooting. Inevitably a number of scenes were cut and some structural changes were made during the course of production" (Pinter, *The French Lieutenant's Woman: A Screenplay,* vii).

Still, there is plenty of evidence that Pinter is deeply involved in the entire filmmaking process, even after the script has been finished. "I have absolute and contractual artistic control over my scripts and act as a consultant to the director in both pre- and post-production work," he says, though he admits that "my post production activity is variable."[44] Normally, he is on the set during shooting and works closely with the director and sometimes the author of the source novel as well—as has been recorded in several interviews with Fowles. Losey has distinguished between "two kinds of writers who work on films. . . . One who is very personal and contributive, like Pinter . . . and others . . . who never make the same creative contributions that a man like Pinter does" (Leahy, 14). As mentioned above, there are also certain traits and patterns that appear in films made from Pinter's scripts that are identifiably his trademarks, no matter who the director is.

Collaboration is a defining element in cinema more than in other art forms, and while Pinter has not always worked with the authors of his sources, most of the times when he has the arrangement has been amicable and successful. Novelists tend to understand that their writing and a film based on their writing are perforce separate entities. Asked to comment on the film script for *Accident,* Mosley's reaction to Pinter's alterations was: "Because I thought that . . . the script [was] a very good script, I made not much more than formal objections to the changes from the book: we were different men, different writers, indeed; how could there not be changes?" (*Efforts at Truth*, 166).

The screenwriter has had a good and creative relationship with most of his directors, too, as detailed below in relation to the various cast and crew configurations.[45] Indeed, when he has good experiences with his colleagues, whether in the theatre or in filmmaking, the author tends to continue the relationship in other projects over a long period of time. Interviews and material in the Harold Pinter Archives in the British Library make it abundantly clear that for Pinter the screenwriter's job is an ongoing one once he and a director start a project. As a matter of fact, the collaborative effort even extends to the author's continuing work on the set during shooting, so even if something occurs in the movie that is not in the script, he is likely to have been involved in the decision to include it. That Pinter generally works well with his directors is further evidenced by the fact that he dedicated his first volume of screenplays to Losey, Clayton, and Anderson; that David Jones (*Betrayal; Langrishe, Go Down; The Trial;* and six plays) directed the playwright in a production of *Old Times* in 1985–1986; and that Reisz (*The French Lieutenant's Woman*) directed several of Pinter's plays, including *A Kind of Alaska* at the Gate Theatre's Pinter Festival in Dublin in 1997, a production of *Ashes to Ashes* in New York in 1999, and three plays during the Lincoln Center Festival (with Pinter in the cast of *One for the Road*) in 2001.

There are parallels with playwriting. When an audience attends a staging of one of Pinter's dramas, there is no doubt that it is a Pinter play, that he wrote it, no matter who directs or designs the set or acts the parts. The collaborative element is present in the theatre just as it is in the cinema; director Peter Hall, set designer John Bury, and numerous actors have talked about Pinter's involvement in various productions of his works from early on.[46]

To complicate matters further, however, even the conclusion of shooting does not mean that an authoritative text can be determined easily. Different "cuts," as the edited film is called, may exist in the hands of the director, the producer, and the studio; European and American variations may be released (sometimes in reaction to the film codes, sometimes because of cultural differences, sometimes owing to marketing strategies, sometimes as a matter of audience taste); new versions can appear on videotape or on television, or both, as well.[47] Thus, there really may be no such thing as a "final," authoritative, cut. In the late 1980s and 1990s, several films were rereleased in versions that were quite different from their original theatrical editions, David Lean's *Lawrence of Arabia* being the prime example. Instead of the multi-award-winning version that premiered in 1962, the 1990 version was the one that director Lean had wanted Columbia Pictures to release in the first place.

To date, seventeen of Pinter's photoplays have appeared in print, including the never-filmed *Proust Screenplay, Victory,* and *The Dreaming Child;* and *Langrishe, Go Down* had only been telecast until the Lincoln Center Festival (although it was published as a screenplay). Even for those that have been published, the printed version is not the shooting script and differs from what appears on the screen.[48] Because of this, in conducting a literary analysis of the films' themes and techniques (that is, to determine the meaning of the movies and the cinematic devices used to express that meaning), I examine each one individually on a shot-by-shot basis. This examination focuses on the technical and cinematic aspects of Pinter's scripts. In the final analysis, then, a scholar has to work with what is available, and when I began this study I decided that ultimately what I was looking at was the finished product, regardless of who was responsible for what portion of it.

Nevertheless, as suggested above, it is clear that there are identifiable patterns and characteristics in Pinter's cinematic work; and from information available in the Pinter Archives and his own and others' accounts of his input, it is obvious that to a large degree his screenplays are the reason that the films with which he has been involved have been so successful. This means not only that an examination of the films can lead to an understanding and appreciation of the meaning and techniques but also that certain kinds of conclusions about his individual input can be drawn with an acceptable degree of assurance. Moreover, the combination of playwriting and screenwriting talent in this one author therefore allows a unique opportunity to demonstrate the differences that exist between the dramatic and cinematic versions of his own works, and by extension it provides for insights into some of the essential aesthetic differences between the media of prose writing, drama, and film.[49]

Pinter may also find writing for the cinema more attractive than writing for the stage because even though some of the steps are the same (working on the script and then, as with a stage production, working with the director, the set designer, the actors, and other crew members toward the performance), once the movie is in the can, it is finished, permanent. It takes on a life of its own, requiring no more attention from the author. It is fixed, unlike the myriad mountings of stage plays by amateur and professional companies, each of which is different from every other staging.

In his interview with Langley, Pinter mentions that when he moves from playwriting to screenwriting, he is not moving from one world to another. He remains, he says, in "one identical discipline: economy." The principle of "economy" becomes more noticeably central to his approach to film as he matures. In commenting on his cinematic adaptation of Mosley's *Accident*, Pinter says, "In this film everything happens, nothing is explained. It has been pared down and down, all unnecessary words and actions are eliminated. If it is interesting to see a man cross a room, then we see him do it; if not, then we leave out the insignificant stages of the action."[50]

As the years have passed, it seems that Pinter's artistic talents increasingly have been channeled away from drama and toward film. Between 1961 and 1973, he wrote an average of almost one screenplay per year, all of them adaptations. He has hardly slowed down since then. Although attaining varying degrees of popular success, his films have all been critically acclaimed and have helped the dramatist achieve a financial security that allows him to be somewhat particular about the production of his plays as well as the choice of stories he wishes to turn into movies.

Thus far, Pinter has not written a full-length original screenplay, that is, a script for a movie that is not based on a preexisting literary work from another genre. In 1981 Leslie Garis asked Pinter why he wrote only adaptations. "Any original idea I may have," he replied, "always seems to go immediately into . . . theatre" (54). In a January 1991 letter, Pinter answered my question about whether he had plans to write an original screenplay with a simple "no," and in 1994 he told me that writing an original screenplay does not interest him and that he may not even have the proper temperament to do so.

Language not only allows us to think about things; it determines how we think about them. In the Vietnamese language, there is no word for the color blue. What we describe in English as blue is seen as a shade of green in Vietnamese. In an Eskimo language there are more than forty words to describe what we call snow in English. One nomadic African tribe's language contains more than four hundred words for the animal that we call a cow— and the concept of cow defines that society's art and economy and all other aspects of its culture.

In the debate over whether heredity or environment is most important in shaping an individual's character, it is likely that both are essential elements. The same is true in the debate over which is true, that language determines what we consider reality or that reality shapes our language. For the cattle people, everything is perceived as it relates to their cattle, because that is the only language that they know; yet obviously the cattle were an important part of their daily lives before that language came into being (the language grew out of their need to express their experiences with the animals). It is highly likely that people cannot think about something for which there are no referents in their language, even given that language develops in reaction to reality. What the people of one culture do is sometimes almost literally unthinkable to the people of another culture, who are operating from a base so different that they cannot conceive of certain "realities" until they are confronted with them. For a native of Cherrapunji in India or Mount Waialeale on the Hawaiian island of Kuaui, the concept of water is quite different from that found among the Bedouin of Arabia, and both the language and the culture of the inhabitants of these locales reflect these differences.[51]

Similarly, we can only see in movies what cinematic language allows us to see, and this language is still in its infancy. There is a vast distance between the patterned images of the experimental films of the surrealists and expressionists such as Dali and Fritz Lang in the early twentieth century, the nonlinear works of Norman McLaren and Ed Emshwiler in the middle of the century, and *Koyaanisqatsi* (1983) in the latter years of the century, though they are clearly related.

In his dramatic works, Pinter gained a reputation for presenting a view of life that made his audiences reconsider the preconceived notions of what drama is and how it is "supposed" to work that they brought with them to the theatre. When his first works appeared on stage, they were considered Absurd, unrealistic, and obscure by critics and the public alike. As the audience came to understand that they were seeing a new kind of drama and began to appreciate it for what it was, not what they expected it to be, Pinter's genius was recognized. His presentation of characters, his thematic development, his use of language (including the famous pauses and silences) went beyond what had preceded him. As an example, the dramatist freely admits that *The Caretaker* could never have been written if Beckett's plays had not already been in existence, but he takes the Chekovian and Beckettian pauses and extends their usage in innovative ways that have redefined stage language.[52]

Pinter's stage play *Landscape* contains one of the writer's most marvelous lines. Beth remembers standing over a man on the beach, a man who "felt my shadow" (10). Later she says, "Shadow is deprivation of light. The shape of the shadow is determined by that of the object. But not always" (28). In *No Man's Land,* shadows are important too. Hirst describes a scene in which "When I stood my shadow fell upon her. She looked up" (46). Hirst also speaks of his photograph album, which, he tells Spooner, includes pictures of girls: "Under their dresses their bodies were white. It's all in my album" (44). How the photographs can show what was under their dresses is not explained. The point of citing these instances is that Pinter perceives things differently than most people do. Like painters such as Rembrandt or Claude Monet, light and its effect on shape are important to the author. Henry Woolf, the childhood friend and acting colleague who was responsible for Pinter's writing *The Room,* claims, though not entirely convincingly for people with good vision, that Pinter has poor eyesight and that this is one of the reasons that he writes about perception, literal and figurative. Since he has difficulty in focusing on peripheral objects, he is more aware of the shadowy borderlines of reality. For him, edges appear soft and fuzzy rather than sharp. At the same time, it is this slight skewing of focus and fascination with light and shifting shapes that allows him to see things differently. Indeed, he sees with a poet's eye. When he reads a novel, the material is like Ralph Waldo Emerson's description of a tree in his essay "Nature." When in a normal posture Emerson sees a tree, it is a tree; when he turns around, bends over, and looks at the tree through his legs, it is something else. It is, of course, still the tree that he saw originally, yet it is also different. So it is with Pinter's film scripts. They are still the novels or plays that he adapts, yet they are different.

In his interview with Bensky, he also said, "I've done some film work, but for some reason or other I haven't found it very easy to satisfy myself on an original idea for a film. *Tea Party,* which I did for television, is actually a film, cinematic, I wrote it like that. Television and films are simpler than the theatre—if you get tired of a scene you just drop it and go on to another one. (I'm exaggerating, of course.) What is so different about the stage is that you're just *there,* stuck—there are your characters stuck on the stage, you've got to live with them and deal with them." This difference between film and stage, he goes on to imply, is part of the reason that he does not write original film scripts; "I'm not a very imaginative writer in the sense of using the technical devices other playwrights do" (Bensky, 355). Taken together, these statements suggest that he is attracted to other writers' material for his cinematic sources because it is a matter of taking what he has been given and simply translating it to the screen. At the same time, it is very clear that his adaptations are extremely imaginative. The challenges of removing the first-person interior monologue of *The Pumpkin Eater,* of fleshing out the subtle character hints of

The Servant, of condensing the lengthy *Remembrance of Things Past,* of capturing the essence of the nineteenth-century romance of *The French Lieutenant's Woman* in a modern idiom, or of the philosophical/psychological underpinnings of *Lolita* all belie the claim of a lack of imagination.

It is interesting that Pinter essentially equated film and television writing in his comments to Bensky. Since his first training in a filmic medium was in television and he finds little or no difference between the two media, it may be that this early work in television was one of the factors that led to his moving into film writing at such an advanced level, though there can be no doubt that the generic medium of film is one with which he naturally feels at home. Louis Marks, the BBC producer with whom Pinter has worked on numerous projects in television and film, told me that the author picked up the three-camera shooting technique in television quickly.

How he has utilized cinematic language can be detailed in examinations of his individual films. He brought some of his techniques from drama, of course, and did so better than other dramatists have been able to do—especially notable is his use of a characteristic dialogue and humor in the exploration of his themes. Pinter's major contributions to the theatre are his use of language (especially its economy), an exploration of the nature of reality, and the concept that the audience need not be given all of the information about the characters, all of which he extends and elaborates upon in his film scripts. What makes him remarkable, however, is the way in which he expands cinematic language as well. His recasting of the narrative structure of *The French Lieutenant's Woman* is a prime example, but the majority of his screenplays are entertaining, enlightening, and thematically and technically interesting, and his use of verbal and cinematic language is innovative and deft.

Pinter is very precise in his word choice, imagery, and overall use of language in his plays; so too is he in his films. British stage director Peter Wood (who directed the first performance of *The Birthday Party*) once claimed that "Harold Pinter and John Osborne pride themselves that they never altered a word."[53] Pinter seems to have tried to cultivate the image of an artist who creates "naturally" (as indicated in our 1994 interview—see the discussion of *Lolita*), one who, like Shakespeare, writes with hardly a "blot." Nevertheless, the existence of multiple versions of all of his scripts in the Pinter Archives is evidence that while he may work intuitively, he is also an extremely careful, even picky, craftsman who reworks his writing continually.

Beginning with *The Homecoming,* part of Pinter's polishing process done in connection with his stage plays was to send the scripts to Beckett for

Steven H. Gale and Harold Pinter in St. Louis, 1988. Pinter is in makeup as Deeley in a stage production of *Old Times*. Courtesy Kathy Johnson Gale.

review before the dramas were mounted.[54] He also admitted in an interview with John Kershaw in an ITV interview early in his career that he was concerned with language: "One of my main concerns is to get things down and down and down. . . . Always paring away" (Kershaw, Interview). This sense of economy comes out in his essay "Between the Lines," in which he explains his need to avoid "Such a weight of words." Speaking to Bensky, he declared, "I want to iron it down, eliminate things" (359). Actor John Normington provides an example of the paring down when he recalls that the first draft of *The Homecoming* was extraordinarily "much more elaborate" than the acting version and that to begin with "some of the speeches were five times as long."[55]

The writer's fine sense of humor sometimes comes through when he talks about his writing. In his interview with Gussow in 1971, he commented on a change in the script of *Old Times* during the pre-London tryouts. The alteration had to do with coffee cups: "I wrote one new line in rehearsal. . . . The line is: 'Yes, I remember.' . . . It came in the middle of the brandy and the coffee and affected the whole structure. In this play, the lifting of a coffee cup at the wrong moment can damage the next five minutes. As for the *sipping* of coffee, that can ruin the act." Although there is humor in the author's exaggeration, there is also a kernel of truth at the base of his claim—the careful blocking and choreography of a scene (evidenced in the 1985 David Jones production of the play in which Pinter acted the part of Deeley compared with Anthony Hopkins's performance in the 1983 production)[56] can make a huge difference in how the audience perceives the action—and it is his awareness of the importance of seemingly insignificant, minute details that can be found in his textual alterations. This awareness, of course, is also one of the attributes that make him a superb screenwriter.

Given this characteristic, it should come as no surprise that he engages in a considerable amount of research in preparing to write a script, since this is a perfectly normal and natural part of the writing process (that much of the material in the archives is dated, down to the month and day, is unexpected, especially since Pinter admits that he is not very good at dates). As a matter of fact, once he begins the process, he always has the script in the back of his mind, and he continually tinkers and adds things. This is demonstrated by the variety of kinds of paper upon which he writes notes to himself—the existence in the archives of notes on a piece of paper from Air Mauritus written while he was on holiday is one of the most notable examples of this habit.

Artists create in the medium best suited to their individual talents and best designed to convey what they are trying to express. Thus, Pinter found drama more conducive to his themes and abilities than prose. As his career progressed, he found that the cinema allowed him artistic explorations not available in the theatre, and he has allocated his energies accordingly. Two of the screenwriter's film scripts contain depictions of movie making (*The Last Tycoon* and *The French Lieutenant's Woman*). In both cases, as is true in many of his scripts, for screen and stage, illusion is foregrounded as part of the author's exploration of the nature of the perception of reality. Since film is a perfect medium for this kind of exploration, it seems a fine fit for both Pinter's interests and talents. Despite Fran Lebowitz's contention "Screenwriting is not an art form, it is a punishment from God," Pinter clearly finds the genre his métier.

The Servant

RELEASED: Venice Film Festival, September 3, 1963; American premiere, New York
Film Festival, September 16, 1963; British premiere, London, November 14,
1963

SOURCE: *The Servant,* by Robin (Sir Robert) Maugham; novel (1948)

AWARDS: British Screenwriters Guild Award (1964); New York Film Critics Best
Writing Award (1964); *New York Times* listing, one of the ten best films of
the year; Silver Ribbon (Nastro d'argento) for Best Foreign Film, Italy
(1966); Las Jornadas Internacionales de Cine (Spain), Castillo de Plata Cine
Club, Irun. Also won British Academy Awards for Best British Actor
(Bogarde) and for Best Black and White Cinematography. Other nomina-
tions included British Academy Award for Best Film and Best British Film;
New York Film Critics Circle Awards for Best Actor (Bogarde), Best
Direction, and Best Film.

PRODUCTION COMPANY: Landau/Springbok-Elstree; released by Warner-Pathe

DIRECTOR: Joseph Losey

EDITOR: Reginald Mills

DIRECTOR OF PHOTOGRAPHY: Douglas Slocombe

PRODUCERS: Joseph Losey and Norman Priggen

PRODUCTION DESIGN: Richard MacDonald

ARTISTIC DIRECTOR: Ted Clements

MUSIC COMPOSER AND CONDUCTOR: John Dankworth

COSTUME DESIGNER: Beatrice Dawson

CAST: Dirk Bogarde (Hugo Barrett), James Fox (Tony), Sarah Miles (Vera), Wendy
Craig (Susan Stewart), Derek Tansley (Head Waiter), Dorothy Bromily (Girl
in Phone Box), Ann Firbank (Society Woman), Harold Pinter (Society Man),
Patrick Magee (Bishop), Alun Owen (Curate), Doris Knox (Older Woman),
Jill Melford (Younger Woman), Richard Vernon (Lord Mountset), Catherine
Lacey (Lady Mountset), Chris Williams (Cashier in Coffee Bar), Brian Phelan
(Man in Pub), Alison Subohm (Girl in Pub), Hazel Terry (Woman in
Bedroom), Philippa Hare (Girl in Bedroom), Gerry Duggan (Waiter)

RUNNING TIME: 115 minutes[1]
BLACK AND WHITE
RATING: Not rated
VIDEO: Thorne EMI

ROBIN (SIR ROBERT) MAUGHAM'S 1948 novella *The Servant* was the source for Pinter's first movie script. Pinter wrote a screen version of *The Servant,* intending it for Michael Anderson; he rewrote it almost completely when Losey decided to do the film.[2] Losey had seen the Armchair Theatre television broadcast of *A Night Out* and wrote to Pinter to express his admiration.[3] Starring Dirk Bogarde as the servant Hugo Barrett, the movie, Britain's entry at the Venice Film Festival and later at the first New York Film Festival, opened in London in November of 1963.[4] Besides *The Servant,* the British entries for the Venice Festival were *Tom Jones* and *Billy Liar* (Francesco Rosi's *Mani sulla citta* won the Golden Lion). In spite of being an official entrant, the film languished in the can and even in England was considered unreleasable. It was actually withheld by the producers, Associated British Pathe (ABP), from the London Film Festival, despite the festival organizers' invitation. Then Richard Roud requested that the film be included in the New York Film Festival in September. This event seemed to be the key, and critical reception when the movie opened in London on November 14 was full of lavish praise.

In his interview with Bensky for the *Paris Review,* the scenarist reveals the novella's source of appeal to him when discussing the repeated theme of dominance and subservience in his plays and its particular application to his short story "The Examination" as a question of "Who was dominant at what point": "That's something of what attracted me to do the screenplay of *The Servant . . .* [the] battle for positions" (362–63). The early confrontation between Tony and Barrett in which Tony invites his prospective servant to sit down is the first indication of this theme, for by forcing the other man to take a seat, Tony temporarily enjoys a one-up position. This seating game appears in several early Pinter dramas (notably *The Room* and *The Birthday Party*) as a means of demonstrating dominance.

Only fifty-five pages in length, the story is narrated by one Richard Merton, who details the moral corruption of his friend Tony during the first two years after World War II. Recently demobilized after five years' service in the Orient, Tony moves into an apartment with his manservant Barrett and Barrett's niece, Vera, who is to work as a maid. Tony's girlfriend, Sally

The Servant (1963). Dirk Bogarde as the manservant Barrett and James Fox as Tony.
Avco Embassy Pictures. Jerry Ohlinger Archives.

Grant, starts to worry about Barrett's influence on Tony, and the theme is
set. Like Tony's ex-nanny, Barrett "insulates" him "from a cold drab world"
(Maugham, 31) to the extent that he eventually rejects Sally, Merton, his
other friends, and his work, even though he has discovered that Vera was
Barrett's mistress, brought along to seduce her employer.

Pinter improved the product as a film. The narrator is discarded, and a secondary conflict grows out of the fiancée's relationship with the manservant, although the fundamental theme of the movie is domination as related to the male characters. Barrett appears infrequently in the novel and often only at second hand when he is mentioned in someone's gossip. He is seldom seen in person. As a matter of fact, he is not even introduced until nearly one-sixth of the way into the book, and when he is presented, it is clear from Tony's remark, "I've given up trying to control him," that the servant dominates his master easily from the beginning (Maugham, 16). There is no sense of conflict between the two men and no tracing of the breakdown of Tony's character. This is because of Maugham's conception of Barrett's nature; like John Keats's Lamia, Barrett, who is described as a snake, is fundamentally evil. Tony is "lazy, and he likes to be comfortable," according to the narrator, so Barrett's method is simple: "He's found out Tony's weakness, and he's playing on it" (20). The basic difference between the novelist's approach and Pinter's is that in the first instance a tale is told, simply and briefly recounting something that has happened, whereas the scenarist *demonstrates* the events taking place, leading his audience to a psychological understanding of not only what has happened but also why it has happened. Maugham's work is less imaginative.

In the novel, Sally is a minor character; in the movie, with her name changed to Susan Stewart (acted by Wendy Craig) and incorporating Merton's role and point of view, she becomes the principal force trying to undermine Barrett's unhealthy influence. She fails, however, and by the conclusion, there has been a role switch between Tony (James Fox) and his servant à la Pinter's *A Slight Ache*, "The Examination," and *The Basement*. The latent homosexuality of the book is toned down, too, making it more ambiguous and thereby emphasizing the theme of domination.[5] In the novel the obscuring of the homosexual element is accomplished by having the narrator return to Tony's flat in a final attempt to woo him away from Barrett, only to find that the servant has introduced another girl into the household to entertain his master and himself; in the movie it is Susan who makes the last attempt, arriving at Tony's in the midst of an orgy. She tries to arouse Tony into realizing the situation by ridiculing Barrett, but Tony is incapable of breaking his servant's hold on him, and the kiss serves more tellingly to demonstrate the reversal of roles that has taken place.

There are additional minor differences between Maugham's original and

Pinter's adaptation, including the move of the apartment from the basement, the inclusion of the ball game on the stairs and the army comradeship talk between Tony and his manservant, the fact that Tony rather than Merton discovers Barrett and Vera together in the film, and Vera's rejoining the two men in the film instead of turning to prostitution. Basically, though, the changes that Pinter makes grow out of his attitude toward the material contained in Maugham's story. The novel has a marked sense of a morality play, with the characters obviously representing several of the deadly sins. Everything is clear-cut and almost preordained, because Barrett is equated with evil. Thus, Vera represents lust, her father stands for avarice, and Tony symbolizes the love of comfort and ease, a combination of sloth and gluttony. When Pinter turns these elements into a psychological study, the tale becomes interesting and moving.

Discussing the alterations that he effected, Pinter says, "I followed it [the novel] up. I think I did change it in a number of ways. I cut out the particular, a narrator in fact, which I didn't think was very valuable to a film, but I think I did change it quite a lot in one way or another, but I kept to the main core at the same time the end is not quite the same ending that it was in the book. I must have carte blanche you know, to explore it."[6]

In fact, Losey was attracted to the script (for which Pinter received £3,000) because of scenes not in the novel—Barrett's rehiring, the final party, and so on—but he was also actively engaged in the rewriting of the script.[7] He noted that Pinter had "already written a screenplay which I thought was 75 percent bad and unproducible, but had a number of scenes which were not changed as they reached the screen. I gave him a very long list of rewrites which enraged him, and we had an almost disastrous first session. He said he was not accustomed to being worked with this way—neither was I, for that matter—but he came to see me the next day, I tore up the notes, and we started through the script" (Milne, *Losey on Losey,* 152).

The changes and additions give Pinter some flexibility to pursue his characteristic interests. The Pinter brand of humor and dialogue both appear in the film (including, incidentally, a scene in a French restaurant that features Pinter and Patrick Magee and Alun Owen, colleagues from the Ian McMaster repertory tour days, in bit parts). The confused, meaningless, yet funny social small talk that the author captures so well in demonstrating the lack of communication between people is evident in Tony's meeting with Susan's parents, Lord and Lady Mountset:

LADY MOUNTSET. That's where the Ponchos are, of course, on the plains.

SUSAN. Ponchos?

LORD MOUNTSET. South American cowboys.

SUSAN. Are they called Ponchos?

LORD MOUNTSET. They were in my day.

SUSAN. Aren't they those things they wear? You know, with the slit in the middle for the head to go through?

LORD MOUNTSET. What do you mean?

SUSAN. Well, you know . . . hanging down in front and behind . . . the cowboy.

LADY MOUNTSET. They're called cloaks, dear.[8]

In addition, as pointed out by John Russell Taylor, "Tony's house is a sophisticated upper-class extension of the recurrent symbol in Pinter's early plays, the room-womb which offers a measure of security in an insecure world, an area of light in the surrounding darkness. But here the security is a trap sprung on the occupant by his own promptings and by the servant who embodies them and knows too well how to exploit them" (*"Guest,"* 38–39).[9] The film, then, fits into Pinter's artistic development perfectly, coming between *A Slight Ache* and *The Lover,* for in his writing for the theatre at this time, the playwright was beginning to shift his attention from examining the disintegration of individuals in the presence of outside, physical menace to exploring the interior, psychological source of that menace.

Considering that *The Servant* was the author's first attempt at screenwriting, the result is especially impressive. Both thematically and stylistically, the film is clearly related to the comedies of menace that he had been writing for the stage since 1957. It also contains many of the elements that appeared in the movie scripts that he wrote over the next several years—a black-and-white film, adapted from a novel (a novella, really), directed by Losey, focusing on the concept of domination, and liberally sprinkled with humorous Pinteresque dialogue. An examination of the opening and closing sequences of the film illustrates how the screenwriter used Maugham's morality tale as his source but turned it into a unique piece of art when translating the prose to a cinematic medium.[10]

Chapter 1 in the novel provides the exposition and introduces the characters. While not much is revealed about the narrator, who has joined a publishing firm, it is clear that he and Tony are from the same social class.

An orphan, Tony had left Cambridge, where he was reading law, and joined Merton's regiment in August 1939; his joining the regiment as a trooper was an indication of his democratic nature, which came through in spite of his upper-class upbringing. The last time that the two men had seen each other was five years previous to the beginning of the story—Tony had just received orders transferring him from their tank brigade to a post in the Far East. His disappointment at the separation from the regiment, which "had taken the place of a family in his life," was evident: "he was standing in the desert with his head tilted defiantly to the sky and his eyes full of tears" (Maugham, 9).

Prior to their reunion, this sketchy outline of Tony's background, combined with his jesting on the telephone when the two men first reestablish contact, is all that is revealed about him to depict his character. A rough physical picture is provided when Merton sits in the bathroom while Tony bathes in the tub in his flat on Ebury Street, but it is only when Tony mentions Sally that he takes on a personality for the rest of the chapter. Merton explains how excited Tony is to have returned to London after a five-year absence, comments on Sally's love for him, and describes the finding of a house for Tony. The chapter concludes with Tony's complaint that his "daily," the housekeeper, cannot cook and the narrator's suggestion that he employ a manservant.

The concluding chapter of the novel finds the narrator making a final visit to Tony's house, as Susan does in the movie, in a desperate last attempt to save him from Barrett's Svengali-like influence. Tony is lost, though, and not simply to a "plain love of comfort" (Maugham, 60). Merton accuses Barrett of destroying his victims "from within": "He helps them destroy themselves by serving their particular weakness." Thus, the double meaning of the book's title becomes evident. Vera, Barrett's "niece"/mistress, has succumbed to lust, Merton claims, and her father to avarice. Yet, Tony is even more completely damned, for, as soon becomes apparent, it is not just the love of comfort that has led to the dissipation and dissolution of his character. When the young girl arrives, it is clear that his very moral fiber has been corrupted by his indulging in illicit and perverting pleasures of the flesh. Early on Tony had asserted that he could get rid of Barrett anytime that he wanted to (31); by the end of the novel it is obvious that he can no more forgo Barrett's services than an addict can reject the source of the addiction.

When Pinter adapted Maugham's novel to the screen, he altered its thematic emphasis subtly and therefore was forced to adjust the presentation of the story as well. The film *The Servant* is not the novel *The Servant*—and it

Pinter's first notes for the opening sequence of *The Servant*. Harold

is better. The focus on Barrett as a corrupting power gives the tale more depth and significance than the simpler morality tale of the degeneration of Tony's character under the influence of Barrett. All that Pinter does in the film script is designed to develop these points, but the twist that compounds the significance of the work is the growing awareness in the film of a subtext. Not only does Tony become dissolute as a result of his experience with Barrett,

4 Up steps. Ring
bell. Door open.
No answer. Sun -
shade. Look at
him from inside
hall. Bell. B writes
No knock h. Opens 1st door.
Empty. walks down.
Open garden door.
Garden overgrown.
5. B. up stairs. All
in fair order. Dark.
Looks out 1st floor
window to back.
Discerns Tony lying
in grass.
6 Garden. Tony's
body in grass.
From grass see
feet approach

Pinter Archives at the British Library. Courtesy Harold Pinter.

but Barrett, too, like Hester Pryne's husband in Nathaniel Hawthorne's *The Scarlet Letter,* gradually succumbs to the very degradation that he is promoting in Tony.

The double-edged-sword effect that Pinter develops depends on the impressions created in the opening scene of the film version. The initial shot in a movie is generally more important than the first lines of a novel or a play, for the visual image so easily can be used effectively to set up the structure and meaning of the whole picture that follows. While the more intellectually oriented content of words must be absorbed over time, the visual image is assimilated immediately and can be recalled throughout the work, more vividly and with less effort than words can be. The words may last longer in the final analysis, but the immediacy of the visual is certainly superior upon first exposure.

The shift from Tony to Barrett as protagonist in the film starts with the opening shot, which becomes a refrain as Pinter returns to it several times. The contrast between the openness of the initial shot and the darkness of the concluding shot, as well as the contrast between the characters, including Barrett at the beginning of the film and then at its end, reflects the movie's theme. Pinter establishes a benchmark immediately and then develops a sense of movement away from that standard throughout the rest of the film. The bearing, dress, purposeful walk, well-groomed hair, and overall demeanor of Barrett in the first few seconds of *The Servant* make the image of him at the conclusion all the more grotesque in comparison.

Although in the published screenplay there is only one exterior shot described in the opening, and the camera instructions are not included (Pinter, [3]), in the film there are two cuts. The first shot is a continuous pan of King's Road, Chelsea, that starts with a 180-degree revolve left from ground level to the tree tops and back to ground level, moves in on the seal of the Sanitary Engineers on the Thomas Crapper building, pulls back to reveal Barrett, and then follows him as he walks through a parklike area until he is about to cross the street. A cut picks him up coming across the street, and the camera follows as he enters the door of Tony's house.

The first shot is a long one, 1 minute and 55.8 seconds long (the average length of a shot in a theatrical film is 10 to 15 seconds).[11] The titles are run over, and music is heard. The music is modernistic and orchestral, primarily strings. No time setting is provided, and the military background described in Maugham's novel has been omitted, yet the time is surely late 1950s or early 1960s. Given this chronological setting, the approximate period of John Osborne's angry young men, the music is appropriate.

As soon as the camera picks up Barrett, the strings cut out and wind instruments, slightly discordant, take over, and as the picture progresses, a kind of Barrett-theme music develops as well, with a saxophone becoming the predominant instrument. The music, the black-and-white film stock emphasizing the shadowy somberness of an overcast October day, the leafless tree limbs, and the wet streets are all reminiscent of the films noirs of the 1940s and 1950s (and somewhat like Elia Kazan's rendering of *A Streetcar Named Desire*), and the atmosphere created by the shots themselves in combination with the film noir allusiveness is one of foreboding that is only partly offset by the initial tone of the music. There are a few bright, light moments in *The Servant,* but in general the grim, bleak film noir mood is unrelieved throughout, with the darkness and shadows reinforcing the darkness of the theme.

Social class and geographical locations as indicators of social class are details that Pinter pays attention to throughout his canon, whatever his medium. Whereas in the novel, when Tony writes that Vera has left Barrett for a bookie (Maugham, 49), no details of her location are provided, in the movie Pinter identifies the area to which she has moved, Wandsworth (Pinter, 46), thereby adding social commentary and simultaneously creating a sense of credibility, since Wandsworth is a lower-class community and the kind of place where a bookie might be expected to live. This detail, then, serves to denigrate Vera's character further.

Similarly, Pinter reenforces Maugham's social commentary by virtue of the establishing shot with which the movie begins. At this stage of his career, the screenwriter was certainly and consciously interested in the possibilities of film to "open out" a text, to "inform" it by involving the real world outside the characters' rooms, but there is more to the employment of this establishing shot than merely placing the story geographically and introducing an element of reality. Pinter has avoided the search for a house to let mentioned in the novel, for example, because that is tangential to his interest and would only diffuse the effect of placing an emphasis on Barrett. By lingering on the scenery in the vicinity of Knightsbridge Square, a nice albeit not posh residential area in west-central London, Pinter visually indicates Tony's social and economic status. This is an important detail, for as Losey says in commenting on the sociopolitical dimension of the story, "All the characters are products and victims of the same thing—class. The same trap. It's a story about the trap—the house and the society in which they live."[12]

Barrett is first seen in what is essentially a head shot, which establishes him as the main character in the film. He is neatly groomed and dressed, wearing a hat and a dark overcoat and swinging an umbrella as he alertly watches the traffic. The juxtaposition of the Sanitary Engineers' crest and Barrett's head is momentarily amusing (the contrast between the staid manservant and the image evoked by the signified profession), but there is also a suggestion that there may be some sort of hidden connection. Nevertheless, Barrett's motions are almost jaunty, and he glances about while he walks down the street, observing things about him, yet it is obvious that he knows where he is going. His movement is quick and deliberate.[13]

Barrett pauses to glance at the sold sign outside the house, which incidentally informs the audience that Tony is just now moving in, and after a cursory attempt to ring the bell, he enters through the front door, which has been left ajar. There is a cut to an interior view of Barrett coming through the door. The camera pans to the staircase, and the first natural noise in the movie is heard in the form of Barrett's nonsynchronous footsteps over. The camera pulls back to include Barrett in the shot—he starts up the stairs, hesitates, looks up toward the second floor, comes back, moves to the front window of the dressing room, and puffs his cheeks. It is significant that he also casually yet purposefully tears the wallpaper on this first trip up the stairs, for this action epitomizes the calculated destruction that he is so ready to visit upon the house's occupant. The camera moves away from Barrett again, passing over the shadow of his head that is cast on the wall, and then moves toward the rear of the house and the conservatory, where Tony is found asleep in an old deck chair.

Symbolically, there are several interesting aspects to this entrance. Barrett is an intruder, an unknown in someone else's house—Pinter's early dramas (*The Room, The Birthday Party, The Caretaker, A Slight Ache*) abound with this situation.[14] Barrett never calls out, but instead he moves through the house almost stealthily, nosing about uninvited, prying, moving through the shadows, occasionally silhouetted by light from the outside or against an open doorway. Furthermore, the stairway has obviously caught his attention. Is there symbolism in the contrast between the white banister bars and the dark top rail, or does this merely represent an interior decorator's color scheme? Does the upstairs represent a potential rise in class? Is each step, therefore, a rung on the cliché ladder of success? Is a distinction being made between a deteriorating mind and normalcy, as in Eugene O'Neill's *Long Day's Journey into Night*? After all, Tony's final appearance is on the floor upstairs, where he lies in a drugged stupor looking down uncomprehendingly through the balustrade. Or, does the upstairs represent a more Freudian component? After all, the downstairs is the formal living area, and it is the upstairs that holds the bedrooms. Still, Susan and Tony will kiss in the downstairs drawing room, and it is in the kitchen that the Tony-Vera seduction starts. But, it is in Tony's bathroom upstairs where Vera's sexuality is first encountered, it is the master's bedroom that Barrett and Vera invade, it is in Vera's bedroom where she and Barrett are seen together, and it is in the master bedroom where the orgy takes place in the film's final sequence. One might, therefore, conclude that to ascribe specific symbolic values to one part of the house relative to other parts of the house is unproductive. The seeming contradictions are probably better recognized as evidence of Pinter's concept of the mixed and uncertain nature of reality.

The importance of the staircase cannot be overemphasized, though. The banister bars are framed in the entrance sequence and many later scenes, often conveying a caging effect. Furthermore, the stairs are a bridge between the formal and the intimate sections of the house. Characters look up or down the stairwell at each other during critical confrontations, as when Susan moves the vase of flowers and when Barrett looks down on Tony and Susan after emerging from his tryst with Vera, Tony passes out at the top of the stairs (seen through and framed by the banister bars) at the end of the movie, and the tag-ball game is played on the stairs. The significance of this last incident is prepared for soon after Barrett meets Tony.

In the novel, the narrator meets Barrett after Tony has already engaged him. In the movie, Barrett and Tony's first meeting is seen. As it is useful for Pinter to skip over the house hunting, so it is important for him to insert this episode. The relative status of the men is determined, a comparison of their natures can be made, and the primary conflict is initiated, all of which the audience is exposed to firsthand.

Tony's house is untidy, and he is asleep when he has an appointment, sprawled out and unkempt, at three in the afternoon (so a clock's chimes announce). Upon emerging from his slothfulness, Tony appears a little uncertain and confused, unfocused particularly in comparison with Barrett, who is fully in control of himself and the situation.

The camera is utilized efficiently in *The Servant*, conveying information graphically but at the same time in a subdued manner. When the camera moves from the drawing room to the conservatory, Tony is at the center of the focus. The unconscious effect of peripherally observed flower pots on the shelves and crumpled papers scattered around the floor is to create a gestalt, a montage that impacts on a subconscious level and colors the viewer's perception of Tony before he ever speaks. When he awakens, his actions and words confirm the impression that has been forming in the audience's minds.

The constant use of camera pans and long tracking shots, the unifying effect of nonsynchronous sound bridges, and the myriad realistic details coalesce in a flowing pattern that sweeps the audience along emotionally. The linking of the visuals and the dialogue supports an intellectual understanding that parallels the emotional content. In one frame Barrett is positioned in a doorway with another doorway visible behind him. Above and behind his head a bare bulb hangs from the ceiling as he stands over Tony. It is almost as though Barrett can open other doors for Tony, bring him enlightenment out of the shadows. And, that Tony needs direction is evident, for he is in the foreground of the same frame, his face in close-up, turned toward the camera, his eyes closed. The implications of the composition of this shot are reenforced by the verbal exchange when Tony admits that he had "Too many beers at lunch" (Pinter, 4).

From the very beginning and for most of Pinter's writing career, he has been concerned with the relationship between characters in terms of dominance. In the Bensky interview, the author admitted that "the question of dominance and subservience . . . is possibly a repeated theme in my plays" (362). In discussing his thematic evolution, Pinter went on to single out "The Examination," which operated as a focal point for him. He realized that the story, which "dealt very explicitly with two people in a room having a battle of unspecified nature," was actually about domination.

Patterns and variations on patterns recur in Pinter's works. The basic plot of *The Servant,* a man and a woman in competition for a second man, is really not much different from the plot of his dramatic masterpiece *Old Times* (1971), in which a man and a woman are competing for the affections of a second woman. The plots are simply devices that function as metaphors to get at something more important that underlies the superficial action. In *Old Times,* Pinter is working on a second level of metaphor in that the theme of dominance is employed to reveal the nature of reality; in *The Servant* the concept of dominance is still his main concern. What he said about "The Examination" is applicable to the movie as well: "the question was one of who was dominant at what point and how they were going to be dominant and what tools they would use to achieve dominance and how they would try to undermine the other person's dominance. A threat is constantly there; it's got to do with this question of being in the uppermost position, or attempting to be. . . . it's a very common, everyday thing." From the reactions of Barrett and Tony at their first meeting, it is also clear that what Pinter means by dominance goes far beyond Stephen Potter's definition in *One-Upmanship*.

The first instance of a clash of wills comes almost instantly. As Giannetti and Eyman rightly note, "Their power struggle is not conveyed in words—which are evasive, oblique—but through the *mise en scène*. Pinter's dialogue is seldom where the real action is. The subtext, or what is implied beneath the words, is what's important. Characters often talk about perfectly neutral subjects, but the manner in which they speak, their hesitations and pauses, is how we come to understand the subcurrents of emotions. . . . This type of emotionally repressed audiovisual communication was refined in two other Losey-Pinter collaborations, *Accident . . .* and *The Go-Between*" (376).

Tony invites Barrett to "Come upstairs," a seemingly innocent request, but instead of following him, Barrett remains standing motionless with a suspicious look on his face (Pinter, 4). There is an implicit cognizance of the distinction between the superior and inferior positions on the stairs, reenforced in the later ball game. Only after Tony suggests that they can sit down does Barrett follow. The servant-to-be then quickly shifts positions with the boss-to-be and leads the way to the stairs, at which point Tony again takes the lead.

In a scene remindful of Goldberg and McCann's inquisition of Stanley in *The Birthday Party*, in which the sit-down game becomes deadly serious as an indicator of who is in control, Tony interviews Barrett. Barrett sits and is shown from the side and from the waist up. During the conversation, Tony walks behind him, reversing the perspective developed in the scene downstairs moments ago. The reversal of physical roles takes on a kinetic dimension as Tony walks about the room, directing the conversation. The camera effectively conveys the tension and the battle for position, rotating to follow Tony, keeping Barrett at the still point of the wheel. Sometimes Barrett is forced to look up at Tony, who is walking up-camera above him; sometimes Tony sits in the foreground, looming over Barrett, who is reduced by perspective in the background and appears small and huddled.

Tony has taken control, as befits someone of his social rank and in this situation. He informs Barrett that he is seeking a manservant (Barrett smiles slightly); he mentions that he has already seen some candidates for the position who were not "suitable" (Barrett clenches his jaw). Barrett mentions that he has served several members of the peerage, most recently Viscount Barr. Tony states that his father knew Lord Barr well, and in fact, they had died within a week of each other. This is an interesting exchange for three reasons. First, if Barr is dead, Tony cannot check Barrett's references. Second, there may be an indication of Barrett's pattern of taking over a household. Third, it seems more important for Tony to exert his dominance by claiming to have been on the same social level as Barr. Ironically, while it is likely that Tony is telling the truth, since the viscount is dead, Barrett has no more opportunity to check Tony's claim than Tony has to check his.

To some extent the inability of anyone, including the audience, to verify certain facts keeps everyone slightly off balance during the entire movie. This is one of Pinter's favorite devices and themes in his plays, too. Whether Vera married a bookie is the kind of question that occurs over and over in the movie, and there is no way of determining the truth, for mutually contradictory facts are offered with enthusiasm and a tone of honesty and sincerity. As John Russell Taylor perceptively pointed out in *Anger and After*, Pinter frequently utilizes the technique of "casting doubt upon everything by matching each apparently clear and unequivocal statement with an equally clear and unequivocal statement to its contrary" (325).

It is interesting to note that at this point in Pinter's published script there is a direction for a shot: "*Exterior. Gardens in the Square. Day. The gardens in the square, seen by* TONY *from the window.* BARRETT's *reflection in the pane*" (5). The use of the reflection here helps set up the numerous reflections in mirrors, windows, and puddles of water that are found throughout the movie with such frequency that they take on the significance of a motif. The distorting effect of such images is discussed later, but the importance of this image is not only that it prepares for what is to come but also that it is an *image*—and the two men are mightily concerned with surfaces, with how they appear to one another. The screenwriter is concerned with how they appear to the audience as well, and Barrett's *reflection* implies a tenuousness of character, a shadowy creature who is not quite real or true (like the shadows in Plato's cave and foreshadowing Anna's presence in the opening moments of *Old Times*).

Doubly interesting is the fact that this shot is excised from the film. Instead, the bracketing shots become part of the rotating camera movement just described. Creating a cinematically more dynamic shot, the moving camera emphasizes the shifting relationship between the two characters without diminishing the inference that Tony is in control.

Due to a small production budget, Losey was forced to make several major cuts in the script. In addition, according to Caute, he edited out twenty minutes of the completed film. Among the cuts were a scene in which Barrett is seen sleeping with his landlady and then hurrying to Fuller's cake shop to satisfy her sweet tooth. Losey apparently regretted having to cut the scene, for he declared that the setup—the walls of Barrett's room were covered with pages from "cheap sex magazines," "pornographic calendars," and the like—was "one of the best I've ever done" (Caute, *Joseph Losey*, 5). The cut reduces Pinter's emphasis on the servant's libido.

The one-upmanship game continues when Tony, who in the novel had complained about Mrs. Jackson's lack of culinary ability, asks Barrett if he can cook. When Barrett replies that he takes "a great deal of pride" in his cooking and that his soufflés have been praised, Tony asks if he knows how to prepare Indian dishes, a more exotic menu. When Barrett answers "a little," Tony reduces that accomplishment by declaring that he himself knows "a hell of a lot" about such food. The scene ends pleasantly with Tony admitting that in addition to doing the cooking, Barrett will be needed to do "everything."

The next scene takes place in a dark restaurant where Tony and his fiancée are discovered dancing. In this scene the couple are at ease, and Tony continues to demonstrate that he is in full control. This is evident first by his explanation of his plans for the future and second by his treatment of the head waiter (Derek Tansley). His ambition, sense of purpose, and self-confidence all come through clearly as he describes his proposal to develop three cities in the Brazilian jungle.

There are several elements in this scene that illuminate Pinter's cinematic approach. To begin the scene, the author has employed a jump cut. Although there are definitely structural, thematic, and character connections in the film, he takes advantage of the medium's ease of transition between scenes to develop his parallel plots and subplots and to increase tension by not resolving plot developments immediately, to illustrate the relationships between the plot lines, and to embrace what is essentially an intellectual theme with a sensation of animation. The physical movement and the vitality of the intense emotional conflict counterbalance the depressing events and the dreary images that he creates to express his theme.

The jump cut keeps the audience a bit unbalanced, so that an understanding of the direction that the plot is taking is delayed, building the impression that there is something wrong somewhere and increasing the audience's uneasiness at not being able to identify the source of the problem easily and quickly. The psychological content is the key, of course, and just as Antonioni was willing to subject his audience to tedious hours in *L'avventura* (1959) as part of his attempt to show how boring life was to a special segment of Italian society, so Pinter is willing to force psychological reactions on his audience in order to reenforce the psychological content of his theme.

All of this is further enhanced when the audience is suddenly thrust not only into a noisy, frenetic dance floor scene but into the midst of a conversation as well. By entering the scene and the conversation in medias res, Pinter has avoided filling in the gaps of how and why the couple is there so that he can concentrate on the pertinent conversation. He has carried over into film his dramatic style, too, in which the audience is exposed to disconnected snatches of conversation and never supplied with a complete context into which the conversation can be placed. This is realistic, of course, this avoiding of Shavian-style exposition, for the characters involved in the conversation share a common background (at least insofar as the progress of the conversation itself is concerned) and therefore do not need to explicate their allusions.

Tony's condescending attitude toward the waiter contrasts with his attentive, almost fawning treatment of Susan. He kisses her hand in the film, though not in the screenplay, and she responds to him coyly when he asks what she thinks of his idea—she says that it is "Cozy," inserting a double entendre as though she is responding to his comment about his needing a rest. With the waiter, however, Tony is curt, abrupt. He refuses a bottle of wine, claiming that it is "corked," thereby demonstrating his self-assured nature. Moreover, he virtually ignores the man and speaks to him in an almost hostile tone, as opposed to the soft tone with which he addresses Susan. While not a major factor in most of Pinter's work, the awareness of class distinction is, nonetheless, a minor constant that runs through the canon, and it is a consciousness of this differentiation that is conveyed by Tony's demeanor. Given Barrett's status, such an obvious distinction on Tony's part makes his subsequent transformation all the more dramatic.

While none of the foregoing scene is included in Maugham's novel, Pinter does change one bit of information that is present in his original. Maugham's Tony had been studying for the bar before entering military service, and on his return he again prepared to become a barrister, a fact alluded to on a number of occasions. Pinter's Tony is involved in developing cities, a creative profession even though it is never made clear exactly what his position is, for whom he works, or what his training is. Of course, none of this is really relevant to the story, but it is suggestive that the Tony in the novel seems interested in the law because he is not interested in anything else and because a law practice will mean a good income (Maugham, 17), whereas in the film Tony appears to be genuinely interested in a career that is a challenge and that will be of service to his fellow man. He mentions that the Brazilian cities will be inhabited by thousands of peasants from Asia Minor—as he says, they are having "a rough time of it" and this will mean "a new life" for them

(Pinter, 6). The somewhat suspect career is replaced by a humanistic one. As a result, he becomes a more admirable if naive character. Pinter is consciously setting Tony up for an Aristotelian fall.

The next couple of scenes reflect Pinter's methods for adapting the novel to the screen. The saxophone music heard at the end of the previous scene is a bridge to the shot of Tony and Susan on a blanket together before the drawing-room fireplace, though it is more romantic in mood than the up-beat rhythm and tone that accompanied the restaurant visuals. The camera movements are an amalgam of typical setups and innovative combinations. In the film script the shot is an interior one; in the film there is an exterior establishing shot of Tony's house, a pan to the drawing-room window, and a cut to the inside of the window. (Incidentally, the screenplay's *"electric fire"* is replaced by an actual fire—a more romantic touch.) It is at this point that Tony informs Susan that he has hired a manservant, something the novel's narrator found out unexpectedly.

The following scene contains the first hint in the movie that Barrett is beginning to seek a dominant position. As Tony and Barrett mount the stairs, moving between working men (who are not mentioned in the scenario), Tony describes the color that he wants the walls painted—mostly white (7). Barrett suggests that other colors would be chic. Tony concedes, "Just a wall" (8), which seems to satisfy Barrett, but Barrett goes on, almost under his breath, to say, "Oh yes, just a wall, sir, *here and there*" (emphasis mine). Just a wall would be seen as a tasteful suggestion; "here and there" goes beyond the suggestion and subtly imposes Barrett's grasping control in the relationship in such a way that Tony seems oblivious to the manipulation. In the novel the redecoration that Merton describes has already taken place when he vis-its the house, and the servant's role in the transformation is communicated secondhand when Tony explains that the compliments for the improvements are due Barrett.

In the subsequent sequence, Pinter has again incorporated material from the novel into the film script, but in an altered form. Tony and Barrett are seen discovering the box room in the film, and Barrett observes that it will be satisfactory for a maid. Tony thinks that a cleaning woman might be more suitable, but Barrett states ironically that maids can be "useful" in much the same manner as when he shifted control slightly with his comment on wall colors. In the novel Tony announces to the narrator that he will be taking in Barrett's niece (23), and this follows Barrett's walking in on Tony and Susan. As a matter of fact, the interruption scene in the novel (Maugham, 20–21) is reproduced in the film with little change. As will be seen below, the minimal change consists of the scene being expanded a bit and seen instead of being described by Sally.

The importance of the scene in developing an understanding of Susan's reaction to Barrett is thus emphasized in the film and prepares for the clash of wills between Susan and Barrett symbolized in the sickroom scene when the placing of a vase of flowers becomes pivotal. In the novel Susan describes the events in the sickroom to Merton immediately after reporting the interruption incident. In the novel this second tale follows the interruption scene, too, but there is a fairly long separation between the maid statement and the interruption.

In the screenplay Barrett's gradual exercising of control and Tony's willingness to let him do so is depicted in two shots, first when Barrett haughtily instructs the painters, and then when Tony asks how the workmen are doing. Barrett informs his master that he is keeping an eye on the workers (9). Incidentally, there are a couple of words of dialogue added in the film that do not appear in the printed script when Barrett announces that he is serving a green salad. Tony asks Barrett to bring him something and Barrett replies, "I was just about to, sir." This amplifies the budding realization that the servant is not only catering to his master's wishes but that he is beginning to anticipate them as well. Ultimately, this pattern will progress to the point that Tony will lose the will to do anything for himself.

Here Pinter inserts another sequence in the movie that is not included in the novel, and this insertion is especially interesting because on the surface it appears to be the kind of scene that Pinter would cut—he shows Tony and Susan arriving at Tony's house. The reason that this scene is included is threefold: one, Tony is seen to be lively and happy in Susan's presence; two, Susan is seen meeting Barrett; three, Susan reacts to the household furnishings, and a bit of Pinteresque humor is added through the dinner-table conversation, which lightens the tension of the rising action. Once more, the contrast between Tony at the beginning of the tale and at the end is established by his portrayal in these early scenes. When Susan and Barrett meet, he is very formal, neat, and precise. She does refuse to let him take her coat, though, so even in this first encounter between the two, Susan is not at ease with the servant. Whether she does not want him to do his job or whether she is uncomfortable in unveiling herself in front of him is not clear. However innocuous the act may be, she may perceive it as being symbolically informed. Her perception is reenforced by the shot of the three as they enter the drawing room, for they are seen in the large, round, fish-eye wall mirror that reflects Tony's taste in decorating and which figures prominently in later shots.[15] The curvature of the mirror distorts the images slightly as Tony is seen in the foreground moving toward the audience, Barrett stands in the background against a wall, and Susan passes from left to right between them.

Whether she intuitively recognizes his nature or is already jealous of his role vis-à-vis Tony is not clear either. In her brusqueness and attempt to ignore Barrett, there is an enlightening parallel with Tony's treatment of the waiter. Her class consciousness sets her apart from Barrett except in the most superficial contact, yet Tony, who displayed the same attitude with the waiter, has apparently begun to consider Barrett in a different light. The social context of the friction between the fiancée and the servant is manifest when Susan examines the decor. Barrett proudly notes that the "simple and classic" is always best. Susan, looking at "a heavy ornament" (Pinter, 10), which in the film is a large, dark, somewhat Reubenesque oil painting of a naked woman surrounded by cherubs and bearded men, observes that, rather than classic, the artwork is "pre-historic." She also has the good taste to choose to sit in the chair that was Tony's mother's favorite. In a sense Susan and Barrett are competing to serve Tony in a motherly fashion, though the tasks that Barrett does (cooking, grocery shopping, housecleaning) are more "motherly"—or wifely— than anything that Susan does.

At this juncture there is a scene in the printed scenario that appears in neither the novel nor the film. Tony and Susan chat over drinks, and Susan jokes about Barrett: "Have you checked his criminal record?" Barrett appears at the door and reminds Tony to ring when he wants dinner served. Susan's joke reenforces the impression that she dislikes and mistrusts Barrett, and his needless reminder prepares for the more noteworthy interruption that is to follow. The cutting of references to incidents in the novel ("Does he bring you breakfast in bed" and "women are no damned good. They can't cook") and Susan's humorous remark is not critical. The preparation for Barrett's subsequent intrusion on the couple's privacy might help explain Susan's vehement reaction, though it is certainly not crucial either.

Removing the scripted scene has advantages. Whereas she had thought the house "beautiful" before Barrett remarked on the "simple and classic" style, in the scene at the dinner table that now follows, Susan comments that the "whole place needs brightening," and she moves to regain some status by declaring that she will "organize a proper spice shelf." Placing these two scenes next to each other emphasizes the link between them.

The inclusion of two typically Pinteresque elements here heightens this effect too. When Barrett serves the wine, Susan says that his white gloves are "ducky." When Barrett notes that the practice is Italian, that the gloves are "used in Italy," the repetition is characteristic of Pinter's dialogue, and Susan's response, "Who by?" is representative of his humor as well, showing a logical break on the one hand and stating the author's contention that one should not assume anything on the other. Directly thereafter, Pinter's fondness for playing with words and sound is widened in the three-way exchange about the wine:

BARRETT: Just a Beaujolais, sir, but a good bottler.

SUSAN: A good what?

TONY: Bottler. (11)

The social discrepancy between servant and master is highlighted in the next scene, in which Barrett is sitting at the kitchen table, picking his teeth with a wooden match, which he flips to the floor. A bottle of beer or ale sits before him, and he smokes a cigarette.

The Barrett theme is heard over, an oboe and saxophone dominating, and connects this scene with the following scene, in which Tony is shown arriving home in the snow and stepping into a puddle of water. Tony has a cold, further evidence that he is losing control, and Barrett ministers to him by pouring salts into a bowl of warm water for the master to soak his feet in as he sits in front of the drawing-room fire. The camera moves from Tony's bare feet splashing in the salt bath to a later time and Susan's stockinged feet in a *"Close shot."* The camera travels along her legs and body, then pulls back to reveal Susan lying on the sofa and Tony sprawled on the floor beside the same fireplace as in the previous shot. It is obvious that Barrett and Susan are trying to win Tony over by appealing to his desire for comfort, even though the nature of the comfort that they provide is different. While Pinter may call for only some of the shots involved in this sequence, the essence is contained in the film script but not present in the novel at all.

Throughout the rest of the scene, Cleo Laine is heard singing "All Gone." In tone and phrasing, the words of the song are reminiscent of the poetry that Pinter wrote early in his career. Ostensibly a love ballad, "All Gone" is definitely not romantic. The opening lyrics may suggest a torchy blues song, but the middle section certainly conveys a different message:

Now while I love you alone
Now while I love you alone
Now while I love you

Can't love without you
Must love without you . . . alone.
Don't stay to see me

Turn from your arms
Leave it alone
It's all gone
Give me my death

Close my mouth
Give me my breath
Close my mouth (42–43)

The morbid imagery functions as a foreshadowing device.

During the scene, Tony's deterioration is further revealed in the dialogue. Susan asks him if he has had any news from his "new frontier," perhaps an ironic reference to the social programs of John F. Kennedy. Kennedy's vision, like Tony's, was to create a grand new world, and the fact that Tony's plans will not be realized encodes the conversation with ironic overtones. That Tony's deterioration is starting to move beyond his physical state to affect his emotional state as well is disclosed in his reply that there is not any news, that the unidentified "he" with whom he is working has encountered some delays. It is interesting that Tony seems incapable of handling any of his affairs (love, business, or household) by himself, relying instead on others both to initiate and to carry through any action. When Tony admits that the whole idea is in a "very preliminary stage," he is showing the beginnings of the debilitating loss of power, purpose, and control that will soon engulf him.

The ascendance of Barrett is mirrored in the fact that the servant has installed Tony's new abstract sculpture in the garden. A line of dialogue has been added in the movie: Susan says to Tony, "you terrible, lazy . . . ," a comment that shows that she understands the source of Barrett's strength. Her reaction is to try to combat the servant's increasing influence by using her sexual appeal, and she kisses Tony. This leads to Tony asking her to marry him, at which point Barrett intrudes unannounced, effectively breaking the mood. Susan will try to reestablish her relationship with Tony, but this is really the turning point, and although it is not clear yet, she has already lost him.

Pinter's screenplay calls for Barrett to walk into the room without any warning. This could lead to the conclusion that the entrance is a mistimed accident or that it is carefully planned, timed to make the greatest possible impression on the couple. In the film there is a shot of Barrett carrying a tray and approaching the closed door from the outside. He hesitates, and though a knock is heard, he tilts his head toward the door and moves his hand as though he is about to knock. In this case his intrusion when there has been no reaction to his knock is indiscreet but does not necessarily indicate any scheming on his part. It does confirm his explanation to Tony later, in both the script and the picture, that he did knock.

More important, however, is how the addition of the shot affects the interpretation of Tony's character. There is a cut back to Tony and Susan in the room, but instead of Barrett coming in, excusing himself, and leaving, Susan lying still, and then Tony standing, Tony jumps up and fairly quickly moves to the other side of the room to turn on the light. Barrett comes in and sets down the tray, and then leaves. The difference is that Tony and Susan are seen acting guiltily, as though they are teenagers caught in a compromising situation by one of their parents. This delineation of Tony's character prepares for later scenes, particularly those relating to Vera, in which his attitude is one of a child's betrayal of a parent's trust and expectations.

As the scene ends, Susan, who has complained about Barrett ("couldn't he live out?"), invites Tony to come home and stay with her. The composition of the shot is telling: Susan's and Tony's heads are in profile facing one another in the foreground, framed by the bookcase door, Susan's face illuminated and Tony's in shadow, while the dark figure of Barrett, centered between them, lurks in the background. A vase of flowers stands on a table in the entrance hall. Over the scene is heard a clock's chimes tolling midnight— and bringing to mind a Cinderella motif when the magic ends and the carriage turns back into a pumpkin.

The scene concludes with Barrett acting solicitous about Tony's health, and the next scene opens with Susan entering Tony's sickroom to voice similar sentiments. Several lines are added in the film, an exchange between Tony and Barrett, mostly Pinteresque semirepetitions (Tony follows Barrett's "I expect you caught a bit of a chill the other day in the rain, sir," with "Yes. Rain. The other day"), and the greeting between Tony and Susan when she enters the bedroom. Nothing tremendously significant appears to have been gained by the additions, although Tony seems to be a little put out with Barrett's overly concerned, even tender, manner (Tony petulantly refuses an offered hot drink) and the entrance is brighter in contrast to the previous shot, with Tony obviously pleased to see Susan gaily come into the room.

The vase-moving sequence features a series of shifting points of view. Susan and Barrett are both shown in one-shots, and as they observe one another, the camera shoots point of view up or down the stairwell accordingly. After she has taken the flowers into Tony's room, Susan knows that Barrett will try to remove them; while lying across the bed but ninety degrees away from the table on which she has placed the flowers, Susan tells Barrett to leave them alone the moment he picks up the vase. She may have won the battle, for Tony supports her by having the manservant leave the vase alone, but Susan has essentially lost the war when he reminds her that Barrett "may be a servant but he's still a human being!" This is one of the scenes, complete with dialogue, that appears in both the novel and the film. The slight alterations that Pinter has made are designed to display Susan's character more fully than is done in the original by placing her in the room with Tony alone at first and changing Barrett's dialogue to third-person reporting by Tony. For instance, Barrett's "I'm afraid we can't allow flowers in our patient's room, can we, sahr?" is cut and replaced by Tony's "he was saying that they're bad in a sickroom at night." By removing some of the sense that Tony and Barrett are acting in concert, Pinter can show Susan to better advantage and delay showing the demise of her dominance. If Susan still has control, the tension from the conflict and the suspense over the outcome are still operating. The symbolic moralistic battle between good and evil continues, and the fact that Tony is still wavering shows him to be of a stronger nature than was evident in the book.

The contest of wills is presented more intensely in the film than in Maugham's telling. Rather than Susan's relating what occurred, it takes place in silence, in the stairwell, out of Tony's view, clearly understood by the two participants, who watch each other so carefully; Susan hesitates, evidencing a momentary feeling of terror, perhaps, when she moves to take the vase, knowing that Barrett is cognizant of what she is doing and why.

The changes in the dialogue are primarily stylistic. Tony's admonition to Susan, "Please try not to cross Barrett every time you come here. If he goes it'll be a cracking bore," becomes "I do wish you'd stop yapping at Barrett all the time. It'll be a bastard if he leaves," for example. The wording, "yapping" instead of "cross," conveys the subtle difference between how Pinter and Maugham delineate their characters, and the general phrasing may be harsher, more 1960s in tone and texture in Pinter's lines, but again, the changes are not vital.

The ultimate temptation, the procuring of fleshly pleasures, is now introduced. In the novel most of what transpires is learned through the narrator's conversations with Tony, Mrs. Toms, and Susan. In the film, Pinter develops the arrival of Susan's replacement (in the one area where Barrett could probably not replace her himself) through a montage of crosscuts. As the previous scene ends, Barrett plays with Susan when he tells her at the door that "it's not very encouraging" and pauses, as though he is commenting on the doctor's visit the day before—and then says he is talking about the weather. When he flips the door closed behind her, Barrett demonstrates that he feels that he is about to gain the upper hand, and when Susan pauses, embracing the lamp post outside (which she will return to later), a horrid look on her face in close-up, the door to Tony's house closed behind her, it is evident that she realizes that she may no longer be able to compete.

The introduction of Vera is Barrett's trump card, and one that he has had up his sleeve for some time—"You got my last letter, didn't you?" he asks on the telephone. The shot of Susan's feet running down the dreary, wet street, which dissolves into a shot of the four young girls descending upon the phone booth creates a linking of the two scenes. The transition from Susan scurrying off in fright amid blowing leaves to the bouncing steps of the girls contrasts Susan's mood and Barrett's state of mind nicely, and when the girls converge on the phone box in which Barrett is standing, the intellectual content of the two scenes is likewise connected. Barrett can feel superior because he is bringing in reenforcements. Ironically, the best reenforcements that Susan will be able to muster are Agatha and Willy Mountset, in a humorous scene described below. Barrett's blank look as the girls' skirts swirl about their legs implies that he is uninterested in sex, and it may be that his alliance with Vera is more to satisfy her lust than to fulfill any sexual needs of his own. He does accuse her of being a nymphomaniac, of course, so there is no emotional tie between servant and girl, yet she can be kept happy, thus ensuring that she will be around to ensnare Tony—and that she has the appetite and the appeal to do so.

To mark the passage of time, to remark on the removal of Susan's influence, represented by her chintz frills being taken off of the dressing table (they have not "seen very much" of her recently), and to prepare for keeping

Vera on "if she's any good," there is a short scene of Barrett serving Tony some mulled claret (recalling a reference in the novel). In the novel, Vera is identified as Barrett's niece; here she is called his sister. Perhaps the betrayal of a sister is more poignant than the seduction of a niece, although it is unlikely that she is either. Next, Barrett is seen standing on the platform at Euston Station as a train pulls in. He turns and moves with the train in the direction of the camera, a slight smile on his lips.

This is followed by a scene in a Soho French restaurant, a scene that easily could have been taken from one of Pinter's early revue sketches. Unconnected social conversations swirl around Tony and Susan, possibly relating to their circumstances, possibly not, yet funny in contrast and in their own right, completely separate from any other context. First, a society man (acted by Pinter) and woman (Ann Firbank) talk about a witty acquaintance who is in prison, a fact revealed in a humorous fashion (she won't see the friend for some time—because he is in prison). Then Susan and Tony enter and are seated.

Another scene at the train station follows, a high-angle shot of Vera running from a candy vending machine to Barrett. The two are some distance away and in the middle of a crowd. Back in the restaurant, Susan gives Tony a present. They are seen in a medium two-shot. Behind them a bishop (played by Patrick Magee, who had acted in the stage version of *The Birthday Party* and later acted in the film version) and a curate (portrayed by playwright Owen) enter. A bit of an Irish jig is heard. Amusingly, in a line not in the published script, the bishop pushes the curate back and says, "Where the hell are you goin'?" The conversation between Tony and Susan is constantly interrupted throughout this sequence when the camera focuses on various other couples in the restaurant as they talk; Pinter obviously did not want to stay concentrated on Tony and Susan too long, and he uses the realistic bits of dialogue that made him famous as a device for shifting the audience's attention momentarily.

The inconsequence of the overheard conversations also dramatically underscores the importance of, one, Tony and Susan's being together and, two, their blithe ignorance of what is slouching toward Knightsbridge while they fritter away their time blissfully oblivious to the future. Barrett and Vera are seen again in a full-body shot, closer, coming down some steps into the camera. Barrett is carrying her suitcase, and she has her hands full with a purse and a plastic bag, which she has trouble balancing. In the restaurant a young woman joins an older woman (there is constant movement of characters throughout the film), and the two women engage in a marvelous paranoid conversation typical in style of Pinter's playwriting:

OLDER WOMAN: What did she say to you?

YOUNGER WOMAN: Nothing.

OLDER WOMAN: Oh yes she did. She said something to you.

YOUNGER WOMAN: She didn't. She didn't really.

OLDER WOMAN: She did. I saw her mouth move. She whispered something to you, didn't she? What was it? What did she whisper to you?

YOUNGER WOMAN: She didn't whisper anything to me. She didn't whisper anything. (21)

The audience never knows who is being talked about, what the background of the speakers is, or what preceded their conversation. Still, the speech patterns (partial repetitions, unidentified references) make the talk seem familiar and sound perfectly realistic, yet at the same time compound the feeling of mystery and sinister plotting. Tony and Susan are seen in the background.

A quick cut to Tony and Susan talking about the Mountsets is followed by a two-shot of Barrett and Vera in a taxi. With each shot as they travel from the station, the servant and the girl appear larger in the frame. The fact that they never say anything contrasts with the innate chatter of the intercut restaurant shots and promotes a feeling of inevitability about their journey and the eventual results of Vera's being brought into Tony's household.

The bishop and the curate are seen discussing a priest; Tony and Susan are seen pleasantly eating behind them. Tony and Susan are intercut again, and Tony describes Barrett as looking like "a fish with red lips" (in the novel Merton says that Barrett looks like a fish with "painted lips"). Back to the bishop and the curate, who get up and leave. Another shot of Tony and Susan follows, the society man and woman in a booth behind them, glimpsed through the dwindling bars. Their conversation occasionally intrudes when Tony and Susan pause.

Barrett and Vera are seen again in the taxi. Vera is eating a candy bar and looking through the windows, her hand on Barrett's leg. Sultry saxophone music accompanies the visuals. Tony and Susan emerge from the restaurant in the next shot, and he hails a cab to take her to Barclay Square before walking off by himself. Neither of these last two shots was in the script, but the juxtaposition of Vera arriving in a taxi as Susan departs in one is a nice connecting touch.

The final shots in the sequence are from the landing at Tony's house. Barrett and Vera are on the stairs moving toward the camera, which tracks them as they ascend and then pans to show them peeking into Tony's room. In the penultimate shot, Barrett and Vera are seen in profile outside Tony's room, laughing. The final shot, from below and through the banister bars, shows Vera preceding Barrett. She enters the room, sits on the bed, and smells a flower that she has taken from the nightstand as Barrett leans against the doorjamb watching her.

In many of his early stage plays, Pinter included items that seemed to have no relevance to anything else in the drama, and his dialogue was filled with conversations joined in medias res in which the speakers understood their shared references, so they did not disclose those references in their conversation, a perfectly normal pattern, even if it did upset some critics and audience members who were not prepared for the withholding of information (or at times a plethora of mutually contradictory bits of information). Moreover, in Pinter's view of the universe, human beings are incapable of either knowing or understanding everything, so it is appropriate for events to take place that the audience may not be fully informed about or can only speculate on in retrospect. The dramatist has explained:

> The desire for verification is understandable but cannot always be satisfied. There are no hard distinctions between what is true or what is false. The thing is not necessarily either true or false; it can be both true and false. The assumption that to verify what has happened and what is happening presents few problems I take to be inaccurate. A character on the stage who can present no convincing argument or information as to his past experience, his present behavior or his aspirations, nor give a comprehensive analysis of his motives is as legitimate and worthy of attention as one who, alarmingly, can do all these things. The more acute the experience the less articulate its expression.[16]

He has also delineated his theory of language and paralanguage:

> Language, under these conditions, is a highly ambiguous commerce. So often, below the words spoken, is the thing known and unspoken. . . . There are two silences. One when no word is spoken. The other when perhaps a torrent of language is being employed. . . . The speech we hear as an indication of that we don't hear. It is a necessary avoidance, a violent, shy, anguished or mocking smokescreen which keeps the other in

its place. When true silence falls we are still left with echo but are nearer nakedness. One way of looking at speech is to say it is a constant stratagem to cover nakedness. . . . I think that we communicate only too well, in our silence, in what is unsaid, and that what takes place is continual evasion, desperate rearguard attempts to keep ourselves to ourselves. Communication is too alarming. To enter into someone else's life is too frightening. To disclose to others the poverty within us is too fearsome a possibility. . . . I'm not suggesting that no character in a play can ever say what he in fact means. Not at all. I have found that there invariably does come a moment when this happens, where he says something, perhaps, which he has never said before. And where this happens, what he says is irrevocable and can never be taken back. . . . There is another factor which I think has considerable bearing on this matter and that is the immense difficulty, if not impossibility, of verifying the past. I don't mean merely years ago, but yesterday, this morning. If one can speak of the difficulty of knowing what in fact took place yesterday one can I think treat the present in the same way. What's happening now? We won't know until tomorrow or six months time, and we won't know then, we'll have forgotten or our imagination will have attributed quite false characteristics to today. A moment is sucked away and distorted, quite even at the same time of its birth. We will all interpret a common experience quite differently, though we prefer to subscribe to the view that there's a shared, common ground, a known ground. I think there's a shared common ground all right, but that it's more like quicksand. Because "reality" is quite a strong, firm word, we tend to think, or to hope, that the state to which it refers is equally firm, settled, and unequivocal. It doesn't seem to be, and in my opinion it's no worse or better for that. ("Between the Lines," 25)

When Pinter combined this approach to his material with an emphasis on certain elements of speech (exaggerated repetition and so forth) that made his dialogue sound "tape-recorder" perfect when it crossed the footlights, the result was a kind of suprarealism in the presentation that was different from traditional realism. A similar sense of realism is effected in *The Servant* by the insertion of the unrelated snatches of conversation in the restaurant. Furthermore, early in his screenwriting career, Pinter commented that one of the things that appealed to him about writing for the cinema was that it allowed works to be "opened out," to show that there was a real world outside the room being viewed, a world populated with real people. His attention to detail is legendary (as when that change in how a cup of tea is poured forced him to rewrite a quarter of a page of dialogue). Parenthetically, this characteristic matches the mise-en-scène element in Losey's directing. The screenwriter's desire to open out the story, to make it more realistic, is contrary to the intent expressed by Maugham's narrator. "This story is about Tony," Merton says in chapter 2; "Therefore I only want to introduce people whose actions affected Tony." The strength of the scenario may in part be attributed to Pinter's insistence on incorporating a perspective that consciously encompasses the world about Tony, for this allows for more character delineation and development in the film than is present in the novel. None of the restaurant intercut with Vera's arrival sequence described above is contained in the novel, but it is important in revealing the innocence of Tony and Susan and in stressing Barrett's Machiavellian scheming.

When Tony arrives home in the scene that follows, he opens Susan's present, a short black silk dressing gown, and hangs the garment on a hook. In the film script he throws it on the sofa—the difference indicates that he still has tender feelings about Susan, which makes sense if they are about to go to the Mountsets' together. Meanwhile, he has to call Barrett several times before the servant appears; up to this point Barrett has always anticipated his master's needs. Tony's tone implies some dissatisfaction with Barrett, especially in contrast with his handling of the dressing gown. Besides not being present even before being called for, there is another change evident in Barrett. For the first time he is not impeccably groomed—a loose lock of hair hangs over his forehead and will for the rest of the film. As the scene ends, Barrett stands at the foot of the stairs, looking at Tony while calling up for Vera to come down. The audience does not witness the introduction of Tony to Vera, however. The scene at the Mountsets' intervenes before Tony and Vera are seen together, at which time it is clear that they are already acquainted.

A series of three scenes focusing on Vera in the screenplay do not appear in the film. They were designed to demonstrate Vera's sexual allure to Tony and presumably were cut as being premature and possibly overly obvious. In their place is an exterior establishing pan shot of the Mountsets' country home.

Following the Mountset scene there is another new shot, a shot of Barrett returning from shopping with some wine bottles. The nonsynchronous sound of clock chimes over links that shot with the next one in the script, in which Vera serves Tony breakfast in bed. She mishandles the tray, demonstrating that she has not had much previous experience as a maid. The contrast between Susan's and Vera's social status is obvious in the opposition of this scene and the preceding Mountset scene.

Vera's sexual nature is evidenced when she returns to the kitchen and an intense encounter with Barrett. This prepares for the ensuing entrapment scene in Tony's bedroom. Tony is found tying a tie and looking in a mirror. Barrett helps his master into a jacket, and while he does so he draws Tony's attention to Vera: "it's her skirts, sir. They rather worry me. . . . they're a little short." Her sexuality is thus highlighted, and the sexual overtones of his remark are further accentuated when Tony finds that Vera is in his bathroom taking a bath. Barrett's preparatory remark followed by the firing of Tony's imagination by the discovery of the naked girl in his bathroom will start Tony on the path to the upcoming seduction in the kitchen.

During the dressing scene, Tony tends to be positioned higher in the frame than Barrett is, he is more animated than his servant, and Barrett lowers his head and speaks quietly and humbly to Tony. Notwithstanding these actions, as soon as Tony leaves, Barrett smiles and moves jauntily to join Vera in the bathroom, where it is revealed that Vera was a "naked girl bouncing about all over" the bathroom because this is what Barrett had instructed her to do. When Vera drops her towel and approaches Barrett, it is obvious that either they are not brother and sister or that they have developed an interestingly unfamilial relationship.

Having established Vera's desirability, Barrett now sets up her availability. The subsequent shot is of Tony watching from an upstairs window as his servant and his maid go off, suitcase in hand, ostensibly to visit their ill mother in Manchester. Tony's preoccupied response to a phone call from Susan shows that his interest has been transferred to Vera.

The decisive nail in Tony's moral coffin is inserted when he returns home from a crowded Chelsea coffee bar that evening. In the novel the narrator is told about the events that follow in fairly graphic detail, but in the film they are seen as they occur. Tony's lonely, agitated state is illustrated in his trip to the coffee house, where he watches a waitress who looks something like Vera—an incident not included in the book. The sexually oriented lyrics of the "Eagle Rock Blues" are heard in the background and follow Tony out of the café. The dialogue between Tony and Vera in the kitchen is essentially the same in the movie as in the novel; that is, the same general things are said and the same general information is imparted, but Pinter has simplified it, pared it down so that the incidental conversation is decreased or omitted, and he expands the scene by adding Vera's suggestive "Can I get you anything. . . . Oh . . . isn't it hot in here . . . Isn't it? . . . So hot." When she gets up on the table, Tony is reminded of what kindled his lust in the first place—"your skirt's too short."

Tony mentions to Merton that the kitchen faucet is dripping: "Each drop fell at regular intervals like the beat of a metronome." In the film Pinter has retained the drip, even focusing the camera on the tap, but the sound is drumlike, almost like a heartbeat, and it increases in frequency as the scene progresses, paralleling the rising passions of the man and his maid. The tension is increased, too, when the telephone rings (it is probably Susan, who was supposed to call) as Tony and Vera face each other. His reflection is seen in a mirrored surface next to him, as though his impulses are split. He does not answer the phone.

While the phone rings, there is a series of shots alternating between Tony (in one-shots) and Vera (in a one-shot, then a close-up, and finally an extreme close-up). As the camera moves closer and closer to Vera's face and records her sensual expressions, and as the water drips faster and faster, the lighting is brought up so that there is a seeming heating up of the physical set that parallels the rise in emotional temperature, which culminates in Vera's "it's hot in here," a metaphorical and literal statement. There is, in fact, an amusing side point in that the light fixture hanging over the table looks like an operating room lamp. Vera certainly will feel even hotter when she positions herself directly below that lamp, and she surely proceeds in the seduction with the skill of a surgeon, yet it may be too much to suggest that the filmmakers purposely try to indicate that she is operating on Tony any more than they are implying that he is butchering a sacrificial lamb.

When Vera does get up on the table, her reflection can be seen mirrored in the glass surface next to her, and when Tony climbs up on top of her, the camera pans to a reflection of them in the same surface, melded together. Pinter's directions are for "*Two figures seen distorted in shining sauce pans*" (32). Although the sauce pans have been substituted for, the importance of these reflections is underscored by the fact that when Tony first enters the room, there is no visible reflection from any of the surfaces.

There is a cut from the couple's reflection to a reflecting puddle of water. The camera pans up to disclose the same location as was seen in the movie's opening shot, though the camera swings to the right before panning over to a straight-ahead view (it was stationary before, looking straight down the square and then panning left), and it is considerably farther back from the end of the square than it was in the initial shot. Although this shot is not called for in the published script, it is effective and appropriate in announcing a new chapter in the story.

There are small differences between the action described in the scenario and that filmed in the subsequent sequence. Barrett, with his overcoat still on, is clearing dishes from the dining room table when Tony comes into the kitchen and reacts confusedly, guiltily, to his servant's presence. Tony sends Barrett off for some brown ale so that he can warn Vera that her brother is back, and the man and the girl embrace passionately, their images clear in an ornate round mirror.

When Barrett returns with the ale, Tony scurries about furtively, and then comes a moment that captures one of the reasons that the medium of film appeals to Pinter. Barrett and Vera confront each other in the kitchen, and even though no words are spoken, there is a knowing communication that passes between them as they glance at one another, she with a slight nod and he with a pleased smile. In the film script, Tony arranges for Vera to meet him at midnight, a segment that does not appear in the film, and Vera speaks to the returning Barrett ("I'm going to bed, I'm tired"). The camera's focusing ability makes the communication between Barrett and Vera clearer than it might be on stage live, as is also the case with Mick and Aston in the film version of *The Caretaker;* the silence of their communication makes it more sinister and deepens the impression that all of what has taken place was planned by the two servants well in advance of the events.

Tony's apprehension about Barrett's reaction to the situation is ironically undercut in the next sequence when Tony knocks on Vera's door and then goes back downstairs to wait for her. The low-angle shot that follows reveals what he would have seen if he had remained on the stairs—Barrett in Vera's bed. The dramatic irony of the embrace between Tony and Vera while the Cleo Laine song plays on Tony's phonograph is enhanced by the audience's realization of where she has just come from to be a substitute for Susan, and Vera's response to Tony's query about whether Barrett is asleep, "His room's dark," is understood as an ironically intended half-truth. The statement is accurate, but it does not answer the question being asked, though Vera avoids an out-and-out lie.

From here on most of what appears in the film is not present in the novel. One of the interesting differences is that Maugham's Barrett affects the narrator like Keats's Lamia. Pinter's Barrett is not as slimy, and the snake-like imagery of the novel is replaced. In fact, some alterations in the screenplay actually decrease this effect, as when a shot of Barrett hiding in an alcove under the stairs while Vera is in Tony's room is deleted. The next shot has been altered, with Vera taking the initiative in an interlude with Barrett rather than the other way around. By reducing Barrett's evil nature, the filmmakers place more responsibility on Tony's shoulders for his own actions. Of course, by having Vera approach Barrett from the rear and playfully put her hands over his eyes, the filmmakers are also demonstrating that she is not merely an order taker, that she is involved in a conspiracy.

When the telephone rings (seen in an added shot, from above and through the banister bars), the servants, as suggested by the pan to the kitchen door that stands slightly ajar, are apparently too busily engaged to answer it. Tony answers the phone and while talking with Susan tears up the note that she has sent him. He tells her that he is to have lunch with his father's solicitor. The subsequent scripted scene, in which Tony visits a nearly hysterical Vera in her bedroom, makes the girl seem to be a victim. The absence of the scene in the film removes this suggestion and retains the appearance that Vera is willingly involved in the assault on Tony. It also reduces any impression that he is the aggressor.

Armed with her knowledge of Tony's luncheon plans, Susan visits the house, much to Barrett's obvious displeasure—displayed in his facial expressions and his slamming the taxi's door after collecting her packages. (There is a minor magic bunny in the reaction shot sequence: Barrett's hair is much more tousled in one shot than in another.)[17] Clock chimes heard tolling noon remind the audience of Tony's whereabouts, but the clock motif that has developed by virtue of the repetition of sounds also signifies the passage of time.

The conversation between Susan and Barrett is reminiscent of Pinter's stage dialogue at about the same time, particularly that in *The Caretaker*. Underneath Susan's seemingly innocuous questions is a tension calculated to throw Barrett off balance through a combination of self-assured commands alternating with double meanings and non sequiturs that appear to have no relation to anything. First, Susan asks Barrett if he likes the flowers that she has arranged in a large crystal vase. When he offers his opinion that the flowers might "be better in a different jar," she responds, "I thought you'd be uncertain." To help put Barrett in his place, she then demands that Barrett light her cigarette; unlike George in Edward Albee's *Who's Afraid of Virginia Wolf?* Barrett acquiesces. Finally, Mick's quizzing of Davies about the old man's background and interior decorating abilities in *The Caretaker* is recalled when Susan asks Barrett if he uses a deodorant and whether he goes well with the color scheme.

The presence of the chimes, a large wall mirror, and the flowers signals the importance of this scene. Susan is confident, and in her confrontational interrogation of Barrett (a device that recurs throughout Pinter's canon), she moves assertively in her attempt to retrieve Tony. She is so sure of herself that she can tell Barrett that "The truth is, I don't give a tinker's gob what you think" (a line altered in the film—in the film script she said that she did not "care"). Barrett is nonplussed, confused, and cowed by her attack to the extent that Susan even dares to ask him straight out, "What do you want from this house?" Unfortunately for Susan, this direct, defensive question reveals to Barrett that she is not completely in control, and when the scene closes with Barrett leaving the drawing room to prepare a luncheon salad for her, he does so with a faint smile.

An interlude at the Mountsets' indicates that Susan may have made some progress in regaining her place in Tony's world, yet the ultimate event that seals her fate occurs immediately. In Maugham's novel, the narrator happens to pass Tony's house while his friend is at his aunt's in Cornwall. Merton's finding a light on in Tony's bedroom leads to his discovery of Barrett and Vera trysting in the master's bedroom. When Tony and Susan return to this scene in the film, Susan's realization of what Tony's relationship with Vera has been leads her to abandon him momentarily. In the prose version that abandonment is permanent, for she marries someone else and moves to Rhodesia; in the film she makes one more attempt at salvaging Tony, but by then it is too late for her to pull him out of his pit of apathy, depravity, and self-loathing.

The idyllic interlude at the Mountsets' is a false dawn of hope in which Tony links himself and Susan ("The best view . . . is from *our* room . . . at the house," emphasis mine). The double irony lies in what is going on in that room between Barrett and Vera and that the servants' actions are what will lead to Susan's abandoning Tony. The omission of one line, "Who the hell's in my room?" is inconsequential. When Tony and Susan enter the house cautiously and Barrett and Vera's voices can be heard from upstairs, Pinter repeats the dialogue from the novel almost verbatim, though he does make a couple of minor adjustments ("bleeding little idiot" becomes "bloody little idiot," for instance) and incorporates a few lines relating to Barrett's cigarette smoking and to Vera's sexual hunger, primarily to cover the time that it takes Tony and Susan to move from the front door to the staircase in a tracking shot.

The close-up of Tony, standing on the stairs, Susan, watching him from a slightly lower level, and Barrett's shadow on the wall between them, seen through the banister (both the physical banister and the shadow banister) as he looks down on the couple looking up at him, is effective in its silence until Vera's voice intrudes with its lecherous suggestiveness. Barrett has been a symbolic shadow between the couple almost from the beginning. Tony moves into the drawing room and rests his head on the mantle; Susan follows and turns on the light as the clock chimes midnight. Tony is now illuminated with the knowledge of his servants' duplicity, and, as they did in Susan's case earlier, the midnight chimes toll the end of his Cinderella innocence.

Susan is upset that servants have overstepped their place in Tony's house, and she is repulsed by the fact that his room and bed have been violated. Her reaction parallels Tony's initial reaction to finding Vera in his bathroom. She crosses to stand under the wall mirror, in which Tony is reflected. After Tony calls Barrett, he stands under the mirror, head bowed. The scene, with the mirror between Susan and Tony, is similar to the earlier scene in which Barrett's reflection could be seen between them, but this time it is the reflection of a defeated Tony that separates the two. Barrett soon enters the reflection, and an image of Barrett and Tony appears while Susan and Tony stand in front of the mirror. The combined dual image of Tony mirrored and his physical body constitute a Tony divided—by Barrett. As Barrett informs Tony that Vera is not his sister, that she is, in fact, his fiancée, he is shown in a shoulder shot. The truth is not delivered by a reflection. Tony moves forward during the revelations so that the reflections in the mirror are no longer present.

The entrance of Vera, called by Barrett as though she is a pet animal, is viewed from Tony's point of view until there is a cut and the camera angle is again such that the reflections in the mirror can be seen between Susan and Tony—and Barrett's action of thrusting Vera at Tony (or Tony's reflection, his other, divided, self) is visible only in the mirror. Throughout, mirrors are used to reflect the characters' interior lives, their souls, and thus to reveal their similarities and the mirror-image reversed characteristics that they share so well.

Vera's entrance into the room is accompanied by the sound of a second clock striking midnight. Lighter, and more highly pitched than the chimes of the first clock, these chimes (the same ones heard when Barrett interrupted Tony and Susan, signaling the demise of her dream) prepare for Vera's echoing confirmation of Barrett's statements. Shot composition during Vera's announcement of the marriage reenforces Barrett's regaining control, at least in his own mind. Her face is seen in close-up while he stands in the background, smiling. It is evident that he is pulling the strings, and his coolness contrasts markedly with her tension and fluster.

The fact that Barrett is not really in control, however, makes this whole sequence remarkable. He may hold the upper hand emotionally, but Tony can throw him out of the household—which he does. It does not make sense that Barrett would have executed a plan that from the start would have been designed to have himself expelled. The key to understanding Barrett's nature and to understanding what is happening here comes later, after Barrett regains his position.

Barrett's experience in the military service must have fostered democratic feelings, for as is noted later, he constantly tells Tony that no one is any better than he is. In essence, Barrett sees himself as Tony's equal. This is not too far from some of Tony's beliefs, voiced to Susan, so the theme of social-class conflict becomes part of the context in which Barrett has striven to take control of Tony and his house; yet he is willing to forgo that position if he can best Tony on other grounds, grounds upon which they are more nearly equal to begin with. His desire to return to Tony later demonstrates that the two men share some of the same needs, or complementary needs (to serve and to be served, for instance), and that those psychological needs can best be fulfilled by one another.

This has been a major thematic strand in Pinter's dramas throughout his career, epitomized by Ruth's situation vis-à-vis her husband's family at the end of *The Homecoming,* which premiered in 1965, just a couple of years after he wrote the screenplay for *The Servant.* That Tony and Barrett in a sense feed off one another is part of the expansion of meaning that Pinter has effected in translating Maugham's prose to celluloid.

With Barrett's and Vera's departure from the room, there is some added indistinct dialogue as they are heard gathering their belongings upstairs. The shots accompanying the voices over are different from those called for in the scenario. Instead of Susan and Tony sitting, Susan remains standing by the mirror—which now is devoid of human reflections. The scene shifts upstairs to show the servants grabbing their belonging, Vera singing the tune of Felix Mendelssohn's "Wedding March" while the sound of the Laine record that Tony has turned on is heard over. The items that the servants carry down the stairs, into the mirror's reflection and out of the house, are a hodgepodge of photo portraits, a radio, paintings, suitcases, umbrellas, and other miscellaneous items.

During the confrontation, which is not present in the novel, Susan remains silent. Tony's betrayal of their relationship has drained her, and when he invites her to go to bed with him after the servants leave, it is clear that

Tony is too self-centered to be able to comprehend that she has been going through the same emotional reaction that he has.

The presentation of the next several scenes in the movie is not in the same order as in the film script. Instead of ascending the stairs to lie on Vera's disheveled bed, Tony is seen in a pub, calling but not talking to Susan. A girl sitting in the pub will reappear in the film's concluding sequence. The shots of Tony coming down the stairs in his house, rummaging about in the kitchen, walking along a London street, and drunkenly trying to play a record in the drawing room are all excised. It was probably determined that there was sufficient evidence of his state of mind without these additional demonstrations.

At this point the scene of Tony mounting the stairs to Vera's bedroom is inserted. The jump cut goes from Tony hanging up the phone in the bar to an uncradled telephone on the floor of the entrance to his house. The camera pans to show the floor cluttered with ashtrays, cigarette stubs, glasses, unread newspapers, and unopened mail to Tony's feet coming out of the kitchen and mounting the stairs. His body is not seen until he arrives at Vera's door. In the pan to the stairway, the camera also picks up a vase on the entryway table; the vase is filled with dead flowers, not just evidence of a servant grown lazy and careless, but a symbol of the fragility of human relationships in general and Tony's destroyed relationships and spiritual decay in particular. The shot of Tony lying on Vera's bed, seen through the banister bars, reemphasizes the situation; he is trapped and at the same time incapacitated by his lustful desires, and the nature of the person who has served as the instrument of his moral destruction is conveyed through the pan of the beefcake photographs on the walls of Vera's room.

David Caute contends that with the script of *The Servant,* Losey "at long last . . . had a screenplay unspoilt by stock studio formulas, melodrama and tedious exposition. For the first time a writer offered him the primacy of the implicit over the explicit, with human conflict percolating through the masking tape of received language, idiom and gesture" ("Golden Triangle"). The Pinter-Losey collaboration has been called the "most critically acclaimed creative collaboration in the history of British cinema,"[18] and the reunion scene that follows is a masterful blend of Pinter's and Losey's talents. The opening shot reveals Barrett at the bar in a fairly busy pub—people are heard talking and seen moving about behind him. He is sitting in the private bar area, next to the decorative frosted-glass partition that separates the private bar from the saloon bar. Tony is seen coming into the saloon bar and calling out for a large Scotch. When he hears Tony's voice, Barrett looks up, and the camera swings to the left, away from the full mirror in which all of this action, it is now realized, has been visible. The camera continues to pan to show Tony sitting at the saloon bar, on the other side of the partition from Barrett, with another man between him and the room divider. In the script, Pinter's directions specifically state that Tony sees Barrett in the mirror, but neither man speaks or indicates the presence of the other. In the film it is clear that Tony, busy first with removing his gloves and then with his drink, does not see Barrett.

After a few moments, the third man begins to speak in a lower-class accent, to no one in particular, about his "bit of bad luck today." Physically, the man is placed between Tony and Barrett, as Barrett has been seen between Tony and Susan a number of times, but, of course, the situation is very different here. Tension is created as the audience waits to see what will happen between Tony and Barrett, and the delay serves several purposes. As is typical in a Pinter work, the audience never finds out what the bit of bad luck was or why it will take the speaker "a good few days" to recover from whatever happened. The episode remains unconnected with the film's plot and from the characters, yet there are parallels.

When the man stops speaking and moves away, for instance, Barrett initiates a conversation with Tony by complaining about the bad luck that he has had in his relationship with Vera, which has been compounded by his experience since leaving Tony's service. The isolation of the bad-luck man and the lack of sympathy from his listeners is humorously emphasized when he turns to Tony as though Tony has spoken to him and says, "You're right there," even though Tony has completely ignored him.

The entire sequence conveys a sense of the loneliness, despair, and lack of human concern for others that appear in some of the author's earlier revue sketches, "The Black and White" in particular. This sense of isolation is reenforced in the course of Barrett's appeal to Tony: Barrett is seen in close-up, staring straight ahead, head slightly lowered (and hair mussed), while in the background a woman is seen sitting by herself during his recital, an inattentive, blank expression on her face that matches the expression on his face during the other man's declaration of bad luck. Although Tony glances at Barrett, he never says anything, paralleling his lack of comment to the other man.

In the novel, Maugham does not directly describe the details of the reunion between master and servant but instead employs an epistolary technique, the incident being described briefly in letters to the narrator from

Sally and from Tony. By expanding the meeting, Pinter accomplishes several things. Most obviously, we can hear Barrett whimsically tell a story that we know to be at least partly false. In the novel it is possible that Tony may not have recorded what Barrett says accurately, and the audience is unable to judge this. In the film, Barrett's own words betray him when he claims to have been "led up the garden path" and that he "didn't know a thing about what was going on between you two until that night." There can be no mistake that he is lying, for images demonstrating the contrary are still fixed in the audience's mind. Furthermore, the self-pitying tone of voice that accompanies his tale makes it even harder for the audience to empathize with him—and makes it easier to consider Tony foolish for accepting the tale as true. And, although the mirrors do not distort Barrett's image as they have in previous scenes, the opening shot of the scene, which turns out to be mirrored, reminds the viewer of Barrett's preoccupation with images and the surfaces of things rather than what lies beneath. The mirror motif is clearly operating metaphorically as a comment on the distinction between appearance and reality.

Barrett's speech itself is important, moreover, for there must be an acceptable rationale provided that allows Tony to renew his relationship with Barrett. At the same time a delicate balance is called for, because the audience must realize that the stated reason is not sufficient for the conclusion to be drawn that Tony has degenerated to the point where he is willing to reengage Barrett. What Barrett can provide Tony must be important enough to Tony that he will willingly overlook Barrett's acts of betrayal. The presence of a bowl of flowers between Barrett and Tony in the scene suggests that this is so and contrasts with the dark, stark image of the dead flowers in the hallway in the previous scene. These are, in fact, close-up shots of Barrett through the flowers, which remind the viewer of similar shots of Susan in the scene in which she confronts Barrett while Tony is at lunch with his lawyer. The pivotal nature of the scenes is thus underscored.

Both in the number of words (269) and in the length of time involved (two minutes and nine seconds), Barrett's speech in the bar is the longest single piece of dialogue in the film. Structurally, it is well conceived. He begins by saying that he wanted to contact Tony, but then goes no further, implying that he is sorry and embarrassed for having hurt his former employer. He quickly shifts to explain that everything that happened can be blamed on Vera (who is not present to defend herself). Not only had she tricked and "besotted" him, he alleges, but she betrayed him, too—by carrying on with Tony without his (Barrett's) knowledge and finally by taking his money and running off to live with a bookie in Wandsworth. Wandsworth is a suburb on the southwest of London, a considerable step down in social status from Tony's Knightsbridge neighborhood. In the movie the point is reenforced by Bogarde's repetition of the area's name as an appalled exclamation of disbelief. Pinter likewise changes the location of Barrett's current position from Lowndes Square to Paultons Square.

Having revealed the shallowness of Vera's character, Barrett asks for another chance, incidentally mentioning how happy he had been in Tony's service ("it was like bliss"). Next, he appeals to his old boss's sense of pity by describing how unhappy he is working for an old lady (his prior happiness makes his present situation all the more poignant by contrast). Again he admits that he deceived Tony, but again he immediately places the blame on Vera, who "done us both." He concludes by asking once more for another chance.

Apparently Tony is convinced of Vera's duplicity and recognizes that whereas he and Barrett are both unhappy now, they were formerly happy, so the logical conclusion is for them to be reunited. Although Tony does not say anything at the end of Barrett's speech in the pub, the following shot is an exterior establishing shot of reflections in a pool of water, with the camera panning up to show the square outside his house. Symbolically, the shot signals another new chapter in the relationship between the two men. Actually, although Susan will make a last attempt to salvage her relationship with Tony, this new chapter is really the beginning of the end, for everything is downhill from now on.

Pinter's scenario calls for an interior shot of the hall in Tony's house. The lack of flowers (it is winter; a time of death and barren desolation) and the changed furnishings indicate that Barrett's influence has replaced Susan's. In the film this shot has been cut, and there is a jump from the exterior establishing shot to a scene in which Tony is sitting at a table working on a crossword puzzle. Since this scene adequately demonstrates the change in Tony and of necessity reveals the settings at the same time, the intervening shot was unnecessary. The Barrett-theme saxophone music makes an audible transition from the pub scene through the exterior square to Barrett's entrance.

In the sequence that follows, it is evident just how much change has taken place in the two men and in their relationship. They have confined themselves to the house, which is littered with their "leavings," and the outside world has been shut out; heavy, dark drapes are open only enough to allow them sufficient sunlight to read by. More overwhelming, however, is the change in the men that the alterations in their environment reflects. They have become a humorous parody of the stereotypical married couple. Tony is an apathetic lay-about, still in his pajamas. At one point he says that he would not mind "going out" for a walk, but he remains inside, unable to make the needed effort. Barrett takes on the role of a shrewish wife, shrilly nagging at Tony because of "all this muck and slime," complaining that he needs a maid and is not used to "working in such squalor." He goes on to bicker at Tony for being in "everybody's" way and for not getting a job while he scrapes and scrimps to "make ends meet"—"butter's gone up two pence a pound." The reference to the price of butter is amusing because it seems to be a non sequitur. It is also a reminder of the description of the habitat in *The Dwarfs* (1960) and an example of the writer's concern with specific, concrete details that underline the ambiguity of the rest of the conversation in which they are found. Even Tony's "man from Brazil" is brought up disparagingly. No longer dressed in a suit (he wears a baggy, dark sweater instead, which he wipes his hands on after picking up a banana peel), Barrett skitters about, hunched over, dumping food scraps and cigarette ashes on a tray. As he leaves the room, he sniffs and then flounces out the door, tossing the bag of bottles that he is carrying by a strap over his shoulder. The camera, meanwhile, has followed Barrett around the room while Tony remains fixed on the sofa.

A shot of the drawing room, empty, is inserted at this point. A dirty plate is seen on the table in the foreground. Then the violence that springs out of frustration and which underlies much of Pinter's writings seems about to burst forth when in the next shot Tony rushes into the camera's field in the hall, shouting for Barrett and swinging a cloth. He throws a towel down and moves determinedly up the stairs, into and then away from the camera, to fling open the door of Barrett's bedroom. He pulls the bedclothes off his servant and sternly demands that he clean up the "tea dregs" from the drawing room carpet. Barrett protests that he was not responsible for putting them there—and Tony goes into the bathroom to run water on the cloth that he has been carrying. He returns to Barrett's bed and calls the servant a "filthy bastard." Barrett storms out of the bedroom, saying that he is leaving. Tony replies, "That's exactly what I want." He pushes Barrett down the stairs, thrusting the wet cloth into his hand, and shouting at him to "Get down and clear it up" (49).

In dialogue that sounds as though it could have been taken from Pinter's revue sketch "That's Your Trouble," the two men refer to the messy house as a "pigsty," and then Barrett's sense of social class comes out, ironically, in an amusingly ambivalent manner. During the exchange, Tony calls him a "creep," and he responds, "Nobody talks to me like that!" In other words, he is Tony's social equal, at least in some respects. He responds to Tony's charge that he is a peasant with "I'm a gentleman's gentleman. And you're no bloody gentleman!" He laughs at Tony when Tony insists that he has not been drinking all morning. Tony threatens to "Knock your head off," and the possibility of violence has been recognized, yet this very recognition permits the situation to be defused, and Barrett, laughing, goes to clean up the mess.

An interlude follows, during which Barrett throws out the spice rack that Susan had installed in the pantry. The camera then tracks Barrett into the kitchen, where the two men sit together at the table. Barrett works on a jigsaw puzzle (not a crossword puzzle in the dining room as indicated in the script; Tony had worked on a crossword puzzle earlier, a form of diversion that may be too intellectual for his base servant), and the sound of children's voices can be heard outside. The same sound has been heard previously in the movie, when Tony and Susan were together outside the house.

Barrett's takeover is further evidenced by the presence of his radio on the cabinet in the background, and the location of the scene in the kitchen rather than in the dining room places the action in Barrett's domain while simultaneously inferring how circumscribed Tony's world has become. It is in this scene that he mentions, listlessly, a desire to go outside, and the noise of the children playing outdoors seems to mock him. Barrett pays no attention, and the sound of the children's voices is replaced by the Barrett saxophone theme as the scene ends, the camera pushing in on the scattered pieces of Barrett's uncompleted puzzle.

Another child's game, a kind of ball tag, is the central action in the scene that follows. In the earlier scene on the staircase in which Tony confronted Barrett about the tea dregs, Barrett threw the wet rag at his employer (who later threw it back, although it had been left on the floor upstairs, another small magic bunny). Still, the violence had been curtailed. In the ball game on the stairway, violence again surfaces, momentarily seriously.

In many ways this scene serves as a metaphor for the entire motion picture. It is also crucial in demonstrating the reversal of positions that takes place. The scene opens with the camera shooting up at Tony, who is standing behind the banister in the second-floor hall (with all of those barlike balusters evoking an oppressive, caged feeling). Tony is holding the ball, which he tosses at the camera (the first few lines of dialogue have been assigned to the speakers in reverse of the order in which they appear in the film script; that is, Tony says "Watch it!" instead of Barrett). The camera then shoots from above so that the whole staircase is in view, and the relative positions of the two players are clear. When Barrett hits Tony with the ball, bringing the score in the game to thirteen to ten, Tony objects, saying that he cannot continue because he has to "bend all the time," since he is positioned above Barrett on the staircase.

Barrett's sensitivity to the social class conflict that is being exhibited comes to the fore again. He disguised his comments as parody while pretending to be a nagging wife, then protested that he was as good as anybody and would not clean up after others or be called certain names.[19] Here he alludes to the disparity between the classes more directly, attributing a symbolic value to their boy's game. "What about me," he asks, "I'm in the inferior position." Suddenly, Tony begins the game anew, throwing the ball past Barrett and knocking over and breaking a vase. The destruction of a fragile and presumably valuable art object may be symbolic of Tony's delicate psyche, the flimsiness of the relationship between the two men, or the apparently perishable nature of Britain's class-stratified society (there certainly are reverberations with the vases and their symbolic values in Pinter's *The Collection*). Tony is unperturbed by the ruination of the vase, and he is pleased that his action has brought the score to fourteen to twelve, but Barrett is outraged because the throw was not *fair*. He refuses to allow this point to be counted, repeats his charge that Tony is taking advantage of being in the "best position," and states (while shaking his finger at Tony) that Tony should be able to play the game "according to the rules."

Barrett throws the ball up the stairs at Tony, who responds by returning the ball "viciously." The ball hits Barrett in the nose, and suddenly there is a subtle blocking movement that changes the situation dramatically. Tony moves down to comfort Barrett, talking like a young boy who has accidentally injured a chum: "What's the matter. . . . It couldn't have hurt." Barrett threatens to leave ("I'm not staying here in a place where they just chuck balls in your face!")—and as he does so, he moves around Tony and up the stairs.

The camera is now at a two-shot distance as Barrett is above Tony for the remainder of the scene. With their physical positions reversed, their standing in the relationship is likewise transposed. First, Tony tries to call the game a draw—"Isn't that fair?"—and he invites Barrett to share a brandy. When Barrett tells him to "push" the brandy ("stuff" it in the printed script),

Tony tries to regain control: "don't you forget your place. You're nothing but a servant in this house!" Barrett, ironically claiming to be "nobody's servant," catalogues all of the things that he does around the house in an attempt to prove that he runs "the whole bloody place"; yet he describes a servant's chores: painting, cooking, washing, cleaning out the bath.[20] Nevertheless, Tony professes that he is grateful—and more importantly, "I don't know what I'd do without you." Now in the superior position figuratively as well as literally, Barrett orders Tony to pour him a glass of brandy, and Tony runs down the stairs to do so. Barrett stands above, watching.

The events revolving around the staircase parallel the plot. In the beginning Tony was clearly superior in standing and in control of both himself and the situation. Through a series of maneuvers, subtle as well as blatant, Barrett manages to put himself in the role of the injured party and as a result effects a reversal in their relative positions in the relationship. Game-playing is certainly involved, too. Barrett uses his inferior position to attack Tony, who has the power to break the rules. He is, after all, a member of the ruling class to whom those on Barrett's level are forced to bow down. But, the rules that Barrett can willfully adjust to fit his transient desires are social rules, so when Tony violates them, his stature is reduced accordingly. He loses the power of the chains of sand that permit him to exercise control over Barrett. As the two men participate in the same activities, they become social equals.

To paraphrase George Orwell, though, some equals are more equal than others. Because Tony has fallen in stature (even if Barrett has not risen), and because Barrett develops and therefore imposes his control on the circumstances that precipitate Tony's decline, it is Barrett who gains power relatively and objectively. Tony's acquiescence as he relinquishes his command (originally symbolized by his former military officer's rank and Barrett's status as a noncommissioned officer) redoubles the strength of Barrett's newly gained position, and Tony's eagerness to please/obey his servant and the easy manner with which the servant assumes command and issues orders demonstrate that the transmogrification has been accomplished and that both parties recognize the change. Even when the two stand in the same two-shot frame, the fair-haired Tony physically is overshadowed by the dark-haired Barrett, and Tony's soft voice is overcome by Barrett's strident shouting. It is particularly appropriate that this microcosmic representation of the plot takes place on the stairs, for since the opening of the film the staircase has metaphorically represented the differences in status between the men and Barrett's ambitions as well, and the bars of the banister reenforce the trapped motif.

In the screenplay, Pinter has Tony run into the drawing room and pour a large brandy while Barrett *"watches him from the hall"* (52). In the movie, Tony runs down the stairs and disappears from the screen as Barrett watches from the top of the stairs. The camera shot is from directly above. After a moment's pause, Barrett turns and walks off camera. There is no cut, as might be expected, however. The shot is held for several seconds, just a view of the staircase and railings from above, with nobody in view. Some of the sense of physical perspective is removed by the absence of the human characters, and the staircase, which has almost become a character in its own right, seems to take on an almost circular configuration—but the flattened perspective is in conflict with the stairs that appear to narrow as they go down. Since the composition of the shot places the bottom of the stairs at the top left of the screen, again contradicting normal perspective, the circle seems to flow back on itself to create a convoluted mobius effect.

The establishment of the new order in the house, and its sinister implications, is depicted in the following segments. First, Tony and Barrett are seen dressed alike in light suits and dark ties, sitting at the dinner table. Tony compliments Barrett on his cooking; Barrett pretends to be self-deprecating about his talents, though he says that being appreciated "makes all the difference." He admits that he sometimes gets the feeling that they are "old pals," a feeling that Tony claims to share. The appellation of "pals" further exemplifies the breakdown of the class barrier, while at the same time it provides for an additional comment on that barrier. Barrett reminisces that he has only had such a feeling once before, when he was in the army. Tony purports to having had the same feeling in the same setting. Barrett's amused grunt indicates that he does not believe that they could have shared that experience, presumably because relations between officers could not correspond to relations between regular soldiers. Throughout the scene, Barrett is the focal point. Tony wants to please him and is quick to follow Barrett's conversational lead. Barrett is also the active member of the pair and holds the master's attention when he moves to pour himself a drink. Looming in the foreground, he does not even bother to look at Tony, a small figure sitting in the background with his eyes fixed on the other.

Next, another game is in progress as the film's mood moves from the quiet domestic dinner-table scene to a horror-movie atmosphere like that of *The Shining*. The game is hide and seek, with Barrett stalking through the house and up the stairs looking for Tony. As Barrett moves up the stairs, he passes the alcove that previously held the vase that was broken during the ball game; now it contains a statuette, which is partly in shadow, as are the participants in the game. Again both men are dressed alike, in dark sweaters that blend with the shadows through which Barrett moves and in which Tony hides. As a result, their pale faces stand out like the hooded face of Death in Ingmar Bergman's *Seventh Seal.*

"Puss, puss, puss," Barrett calls enticingly as he moves after his terrified quarry. The camera crosscuts between the face of the approaching Barrett and the silhouette of Tony behind the shower curtain (possibly an homage to Hitchcock's *Psycho*). That there may be more than merely a childish game involved is indicated when Barrett calls out, "You've got a guilty secret . . . but you'll be caught. I'm coming to get you, I'm creeping up on you!" When Tony makes a noise, alerting his pursuer to his hiding place, Barrett turns to the camera and moves menacingly toward it as it pulls back. There is a cut to the point of view of a subjective camera, shooting over the backs of Barrett's hands as they reach out for the shower curtain and then open it. The look on Tony's face when the curtain is jerked open mirrors the look on Skat's face when Death cuts down the tree in which he has taken refuge in *The Seventh Seal.*

At this point, Barrett's position is fully established. Structurally, the remaining scenes collectively render the story's conclusion as they are used to demonstrate the degree and the extent of the control that Barrett has assumed over Tony. There can no longer be any doubt that the former servant can impose his will on his erstwhile master.

In the first of the concluding scenes, Barrett is seen shuffling down the dark entrance hall on a rainy night. He opens the front door, and a soaking wet Vera comes in begging to see Tony. Barrett is about to eject her when Tony enters and says that he will talk with the girl. Vera is shown between the two men, running from Barrett to Tony; Barrett trips her. There is a cut to a two-shot of Tony, in left profile, sitting in a chair, and Vera kneeling in front of him. He listens to her, stone-faced, as she tells him that she has to go to the hospital and needs some money. "What about what you did to me?" Tony asks. "He made me," Vera responds, "I love you, though." Tony turns and embraces Vera, only to be interrupted by Barrett ("Playing games with little Sis again, are you?"), who pulls Vera away and pushes her out into the hall. He pauses there and turns so that he is speaking back in Tony's direction. "Get back to your ponce," Barrett commands Vera, obviously for Tony's sake. He smiles at the woman and then escorts her down the hall and back out the front door. Before she leaves, however, he steps outside with her, holding the door almost closed behind him. For a moment the camera shows only the almost closed door at the end of the hall. After Vera's departure, Barrett comforts Tony by placing a cigarette in his mouth and lighting it. He then slams the cigarette box shut and spits out the expletive "Slut!" as though he is closing the chapter in Tony's life concerning Vera.

Barrett now has the power to deny Tony some things that he wants. By tripping Vera so that she must beg Tony for an audience, Barrett has made sure that her relative position is made clear. This position is reenforced by her kneeling before Tony's chair—Tony clearly has the power to accept or reject her. Then, when Tony and Vera are on equal standing in the embrace (Tony having moved down to her level), Barrett asserts himself to demonstrate his position over Tony. By expelling the girl he demonstrates his power to deny.

The comment about the ponce that is directed at Tony and the momentary hidden conference (or implied conference) outside the front door, however, indicate that the show of power may literally have been a show of power. From this sequence of events it might be inferred that they had planned this charade to show Tony where the power really lay. Vera's reentrance in the final scene makes the sense of conspiracy in this scene credible. The printed script contains an exchange between Tony and Vera in which Tony tells her to go to her bookmaker for money and Vera claims that Barrett's accusation is a lie. By removing this dialogue so that the sole reference to the situation comes from Barrett, Pinter simultaneously weakens Tony's character (he is too much of a weakling to mention the past and is willing to accept her back without question) and strengthens Barrett's (who has the power to feel free to direct even Tony's thoughts by introducing the reference to the "ponce"). Again, this not only suggests the relative positions of the two men but also bolsters the implications that the return of Vera was a staged event.

In the next scene, having demonstrated his power to withhold, Barrett now illustrates his ability to provide something that Tony wants. Whereas Vera knelt before Tony in the previous scene, Tony kneels in front of Barrett in this scene as the servant plays solitaire. To start the scene, the camera pans down from a painting of an eighteenth- or nineteenth-century battle. Given the military history of the film's two main characters, the portrayal of a heroic flag carrier leading a charge serves as an ironic comment on what has been happening in Tony's house.

The camera focuses on the cards, the ornate faces of which resemble tarot cards. Barrett's voice is heard nonsynchronously as he produces a medicine bottle with no label on it. "I've got something special for you," he tells Tony, "from a little man in Jermyn Street." Tony resists, but not for long or very strongly. His expression after he sips the drink is one of coy pleasure, and Barrett takes the opportunity to remind his employer that he can "still think of things that'll please you." "My only ambition is to serve you," he continues. He condescendingly admits to making a few mistakes ("I'm only human"). Tony tries to use this comment as a transition to discussing Barrett's lack of housecleaning, but the liquid that he has drunk has destroyed his ability to think, to concentrate. His labored, faltering speech contrasts with the crisp, articulate dialogue of the movie's beginning, just as his confused expression is brought into sharp relief by Barrett's quick movements and animated voice as the scene ends. Most of the action has been framed within a two-shot composition. A shot of an irritated Tony posturing like a chimpanzee has been excised; it is more effective to end the scene with a bewildered, apathetic Tony.

The opening scene began with a pan—so does the final segment. In this case the camera is focused on a painting of a partially clad woman. The love song that has become a motif for Tony's apathy is heard over.[21] And, as in the previous sequence, the initiating event is the arrival of a woman. This time it is Susan who has come to see Tony.

As the final sequence develops, it takes on an eerie quality reminiscent of Robert Wiene's *The Cabinet of Dr. Caligari* (1919), with overtones from Fritz Lang's *M* (1931, starring Peter Lorre) and any number of French and American films noirs. Interestingly, in turn this sequence may have influenced the 1970 British film *Performance,* which was codirected by Donald Cammell and former photographer Nicolas Roeg, who worked on two of Pinter's later films. The sequence takes place the night following Vera's visit. It begins with Tony sitting and listening to the record of Laine singing "All Gone." He has a drink in his hand.

Barrett enters to announce that Tony's "other one" is there. He grasps Tony's face, as though he has to shake him to get his attention. Although he has told Susan that they are expecting visitors, Barrett admits that he took the liberty of showing her into the drawing room because she is a "lady."

When Tony greets Susan in the drawing room, either he is too weak to stand or he cannot look her in the face, so he lowers himself into a chair with his back to her. In the screenplay, he slams the door when he comes in, but in the film he has already entered the room when he is seen. He will react angrily, calling Vera a liar—announcing, in fact, that "they're all liars"—but his weakness is better conveyed by his swaying gait, and the door slam would not fit his attitude toward Susan. Susan stands behind the chair and announces that Vera has been to see her. For a moment she is framed against another painting, then she moves and the physical relationship between her and Tony approximates that of the two figures portrayed in the painting, one standing, one sitting, both partially nude. The light from the floor lamp beside Tony's armchair keeps the two characters' faces in shadow.

Tony struggles to his feet to tell Susan that she does not "want" to be there as the sound of a car driving up off camera is heard. The Laine song begins again, though as the film's theme rather than on the phonograph, along with the sounds of Barrett ushering a group of women into the house. Susan stands in the foreground, bathed in white light, while Tony moves haltingly behind her deeper into the shadows. One of the women walks into the room for a moment, looking for Tony; then Barrett's voice is heard calling Tony to join them ("we're waiting for you"). Susan asks her fiancé what is wrong with her and he answers that nothing is wrong and invites her to join the party. As Tony leads Susan into the bedroom, the jazz music begins to override the Laine ballad.

With the couple's entrance into the bedroom, Barrett, who is kneeling and taking a still picture of something outside the frame, demands, "Where's my drink?" even though when he gets up he has a glass in his hand. He asks Susan (whom he addresses condescendingly as "Luv") if she would like one, then laughs when she does not answer. Barrett's clothing—a fancy robe over his white shirt and dark trousers—is the costume of a relaxed, self-assured master of the house, not that of a servant.

In the meantime, Tony has picked up a crystal ball from the bureau top (on which there are also a lighted candle and a clock that reads a little after nine twenty). Tony has passed between Barrett and Susan in the background to go to the bureau. Now as Tony comes forward, Barrett moves back between him and Susan. When Barrett addresses Susan, all three are framed in a line. Susan stares straight ahead. Tony is insensitive to what is happening, for his head is down as he stares at the crystal ball. This is the last time that all three of the principals are seen together in one frame, and it captures their characters for a moment. Susan is aloof and will not even acknowledge Barrett's presence. Barrett is in control of the situation, yet he no longer reveals any sense of decorum or self-dignity. Tony is oblivious to everything, including the fact that he is cut off from Susan and that Barrett has replaced him as master of the household.

Tony's state of mind is clearly elucidated when he holds the crystal ball up to eye level to peer into it and the camera pushes in for a close-up of his head and shoulders. Because he is holding the ball at eye level, his head cannot be seen and it appears that the crystal is his head—but his head appears in the crystal, upside down, just as his world has been inverted physically and psychologically. It is an arresting, Magritte-like image. There is a cut to Tony's point of view, and we see as through the crystal ball; the room appears upside-down. When Tony lowers the ball, still in the same shot, the scene that is revealed looks like a cabalistic harem. Barrett is reclining on the floor next to a woman, while other women are visible lounging in the dark background behind them.

The next series of cuts suggests the kind of world that Tony inhabits now, the world that he perceives, whether through the influence of a transforming device that parallels Barrett's influence or the effects of the contents of the unlabeled bottle that Barrett provided for him earlier. The world that Tony sees is a glimpse of his distorted and upside-down future. First, there is a two-shot of a woman and Barrett looking at, and laughing at, some photographic slides. Then there is a shot of the woman from the bar sitting expressionlessly. A quick shot of Vera sitting in front of a mirror, slowly, sensually combing her hair, follows. The shot is from behind, so that her back and her face in the mirror are observed simultaneously, perhaps an indication of the dual role that she has been playing. Next there is a close-up profile of the woman in the dark hat who was looking for Tony earlier in the scene. As he moves past the bed that she is sitting upon, she reaches up and pulls him down onto the bed. She kisses him and he lies on his back while she cackles, his head hanging over the foot of the bed so that he is now literally upside-down. Tony glances up at Susan, who appears to be observing him as dispassionately as Teddy observes Ruth with Lenny and Joey in *The Homecoming*.

With a look of resignation, Susan moves away. Seeing her move, Barrett gets up and announces that he and Tony are "going to Brazil in the morning" and offers her a cigarette in much the same way that he had offered her a drink earlier—casually, as though he relishes being in control, being in the position to make such an offer, yet knowing that the objects being offered are insignificant and that they have value only in their symbolism. It is obvious that he does not care whether she accepts his offer, for the process of the offer and the tone of his voice indicate that this is his way of dismissing her. She has been defeated, so she no longer represents a threat to his designs for taking over the household. The drink and the cigarette are Barrett's way of acknowledging the fait accompli.

That Barrett's actions have been deliberate and predetermined is again reenforced throughout the remainder of the film's closing sequence. He walks over to Vera, making the conspiracy connection quite clear. As Vera takes a picture of them in the mirror (the camera is shooting as though through the mirror, emphasizing the reversal that has taken place), Susan walks up behind them. For a moment Susan is framed in the arched doorway, her head in shadow so that her torso appears headless. Her quiet seriousness contrasts with the giggling of Barrett and particularly of Vera.

Barrett pours a drink, then blows cigarette smoke in Susan's face. There is a cut to a close-up of Tony watching helplessly. After a glance at Tony, and with Vera's double image behind her, Susan slowly moves to Barrett and kisses him. After a moment, Barrett reacts passionately, pulling her to him tightly. Susan pulls away. Vera's mirror image is seen smiling while Barrett laughs. In a close-up, Tony's head droops in recognition of his defeat.

The Laine song begins again, and Susan and Barrett are seen reflected in the mirror, embracing; Vera moves out of the mirror to Tony, and the camera follow-pans after her as she passes Susan and Barrett, the characters rather than their images. The mirroring, the two-sided nature of the reality in Tony's house is thus underscored by the views of the characters in reflection and then in the flesh in the same shot. The concept is further amplified by the smile on Barrett's face, both as it is reflected in the mirror and then as it is seen while Vera walks past him, and by the next cut, from behind Barrett, showing Susan's distorted features as she reacts with horror and revulsion to what is happening. There has been speculation about the possibility that Susan is attracted to Barrett or the moral degradation that she witnesses, or both. Her expression when she kisses him (like Jimmy Stewart swallowing the foul-smelling and -tasting magic potion in *Bell, Book, and Candle*) suggests that no such attraction exists.

Susan pushes away from Barrett while Tony, who has struggled to his feet and tried to walk toward them, falls at their feet. The words of the song "Leave It Alone" repeat while the camera cuts back and forth from Tony's face as he lies on the floor to the laughing faces of the women in the bedroom watching him. Tony manages to struggle to his feet once more and lashes out in physical violence, the kind of outburst present even in Pinter's earliest dramas, *The Room* and *The Birthday Party*, that in essence signals the death throes of the protagonist. Tony kicks a serving cart and throws the record player to the floor, all the while shouting for Barrett to "Get 'em all out." This ineffectual physical and verbal outburst is the final manifestation of Tony's loss of authority and of his inability to command what is happening because he cannot actually effect his desires himself. When Tony collapses again, Barrett patronizingly, as though to humor his master, ushers the women out—including Susan. "And you. Come on," he says to her contemptuously. As the woman in the black hat exits, Barrett invites her back "tomorrow night" and tells her to "bring John."

The departures are viewed from the staircase-hallway as the camera cuts back and forth, looking down from Tony's vantage (he has crawled out to the landing to look down through the balustrade bars) or up from Barrett's (who whistles during the ejection). Tony accepts a drink from the black-hatted woman and then collapses once more. There is one additional shot of the glittering glass eyes of the woman's fur stole as she picks it up off the bed.

After the last of the outré women leaves, there is a brief exchange of glances between Tony and Susan, each in close-up. While the camera is focused on Tony, there is the sound of a car pulling away. When the focus is on Susan, Barrett's voice is heard. Standing at the foot of the stairs, Barrett demeaningly whistles and clicks his tongue for Susan as though he is whistling for a dog to come. He speaks the last words in the film: "Come on." Tony's head is seen in the foreground as Susan descends the stairs to confront the waiting Barrett. The two stand face to face, the camera, in extreme close-up, showing her left hand touching the heavy metal bracelet that she wears around her right wrist. The camera pans up to her face and she lashes out savagely, striking Barrett's cheek with the bracelet. Reaction shots of the two are revealing. Barrett looks at Susan in pain and with momentary fear. Susan looks back, haughtily dismissing him with a flicker of her eyelids, even though the blow represented her acknowledgment that he has defeated her. When she moves past him, Barrett makes a final servantlike gesture, pulling her wrap up over her shoulder and holding the door for her. Susan runs through the door, and with both hands Barrett slams it shut behind her. He remains leaning against the door, pushing with his hands and his forehead pressed against it as though to keep out any further intruders.

The camera cuts to Susan running down the steps to a tree, which she clings to, sobbing. Back inside the house, Barrett, shot from above, is shown bolting the door. He hesitates for an instant, listening. Outside, as can be seen through a window above the door, a quiet, peaceful snow has started.

Barrett turns off the hall light and then climbs the stairs with a complacent though anticipatory look on his face. While he mounts, his hand trails languorously, lovingly along the banister. As he passes out of the upper right of the frame, his fingers rhythmically stroke the rail. Tony is seen through the bars, partially supine on the hallway floor. His dark shape blends with the shadows—only the bars pick up the off-camera light, which emphasizes their cage-like nature, and his face is half-lit with a pinpoint spotlight. Tony sets his brandy snifter down and slowly reclines. Vera's raucous laugh welcoming Barrett is heard as Tony lays his head and open hand on the carpet. Vera's presence, of course, once more corroborates the conspiracy element. The camera pans down to show the grandfather clock in the entry way on the level below Tony. The clock face, seen through the stairway balustrade, is illuminated—the clock has stopped. After a moment the screen goes black.

In their discussion of the film, Beverle Houston and Marsha Kinder state, "*The Servant* begins punctually with the appointed meeting between master and servant; it ends at some unlocatable time" (22). As Joanne Klein notes, time, an enduring concern in Pinter's work, "remains familiar and intact to the extent that other social artifices in the story retain these qualities, and it disintegrates as these societal conventions founder" (12). Tony, at least, has become frozen in the kind of timeless no-man's-land that the author later describes in his play of the same name (1974).

In transposing *The Servant* to the screen, Pinter faced the problems of adapting a work in one medium to another, from prose to film. His success in creating the adaptation to some extent grew out of the fact that he had very few limitations placed on him by the original story (the reverse would be true when he worked on *The Proust Screenplay*). Maugham's novella provided the main idea for the film, yet because it is so short and relatively undeveloped, Pinter both had to translate the words into visual images and expand the story to a sufficient length for a feature motion picture. Some screenwriters might have found this troublesome, but Pinter was well suited to this situation, since it permitted him to exercise his imaginative powers to their optimum. Truly, part of the power of the picture derives from the fact that he was allowed to develop the characters and their conflict more clearly and fully than they had been developed in the book. His decision to delete part of what was there, in the figure of the narrator, was appropriate, too, for film relies on the visual. In effect he substituted the camera for Merton.

At first the significance of the action is not as clear in the movie as it was in the original, because the omniscient narrator is not present to explain what is happening and how it relates to other events, but ultimately Pinter's approach is more effective, for he demands that the audience come to its own understanding of the characters and events. It is almost always more efficacious for viewers to reach a conclusion without having it drawn for them; if they arrive at a conclusion based on their own logical analysis of the evidence, that conclusion is theirs. And, there is no doubt that Pinter provides sufficient clues for this to happen, yet he does so by presenting information only where it is revealed naturally as the plot unfolds. Moreover, he takes advantage of the immediacy of the impact of film and manipulates and orchestrates the visuals so that they constantly either carry the meaning of the film or reenforce it.

In the prose version of *The Servant*, Maugham is primarily concerned with the moral decay that his protagonist experiences. He illustrates Tony's deterioration by using a subtext that revolves around the post–World War II class struggle in England, and the combat between master and servant functions effectively on several levels to both foment and reflect the author's commentary on declining morals in modern society. After all, with a bow toward Aristotelian tragedy, if a man of Tony's intellect and social status can be so easily destroyed, the prospects for those of lesser talent and inferior backgrounds are gloomy indeed.

At the beginning of chapter 10, Maugham explicitly states what has transpired when the narrator observes, "The screen of convention which stood between [Tony] and Barrett had been shattered" (51). Merton's explanation of how Barrett effected this by destroying his victims from within comes near the conclusion of the novelette. When the narrator walks out of the house into the cold darkness, Tony has rejected his entreaty to leave: "I'm staying. . . . Have a good time in prig's alley" (62). And, conscious of what he is doing, he is ready to join Barrett and the young girl in their depravity. The terrible implications of Tony's decision almost overpower the narrator, whose mind fills with a sense of calamity as he winds his way home.

Throughout his career, Pinter has been intrigued with the concept of domination. This has been one of his main themes from *The Room* through *Ashes to Ashes*. Clearly, it was the question of dominance and subservience that attracted him when he decided to write this screenplay. He willingly incorporated Maugham's themes of moral decay and class struggle in his scenario, but for the screenwriter it must have been the theme of domination that appealed the most. His imagination is always captured by what lies below the surface. He concentrates on the underlying rather than the proximate causes for people's actions. Thus, even though the social elements are interesting and useful as metaphors for expressing and exploring his main themes, there is no doubt that he focuses his attention on the fundamental, elemental aspects of human nature and the human condition that transcend time and place—the threat "constantly there."

The Servant may be set in mid-twentieth-century England, but its meaning is applicable in other times and other places. When the film ends, then, ' the audience has witnessed a reversal that has taken place in the relationship between an upper-class British master and his lower-class servant. The reversal is engineered by the servant and accomplished by his exploitation of his master's prurient desires, but the details are really inconsequential. What matters in Pinter's version of The Servant is that basic human interaction and the nature of dominance are examined.

There is not much material in the Servant box in the British Library archives, but the most interesting items are two loose 4 x 8 pages with the first eight scenes of the screenplay handwritten on them. This is clearly Pinter's first organized work on the script, and most of the scenes are retained intact in the final version, evidence that he starts writing with a fairly well-developed vision of the screenplay in mind. Nevertheless, it is evident that the process is evolutionary in nature, too, as he constantly reworks and refines his material from individual words to entire segments. An examination of the materials gives a hint of the process that the writer went through in developing his screenplay, a process considered in more detail in the analyses of some of his later films.[22]

As might be expected, the screenplay parallels Pinter's stage plays stylistically as well as thematically. Although never presented in a completely realistic mode, his story depends, especially in the beginning, on a semblance of realism to establish a touchstone against which later events can be compared and contrasted. The early scenes convey a sense of spontaneity, a feeling that they have not been carefully prearranged. The camera setups and movement, including occasional hand-held shots, and the gritty visual images all contribute to the appearance of an objective viewpoint through which the surface of concrete reality is conveyed. As the film proceeds, however, the style becomes progressively more formalistic, a movement that culminates in the final, nightmarish sequence. Surface reality is presented subjectively in order to reveal the true essence of the reality that lies below the surface. As a result, the audience experiences very different realities when Tony and Barrett first meet and then when Tony peers into the crystal ball, and the expression of these realities is complemented by the difference in cinematic styles employed at different times in the film.

There are a number of cinematic techniques utilized in The Servant that are essential in bringing out the meaning of the story. The over-the-shoulder shot is typically used to emphasize one character's domination over another, and the movie is full of such shots. The five basic camera angles are all expertly used to reenforce the status of the characters and the shifts in their relationships. The bird's-eye view from the top of the stairs mirrors the distortions taking place within the house; the high-angle and crane shots, particularly in establishing shots, produce an omniscient point of view to suggest a generality in the events filmed (by implication, the members of the audience are subtly persuaded that they, too, are vulnerable) or to reduce the stature of one character in relation to the other. Early in the film this type of shot creates an ironic and foreshadowing quality when Barrett stands over Tony. Tony is clearly aware of the symbolic value, as demonstrated by his attempt to quickly reverse the situation. Low-angle shots are used in conjunction with the high-angle shots when the camera positions are alternated to underscore the characters' relationships. Consequently, the shots operate simultaneously as a statement and as a demonstration of the relationship. The sense of distortion and disorientation is further stressed by the occasional use of oblique-angle shots when the camera is tilted laterally.

Closely allied to the use of high- and low-angle shots to illustrate relationships are several additional characterizing devices that are employed harmoniously to augment or enhance the impressions constructed by the shot angles. Besides high- and low-angle shots, and sometimes in conjunction with them, director Losey also frequently employs selective focusing to communicate the characters' relationships. The focus-shifting technique underlines Tony's or Barrett's relative status at a particular point in the movie by putting one of them in focus, in either the foreground or the background of a shot, while the other is out of focus; then there is a switch so that the first goes out of focus while the second is brought into focus. This technique likewise indicates the flux and transitory nature of their relationship.

The choice of black-and-white film stock is itself an important feature, for traditionally this aligns films with a documentary approach to their subject matter, but it is also appropriate as a means of emphasizing the psychological, interior conflict that is taking place. There are shadows within shadows; lines and planes melt into one another. Black-and-white symbolism, good versus evil, may be suggested, too, but the idea of confusion, of merger rather than clear delineation, of a lack of exactness and definition that exists outside the physical world as the characters engage in mind games is much more important in conveying the content of Pinter's film script. It is interesting to note that available lighting, which is favored by realist filmmakers, is often utilized in this film, but the low-key lighting certainly creates expressionistic effects. Consequently, the conventional psychological symbolism associated with darkness (fear, the unknown, evil) pervades this movie.

Finally, among the most commonly used lighting effects in *The Servant* are pin lighting and half lighting. Oftentimes the elements of the mise-en-scène indicate entrapment and bewilderment. The composition within the frame alternates between open and closed forms. In the bar and the restaurant scenes, for example, the open form gives the sense of life extending beyond the confines of the frame and of the point of interest of the protagonist.

Similarly, the open form is also used in most of the scenes in which Susan and Tony are together, and a sense of freedom, of sociability, of openness, and of potential is thereby conveyed. Conversely, the majority of the scenes between Tony and Barrett are composed of a series of closed-form shots that accentuate the tight focus of their combat almost to the exclusion of all else. The men are limited in their concentration, and an atmosphere of doom and destiny encompasses them. This is especially true in the film's later segments. Frequently, too, the characters are positioned one in the center of the screen and the other off to one side, though in a medium shot so that their surroundings are evident. As the story nears its climax, the surroundings that are visible become increasingly darker and more cluttered. A jumble of items appears to engulf Tony in several scenes (remindful of the condition of Aston's room in *The Caretaker*), the visual overload corresponding to his confused, disordered mind in much the same manner that the motif of bars (as in the myriad of sequences shot through the balustrade) visually expresses his entrapment. With a pin light, Tony's face is brought into dominant contrast so that he is isolated from the background and at the same time besieged by his environment. Further underscoring his plight is the fact that in many of these takes the character's face is lighted only from one side so that the effect is one of division and ambivalence. As in Bergman's masterful *Persona* (1966), there are instances when Tony's and Barrett's faces appear to be two halves of a whole. By the end of the film, their faces, or at least Barrett's face, tend to be more fully lit.

How much of the cinematic quality and the techniques, some of which are called for in the published screenplay and some of which are not, can be attributed to Pinter and how much can be attributed to Losey is problematical. Foster Hirsch points out that "Pinter's coolness, his utter ironic detachment from his characters, his dry wit, his love of nuance and innuendo, emphasized qualities that had been present in the Losey iconography from the beginning" (25). Still, Pinter's later films and Losey's prior efforts can be examined for some clues. The script foreshadows the author's subsequent film work, and Losey's collaborations with Pinter are superior to anything else that the director did. This leads to the conclusion that while Losey was a gifted and experienced director when he made *The Servant,* it was Pinter's script that raised the film to a level that the director had not previously reached. The film version of *The Servant,* then, provides an excellent illustration of how capably Pinter translates from prose to a cinematic medium and foretells some of his later triumphs. In the transformation a minor masterpiece has been created.

The Caretaker (The Guest)

RELEASED: February 1964 (first screened at the Berlin Film Festival on June 27, 1963)

SOURCE: *The Caretaker,* by Pinter; stage play (premiered April 27, 1960)

AWARDS: Berlin Film Festival Silver Bear (1963), Edinburgh Festival Certificate of Merit (1963)

PRODUCTION COMPANY: BL; Janus

DIRECTOR: Clive Donner

EDITOR: Fergus McDonnell

PHOTOGRAPHED BY: Nicolas Roeg

PRODUCERS: Charles Kasher (executive) and Michael Birkett

PRODUCTION DESIGN: Reece Pemberton

SOUND RECORDISTS: Robert Allen, Peter Bridge

EFFECTS SCORED BY: Ron Grainer

CAST: Alan Bates (Mick), Robert Shaw (Aston), Donald Pleasence (Davies)

RUNNING TIME: 105 minutes

BLACK AND WHITE

RATING: Not rated

VIDEO: Lion

FIRST SCREENED AT THE Berlin Film Festival on June 27, 1963, *The Caretaker* was released publicly in February 1964.[1] In the United States, the film appeared under the title *The Guest* (perhaps to avoid confusion with Hal Bartlett's *The Caretakers,* which had been released in 1963). Pinter's second film, *The Caretaker* was the first from a screenplay based on the adaptation of one of his own stage plays. Critically acclaimed, it was awarded the Berlin Film Festival Silver Bear (in 1963) for "Clive Donner's balanced direction of Harold Pinter's remarkable script and the ensemble performances of three fine actors" and the Edinburgh Festival Certificate of Merit (1963)— the only British film so honored.[2]

In light of its success, it is ironic that there had been some difficulty in securing backing for the film. The production cost of £30,000, with no guarantee of distribution, finally was privately financed by a group of backers (Caretaker Films, Ltd.) that included Richard Burton, Leslie Caron, Noel Coward, Peter Hall, Peter Sellers, Elizabeth Taylor, and the continuity girl (Lee Turner). Ironically, Pinter's combined success with the stage and film versions of *The Caretaker* (which premiered on the stage on April 27, 1960) brought him his first real sense of financial security (over the years it has been estimated that he has earned an average of £250,000 per film script).[3]

This black-and-white film is notable for its distinguished crew and cast. Directed by Donner, photographed by Nicolas Roeg (who later turned to directing), and edited by Fergus McDonnell, it features the New York stage cast of Donald Pleasence, whose superb acting beautifully brings Davies to life, Robert Shaw as Aston in a performance nearly equaling Pleasence's, and Alan Bates as Mick (Pleasence and Bates were reprising their roles in the original stage version). In fact, Pleasence believed that he achieved his finest performance in this film (Knowles, "1994–1995 and 1995–1996," 156). The motion picture is an excellent cinematic translation of the play. Donner's direction is nearly flawless, with the exception of two scenes in which Mick attacks Davies, which are a little too dark to tell what is going on, so the audience's terror is not increased precisely because they cannot see what is happening, and also the pacing of the ending is a little slow.

Stanley Kauffmann's review of the movie emphasizes the effect of exchanging a stage for the screen:

> It is a fascinating, funny, eerie film, a work of murky evocations boiling out of grubby naturalistic minutiae [the film was shot in five weeks at 31 Downs Road, a derelict house in Hackney, not far from Pinter's childhood home, and at 36 Dover Street, London]. That is, of course, the Pinter method, but in this film we are seeing that method used at its best so far. . . . One feels that, at last, the work has been fully revealed . . . the smallest subtleties of expression can buttress his naturalistic mode, where magnified presence can lend greater implications to silences and hints and physical objects, where the skillful placement and shifting of the audience by camera movement and angle can underscore his interest to draw us into confined areas, literally and figuratively. ("The Guest," 213)

Gerald Nelson, commenting on this film, says that compared with his stage work, Pinter's work in the cinema shows both greater freedom and

The Caretaker/The Guest (1964). Donald Pleasence as the tramp Davies and Alan Bates as Mick. BL/United Artists. Jerry Ohlinger Archives.

control of movement in creating "real human personalities" (33–34). Along the same lines, Penelope Gilliat notes Davies's defensive use of language in the motion picture, stating that the old man is "haunted by suspicions of malevolence, but he has no one to ask about them; so when he is talked to he often says 'What?' not because he hasn't heard, but as a hopeless way of gaining time and puzzling out how much ground he has just lost" (24). Indeed, there is characterizing repetition in the tramp's talk. He is trying to grab hold of reality, and Aston finishes many of Davies's tortured efforts at expressing his thoughts as part of his attack on that reality.

These comments are reenforced by Pinter in "Filming 'The Caretaker,'" an article that he cowrote with his director. Pinter sees the situation as cinematic: "It seemed to me, that when you have two people standing on the stairs and one asks the other if he would like to be caretaker in this house, and the other bloke, you know, who is work-shy, doesn't want in fact to say no, he doesn't want the job, but at the same time he wants to edge it round . . . . Now it seems to me there's an enormous amount of internal conflict within one of the characters and external conflict between them—and it's exciting cinema" (19).

Pinter is in agreement about the work's being "fully revealed," and he goes on to acknowledge the superiority of the film in conveying the bond between Aston and Mick as well: "You can say the play had been 'opened out' . . . that things . . . crystallized when I came to think about it as a film. Until then I didn't know that I wanted to do them [films] because I'd accepted the limitations of the stage. For instance, there's a scene in the garden of the house, which is very silent; two silent figures with a third looking on. I think in the film one has been able to hit the relationship of the brothers more clearly than in the play" (19).

The writer is also of the opinion that the mechanics of moviemaking, things such as close-ups and focusing techniques, are responsible for a cinematic version that is more intimate than the play at the same time that they allow him to establish the relationships between the characters more clearly. In the screenplay, it is obvious that Pinter exults in the possibilities that the film medium provides for him to go beyond his own original text. There is a corroboration of André Bazin's claim that the function of cinema is "to bring to light certain details that the stage would have left untreated" (251). Arnold P. Hinchliffe points out that the significance of the final glance between the two brothers, Aston and Mick, at the end of the drama when the intruding tramp, Davies, is rejected is more emphatic (especially the hint of triumph on Mick's part) than it is on stage because of the camera's focusing ability—in the play there is only a slight indication of Mick's underlying emotional reaction (175 n. 16). In the drama, the stage directions read: *Aston comes in. He closes the door, moves into the room and faces Mick. They look at each other. Both are smiling faintly* (Pinter, *The Caretaker*, 75). On stage there is only a slight implication of collusion; there is nothing to direct the audience's attention specifically to the men's faces, so the quick look that passes between them might easily be missed by the viewers. On the screen the expressions are carefully framed. Since this glance epitomizes the brothers' relationship, it is easy to see why Pinter feels that in the movie the essence of the work is captured "more clearly than in the play."

An illustration of what Pinter says is found in the film when Mick hears Aston coming and leaves the room to cross the landing and go into the empty room across the hall. When Aston comes upstairs, he pauses on the landing and looks at the door as though he knows that Mick is in there. There is a cut to Mick, seen from the back, as he leans against the door, listening to

Aston, who is on the landing. Cut back to Aston, who then goes into the room with Davies. This movement and relative positioning emphasizes the related interactions between the characters in a way not easily duplicated on stage.

The opening out is enhanced by the naturalistic capabilities of a cinematic medium, too. Pinter is aware that the proscenium arch defines action as prescribed, transpiring in a closed form. The audience does not assume that action occurs simultaneously in or is extended into the wings. In film the frame corresponds (albeit constantly temporarily) to the proscenium arch, yet a number of shots establish a sense of movement and expand spatial awareness by presenting fragments of space in a fluid manner, moving the camera to different lateral positions and/or closer or farther back. Because the viewing distance from the audience to the stage remains constant, live drama can seem more static and prescribed. Of course, film presents the audience with a two-dimensional image, so it suffers some limitations in representing real-world space, but movies can suggest broader spaces than can drama. For example, Mick's parked car in the street outside the apartment building implies the existence of a surrounding city, even if the city is not focused upon or even seen.

Says Pinter, "What I'm very pleased about myself is that in the film, as opposed to the play, we see a real house and real snow outside, dirty snow and the streets. We don't see them very often but they're there. . . . and these characters move in the context of a real world—as I believe they do. In the play, when people were confronted with just a set . . . they often assumed it was all taking place in limbo, in a vacuum, and the world outside hardly existed, or had existed at some point but was only half remembered. Now one thing which I think is triumphantly expressed in the film is Clive's concentration on the characters when they are outside the room" (Pinter and Donner, 23). In other words, that "there is a world outside" is important to the meaning of the work, and in the writer's opinion this world is better indicated in the film than in the stage version.[4] Ultimately, it must be remembered that Pinter thinks of his characters as being "real." While Davies may represent the existential Chaplinesque/Beckettian tramp on the road of life, at the same time he is a *real* tramp who probably does "stink the place out" literally and who becomes characterized by variations on the tramp's "Thank you, mister" every time he is given something, be it money, cigarettes, or clothing. Aston's acquaintance with the names of tools and their functions and Mick's knowledgeable recital of bus numbers (after the manner of Pinter's amusing review sketches "Trouble in the Works" and "The Black and White") and his tracing the highway route to Sidcup (added in the film) link them to the real world.

The opening out also reflects the dissimilarities in the two media with which the screenwriter is working. Although the inclusion of outdoor scenes in the movie sacrifices some of the emotional intensity evoked by the sense of confinement of the stage version, Pinter has been able to concentrate on other devices to achieve a like effect on film. The closed-in, claustrophobic sense of the stage set is replicated on screen by shooting through piles of junk and by compressing Aston and Davies on the beds in close-ups and tight two-shots of the men crushed against the walls under the down-pressing shapes of the dormers.

There are other instances that reenforce the meaning gleaned from this episode: Mick's sudden attack on Davies is more startling as he appears in the frame without warning; the younger brother picks up the old man in his van to take him down to Sidcup to recover the papers that the tramp claims will establish his identity—then he merely drives around a traffic circle and lets his passenger out, showing Mick's unwillingness to be *obviously* responsible for his rival's removal and simultaneously drawing attention to the ritualistic circularity of action and conversation that fills the drama. This scene also functions (as the curtain does on stage) to break the tension generated by Aston's hospital speech at the end of act 2. And, finally, shots of Mick's sometimes furtive activities, moving from one room to another and watching through partly open doors when Aston comes home, plus the older brother's realization that this is being done, help make the relationship between the brothers more comprehensible (the fishpond scene, introduced in the movie, implies that they may be working together).

Because some of the action now takes place outside the room, dialogue must be added, cut, or rearranged in order to accommodate the differences in setting. Partially, too, the dialogue alterations (e.g., the removal of some lines from Aston's hospital monologue) are necessary because of the kind of flow of action demanded by film. As a matter of fact, the screenwriter seems more willing to substitute pure action for words in some cases, as when Aston wordlessly places the ladder under the bed or when he shakes the blanket—making Davies sneeze—without the preceding comment that it might by dusty, which was included in the stage version. In addition, the author uses the camera's focusing ability for comic effect, as when Davies, in the foreground, close up, notes that there is a "good bit of stuff" in the room, and the piled junk seen behind him almost seems to be closing in, or when the tramp asks, "Is this in use at all?" while he and Aston unload the buried bed. All in all, while the transference to film has weakened some aspects of the theatrical version of *The Caretaker,* it has strengthened many others, so that Pinter has managed to retain the essence of his play on the screen, which, according to Knowles, Pinter states is about victory, not defeat.

As is typical with most of Pinter's scripts, the plot of *The Caretaker* is simple.[5] In fact, Pleasence, who created the role of Davies in the original production and then gave up a part in George Stevens's *The Greatest Story Ever Told* in order to reprise the part in the film version, has comically reduced the plot to a six-word summary: "boy meets tramp, boy loses tramp."[6] As is also typically true of Pinter's dramas, a minimal plot provides few clues, but this does not mean that it contains a simple meaning—instead, a number of possible alternatives come into play. In *The Caretaker,* two brothers, one a former mental patient (Aston), and an old tramp (Davies) become locked in a battle of wills when the recuperating brother rescues the tramp from an unpleasant situation and invites him into his room, which is in a house owned by the younger brother (Mick). The drama evolves in a series of confrontations between these three characters as they try to establish relationships with one another. The result of these confrontations is the expulsion of the old man.

In choosing a play, his own *The Caretaker,* to transform into a film for his second attempt at screenwriting, Pinter faced a different set of problems than he had in adapting *The Servant* to the screen. Many of the visual images were already incorporated in the stage play script, and the drama was the right length for a feature film. However, stage drama depends much more heavily on dialogue than film does; indeed, stage plays tend to become wooden when presented on film exactly because of the importance and preponderance of words.

Ordinarily, either a filmed play is relatively static, with long takes of characters delivering dialogue, or the dialogue is delivered in a series of short takes; the latter approach is unsatisfactory because the spoken lines are chopped up and the camera seems to jump around. Added to this is the fact that drama takes place in a confined space, both literally and figuratively. Stage sets tend to be indoors, and there are often not many scene changes. In the stage version of *The Caretaker,* for instance, everything takes place in one room. A stage play is an excellent vehicle for presenting intellectual and psychological themes because of the predominance of words and the nature of the set. In contrast, film can more easily produce emotional reactions in the audience because of the immediate impact of visual images that are not, cannot be, first filtered through the observer's mind as words are. This is the essence of montage.

According to the proponents of one critical theory, the opening shot, certainly the opening segment, of a film should contain the essence of what that film is about. That is, the initial sequence should visually symbolize the core of the film. Therefore, an analysis of the beginning of a movie provides for an insight into the meaning being expressed and an understanding of the techniques utilized to express that meaning. There are literary parallels, of course: the importance of "Air #1" in John Gay's *Beggar's Opera* and of act 1 (even scene 1) in Oliver Goldsmith's *She Stoops to Conquer* are obvious theatrical examples. Edgar Allen Poe understood this principle when he wrote a book review of a Charles Dickens novel after reading only the first chapter.

The initial shots in *The Caretaker* are significant in establishing the meaning that Pinter will develop during the course of the film. They convey the movie's thematic kernel. The importance of the house; Mick's potential strength, watchfulness, and patience; his ability to coerce Davies into forcing himself out of his refuge; the relationship between the brothers; the underlying tensions; the ambiguity of the situation; the gritty reality of a theatrical world opened out—all of this is suggested or prepared for through the use of cinematic devices in the opening sequence of the film. When we see Mick cross a street, for example, we are outside the house and the room that is the only locale in which the stage play takes place. When Mick enters the building, climbs the stairs, and goes into the room tracked by the camera, besides the sense of menace described above, a sense of the size of the house and the existence of other rooms is imparted to the audience, so that Aston's shutting himself off is more starkly recognized.

The first scene in the movie is both a departure from the original stage script and an opening out of that script. The titles are run over a shot of Mick's car parked outside the building in which Aston lives. It is night. The eerie sound of a train passing is heard over, establishing a feeling of foreboding. Since Mick is his brother's keeper, all of the action takes place in or about his house; the intruder/guest Davies is a tramp, and tramps are associated with trains. This all sets the stage for what is to follow.

As the scene develops, Mick emerges from the car, the interior of which is so dark that he has not been seen previously. Not only is he watching the house, then, but he appears somewhat menacing, too. His leather Teddy-Boy-style jacket along with the cascading, atonal music that accompanies him as he crosses the street support this impression.

On-screen movement is one of the filmmaker's primary tools. Although a subtle element, it can be an important component in the conglomerate development of a montage, with a potentially profound and powerful effect on an audience's subconscious. It is revealing to see how movement is utilized in this sequence, which was not included in the stage version. The first indication that the audience has that the car is occupied is when there is a flicker of Mick's hand, lifting a cigarette to his unseen mouth, observed through the driver's-side window. A beat later this is followed by the casual tossing of the cigarette out of the window. The audience is now aware that someone is present, but tension is created, because neither the identity nor the intent of the person can be discerned. While the disposal of the cigarette may be merely a continuation of the process of drawing attention to the automobile (although the car is in the foreground, the house across the street in the background is lighted so that it is the dominant feature in the frame), littering is also a minor, thoughtless, antisocial act, so it may increase minimally the audience's concern about who is in the car and what is being done in there. Perhaps there is a nod as well to the gangster- or cowboy-film convention of a character purposefully discarding a cigarette just before initiating a violent action, an action that often involves gunplay.

When Mick gets out of the car, he momentarily moves offscreen, then walks quickly left to right across the frame and again offscreen for an instant before reappearing and walking across the street, his back to the camera. Mick's face is seen so briefly, and in profile, that it is difficult to determine what he looks like. His disappearance from the screen increases the mystery, and his movement away from the camera further distances him from the audience both physically and psychologically. At the same time, it appears that the threat is withdrawing.

Collectively, Mick's movements are sending mixed signals, thereby intensifying the audience's subconscious discomfort. A left-to-right movement across the screen is considered natural and therefore comforting; movement to offscreen is disturbing and suggests that the character does not abide by socially imposed restrictions—he determines his own course and limitations. The movement away from the camera is confusing, because the threatening figure is retreating, but this movement likewise reduces the audience's ability to verify the nature of the character. The totality of the effect is remindful of the circular pattern of menace, communication, and verification in Pinter's stage plays (see below).

The ambiguity is compounded when Mick mounts the steps, for an upward movement in film signifies positive attributes, such as freedom, strength, control, and hope, but there has been a cut and the camera has been placed to the left of the stairs (i.e., a directorial choice has been made) so that this movement is simultaneously from right to left. Lateral movements are diminished by vertical movements, yet the right-to-left progression conveys the unnatural, further stimulating a sense of tension. The right-left movement can also imply that Mick is a man of action and represent the character's determination, so there is an internal tension between these contradictory impulses.[7]

When Mick arrives at the top of the stairs, there is another cut and he is shown in a medium close-up—but the closed form and the tight framing, together with his three-quarter-turn positioning, are confining and retain an atmosphere of mystery because he is still partially concealed. Again, the audience may even feel that the character is antisocial, consciously avoiding them or hiding something. Mick's threatening anonymity is undercut, however, when he produces a set of keys and unlocks the door. The discordant musical tones that accompany him on his walk across the street indicate that he is up to no good, yet it is suddenly apparent that he belongs here. As is revealed during the course of the movie, Mick is a complex character, and all of the contradictory and unsettling features in the opening segment demonstrate this while concurrently containing the thematic kernels. The entire sequence, from the first movement observed through the car window to Mick's entrance into the house, takes approximately thirty-four seconds. The details and refinements of the plot and themes that constitute the movie proper are dealt with in much the same cinematic manner.

In Pinter's early plays there was a thematic cluster that paralleled the effects created through the movie's opening and to which the meaning of the stage version of *The Caretaker* is clearly related. The controlling image in the dramas is of people in a room—a room with a door, and outside that door something is snuffling about, an intruder trying to get in. In order to assuage the feeling of menace, to verify whether what is outside the door truly is a menace, characters try to communicate with one another. Communication, though, is inefficient, in part because the inhabitant of the room is fearful of revealing his or her personal vulnerability and does not want to expose any potential weakness through the communication with whatever is on the other side of the door. A circular effect is created as the lack of communication intensifies the menace and the resultant increased need for verification, which in turn weakens the ability to communicate. This circularity feeds on itself and creates an impossible situation for the inhabitant.[8]

In the three "comedies of menace" that precede *The Caretaker* (*The Room, The Birthday Party,* and *The Dumb Waiter*), the world pictured in Pinter's plays is a place in which an a priori underlying terror of loneliness combines with a young Jew's knowledge of the atrocities of Adolph Hitler's Germany and Hackney alleys full of neo-Nazi thugs waiting to "carve up" students on their way home from school, which creates a feeling of omnipresent menace.

This is a description of a Beckettian world as well, yet it is a recognizable world. People are existing on the edge to the extent that they will accept any possibility that is offered that might fulfill their individual psychological needs. This is clearly expressed in Davies's fears, in the inadequacy of his verbal attacks on minorities such as blacks (in which group he includes East Indians), the Irish hooligan, and the Scotch git (Davies is a Scottish name!) of whom he is so afraid that he is incapable of expressing himself articulately. He is likewise left speechless when Mick asks him if he is a foreigner. His broken phrases mirror his shattered sense of identity, which cannot be established because his papers do not exist. He is in a state of desperation that pushes him to an existential acceptance of an any-port-in-a-storm mentality. Such content is suitable for a stage production because the cluttered, dark room full of isolated items reflects the minds of the characters and their psychological states. The single set also intensifies the confined nature of their situation. Even though both Mick's and Aston's occasional excursions outside demonstrate that the room does not exist as a closed system, for Davies it represents a fortuitous sanctuary cut off from the world, and he does not want to leave it. One of the writer's challenges in adapting the work for the screen was to bring in the outside without diminishing the sensation of confinement.

Pinter accomplishes this in several scenes. Opening out the script has advantages beyond showing that there is a world outside Aston's room. The shot of Mick and Aston in the back garden makes the shed real, not merely a figment of Aston's desires, and it shows that progress is being made. Aston has talked about building the shed, and in this shot he touches the wood that he will use (although there is no dialogue heard, the men are together, in much the same physical relationship as Aston and Davies were earlier), and Davies, watching through the window, obviously sees a threat in their togetherness.

The final meaning of the play has been simply expressed by Pinter. Terrence Rattigan claims that "When I saw *The Caretaker* I told Pinter that I knew what it meant. 'It's about the God of the Old Testament, the God of the New, and Humanity, isn't it?' Pinter said blankly, 'No, Terry, it's about a caretaker and two brothers.'"[9] This statement becomes meaningful when joined with Pinter's assertion in Charles Marowitz's "Theatre Abroad" article in the *Village Voice* that the play is "about love."

Love in a Pinter play differs from the conventional definition of love. From *The Room* through *The Homecoming*, what Pinter calls "love" really amounts to an individual psychological need that must be fulfilled for the emotional well-being of the organism. In psychological jargon, this need is categorized as a primary appetite (something that is necessary for homeostatic balance). When "love" is equated with "need," a certain pattern falls into place. This is as close as the author has come to supplying a definition of what in his subsequent dramas becomes his major thematic element, and it provides an understandable basis for his characters' actions. Thus, when Pinter talks about love, he means a psychological *need* for acceptance or affection or emotional attachment. What he is saying in *The Caretaker* becomes clear when one realizes that Davies, Aston, and Mick all need to satisfy a primary appetite for acceptance, affection, or emotional attachment, and their actions are designed to fulfill their needs.

In terms of the action of the play, all three of the characters have individual needs for attachment of some kind, and everything that they do is aimed either at creating such a relationship or maintaining one that already exists. Aston turns to a stranger in the hope that he can establish a relationship that will not end in his being betrayed. He is a character whose need for human contact has led him to disillusionment, since his overtures to others have been rejected because of the unusual nature of those overtures, yet he keeps trying to establish a relationship with someone, and ultimately the union between him and his brother is stronger for his efforts.

His talk is slow, quiet, monosyllabic in the beginning, but as he gets better his speech changes, becoming quicker, louder, more assured. He moves from ready acquiescence to steadfast refusal of Davies's demands. His tinkering with things represents his trying to make connections, to bring his fragmented mind back to unity. At the end he reestablishes and redefines his relationship with Mick. He is more able to take care of himself; perhaps he is actually going to build the shed. He gets things working now. And, the matter-of-fact tone of his description of the event in the hospital builds powerfully, movingly (a parallel with Mick's less emotionally loaded but more lyrical description of decorating with teal blue and copper).

In the long run, though, Aston's role is basically that of an object over which his brother and his newfound "friend" battle. Davies tries to form alliances with both Aston and Mick but fails. In the final analysis it must be admitted that Davies remains an enigmatic, chameleon-like, existential figure who tries to fulfill his own needs for companionship and easy security by changing to fit the requirements needed to fulfill the needs of others so that they will form an alliance with him (there are traces of Davies in both Stella in *The Collection* and Ruth in *The Homecoming* in this respect). He allows those around him to play out their own fantasies because he is so indefinite, taking on the shape that they need. The irony is that his changeability and lack of selectivity ultimately cost him what he most desires.

Mick, who displays his acuity during his games with Davies when he tricks the old man into contradicting himself, is aware of the tramp's changeable nature, and this allows him to manipulate the old man. He recognizes Davies as a threat to the union between himself and his brother and strives to displace the tramp so as to keep his own position secure.

Mick's strategy in expelling the tramp indicates that his protective stance regarding Aston derives from fraternal affection rather than merely from a perception of duty. It is clear that Mick recognizes Davies as an opponent from the very beginning, and it is also clear that he would have little trouble driving the intruder out with physical force. His immediate reaction to the presence of a guest in his brother's room is an attack that completely overpowers his victim. Still, he does not try to force a withdrawal. Instead, he initiates a plan whereby Aston will himself eventually reject the old man voluntarily and therefore will not turn against his brother for having banished his friend, and so that banishment will not in itself make the tramp more appealing. Mick understands, as the song in *The Fantasticks* suggests, that children are most likely to put beans in their ears when they are told not to do so.

If Mick were simply being protective, he would have removed the threat to his relationship with Aston instantly and permanently by force and the implication of future violence or even legal recourse, but he undertakes the slower, more devious procedure because his brother's feelings are important to him. He wants to be sure that his actions do not cost him the relationship that he has with his brother, a relationship that is emphasized by the fact that they always refer to each other as "brother," never by name. The motivation, then, is fraternal affection, and they must unite in overthrowing a potential usurper. This will bring them closer together, a psychological ploy that politicians sometimes exercise.

Finally, as mentioned above, when Mick leaves the stage for the last time, having defeated Davies, the two brothers smile faintly at each other. Clifford Leech sees this smile as a token that things are again as they should be—the family tie has been restored and there is hope for the future: "They are brothers, and . . . they are together for a moment, in silence . . . as they smile . . . there is understanding and affection" (29). Director Peter Hall has pointed out the importance of specific actions in Pinter's plays.[10] If the author calls for an action, it is not merely a piece of "business" but something that has a direct bearing on the meaning of the drama. The called-for smile, then, is meant to be significant. This last glance between the two brothers helps emphasize the theme of need, for it signifies their dependence upon each other, thereby placing their actions and motives in perspective. They have proven their affection to each other, and Mick's going out indicates a realization that the situation is now secure. He can rely on his brother to expel Davies, so his own presence is no longer necessary.

Whereas some critics claim that the glance suggests a conspiracy of or at least collusion between the brothers against Davies, it actually signifies their recognition that the ties between them have been reestablished. They have not acted in union to entrap and torment the derelict; they have found that their relationship with each other is valuable and that it can withstand considerable outside pressures that threaten it, whether those pressures are in the form of electrical shock treatment or an intruding tramp.

In interpreting the play, the items to be considered include the questions of identity and verification clustering around Davies; Aston's attempted reorientation, as well as his suggested Christ-figure qualities and his role in the society-versus-artist confrontation; and the problem of communication and interaction between individuals. The last element is probably the most important in determining the ultimate meaning of the play, for the actions of the three characters are reasonable given that each is trying to establish an attachment with one of the others. Simultaneously, each is trying to protect that relationship from an outside interference, the third member, which threatens to destroy it by forming a new pairing.[11]

It is evident why the tramp had to go, though. In the relationship between the two brothers, an outsider could weaken their bond, and their power to help one another might be diminished as a consequence. In John Arden's words, The Caretaker is "a study of the unexpected strength of family ties against an intruder" (29). Aston is dependent on Mick to provide a sanctuary where no one will bother him and where he can work things out in peace. Mick is his brother's keeper, his caretaker.

Interviewed by Kenneth Tynan, Pinter is even more explicit about how the drama might have ended and how it does end, incidentally recognizing that his dramatic techniques have improved since he wrote his first stage plays: "I think that in this play . . . I *have* developed, that I have no need to use cabaret turns and blackouts and screams in the dark. . . . I do see this play as merely . . . a particular human situation, concerning three particular people." The "human situation" is the confrontation of various characters with various psychological needs.[12] The tramp is important only if he functions as a satisfactory agent; he ceases to be important when this requirement is not met. Since his loss is not traumatic, he can be ousted easily. When both brothers are cognizant of this, the play ends. And, when the writer turns the play into a film, he moves even further away from those "cabaret turns and blackouts."

As indicated in the introduction, an interesting phenomenon of Pinter scholarship is the lack of consideration of how the dramatist's stage plays differ from his film version of the same works. One of the differences between how Pinter approaches adapting someone else's work to the screen and how he approaches adapting his own stage plays is that when he uses another author's writing as the basis for his screenplay, he picks out the thematic elements that most appeal to him and emphasizes them. While he may well be being true to his source, then, that truth may be established in much the same way that he creates realistic dialogue.

From the beginning of his career, critics have commented that Pinter has a tape-recorder ear and that he accurately reproduces realistic-sounding dialogue on stage. The key, though, is that he selects certain quintessential elements and amplifies them.[13] Real language literally reproduced on stage does not sound as real as Pinter's artificial dialogue;[14] in a sense he has created a suprarealistic dialogue that captures and expresses the essence of normal speech. In his cinematic adaptions of novels, his intent likewise is to focus on those components that comprise the essence of the work rather than trying to faithfully reproduce the novel on film detail by detail. In adapting his own works, although he may exercise the opportunity afforded by the medium of film to open them out, to augment with cinematic techniques and devices what was already there, basically he relies on what is there and does not try to focus on certain elements in order to express the essence of the drama.

Therefore, the meaning of the film version of *The Caretaker* is the same as the meaning of the stage version. And, as might be expected, the archival material is not especially helpful in tracing Pinter's artistic decisions, precisely because the stage and film scripts are so similar.[15]

At the same time, as Giannetti has observed, "Since plays stress the primacy of language, one of the major problems in adapting them for the screen is determining how much of the language is necessary in a predominantly visual art like movies" (220). In *The Caretaker* do visuals merely tend to illustrate the language, or is visual expression substituted for verbal expression so that spoken information is replaced by visual images that not only convey the same meaning but carry the same emotional content as well? The symbolic importance of Aston's room is continually reiterated by shots that emphasize clutter, which reflect his state of mind. As the film progresses, the suffocating, towering piles of junk are not foregrounded as they were in the opening shots. The surroundings seem to become simpler, less congested, more clean, though sparse and even barren. Pinter creates an illusion of reality that cannot literally be felt.

As a matter of fact, the film confirms, emphasizes, and further elucidates the meaning distilled from the drama. This raises an interesting critical question: is the information gathered from this extraneous source (the film) valid in interpreting the play? Or, are the film and the play separate, though related, entities that perforce must stand on their own? In examining the play after having viewed the film, are elements introduced that are foreign to the original? And, if this the case, how does a critic confront this?

Again, the plot and the themes are dealt with in much the same way in the movie. For instance, in the theatrical version, the stage directions suggest that Davies is following his host like a scared, lost dog when they first enter the room at the beginning of the play: "ASTON *and* DAVIES *enter,* ASTON *first,* DAVIES *following, shambling, breathing heavily*" ([7]). In the film, which shows the two men walking down the street on their way to the room, this comparison is certainly indicated by Davies's shuffling back and forth after Aston. (Pinter is the stocky man in a mackintosh who walks past Davies in this scene.) The most interesting thing about the opening sequence of the film version of *The Caretaker,* then, is that in adding it Pinter not only symbolically captures and conveys the essence of his stage play, but in doing so he demonstrates that he understands how film functions and that he can control this medium as surely as he controls the dramatic medium.

Possibly an early indication of Pinter's use of art objects as metaphors (despite his contention that he does not use symbols) might be seen in the introduction in the play of the mysterious and conspicuous figure of Buddha that Mick smashes (much as society crushes Aston). This is the statue of a sensitive man; yet the statue in the play appears to have no significance other than its mere existence. Like the stove, it has no connection; it is absurd—unless it represents the uselessness of religion or the meaninglessness of symbols, or both. At the same time, the film is filled with containers (the bucket hanging from ceiling) that exclude rather than include, and the Buddha, like Davies, does not belong in the dark, compressed, junky world that Aston inhabits: bright and pearly white, the statue is in the background in many shots, accentuated by the lighting. Thus emphasized, it may be seen as representing Aston's past, the purity and sublimity of his thoughts when he saw what others could not.

Mick gets so emotional at the end of the movie that he goes too far and breaks the object ("Look, ummm," he says, as he stands in the doorway about to leave, the hesitation indicating that he feels bad about his action, though he never completes his apology), but breaking the statue also demonstrates that Aston can break/has broken from his past—the possibility of the break having been implied by his bringing Davies home in the first place. There is also an indication that he can move on in his life, since the Buddha, having been smashed into smithereens, cannot be brought back; Aston will not go back either. The irony is that Aston's initial enlightenment about what the world should be like ideally has been replaced by a pragmatic enlightenment about how to survive in the real world. The destruction of the statue thereby takes on the suggestion of a signal between the two brothers, a physical representation of Mick's statement that the Davies affair is closed. Aston's lack of reaction seems to be a concurrence.

One of the unexpected complications in examining a literary text can be trying to determine what is the authoritative text. Various editions may differ, either because of changes or deletions made by the publishers or because of alterations made by the author. In examining the stage version of *The Caretaker*, I discovered that several different editions had been published—with little or no notation that any changes had been made.[16] In the introduction I mention that filmmaking exhibits this problem as a matter of course, for there are often several different cuts produced before the final version is decided upon. This practice may be analogous to out-of-town tryouts in live theatre, but the cuts remain fixed as concrete products while the tryouts are transitory. Complicating the problem that the existence of diverse cuts of the same movie can create for someone who wants to analyze the film is the situation that occurs when a film is censored (and both censored and uncensored versions are distributed), when different versions are released for, say, the European market and the American market, or when the movie is edited to be shown on television.

An analysis of *The Guest* involves this last case. It is difficult enough to compare a film with its dramatic original to assess what changes might have been made in transferring the play to the screen and why the alterations were made (and whether they are effective). It is even more difficult when the theatrical release differs from the telecast version. When *The Guest* was shown nationally in the United States on the Turner Broadcasting System, a number of cuts had been made, presumably though not necessarily to fit the film into a time slot of given length (complete with commercial breaks). Davies's walking about the streets and slouching in an alley doorway after Aston has thrown him out of the room is a poignant and telling moment—but it is one of the sequences that is deleted from the television version. It is amusing that some of the deletions made for the television presentation were among the segments specifically added to open up the production, Mick's driving Davies around the circle being one of the most obvious excisions to end up on the television editor's cutting-room floor.

The quality of the exceptional original play comes through to help make *The Caretaker* a fine movie; it makes one wish that Pinter would write more plays and that they would be made into movies. He could do both.

The Pumpkin Eater

RELEASED: July 15, 1964

SOURCE: *The Pumpkin Eater,* by Penelope Mortimer; novel (1962)

AWARDS: British Film Academy Award for Best Screenplay, 1964; British Film Academy Award for acting (Bancroft); nominated for Academy of Motion Picture Arts and Sciences Award for Best Actress (Bancroft); British Academy Award for Best Black and White Cinematography and Best Foreign Actress (Bancroft); nominated for Best Film and Best British Film; Cannes Film Festival, nominated for Best Female Performance

PRODUCTION COMPANY: Royal International–Columbia Pictures

DIRECTOR: Jack Clayton

EDITOR: James B. Clark

DIRECTOR OF PHOTOGRAPHY: Oswald Morris

PRODUCER: James Woolf

ARTISTIC DIRECTOR: Edward Marshall

ART DEPARTMENT LIAISON: David Fiockes

MUSIC: Georges Delerue

SOUND RECORDISTS: Peter Handford and John Aldred

COSTUME DESIGNER: Motley

CAST: Anne Bancroft (Jo), Peter Finch (Jake), Richard Johnson (Giles), Frances White/Kate Nicholls (Dinah), Fergus McClelland (Fergus), Sharon Maxwell/Mimos Annis (Sharon), Kash Dewar (Mark), Elizabeth Dear/Sarah Nicholls (Elizabeth), Gregory Phillips/Rupert Osborn (Pete), Michael Ridgeway/Martin Norton (Jack), Alan Webb (Mr. Armitage), Sir Cedric Hardwicke (Mr. James), Maggie Smith (Philpot), Mark Crader (Youngest Child), Faith Kent (Nanny), Cyril Luckham (Doctor), Eric Porter (Ingram), Yootha Joyce (Woman in Hairdresser's), James Mason (Conway), Gerald Sim (Man at Party), Janine Gray (Beth), Rosalind Atkinson (Mrs. James), John Junkin (Undertaker), Anthony Nicholls (Surgeon), Leslie Nunnerley (Waitress at Zoo), Frank Singuineau (The King of Israel), John Franklin Robbins (Parson)

RUNNING TIME: 110 minutes
BLACK AND WHITE
RATING: Not rated

PINTER'S ACCOMPLISHMENT in the script for *The Pumpkin Eater* can be measured somewhat by what he keeps and what he discards from his source. Unlike *The Servant,* in which the screenwriter opened out his source psychologically and thematically, and *The Caretaker,* where the physical outside world was incorporated, in his third film he narrows his focus and reduces the thematic and symbolic content.

In Penelope Mortimer's 1962 novel *The Pumpkin Eater,* the main character examines her life during her marriage to Jake Armitage. She traces the events that, over a period of about thirteen years, lead to her coming to grips with reality, her own nature, and her relationship with reality.

The plot of the novel is simple and straightforward. Jo Armitage, who has a great many children from three previous marriages, marries and has more children. Her new husband is unfaithful to her, but the couple stays together. The wife seems obsessed with having more and more children. Finally, her husband convinces her to have an abortion and to be sterilized, something that he is motivated to do because he is having an affair with another woman, a woman who would break off the relationship if a child were born to his wife. The wife finds out about the affair and flees to the new home that they are building, but the husband and children seek her out and she returns to the family.

Narrated in the first person, significantly by a narrator whose given name is never revealed, the story is framed by the wife's avowal of honesty in reporting the events described. The story begins in medias res with the narrator recalling her childhood for a doctor, and the opening passage contains within it what will finally develop as one of the book's primary themes, honesty: "Well, I said, 'I will try. I honestly will try to be honest with you, although I suppose really what you're interested in is my not being honest, if you see what I mean'" (Mortimer, 9). Chapter 2 begins a flashback to thirteen years previous, when the narrator was about to become Mrs. Jake Armitage (the only name by which she is ever identified, thus signifying that her identity is defined in terms of someone other than herself, a man, her husband). The rest of the novel then moves back toward the present at which the story began. At the book's conclusion, whether the narrator is addressing the doctor or, more likely, the reader is not clear, but the important point is

The Pumpkin Eater (1964). James Mason as Conway and Anne Bancroft as Jo Armitage at the zoo cafeteria. Royal Films International. Jerry Ohlinger Archives.

that she ends by talking about what she began by talking about—honesty: "I have tried to be honest with you, although I suppose that you would really have been more interested in my not being honest. Some of these things happened, and some were dreams. They are all true, as I understand truth. They are all real, as I understand reality" (222). The significance of the frame is not in the similarity of the passages but rather in the three concluding sentences.

In crafting her narrator's story, which, according to Mortimer, is factually based, the novelist carefully intertwines a series of events revolving around the concepts of fertility, sexuality, and salvation that have attained symbolic significance for Mrs. Armitage. In fact, in her journey to self-understanding, and a corresponding understanding of the universe, the narrator constantly is involved with symbolic values that pervade her life. Married for the fourth time, for much of the novel she seems driven to have children, although with the exception of her daughter, Dinah, she normally refers to the children abstractly; still, it is children or the having of children that defines her identity. When she marries Jake, she allows, with some minimal protesting (but nevertheless she allows), the three eldest children (products of her first marriage) to be shipped off to boarding schools by the sea. Interestingly, the number of children that she has borne is never revealed. Why this is so is not made clear, though in some numerologically oriented societies, counting possessions is considered to be tempting fate (presumably only the gods truly possess by the number). At the same time, an indeterminate number simultaneously has a more generalized effect and allows for an impression of greater vastness than does a fixed number. The doctor recalls that Mrs. Armitage has "a remarkable number" (12), and throughout the novel other characters, including her father and mother, comment on the large number involved, yet the narrator does not count them. Instead, she refers to her children in dispassionate terms. She has "surviving" children (25); "other," "various," and "Jake's" children (32); "a bodyguard of children" (43); the "younger" children (44), "the violinist's" children (110); "older" children (111); "some" children (113); "the boys" and "children of varying sizes" (139); "great bored ones," and "small, manageable ones asleep with their teeth cleaned" (140); the children are also referred to as "one," "its" (44), "they" (140), and so forth—emotionally detached, nonpersonal appellations. She must have fewer than fifteen (she has fewer than her grandmother did, and her grandmother had fifteen), but at least eight different children can be distinguished, and the total is probably higher.

Mrs. Armitage's goal seems to be to continue bearing children until she dies of old age. Her mother and Jake are appalled at such a thought ("Have you no consideration for other people? In my mother's day there was no proper prevention, but how can you contemplate—," her mother rails when informed that her daughter is pregnant once more [130]).

The doctor presents the narrator-patient with a Freudian interpretation of her need to have children: "Don't you think sex without children is a bit messy. . . . you're an intelligent woman. Be honest. Don't you think that the people you most fear are disgusting to you, and hateful, because they are doing something for its own sake, for the mere pleasure of it?. Something which you must sanctify . . . by incessant reproduction? Could it be that in spite of what might be called a very full life, it's sex you really hate? Sex itself you are really frightened of?" (64). There is evidence that the doctor is partly right, as indicated in three incidents in Mrs. Armitage's past, two of them in her youth, revolving around people whose only interest in sex was hedonistic. She tells the doctor at one point, when he asks her what the first thing she hated was, that "it was a man. Mr. Simpkin . . . [and] Ireen Douthwaite. . . . and a woman called Philpot" (13). Later, she explains that Mr. Simpkin was an older man who tried to seduce her when she was about fifteen (92–97). Irene (Ireen) was a precocious schoolmate who stayed with the narrator at about the same time, and who obviously flaunted her sexuality, both distracting the narrator's father and seducing her erstwhile boyfriend in the process (68–87). Philpot was a friend of the Armitage family who lived with them for a while and with whom Jake had the first affair that his wife found out about (27–44).

Still, the drive to have children is most likely a manifestation of Mrs. Armitage's maternal spirit. In other words, her urge is symbolic of her nature, and her nature embodies the primal female principle of fecundity. The childbearing impulse and the resultant children thus are both the urge functioning and symbols of the urge. Because one of the themes of the novel is the concept of betrayal, it is noteworthy that two of the earliest and most romantic betrayals that the narrator encountered were aimed at her male partners, instigated, more importantly, by females who were supposed to be her friends and thus also aimed at herself. Furthermore, her own mother is not supportive of her pregnancy (motherhood). The women in the novel are ambivalent toward others of their own sex, a result of the distortion of traditional sexual roles that confronts Mrs. Armitage. The conflict that batters the narrator's identity is the subconscious realization that her fertility and effective functioning as a minor earth goddess are out of place (or time) in the modern world.

This is further demonstrated by her relationships with her husbands. She divorced her first husband because he was "pretty hopeless with children" (62). She then married the Major, who was "very interested" in children, but he could not support her—he had to go to war, where he died (63). Her marriage to Giles, the professional violinist, ended when she replaced him with Jake (64). According to the doctor, Giles "didn't want any more children, and sex without children was unthinkable" to her. Mrs. Armitage vehemently denies this premise, yet she never offers any alternative rationale or explanation for her action. Earlier in the novel, when she met Jake's father, it was established that Jake liked children and the fact that he was inheriting a family (18). His actions toward the children throughout the tale seem to confirm this, although he certainly also feels that there must be a limit to the number of children produced in one family. Mrs. Armitage explains in her first visit with the doctor that "Jake doesn't want any more children" (12), and when she later describes her conversation with her husband following her declaration that she is pregnant again, Jake's reaction is that enough is enough: "when we could for the first time start planning a happier, more sensible life, just at the point when we could start thinking of a little freedom—[she's] pregnant again" (145). Whereas children symbolize fulfillment and give meaning to Mrs. Armitage's life, they have come to symbolize entrapment for her husband.

The conflict between the narrator and her husband revolves around the children, and the couple's attitudes symbolically reflect the underlying conflict in the novel. She is caught in the midst of the sexual revolution, and the fact that in a man's world "Women aren't important" (148) frustrates her because she is delegated to a role, childbearing, that the delegating modern world does not appear content to let her fulfill. That this is a modern condition, shared by other women, is corroborated by the letter that she receives from the lower-class Meg Evans (147–48).

Mrs. Armitage represents a traditional, family-oriented society, whereas Jake is a representative of a contemporary, technological society. Her simple, earthy, humanistic cosmology is contained in the world of childbearing; his is symbolized by his profession—he works in the cinematic arts, a highly technological world. The clash between these two cultures results in a perversion of the natural order of things (i.e., her abortion), which leads to chaos.

The second symbol cluster in the novel is less crucial, less pervasive, and less obvious than the symbolism of the children. It is apparent because it operates symbolically for the narrator to the extent that for most of the story she is not even aware herself that it is functioning as a symbol. The second symbol is an equation of dust with evil that grows out of her childhood experiences with Simpkin and Ireen.

The tower is the final symbol in Mrs. Armitage's life, and it is both the most obvious and the most momentous symbol in the novel. She initially alludes to the tower that she and Jake are building on their land in the country (which was given to them by her father) in her first discussion with the doctor (11). During the course of the story, she mentions the tower over a dozen additional times (47, 103, 104, 124, 142, 151, 155, 157, 174, 180, 192, 202, 212–21). Many, but certainly not all, of these references come at times when she is under stress, and the tower takes on positive connotations as a representation of hope and as a place of refuge, freedom, and peace.

In some forms of the divinatory card game of tarot, the figure on one of the cards is a tower, which indicates "Catastrophe, undeserved disaster."

After all, one can fall from or be imprisoned in a tower, so it is not surprising that such a structure can symbolically suggest a "life style and ideas upset, permitting new enlightenment . . . [reversed:] Oppression, perhaps false imprisonment. But through misfortune, freedom of body or spirit is gained" (Brent, 57; see also Gibson, 187). One version of the card includes certain ambiguously contradictory symbols—a dove of peace on the left above the tower, the mystical eye of knowledge centered above, and a serpent above right, among others.

While some of the disaster, downfall, and destruction leading to a spiritual rebirth obviously apply to Mrs. Armitage's tale, in the novel itself the symbolism is mostly positive. When things go wrong for the narrator, even the building of the tower reflects this condition (Mortimer, 47); yet more often the tower is connected with hope and salvation. When Jake returns from a location shoot in Africa (and, ironically, the affair with Beth), Mrs. Armitage is happy and shares her joy by telling him that the tower is finished (124). She continues and expands this reward association by arguing that once the baby is born they can repair to the tower in the summer (summer being a time of relaxation and ease [142]). After the abortion, this reward concept is extended, though again with a tinge of irony, when the narrator tells herself that she and Jake can now go to the tower, and she realizes that "for the first time in my life I could make love without danger. Danger? For the first time in my life I could make *love*" (155, emphasis mine). Her subconscious equation has been that sex is evil (an idea initiated by and represented by Simpkin) and a danger to be avoided. Therefore, she could justify sex, even with Jake, only when it led to children. However, since because of the hysterectomy she is no longer capable of conceiving, she can now experience sex as an expression of love, and it is in the tower where this can take place.

Tower symbolism, in addition to obvious Freudian implications, frequently involves concepts of security (a defensible military position), spirituality (a religious place in the heavens, thrusting up close to God), or sanctuary (probably a merging of the military and religious connotations). Mrs. Armitage's tower embodies all of these attributes. In the hospital room she is revitalized by thoughts of her love for Jake, thoughts that are clearly linked to the completion of the tower (157). When she finds Beth's letter and learns of her husband's duplicity (159–60), the tower takes on the association of a place of salvation.

At first, her reaction to the knowledge of the affair is that even her children have failed to make her life meaningful ("lacking now my own instincts, values and beliefs, I had nothing to offer them, and what they offered me—dependence, love, trust—seemed a monumental responsibility which I could no longer bear" [174]), and she sees the tower as "a folly" (in England historically a towering structure built on an estate for no practical purpose was called a folly).

She has been exposed to overwhelming evil in the form of the abortion, compounded by her husband's motivation, and this becomes the key to understanding the novel. She recognizes a new reality: "We were back at the beginning again. There was no end. You learn by being hurt. Where I had been viable, ignorant, rash and loving [this self-evaluation is strongly confirmed by Giles (180–81, 196–97)] I was now an accomplished bitch, creating an emptiness in which my own emptiness might survive. We should have been locked up while it lasted, or allowed to kill each other physically. But if the choice had been given, it would not have been each other we would have killed, it would have been ourselves" (171).

Jo has been initiated (the abortion, which will not heal, is clearly the physical as well as the psychical wound of the ritualistic pattern that has stimulated her awareness), and she now sees reality and herself in a light of new understanding that must necessarily lead to change. Part of her new knowledge relates to her battle with evil. She has passed through a period of self-recrimination in which she blamed herself for everything that has transpired and wanted to punish herself: "In the darkness I covered my face with my hands, pressing . . . against my jaw and forehead longing to break the bone. Nothing I could do to myself would hurt enough. Everything was an indulgence, courage and cowardice, punishment and crime, honesty and deceit; everything was corrupt. . . . I might as well stay . . . revelling in disgust; I might as well give in. Avoid evil? There's nothing else in me" (203–4). Then Giles's admission that Jake has been trying to contact her reverses the momentum.

At her father-in-law's funeral, Mrs. Armitage has a revelation. Overcome by grief for her own position and confronted with death, she feels diminished and lost. "Who was I," she wonders, "to come to terms with evil? What arrogance." But, she likewise realizes that "it's arrogance that keeps one alive: the belief that one can choose, that one's choice is important, that one is responsible only to oneself." "Without arrogance," she concludes, "what would we be?" (211).

Mrs. Armitage's transition to an acceptance of a new reality without equating it with evil actually began when she spent the night at Giles's and revealed that "I feel pity—pity for everyone" (195). Like Samuel Taylor Coleridge's Ancient Mariner, she cannot come to terms with her new reality until she can bless unaware the equivalent of the sea snakes. The actual transformation takes place in the tower to which she has fled, like a hermit, alone. In fact, in the novel's concluding chapter, she depicts the tower as a "cell" (212), evoking an image of a hermit or a solitary nun. Because of the religious setting in the previous chapter, in which she describes Jake standing "alone, isolated, as he had chosen" in the graveyard (211), the implications are religious rather than penal, and she underscores this while concurrently evoking the positive symbolism of the tower when she observes "the wall of sky that rose ten feet away from my lookout window" (212). Earlier she had related the tower to the quiet peacefulness of nature (192–93). Now she meditates in this surrounding. She reviews her life, caught between a past that is over and a fearful future, "a perfect circle of isolation captive between yesterday and tomorrow, between two illusions. Yesterday had never been. Tomorrow would never come" (212).

Slowly she reconciles herself with her new reality, but in so doing she transmogrifies that reality and realizes that it is acceptable. In her children's memories and dreams of her, she knows, she remains forever firmly captured. She is still identifying herself, defining her existence, through her children, of course, but in the tower she is cut off from them: "there were no children to identify me or to regulate the chaos of time. . . . I was alone with myself, and we watched each other with steady, cold, inward eyes: the past and its consequence, the reality and its insubordinate dream" (214–15).

Salvation is at hand, though. After a three-day, Christlike entombment in the tower, she knows that she loves Jake, but she also has come to realize that she has overreacted and rejected things that should not, perhaps cannot, be discarded: "I was still on about avoiding evil: avoiding the messes in the street, the dust, the cruelty of one's own nature, the contamination of others. I still believed that with the slightest effort we could escape to some safe place where everything would be ordered and good and indestructible" (219). The final component needed for her salvation, for her transition from one stage of life and her reentrance into life at another level, comes in the shapes of her children, sent ahead by Jake, cresting the hill below her. The image conjured up is that of the sun rising, the symbolic dawn of a new day. Jake's love has been unsteady, but it is her saving grace and is evidenced in her children: "I accepted him at last, because he was inevitable," she says (221).

Since the tower is the location of this transformation, in its completion it has also come to represent fulfillment, and the narrator can accept a life in which she no longer has to bear children.

The structural use of the three symbols, children, dust, and the tower, is interesting because Mrs. Armitage is whole (in sacred geometry, numerology, *one* is the symbol of unity), becomes divided (the number *two* represents duality), and becomes complete again (*three* stands for the triangle, which contains all things, being a union of *one* and *two,* and is a form of the circle). She has, then, ended up where she started, yet paradoxically she is more complete because her knowledge is fuller (she has been exposed to the experiences of a Blakian world), and her spirit is tempered and purified, not corrupted as she had feared that it would be.

The final symbolism of *The Pumpkin Eater* resides in the novel's title. Taken from the Mother Goose rhyme ("Peter, Peter, Pumpkin Eater, / Had a wife and couldn't keep her. / He put her in a pumpkin shell / And there he kept her very well"), the title is intriguing because the tale is presented from the wife's point of view, not the husband's. There are sexual connotations to the rhyme, as well as fertility symbolism. The pumpkin is itself a symbol of the fall harvest season, and it is filled with numberless seeds for the future. Consequently, the implication is that Peter can hold onto his wife by keeping her pregnant, a state with which she is apparently satisfied.[1] In the novel the wife is happy until her husband refuses to keep her pregnant. After her hysterectomy she becomes an empty shell.

Ultimately, therefore, the title reenforces the theme of chaos created by the imposition of the restrictions of a modern, and possibly a technological, world on the natural order of things. Furthermore, the nursery rhyme's focus is on Peter, not his unnamed wife. Thus, the novel itself becomes symbolic, for society does not seem to know what to do with those whose traditional values, values that used to be paramount and needed for racial survival, are no longer prized or respected. The options seem to be to lock away the offender or to surgically remove the offending values, which are represented in this case by Jo's maternal instincts and therefore might stand for all of a society's values that are brought into question by a change in social circumstances. As a symbolic novel, Mortimer's work seems to demonstrate that traditional values are out of place in a modern world.

In the end the novel's heroine achieves salvation not because she has acquiesced and accepted the dictates of a male-dominated, technological society at the expense of her maternal instincts. Instead, she is now secure in the love of her husband and children, not requiring ever more children to continually define herself. She has attained liberation from an obsessive need to procreate for definitional purposes that grew out of her childhood experiences; in doing so she realizes internal and external completeness. She becomes part of a closed whole rather than an open-ended, ever-expanding something that even she could never define. The now finite number of family members gives her a sense of stability and oneness with her identity as a person, not as a breeding machine, and she has been accepted as such by Jake and the children. Totality is evident in her reaction to Jake's "inevitable" reappearance, and the sense of unity is emphasized by the tower, a giant number one pointing upward and standing outlined against the sky.

Typically, the film version of *The Pumpkin Eater* received mixed reviews. It is considered by some to be one of Pinter's less successful ventures artistically, as indicated in the reactions of Hollis Alpert and Philip T. Hartung, who call Pinter's script "obscure" (Alpert, "Sour Smell," 34; Hartung, "The Screen: Had a Wife," 332). In a *Newsweek* review, Pinter's "glittering screenplay" is noted, but the reviewer decides that there are "irrelevant snatches of dialogue, and [a] whole bag of vogueish tricks" (102). However, most reviewers, like the *New Yorker*'s Brendan Gill, praise the "very attractive" movie and allude to Pinter's "dazzling screen play" (148). Knowles finds *The Pumpkin Eater* to be a feminist film about a woman trapped in a society shaped by males: Jo, he claims, seeks "the mutuality of her husband to sustain her role as wife" (*Understanding*, 95). Elsewhere, he labels the picture an "outstanding feminist film before its time" ("1994–1995 and 1995–1996," 156). Directed by Jack Clayton, *The Pumpkin Eater* brought Pinter a British Film Academy Award for best screenplay of 1964 and a British Film Academy Award for acting to Anne Bancroft in the role of Mrs. Jake Armitage.[2]

In retelling Mortimer's story of the conflict between the husband (played by Peter Finch), who wants to escape from the mundane world of work and family into the arms of other women, and his wife, who would be content forever having children, Pinter brings his own artistry into play.[3] Joanne Klein has pointed out that "Pinter's discovery of subjective, non-linear structure as a device for exploring" the themes of the interaction of past and present and its effect on individual perception grew out of his need to insert a flashback at the opening of *The Pumpkin Eater* to explain Jo's current mental state carried over into his stage plays (41).

Moreover, the screenwriter's characters are "complex, psychologically plausible" (Peacock, 44), and are contained within concrete, real settings.

Although he was not speaking about filmmaking in "Writing for the Theatre" in 1962, the author's words certainly are applicable to his script of *The
Pumpkin Eater*: "The context for me has always been, for me, concrete and
particular, and the characters concrete also" (Pinter, "Writing for the Theatre," 80). It is this combination that makes his psychological studies, such
as *The Pumpkin Eater* and *Lolita,* so effective and so stunning in their impact. It is the opposite of *The Cabinet of Dr. Caligari,* in which everything
about the world in which the protagonist operates seems out of kilter, and
only he appears to be normal. In Pinter's works, the world in which the main
character appears is a real, concrete world, and the protagonist is real and
concrete as well. The contrast between the seemingly normal exterior and
the revealed interior of the protagonist is emphasized by the very normality
in which he or she is trapped; the contrast is accentuated and at the same
time more acceptable because of this juxtaposition of "reals." This technique is reminiscent of Alfred Hitchcock's primary cinematic vision—the
everyman figure caught in a *Rosencrantz and Guildenstern Are Dead* situation where the protagonist has no idea why he or she is being pursued. The
effect is generalizing; it is applicable to any member of the audience: "There
but for the grace of God. . . ." And, again, it is the aura of normalcy of the
protagonists and the world that surrounds them that allows for this feeling
to be developed.

One element that Pinter introduces into the adaptation is his characteristic approach to language. A bit of after-party conversation exemplifies the
screenwriter's contribution to the dialogue, especially representative in its
use of repetition:

CONWAY (*his voice coming out of the silence*). I call myself a tradesman,
    because it's the only thing left to respect, in my honest opinion. In
    my honest opinion, an honest tradesman is the only thing left to
    respect in this world. That's my honest opinion.

JAKE. You'd say that in all honesty, would you?

CONWAY. In all honesty, Jake. In complete honesty, boy. Ask Beth. Ask
    Beth if I mean what I say. (*Pause.*) Ask her! (*Five Screenplays,* 100)

Elsewhere, the use of non sequiturs is evident, representing the lack of
connection in modern life, as when Jo is confronted by a strange woman
while at the hairdresser's: "WOMAN. To tell you the honest truth, my life is
an empty place, to tell you the dog's honest truth. Your eyes are more beau-

tiful than in that picture. I bet you didn't always have things so good, that's why you appreciate, don't you? I never dreamed I'd meet you like this and I mean you're so kind, you're so full of sympathy for me. My husband doesn't come near me any more, no, nowhere near me. Don't you think I'm attractive any more? I think I'm still attractive" (91–92). Pinter's customary use of pauses and silences is evident in a scene that does not appear in the novel, when Jake invites his wife to accompany him to Morocco for the shoot but she ignores him (84–85).

Finally, the idea that nothing may be taken for granted, a characteristic theme in Pinter's dramas, is expressed with humorous effect in a talk between Jake and his father. The elder Mr. Armitage asks, "Do you like children?" "Of course I like them," his son answers, "Of course I do." Mr. Armitage can only query, "Have you actually known any?" (67).

For Pinter, part of the appeal of Mortimer's novel may have resided in the style and humor of her dialogue. Two of the passages cited above, for instance, are almost identical to passages in the novel, though Pinter has altered them slightly to make them his own.[4] It is the alterations that give the passages their punch.

Two other things about the novel that may have interested Pinter are the nervous breakdown that the wife is suffering and the fact that the story is told entirely from her point of view, negating any chance for verifying the true motivations behind the actions of the other characters. The film is more objective than the novel in its treatment of motivation, and critics such as Ian Wright in the *Guardian* and David Robinson in the *Financial Times* agree that there is a clash between the dialogue and the visual presentation that makes it seem too "stagy." Leslie Halliwell, however, feels that there are sufficient "brilliantly-handled sequences" to give the film a "feel of life" (792). It is interesting that by and large critics have looked at the meaning of the film without distinguishing how it differs from the original.

The strength of Pinter's screenplay lies in his choice of the cinematic images that he uses to replace the symbols of fertility, sexuality, and salvation that appear in the prose original. When Jo becomes pregnant and then undergoes a hysterectomy, the author inserts a typically Pinteresque symbol that was not included in the novel—the sailless windmill in which Jo lives after the operation. Neither the structure nor its inhabitant can any longer fulfill a primary function. This symbol replaces the novel's tower and is not only more visually effective, with the stark, broken blades silhouetted against the sky, but its symbolic significance is more telling as well. There may even be an allusion to the romantic fantasies and idealism of Cervantes' Don Quixote.

There are indications that Pinter tried to retain some of the novel's symbolism. A shot of Jo at the dust bins (*Five Screenplays*, 80) is included, and she is seen washing dishes or cleaning up a number of times. The published script also calls for a shot of a salesman demonstrating a Hoover vacuum cleaner in the Harrod's segment (81),[5] and Jo is using a vacuum cleaner in a scene with Philpot (73–74); neither shot appears in the motion picture, and neither is necessary, given the reduction of the dust symbolism.[6] Conversely, and incidentally demonstrating the fluid nature of filmmaking, in the movie Jo hears bits of Jake's telephone conversation after the psychiatrist leaves. This action is included in the novel (Mortimer, 54) but not in the published script (*Five Screenplays*, 84). Evidently, during the shooting it was determined that the inclusion of this dialogue strengthened the scene, perhaps by stressing the possibility of Jake's betrayal.

From the beginning of his career, Pinter frequently has claimed that he does not deal in symbols. "I have never been conscious of allegorical significance in my plays, either while writing or after writing," he says. "I have never intended any specific religious reference or been conscious of using anything as a symbol for anything else" (Hewes, "Probing Pinter's Play," 56, 58, 96). "I start off with people," he states in "Writing for Myself," "who come into a particular situation. I certainly don't write from any kind of abstract idea. And, I wouldn't know a symbol if I saw one" (10). Elsewhere he states, "All I try to do is describe some particular thing, a particular occurrence in a particular context. The meaning is there for the particular characters as they cope with the situation. My plays are often interpreted symbolically. Well, you can make symbolic meat out of anything" ("Pinterview," 69).

Although these statements are not necessarily the whole truth, despite the existence of some symbolic material, they do represent an attitude that is consistent with much of what the author has accomplished in adapting *The Pumpkin Eater*. Primarily, Pinter has done away with the theme of sin, which was so heavily symbolized in the novel. He does this by deleting the character of Mr. Simpkin and removing the heroine's interior monologues and her dialogues with the psychiatrist. Not only does the removal of Simpkin break the sex-sin connection, but doing away with the dialogue about dust effectively destroys the dust-evil equation. As mentioned above, he does insert the windmill in place of the tower, with a symbolic consequence, and the children still represent fulfillment and give meaning to Mrs. Armitage's life while at the same time representing entrapment for Jake. Yet, by shifting the emphasis away from the metaphysical, Pinter focuses more narrowly on an especially modern problem. This problem is again epitomized in the figures of the children, who clearly come to symbolize the underlying conflict in the movie—the conflict between man's technological universe and woman's familial universe and the attendant concept that women are not important in a man's world. Thus, the wife is delegated to a role that the contemporary world will not let her consummate.

Actually, of course, Mr. and Mrs. Armitage function as symbols themselves, too, Jake exemplifying the technologically oriented modern world and Jo personifying the traditional, family-oriented world. On another level, though, Pinter is writing about particular people in particular situations, just as Shakespeare did when he created the characters of Hamlet and Lear and Othello. The two positions are not mutually exclusive.

Among the differences between this film and Pinter's first two motion pictures is a shift from the objective point of view. Although the interior monologues are gone, Pinter retains the flavor of the novel by doing things such as posing the protagonist on the inside of a window looking out in the opening sequence and then switching to an interior shot and by using a hand-held camera to film subjective, point-of-view shots in the Harrod's sequence (Mrs. Armitage's feet and the floor are seen as the camera threads through merchandise displays and groups of shoppers). Pinter calls for many of these shots ("*Row of gleaming refrigerators. . . . Shoppers hustling by. . . . Another angle: shoppers passing, glancing at* JO *curiously*" [*Five Screenplays*, 81]), and his insertion of a technician tuning a piano while Jo walks by in a daze suggests that she is out of tune, out of harmony with her surroundings. The use of subjective sound linked to these visuals reenforces the effect (we hear only the sounds that she is making, as heard by herself). In contrast, nonsynchronous sound is employed for bridges between scenes. Another effective use of sound is Jo's laugh after her abortion, which echoes in her cry at her breakdown. Dialogue is utilized as well to connect times and events in her life, as when the lines "Do you want one?" "I'll have one" when Jo was pregnant (the squirting can scene) are repeated at the end of the movie. Pinter also follows the flashback structure of the novel, though not always in the same order, and certainly not in the same ratio.

With the removal of Mrs. Armitage's appointments with her psychiatrist and her position as narrator as well, Pinter also deletes the honesty frame set up in the novel.[7] To indicate flashbacks, then, is more difficult in the movie, and the heroine's hairstyles, clothing, and activities are often the best clues that a change in time is being signaled—Jo laughs and is involved with the children to a greater extent in the earlier time periods than in the later, when she appears much more stoic in bearing and demeanor, hair and clothing included.

In translating Mortimer's detailed novel to the screen, Pinter's approach had to be considerably different from the one that he took in his cinematic transformation of Maugham's *Servant*. Whereas in the former case he was essentially working with a skeleton that had to be fleshed out and with words that had to be expressed in visual images, in his adaptation of *The Pumpkin Eater*, he was provided with more material than he could use. Again, it is interesting to see what elements he chose to discard and which he retained, as well as how he utilized that which he retained. Some of his decisions are obviously related to the themes developed in the film; other decisions reflect the difference between the media of his source and his product. Pinter captures the sense of conflict between Jo's desires and Jake's, her needs versus his, by showing her thriving in the midst of the family's activities. Everything focused upon revolves around her, as in the scene when she meets Jake and the children are noisily rushing about her, like water streaming around a rock as the waves roll in and recede; Jake seems nearly overwhelmed by the children and the commotion. In contrast, the scenes with Jake trying to work at his typewriter while noisy kids interrupt and play two radios simultaneously set the rationale for his break with his wife. The maternal, organic, would-be earth mother, fertile and fecund and happily emotional, is unbothered; the analytically mechanistic world exemplified by filmmaking that has replaced her world cannot function in these tumultuous conditions. While Jo's organic environment exults in clamor and movement, a sterile, antiseptic atmosphere is required for Jake's habitat. The implications of the scene are not fully developed because even Mrs. Armitage does not understand why the break has occurred.

Amusingly, the screenwriter takes advantage of cinematic technology to strengthen some of the novel's emotional renderings. Jo's isolation is symbolized by her constantly being seen behind windows and curtains; this distances and separates her from whatever it is that she is watching. There are numerous fades, which nicely communicate the heroine's mental state and the lack of a distinctive line in the mind between past and present. There are jump cuts that produce strong emotional effects, too, as when the camera moves from the barn setting to the bedside of the dying father. Additionally, Pinter uses the positioning of his characters within the frame to convey meaning, as in the scenes of Jo's depression when she is seen isolated in long shots, viewed from the back as she stands alone, or when the camera shoots up at her through the window. The subjective first-person narrative is replaced by an objective camera, but the result is interpretable because of the juxtaposition of uninflected (unrelated) shots that are used to tell a story by their arrangement. In her happy past, Jo was busy and involved with the noisy action. When she is between the past and the depressed present, as at the party, she is seen isolated in the crowd, not connected with the conversation or action; she moves while her guests stand.

"Jo is entrapped by sex, gender, and society as well as her own psychology," according to Knowles. He goes on to describe her:

> Staring from the window, she hears, then sees, her family climbing the brow of the hill: "*fanning out like trappers, converging on house*" is Pinter's revealing camera direction. As they invade the house with noise and food, Jo cannot escape their united expectations. The camera work is crucial here. Going from Jake's face to Jo's, complex thoughts, feelings, and apprehensions are signaled. Jake's chummy smile, with deliberate naiveté, oblivious to his own insidious shallowness, in part masks his habitual unconscious blackmail in using the children. Jo's generosity of spirit, her love and responsibility, complies with the symbolism of circular, all-encompassing domesticity. But just before the credits her smile is troubled, the light darkens, and she looks slightly down with the final image of tear-stained apprehension—an image that recalls the epigraph for the novel. (*Understanding,* 134)

When Pinter abandons the novel's opening segment, however, he effectively does away with the symbolic linking of dust and sexuality that is developed throughout the novel. He also removes part of the exposition, but this allows him to concentrate on Jo as an individual and on her problem in a way that is appropriate. The psychiatrist is not seen, so Jo is central—and, after all, it is her story that is being told. The picture of Jo that is presented gives the audience a good indication of her state of mind, yet it does not force the audience to the inference that she is mentally ill, just that she is disturbed about something. In truth, her mental condition is better depicted in the film than it was in the book, for her appearance on the screen is very affecting. At the end she lets down her hair and returns to the younger look that characterized her in the early years of her marriage. Furthermore, in retrospect the austere woman at the movie's opening contrasts markedly with the soft, warm mother of the flashbacks, so that in the film the difference is more striking than in the book.

Similarly, in deleting the visit with the doctor, Pinter avoids including some dialogue—which would have made the picture too talky. While the film moves slowly at the beginning, then, this is the author's intent, for it mirrors Mrs. Armitage's mental state; dialogue might have sped things up, but the audience would have been told about rather than being forced to experience her trauma, a good example of the difference between left brain–right brain appeal that is inherent in the nature of the two media. The world of a disturbed woman is explicitly and graphically portrayed through the use of freeze frames (at the hairdresser's, for instance) and by having the main character stare at the camera—a position normally avoided because the effect is too intimate, personal, and possibly intimidating.

Likewise, in the novel Mortimer did not provide names for the children in order to convey the fact that mystic significance accrues when something is numbered or named, for that makes them important as individuals, whereas to Mrs. Armitage the importance of her children lies in the congregate, in her conception of them as a part of her own holistic being. This is perfectly delineated on screen by the crowded bustle that literally can be seen and heard.

It is worth noting that when the psychiatrist does appear in his diminished role, he is seen by Mrs. Armitage observing him through the balustrade as he talks with Jake. This sets up resonances with the myriad of stair shots in *The Servant* and underscores the subthemes of dominance and betrayal that may have caught Pinter's attention. When Jake closes the door behind the doctor, it is reminiscent of Barrett's closing the door after Susan.

Besides Mr. Simpkin, two other characters are cut in the movie version: Irene and Mrs. Armitage's first husband. These cuts were probably made purely on the basis of economy and simplicity. First, there is no need to include Irene, for she is tied to the sex-dust-sin theme; second, the first husband's attitude toward children probably would have made the main theme too obvious.

In some ways *The Pumpkin Eater* might be seen as an indictment of the art world. Certainly those in the film industry are not portrayed as admirable characters, and the easy money and easy morals of the film world are castigated. But, there is no blanket condemnation of the art world—Giles is a musician, after all. A claim could be made that the movie is a feminist complaint about a masculine world in which men are in control and women defer to them (as witness Jo's mother), yet the same kinds of objections arise—several women, notably Philpot and Beth Conway, are not models of decorum. In the end Mrs. Armitage finds happiness by acquiescing, accepting the time and place in which she lives. Her acceptance may be ameliorated a bit by a feminine impulse, an artistic sense of completion because the family is no longer expanding and things are settled. The expansive mode is in the past. Instead of running helter-skelter, Jo can now rest in the warm comfort of her nest, her brood close at hand.

Finally, by focusing on only one of Mrs. Armitage's neuroses and by making Jake's character more sympathetic, by doing away with much of the metaphysical content of Mortimer's story, and by masterfully substituting filmic spatial equivalents for verbal ideas, Pinter has created an emotional, subjective, impressionistic film.

The Quiller Memorandum

RELEASED: London, November 10, 1966

SOURCE: *The Berlin Memorandum,* by Adam Hall; novel (1965)

PRODUCTION COMPANY: Twentieth Century–Fox, Paramount, National General
    Corporation, The Rank Organization

DIRECTOR: Michael Anderson

EDITOR: Frederick Wilson

PHOTOGRAPHED BY: Erwin Hillier

PRODUCER: Ivan Foxwell

ARTISTIC DIRECTOR: Maurice Carter

SOUND: Archie Ludski

MUSIC: John Barry

SET DECORATION: Arthur Taksen

COSTUMES: Carl Tom

SPECIAL EFFECTS: Arthur Beavis, Les Bowie

CAST: George Segal (Quiller), Alec Guinness (Pol), Max von Sydow (Oktober),
    George Sanders (Gibbs), Senta Berger (Inge), Herbert Stass (Kenneth Lindsay
    Jones), Robert Flemyng (Rushington), Peter Carsten (Hengel), Hans Schwarz
    (Barman), Victor Beaumont (Dorfman), Gunter Meisner (Hassler), Robert
    Helpmann (Weng), Konrad Thoms (School Porter), Edith Schneider (Frau
    Schroeder), John Rees, (Man A), Philip Madoc (Man B), Harry Brooks (Man
    C), Ernst Walder (Grauber), Bernard Egan (Man F), Paul Hansard (Doctor),
    Sean Arnold (Man H), Janos Kurucz (Man I), Carl Duering (Barman), Philo
    Hauser (Nightporter), Brigitte Laufer (Assistant), Nikolaus Dutsch (Man J),
    Ves Delahunt (Nagel), Peter Lang (Man K), Herbert Fux (Man L), Peer
    Goldmann (Man M), Malte Petzel (Man N), Axel Anderson (Man O),
    Wolfgang Priewe (Man P), Claus Tinney (Hughes)

RUNNING TIME: 104 minutes

COLOR

VIDEO: CBS/Fox

ANOTHER NOVEL IS the source of Pinter's next scenario, *The Quiller Memorandum*. The author's first script to be filmed in color—undoubtedly in an effort to appeal to a wider audience—it was adapted from Adam Hall's *Berlin Memorandum* (published in the United States as *The Quiller Memorandum*).[1] *The Quiller Memorandum* opened in November 1966 with an international cast including Sir Alec Guinness, Max von Sydow, George Sanders, Senta Berger, and George Segal (as Quiller). Major actors, Guinness, von Sydow, and Sanders reportedly accepted their minor roles in the picture because they felt that their characters were so interesting and well written. The film version of the 1965 spy thriller concerning a Western agent who infiltrates a neo-Nazi underground organization was directed by Michael Anderson (for whom *The Servant* was originally intended).

There are a number of elements in Hall's book that might have attracted Pinter's attention, including the theme of domination and the Hitler/Jew back-

The Quiller Memorandum (1966). George Segal as Quiller. Twentieth Century–Fox. Jerry Ohlinger Archives.

ground (which is mirrored in the images that the screenwriter uses twenty-four years later in his script for *The Handmaid's Tale*). Over the years, he has paid increasingly more and more attention publicly to the Holocaust, as evidenced in his scripts for *Reunion* and *The Diaries of Etty Hillesum*. The interrogation of Quiller by the opposition looks back to Pinter's short story "Kullus" and forward to his one-act play *Mountain Language*, too, in terms of thematic content and the author's fascination with how language functions and is used. And, Knowles declares that the major difference between Pinter's and Hall's versions of the story is Pinter's stress on game-playing (*Understanding*, 99).

Pinter's spy movie is a cut above the typical examples of the genre (the James Bond movies were extremely popular at the time). The film also represents the only time to date that there has been a disagreement between the screenwriter and the source's author over the nature of the adaptation. Clearly, there are problems with the original, *The Berlin Memorandum*. It is hard to believe, for instance, that Inga could have been a child in Hitler's bunker during the war. Even so, for those who glory in the minutiae and convoluted intellectual mysteries of the best espionage novels, in some ways the screenplay is not as intriguing as the novel.

It is true that the screenwriter simplified the narrative and deleted most of the technical espionage material, and Joanne Klein dismisses the movie as "hack writing for popular markets." She finds that Pinter's approach to the "problematic complexity and introversion of Hall's narrative lacks the ingenuity of his other adaptations" (48). The result, she claims, is a "relatively simplistic spy movie" (49). Nevertheless, scholars like Bernard Dukore would argue that the film is underrated.[2] In fact, Dukore points out that the screenwriter "very capably adapted *The Berlin Memorandum* to the dramatic medium of cinema, abandoning what is narrative and expository in nature and substituting dramatic action, visual imagery, and montage" ("Pinter's Spy Movie," 15). Happily, these are characteristics common to the writer's film scripts.

As opposed to his screenplays of *The Pumpkin Eater* and *Accident,* in adapting Hall's work Pinter retains so little of his source that it is easier to note what he preserves than it is to catalogue what he deletes. The general idea of a resurgence of Nazism, the figure of Oktober and the grilling scene, the shadowing, and the bomb under the car are virtually all that is kept intact. The motivational element of Zossen (the character used as bait to involve Quiller), the particulars of Quiller's plan, the first-person narrator and the attendant psychological explanations and spy-world trappings, the visit to the girl's room, the code, and the murder of Dr. Solomon Rothstein are all vital matters in the novel—and all are missing from the movie.

Conversely, Pinter has added the opening sequence, in which we see K[enneth] L[indsay] J[ones]'s murder, and the scriptwriter has altered the settings and happenstances of Quiller's meeting Pol and Inga significantly (changing the characters' intents and the themes of the novel along with the plot—and, incidentally, the spelling of the woman's name). Among the other massive alterations that the screenwriter implements are the invention of the swimming-pool sequence. He also introduces a new method of administering the knockout drug to Quiller and combines some of the characters (Oktober and the narcoanalyst). Other characters, such as Frau Schroeder, are added to the film. As is often the case, too, there are differences that apparently were generated during the shooting of the movie. In at least one instance, a scene is included in the film that is not contained in the published script: a car chase is inserted after the Gibbs-Rushington scene that follows the interrogation scene (*Five Screenplays*, 176).

Most notable, however, is the change effected with Inga, whose profession as a schoolteacher at a nameless school (called the Star of David School in the book) becomes elemental in the film and whose background is diminished to the point where the reasons for her actions become obscured. The change in Inga's character also affects the tone of the story and the audience's reaction to the character.

The impact of these changes is evident in subtle ways. In the original the fact that Inga's hair is blond is important symbolically. Not only is the tale a "clinical portrayal of move and logiccounter-move" among espionage agents,[3] but it is also a psychological thriller having to do with the psyches of a nation and of the individuals involved in the action. Symbolically, then, Inga's hair obviously represents the Aryan mystique that created Hitler's bunker, a location from which she is unable to escape. Berger's red hair in the film carries no such metaphorical content.

Along the same lines, the painting in Oktober's base is carefully delineated in the novel: "Her skin was the shade and texture of a wax rose, quite flawless, and her hair fell across her naked shoulder in blond rivulets. Her regard was innocent, the eyes wide and frankly gazing, too young to have learned that you must sometimes glance away. She leaned across the white chair without coquettishness, insouciant, her small breasts barbed with nipples of carmine, her thighs heavy with pubic hair" (70). The symbolism is literally spelled out: "Hypocrisy. Schizophrenia. They've always been like it." In the film script the painting is simply described as "an oil painting of a nude blonde, leaning across a chair" (*Five Screenplays*, 165); in the film the canvas is merely Quiller's focal point during the grilling, and the portrait of a female body elicits his answer of "Inge" when he is asked his name (171). This difference is a result of Pinter's having removed the narrator convention and thereby diminished or expunged the symbolic element.

Apparently, Hall was not amused by the changes. In 1994 Christopher Hudgins learned that Hall was living in the Phoenix, Arizona, area. He asked a friend, a detective novel writer who had shared a podium with Hall at a mystery writing seminar, if he could set up an interview with Hall to discuss Pinter's adaptation. Hall refused on the grounds that he was terribly upset with the adaptation and with the casting of the film (especially the casting of Segal, whom Pinter has praised for his work in the movie).[4] Hall contends that Pinter destroyed the kernel of his book, that the screenwriter created something with which he (Hall) is very much displeased. When Pinter was asked about this reaction, he was a bit surprised. He had not realized that Hall had such a negative opinion of the film. He went on to say that Hall was the only author with whom he had not spoken in some detail about the adaptation that he had made. He was of the opinion that all of the other novelists had been very pleased with the adaptations of their works, and he mentioned Fowles in particular as having been more than satisfied, an assessment unquestionably supported by Fowles's comments in "HORS D'OEUVRE." Pinter agreed that he had changed the book considerably, that the film was not Hall's book picturized. Nevertheless, in the final analysis the film is true to some of the spirit of the novel, and it is true to some of the vision of Quiller as well.

In an act of unwilling self-policing, at government request, the U.S. film industry reportedly agreed to cut all allusions to the villains as members of a neo-Nazi terror organization, as was done by the American distributor when the film was shown in West Berlin (the audience there assumed that the villains were Communists), though the deletions were not made in the American cut.

In West Germany the changes had been made at the request of Ernest Krueger, the head of a German film industry group, who claimed that his organization considered "that the presentation of a radical right secret terrorist group in Berlin is unrealistic. It is also inopportune because of our image toward East Germany and the Communists, who are raising charges of neo-Nazism against us at the moment" ("Cut Radical Right," 18).[5] Some

THE QUILLER MEMORANDUM   **139**

of this political maneuvering is understandable, for *The Quiller Memorandum* was filmed at the height of the cold war. An incident that took place during the shooting demonstrates how touchy things were at this time. East Berlin border guards in a helicopter spotted a truck with a camera crane heading for the Wall and delayed it for twenty hours until they were convinced that it was, indeed, a film company camera crane and not some kind of weapon.

The villains, however, are quite clearly identified as neo-Nazis in the movie. When Quiller receives his assignment, for instance, his contact identifies the enemy as "quite a tough bunch. Nazi from top to toe. In the classic tradition" (*Five Screenplays*, 142), and later the agent poses as a journalist researching an article "about the present day Nazi question in Germany" (154). Obviously, being set in postwar Berlin and dealing with surreptitious military and fascist indoctrination of German youth, the film gains added meaning by drawing on history, and the characters' motivations are better understood when it is seen that the underground group is trying to revive a tradition that had given meaning and structure to their lives. It is ridiculous to try to ignore the historical facts of Nazism, World War II, and the rest. The agreement is simply another instance of the industry's current exercise in catering to oversensitive ethnic groups; the attempt to please everyone perforce demands a complete disregarding of reality.[6] In the cut shown nationwide on American television in 1971, the references were retained.

With the exception of Joseph Morgenstern, who finds the protagonist to be real and adult in comparison to the regular portrayal of spies in the Bond mold,[7] *Variety*'s Rich,[8] and Dukore, the consensus among movie critics is that this film is only of average interest, even as an adventure piece. Nonetheless, the action moves fairly well, and the picture rises above its genre because of Pinter's taut dialogue and cynical humor. The movie is one of the few examples of his working within an established genre, and cinematically the interest lies in how he expands the built-in limitations to create a better-than-average spy film.

Where *The Quiller Memorandum* is weak is where the conventions of the genre are adhered to. The escape-fight scene in the enemy's stronghold does not seem realistic, nor does the suddenness of Inge's declaration of love (194). Quiller's escape is not accounted for satisfactorily in the movie either—while the audience is informed that the protagonist did not receive the full treatment from Oktober, no rationale is given for his simply finding himself lying at the river's edge (Quiller's ruminations about his fate in the novel cover several pages, and Hall's narrator presents at least three reasonable explanations for what has occurred). Immediately following this scene, there is a sequence in the printed script that takes place in a bar. Quiller asks the barman to call a taxi, and the underlying animosity between the German and the American is palpable (176–78). This scene is cut, and a car chase is inserted in its place, something that might be expected in the genre. *The Quiller Memorandum* is probably one of Pinter's weaker screenplays precisely because of its generic character. It is about events rather than about people or relationships between people.

Fortuitously, there are some minor Pinter touches in characterization (verification problems) and dialogue. The opening conversation, for example, is pure Pinter:

GIBBS. What exactly is he doing now?

RUSHINGTON. He's on leave, actually. On vacation.

GIBBS. Ah.

> *They eat.*

> Well, perhaps someone might get in touch with him.

RUSHINGTON. Oh yes, certainly. No difficulty about that.

GIBBS. Ask him if he'd mind popping over to Berlin.

RUSHINGTON. Mmmm. I think so.

GIBBS. Good.

> *They eat.*

> Shame about K.L.J.

RUSHINGTON. Mmmm.

GIBBS. How was he killed?

RUSHINGTON. Shot.

GIBBS. What gun?

RUSHINGTON. Long shot in spine, actually. Nine point three. Same as Metzler.

GIBBS. Oh, really?

> *They eat.*

> How's your lunch?

RUSHINGTON. Rather good.

GIBBS. What is it?

RUSHINGTON. Pheasant.

GIBBS. Ah. Yes, that should be rather good. Is it?

RUSHINGTON. It is rather, yes. (140)

The discussion of the 9.3 caliber bullet that is juxtaposed with talk about pheasant and the Lord Mayor's Midsummer Banquet question about news from Berlin that is juxtaposed with Quiller's beaten body lying at the river's edge grow out of Pinter's preoccupation with the cold war (a preoccupation also underlying *The Birthday Party*, according to Knowles [*Understanding*, 99]). Like W.H. Auden, the screenwriter recognizes the close proximity of the ordinary with violence. As Pol says about the neo-Nazis, "They're difficult to recognize—they look like everybody else" (Pinter, *Five Screenplays*, 143). Thus, as Knowles notes, Anderson provides two frame images: the Nazi Olympic stadium and the postwar school playground (*Understanding*, 100). The link between these two worlds is embodied in the line "atrocity begins in the mind," which implies a chain of cause and effect from the playground to the gas chamber. Quiller's comment to Inge reflects Pinter's understanding of the insidiousness of evil: "They want to infiltrate themselves into the mind of the country, over a period of years. But they're not in any kind of hurry, this time" (*Five Screenplays*, 159).

The variants of the script that are housed in the Pinter Archives reflect interesting, wide deviations in the stages of composition. Some, as would be expected, are simple: the alternate spellings of the main female character's name as Inge in the 1966 version and as Inga in a version titled *Berlin Memorandum*.

The changes in the *Berlin Memorandum* typescript are most revealing. The fifty-one pages (containing 136 scenes) are filled with handwritten alterations (including some on the reverse of pages). Again, many of the changes are simple. On the first page, for example, the directions "puts phone down deliber.—slowly opens door" are added, the word "restaurant" is changed to "club," and the word "sir" is deleted in two places. In addition, Pinter's habit of not naming his characters in early versions of his scripts is apparent in his labeling Gibbs and Rushingham "1" and "2," respectively.

There are more important changes, too, of course, and clearly Pinter has certain specific purposes in mind when he writes and rewrites, even though it may take him several tries to find what he considers the best method of expression. The holographic changes indicate that the thinking and experimentation with possibilities may have taken place over a considerable period of time. For instance, the long opening section, in which Pol and Quiller meet in Quiller's theatre box at a musical review and in which Quiller is informed of Jones's death, is preceded in the film by a dark enactment of the murder (which is not delineated in the novel). This is consistent with Pinter's practice of presenting action rather than narrative. Instead of meeting Pol (called "Man" in the first four references, then "Pol" subsequently) at a place of musical entertainment, the screenwriter locates the first contact in the bird house at the Berlin Zoo, a suitable setting for the kind of spy world that he is replicating. In the film, the communication between Quiller and Pol takes place in the Olympic Stadium. This backdrop is fitting in its own way, too, reflecting the German enthusiasm for sports and health-oriented activities, the hollow German victories in Hitler's 1936 Games, and the disparity between the ostentatious grandeur of the Third Reich and the grey decay of contemporary Berlin. The ironic contrast between the stadium and its surroundings recalls Ozymandias's statue in Shelley's poem. The code word permitting recognition changes from "Windsor" (the C Group: "care," "call," "cavil") in the novel to an exchange about praying mantises in this adaptation—less unobtrusive but likewise more literarily appropriate to the world of fictional espionage. In the film, recognition is accomplished through the more mundane vehicle of a package of cigarettes (Chesterfields, which were used as the identity establisher in the Hengle sequence in the *Berlin Memorandum* script). Furthermore, the length of the exchange is reduced considerably.

Similarly, the event concerning the Local Control cover agent who follows Quiller is handled differently. In the novel, Quiller merely stops the unidentified man on the street and delivers a message. In the *Berlin Memorandum* version of the script, the cover agent is named Hengel and the meeting takes place in a bar, after which Quiller goes to another bar, Chez Nous, which features female impersonators (7–8). This latter touch reenforces the theme of decadence and corruption that Pinter focuses upon, yet in the published and film versions, while the Quiller-Hengel scene is retained virtually intact, the Chez Nous scene has been deleted.

Quiller's meeting with Fraulein Inga Lindt occurs in chapters 4 and 5 of the novel, when he sees her at a war-crimes trial at the Neustadthalle. Pinter's placing the meeting in an elementary school classroom conveys a more subtle judgment of evil and corruption (*Berlin Memorandum* script, 12; *Five Screenplays*, 153). As he develops the plot, it is at this school where Inga/Inge is going about her business of surreptitiously brainwashing children and converting them to the cause of neo-Nazism. Quiller's false profession as a NATO representative for the Red Cross in Hall's book is changed to that of a newspaper reporter for the *Philadelphia World Review,* a fictional newspaper, in Pinter's script. This transformation carries with it some amusing implications: not only does it establish a rationale for Quiller's propensity to ask questions, but it also plays into Inge's character, for she is seeking public acceptance of her cause while simultaneously she is anxious to avoid publicity.

Inge's schizophrenic character mirrors the old Germany–new Germany dichotomy that underlies the action, and it represents the ugly, hidden nastiness that is always close to the surface, much like the violence that is pervasive in Pinter's stage plays. It is something that occasionally breaks through with great force and, in this case at least, attempts to take back control. The question of dominance is another of the playwright's primary concerns that runs throughout his canon. In connection with "The Examination," Pinter considered the question of who was "dominant at what point and how they were going to be dominant and what tools they would use to achieve dominance and how they would try to undermine the other person's dominance. A threat is constantly there; it's got to do with this question of being in the uppermost position, or attempting to be. . . . it's a very common, everyday thing."[9] The theme of dominance has been a primary one in his films since his first movie, *The Servant,* and while at this point in his career Pinter was concerned with individuals as individuals, his later political pronouncements have demonstrated that this topic can be discussed in political terms as well, so *The Quiller Memorandum* is reasonably situated in his canon.

There is one final set of significant differences. At the conclusion of the novel, Quiller assumes that Inga, in a desperate attempt to remain true to her allegiance to the dead Reich and to save her life, has given Oktober the secret, but fake, telephone number that Quiller had whispered to her. The hints about Inga's fate are ominous, but there is no final resolution. The novel ends with Quiller listening to his taped report being radioed to London: "My voice sounded very tired on the tape. I must be getting old, getting old" (189). In the film, Inge says that she tried the number but found that it was not in operation. She has managed to escape the roundup of Oktober's gang, and the movie concludes with Quiller saying good-bye to her at the school. There is a suggestion that she will continue to work toward her goal of converting the young:

QUILLER.Good-bye.

INGE.Good-bye.

> *He goes to the door. As he closes door, he sees her placing books into her bag.*
>
> *Exterior. School. Playground.*
>
> QUILLER *walks away through playing children.*
>
> INGE *comes to the top of the school steps.*
>
> *She calls to the children.*
>
> *They collect around her.*
>
> *They talk eagerly to her. She listens to them, smiling.*
>
> *She glances up.*
>
> QUILLER, *in the distance, walks through the school gates.* (216)

Quiller's reaction to Inge and hers to him seem oddly ambiguous, given their previous relationship. Although not contained in the printed script, in the movie the ambiguity of the ending is reduced when another woman passes by Inge, the suggestion of conspiracy thereby being reenforced.

The original ending of the *Berlin Memorandum* script is explicit:

135.

H. - Well, that's that, for the time being.

Q. - What are the details?

H. - Not many. We've got them all. Got Oktober.

> pause.

Q. - Any shooting?

> Hughes looks at his transcript.

H. - ["Yes, a bit." typed over with x's] A little, I think. . . . Yes. . . . That's right . . . A girl started shooting away . . . She's dead . . . otherwise all sage [*f* handwritten over *g*] and sound. No bones broken.

> Silence.

135. (cont.)

H. - Eh, by the way, I came across something that might interest you.

Q. - What?

H. - Last report we got from KLJ. It was stuck away in the files.

> H. takes a piece of paper from folder.

He reads.

"Tags now a nuisance. Time wasted in flushing.

But have got a line on base, will confirm soon.

Things very tricky now. Request no contacts any account. May not signal for a time. KLJ."

H. - Funny, isn't it?

Q. remains in the same position, still, his legs up on chair.

Mind you, we lost a pretty good man there.

136. Close Up of Quiller lying in chair, his eyes looking at nothing. (51)

There are two pages 51. The first ends with "no bones broken./Silence."; the lines from and including "Any shooting" are crossed out by hand. The second page 51 starts with "135. (cont.)."; all of it is crossed out by hand. On the back of the first page 51 is handwritten:

Q. - Did they find a girl.

H. - No, no mention of a girl. No girl.

Q. - Are you sure?

H. - Twenty men. No girl.

This is crossed out by hand, and under it is written in a slightly different style (though still in Pinter's hand): "Quiller walks to window/looks down, sees people/walking to work" with a line under the section, and under the line is written: "next shot—children in playground." This direction line, the final one in this version, is a repeat of the line used when Quiller first approaches Inge's school.

Apparently the screenwriter felt a need to resolve Inge's fate rather than leaving the audience hanging. Subsequently, he seems to have decided that it would be better to leave the question undecided. This led him to the children-in-the-playground shot, and from here it appears that he determined that the more darkly sinister ending of the insidious menace continuing under an innocent guise was in keeping with the themes that had structured the story in the first place—and coincidentally, it correlates with his view of the omnipresence of menace that pervades his dramatic writing from *The Room* onward.

In comparison with Pinter's earlier screenplays, it is interesting to see how closely the director followed the script. Admittedly, the published version is not the shooting script, but examples of Anderson's attention to Pinter's directions are found throughout, as in the scene where Inge is in bed when she receives Quiller's telephone call (179). There are alterations (additions and deletions), as indicated above, but most of what Pinter calls for in the screenplay appears exactly as he wrote it, whether because Anderson was less capable than his predecessors or because he recognized that the writer had already presented him with what he needed.[10]

The Basement
(The Compartment)

RELEASED: Televised on BBC-2 Television, February 20, 1967
SOURCE: Original screenplay by Pinter (1963)
DIRECTOR: Charles Jarrott
CAST: Harold Pinter (Stott); Kika Markham (Jane); Derek Godfrey (Law)
BLACK AND WHITE

THE COMPARTMENT WAS originally intended to be one of the segments in a Grove Press film project, "Project I: Three Original Motion Picture Scripts by Samuel Beckett, Eugene Ionesco, Harold Pinter," when the script was written in 1963. Neither *The Compartment* nor Ionesco's *Hard Boiled Egg* were filmed; only Beckett's *Film*, starring Buster Keaton, has been made into a movie short. Under the title *The Basement*, Pinter's proposed contribution was telecast by BBC Television on February 20, 1967, with the author in the role of Stott. The director, Charles Jarrott, had also directed Pinter's previous teleplay, *Tea Party*.

As he had when writing for radio, Pinter found that he could be more experimental with his television scripts than he could be with commercial feature-length film scripts, a medium in which relatively high finances play an important, sometimes overriding, part. In his stage play *The Collection* (1961), Pinter had used the equivalent of quick cutting to establish the parallel plot lines between the two couples; in the even more successful drama *The Lover* (1963), he had played with nonverbal visual sequences; and in *Tea Party* (telecast in 1965), the author had demonstrated that he could be quite imaginative in the use of the camera by calling for shots from "Disson's *point of view*," soundless sequences, and so forth. This developing versatility was given freer rein in the television plays than in the screenplays, and with *The Basement* he achieved effects that would be difficult to reproduce on stage—which may be why the play version has not been mounted often.

The work harks back to the writer's prose poem "Kullus" (written in 1949) and his only published short story, "The Examination" (1959, later read by Pinter on a BBC Third Programme broadcast on September 7, 1962), and perhaps looks forward to *No Man's Land* (1974) in terms of a confrontation between two men in which positions shift. Reflecting the author's concern with the concept of domination, his setting a contest of wills in a single room, and the easy maneuvering between reality and fantasy in the minds of his characters, *The Basement* is still unique in the author's canon for several reasons. First, of course, it is the only original film script that he has written. Second, the theme of the screenplay was well suited to a cinematic medium, both in the quick movements and in the circularity that he was trying to express. Third, for the first time Pinter conclusively demonstrated that he was able to subordinate the verbal to the visual—the printed text consists of approximately equal portions of dialogue and combined camera directions and set descriptions. Fourth, it confirms what has been obvious since he wrote *The Servant*: not only does he have the ability to translate thoughts into visual images, but he sees original material visually as well. Fifth, freed by the camera, the writer is no longer confined to a small, interior set.

The title *The Compartment* comes from a line in Pinter's novel *The Dwarfs,* in which Len says, "I have my cell. I have my compartment. All is ordered, in its place, no error has been made" (29).[1] The choice of this title may represent to some degree the writer's frustration with this project. It seems that he did not want to write this screenplay in the first place. Documents in the Pinter Archives, box 2, include a communication to an unidentified person ("you bastard") in which Pinter complains, "In case you haven't got my point (!) I'm very unhappy in having to do it at this stage." Apparently he felt that his original narrative version about a female narrator living in her compartment was unfocused: "I trust it will possess a unity and clarity when finished - both as a script and as a film. As far as I'm concerned, these are just very rough working notes and images. It will unquestionably go through many changes - Christ. But there's a <u>kind</u> of whisper of a <u>kind</u> of structure - for me! And for me alone, I'm sure. One thing is certain—there will be three characters." He followed his typical pattern of not naming his character in early drafts of the project, for later he writes that he is weary of using *A., B.,* and *girl* as titles for the characters and gives them their names.

Circularity is the key thematic element in this work.[2] The script for *The Basement* is basically simple, because Pinter's purpose is to examine an uncomplicated concept. The author's techniques, such as limited setting and

THE COMPARTMENT.

In due course I made my way back to the compartment. There I found
her engaged, without haste, at her task. ~~Shxxxxkxkyxxxxximxdxxx.~~
The cold of the place was not countered by fire. I did not, upon
entering, venture the inquiry : was the lack of fire by intention or
by accident ?*~~I doubted~~ if I was in a position to ask, or she to
answer, such a question. That I might, in time, achieve such a position
was my purpose and trust in entering the compartment. Naturally, this
development was dependant upon her inclination to reply to queries of
this nature. In the past, I had had reason to believe her inclinations
to be mutually beneficial ; whether this still remained so, I could
not yet attest.
        It was evident, upon entering, that the formulated
policy was still strictly adhered to. The symptoms were apparent and
in no way changed. Nor had I expected change. There was , however, an
innovation ; a seat, set by the window, but not limited to its
boundaries, for I observed it at both corners of the compartment, on
the window wall, and along the adjacent walls to their centre, where
it stopped abruptly. As to the wall to my right, the cessation was
compulsory, in that the grate obstructed its progress. As to the wall
to my left, the reason for cessation was less clear. For this wall
was quite bare. However, I reserved this query for a further occasion.
It must be added that although the seat was not limited to the window,
it remained a windowseat. At least, so I was obliged to consider it.
For it began from the window, as from a source, and began nowhere else.
Truly I was unable to comprehend the reason for its continuance, and
was compelled to view this factor as an irrelevance, but whether as
a deliberate irrelevance, or in the nature of an error, I could not, at
that point, determine.
        That I had interrupted an extent of activity
I did not doubt, though I was at first unable to define its nature.
Not that the girl seemed in any way disturbed by my entrance. Yet
her manner, although not concerned, showed some element of curiosity.
I not only allowed this curiosity but indulged it. It seemed to me
essential as a beginning to any common understanding between us. And
as such it was welcome. It was not long before that I had invited
Kullus to participate in an examination, which had, for my purposes,
failed. If she desired to mock at this failure, I was content that
she did so, for I looked further, required her allegiance, and hoped,
by craft, to obtain it. And so, as she was curious, so was I deferenti
and appreciative.
        Soon, however, I observed that her curiosity
waned with my increasing deference., and brought myself to inquire,
with some concern, the reason for this. Here I learnt a fact as
encouraging as it was surprising. It was not the failure of my
examination at which she was curious, but rather the attempt itself.
My deference had therefore been misinterpreted, and she was tending
towards disbelief in my initiative, when, fortunately for our potentia
alliance, I had spoken. She recalled an earlier conversation between
us, on which occasion I had been unable to conform to her suggestions,
with respect to Kullus. It was therefore with a new admiration she
~~rxxxxxxxxxxpxxxxxfxpxxxd~~

*it was
doubtful*

?

The Compartment. Manuscript of the prose version. Harold Pinter Archives at the
British Library. Courtesy Harold Pinter.

characterization allowing for easy focus and concentration of thought, remain the same as in most of his other dramas up to this time. But, since *The
Basement* is a screenplay (and so designated in the published version), it
relies on visual effects to a large degree and is perforce less dependent upon

you a bastardised x idea of what's in store.
In case you haven't got my point (!) I'm very
unhappy in having to do it at this stage.

Now I haven't the slightest idea of how to go about
it.

TITLE : (you bastard) : THE COMPARTMENT.

Rain. Front yard of basement flat. Steps going down.
Man (A). Standing. Girl, by walb. Rain.
They are still. Man is looking in a lighted window.

In room. Man (B) lying in chair, reading, listening
to music. kxrxgx Large basement flat. Overfurnished,
but very comfortable. Fire in grate. Pictures, etc.
Ease.

A comes in. B. greets him warmly. They are old
friends. A quiet, charming. A. tells og friend
outside, can they stay night. Girl comes in. A. and
girl , while B. is talking, undress and get into
B's bed. B. sits by fire, puts coat over his lamp
to shade the light.

Beach. Sun. Girl and B. B. speaking enthusiastically
of A. Old friend. Enumerates his virtues. They
walk along beach to A. asleep in sand. Admire his
repose, etc. Girl pleasant but reserved.

The three of them at a cafe. Very gay. Girl dances
with B. A. teases them.

Night. Room. A. and girl in bed. B. on floor. Girl
and B. exchange looks.

Day. Room. Girl cooking. B. whispering to A. Tells
him he is doubtful of girl's character, must speak
as a friend, etc.
A. takes a picture off a wall.

Undated letter from Pinter to an unidentified person with the opening of *The Compartment* sketched out. Harold Pinter Archives at the British Library. Courtesy Harold Pinter.

The Compartment. *No frant*
window

I. Night. *large basement window*
Front yard of a basement flat, at the foot of a
short stone flight of steps. There are lights in
the basement window. The upper storeys of the
house are dark.
Rain falling.

2 — Stott is standing in the centre of the yard,
looking into the room. Behind him, close to the
wall, is a girl. She clasps her raincoat to her. *She wears a raincoat*
2.
The room is lit by a number of lamps. Law is lying
in low in an armchair, reading.
The room is very large. It is comfortable, relaxed,
overfurnished: numerous sidetables, plants, a screen,
armchairs, paintings, bookshelves, a large bed.
There is a full fire in the grate.
Silence.
3.
Stott still.
4.
Law in armchair. He is smiling at his book.
He giggles. He is reading a Persion Love Manxual,
with illustrations.
5.
Jane huddles against the wall. Stott is no longer
in the yard. She clasps her elbows.
6. *Doorbell.*
Room. Law looks up from his book. He closes it, puts
it on a sidetable, stands, goes to front door.
Silence.
7.
Int. Small hall. Front door, closed. Law comes into
hall, shaking a raincoat. He hangs it up. *Looks inside it. Smiles.*
8.
Stott warming his hands at fire. Law comes to him,
laughs.

Law   - ~~You haven't changed.~~ You haven't changed at all.
        I'll get you a towel. *You've Got a new raincoat, I see.*
              Law goes to bathroom.
9.   *about him at the room.*
Stott looks up at ~~room. He looks at bed.~~
IO.   *99 — The room from Stott point*
Law in bathroom, at airing cupboard. He swiftly discards
a number of towels, chooses a soft one with a floral
pattern.

The Compartment. Manuscript page from an early version of the screenplay. Harold
Pinter Archives at the British Library. Courtesy Harold Pinter.

verbal expression for relaying the meaning of the work to the audience. There is, for example, even less verbal imagery than usual, and it lacks the witty wordplay of the works in the comedy-of-manners-style that preceded it.

The plot is spare. Tim Law is reading in his comfortable flat one winter's evening, when an old roommate, Charles Stott, arrives. Stott brings with him a young girl, Jane, with whom, after brief amenities, he climbs into bed and begins making love. The rest of the play traces Stott's taking over Law's flat and then Law's replacing Stott as Jane's lover. The putative object of the conflict, and the tool for establishing dominance, is the woman who is to be possessed in the flat.

From the very beginning of his career, Pinter has incorporated into his writing images from events in his life. For instance, *The Room* introduces this creative pattern, the subject of menace with the related concepts that are explored, and the techniques that Pinter was to utilize for several years. The author's conception of that play and its subsequent evolution in his mind are typical—he started off with an image from his memory and proceeded from there.[3]

It should be no great surprise, then, when similar images surface in his other plays; at one point in *The Basement,* the broken milk bottles that figure so prominently in the writer's memories of his childhood reappear in a duel between the two antagonists. Another connection with the author's past is the name of the character Law, which was the name of one of his childhood friends. There is also a competition in which Law and Stott are supposed to engage in a footrace, but when Jane acts as starter, Stott merely watches as Law runs off. Billington, in his *Life and Work of Harold Pinter,* traces this back to an actual event in Pinter's life. According to Donald Pleasence, while *The Caretaker* was being performed in a pre-Broadway tour in New Haven, Connecticut, in August 1961, he, Pinter, and Robert Shaw "used to go out every night after the show. We'd go to a bar and then have ham and eggs in a diner. We made this particular one into a replica of the Hemingway diner in *The Killers*—a favourite story of Harold's. . . . one night Robert challenged Harold to a 100–yard sprint. Robert was always very serious about sport, but Harold of course was a champion runner at school. I don't think Robert knew this. He was quite sure he was going to win. I was the guy with the handkerchief starting them off. Anyway, Harold went off from the starting place like an electrified rabbit and Robert just stood stock-still in amazement. When I asked him why, he just said, 'Oh, fuck it—I just didn't want to show him up" (Billington, 193).[4] Billington says that Pinter confirms this story but is of the opinion that Shaw quit because he knew that he was going to lose. Billington then points out that the tactic of gaining the upper hand by refusing to participate is utilized by Stott in *The Basement*. He might have added that this is a strategy employed by many of Pinter's characters (see "The Examination," etc.).

The footrace is included in a sequence of quick cuts, alternating short related winter scenes with summer episodes (Pinter, *Basement*, 103–4), that illustrates Esslin's appraisal of *The Basement* as a nonrealistic dream structured like the movements of a symphony on the themes of fighting for possession of a girl and a room, as Law imagines how Stott, whom he envies, would defeat him and how in turn he would try to reverse the process (Esslin, *Peopled Wound*, 175–76). In fact, despite Pinter's early worry about structure, what he ends up with after producing scripts with the number of scenes ranging from 11 to 22 to 77 to 96, and possibly even more, is exactly the kind of structure that would be expected in cinematic cutting.

A comparison with the full-length stage dramas that Pinter was writing at the time is instructive. *The Homecoming,* one of the author's two greatest dramas, was written in 1964 and first performed in 1965. The original published edition was seventy-six pages long. It is composed of two acts, which contain eight scenes in toto.[5] All of the action takes place in one room. *The Basement* was written two years earlier and telecast two years later than *The Homecoming.* The published version is about one-third as long as *The Homecoming* at twenty-three pages in length. It contains fifty-two scenes and a total of 98 shots. Eighteen of the shots are specified exteriors, and there are 80 interior shots, 44 of which are not specifically designated interiors but are obviously parts of interior scenes. The exterior shots include outside the front door of the flat, a cliff top, a cave, the backyard, a beach, a bar, and a field. The interiors include the front area, a room, a hall, a bathroom, and the kitchen.[6] Nine of the shots are called for as taking place in winter (the screenplay begins and ends with winter scenes), although, given the sequences, the total number of winter shots is 81, and 6 are called for in summer, with the total summer shots adding up to 14.[7]

There is a fluidity and connectedness in the alternating sequences, which move between exterior and interior, night and day, winter and summer, all neatly epitomized in the mirror-image opening and concluding shots and unified by the intercut shots. *The Compartment* is most notable as a successful exercise in which Pinter experiments further with the possibilities inherent in screenplays. As D. Keith Peacock might say, in this piece the iconic narrative of the author's earlier works is replaced by indexical images and the symbolic signs of cinematic grammar. Significantly, the intertwining parallels of possession and dominance may have laid the groundwork for the mindset that led to Pinter's innovative approach to adapting *The French Lieutenant's Woman* fourteen years later.

Chase observes that "the author of an original screenplay is more likely to be able to negotiate himself into a situation where he is able to retain some authority over his work than the adapter is. The author of an original screenplay brings the product of his own imagination, complete, . . . to the marketplace, while the adapter comes there to sell his services to a producer or studio" (66). With his three adventures in filmmaking prior to *The Basement,* Pinter was fortunate: "I have had absolutely no restrictions in working; there was mutual respect and mutual objectivity. But I was in each case adapting a work for the screen, even when, with 'The Caretaker,' it was my own. With 'Project One' I had nothing to refer to: there was complete freedom of choice, no existing framework" (Langley, "From 'Caretaker' to 'Servant'"). As noted in the introduction to this book, the screenwriter has explained why he has not written any more original film scripts. Still, since he apparently finds *The Basement* a reasonably successful endeavor and admits that he appreciated working on that script because of the "freedom of choice," it is too bad that he has never written another original screenplay.

Accident

RELEASED: London, February 9, 1967; United States, April 1967

SOURCE: *Accident,* by Nicholas Mosley; novel (1965)

AWARDS: Cannes Film Festival Special Jury Prize, 1967; Movie Critics of the Foreign Language Association Award, Best British Film, 1967; National Board of Review Award (Ten Best Films of the Year List), 1967; UNICRIT Prize, 1967; Premio di Selezione di Sorrento Award, 1967; Grand Prix de l'Union de la Critique de Cinema (Belgium), 1967; nominated for British Academy Award for Best Film

PRODUCTION COMPANY: Royal Avenue Chelsea Productions, Ltd., distributed by London Independent Producers, Cinema 5

DIRECTOR: Joseph Losey

EDITOR: Reginald Beck

PHOTOGRAPHED BY: Gerry Fisher

PRODUCERS: Joseph Losey and Norman Priggen

ARTISTIC DIRECTOR: Carmen Dillon

SOUND: Simon Kaye and Gerry Humphreys

MUSIC: John Dankworth

COSTUME DESIGNER: Beatrice Dawson

CAST: Dirk Bogarde (Stephen), Stanley Baker (Charley), Jacqueline Sassard (Anna), Michael York (William), Vivien Merchant (Rosalind), Delphine Seyrig (Francesca), Alexander Knox (Provost), Ann Firbank (Laura), Brian Phelan (Police Sergeant), Terrence Rigby (Plain Clothed Policeman), Harold Pinter (Bell), Nicholas Mosley (Hedges), Maxwell Findlater (Ted), Carole Caplin (Clarissa), Freddie Jones (Man in Bell's Office), Jill Johnson (Secretary), Jane Hillary (Receptionist)

RUNNING TIME: 105 minutes[1]

COLOR

RATING: Not rated

IN *ACCIDENT,* the second Losey film for which Pinter wrote the screen-

Accident (1967). Jacqueline Sassard as Anna and Dirk Bogarde as Stephen, filmed at Magdalen College, Oxford University. London Independent Producers. Jerry Ohlinger Archives.

play, the relationships between an Oxford University don named Stephen (Dirk Bogarde again, in what many critics consider his best performance), his wife Rosalind (portrayed by Pinter's first wife, Vivian Merchant), their friend Charley (Stanley Baker), and two of Stephen's students, the aristocrat William (Michael York) and the Austrian princess Anna (Jacqueline Sassard) are probed.[2] First shown in London on February 9, 1967, and in New York on April 18, *Accident* was England's official entry in the Cannes Film Festival and was honored as one of the ten best films of the year by the National Board of Review.[3]

The adaptation, from the novel published in 1965 by Nicholas Mosley (who, incidentally, appears as Hedges in the film, along with Pinter, who acts the part of Bell) and sent to Pinter by Losey,[4] opens with a shot of the don's house. There is the sound of an approaching car and then a crash. But, the camera pushes in on the house instead of panning to reveal the accident. Stephen emerges to investigate and finds William dead and a drunken, licenseless Anna in the driver's seat. When Anna steps on William's face, shockingly reacted to by Stephen with a shout of horror in the film, a shout that is repeated later, she is in reality walking on the dead boy just as she did in essence when he was alive. She is likewise carelessly stepping on his aristocratic face, as she has carelessly treated the other men in the story. Stephen carries her into the house before the police arrive and conclude that William was alone. There is a flashback.[5]

The flashback, which in real time takes place over the course of the night as Stephen waits to take Anna home the next morning, details the events leading to the accident: the don has been attracted to his sloe-eyed student but is torn by his responsibility as a teacher because of William; he loves his pregnant wife and children but desires one last fling (and involves his lonely ex-girlfriend, Francesca, played by Delphine Seyrig, who had acted in Pinter roles on the French stage);[6] Charley, a fellow don, seduces Anna; the unaware, callow, athletic William is caught in the middle, too young for his fiancée, Anna, yet arousing middle-aged envy in Stephen and Charley. With the girl now dependent upon him because of his damaging knowledge that she was driving, Stephen might take advantage of her. The movie ends as it began, with another automobile accident in front of the house (*"Identical shot as at the beginning of the film"* [Pinter, *Accident*, 284]). This time it is broad daylight, and obviously the accident is caused when the family dog runs across the road in front of the oncoming car. In essence the two accidents are the same, but the camera's concentration on Stephen instead of the crash in the first instance provides the meaning of the film, for the wreck is one thing and what the don makes of it is something else. After the second collision he does not bother to investigate.[7]

Reporting on *Accident* for the *Saturday Review,* Hollis Alpert remarks on the atmospheric qualities of Pinter's script, which "is of the evocative kind that concentrates on images rather than dialogue" ("Where It's Happening"). Judith Crist comes to the opposite conclusion, citing the author's use of language and the excellence and importance of the dialogue: "Mr. Pinter proves his genius for capturing the essence of our society in the small-talk veneer of our lives, in probing to the heart of the matter with needle-pricks that barely blemish the skin, in turning the commonplace into a portentous suggestion of all the human agony that feeds on its own secrecy" ("Agony beneath the Skin," 29). Andrew Sarris disagrees with both Alpert and Crist, calling the movie a "slice of stilled life" in which the "dialogue is almost turgid in its terseness" ("Accident," 31).

Brendan Gill relates the scenario to Pinter's stage work: "Mr. Pinter is fantastically clever at presenting family scenes that, under a smooth surface, are . . . charged with the ability to ravage and destroy. . . . [He] appears to believe that evil is an entity and that man is capable of being invaded and possessed by it. . . . Pinter conveys this progressive, irreversible disaster with words." Gill also makes the point that in *Accident,* as in *The Servant,* "a house played a role so important that it became, in effect, one of the leading characters" (150). And, Pauline Kael, who normally dislikes Pinter's films but approves of this film in spite of its faults ("*Accident* is the best new movie around"), feels that the "sensual" dialogue ties the movie to the author's dramatic masterpiece *The Homecoming,* which it resembles in many ways: "each has its philosophy professor; each has its enigmatic female—the respectable whore to whom all the important male characters are attracted. Each is a satire of home, and in both movie and play Pinter's peculiar talent for dislocating family life and social and sexual relations to a kind of banal horror has some recognizable truth in it and his cadences are funny and reverberating" ("Comedy of Depravity," 131–32). In addition, the author's stage dialogue is characterized by his use of silences and pauses to punctuate and express underlying tensions at moments of psychological stress. This is evident in *Accident,* for example, when Charley and Stephen recognize the emotional conflict that is evolving:

CHARLEY. They're staying.

> *Silence.*

> Which room . . . is everyone in?

> *Pause.*

STEPHEN. How the hell should I know?

> *Pause.*

CHARLEY. Splendid day. (252)

Pinter's philosophy of life and its representation in film and drama, along with his spare approach to writing, are exemplified in *Accident.* Discussing the cinematic medium with John Russell Taylor, he is most interested in the verification of characters and Losey's techniques for exposing this concept:

I do so hate the becauses of drama. Who are we to say that this happens because that happened, that one thing is the consequence of another? How do we know? What reason have we to suppose that life is so neat

and tidy? The most we know for sure is that the things which have
happened have happened in a certain order. . . . it is this mystery which
fascinates me: what happens between the words. . . . when no words are
spoken. . . . In this film everything happens, nothing is explained. It has
been pared down and down, all unnecessary words and actions are
eliminated. If it is interesting to see a man cross a room, then we see him
do it; if not, then we leave out the insignificant stages of the action. I
think you'll be surprised at the directness, the simplicity with which
Losey is directing this film: no elaborations, no odd angles, no darting
about [the camera work was by Gerry Fisher].[8] Just a level, intense look
at people, at things. As though if you look at them hard enough they will
give up their secrets. Not that they will, for however much you see and
guess at there is always something more.[9]

Interestingly, the scenarist's fascination with the presentation not only of
language but also of the meanings present between words echoes master
director Bergman's thoughts on the subject, that a "dialogue is like a musical
score. . . . Its interpretation demands a technical knack . . . how it should be
delivered, its rhythm and tempo, what is to take place between the lines"
("Bergman Discusses Film-Making," 16).

Mosley's novel is a more complicated source than was either *The Servant* or *The Pumpkin Eater*, both thematically and stylistically. Pinter has
called the book "A most brilliant and singular piece of work" and claims
that he was unable to put the novel down once he began it.[10] When he tele-
phoned Mosley to talk about an adaptation, Mosley thought that one of his
friends was playing a joke on him when the caller said, "This is Harold
Pinter." The book had been optioned by Sam Spiegel as a possible "vehicle"
for Richard Burton and Elizabeth Taylor, Pinter informed the novelist, but
the project had fallen through, so he and Losey wanted to have a go at it.[11]

It is easy to see why the screenwriter was attracted to Mosley's themes
and subthemes, for they are similar to those that have fascinated him throughout his career—the class warfare that served as a frame for *The Servant*, the
question of dominance in relationships, betrayal, the nature of love versus
need, and so forth. Speaking of Pinter's previous work, Mosley has said that
the dramatist's "very great talent was in showing how people in a sense were
indeed on their own with responsibilities tied like tin cans to their tails; their
shows of communication were not much more than the playing of games."
He also suggests that "Perhaps what had drawn Harold to *Accident* was that
much of the book was like this: Stephen and Charley were sophisticated

people who recognized that of course much of human behaviour is to do with playing games" (*Efforts at Truth*, 166). And, Mosley notes, ultimately his book is optimistic, which coincides with the underlying tenor of most of Pinter's writing.

There are more thematic elements explored in this film than in the previous two sources, and they are carefully interrelated in Mosley's novel, possibly because of the underlying philosophical concepts that he explores. As Steven Weisenburger explains, "By the term *accident* Mosley signifies both the constituting event of this novel—William's fatal car crash—and a specific definition in philosophical discourse: the accidental is that which participates neither in substance nor in essence, and which therefore obeys none of the causal rules of substantial being. It is purely fortuitous, not in the modern sense of probabilistic chance but in the oldest (Hellenic) sense: during 'an accident' events 'just happen.' In ethical philosophy the idea is also linked to Indeterminism, the theory that events sometimes unfold absolutely without cause" (193).

This last certainly relates to Pinter's pronouncements about reality and causality and perhaps to the concluding accident in the film, and in fact it may be the screenwriter's demonstration of the principle.[12] In the first conversation between Stephen and Anna in the book, the two discuss the existence of the universe and of the individual self, which leads to their observations on the possibility that the world may end because, it is implied, of the threat of nuclear destruction. Stephen opines that the contemporary world has a choice about whether or not it will continue to exist, whereas before, "it was just accident" (29–31).

Later, during an interval between flashbacks when the narrator is explaining why he is writing this novel, Stephen says, "An accident is different from reality" (61). Abstract or academic philosophy is clearly not Pinter's primary interest (as evidenced by his treatment of it in *The Homecoming*). He is concerned with the pragmatic, which may well have a philosophical base, yet it is not the base that interests him but rather the practical application of the philosophy in his characters' quotidian lives. It is not surprising, then, that another of his alterations is to cut the philosophy professor's debating morality with his colleagues (as in chapter 26). The novel is more intellectually engaging; the movie is more vivid. This is partly because the film version is simpler as a result of the reduction in abstractions, subthemes, subplots, and extraneous characters and events.

It is also interesting, given the reference to Aristotle in the novel, a reference retained in the film, to consider the ancient Greek philosopher's two definitions of the concept of accident.[13] Aristotle defined an accident as either (1) something that occurs which was not intended and is an "unexpected conjunction" of events or (2) "a property which does attach to the sort of thing the something is," yet it is not a property that follows by virtue of the essence of the thing. The second definition is related to the concept of eternal accident; it is in the abstract domain of mathematics and logical entities (he uses the example of a triangle, the angles of which must add up to 180 degrees but which by "accident" may have angle a equaling 50 degrees with angles b and c equaling a total of 130 degrees) and probably is not relevant, though on an abstract level, in which properties are applied in human terms, it might be argued that Mosley is positing a theorem germane to a definition of human nature. In other words, Stephen's character is such and such, and William and Anna are relevant in the sense that they bring out that nature, but his nature is fixed, and if the roles of the two lesser characters were reversed, the result would still be the same insofar as initiating Stephen's actions, which are based on the kind of person that he is.

The first definition, however, is clearly applicable. This kind of accident is temporarily emergent. It is on the plane of contiguous temporal happenstances, which fits the events in the story. Like the spider and the moth in Robert Frost's "Design," there is an intersection in time of a series of people and events. An extension of this category of accident is the idea that substances of "subjects" have "accidents" attaching to them that are to be "truly asserted" of the subject but are not essential to the identity of the substance as the type of substance that it is. Aristotle's example is that "a musical man *might* be pale." Being pale is truly asserted of the certain musician, but this quality is not essential to the person's identity as a man or as a musician. The accident in *Accident,* then, does not define Stephen (or any of the other characters), but it does reveal his nature.

The style of Mosley's novel is similar to the style that Pinter used in his own novel, *The Dwarfs,* which he worked on from 1952 to 1956, ten years before he read Mosley's oeuvre.[14] The short, fragmented, somewhat repetitious sentences, incomplete thoughts, a minimum of dialogue and descriptive passages, and impressionistic imagery (yet the effect is distanced, not always lifelike) combine almost like a cinematic montage, a collection of quick cuts (some without apparent antecedents) in both works.

Another element in *Accident* that is present in Pinter's other films but which is especially pertinent in this one is the use of art objects for symbolic purposes. While he has said that he has "nothing to do with the use of art objects in any film. That's entirely to do with the director and designer,"[15] objets d'art, particularly paintings, do figure prominently in his films, and examples have already been given of the collaborative nature of his filmmaking experiences and of his artistic control. At times the art objects incorporated into the motion pictures made from his film scripts operate in a fairly traditional manner, merely setting the time and locale of the event or serving as a plot device; sometimes they function as simple characterizing devices. The decor of a character's habitat conveys a considerable sense of the person—whether it is frameless Alexander Calder posters or gilt-framed etchings of eighteenth-century hunting scenes. The use of artworks for setting and characterization purposes is evident early in *The Servant,* for instance, in the social context of the friction between Tony's fiancée, Susan, and his manservant, Barrett, that is manifest when she examines a particular painting (see the *Servant* chapter, above).

In *Accident,* much of the artwork is utilized conventionally by the filmmakers and is what might be expected in the office and home of an Oxford don. There is a Persian throw rug in the hallway and a landscape painting on the wall of his study. In other rooms there are pictures of city street scenes; small, golden, sitting-dog figurines on the living-room mantel, along with a clutter of knickknacks, small photos, and other statues; a dark, Rembrandt-like oil portrait in the bedroom; and a framed landscape and colored prints in the dining room. As in *The Pumpkin Eater,* the varied collection of artifacts suggests a catholicity in the inhabitants' artistic taste and a fondness for items with which the possessors have personal connections. In the case of the don's family, though, there is more homogeneity and a sense of settled comfort—the decorations primarily seem to be eighteenth- to early-twentieth-century British in origin and subject matter. In *The Pumpkin Eater,* the artifacts were a jumble of everything from classical Greek or Roman to contemporary African and appeared to have been chosen to reflect the film director husband's world travels rather than specifically to complement the personalities of the husband and wife, albeit this may well have been an unintended result. In Mosley's novel, the narrator twice describes the sitting room "with yellow carpet, black curtains, heavy gold pelmet" (8, 20); Pinter's screenplay calls for the interior of the house to contain a *"careless mixture of contemporary and antique furnishing, none of it expensive"* (224). There is no art in the filmed kitchen, just hanging utensils, pots and pans, as though the room is considered purely functional.

In contrast, in the movie Stephen's office at the university (identified as St. Mark's College in the novel [13]), virtually undescribed by Mosley and Pinter, is filled with photographs (presumably of famous philosophers), paintings, etchings, and books and is a much more human and individualized environment. When Stephen visits the television office, similarly described by both Mosley and Pinter as being composed of wood and glass, with contemporary furnishings, and filled with cubicles (Mosley, *Accident*, 92–93; Pinter, *Accident*, 254), the emphasis is again on the sterilely functional. The filmed version of the office complex is full of straight lines and no ornamentation. Francesca's flat is filled with small, framed pictures and colored prints of Paris scenes, indicative of a woman of her age (late thirties) and background of relatively good taste but moderate means in the early 1960s. Stephen's spare bedroom, where Charley and Anna consummate their affair, is adorned with only a few incidental pieces of art: some small painted boxes, bowls, and porcelain candlesticks on the bureau. There are no candles in the candlesticks, so they are for decoration, not function, as is likely the case with the boxes and bowls, meant only to give the room a more homey feel than it would have if it were complete bare of ornaments. The art in the bathroom is likewise not especially significant. There is a covered, decorated basket on the floor, a couple of small pictures on the wall, and some figures painted on the wall over the bathtub, obviously meant for the amusement of the children.

In a couple of instances, artwork is used for a humorously ironic effect. In Stephen's internal monologue, remarks about the nature of the aristocracy occur occasionally in the novel. "I was rather fascinated by aristocrats at this time," Stephen admits (Mosely, 23), and later he comments on Anna and on William's family. Because Pinter abandoned the device of a narrator, yet evidently felt that the aristocracy subtheme was important, he retains it by putting it into the dialogue in several scenes. In fact, there is an expansion of the implications of Stephen's thoughts when they are taken out of the first-person narrator's narration and imbedded in the character's dialogue. When William and Stephen talk in the don's room at the college, Stephen observes that "aristocrats were made to be. . . . Killed."[16]

Although it is not called for in the script, in the film there is a pan of the gargoyles on the roof of the building while the voices are heard over. The statues, frozen in their humorous grotesquery, seem thus to be equated with the aristocracy being spoken about—ancient, hideous beings, stiff and unfeeling though expressing emotion, above and separate from humankind.

Since historically many of the visages are of former popular dons or scouts (dormitory servants), there is a further ironic undercutting of the role of the aristocracy.

At the opposite end of the ironic scale is the restaurant at 19 Mossop Street where Stephen and Francesca are seen eating in a wonderfully evocative shot from outside a rain-streaked window. When the two enter the restaurant, they pass a painting of a large, naked Adam and Eve (with an apple). Since it may have been the sin of fornication that resulted in the acquiring of the knowledge of sexuality that is represented in the biblical apple, the backdrop is appropriate. The shot of the couple dining is humorously enhanced by the poster that hangs on the opposite wall. It reads, "Have your Meals Here and Keep the Wife as a Pet." There is no dialogue to detract from the debasing message that is ironically further diminishing since Stephen and Francesca are not husband and wife, in fact Stephen's wife is allotted pethood status because she is not there but at home about to have a child, and the dining scene is as erotically charged as that in Tony Richardson's *Tom Jones*. The sign is not called for in the script, but the shot through the window may have been intended by Pinter, for the dialogue is indicated as being voice-overs (*Five Screenplays*, 258).

There is a more important utilization of art objects in Pinter's films than those outlined above, however. This is the linking of the thematic relationship between the plot and the objects. The first notable appearance of an art object in Pinter's writing was the use of the statue of Buddha in *The Caretaker*. Other instances of this kind of usage are found in *The Servant* when the penultimate scene in the film begins with the camera panning down from a painting of an eighteenth-century battle and the final sequence also begins with the camera panning from a painting.

Often, in a piece of literature, there is a key image, phrase, line, or scene that sums up the meaning of the entire work. Hal's son/sun and Hotspur's "methinks it but an easy leap" speeches in Shakespeare's *Henry IV*, part 1, Vladimir's line "Hope deferred maketh the something sick" (a corruption of Proverbs 13) in Beckett's *Waiting for Godot*, and Anna's comment that "There are some things one remembers even though they may never have happened" in Pinter's *Old Times* are examples of this. In *Accident*, a key sequence occurs in the first flashback scenes. After the police leave, Stephen watches Anna as she lies in bed. She kicks her shoe off; there is a shot of her shoe followed by a shot of her shoe on William's face in the car, which leads to a flashback to the time when William is in Stephen's room, the first time that

Anna is discussed. The physical relationship of the two men in the frame, the student-teacher relationship, the books, the centaur statue, the liquor, and the white goat in the quadrangle are all important signifiers that are combined in this sequence.

Finally, one of Pinter's most interesting utilizations of art objects is metaphorical in nature. In fact, at times the objects form a kind of subtext in *Accident*. The scene in Stephen's room at Oxford when Anna is first seen through the window is fascinating. In the novel, the description of the event is straightforward: "The first time I saw Anna she squatted down by the goat to talk to it. The shadow of the rope made a thick line on the grass. A big blonde girl in a tartan skirt. The goat was tufted" (14). Unobtrusively in the background in the filmed version, though frequently centered in the frame, is a statuette of a satyr. When Anna is observed, she is petting a goat in the middle of the college quadrangle, but, barely out of focus in the foreground, the statuette is visible, standing between Stephen and William. Interestingly, there is a goat in the novel, but the satyr is unique to the motion picture. Furthermore, the satyr does not fit with other art objects in the room. Perhaps the idea for the introduction of the statue into the shot comes from Stephen's description of a party (cut by Pinter) in which Anna reminds him of "a golden age with satyrs and nymphs and fauns" (Mosley, 37).

Whatever the case, because of the film's sexual theme, the seduction of Anna by the unfaithful Stephen while William unknowingly assists, the combination of satyr statue, goat, and supposedly innocent female at the center of the triangle created by the two competing males who lean out to watch her is symbolically appropriate, and the statuette serves metaphorically to capture the film's thematic essence.[17] Unlike Pinter's earlier use of art objects, in this case the artwork itself is never focused upon. It is only with repetition and in retrospect that it gains significance, along with several other art objects employed similarly. The iconography is subtle and achieves its effect through accumulation, which through a collective preponderance of related items provides a substructure for the film.

Another instance of art objects serving as metaphors is found in one of the most famous sequences in the motion picture, the rugby scrum in the corridor of Lord Codrington's country house. Stephen describes the scene thusly in the novel: "a long stone corridor with high windows and cream paneling. There were family portraits on a wall—men in full armour and wigs, fleshy faces like women, a few recent ones dry as match sticks. . . . There was a green baize door at one end and at the other an archway like a cloister. . . . Above us were the portraits of plumes and horses and shining metal. . . . Beyond me gothic vaulting like a church" (89). Pinter's stage directions are similar: "*A large stone corridor. High windows. A green baize door at one end. An archway to the main body of the house at the other. Large family portraits on the walls*" (269). In the film, the corridor, shot at Syon House (presently the home of the eleventh duke of Northumberland, designed by eighteenth-century architect Robert Adam and located about midway between London and Heathrow Airport), contains marble columns and has a domed ceiling decorated with five rows of painted octagonal designs. Heraldic crests are embossed on the wall on either side of the doorways. There are embroidered chairs and marble urns, and large silver bowls sit on a table. The floor is tiled with a black-and-white checkerboard interlaced with a geometric design. But, instead of family portraits, the hall is lined with marble busts and statues on pedestals, statues of draped male and female Greek or Roman patricians. At the opposite ends of the corridor are a larger-than-life-size copy of the restored *Apollo Belvedere* and a life-size copy of *The Dying Gaul*. Art historian Robin Middleton has described the niche in which the *Apollo Belvedere* stands as being architecturally "large, soft, [almost] intimate," and the niche of *The Dying Gaul* as being "hard and strong, elevated,"[18] with the dynamic pattern of the ceiling and floor leading from the *Apollo* to the *Gaul*. Into this gladiatorial arena come the combatants.

Pinter has been interested in sports throughout his life, and there are numerous sporting incidents and references in his works.[19] In this case, the event takes on an added significance because of the art objects in the setting that metaphorically underscore the movie's thematic content. It was not happenstance, first, that this location was chosen and, second, that Stephen, the commoner who reacts emotionally throughout the film, defends the goal under *The Dying Gaul* that is being attacked by the aristocrats who come from the direction of the *Apollo Belvedere*. To reiterate, if something is seen on the screen, it is there because someone chose to put it there for a specific purpose. Just as the triangular shot of Stephen and William looking out the window at Anna with the satyr statue positioned between them was no accident, the use of this setting and the camera angles aligning the characters with the statues (low angles from in front, the statues towering above and behind the two men) were designed to express a symbolic content.

The rugby game degenerates into a brawl between the players. During the action, Stephen and William grapple and Stephen purposely knees his pupil in the face (a precursor to Anna's insensitive step). The mock combat between the two males occurs under the statues of *Apollo Belvedere* and *The Dying Gaul*, the presence of which suggests the division between the classical and the pagan, the intellectual and the emotional. The *Apollo Belvedere* is one of the best-known, and some art critics say the most notorious, Roman copies of a Greek statue.[20] Embodying the lyrical, harmonious qualities of Praxitelean beauty, the *Apollo Belvedere* was probably sculpted in the late fourth century B.C. There is a sense of cerebral, Platonic removal from feelings in the aloof blank stare of the demigod-like figure. Copies of the marble statue became especially popular at the time of the Greek Revival in the eighteenth and nineteenth centuries because it was seen as the perfect example of the admired Greek spirit.

The artistic style of *The Dying Gaul* is more realistic than that of the posed, idealized *Apollo Belvedere*. The life-size Roman copy was modeled after a bronze original cast between 220 and 230 B.C. in Pergamum in northwestern Asia Minor to celebrate the Greek leader Attalus I's defeat of the Celtic Gauls. The partially supine figure, with its clearly delineated musculature and non-Greek but very human facial features, conveys a more solid, animalistic quality than does the *Apollo Belvedere*. The pathos of the fallen warrior's exhausted struggle to rise comes through because of the dignity resident in his demeanor and the configurations of his body. Obviously, in the battle between Stephen and William, these are the warring elements.

The existence of this room in the real world may be fortuitous, but a conscious, agreed-upon choice was made to use it in the film. Further choices were made in the camera angles used in the sequence and in positioning the characters so that the artistic contents of the room assume a metaphorical quality in reflecting the movie's themes.

An interesting juxtaposition occurs when the rugby scene is followed by another sports event, the cricket match on the field at Magdalen College. Although the match takes place much later in Mosley's novel, Pinter moves it to this point in the film and incorporates some of the events that occur elsewhere in the original. Not only does the restructuring compress and omit some unnecessary action, but by moving out of doors, Pinter makes this event seem much more civilized and less confined by ancient, cold marble. In contrast to the statues, the grass and trees provide a natural setting in which occurrences are more normal—and Anna announces that she is going to marry William.

The significance of art objects in relation to the film's thematic content is clear, and the use of plastic art objects in a nonplastic medium in order to explore the movie's theme gives an added dimension to the film by incorporating material from another medium. It reveals not just how the filmmakers thus reflect, emphasize, or express the theme of the film but something about the nature of the media themselves and the relationship between them as well. The artist's conscious recognition of this is demonstrated by Anna's removing a carving from the wall of her room as she leaves to return to her homeland. No mention of the carved decoration is made in either the novel or the film script; yet in the minds of the filmmakers, it clearly was important to include this piece of art as an object that Anna consciously feels defines her and which she cannot leave behind. Pinter insists on exactitude in his plays; this is not the case in the movies. Where he demands that actors refrain from engaging in uncalled-for "business" on stage, the difference between his film scripts and the finished movie varies considerably, in relative terms. Not only are shots, even scenes, inserted or deleted, but even the words are changed throughout, though admittedly only in minor ways, as is mentioned in the discussion of *The Servant*.

It has been noted that many elements in the films made from Pinter's scripts are added or deleted during the prefilming or filming processes and that the author engages in the discussions about these alterations, plus the fact that a number of the changes are not reflected in the published screenplays. Sometimes Pinter even leaves out items that are present in his sources.[21] Thus, that the use of certain pieces of art is not called for in the scripts is neither startling nor an indication that Pinter was not involved in introducing them into the mise-en-scène.

Pinter has always been consciously concerned and thoughtful about the art of filmmaking. With this movie, for instance, he learned that opening out is not always an asset in film:

> At first we thought of perhaps trying to do it the way the book does, to find a direct film equivalent to the free-association, stream-of-consciousness style of the novel. I tried a draft that way, but it just wouldn't work. . . . suppose a character is walking down a lane. . . . You could easily note down a stream of thought which might be perfectly accurate and believable, and then translate it in to a series of images: road, field, hedge, grass, corn, wheat, ear, her ear on the pillow, tumbled hair, love, loved years ago. . . . But when one's mind wanders and associates things in this way it's perfectly unselfconscious. Do exactly the same thing on film and the result is precious, self-conscious, over-

elaborate—you're using absurdly complex means to convey something very simple. Instead, you should be able to convey the same sort of apprehension not by opening out, proliferating, but by closing in, looking closer and closer, harder and harder at things that are there before you. For example, it seems to me that *Marienbad* works very well in its own terms, on the level of fantasy. But there is another way of doing it, and one I personally would find more interesting to explore. In a real, recognisable Paris an ordinary, reasonably attractive woman sits at a café table, wearing what she would be wearing, eating and drinking what she would be eating and drinking. An equally ordinary, everyday sort of man comes up to her. "Excuse me, but don't you remember we met last year at Marienbad?" "Marienbad? Impossible—I was never in Marienbad last year . . ." and she gets up, walks out to an ordinary, believable street and gets into a real taxi. . . . Wouldn't that be just as strange and mysterious and frightening as the way the film does it? Perhaps more so, because the very ordinariness of the surroundings are apparent normality of the characters. (Taylor, "Accident," 183–84)

To some extent, this is what the screenwriter does with the restaurant scene. Pinter continues:

It's something of that sort of feeling we're trying to get here. In the book, for example, there is a scene in which Stephen, coming home, sees a car outside his house and Charlie . . . standing by it. To convey what effect this has on him the novel needs a couple of pages of free association. But in the film, it seems to me, all that can be conveyed just by the shot of what he sees, photographed in a certain way, held on the screen for a certain length of time, with the two characters in the sort of relationship to each other that we know to exist already. It's just the same as the way that a novelist may need five or six pages to introduce a character, to tell us what we need to know about his appearance, age, bearing, education, social background and so on. In a film the actor just walks into a room and it's done, it's all there—or should be. So in this film everything is buried, it is implicit. There is really very little dialogue, and that is mostly trivial, meaningless. The drama goes on inside the characters, and by looking at the smooth surface we come to see something of what is going on underneath. (184)

As Pinter says, "in this situation, something happens: the young man is killed in an accident. And this changes things, it makes all the unlocalised, unformulated guilt sharper, nearer to the surface. But still the unforgivable, unforgettable things are never said, things are never actually brought to a showdown" (Taylor, "Accident," 184).

Set designer Carmen Dillon understood the nature of the characters in the film script, which is very similar to the nature of Pinter's stage characters. From the beginning of his career, the author's characters have seemed superficially rather commonplace, and their dialogue has sounded quite ordinary. Beneath these elements, however, there has always been a great threat of physical violence bursting out (vide Bert in *The Room,* Mick in *The Caretaker,* James in *The Collection,* and on and on). That, in fact, has been one of his trademarks—the seeming normalcy with fear and anger lurking just below the surface. According to Dillon, *Accident* is "very much a film about people who appear to be ordinary, and perhaps are, though during the film we learn what depths of violence and uncontrollable emotion they constantly skirt. So in the sets we have concentrated on making everything look used, lived in, believable as a background for them." While Dillon notes that *Accident* is far less mannered than any of Pinter's recent plays (no mirrors, no cages), the designer did not see the sets as realistic: "No . . . a step down from strict realism, a toning down or selection. In colour, for instance, we are limiting our range beyond what basic realism would dictate, trying to make a colour film almost monochrome, with just occasional accents of colour."[22] Photographer Gerry Fisher agrees: "there is always a purely economic pressure to make films in colour, because of the eventual possibility of sale to colour television. . . . But I think anyway the decision was the right one: it makes it all much more interesting to use colour in this way, to make points by its absence rather than its presence" (Taylor, "Accident," 179).

The actors were certainly satisfied with the script. Stanley Baker, echoing Dillon's observations regarding the nature of the characters, said that "The script is extraordinary: to read the dialogue you would say that the most of it was just slight exchanges of small talk, that there was nothing to it. But once we get together, so many characters in a room, and start to say the lines and live the action, suddenly everything becomes clear, you know just what is going on behind the masks, just what violent emotions the clipped civilised conversation covers." Bogarde echoed Baker: "The script is fantastic—I think the best script Harold has done. It's so sharp, and spare, and pared down." Bogarde also recognized that "the whole film is based on strange time-shifts, a bit like what Alain Resnais does in *La Guerre est finie,* only more consistently. In fact the whole action is seen as refracted through my [character's] mind . . . , and so one memory sets off another, and scenes that take place in widely different times and places actually appear on the screen simultaneously" (Taylor, "Accident," 182). Likewise, he understood that "because the structure is so complex the visual style will be very simple and direct" ([183]). The sense of a common perception of the project is underscored by this statement, for it closely resembles Losey's vision, which is summed up in the director's statement that "There are certain scenes in this picture that just must be shot in dazzling summer heat" (179).

That the realization of this vision was successful is seen Knowles's conclusion that the "style of the film was in direct contrast to the baroque [of the settings such as Syon House], with Losey's direction stressing the linear and horizontal throughout—fields, the front elevation of Stephen's Georgian country house, dining tables, and cricket field. This visual style complemented Pinter's dialogue, which was almost wholly and deliberately concerned with reflecting social surface and exchange" (*Understanding,* 103–4).

One difference between the novel and the screenplay that Pinter introduced is so substantial that the screenwriter felt a need to write an apologetic letter to Mosley to explain why he had effected the change. The letter also reveals some of Pinter's thoughts about the nature of adaptation and the close, collaborative relationship that he had with his director:

> there's one major deviation, change—it might be said distortion—the fact that Stephen sleeps with Anna, and that Charley knows nothing about anything at the end.
> . . . I worked very hard to follow your ending at all points to begin with and in fact finished a complete first draft following that course. Then there was something *wrong.* This, of course, could have been entirely my fault, my inadequacy, probably was, but the long debate between Stephen and Charley simply did not work, convince, sustain itself in dramatic terms. A novel is so different. You have so much more room. A dramatic structure makes its own unique demands. They're unavoidable. Anyway, the more the whole thing grew in me the more one fact sank in and finally clarified itself—that is, that Stephen, ultimately, must be alone in final complicity with Anna, or so it seemed to me. And, in many long discussions, to Losey. It seemed to follow; it seemed to be logical. Dramatically, it economised and compressed, and by narrowing the focus achieved a greater intensity. . . . Charley finds himself staring at a blank wall. And Stephen has to, will have to, carry his own can, alone, with whatever the can holds.[23]

When Losey began the film, he, too, wanted to make it as a "continuous texture, without defined sequences, and without exits and entrances" (Taylor, "Accident," 182).

A brief, chronologically ordered discussion of the elements in Mosley's novel that Pinter retains and those that he deletes is instructive. When Mosley's Stephen first sees Anna, he is alone in his office at the college; she is squatting down by the white goat in the courtyard (14). Pinter quickly sets the triangular theme by introducing William into the scene, as discussed above: "WILLIAM *and* STEPHEN *are sitting by the open window. The window looks down to a quadrangle. On the grass a white goat is tethered. The scene is framed between them, below. . . . From the same viewpoint,* ANNA *appears in the quadrangle. She stops and talks to the goat"* (229, 230). In the novel, Mosley introduces the teacher-student relationship between Stephen and Anna before the don's relationship to William is established (14, 23). Pinter reverses this order. If Stephen's relationship with Anna is set first, then he is guilty of betraying his student. If his relationship with William is established first, then he is betraying a friend, and the dramatist-screenwriter has always been more interested in interpersonal relationships between individuals than in abstract professional ethics.

The heraldic stone lions that stand on either side of the front door of Stephen's home (Mosley, 18) are omitted by Pinter, who included many other specific descriptive details from the source. Presumably this is because such decorations would align the protagonist too closely with his aristocratic students (it may be that Mosley used this detail to show how much Stephen desired to emulate the aristocracy).

The reasoning that led Pinter to exclude the lions may also have been operating in his decision to change the name of the don's son from Alexander to Ted, a more plebeian name. Also omitted is the development of several minor characters, such as Tommy Parker (Mosley, 27), who do not add to the plot or to the thematic lines that Pinter concentrates upon. They may be intellectually interesting and tangentially relevant as part of the overall milieu and therefore suitable for the more leisurely medium of the novel; in Pinter's film there is no need for them because he can set the milieu easily and swiftly with a few visible images, so he excises them or brings them on only in sort of minor crowd scenes, as in the gathering of the academics in the library, which is sufficient to serve his purposes.

Along the same lines, Pinter deletes a good portion of the novel's dialogue, such as Stephen and Anna's allusions to how the existence of the atomic bomb affects people's views of life (Mosley, 31). The screenwriter, as he does in his dramas, is always narrowing down, focusing on only those elements that have a direct bearing on the theme that he is exploring. Ironically, this contradicts Kael's constant assertion that Pinter's film scripts are too talky, but again, his conscious approach, as indicated in his assessment quoted in the introduction above, is worth repeating because it is a key to recognizing a significant stage in the author's development as a screenwriter; most of his previous public comments on the subject of writing for the cinema were limited to remarks similar to his expression of excitement at the ability to "open out" *The Caretaker* in this medium.

Accident is an especially important film, then, because of the author's articulation of his conscious understanding of one of the major characteristics that differentiate film from drama which comes in connection with this movie: the paring down so that "everything happens, nothing is explained." Additional prime examples of Pinter's deleting extraneous people and sub-themes are the Woodstock Road party scene and the subsequent ruminations about Charley's background (Mosley, 36–46), Stephen's reading the lesson at church and his digression on Angus MacSomething-or-other (58–70), the long conversation between Stephen and Anna about her marrying William (137), and Stephen's visit to Laura and Charley's (139).

Incidentally, since the church-going excursion has been excised, in order for Stephen to arrive at his house after William, Anna, and Charley do (Mosley, 72), Pinter must make a small alteration. He inserts a scene in which the don, his son Ted, and his dog Mike are out for a walk (Pinter, 240–41). Because they walk near where the accident will take place and the dog is seen running across the road, as it does at the conclusion of the film, there is a foreshadowing that strengthens the possibility that a similar action was the cause of the car wreck. In Mosley's novel, the philosophical concept of accident is a major concern. In Pinter's film version, the accident is important chiefly because it is the initiating event for the story; the relationships between the characters are what concern him, as opposed to trying to put an abstract concept into human terms.

At the same time, Pinter does add bits and pieces to the screen version of the story. Typically, these additions are amusingly phrased social commentary. The humorous depiction of the dons and the provost talking about "A statistical analysis of sexual intercourse among students" at the fictitious Colenso University, Milwaukee, is contained in the novel (149–500), and Pinter retains the passage almost word for word, but it is Pinter who adds the final joke when he has the provost say, after a pause, "I'm surprised to hear Aristotle is on the syllabus in the state of Wisconsin" (233). In what is probably a concession to his audience's presumed lack of training in the classics, the screenwriter changes Mosley's reference to "Aristotle's Analytics" to a simple reference to Aristotle. Because he has also done away with the character of Parker, he ascribes the first part of the Wisconsin dialogue to Charley—who incorporates some of the Parker character.

Speaking of Charley, in the film Pinter omits most of the details of the characters' pasts, including Stephen's and Charley's, along with the development of Charley's character, because the screenwriter has been forced to abridge and condense events (such as the humorously described costume party [Mosley, 66 ff.]) and characters because it would not be possible to include everything that is found in the book in a 105-minute-long movie. The characterizing detail of Laura's glasses (121) is another example of a deletion due to the time limitation.

Contrarily, the characterization of Francesca is expanded and she is made more attractive in the film than in the novel. Because of the difference in style of the presentation of this sequence, the quality of fantasy is enhanced and the possibility arises that the meeting was wishful fantasizing on Stephen's part rather than a literal event. This possibility is belied by the detail of his straightening his tie while he is in the telephone booth waiting for her to answer; this is a real, human touch.

Likewise, the restaurant scene is transformed in the movie (see Mosley's bare description, p. 100). Francesca's nature and the adventure that Stephen shares with her are important in enhancing Pinter's delineation of his protagonist in ways that do not apply in Mosley's work. When something is essential, such as the storytelling episode on Stephen's lawn (Mosley, 74–75), the script is often virtually the same as in the novel (Pinter, 243–45), though the dialogue may be split differently. Despite the fact that the establishing shot of the group on the lawn is evocative of the opening shot of the wild-strawberries sequence in *The Seventh Seal,* Pinter's hallmark as an adapter has been to capture the essence of his source and to translate that into images that at the same time both contain that essence and go beyond it to create something new.

Pinter also changes the next joke that appears in the novel. Where Parker reads, "Book-maker found in undergraduate's bed," and the provost asks, "Might it not be a misprint for book-marker?" Charley reads, "Bus driver found in student's bed," and the provost asks, after a pause, "But was anyone found in the bus driver's bed?" (Pinter, 233–34). With his interest in sports, it is surprising at first glance that Pinter does not include some of the jokes in the novel that revolve around sports (e.g., Mosley, 151), yet since these jokes do not advance the plot or themes that Pinter is concentrating on, it makes sense that he has omitted them from the scenario.

Almost always the alterations that the screenwriter makes improve the product, as when he has the reading aloud of Laura's letter to Stephen take place in front of Anna and Charley in Stephen's kitchen; in the novel the lovers have gone before Stephen opens the envelope. The effect of the letter is considerably more pronounced on both the characters and the audience in Pinter's version, especially since in the movie it is Charley who reads the letter rather than Stephen. Similarly, in the book Charley contends that Anna was interested in him only for sex and that sex is different from love (Mosley, 41); in the film Charley is in love with Anna and believes that she is in love with him as well. Again, the impact on the characters and the audience is enhanced by Pinter's alteration.

The exteriors of the film may be flooded with sunlight, but the interiors are drab and almost colorless, an overall effect for which Losey was striving.[24] In an interview with Tom Milne, Losey noted that "on the interiors of the house, and also the colleges, the effort was primarily to remove colour, or at least colour that would be at all obtrusive; and at the same time to get cluttered interiors that were not purposeless, giving an overall sense of disorder" (Milne, *Losey on Losey,* 112). Stephen's isolated country house is a tangle of narrow stairs and warrenlike rooms, offering neither comfort nor any sense of real domesticity. Enormous amounts of alcohol are consumed throughout the film, ostensibly to blot out the emptiness of the characters' lives, but to no avail. As with Stephen's brief fling with Francesca ("a real lost night, which instead of relieving frustration, makes it worse," as Losey observed [Milne, *Losey on Losey,* 117]), the endless scotch and lager consumed by Stephen, William, and Charley will bring them no solace.

Significantly, Anna and Rosalind refrain from overindulging in alcohol. Rosalind is expecting, and Anna wants to retain control. Wheeler Winston Dixon notes that although the film appears to focus on three men lusting after Anna, *Accident* is actually a demonstration of Anna's dominance (34). And, of course, dominance is a theme that has intrigued Pinter throughout his career. An example of how Anna controls those who seek to dominate her comes when Charley orders her to "get the letter" that his wife has written Stephen. Anna does not respond, forcing Charley to retrieve the letter himself. At the same time, although Anna offers to cook Stephen's eggs for him, clearly she is not the domestic drudge that Rosalind has allowed herself to become. By the conclusion of *Accident,* Anna has obtained all that she wants from Stephen and Charley, and she leaves Oxford for her home in Austria. Charley's attempt to make her remain is fruitless, and Stephen knows that "there's nothing to keep her here" (Pinter, 282).

William is not as alive as a character in the book as he is in the motion picture; the narrator's first-person point of view focuses on himself, naturally. Still, even in the movie it is evident that William is not an important character per se. Mosley's William suggests that Stephen invite him and Anna for Sunday afternoon (47); in the film, Stephen suggests the outing to William. The effect is to place the responsibility on Stephen and thereby to emphasize his conscious desire to be around Anna. In the novel the narrator explains his almost Lolita-like attraction to Anna and others like her: "I fell in love with these girls for what they were not, for the dream, the unattainable" (66). The closest that Pinter comes to explaining Stephen's behavior in this regard is in the storytelling exercise on the lawn, taken nearly verbatim from the novel. Pinter has seldom disclosed his characters' motivations, preferring to leave it up to his audience to deduce what lies behind the actions that are seen.

Dixon concludes that "The world of *Accident* is a world of fatal and continual moral compromise in which every character is guilty of some sort of manipulation and/or vanity, and no one is entirely free of blame" (36). This ubiquity of guilt certainly ties in with Pinter's early vision of the world as expressed in Stanley's interrogation in *The Birthday Party.*

Beyond this, the tale is about the various lines of the characters' lives that converge to bring about the fatal car crash. The crucial question is, Is Stephen responsible for the convergence of the lines? He invites William and Anna to his home and in a sense panders for Charley. There is dramatic irony cinematically expressed when Stephen tells William that Anna can sleep in the spare room—when he, she, and the audience have seen her bedded with Charley there. Isolating the obvious elements in Stephen's character that lead him to do things that ultimately come together at the accident scene (not unlike Frost's spider, heal-all, and moth), Pinter emphasizes the intersection of lives that leads to this event more clearly than is done in Mosley's presentation of the story.

There are numerous additional examples of the coupling of effective cinematic technique with material from the novel that enriches the film. The movie contains a use of mise-en-scène to convey relationships much as was done in *The Servant* (i.e., the positioning of the characters within the frame in relation to each other to demonstrate a sense of dominance, and so forth), though the writer was working with a more complicated source than he had in earlier films. An incisive moment occurs when the characters of Rosalind and Anna seem to mix on the stairs: when Stephen and Rosalind go upstairs after the party, she appears to be Anna (though when Stephen climbs in bed with his wife and discovers who she is, his "I love you" sounds like a sigh of relief). Later, when Anna comes down with Charley, at first it appears that she is Rosalind. Another nice cinematic mix occurs when Stephen sees Laura and tells his wife about it—there is a flashback within a flashback as Stephen caresses Anna's face as he had Rosalind's.

And, an almost insignificant detail in the set signifies the initiating theme of the story: Stephen and Charley are both immersed in midlife crises. After all, Stephen is looking at television as a possible new venue in which to prove himself, and he visits an old conquest (Francesca). This midlife crisis is manifest in Stephen's disdain for and displeasure with the aristocracy, too. In his office he asserts that all aristocrats should be killed (a thought that is repeated at Lord Codrington's—"Isn't it true all aristocrats want to die?" [Pinter, 270]), and in the scrum Stephen and William fight as though they are trying to kill one another (Stephen is seen *pressing his fingers on the back of* WILLIAM'S *neck*" [Pinter, 271]). During the game, Stephen also attempts to usurp the place of his "betters" (Apollo might represent the artist; the Gaul might represent the common man). On the surface, this may seem to be a kind of class war, but Stephen's motivation is different from that of Barrett in *The Servant;* it is almost incidental—more significant is the old-men-and-ladies exception that William states. The detail has to do with the meadow-gate scene, which effectively captures the sense of Stephen's Prufrockian dilemma visually: does he have the strength to force the moment to its crisis? Also, the gate, which is shown for several seconds after Stephen and Anna walk out of the shot, is marred by a broken slat; like Stephen's relationships with his wife and the girl, the connection is incomplete, broken.

Jack Kroll finds *Accident* a "compelling" film (97), and Philip T. Hartung, praising Pinter's "bright, spare dialogue" and commending the use of flashbacks for character revelation, calls the motion picture "the best of the Loseys" ("The Screen: A Successful Accident," 177). Milne may well have identified the reason that some critics disagree about the quality of the film, a failure that resides in those critics themselves, when he summarizes the nature of the movie: "nothing is signalled, nothing given away. . . . you have to do your share of the work" ("Two Films," 59).

Calling *Accident* a "brilliant study of corruption," Gill designates the Losey-Pinter collaboration as the explanation for its success. He pronounces the two men "an exceptionally gifted and intelligent team" (150). Commenting on his collaboration with the screenwriter, in 1967 Losey stated: "With Harold now, it's a question of detailed discussion of intent; then he usually writes a first draft, which I comment on, and which he then rewrites; and there may or may not be small rewrites during the course of shooting—more often than not there aren't. I may ask for additions, there may be tiny things within a scene—[and] he's very often around during shooting" (Milne, *Losey on Losey*, 152–53). Pinter was, indeed, "around" during the lengthy production of *Accident,* and it is possible to follow the screenwriter's thought processes through the stages of his developing script to see why he makes some of the changes that he makes.

There are three notebooks in the Pinter Archives *Accident* box. Notebook 1 is handwritten, worn as if used a good bit, and labeled "*Accident 7/ 6.*" It begins "56?" then includes scenes 57 through 74. There is a lot of unlabeled dialogue, then numbered scenes. The entries from the second morning start a new series, labeled "scenes 1–44." The notebook includes what seem to be revisions from an earlier script, which is not included in the collection. It is still a rough draft, which nevertheless provides a good many detailed set or shot directions. For example, after the scene with the police in Stephen's living room:

64　Dog asleep inside door.

　　Out into back garden.

　　Dustbins.

　　Clouds.

　　Black trees. Looks about.

65　Upstairs. Quiet.

This describes an early version of a scene where Stephen is looking for Anna first in the backyard, where she has hidden herself from the police.

The notebook also includes a scene outline, labeled 1–16, of Stephen's early contacts with Anna and William, together with dialogue more closely related to the novelist's depiction of "Charley" ("Charlie" in the novel) and

Stephen having a conversation about its being Anna's decision whether or not to give herself up, particularly since she might go to prison. As Stephen tells her, "We'll do it all for you" (echoing Goldberg in *The Birthday Party*), Anna "slowly becomes limp." The notebook ends with a scene in which the doctor announces the good health of Stephen's wife and baby and which is scratched through.

Notebook 2 begins with Pinter's note to himself, "More flagrant—objective and subjective jumps of action." This is in keeping with his general approach to screenwriting, and he puts this into practice by including a good deal of emphasis on Anna's talking to the dog and the children at Stephen's house. This notebook also includes material from Stephen's scene with Francesca. Pinter writes that the lines in the Francesca scene should be "distributed over scene so as never to be synched sound but becomes a disembodied comment on the action."

Notebook 3 includes a variety of scenes that are omitted from the film. Of particular interest are a scene in church with cuts to William, the house and the car, and Charley and Anna; a scene with Stephen and a young Francesca in the front of a car, which is in the novel but not incorporated into the film; and a scene labeled 29 that refers to "Interrog. of Anna. Her paroxysm." The ending, labeled "(D)," occurs at the porter's lodge and includes "Message on paper—baby okay."

In a section written with a different pen, notebook 3 includes with "332" an alternate ending featuring just Stephen and Anna, showing her kissing him and him assuring her that "It's all right." In scene 413, Charley refuses to shake her hand as she goes out the door. Stephen closes the taxi door for her and walks to the office, where the porter delivers the line about the baby.

Written in longhand on another group of separate pages are comments about the opening, including and calling for "subjective camera through first scene." A description of the house and study and a possible transition to the past is written on another page—William and Stephen in sunlight, Stephen with his feet up; Charley at the party is described as "Sober. intelligent. drunker and drunker."

Three two-page groupings, typewritten, apparently from different times, include a scene where Stephen labels aristocrats useless and another with Charley and Rosalind in the kitchen where he turns down her offer of a second beer but chugs one and gets another as soon as she goes out. A second version of this scene follows, where she pours Charley another glass of beer, saying "This'll kill you."

Elsewhere there are notes for several shots not in the film or the published version. For example, page 14, scenes 145 through 153, are details of Stephen's first seeing Charley at the house when he and Anna engage in a mock gun battle with Stephen; Stephen plays and drops down, runs around the car, pretending to shoot Charley who "dies"—his final words are "I never had nothing to do with it." On page 22, the directions for the Francesca scene have been changed to "The words are fragments of realistic conversation. They are not thoughts." The scene with Anna in the bedroom is a good bit more graphic in this version: Stephen "thrusts his body between her legs, fixes his elbows on her arms, and presses his thumbs on her cheeks."

Perhaps most interestingly, this manuscript includes three scenes very different from either the published or film versions and much closer to the novel. In scenes labeled 34–37, Charley comes to Stephen's house the night of the accident, as more briefly suggested in what appear to be the earlier manuscript pages, though the phone call to Charley is scratched out there. Stephen tells Charley of his finding the couple, including the facts that Anna stank of liquor, that she fell on him from her driver's position, and that she hid herself from the police. Charley says, "Yes, she might go to prison." Stephen answers, "She . . . can give herself up, but it's really up to her, isn't it." Charley asks, "You mean we can't force her to give herself up," and Stephen responds, "No," after which they argue. Charley goes off to a bedroom, Stephen sits in the hall, and at morning light Charley appears with "Anna, dazed, her mouth slightly open," and puts her in a chair. In an interrogation scene vaguely reminiscent of *The Birthday Party,* Charley tries to get her to say whether or not anyone knew she was with William. Then Stephen repeats the question, telling her that William is dead. "Anna's head jerks back, hits the back of chair. Her head goes from side to side," almost a description of a fit, the "paroxysm" referred to in an earlier version. At this stage, Stephen places his thumbs on her cheeks, brutally pulling them back, "her hands clawing," and Stephen pressing between her knees, his elbows on her arm. Finally, he says, "We'll do it all for you," and Anna slowly becomes limp; her eyes close. Charley takes her back in this version, and then there is a cut to Rosalind's room in the hospital.

A second scene gives more details about Anna's and Stephen's leave-taking in her dorm room. Charley is packing Anna's bags, sympathetic about Stephen's newborn's health. Stephen comments that "They're sending her [Anna] home by air," and "there'll be an inquest." Charley goes out with her bags as Anna enters. She, too, is sympathetic about the baby; monosyllabic good-byes follow, as in the novel, with no thanks offered from Anna. Stephen puts "his arms on her shoulders, holds her loosely at arm's length (again a Goldberg echo), turns, and goes out the door. "Anna remains in middle of room, not moving."

The third scene is in the provost's room, where Stephen discusses the possibility of his resignation, almost exactly as in the novel. The provost pours Stephen a second glass of sherry, "clearing throat and wiping nose before he pours." Stephen's last line is "Thank you. I'd be very glad of one," in response to the offer of a second glass. Though these scenes are more specific about the implications of these events than the published script or the film, there is no interior monologue about the theme of confrontation, the joy of living and going on, as in the novel.

A neat, typed script, apparently a final draft, contains only a few changes in ink (e.g., the ticking "petrol pump" after the accident is scratched out and "ignition" is substituted). At the conclusion of this version, as in the published script, the last shot is of Stephen with his children (there is no third child as in the novel).

The collaborative element in filmmaking may be found on a page in longhand, labeled "Time lapses and transitions for Sunday at Stephen's sequence; Joseph Losey 1st August 1966." Hudgins believes that this is a page from Losey's notes on shooting the script, to which scene and page numbers refer. It includes notations such as "p. 44 scene 182b (already shot). Rosalind and William exit. Camera zooms into Stephen and Anna tiny figures in remote background coming through cornfield," with a check in the margin. Another interesting notation is for scene 337, page 89, a description of Stephen and Anna standing by the bed with the window open at night. Scene 338 follows: "Long panning shot, down. As camera comes to Anna in room she pulls back and exits (Already shot)." Then, also labeled scene 338: "(new shot) The empty bedroom. The window at dawn. Probably same position as 337. Then cut to 339 as already shot."

With the script for *Accident*, several things become clear. Pinter continually reworks his materials, trying to produce the most effective screenplay possible and always endeavoring to remain true to the essence of his source. He is also becoming increasingly more adept at working with cinematic elements in his adaptations. This is a pattern that has continued throughout his career.

The Birthday Party

RELEASED: 1968
SOURCE: *The Birthday Party,* by Harold Pinter; play (1958)
AWARDS: nominated for New York Film Critics Circle Award for Best
    Screenwriting
PRODUCTION COMPANY: Palomar Pictures/Continental
DIRECTOR: William Friedkin
FILM EDITOR: Anthony Gibbs
PRODUCERS: Max Rosenberg, Edgar J. Scherick, Milton Subotsky
CINEMATOGRAPHER: Denys Coop
ART DIRECTOR: Ed Marshall
CAST: Dandy Nichols (Meg Bowles), Robert Shaw (Stanley Webber), Patrick
    Magee (McCann), Sydney Tafler (Nat Goldberg), Helen Fraser (Lulu),
    Moultrie R. Kelsall (Petey Bowles)
RUNNING TIME: 123 minutes.[1]
COLOR
RATING: G

PINTER'S FIRST THREE DRAMAS, *The Room, The Birthday Party,* and
The Dumb Waiter are known collectively as "Comedies of Menace." They
are hilariously funny, but in this thematic cluster the playwright explores
possible reactions to the existence of menace.[2] First, one can seek sanctuary,
as in *The Room,* but menace intrudes, so flight is taken, as in *The Birthday
Party.* In Pinter's universe, menace cannot be avoided. *The Dumb Waiter*
makes this clear when even the menacers are menaced.[3]

Like *The Room, The Birthday Party* grew out of an experience that
Pinter himself had. In a letter sent to a friend during one of his tours as an
actor, about three years before the drama was written, Pinter describes his
rooming house: "'I have filthy insane digs, a great bulging scrag of a woman
with breasts rolling at her belly, an obscene household, cats, dogs, filth,

teastrainers, mess, oh bullocks, talk, chat rubbish shit scratch dung poison, infantility, deficient order in the upper fretwork.' Now the thing about this is that was *The Birthday Party*—I was in those digs, and this woman was Meg in the play; and there was a fellow staying there in Eastbourne, on the coast. The whole thing remained with me, and three years later I wrote the play."[4]

The dramatist's first play to be mounted professionally, *The Birthday Party* premiered at the Arts Theatre, Cambridge, on April 28, 1958, and became the first Pinter play professionally performed in America when it was staged at the Actors Workshop in San Francisco on July 27, 1960. It was televised on Associated Rediffusion-TV (ARD) in 1960.[5] The three-act play was begun immediately upon the completion of *The Room* in 1957, and many of the thematic and technical elements present in his first play reappear. In the characters there are numerous echoes too, though they are presented in different aspects: Rose's motherliness and playacting show up in Meg; Petey is Bert without violence; there is a song about Reilly; and Goldberg and McCann are Riley broken down into more identifiable terms.

The undefined cause of menace becomes extremely general in nature in *The Birthday Party* as a result of the self-contradictory possibilities suggested by the tormentors. It is evident that the terrors undergone by the participants in the drama are representative rather than the portrayal of a single individual's plight. Perhaps because the horror is intensified, by contrast the characters' dialogue sounds much more realistic and the horror comes through much more strongly. Humor becomes more important for the same reason, and the element of irony is also more prevalent.

As in *The Room,* the theme of the threat to a person's security by unknown outside powers and the disintegration of his individuality under the onslaught of the attacking force is carried throughout *The Birthday Party.* There is also the generalizing effect that allows the meaning of the play to extend to all members of the audience. This includes the idea of verification, which contains within it the problems of identity.

Ultimately, it is through Petey that we understand that Goldberg and McCann are not merely businessmen stopping for a night who become unwillingly involved in Stanley's mental breakdown. Petey knows that these men are actually representatives of a force that is seeking Stanley and that their intentions are not innocent. As a matter of fact, he goes so far as to try to stop them from taking Stanley away with them at the end of the drama. It is this action that gives us the perspective to see the two menacers truly as menacers, inasmuch as Petey immediately comprehends Goldberg's threat (that he might to go with them to see Monty) and subsequently refrains from attempting to protect their victim, demonstrating that there is truly something to be wary of.

Before the audience's suspicions are confirmed, however, Pinter amplifies the terror of the situation by creating a context that is absurdly funny, as in Meg's misunderstanding of the word *succulent* and her response when Goldberg offers the compliment that she will "look like a tulip" in her party dress and she asks, "What colour?" Having provided a background through colloquial dialogue and interactions between the characters, Pinter is now ready to amplify his hints of terror.

Ignored on the spoken level, the news that two men are seeking lodging at the Bowles's rooming house has a causal effect, and things are suddenly no longer as they were. A concern with identity emerges, and Stanley asserts himself by asking Meg who she thinks she is talking to and then proceeding to tell her: "I've played the piano all over the world. All over the country. (*Pause.*) I once gave a concert. . . . (*reflectively*) Yes. It was a good one, too. They were all there that night. Every single one of them. It was a great success. Yes. A concert. At Lower Edmonton."[6]

The pattern of contradiction in this speech is conducive to humor as each positive statement is lessened by another positive, albeit not so grand, statement: the world becomes the country, which becomes Lower Edmonton; everyone attended—except his father, who was nearly there because Stanley "dropped him a card," only the address was lost. The progression of the dialogue in this scene is a fine example of Pinter's dramatic technique in revealing multiple layers of meaning as related to characterization, and the interplay is a serious attempt by the characters to assert their superiority over one another.

The confrontation scene between Stanley and the two intruders is the crux of the play. As demonstrated by the catholicity of the list with which they assail him, it is not a particular that is important; since there is no way to escape the all-encompassing catalogue, the stress is on the idea of inevitability that ultimately defeats Stanley. The crimes attributed to him are mostly antisocial—murder, failure to keep a clean house, refusal to marry. The catalogue of cliché awards that Goldberg and McCann offer Stanley for his rehabilitation likewise reflects socially desirable goals and prizes.[7]

Though there is an artist-versus-society motif in *The Birthday Party*, the meaning need not be so limited. Because neither the original deed that stimulated the menace nor the source from which the menace comes is identified, and because of the generalizing effect created by the inclusiveness of the sins attributed to Stanley, the implication is that everyone is vulnerable to such terror. The meaning of the drama does not depend on our knowing what Stanley did. All we have to know is that at some time in his past, he, like all of us, did something—he is guilty. In this sense, he is related to K in Kafka's *Trial*.

There are other literary links. The connection between the stage play and Pinter's early interest in American gangster films and Ernest Hemingway's "Killers," which was so obvious in *The Caretaker,* is clear here, too, as is the atmosphere of *Boomerang!* The humorous but terrifying verbal exchanges between Ben and Gus in *The Caretaker* and the parallel dialogue between Goldberg and McCann and the two intruders and Stanley contain the Yiddish phrasing and quality of film comics such as Laurel and Hardy and particularly Abbott and Costello, as well as the cross-talk acts popular in Britain in the 1930s through the 1950s, acts such as Flanagan and Allen and Jimmy Jewel and Ben Warris. Moreover, Pinter's cinematic eye was apparent in the stage version of *The Birthday Party* when at the end of act 2, after Stanley has tried to rape Lulu, Goldberg and McCann converge on him in the darkness and only his face is clearly visible in the light from the flashlight.

The film version of *The Birthday Party* opened in New York in December 1968; it was the second of Pinter's stage dramas to be converted to film. One of ABC Film's first distribution projects, the venture was financially unsuccessful. A profit-and-loss analysis published in May 1973 contains figures that are revealing.[8] Still, it was an excellent and faithful transfer of the play. The movie clearly traces the disintegration of a sensitive man's character as Stanley is exposed to the presence of menace. The film was directed by William Friedkin and starred Robert Shaw (whose *Man in the Glass Booth* Pinter had directed the preceding year) as Stanley in his second Pinter film, Dandy Nichols perfectly cast as Meg, Sidney Tafler as Goldberg, and Pinter's old friend Patrick Magee, also reappearing in a Pinter film, this time in the role of McCann.[9]

Early reviewers such as the *New Yorker*'s Kael ("Frightening the Horses") and *Newsweek*'s J[oseph]. M[orgenstern]. react to the movie much as early drama critics reacted to the author's first stage plays—they do not understand and do not know how to react to something that does not follow established patterns and their preconceived expectations. Some critics (Morgenstern and Kauffmann ["The Birthday Party"]) fault the director. Others, such as Harold Clurman, not only praise the director and the camera work (a common thread among the reviews) but also appreciate Pinter's

The Birthday Party (1968). Dandy Nichols as Meg and Robert Shaw as Stanley. Palomar Pictures International. Jerry Ohlinger Archives.

screenwriting: "This . . . is as fine a film version of the play as I can imagine" (Clurman, 30).

The opening out of the play begins immediately with a shot of Petey setting out his deck chairs to the nonsynchronous sound of sea gulls. The titles are run over, and the sea gulls' calls become a mysterious rasping sound that is later shown to be the sound of McCann tearing a newspaper into even strips. At the same time, the image on the screen becomes one of a street seen in the side rearview mirror of a moving car. The image widens to show the car and then the car's point of view as it is driven through a seaside resort. Although Clurman is disappointed that the allusiveness of the film is diminished because we "behold mystery concretely," whereas on the stage it "exists covertly, phantomlike," he believes that the film presents buildings that are "haggard, the sea seems dead, the streets are inert, the beach chairs ghostly. They are all dyed with the hue of mortality" (29).

There is a cut to a promenade along the beach. The light on a lamppost goes off. The final act begins with what is nearly a reversal of the opening sequence, with the lamppost pointing in the opposite direction and a shot of the deck chairs in a line. The film ends with thirty seconds of blank screen.

Following the opening sequence, the location shifts to the interior of the boardinghouse, and there is a close-up of Meg spilling Kellogg's Corn Flakes as she pours them into a bowl (there is even a shot of Meg serving Petey breakfast in the living room seen in a mirror, reminiscent of shots in *The Servant* but adding little to this film). Soon, the reality of the presence of an outside world is brought back into play when Stanley breaks away from the cloying, adolescent attentions of his landlady and goes out the front door. The sound of an airplane passing overhead is heard in this exterior shot.

Esslin's contention that *The Birthday Party* is about Stanley's attempted escape from his gangster past is given some credence by the camera angles and close-ups of the lodger as he reacts to Meg's announcement that two men are going to be staying in the house. The force provided by these shots makes the possibility of a gangland connection seem real. The same is true of Stanley's description of his piano-playing career, especially the concert that he gave in Lower Edmonton, as the camera tightens on the emotions crossing his face in close-up. A similar effect is achieved in the same manner when Meg is seen reacting in terror to Stanley's threat about a van and a wheelbarrow—the camera circles and tracks the characters to produce an emotional impact not possible on the stage.

This is the key to the difference between the stage and film versions. Certain bits of business that occur in the motion picture may well be used on stage, as when Stanley drops his cigarette, but it is the use of cuts, angles, and shots (especially close-ups, two-shots, three-shots, and combinations of medium shots) that distinguish the film from the drama. The immediacy and intensity of live theatre is lost, but this is compensated for by cinematic techniques. The inquisition scene, for instance, is made excruciatingly graphic, and the action of the fight is also effectively enhanced and made more violent by the use of the camera.

Other examples are found throughout the film. The concept of eyesight is extremely important in the play and the film, as evidenced by the handling of Stanley's glasses and the many references to sight and seeing and the game of blind man's buff, but in the film the eyeglasses are focused upon in close-up shots several times (as when Stanley drops them in the kitchen and when McCann breaks them), and twice in the movie Stanley's point of view is taken by the camera, first when McCann removes the glasses and everything is seen out of focus and second when the blindfold is put over Stanley's eyes in the game and the screen goes black momentarily. These effects would be hard to duplicate on stage.

Sometimes the camera allows Pinter to expand on his themes in additional ways not readily available to him as a playwright. When Meg goes to the front door to greet Lulu, in the live theatre she goes offstage and Stanley is seen listening to the conversation taking place in the hallway. The depth of his fear is better expressed in the film through a reversal when the camera picks up Meg and Lulu in the hallway and Stanley is seen surreptitiously peering around the corner of the door at them. Stanley's attitude is more pronounced in this instance, for both the spyer and the spied-upon are seen in the same shot. Likewise, he looks through the serving hatch when Goldberg and McCann arrive; he is seen from the back, and the effect of hiding is amplified by the view of the room in the background framed by a small portion of the kitchen and the hatch itself. The caging effect is definitely enhanced in the blind man's buff game sequence with a high overhead shot of the blindfolded Stanley stumbling around the small, boxlike room.

Additional hints of the menace about to pounce are more pronounced in the film because the camera can move out of the one-room setting. It does so when McCann first arrives, and like Barrett in *The Servant,* he is seen casing the house, moving from room to room—not the action of an innocent traveler. Furthermore, the confrontation between Stanley and McCann in the hallway, McCann's paper-tearing scenes, and the "sit down" contest all gain intensity from the close-ups and two-shots employed, particularly as the camera moves back and forth between the combatants and then pushes in to a tight shot at a crucial moment. Similarly, the implied threat ("I never took liberties") lying behind Goldberg's funny story ("I'd tip my hat to the toddlers, I'd give a helping hand to a couple of stray dogs, everything came natural") is accentuated by the close-up of Stanley during the monologue.

At times the camera merely makes things more visible. This is the case when McCann puts the strips of paper back together. Shot from a high angle, the weirdness of the act is emphasized, as it might not be on stage, where it would not be so clearly seen. And, while the unexpected that occasionally occurs during a live performance is avoided with film, there are still errors caught by the camera, such as the magic bunny that occurs in the toy-drum scene at the end of act 1: Stanley is wearing his glasses in one shot and not wearing them in the next.

Harriet and Irving Deer reach a conclusion similar to that expressed by Clurman regarding the creation of an illusion of lifelessness when they note that the bookend conclusion of the film, in which the intruders drive off with Stanley, is enhanced by the camera: "What stands out is the pattern, rigid, neat, but most of all empty, not a sign of life anywhere. McCann and Goldberg, like the bogey-men Stanley taunted Meg with, have brought order and peace to the world, but they have done so in the most ironical fashion, by depriving it of any of its vitality or life" (30).

Pinter makes a few very minor changes in the script. In the play Petey tells Meg that the two men approached him "last night." In the movie, they talked with him "this morning," which makes sense because he does not now have to explain why he did not alert her to their pending arrival earlier. There are very few additions to the stage script dialogue (literally only a few lines, including a new scene when Meg takes Goldberg and McCann upstairs to their room and in the inquisition scene), so most of the alterations are cuts in dialogue, many of them having to do with Lulu. It is likely that the majority of these cuts are made to accommodate the time taken up by opening out the production and the screenwriter's insertions of action shots and the exterior scenes and the movement of the camera into the hallway, the stairwell, the upstairs bedrooms, and the kitchen.

Unfortunately, although nothing essential is removed, a lot of the humorous dialogue of the stage play is missing, and to a large extent the humor is essential to understanding the nature of the characters. For example, the credibility of Goldberg's family-oriented, philosophical pronouncements is diminished by the many names that he is called and by simple statements that are contradictory. In reminiscing about his "old Mum," he immediately begins talking about a young "bird" that he went out with, but with whom he took no "liberties" (a characteristic that apparently no longer applies, as will be seen shortly), and then he remembers his mother calling him to come in to eat, "quick before it gets cold." "And there on the table what would I see?" he asks, "The nicest piece of gefilte fish you could wish to find on a plate." Of course, gefilte fish is normally eaten cold.

The character of poor Lulu suffers most from the deletions, a process that began even before the film script was written, for Pinter changed her role between the first publication of the play in 1959 and a revised edition published in 1965. The lovely exchange between the girl and Goldberg is abridged in the later version so that her line "You didn't appreciate me for myself. You took all those liberties only to satisfy your appetite" (84) is no longer followed by his "Now you're giving me indigestion." In the motion picture, whole sections featuring her and Goldberg, many of them quite funny, are missing. Another unfortunate deletion is Meg's reference to the wheel-barrow at the end of the movie.

All in all, though, *The Birthday Party* serves as an excellent example of how Pinter uses cinematic techniques to bring his stage work to life on the screen. Incredibly funny and frightening, *The Birthday Party* is not suffi-ciently appreciated as a play or as a film. And, it is Pinter's script that gives the movie its power, not the technology of filmmaking.

The Go-Between

RELEASED: 1971

SOURCE: *The Go-Between,* by L.P. Hartley; novel (1953)

AWARDS: Cannes Film Festival Palme d'Or (1971); British Film Academy Award, Best Screenplay (1971); Society of Film and Television Arts, Best Screenplay; INTER Film Award; also nominated for Academy Award for Best Supporting Actress (Leighton); British Academy Awards for Best Supporting Actor (Fox), Best Supporting Actress (Leighton), Most Promising Newcomer (Guard), and nominated for Best Film; nominated for New York Film Critics Best Supporting Actress (Leighton); Society of Film and Television Arts, Best Film

PRODUCTION COMPANY: Columbia/World Film Services, presented by EMI/MGM

DIRECTOR: Joseph Losey

EDITOR: Reginald Beck

PHOTOGRAPHED BY: Gerry Fisher

EXECUTIVE PRODUCER: Robert Velaise

PRODUCERS: John Heyman and Norman Priggen

PRODUCTION DESIGNER: Carmen Dillon

ARTISTIC DIRECTOR: Carmen Dillon

SOUND: Garth Craven

MUSIC: Michel Legrand

COSTUME DESIGNER: John Furniss

CAST: Julie Christie (Marian), Alan Bates (Ted), Margaret Leighton (Mrs. Maudsley), Michael Gough (Mr. Maudsley), Edward Fox (Trimingham), Dominic Guard (Leo Colston), Richard Gibson (Marcus), Simon Hume-Kendall (Denys), Amaryllis Garnet (Kate), Roger Lloyd-Pack (Charles), John Rees (Blunt), Keith Buckley (Stubbs), Gordon Richardson (Rector), Michael Redgrave (Old Leo Colston)

RUNNING TIME: 116 minutes[1]

COLOR

RATING: PG
VIDEO: Anchor Bay Entertainment

IN 1969 PINTER COMPLETED his adaptation of L.P. Hartley's 1953 novel *The Go-Between*, the film script that earned him his most prestigious award. The third collaboration with director Losey, this film brought the screenwriter a Palme d'Or (Golden Palm) for the best picture at the 1971 Cannes Film Festival, along with rave reviews that established his reputation internationally.[2] Whereas Pinter's early plays were often rejected by public and critics alike, ironically, it now seemed that the author's name was sufficient to insure acceptance. To some degree, that acceptance can also be measured by the fact that he received seventy-five thousand dollars plus 5 percent of the profits for his work, figures that are astounding when compared to the provisions made just seven years earlier when he wrote the screenplay for *The Caretaker.*

In *The Go-Between,* the narrator, Leo, relates how he found his old diary and the memories that it evokes: in the summer of 1900 he stayed with a school chum in Norfolk, where he was the go-between for a pair of lovers, carrying their messages back and forth; he discovered them making love, and the man committed suicide. In the epilogue, Leo returns to Norfolk and renews his acquaintance with the girl, who is now an old woman.

Just after the filming of *The Go-Between* in 1970, Pinter discussed "his pleasure in working with the gifted Losey. He spoke with great empathy about the rigors to which a difficult location had subjected their talented actors. He told [the interviewer, Lois Gordon] that he had begun L.P. Hartley's novel late one night when he was at home alone and was unable to put it down; it had moved him deeply" (Gordon, x).[3]

The screenplay is not an entirely faithful cinematic treatment of Hartley's novel, but, as with Pinter's adaptation of *The Servant,* it was not meant to be. The major theme has been changed, subordinated really, and despite the accolades that it received, *The Go-Between* is not as cinematically successful as the earlier film, because first, the original is better and, second, Pinter's choice of subject matter to emphasize is less compelling.[4] Losey sees the film as a "study of people trapped by their class and by society in a improbable situation."[5] According to Esslin, the adaptation is even more "laconic and elliptic than *Accident,*" and "Pinter has telescoped the action into the last visit and brilliantly parallels the narrator's arrival, inspection of the place as it now is and meeting with the old lady, with the flashback of the ancient events, so that the whole culminates in the complete fusion of past and present in the mind of the spectator, who has been gradually drawn into a complex pattern of past and present images and relationships" (*Peopled Wound*, 205).

Unfortunately, while *The Go-Between* is a fine film, Esslin's evaluation may be slightly overenthusiastic. There are bits of Pinteresque humor (the villagers bothered by an insect while sitting and watching the cricket match), yet in adapting the novel to the screen, Pinter has changed the focus, and some critics contend that he has thereby weakened the end product. As Arthur Schlesinger Jr. points out in a review of the film for *Vogue*, "The boy in *The Go-Between* not only undergoes an initiation into maturity but is permanently traumatized" by his experience. If the viewer is aware that this is the essence of the story before seeing the film, it is possible to follow the plot line to such a conclusion. However, to an audience unfamiliar with the novel, the movie is somewhat mystifying and unconvincing—the meaning is hinted at, but it remains undeveloped. Unlike the experience of the Dean Stockwell protagonist in Losey's first film, *The Boy with Green Hair* (1948), in this case the boy's awareness of the initiation appears to be minimal, so the hinted-at trauma does not seem completely justified. It is only in retrospect that we see that the dry, staid character of the adult Leo is a result of the emotional stunting caused by the experience in his childhood. Even so, it is fascinating to see how well the author understood the craft of screenwriting even at this early stage in his screenwriting career.

In part, what problems there are with the script are a result of Pinter's shifting of the thematic emphasis: in Hartley's book the focus is on how actions based on class distinctions impact upon individuals; in Pinter's screenplay the focus is on that impact over time on those not directly involved in the application of those distinctions. More particularly, the screenplay is about how a young man is initiated into the enigma of adult sexuality and the tragedy that results, destroying the couple involved in the affair (beautiful Julie Christie in the role of Marian, Alan Bates in the role of Ted) and traumatizing the boy (Michael Redgrave as the older man, Dominic Guard as the young Leo).

Much of the attraction of the motion picture lies in its beautiful, leisurely evocation of a special time in British history. It elicits the kind of sense of time and place for which Merchant/Ivory would later become renowned. It is a masterly depiction of stately Edwardian elegance, almost devoid of action rather than filled with the multiple meanings of a Pinter stage play—so much so that the magnificent house and surrounding countryside where

The Go-Between (1971). Julie Christie as Marian and Alan Bates as Ted. Note what appears to be a twentieth-century bus in nineteenth-century Norwich. The bus in the background of the publicity shot did not appear in the film. Columbia Pictures. Jerry Ohlinger Archives.

the action takes place almost assume the importance of principal characters. Melton Hall, a derelict manor built in the 1660s, was beautifully transformed into a gracious and captivating representation of the turn-of-the-century Brandham Hall by art director Dillon, who had previously worked with Pinter and Losey on *Accident*. Indeed, Hartley was pleased with the house and garden, which closely replicated that which served as the basis of his semiautobiographical novel.

Shot entirely on location in the county of Norfolk by Gerry Fisher, who had also photographed *Accident,* the film gains much of its atmosphere from the countryside, especially that around the nearby villages of Melton Constable, Hanworth, and Heydon, and the flavor of 1900 captured during Leo's shopping trip in town, shot in the ancient cathedral city of Norwich.[6]

Finally, though, there are imbedded in the film links to the playwright's dramas that deal with the subjects of memory, the past, the relationship between the two, and their reality as they create the present or are created in retrospect by the present—in the manner again of T.S. Eliot's "Time present and time past / Are both perhaps present in time future, / And time future contained in time past" (lines 1–3 of "Burnt Norton") or Mary Tyrone's observation "The past is the present. . . . It's the future too" in O'Neill's *Long Day's Journey into Night.*

The themes in *The Go-Between* are the same as those that structure *Landscape* and *Silence,* two stage plays that Pinter wrote the same year that he wrote this screenplay (intriguingly, there is even a phrase in Hartley's novel, "the landscape of a dream," that resonates with the title of the play that marked a major shift in Pinter's dramatic themes and style). Moreover, the plays of memory, in which the dramatist examines the workings of the mind and the interconnections between memory and time, are essentially capped by *Old Times,* which opened the same year that *The Go-Between* was released.

Pinter recognizes that these subjects have assumed primacy in his writing, that as in his stage plays, time becomes increasingly part of his creative focus in his film scripts. He tells Gussow that "The whole question of time and all its reverberations and possible meanings really does seem to absorb me more and more" (*Conversations,* 209). Elsewhere he says, "I think I'm more conscious of a kind of ever-present quality in life. . . . I certainly feel more and more that the past is not past, that it never was past. It's present" (quoted in Houston and Kinder, 198). And, specifically relating his ongoing concern with time and this film, the screenwriter tells John Russell Taylor, "What I find exciting about the subject is the role of time: the annihilation of time by the man's return to the scene of his childhood experience."[7]

The opening line of both the novel and the film is "The past is a foreign country: they do things differently there."[8] The promise of this exquisite line is never fulfilled, however, and *The Go-Between* is not Pinter's most successful effort, although it certainly rises well above the level of most motion pictures, and it stands at an important point in his development as a screenwriter.

The contents of the *Go-Between* box in the archives reveal what Pinter was trying to do with this script. Included are notes on passages and scenes from the novel. In these notes, the screenwriter highlights those things in the novel that apparently seemed central or filmically useful. For example, there are direct quotes, with the page numbers that Pinter used as references.[9] These selections are a fascinating blueprint of how Pinter reads, how he identifies the core of the script that he creates for himself as he begins a project. Much of what is included does not specifically emerge verbatim in the completed script (though some of it does), but as Hudgins has observed, it "reveals a good bit about Pinter's understanding of the novel and, implicitly, about our own intended response to the more visual medium of the film itself" (conversation with Gale).

More importantly, there are clear indications that Pinter was wrestling with how to merge past and future. Among the materials is a draft outline, with chapter references to the novel, labeled 1–104 in ink, which is a scene chart that begins with chapter 2 of the novel (scenes 1–11) and concludes with "103, Mrs. M Leo Outhouse," the scene in which the young boy sees Marian and Ted making love, and "104 Return to Village." Although there is a good bit of detail suggested about the scenes from the past, this outline includes almost nothing about the present scenes, how Pinter is going to handle the memory framework, and the like. While Hudgins feels that the chart may refer to an already completed script or may be an outline for the script to come, he is convinced that it is an "intermediate stage, where Pinter begins to see how he will shape details of the novel he finds central into a script" (conversation with Gale). For instance, the following jottings come from the screenwriter's reading of chapter 9: "[scene] 47 Ted—tell her it's all right/Envelope—blood ('No blood on this')/Sliding down haystack./ 48 Marian-Trimingham on terrace." There are also notations that indicate that at this point in the process Pinter is not quite certain how he wants to make use of a particular scene, where he wants to place it chronologically, or even if he wants to use at all. For example, for scene 92 he wonders: "Destruction of the belladonna? Moving downstairs, etc.? Preparation—spell?"

A separate sheet includes handwritten comments on the concluding scene from the present: "1st man" is connected by a curved line to "Church," which is linked by a similar line to "viscounts—# of tombs. Man meets man," and then an arrow pointing toward "grandson." The next two notes are simply "lodge" and "meet old lady." This is Pinter's first description of the modern sequence at the conclusion of both the novel and the film.

On three pages of yellow legal-pad sheets, the author sketches a sequence that is his broad solution to the modern scene problem. It begins "Split Epilogue into front and back—which consists of man's entrance into village into meeting with old lady." A second note at the head of a major section is "injection of present into boy's story/voice—over solitary boy scenes." This is the impetus for the varied, restrained "intrusions" of the present scenes into the memory scenes (i.e., the scenes from the past) that make up the bulk of the novel and the movie. The technique foreshadows and broadly parallels that which Pinter uses later with such great inventive effectiveness in *The French Lieutenant's Woman.*

A final section concludes: "Present treated as past silent: 1) Presentation of places to be seen later in the past/ 2) Establishing of main voice of him and old lady's voice/either in narrational mood comment or selected dialogue heard close." An illegible section follows, and then "extraction of dialogue over long shots" concludes the plan.

Additionally, a longhand script outline and notes include many camera directions. On these pages Pinter often labels his scenes either "past," "present," or "neutral" ("neutral" meaning that one cannot tell, at least at first, whether the scene is set in modern or memory time). Similar labels are used in the published script, though it includes only one example of the "Time Neutral" label. The concept is used very effectively in the film and earlier versions of the script. For example, Pinter describes the first of three shots thus:

Street (MOD)
Street neutral
Street 1900.

The modern shots typically include automobiles, tractors, telephones; the memory shots often include horses, antique farming equipment, carriages, dirt roads; the neutral shots have no telltale indicators.

This section is followed by the notation "Carry on action with occasional interpolation from the old man, Leo's introduction to house, etc." It ends with the boys looking at the beautiful young Marian in her hammock, and then the old lady's voice comes over. There is also an early description of the film's concluding scene:

Square (Mod)
Pan to st. (neutral)
2 Neutral street—to 1900 square
train and old man
pony cart and boy
. . . square > modern
see old man .

In a typescript ending at 151, with some scenes and lines deleted by pen, two early scenes are of interest. As Marcus welcomes Leo to his summer home, he says that he hopes that Leo does not have a disease or snore or else he will kick him out of bed. Leo ups the ante: "I hope that you don't have nightmares and froth at the mouth. Otherwise I shall ~~kick you out of bed~~ — beat you to death." Pinter has drawn a line through the whole passage. A second scene, ironically in Marcus's sickroom, describes Leo getting "prayer-buggins" (prayer books) and details a conversation in which the boys belittle religion. This scene is absent from the film.

There is also a bound script, labeled "for Joseph Losey/January 27 1969." This seems to be the revised, final version of the script. A few scenes are cut, and Ted's language is enriched, taking on a more rural tone. For example, in this script he says, "That ain't hard to make her cry," where in earlier versions he said, "It isn't hard . . ." Pinter also gives his speech a more rural flavor grammatically, with "She do" as opposed to "she does," and so on. Schlesinger finds that Pinter's careful use of language is such that the screenwriter's "capacity to evoke genuine mystery by words" is the reason this film is so outstanding.

Pinter's treatment of the narrator in *The Go-Between* is different from that in *The Servant*. Whereas he discards the narrator in *The Servant* (the camera takes the narrator's place), he substitutes voice-overs in *Accident* and again in *The Go-Between*. The movement back and forth in time that predates Pinter's work on his stage play *Betrayal* (1978) and his screenplay for *The French Lieutenant's Woman* (1981) cannot be dealt with so easily, though. The techniques employed in *The Go-Between* (flashbacks, voice-overs) are fairly standard, and while they serve his purpose of transmitting thematic information, they are not what the writer was looking for. But, his experimentation in trying to develop an acceptable approach to the dilemma of managing time in the *Go-Between* script surely led to his innovative and extremely successful method in *The French Lieutenant's Woman*.

The chronology of the novel is straightforward. There is a prologue set in the present, in which the narrator explains how he came upon the diary that he had written during nineteen days in July just before his thirteenth birthday, fifty-two years earlier. This is followed by the story, told as a flashback. The book ends with an epilogue in which the narrator uses the plot device of visiting the tale's heroine in the present to tie up all of the elements. Pinter, however, layers time by intercutting between the present and the past and by overlapping dialogue from one period and images from the other so that the images on the screen are memories flowing through Colston's mind, punctuated by brief returns to the present. Hartley refers to the present only at the beginning and end of the novel; Pinter inserts flash-forwards through-out the film version, a reversal of the common cinematic pattern of using flashbacks for jumps in time. The story unfolds intercut with the old man's trek back to Brandham Hall. Pinter's approach may well be more effective in demonstrating the influence of the past on the present—although he takes a completely different tack in *Betrayal*.

Marya Bednerik claims that "From the linear novel with its present-day prologue and epilogue and its emphasis on heredity and environment as the causal factors in the formation of identity, Pinter's cinematic reconstruction with its use of flash-forwards and multiviewpoints changes the novel's Aristotelian structure, which demonstrates a deterministic view of character. Pinter shifts away from the tenets of naturalism in which heredity and environment are the major factors in constructing character into a quantum universe where identity is a series of assigned roles" (49).

The film opens with the credits over raindrops on a window. It is only in retrospect that the viewer understands that the window is that of a car in which the character who was the narrator in the novel is riding on his way to visit the woman in the present (though no date is ever provided) for whom he served as a go-between so many years before. There is an abrupt imposition of the harsh framing notes of a piano concerto (which are repeated at the end when the car drives away) over the images, as a long shot of Brandham Hall comes into focus and the narrator's voice-over is heard in the "the past is a different country" pronouncement. A cut to the young Leo and Marcus being driven through the countryside to the manor house, which they spy in the distance, follows.

Several elements imbedded in this opening sequence exemplify Pinter's approach to adapting Hartley's novel. To begin, the intercutting of past and present, which is Pinter's invention, and the use of voice-overs run through the film. Not only do these carry the thematic and plot threads of the original, but they also operate to emphasize the thematic points that the adapter wishes to focus upon, particularly the impact over time. An additional advantage of these devices is that they facilitate the condensation of the novel's 308 pages into the cinematically manageable 80 published pages of script.[10]

The film script is closer to the original than many of Pinter's adaptations of other writers' works. For example, the opening line signals that large sections of dialogue are incorporated into the screenplay almost verbatim, as in the playful tussle between Leo and Marian in the garden and their confrontation with Mrs. Maudsley (Hartley, 276–84; Pinter, 354–58).

Mirrors are seldom used in this movie, in contrast to the earlier Pinter-Losey collaborations. Leo's face is seen in a mirror over his shoulder as he combs his hair in one scene, the village is reflected on the car doors in another, but this is not a film about the youthful protagonist's interior life. Instead, it is about what he sees (and does not see) going on about him; later the events assume psychological ramifications, but, with the exception of Ted's suicide, not when they are actually taking place. Things are often observed from afar in this film, as though voyeuristically. This perspective is appropriate for the theme of dual initiation into the adult worlds of sexuality and class distinction found in the novel, and it keeps the class-consciousness element in play even though Pinter diminishes this line in his screenplay. Although the script does not contain directions that the credits are to be shown over the car window, windows appear frequently in the movie as places from which Leo observes a country more foreign to him than the past. His first view of Marian and the assembled adults, when he looks down through the upstairs window, is static and stylized, much like scenes from *Last Year at Marienbad,* filmed ten years earlier. Parenthetically, Marian is seen several times in attitudes resembling a Francisco de Goya maja or a figure by Eugene Delacroix or Jean Auguste Dominique Ingres. The nineteenth-century affiliation, style, and pose are equally germane.

Hartley's use of symbols is fairly obvious (the designation of belladonna as a symbol for evil is a case in point; the association of the color green—as in inexperienced—with Leo).[11] Pinter's is more subtle. The staircases function not only as a passage between the boy's upstairs room and the downstairs, but also as maze through which Leo must approach the adult rooms and the world downstairs. His first view through the balustrades introduces a different motif from the one that reenforces the meaning in *The Servant* and *The Pumpkin Eater.*[12] Rather than implying a sense of being caged, Leo's self-chosen vantage point is voyeuristic, which indicates separation. He is not kept away from things, but he is not part of them, either. The railings do not restrain him, and he can see through them into a world that is not his but in which he is accepted and in which he participates.

The symbolic use of windows, doorways (through which the activities of the upper class are glimpsed and through which only those who are invited—as in the case of the smoking room—can pass, and before which Leo occasionally pauses before passing through), staircases, and other passageways is part of what composes the metaphor of class distinctions in the film. The Maudsley family portraits in the stairwell (not mentioned in the novel) go unnoticed by the boy, yet they are part of his initiation into upper-class life, as is his presentation to a viscount.[13] It is germane, then, for Marcus to tell him to leave his clothes "wherever they fall." After all, "the servants will pick them up. That's what they're for" (Hartley, 45; Pinter, 293). Clothing is part of Hartley's means of depicting the class differences, as suggested above, and it is used in this manner in the film as well. The leisurely lines of carriages rolling through the landscape with the languorous women in frilly white frocks carrying parasols and the men dressed in white linen suits and Panama hats is especially evocative of the time, place, and situation being depicted. Ted's rough, sweat-stained garments make a nice contrast, but the most effective contrast is found in the pavilion tent between innings at the cricket match, when the gentlemen all sit on one side of the table dressed alike in their blazers while the villagers and farmers sit across from them in a jumbled array of outfits.

There are minor differences between the novel and the screenplay too, of course, as when the name of one of the Maudsleys' horses, Dry Toast, is given to Marcus's dog and when Leo does not misinform Marian about the time that Ted sets for one of their meetings (Hartley, 239, 254). The lunch at the Maid's Head in Norwich is moved chronologically, as is Leo's mother's letter (which is delivered in a voice-over). Many sections are deleted. The scene of Ted with the horse (Hartley, 86) and the dialogue in Ted's kitchen while he is writing a letter to Marian (Hartley, 90) are cut, which is dramatically better, because these superfluous details are excised rather than needlessly stretching the film out. Other sections are condensed. The focus on the concept of viscounts and family history associated with Leo's meeting Trimingham in church and later (Hartley, 69–70; Pinter, 306), Trimingham asking Leo to carry a message for him to Marian (Hartley, 75–76; Pinter, 306), and the long passages related to the planning for and buying of Leo's clothes are reduced drastically. They may be important in regard to the class distinction motif, but they are less significant in Pinter's emphasis on the impact of others' actions upon our lives. Likewise, it is sufficient to reproduce Ted's singing of "Take a Pair of Sparkling Eyes" and Leo's rendition of "Angels Ever Bright and Fair" to contrast the two characters relative to the major theme while simultaneously providing a picture of turn-of-the-century life in upper-class England without including Leo's "Minstrel Boy" (Hartley, 160) or Marian's "Home Sweet Home" (Hartley, 164). Again, the dramatic effect is enhanced with these reductions.

At the same time, the absence of the narrator has an impact on the meaning of the film. Leo's reaction to Ted's harsh words in the kitchen is missing (Pinter, 311), for instance, so we have to determine from the action itself what that reaction is instead of hearing it from the narrator.

Whether the novel's meaning is conveyed in the film is another question. There are times when there is no need for this to be done, times when the meaning expressed by the novelist would not correspond to the point that the screenwriter is trying to make, and times when that information would be helpful for the audience. There are instances when something retained in the movie does not carry the impact that it did in the novel because something else has been cut. Furthermore, it is difficult to express imagistically on film Leo's uncomprehending innocence and youth (though Pinter captured emotions and concepts in *The Pumpkin Eater*). While the reader is specifically informed of these considerations in the novel (Hartley, 110–11), the removal of the narrator reduces the motion picture audience's awareness of them. Similarly, the significance of Ted's explanation that the mare is ill because she has been "spooning" is lost because Marcus's comments about humans spooning have been cut. The picture of Leo as an uninitiated youth is captured in Pinter's version, but the boy's ignorance and inability to connect human and animal activity is diminished. At the same time, Leo's spooning lesson from Ted is paralleled by Marcus's dissertation about why Leo's wearing a school cap would be a faux pas. Because of the surrounding cuts,[14] this part of Leo's initiation into the world of the upper class is actually more effectively achieved in the screenplay. What remains, then, is put into focus by the film much as the movie projector's bright arc light incandescently casts the images onto the screen.

In the novel, the theme of class is uppermost, and the introduction to adult sexuality almost assumes a secondary importance. This is partially because Leo is clearly aware of the class elements. He comments on them, and they are reenforced by the descriptive passages and by the narrator's musings. Pinter has reversed the equation. Leo is still caught like Rosencrantz and Guildenstern in the midst of events that are beyond his understanding, but the action foregrounds the initiation theme. In turn, the class elements become secondary in part because they blend in as part of the setting, because they are not commented upon, and because many of Hartley's events, descriptions, and conversations related to this theme have been deleted. This is Pinter's technique: he pares things down, he combines, he condenses, and he focuses on what he considers the major thematic element.[15]

This narrowing of scope can be seen in the removal of one of Hartley's subthemes as well. The clash between the British and the Boers, epitomized by the Boer War (1899–1902) is another division that the novelist mentions frequently. Virtually all references to the Boers and the war being fought during the time in which the novel is set have been removed; what remains is too incidental to be of any consequence. Besides being a distraction in the movie because it could not be developed to any great extent, this subtheme is not relevant to Pinter's main interest, the topic of Leo's initiation (the English-Boer conflict is merely another part of the adult world that the youngster does not comprehend). It does not have the universal application that the primary theme has, so he eliminates it. The novel is a time piece and includes exact dates; the film is timeless and few exact dates are given.[16]

In like manner, the magic motif that runs throughout Hartley's work has been reduced considerably. There are still plenty of references to Leo's practicing of magic in the film, but they are more on the order of child's play than the important thematic indicators that they are in the novel. Whole segments such as the fairy ring (Hartley, 149) are excised, because the screenwriter is not interested in the supernatural even as an ingredient used to underscore psychological components. Hartley uses the spells conjured up out of Leo's books to contrast with the natural. In the discussion about horses' spooning, Ted accentuates the natural. When asked, "Could you be in love with someone without spooning with them," he answers, "It wouldn't be natural" (125). For the farmer-lover, love and sex are naturally linked. He makes similar statements elsewhere in the novel, and he is referred to as being a "natural" man by other characters.

Pinter has removed these references (e.g., 322–23). Perhaps the stock shots of a massive herd of stately deer moving through the grounds of the estate that are inserted in several places are meant to take the place of the references to what is natural. Whether these deer are meant to represent the upper class, who keep their own herds of game within the controlled boundaries of their property, or Ted's wildness, which exists within and despite these limits, is unclear. Both meanings may be intended, for the intercut shots do not come at patterned times. They may appear when Leo is involved in an activity that reflects his hosts' class standing, or—more often—they may be interjected when Ted is part of the action, as before and after Leo's first sighting of the farmer in Norwich and when the boy is on the way to the farm.

As is the practice in filmmaking, the script is not the final pattern for the movie. Many sections, long and short, in the published version of the script are rearranged or do not appear in the film.[17] A shot of a falling rook that has been gunned down by Ted, taken from the novel, is included in the screenplay (Hartley, 189; Pinter, 338) but does not appear in the film, although the nonsynchronous firing of the gun is heard (as is the call of the rooks, a sound used a number of times in the farm scenes); a description of Ted shooting rabbits in the novel ("he was standing with his gun watching for the rabbits and other creatures that clung to their shelter till the last moment before bolting out" [108]) is embellished by Pinter, who adds *"Close-up of* TED *with gun./He shoots./Close-up of rabbit./The rabbit is flung into the air"* (318–19), which is in the film. Following Ted's shooting of the rabbit, the image of his bloody hand carelessly smearing blood on an envelope carried from Marian is connected with this latter scene and serves as a foreboding of what is to come.

There are additions in the movie of scenes, individual words, and lines, too, naturally. It is impossible to tell who is responsible for most of these alterations. The inclusion of stock shots such as the herd of deer falls into this category, and the most important incorporation of stock shots may come just before and after Leo asks Marian, "Why don't you marry Ted?" and she replies, "I can't" (Pinter, 350). One of the shots of the deer herd occurs prior to this scene, and a shot of a flock of geese landing in a pond follows it. The effect is of natural occurrences bracketing a human event that is unnatural, the joining of two people, Marian and Trimingham, who are not in love.

Several critics have cited the importance of nature in relation to humanity in Pinter's screenplays (the fields in *Accident,* the undercliff in *The French Lieutenant's Woman*). Besides the deadly nightshade, Losey took symbolic advantage of another piece of nature that he found on location, a large, ancient tree that stands at about the midpoint between Brandham Hall and Ted's farm. Leo must go past this tree on his messenger's errands, and it comes to stand for a tree of knowledge under which he pauses for moments of reflection and revelation. The relationship between nature and humanity is underscored in *The Go-Between* in Pinter's screen direction as the old Leo leaves Brandham Hall for the last time: *"The elms have been cut down"* (367).

Even more important than the addition of stock shots, and so forth, is an alteration that occurs near the end of the film. In the novel it is revealed that Marian's grandson's name is Edward ("a family name," she claims [307]); he is unnamed in the film. When Colston visits Marian, she asks, "Does he remind you of anyone," and Leo responds, "Well, yes, he does. . . . His grandfather" (308). There is little doubt that Ted was the grandfather, but this is never directly stated. In the screenplay, the same exchange occurs in a voice-over that takes place in the lavatory in the past (359). In the film, Leo's response is "Of course. Ted Burgess."

Finally, in the novel's concluding paragraphs, Hartley's narrator says that he is going to be Marian's go-between one more time, that he is going to carry a message for her to her grandson (311). Most of the dialogue from this section is missing from the conclusion of the movie, and it is evident from the break in the dialogue and the look on Colston's face as he is driven away from the Hall (in the script the look is described as "*impassive*" [367], but in the film it is haunted) that it is unlikely that he will fulfill this final errand.

Pinter does add another touch of his own to the story. The realistic, humorous buzzing insect scene speaks for itself, much as the cricket game does. The discourse on cricket (Hartley, 138–39) may have been one of the things that attracted Pinter to the book, but the screenwriter was satisfied with presenting only that action which would be meaningful to cricket fans but not incomprehensible to nonfans, and he did not dwell on it. Losey wanted to excise the cricket match, but later he admitted that even Americans who knew nothing about the game found it amusing.

There is a minimal pattern in the intercuts from the present. The most obvious of Pinter's use of cinematic devices, these insertions tend to occur when key information about the affair is about to be introduced in the flashback that immediately follows. However, this is not always the case. Sometimes it seems as though Pinter is merely trying to remind his audience that the time portrayed in the flashback is not the time of the film. The use of the flashback makes the action of the past come alive naturally so that it seems to be more than simply a story that is being told—it was lived by the characters and it is vicariously realized by the audience. Still, the insertion of the present scenes does not follow the pattern without exception; there are times when no key development takes place. On these occasions it appears that by inserting moments from Colston's pilgrimage in the present, the author is reminding the audience that this is a remembered story, and it is remembered through one man, who was a boy when the events transpired. Moreover, the remembrance is filtered through the old man's retrospection. In his stage plays, Pinter has dealt with the malleability of memory as well as the intrusion of the past into the present.[18] Not only would this aspect of the novel have appealed to him, but it is in keeping with his examination of the nature of the phenomenon. When he comes to use intercutting in *The French Lieutenant's Woman,* Pinter demonstrates how masterful a device it can be when perfected.

The Homecoming

RELEASED: 1973
SOURCE: *The Homecoming,* Pinter; stage play (1965)
PRODUCTION COMPANY: American Film Theatre
DIRECTOR: Peter Hall
EDITOR: Rex Pyke
CINEMATOGRAPHER: David Watkin
PRODUCERS: Ely Landau, Otto Plashkes, Henry T. Weinstein
PRODUCTION DESIGNER: John Bury
ART DIRECTOR: Jack Stephens
COSTUMES: Joan Bridge, Elizabeth Haffenden
CAST: Cyril Cusak (Sam), Ian Holm (Lenny), Michael Jayston (Teddy), Vivien
    Merchant (Ruth), Terrence Rigby (Joey), Paul Rogers (Max)
RUNNING TIME: 111 minutes[1]
COLOR
PG

PINTER WROTE THE SCREENPLAY for *The Homecoming* in 1970, the third of his dramas to be adapted for the screen. Released in 1973 as part of the highly touted American Film Theatre program,[2] *The Homecoming* was directed by Peter Hall, who had directed the stage version in 1965, and included four of the original cast: Paul Rogers as Max, Ian Holm as Lenny, Terrence Rigby as Joey, and Vivien Merchant as Ruth. The newcomers were Michael Jayson, who replaced Michael Bryant in the role of Teddy, and Cryil Cusack playing Sam, a part originally created by John Normington. Cinematographer David Watkin was responsible for the excellent photography.

The playwright's third full-length play, the two-act *Homecoming* is at the same time his most representative, his best, and his most important drama and is challenged in his own canon only by *Old Times*. It was first presented by the Royal Shakespeare Company at the Aldwych Theatre on June 3, 1965, where it ran for a year and a half, closing to take the original cast to New York for the American premiere in 1967. There it won the New York Critics Antoinette Perry Award for Best Play of that year, and also earned Pinter the Award for Best Playwright.

The final play of consequence in Pinter's second major period of writing, *The Homecoming* is funnier and less conventional than its predecessors because the characters are more desperate in their needs, closer to the "extreme edge of living," so that their actions are more exaggerated and even further from normal behavior. They have not reached the point where they have to protect viable relationships—they are still trying to create them. A pattern repeated many times during the play is that of two characters sparring with each other, calling names, showing no respect, threatening physical violence; but this is all done half-seriously, half-playfully, as though it is the only way that the participants know of expressing affection for each other. In this family the ritual pervades all actions to such an extent and with such intensity that it goes beyond the customary exchanges between father and sons or siblings.

As is typical in Pinter's stage writing, the plot is not complicated. It was inspired by a boyhood friend of Pinter's from Hackney who went to Canada to teach and secretly get married before returning home to surprise his family. In *The Homecoming,* a philosophy professor returns to his London home after being away in Texas for six years, bringing with him a wife whom the family has never been informed of.[3] Once in the house, the husband and wife confront the father, the uncle, and two brothers who still live there, and the actions and reactions between the various members of the group eventually lead to the professor's returning to his job while the wife remains behind, ostensibly to help support her new family by becoming a prostitute.

Because of difficulties in communication and the resultant frustrations, because of the emotional needs of the characters and their resultant vulnerability, affection is not expressed in a normal fashion. There is a series of minor details that, taken in toto, implies that the men are emotionally attached: most obviously they live together—first, Max could kick the others out; second, Sam, Lenny, and Joey all work, so they probably could support themselves singly; third, a wall is torn down to provide a larger living room so that they can all get together freely.

Nevertheless, the family members act barbarously toward one another. For example, the lovemaking scene in the final act is both shocking and hilarious, but it is useful in helping the audience determine the meaning of the play, for the characters' desperation is exposed, and they seem willing to agree to anything, no matter how unusual it may appear on the surface, in hopes that it may lead to solving their unhappy situations. They will and do play, whatever the game. Thus, the first overt clue that *The Homecoming* is concerned with the theme of need comes at the end of act 1, when Max welcomes his boy in a manner as extreme as his rejection had been: "Teddy, why don't we have a nice cuddle and kiss, eh? Like the old days?" Teddy agrees, and the first half of the play ends with the two men facing each other, Max happily exclaiming, "He still loves his father!" (44); lines of affection have been tentatively reestablished. Ironically, in today's climate this dialogue is interpreted as evidence of past child abuse—but this accusation falls into the same category of exchange as the name-calling between Lenny and Max in the opening sequence, when Lenny says, "Why don't you shut up, you daft prat?" and Max answers, walking stick raised, "Don't you talk to me like that, I'm warning you." It is not to be taken any more literally than Lenny's Walter Mittyish flights into fancy concerning women, which relate to Pinter's verification theme and imply Lenny's view of women. It makes no difference what the "truth" of the matter is, whether or not the girl had the pox; all that is important is how the characters react to a given statement.[4]

The keys to the meaning of the drama are found in four exchanges, one early in the drama, two related descriptions that occur two-thirds of the way through, and one near the conclusion. First, a picture of uneasiness simultaneously created and held in check by love comes from Lenny's treatment of his father. The dialogue between father and son is revealing:

> MAX. Mind you, [Jessie] wasn't such a bad woman. Even though it made me sick just to look at her rotten stinking face, she wasn't such a bad bitch. I gave her the best bleeding years of my life, anyway.
>
> LENNY. Plug it, will you, you stupid sod, I'm trying to read the paper.
>
> MAX. Listen! I'll chop your spine off, you talk to me like that! . . . Talking to your lousy filthy father like that! (9)

Max contradicts himself and reveals his unflattering impression of women, which includes a reversal of a wife's customary complaint about wasting the best years of her life. Lenny displays no respect for his father, and instead of answering the image painted by the old man by standing up for his mother, he wants Max to be quiet because he is trying to read the newspaper. Max's choice of words in describing himself keeps the tone of his exchange with

Lenny amusing instead of serious. The two men threaten, but they do not mean to call anyone's bluff; they tolerate each other. After all, Lenny continues to live in the house, and his father allows him to remain.

The intensity of the language used raises questions about this family unit, though, which by definition should be close. Lenny's words are outrageous, but they are immediately undercut by Max's calling himself a "lousy, filthy father." If he can call himself that, Lenny's expletives lose their impact. And, Lenny's response, "You know what, you're getting demented," is within the parameters of the name-calling, yet after a pause he continues by asking, "What do you think of Second Wind for the three-thirty?" which indicates that none of the verbal abuse is to be taken seriously. This episode is an example of male bonding taken to the extreme, a situation in which the form is present but the meaning has been lost. There is a serious game being played, and the presence of potential crisis comes from the expression of the unconventional thoughts in an uncommon manner. But, as in Pinter's preceding two dramas, *The Collection* and *The Lover,* the emerging pattern of action implies that need is the essential element that defines the game, for it is specific needs that ultimately determine the characters' actions. Later, in talking with Lenny, Teddy paints an attractive picture of Ruth's role in their life in America: "She's a great help to me over there. She's a wonderful wife and mother. She's a very popular woman. She's got lots of friends. It's a great life, at the University . . . it's a very good life. . . . It's a very stimulating environment" (50). Ruth's description of America differs markedly, indicating that her life there has not been so rosy: "It's all rock. And sand. It stretches . . . so far . . . everywhere you look. And there's lots of insects there. *Pause.* And there's lots of insects there" (53). It is clear from the picture that she presents that she has been living a lonely, barren life.

Existentially, it could be said that Ruth is continually in the process of "becoming." She has been placed outside traditional boundaries by the failure of conventions such as marriage to meet her requirements so that anything she does is acceptable to her if it brings her closer to satisfying those requirements. This is demonstrated in her businesslike bargaining over the details of her contract and place of work—almost like Millamant in William Congreve's *Way of the World*—when they are talking about setting her up as a prostitute.[5] Finally, the whole play is epitomized in Ruth's farewell to her husband. She feels no real affection, antipathy, or guilt for him—she has done what she had to do, and as he moves to the front door to leave for America without her, she calls to him:

RUTH: Eddie.

TEDDY *turns. Pause.*

Don't become a stranger. (80)

She does not hate him, but he can be released because he cannot fulfill her needs. In the power struggle, Ruth is the strongest; new lines of attachment are established, and at the end of the play she sits with her new family arranged about her as in a traditional family portrait.

The Homecoming is Pinter at the top of his game. He utilizes his tools well: the setting concentrates the action as the six characters are joined together for unavoidable confrontation in the confining, barren set; the humor and irony enhance the terror involved in the underlying conflicts; the images of corruption produce vividness (note Max's description of his wife and Lenny's description of the girl "falling apart with the pox" in act 1, for instance); and the realistic language (phrases and patterns) emphasizes the movement from reality to unreality through contrast. All of this is done as a means of dealing with interpersonal relationships.

The basic structural device in the play is the framework of a power struggle in which sex turns out to be the deciding agent. In a series of skirmishes throughout the drama, the characters meet, compete, and attempt to gain dominance over one another, with Ruth using her sexuality to emerge victorious. There is a tension set up by the alternating tonalities (humor versus horror, for example) of the continuing confrontation. Through the form of verbal fencing, the weaponry of the power struggle, Pinter exposes the characters and their beliefs, thus providing the meaning of the play.

The reason for the power struggle is essentially the same one that motivates the majority of Pinter characters in one guise or another. Although the writer tends to exaggerate when explaining his works to interviewers, many of his exaggerated comments are based on a valid core, and often the basic thought is applicable to the work in question. When asked by Henry Hewes what *The Homecoming* was about, he replied: "It's about love and lack of love. The people are harsh and cruel, to be sure. Still, they aren't acting arbitrarily but for very deep-seated reasons."[6] Elsewhere he has insisted that his writings deal with "the terror of the loneliness of the human situation."[7] The need to love and to be loved, a primary appetite, is at the center of the characters' actions. It is also the cause of all their troubles. Asked whether the family represents evil, Pinter contends, "There's no question that the family does behave very calculatedly and pretty horribly to each other and to the returning son. But they do it out of the texture of their lives and for other reasons which are not evil but slightly desperate."[8] This brings to mind the earlier equation of love and need in connection with *The Caretaker*. If the people in the drama are desperate in their needs, then everything they do may be aimed at satisfying themselves.

When applied to *The Homecoming*, these statements explain much of why the characters do what they do. Pinter's description of Ruth is pertinent: "The woman is not a nymphomaniac as some critics have claimed. . . . She's in a kind of despair which gives her a kind of freedom. Certain facts like marriage and the family for this woman have clearly ceased to have any meaning."[9]

In a family in which individuals feel these needs so vitally, there has been a breakdown in the ability to communicate between the individual members, and as a result they have resorted to game-playing and rituals in an attempt to get through to one another. Unfortunately, the game-playing and rituals only serve to compound the problem and make expression of feelings more difficult because the stylized forms get in the way of the players, somewhat along the line of Pinter's *The Lover* (1963), intensifying the very problems they are meant to alleviate. According to Pinter, "The game is the least of it. What takes place is a mode of expression, a chosen device. It's the way the characters face each other under the game that interests me."[10] The game, essentially, is the continual battle for emotional security.

Pinter's canon is of a piece. When the dramatist wrote *The Room* in 1957, he was interested in exploring the effect of fear, of physical menace, on an individual. By the time he completed *The Homecoming* in 1965, the subject of his works had become psychological need, and the actions of the characters in the play are centered in those needs.[11] While the conclusion of *The Homecoming* is astonishing if taken out of context, as in the "comedies of menace," the movement from a realistic beginning has been smooth and logical, each step being a bit more absurd than the one before it, yet each is based on its predecessor.

Film critics, such as Paul D. Zimmerman of *Newsweek*, have agreed that the film version of *The Homecoming* is "more relevant and penetrating than when it first reached Broadway," being both funnier and more frightening because of the "harder, more savage tone" given by Hall's direction. The acting is again superb, with Rogers dominating the outstanding cast and Merchant and Holm providing fitting support. Zimmerman concludes that the American Film Theatre production nourishes "both the theatre and film," in part because Hall shies "away from . . . cinematic razzle dazzle." "Close-up," says Zimmerman, "compensates for the loss of intimacy of a live performance," and the "absence of 'exteriors' contributes to the dramatic tension inherent in [this work] about people trapped together" (113).

Jay Cocks, writing for *Time,* also comments on the film's tension. Calling Pinter's film scripts "probably the best scenario writing now being done in English," he credits the immense artistic success of this film to two factors. First, the strength of the original. "No one writes this well originally for films," Cocks asserts. The second factor that Cocks cites is the appropriateness of the performances to the material: "Each inflection, every pause and gesture, seems to have been measured by caliper, but this precision never becomes deadening. Instead it draws everything taut, gives an almost musical tension" ("Fire and Ice," 70). Interestingly, there is no music in the film, with the exception of the jazz record that Lenny plays in the dance scene. Kauffmann, who also makes a musical allusion in his review of the movie, is in agreement with Cocks: "A fine play is now a fine film. It's a safe bet that generations to come will be glad that it exists" ("The Homecoming," 33). Pinter seems pleased with the transference to film, too, saying that the movie is "very good."

As is the case with *The Caretaker* and *The Birthday Party,* Pinter's *Homecoming* screenplay does not vary greatly from his stage script. Actually, with the exception of a very few lines deleted, it is practically a word-for-word adaptation. Again, he has no need to seek the essence of the material with which he was working—he had already done that in writing it for the stage. The challenge, therefore, was to translate the existing work into cinematic language. Indeed, the product is much what one would anticipate, given the writer's comments about the differences between directing stage and film productions: "On the stage one of the challenges that faces a director, a writer and the actors is how to focus the attention of the audience, how to bend the focus, how to insist that the focus of the audience goes in one specific direction when there are so many other things to look at on the stage. With a film the audience must attend only to the particular image you're showing them. They have no chance to do anything else."[12]

In his speech accepting the Shakespeare Prize at the University of Hamburg in 1970, Pinter talks about revisiting his plays in subsequent performances, about the chance to "wring the play's neck once more," to reexamine a drama before his protagonists "withdraw into the shadows" ("Speech: Hamburg 1970"). Despite this opportunity, the essence of *The Homecoming* remains virtually the same on celluloid as it was on the stage, a testament to the genius of the original. The expected minor deletions and additions are present to open out and to accommodate for other alterations, but they do not significantly change the nature of the material.

John Bury, who had designed the set for the original stage production of *The Homecoming* for the Royal Shakespeare Company, was called upon to design the set for the film as well. Although the differences between the sets seem minimal, they reflect the differences between the media and how those differences subtly affect the production.[13] For the stage presentation, Pinter and Hall wanted the single room to contain an area that was not in full sight line: the "window was out, so was the bottom of the staircase" (Lahr, 32–33). In an interview with John Lahr about his design, Bury says, "The non-use of the door made the door far more real than if you had a stage door" (33). He goes on to say that having a stage that contains only the absolute essentials is a means of insuring that "a movement means the thing it ought to mean." This is exactly what Hall and Pinter desired. Hall told Lahr that he wrote a brief to Bury saying that he did not want a naturalistic set that "tries to kid the audience that they're not in a theatre"; "'we will have nothing on stage except what is necessary' because what is necessary will speak that much more eloquently" (11–12). Only "a few pieces of furniture" are placed on stage (12). In this way, the reality of the play becomes a suprareality.

The sound design is equally simple and spare, and Watkin's lighting is praised by a number of reviewers. Cocks calls it "crucial" in this film, because the "low, somber tones" give the movie "a tangible but evasive air of menace that perfectly matches the shadows and undertones of Pinter's language" ("Fire and Ice," 70), and it is the author's language that sets him off as the foremost English-language playwright of his generation, perhaps of the century.

The reality of the film is also the reality of the photographic image: there is an outdoors, there is a kitchen, there are pictures on the wall, all captured in detail. The opening out begins audibly with the sound of Max rummaging through the kitchen drawers as the credits roll over a black screen. Visually, the opening out occurs with the first shot in the film—Max's hand pushing utensils around in the drawer. In addition, as opposed to the stage production, characters are seen in the hallway and going up and down the staircase, there is a shot of Lenny in his room, there are shots of the family eating lunch in the kitchen, and there are a few additional exterior shots: Ruth and Teddy arriving in a taxi at the family home in North London, the camera tracking Ruth as she walks out the front door and down the street and then comes back, Joey working out in the backyard, and the exterior establishing shot of the building.

As in the *Birthday Party* film, the magnifying effect of the camera is in play throughout the movie to show the characters' emotions in close-ups and through the use of angles, juxtapositions, and the like. Kauffmann comments that "The power of enclosure, of making related series of enclosures, is native to film" ("The Homecoming," 22). The critic also provides an example of effective use of the camera when it is proposed that Ruth stay behind and support the family by becoming a prostitute: "Her first comment is to ask how many rooms there would be in the flat, and there is a quick glimpse of her husband's face before we go to the reply from his brother. That glimpse is not a banal reaction shot: it's like a beat before a leap" (22).

Enoch Brater speaks of the use of cuts in the movie that are utilized as a "theatrical analogue for . . . theatrical effects": "When the camera centers its attention on one speaker, close-ups and medium shots exaggerate each individual's isolation, transforming Pinter's stage monologues into cinematic soliloquies. . . . the series of close-ups extends the inner world of each actor [so that an] audience which comes prepared to see the group . . . finds instead the individual drawn in sharp relief" (445–46). Brater concludes that this use of cinematic devices, "making cinematic precision to amplify the ambivalence of the script . . . brings a more humanized dimension . . . to the play" and results not in a filmed play but rather in a "sophisticated film based on a play" (447).

There are innumerable examples of how the camera is used imaginatively to replicate the effect of the famous Pinter stage pause through a series of shots. For instance, when Ruth and Lenny engage in their verbal combat, on stage the two simply say nothing for a moment, and the audience watches them both. On film, the camera holds on the speaker, then moves swiftly to the listener, then jumps back and forth between the two characters.

One of the most obvious demonstrations of Pinter's directorial focusing is the famous cigar-lighting scene. It is more effective on film because instead of the four men standing in the middle of a large stage, the audience sees them all captured in a medium shot that demonstrates the nature of their relationship. The composition of this shot is magnificent. All four men are seen within the frame. The two sets of brothers stand in a grouping of four, yet they are isolated in their own individual circles. Teddy is on the left, facing Lenny but staring past him. Lenny is in the center of the picture, in front of Sam, who is slightly farther downstage than Teddy and facing the same way—that is, with his back to both Teddy and Lenny so that he is facing away from both of them. On the right, slightly upstage from Lenny and standing behind him but facing the same direction, is Max. They all seem lost in their own smug thoughts, in

The Homecoming (1973). Michael Jayston as Teddy, Ian Holm as Lenny, Cyril Cusak as Sam, and Paul Rogers as Max. American Film Theater. Jerry Ohlinger Archives.

celebratory, ritualistic poses that serve to highlight the phallic nature of the slightly upward-tilted cigars that they are smoking. No one, son, brother, father, or uncle, is looking at anyone else. They are a family unit, photographed together in the living room of the house, the center point of the home that they share (or shared), and they are sharing a moment together, but they are separated within that unit and that moment.

   The Homecoming as a motion picture displays many of the positives and negatives inherent in filming a stage play. Some of this may be due to the direction by Hall, who was great in working on the live stage performance but who might have been too wedded to retaining everything on film. On the screen some of the magnificently inventive and funny monologues are a little wordy because of their length, and occasionally they take on a wooden character due to being presented in static shots. In many cases the shots come in concert with certain stage directions, such as "pause." The couple of times when the camera is used to convey physical action in ways not possible on stage, the fight between Max, Joey, and Sam in act 1 and Sam's collapse at the end of the drama, are not especially successful. There is a lot of motion, but nothing is gained by it.

Conversely, the effectiveness of the movie comes from the movement of the camera during dialogues, in the close-ups, the two-shots, and the shifting back and forth between the characters as they talk. The characters' lines are frequently very humorous, and the combinations and contrasts of words and ideas is highlighted by the use of the camera. And, there are some exquisite bits of cinematography that demonstrate how the screen can be superior to the stage in communicating the nature of the relationships between the characters. A prime example is the dance scene in which Ruth and Lenny are seen kissing in an extreme close-up while Teddy, in deep focus, is visible between the two of them in the background, an actual triangle being formed by the figures. As good as it was in the original, the "We'll put her on the game" sequence benefits from being filmed, too.

There have been three avatars of *The Homecoming*. The stage play is the most emotionally moving. When trying to retain the flavor of the drama on the screen, things such as the use of titles in the opening act ("Summer. A House in North London. Evening.") and again midway through ("Evening") get in the way more than they enhance the production. The televised version exposes one of the major weaknesses of that medium: the cropped frames mean that much of the advantage gained by using a camera to illustrate the characters' relationships is lost because the frames are cropped and some of the characters are partially or completely cut out of the picture. Letterboxing would be useful in countering this effect.

The screenplay for *The Homecoming* follows the pattern of the film scripts for *The Caretaker* and *The Birthday Party*. The motion picture version is a quite effective recreation on the screen of the stage production. Pinter does very little in the way of rewriting the script. What he does do is take advantage of the camera's magnifying attribute to focus the audience's attention exactly where he wants it and to enhance the audience's ability to discern the emotional impact of actions on the individual characters. Nonetheless, it is the greatness of the original play that carries the film.

This is the last of his own plays that Pinter adapted for the screen for nearly a decade, perhaps because by this time he had begun to emerge as a major force not just in contemporary drama but in the modern cinema as well. Since then his work for the cinema has increased in quality, and his fame has been in corresponding ascendance.

The Proust Screenplay (Remembrance of Things Past)

RELEASED: Not filmed
SOURCE: *À la recherche du temps perdu* (*Remembrance of Things Past*), by Marcel
Proust (1913–1927; translated, 1922–1931)

IN A BOOK ABOUT HOW TO WRITE film scripts, French screenwriter Jean-Claude Carriere notes that "usually, at the end of the shoot, scenarios are thrown into the studio dustbin. They are torn, crumpled, dirtied, abandoned. Very few people keep a copy, and even fewer still have them bound, or collect them" (11). From early on, Pinter's attitude toward his screenplays has been just the opposite; in fact, he has said that he thinks that screenplays should be "publishable." *The Proust Screenplay* is a fine example of why he may have attached more importance to his film writing than is typical—he is aware that he is producing art, not the mere skeleton for technological exploitation. He told interviewer Stephen Menick that he accepted the assignment to write the film adaptation of the Proust novel because "it was the greatest excitement to do so. What you see here [the screenplay], whatever this is worth, it's something based on absolute devotion" (47); "I wanted . . . to try to express it in terms that would be true to it, so that the thing would work in itself and yet have a truth of a different nature" (46).

Pinter is as serious about his film scripts as he is about his play scripts. Others recognize the value of his scripts, too, even those scripts that may never be "realized" as shot films: "In its published form, Pinter's text of the theme of time in Marcel Proust's *À la recherche du temps perdu* . . . is as perceptive as that contained in any recent volume of explicit critical analysis" (Armes, 35). One critic called the screenplay "uncomparably the best adaptation ever made of a great work and . . . in itself a work of genius. . . . a recomposition in another art" that "rises . . . to the level of his best theater work" (Kauffmann, "The Proust Screenplay," 22).

In his introduction to the published version of the film script, Pinter recalls that in early 1972 Nicole Stephane, who owned the film rights to *À la recherche du temps perdu,* approached Losey about the possibility of directing the film version of the book. Losey in turn asked Pinter if he was interested. The writer, who had read the first volume, *Du côté de chez Swann,* was greatly interested. He proposed that Barbara Bray, a script editor at BBC Radio whom he knew to be an authority on Proust, work with them on the screenplay. The manuscript was finished in 1973.[1]

In his interview with Gussow, Pinter mentioned that he was "going to enter into a film which is going to be the most difficult task I've ever had in my life—and one which is almost impossible" (Gussow, "A Conversation," 132). In a letter written at about the same time as the interview, the author answered a question regarding his current projects by stating that he was "not working on any play," but "I'm trying to write a screenplay of 'A la recherche du temps perdu' at the moment!" and in several subsequent letters he referred to the complexity of his task.[2]

Pinter read Proust's work daily for three months and even visited the French locales, such as Illiers, Cabourg, and Paris, about which the novelist had written. The job of translating the novel to the screen took five months, and the problems presented by the work were immense. Chief among these was that of reducing Proust's work to screenplay length. The length of the screenplay itself, published in 1977 by Eyre Methuen in Great Britain and Grove Press in the United States, underscores the magnitude of that task. The average length of Pinter's first fourteen published screenplays is 79 pages. Not counting *The Proust Screenplay,* the average length is 71 pages. *The Proust Screenplay* is 174 pages long (and this is without the 24 pages that Pinter cut from the manuscript). That is two and one-fifth times the average; the next longest of Pinter's screenplays is *The French Lieutenant's Woman* at 103 pages. In fact, Pinter has replied jokingly to the question of what specific problems he faced in converting the novel to film by saying that the book is 4,722 pages long and each page presented a specific problem. Despite—or perhaps because of—this inherent set of difficulties, Losey, the director of several earlier Pinter films, felt that the manuscript was "the absolute height of his [Pinter's] achievement."[3]

Filming the screenplay did not prove to be easy, either. One of the reasons that financing was impossible to find (Pinter thinks that it was *the* reason) was the length of the film. The screenwriter recalls that he read the screenplay with his son David, "acted the whole thing out," and found that with all the silences it timed out at three hours and thirty-five minutes. Acknowledging that the picture could well have been epic in length, as much as eight or nine hours, Pinter says, "I should point out . . . that the length, the three and a half hours, was an artistic decision . . . if it was going to be an eight-hour film then it was going to be an eight-hour film. . . . In fact, the whole structure of the film is the structure that was *found,* not predetermined in any way."[4] He also recognizes that three and a half hours is a long film, that a film of that length will be costly to shoot, and that financiers want to be certain that they will get their money back.

Losey called *Remembrance* the "best screenplay I've even seen or known of" but notes that he had a twenty-one-week shooting schedule for the film.[5] At the time that he was interviewed, Losey felt that with luck the film would be released in 1977, the finished product to run between three and four hours.[6] At this point, of course, there is little hope that the project will ever be realized, although a radio version of the script was presented in a successful two-hour BBC Radio Three production of a version adapted by Michael Bakewell on December 31, 1995.[7] If nothing else, this was a tribute to Pinter's verbal abilities, even though the idea of a film script, the essence of which is its visual images, being performed in a pure sound medium is deliciously ironic and perverse. In another ironic twist, in its latest incarnation, the screenplay was turned into a stage play by Pinter and Di Trevis and staged in 2000 at the Royal National Theatre in London under Trevis's direction.

According to Ronald Knowles, John Walsh, a critic for the *Independent,* visited the studio set and was apprised by the BBC technical staff of the secrets of radio sound:

> Obviously, a sound production could make much of such things as the bells at Cambray, or a tinkling glass, let alone the Vinteuil Septet which really came into its own on the airwaves, but what of the camera focus on the visually erotic in the screenplay? "Rustling," apparently, is the answer. BBC personnel explained to Walsh that "sex . . . is a problematic business, because you have to imply so much through mere silences and tiny squeaks. Period costume sex is easier because you can suggest that crinolines and pantaloons are being rudely adjusted all over the set. Hence the entire cast of *A La Recherche* were holding up things called 'practice skirts' to rustle whenever things are hotting up." One thing puzzled Walsh: "What about the scenes of Sapphic rapture between, say, Albertine and Andre? Did they have a different rulebook for lesbian sex on the radio? 'It's a grey area' said the Radio Three lady.

'We usually settle just for lots of giggling.'" (Knowles, "1994–95 and 1995–96," 165)

In a 1980 interview, Pinter revealed that he begins writing his plays without knowing how they will end (as he recounts in regard to how he came to write *Old Times*).[8] Obviously, this is not normally the case when he writes an adaptation—and this practice may affect how he structures his works and why, when he has composed plays and film scripts at the same time, the plays seem more lyrical in tone and imagery than the film scripts. Peacock points out that many of the striking, almost stylized images in this screenplay are characteristic of Pinter's screenplays and reflect similar passages in his stage dramas.[9] It is noteworthy, then, that the screenwriter was nearly overwhelmed by the amount of material that he had to work with, and he and Losey had a number of conversations about how he should begin. Menick reports that Losey told Pinter that "There's only one thing to do. Go home . . . and start. Just start." Pinter responded to Losey's suggestion: "I was immediately plunged into . . . the question of what caught me . . . what I was aware of in terms of film. . . . I suddenly went straight into images. I actually threw a lot of images down on paper and found myself left with them. And that's how I got started" (46).

As he had in previous film scripts, disdaining the voice-over, Pinter relies on images and sounds held together by the device of a serial montage. Since he cannot recreate on screen the taste of Proust's madeleine (the famous *evocateur* of memory in volume 1, *Swann's Way*), the screenwriter relies on things such as sound to bridge time. For instance, when Marcel feels lonely in Balbec, he knocks three times on the wall separating his room and his grandmother's room. She responds with three knocks and comes to him (*Harold Pinter Collected Screenplays 2*, 35–36). After his grandmother's death, Marcel remembers her and is "*overcome with grief*" as "*three knocks are heard on the wall*" on the soundtrack (87–88).

While many lesser characters have been cut (the painter Elstir, the novelist Bergotte, and the musician Vinteuil, for example), Losey reported that there are still forty-nine "important speaking roles" left, and the movie would be filmed on sixty-seven different locations.[10] Despite being disappointed that the screenwriter deleted Tante Leonie, a character rich in comic potential and the one who gave Marcel the madeleine, an episode also not included in the screenplay, Mary Bryden is of the opinion that Pinter's embracing of the "twin structuring principles of disillusion and revelation" led to his "recognizing the overlapping swathes of narrative and reflection, past and present, impulse and curtailment within Proust's writing . . . [so that] Pinter's screenplay is restless and mobile, juxtaposing flashes in time and place, revealing to the viewer Marcel as viewer of his own life-reel" (Bryden, [186]–87).

Considering Pinter's preoccupation with the interworking of time and memory in many of his plays and films, especially in works such as *The Go-Between* and *Betrayal,* it is easy to see why *À la recherche du temps perdu* would appeal to him. In the novel the protagonist finds that he can evoke "the very quality of past experience by simply yielding to the undertow of free association," according to Walter James Miller and Bonnie E. Nelson. This leads to the hero's living "subjectively on three levels of 'sensation': recollection, immediacy, anticipation." As a result, "The present becomes for him mainly a stage for past and future" (30). Additionally, the cinematic perspective intrigues Pinter, and this element is included in the equation. Kauffmann says that in early 1974 Pinter wrote to him about a book that he and Bruce Henstell had edited, *American Film Criticism,* which was published in 1972. Kauffmann records in "The Proust Screenplay" that Pinter was "particularly struck" by one of the pieces in the volume, Paul Goodman's essay "The Proustian Camera Eye," so the screenwriter may have felt a kinship with the novelist (and there was a link to Beckett, who had written about Proust).

As might be expected, critical reaction to this script has been minimal because critics do not know how to handle it; since it has not been filmed, the work is not considered complete, yet there is interest in seeing how the screenwriter approached a major piece of literature. The consensus among scholars seems to be that Pinter's use of sound—and silence—and his deletion of the madeleine episode are master strokes. Among the earliest essays published about *The Proust Screenplay* was David Davidson's "Pinter in No Man's Land: *The Proust Screenplay*" in 1982. Davidson contends that Pinter failed to create an innovative filmic language equivalent to Proust's literary language, and thus the critic finds the screenplay almost completely devoid of value. He seems to dislike Pinter's effort primarily because only Proust can be Proust. The only exception, he notes, is the use of point-of-view shots.

Still, the importance and quality of the script have not gone unnoticed. Faber and Faber published a reprint in 2001. And, there have been several thoughtful studies in which Davidson is shown to be mistaken. In "*The Proust*

Screenplay: Temps perdu for Harold Pinter?" (like Davidson's piece, also published in 1982), Mark Graham produces a fine partial shot-analysis of the film script in which he considers the cinematic methods employed by Pinter to convey Proust's fusion of objective reality and subjective perception of present and past through memory.

Two later examinations echo Graham's conclusion that Pinter's work is praiseworthy. Stephanie Tucker demonstrates that while an audience unfamiliar with *À la recherche* might be confused by the juxtaposition of the opening scenes, Pinter's "interspersing these images with shots in which '*a middle-aged man* (MARCEL)'" appears prominently makes it clear that "the fragmented images are Marcel's—from his childhood, his youth, his adulthood" (39). She explains, too, that Pinter conveys the novel's first-person point of view. Tucker also concludes that at the beginning of the film script Pinter moves from a detail to the whole and at the end he uses the yellow patch from Vermeer's painting *View of Delft* to reverse this structure so that "lost time resides in the cinematic present" (47). Without doubt, one of the best critiques of Pinter's film script to date is Thomas P. Adler's "Pinter/ Proust/Pinter." Adler analyzes the relationship between the structure of and ideas in *The Proust Screenplay* and Pinter's contemporaneous stage plays, notably *Old Times* and *No Man's Land.* This involves a comparison of Proust's and Pinter's theories of memory, as gleaned from their writing. Starting from the assumption that we "feel that the cinema, unrestricted spatially and temporally and fully able to visualize thought, would be the most ideally suited of all artistic media for accomplishing the Proustian play of mind and memory," Adler concludes that in his script Pinter conveys cinematically the manner in which Proustian involuntary memory functions, despite Proust's belief that, as an outgrowth and extension of photography, film can simulate only voluntary ("intellectual and visual") memory (132). He also includes a useful outline of the chronological structure of Pinter's script.

Losey regards the novel as "a work that concerns itself profoundly with bisexuality" and indicates that the film would, too. The transformation from homosexuality to heterosexuality is shown, therefore, although the screenwriter stays away from discussions of whether or not Albertine is Albert. The essence of the book, and the elements that probably attracted Pinter most, however, can be found in *Le temps retrouvé,* the final novel of Proust's lengthy series. Bits of it are scattered throughout the film and are used to pull everything together at the end. The final lines of the screenplay, recalling the opening of *The Go-Between,* can be seen as the key to the film:

Vermeer "View of Delft."

Camera moves in to the yellow wall in the painting.

Yellow screen.

Marcel's voice:

"It was time to begin."

Time, in fact, is Pinter's theme. "The subject was time," he says in his introduction (x). "*In Le Temps Retrouvé,* Marcel, in his forties, hears the bell of his childhood. His childhood, long forgotten, is suddenly present in him, but his consciousness of himself as a child, his memory of the experience, is more real, more acute than the experience itself" (viii). The sound of the bell referred to occurs in both the opening and closing shots of the movie.

Pinter admits that the final line came about because Bray insisted that the ending that he and Losey had agreed upon lacked something: "I suddenly realized that that was the crucial and absolutely essential sentence—in that, if we've just seen the damn thing, or read the damn thing, well, now he's going to do it, now he's going to write it."[11] That this was already inherent in the screenplay is indicated by the fact that the opening scene in the film script is the final scene in the book.

The effect on Pinter of the experience of writing this screenplay was crucial. The themes revolving around the nature of time that are contained in the original obviously fit into his understanding of the way that memory works, and they reenforce his conception of how personal experience can be transposed into art, which he had recognized in working on *Betrayal.* In his introduction to the published script, Pinter says that "the architecture of the film should be based on two main and contrasting principles: one a movement, chiefly narrative, towards disillusions, and the other, more intermittent, towards revelation, rising to where time that was lost is found, and fixed forever in art" (vii).

Thus, the screenplay opens with a serial montage, the cinematic equivalent of a prose stream of consciousness. There is a series of eight shots in which the sound of the garden gate bell is heard over a yellow screen. This is followed by images of the countryside and a line of trees seen from a railway carriage (even though from an unmoving railroad car, in its applicability it is an image harking back to *The Dwarfs;* see also shot 27, etc.), the sea, Venice, and the dining room at Balbec interspersed with repeated shots of the yellow screen (3); the significance of the yellow screen becomes clear with his focusing on Vermeer's painting. In the meantime, however, the other images in the series take on significance when they are repeatedly intercut with the action of the narrative. It becomes clear that they are images from Marcel's past that the character must come to recognize. Once this occurs, Marcel can determine the pattern contained in the images, and out of this context he can transform them into art. Which is exactly what Pinter does. No wonder he declared his time working on this adaptation "the best working year of my life" (*Harold Pinter Collected Screenplays 2,* x).

The Last Tycoon

RELEASED: 1976 (1977 in Britain)

SOURCE: *The Last Tycoon*, by F. Scott Fitzgerald, novel (1941)

AWARDS: National Board of Review Best English-Language Film (1975), Ten Best Films list; Academy of Motion Picture Arts and Sciences Award nomination for Best Art Direction; New York Film Critics Circle Award nomination for Best Screenwriting

PRODUCTION COMPANY: Tycoon Productions, Academy Pictures, distributed by Paramount; CIC in Britain

DIRECTOR: Elia Kazan

EDITORS: Richard Marks, Ronald Roose

CINEMATOGRAPHER: Victor J. Kemper

PRODUCER: Sam Spiegel

PRODUCTION DESIGNER: Gene Callahan

ART DIRECTOR: Jack Collis

SET DECORATION: Bill Smith, Jerry Wunderlich

MUSIC: Maurice Jarre

COSTUMES: Anna Hill Johnstone, Richard Brunno

CAST: Robert De Niro (Monroe Stahr), Tony Curtis (Rodriguez), Robert Mitchum (Pat Brady), Jeanne Moreau (Didi), Jack Nicholson (Brimmer), Donald Pleasence (Boxley), Ray Milland (Fleishacker), Dana Andrews (Red Ridingwood), Ingrid Boulting (Kathleen Moore), Theresa Russell (Cecilia Brady), Peter Strauss (Wylie), Tige Andrews (Popolos), Morgan Farley (Marcus), John Carradine (Guide), Jeff Corey (Doctor), Angelica Huston (Edna), Brendan Burns (Assistant Editor), Seymour Cassel (Seal Trainer), Eric Christmas (Norman), Peggy Feury (Hairdresser), Betsy Jones-Moreland (Writer), Lloyd Kino (Butler), Sharon Masters (Brady's Secretary), Diane Shalet (Stahr's Secretary), Bennie Bartlett

RUNNING TIME: 125 minutes.[1]

COLOR

RATING: PG

S.J. PERELMAN, ONE OF America's premier humorists, spent a goodly portion of his life writing movie scripts in Hollywood. His reaction to that experience was not funny. In an interview he expressed his impression of the city and the film industry: "a dreary industrial town controlled by hoodlums of enormous wealth, the ethical sense of a pack of jackals, and taste so degraded that it befouled everything it touched. I don't mean to sound like a boy Savonarola, but there were times, when I drove along the Sunset Strip and looked at those buildings, or when I watched the fashionable film colony arriving at some premier at Grauman's Egyptian, that I fully expected God in his wrath to obliterate the whole shebang. It was—if you'll allow me to use a hopelessly inexpressive word—*degoutant.*"[2]

Despite the fact that there were good writers involved in filmmaking, Perelman goes on to say, "it was a director's medium rather than a writer's. . . . I always felt that the statement attributed to Irving Thalberg . . . beautifully summed up the situation: 'The writer is a necessary evil.' . . . I consider that a misquotation. I suspect he said 'Weevil.'"[3]

Perelman's brother-in-law, Nathanael West, wrote *The Day of the Locust,* a novel in which many of the same sentiments were expressed, but probably the most famous novel about Hollywood moviemakers is F. Scott Fitzgerald's unfinished work, *The Last Tycoon.* Orson Welles's depiction of Hollywood echoes Perelman and might serve as an introduction to Fitzgerald's novel: "Hollywood is Hollywood. There's nothing you can say about it that isn't true, good or bad" (Megahey, *With Orson Welles*).

Shooting was begun on *The Last Tycoon* in 1975. On November 1, 1965, *Variety* had carried a story stating that Lester Cowan would produce the motion picture for MGM from a script to be written by Irwin Shaw, and Karel Reisz and Mike Nichols were rumored to be in the running for the movie's director. Apparently Nichols was chosen, but the film was turned over to Elia Kazan by producer Sam Spiegel when Nichols was delayed in editing his picture *The Fortune.* Kazan had directed *Boomerang!,* one of Pinter's fondly remembered movies from his youth.[4] Based on Fitzgerald's unfinished novel (1941), *The Last Tycoon* is the story of a Hollywood producer, Monroe Stahr, as told by Cecilia Brady, the daughter of his film-producer business rival. The themes evolving in the story when the novelist died include the conflict between art and economics, business ethics, the vulgar debasement of the American dream, the concept of appearance versus reality as exemplified in the make-believe world of the movies, and the power struggle between Stahr and Pat Brady. The last two in particular would appeal to Pinter.

The Last Tycoon (1976). Robert De Niro as the isolated Monroe Stahr. Paramount Pictures. Jerry Ohlinger Archives.

Too, Knowles has commented on Fitzgerald's "metafilmic possibilities" and the "concept that pop images shape reality" as elements of the novel that Pinter seized upon (*Understanding*, 157)—elements that may have prepared the screenwriter for the problems that he would face in adapting *The French Lieutenant's Woman*. Pinter uses Stahr's explanation to the inept Boxley of how to write a screenplay as a key metaphor for the film and as a means of dealing with the problem of the unfinished novel. When Boxley asks, "What Happened?" after the girl in Stahr's story says that she has never owned a pair of black gloves, Stahr replies: "I don't know. I was just making pictures" (Pinter, *The Last Tycoon*, 229).[5]

Considering that the much-heralded film version of *The Great Gatsby* failed when it was released in 1974, and that critics attributed its failure partly to the fact that its British director did not understand the American character (or audience), it is surprising that another Fitzgerald source would be used so soon and then given to a British screenwriter to adapt, to boot. Even given the formidable Kazan-Siegel team, the choice of Pinter as scenarist is a tribute to his growing reputation as a major film-writer. As Joan Collins points out in her introduction to the televised version of the film, the project was so highly regarded that Robert De Niro, Robert Mitchum, and Jack Nicholson were eager to be connected with it.

In 1941, in his foreword to *The Last Tycoon,* Edmund Wilson wrote that the novel was Fitzgerald's "most mature piece of work." He went on to say that "*The Last Tycoon* is far and away the best novel we have had about Hollywood" (x). Just as Shakespeare's interest in the workings of the theatre was incorporated into his writing throughout his career, Pinter has shown a lifelong fascination with the cinema that has found its way into his canon. Besides the evidence of this interest that can be found in his stage writing, when he started work on the script for *The Last Tycoon,* he had already written a screenplay in which moviemaking was dealt with (*The Pumpkin Eater*). It is no wonder, then, that this novel appealed to him as a source for another film. As incomplete and imperfect as Fitzgerald's work is, it is still recognized as the most important novel about filmmaking.

Fitzgerald's novel is about the desperation, shallowness, lack of values (especially a disregard for or insensitivity to artistic and humanitarian values), and the general weakness of character of those who work in the film industry. In the completed six chapters of his work, the novelist uses the persona of Cecilia Brady to both narrate and create a frame for the story of Stahr, her father's business partner and the most powerful man in Hollywood—and reportedly modeled after Thalberg. Cecilia loves Stahr, but his only interest is his work, until he meets Kathleen Moore, who reminds him of his dead movie-star wife. At the end of chapter 6, Stahr has fallen in love with Kathleen, but she has married another man. Up to this point the main characters are engaging. Even though they exhibit some minor character flaws, by and large they seem to be nice enough people who have some talent for what they do. This is particularly true of Stahr, who demonstrates acumen and compassion.

Fitzgerald's plans for the rest of the story have been generated from his notes and outlines and from "reports of persons with whom he discussed his work" (editor's note, 1986 ed., 128). The tone changes dramatically. What seemed to be a love story turns into a tragedy. It is not a tragedy about star-crossed lovers, however; it is a tragedy born out the despicable nature of the inhabitants of the film world. The tale becomes grimy and vulgar. Troubles at the studio are compounded by management betrayal. Stahr and Kathleen have an affair and are subjected to blackmail by producer Brady, who learns of their dalliance. Fearing that Brady will eventually murder him, Stahr contracts with gangsters to murder his partner. Stahr changes his mind but is killed in a plane crash before the order can be rescinded and Brady is murdered. The whole experience leaves Kathleen a devastated outsider who can never belong to the Hollywood world. And, it turns out that Cecilia has tuberculosis and has been putting her story together in a sanitarium.

At this point in his career, Pinter had seldom expressed a disparaging attitude toward filmmakers (though he had been annoyed by some decisions that were made on a purely financial basis). His interest in filmmaking has been evident since his youth, however, and a novel about the film world would naturally be of interest to him, as might be the involvement of Jews in that business. The themes that Fitzgerald was developing, especially the concept of appearance versus reality and the power struggle between Stahr and Brady, might have appealed to Pinter as well. Reflecting his interest in dominance, early in the movie a studio guide points out Stahr's office high up in a building—a classic camera angle to denote power. Later, Brady looks down on Stahr from a window above, assuming, as Katherine Burkman and Mijeong Kim say, "the power that he will now wield against his victim" (60).

Certain images in the novel might have caught his imagination, too, as he thought about converting the prose into cinematic images. There is no question, for instance, that the scene of the floating Shiva head is more impressive and imposing in the moving picture than it is in when presented in the prose narrative; the same is true of Stahr's roofless house at the beach, which achieves a symbolic status.

From a critical point of view, it is also intriguing that the screenwriter had a unique choice to make in deciding how he would handle the tale. Since Fitzgerald did not complete the novel, would it be more effective to end the film where the novel ends, or would it be better to take into account the synopsis, notes, and so forth about what Fitzgerald might have intended? And, what reasons might there be for Pinter's choice? Pinter accepted the challenge by continuing the film beyond the point where Fitzgerald's novel ends, but he does not include much of the material found in the synopsis, notes, and so forth. After what would be the end of Fitzgerald's chapter 6, Pinter extends the film for another twelve minutes and thirty-five seconds, ten minutes and twenty seconds of which is additional action.[6]

The ending of the film is enigmatic.[7] The morning after Stahr is beaten by Brimmer in a fist fight and Cecilia has comforted him during the night, Brady informs Stahr at a board meeting that the bosses in New York have taken away his power. The importance of Kathleen in his life is emphasized in the additional material, when Stahr glances at the telegram while in Cecilia's pool-side guest house and then by the voice-overs of Kathleen speaking when Stahr goes to his office. In spite of what has happened to him moments before, his concentration is on the girl. His illness is referenced, too, for he is seen taking pills several times (once hiding the act from Cecilia), and the doctor's voice is heard again asking him if he feels any pain. Absent from the movie are the confrontation between the management and the writers, the murder plot, the affair with the now married Kathleen, the plane crash, and Stahr's death.

Instead, Stahr restages the woman with the gloves and nickel story with which he had beguiled Boxley. This time, though, we see the woman—it is Kathleen, wearing white gloves, and after burning a letter she turns lovingly to a man whose face is not seen but who is not Stahr. Stahr says aloud and apparently directed to her, "I don't want to lose you." He then appears on the studio lot, walking to an empty sound stage. The words "I don't want to lose you" echo over. Does he refer to Kathleen or the studio? Stahr pauses outside the open door of the sound stage, then disappears into the dark interior. End of film.

Although Leonard Maltin calls *The Last Tycoon* and Joan Micklin Silver's television version of *Bernice Bobs her Hair* "the best Fitzgerald yet put on the screen" (643) and the film won the National Board of Review Best English-Language Film Award in 1975, Pinter's adaptation generally has been dismissed by the public and critics alike. Ingrid Boulting (of the British film family, a South African leading lady) is introduced in the role of Kathleen Moore. Kazan's direction of his actors is not particularly exciting. Boulting, Russell, and even De Niro seem to be struggling at times.

Among the critical complaints are those by reviewers such as Kael ("The Cinema") and Kauffmann ("The Last Tycoon"), who are upset that the novel's opening section is deleted and who, because they do not understand it, find the ending unsatisfying because it does not explain what happens to Stahr. Colin L. Westerbeck Jr. thinks that Pinter "has failed miserably" in trying to repair an incomplete novel (52). Michael Adams maintains that the "*Casablanca*-style" nightclub scene is a ludicrous failure because "fifty-one-year-old Tony Curtis and forty-eight-year-old Jeanne Moreau [are] both well overage for the 1930s romantic leads" (301). However, given the ages of some of the other name actors in the cast (Mitchum, Pleasence, Ray Milland, Dana Andrews, John Carradine), Curtis and Moreau do not seem out of place, for the studio bosses may well have seen them as alter egos from a time gone by, through which they are trying to live illusively. Burkman and Kim's counter to Adams is, "Surely the insipid nature of the film and the aged actors were purposeful on Pinter's and Kazan's part, giving, as they do, an extraordinary sense of how Stahr is trying to revive and hold on to the past" (65). And, Pinter has admitted his appreciation for actors such as William Bendix, Alan Ladd, Brian Donlevy, Franchot Tone, and Elisha Cook Jr. Asked by Gussow if he had any favorite actors, he replied: "I fell in love quite a lot in those days, people like Veronica Parker. I was crazy about Gene Tierney. Lana Turner. And an English actress called Patricia Roc. . . . Henry Fonda . . . Anthony Quinn, and Dana Andrews. I was very pleased when we did *The Last Tycoon* many many years later, we had a hell of a cast list. De Niro and Robert Mitchum and also Dana Andrews, Ray Milland and John Carradine!" (*Conversations,* 138, 139). Furthermore, the "miscasting" seems too obvious, and Pinter's acumen in exploiting this kind of device in his other films would give credence to the idea that this was a purposeful decision on the part of the moviemakers. Using movie stars from the period being depicted is a nicely ironic fillip—we see what has come of the youth and power of those who so intensely pursued these fleeting qualities. Pinter's *The Last Tycoon* may be a forgotten film, yet the readers of the novel cannot be disappointed by it.

In adapting Fitzgerald's work, the screenwriter was again faced with the problem of what to do with a narrator. In this movie script he simply discarded the device and treated the story straightforwardly, incidentally reducing the importance of Cecilia's character to that of a bit player. Since *The Last Tycoon* is Stahr's story, anyway, this decision is reasonable. One of the things lost through this approach, of course, is Cecilia's commentary—her filling in of details, her insider's observations, her insights, and her interpretations of what has happened and is happening. This is offset by the reduction of the number of elements that the author has to worry about, simplifying his task and the text, and the change has the added benefit of allowing Pinter to emphasize the present tense in his presentation.

Another element in the novel that Pinter eliminates is the role of Pete Zavras, the suicidal camera man who has meaning when seen in the context of Fitzgerald's intended ending but would serve only to show more of Stahr's effectiveness in understanding and manipulating people in the film; these components of Stahr's character are already demonstrated in the sequence dealing with Rodriguez, the leading man actor (played by Curtis) who cannot sexually satisfy his wife (the nature of the case is more clearly spelled out in the novel).

The beach house, or rather the frame of the house, is entirely roofless in the film, as the screenwriter does not include the one room in the house with a roof that Fitzgerald's characters make use of. Stahr brings in sets, but the house is not real; it is unfinished. Man's intrusion on nature is dwarfed by the sea in front of it and the canyon bluffs into which it is fitted; the swimming pool under construction seems laughably small in comparison to the ocean that lies just a few yards beyond it. The house symbolizes the shallow incompleteness and insubstantiality of the Hollywood film world, as well as the hollowness of Stahr.

Like Gatsby, when Stahr realizes his dream, he also realizes that it has no substance. If the title of the novel refers to Stahr in the role of a robber baron who is out of his time in the early part of the twentieth century, unquestioningly in control of a new artistic technology but ultimately defeated by those for whom the safe bottom line is all important, then there are reverberations with Arthur Miller's Willy Loman, who was caught up in a dream of Dave Singleman but who did not have the personality to be a single man and who lived in a time when drummers could no longer compete. Stahr's downfall in the movie can be traced to the combination of his romantic attitude toward art and toward Kathleen. For artistic reasons he is willing to make a film that will lose money; when Kathleen comes into his life, he is willing to put her ahead of his business—which up to then was his life, as he confided to Cecilia early on.

In line with his commentary about Hollywood, Pinter creates a new role, that of the studio guide, a cameo played by Carradine, whose effusive and avuncular tour is an effective means of showing what the studio is like (including the device of exposing the earthquake mechanism, an ironic foreshadowing) and how much the public is entranced by the world of the silver screen. To the outsider, the industry is glamorous. But, Minna Davis's dressing room as an altar is counterbalanced by the intercuts of scenes from her movies when Stahr enters his empty bedroom. The movie actress is dead, yet the movie goddess lives on except in the reality of her widower's loneliness.

Pinter inserts an episode in which Eddie the film editor dies while watching a rough cut. No one knows that he has died because they did not hear any sound from him—the explanation that one of the characters offers is that the editor was a professional who "didn't want to disturb the screening." The ridiculousness of this motive and the callousness of those in the room at the time of the man's death are indictments of a Hollywood that Perelman would have recognized.

In an interesting sequence, Stahr's lie to Cecilia about the man with whom he left the dance to see a changed part of Hollywood is connected with Brady's naked secretary in the closet and then with another film-within-a-film in which Rodriguez plays the Humphrey Bogart part in a musical version of *Casablanca* and in the role of the boss who kisses the "talent."

There is much less of Pinter's typical humor and dialogue in this film than in his other screenplays. An ironic moment occurs when the telegram is delivered to Stahr, who is in the screening room and obviously watching a cartoon, as attested to by his facial expressions and the music and sounds from the film and laughter from others in the room, all heard over. At the premiere Didi does say thanks for "changing that *fucking* director," and the "New York is loyal" exchange between Brady and Fleischman is typically Pinteresque, but the more powerful Pinterese of his plays is missing. Still, there is a more dramatic structure to the film than there is in the novel; the film is less leisurely.

The emphasis of the film script is on the love story. Interestingly, the music (and the use of woodwinds) is reminiscent of the love sections in *The Servant*. The opening sequence of *The Last Tycoon* apparently is unrelated to the love theme. In place of the plane ride to Tennessee, the movie begins with a segment from a black-and-white gangster film in which a mob hit is depicted. There is a cut to Stahr in the screening room describing what needs to be done with the film-within-a-film scene to make it more appealing to the public. This visual demonstration establishing Stahr's control, power, and perspicacity is quicker and more effective than the segment that opens the novel. While the filmed kiss in the automobile is effective, it lacks the intensity conveyed in the novel, an intensity born not of lust but of emotion. Ironically, then, since it is the love story that is accentuated in the film, it is also clear that the prose version conveys the feelings of love more accurately and surely than the motion picture does. Kathleen's narrative about her past is broken into different scenes, yet her voice and story effectively unite the tale.

The morning after they make love, the scene showing the lovers driving their cars out of the parking lot in opposite directions nicely captures the separation and sense of aloneness that occurs. The close-up shot of Stahr silently reading Kathleen's letter with the illuminated portrait of his dead wife in the background and the nonsynchronous sounds of waves over provides an effective juxtaposition and lends suspense to the scene. Kathleen's voice-over reciting what is in the letter after he has read it is effective.

Instead of the dialogue and descriptions that Fitzgerald uses to tell his story, the screenwriter relies on images and cutting, montage. The difference between prose and cinematic narrative is seen in the segment in which Stahr acts as a problem solver for his leading man, Rodriguez. In the novel we are privy to Stahr's thoughts as he helps the actor confront his problem. In the film the problem is never verbally identified, yet the seemingly suave Rodriguez's shirt is stained by underarm perspiration, and the impotence in his real life that is sardonically contrasted with his screen image is exposed when his agitated whispering and sweat give meaning to the line "She's my wife." Another ironic element is subtly underscored when Stahr's doctor is seen in the anteroom as Rodriguez exits. Stahr has been seen taking medicine previously, and the doctor has warned him to stop working so hard; the use of the camera to juxtapose an example of his success in solving the problems of others while being unable to solve his own problems is telling. Similarly, the image of Marcus's servant bodily picking up the old man is quite a bit more striking than the description of his weakness in the novel.

One episode that works considerably better in the original than in the adaptation is the confusion over which girl is Kathleen. Fitzgerald intentionally does not provide enough information for the reader to be able to realize that the girl with the silver belt with whom Stahr first meets is not the girl whom he is seeking. It is not clear that a mistake was made and that it was not merely a matter of his inability to see her well during the flood. Instead, it seems that he has been pursuing someone who is not worthy of the pursuit. The revelation that Edna is the "other" girl is surprising. On the screen the mix-up does not work well because the audience has already seen Kathleen and knows that Edna is not she.

Filmmaking has been a Hollywood subject almost from the beginning of the industry. One of the earliest films to show filmmaking was *The Story the Biograph Told* (1903),[8] and *Uncle Josh at the Moving Picture Show* (1902) was among the first motion pictures featuring a film-within-a-film. *Biograph* is about a comic mishap that occurs at the motion picture studio when a boy makes an unscripted film of a couple kissing. *Uncle Josh*, a movie about a man attending a motion picture screening for the first time, is notable because it includes three films-within-a-film.

On one level *The Last Tycoon* is about filmmaking. On another, it is about the creative process. On still another, it is about human relationships. Over the years, Pinter has demonstrated an interest in all three of these subjects many times.

Peacock contends that the "counterpointing of reality and fiction, the iconic and the indexical, offered by the symbolic context of filmmaking, is central to the screenplay." This would relate *The Last Tycoon* to *Remembrance of Things Past* and *The French Lieutenant's Woman*. So, too, would Peacock's subsequent assertion that "the audience is made aware both of the manipulation of reality demanded by the studied construction of an artifact (in this case a film) and of the danger inherent in Stahr's total immersion in a fantasy world. . . . The awareness of the mechanics of the film's creation and of its status as a product aimed at a paying audience is intended to distance the spectator from the action" (193).

Pinter acknowledges his own realization of this fact in one of his additions: the black-and-white restaurant scene and Stahr's criticism (in a color shot) that the tip-off signal for the gangland slaying is "too obvious" (Peacock, 193). According to Knowles, "Past actuality makes illusion more 'real' as the cinematic imagination of the visitors [to Minna Davis's dressing room] reenacts and replays a celluloid death. Further shots amplify this self-reflective mode, including the guide's explanation of how the illusion of the San Francisco earthquake was achieved" (*Understanding*, 157).

In a sense, everything in the film is about illusion, from the very opening sequence in which the black-and-white scenes from a movie being made by Stahr are seen, and given that the illusion is Hollywood based, it is fitting that the point of view is that of a camera. As John F. Callahan points out, "The camera is the narrator and there is the added touch of shooting Stahr as he would have liked to have shot himself—in motion, a personification of the moving picture" (209).

Burkman and Kim have demonstrated that Pinter took what Fitzgerald was developing into a melodrama and made it a tragedy, a tragedy based on illusion. This is distilled in the final scene, they find, when Stahr "takes final control of illusion in this moment of tragic victory": he addresses the camera and thus "writes" his own exit (67). There is, then, a sense of triumph as the erstwhile king controls again—and perhaps at the most consequential point in his life. Pinter has created another original and transcendent work of art. He has transformed a source that has merit into something that not only fully realizes that inherent merit but also has more depth of meaning and culminates in a positive statement about the dignity and strength found in human life.

The French Lieutenant's Woman

RELEASED: 1981

SOURCE: *The French Lieutenant's Woman,* by John Fowles; novel (1969)

AWARDS: 1981 Academy of Motion Picture Arts and Sciences nominations for Best Picture and Best Screenplay Based on Material from Another Medium (also Best Actress, Meryl Streep; Best Art Direction; Best Costume Design; Best Editing; British Academy Awards for Original Film Music and Best Actress); nominated for a Golden Globe (Best Screenplay–Motion Picture); 1982 Donatello Award (Italy) for Best Foreign Screenplay (Best Actress nomination, Streep)

PRODUCTION COMPANY: Parlon Productions; United Artists

DIRECTOR: Karl Reisz

EDITOR: John Bloom

CINEMATOGRAPHER: Freddie Francis

PRODUCERS: Leon Clore, Geoffrey Helman

PRODUCTION DESIGNERS: Allan Cameron, Norman Dorme, Assheton Gorton

ART DIRECTORS: Allan Cameron, Norman Dorme, Assheton Gorton

MUSICAL DIRECTOR: Carl Davis

COSTUME DESIGNER: Tom Rand

CAST: Meryl Streep (Sarah Woodruff/Anna), Jeremy Irons (Charles Smithson/ Mike), Hilton McRae (Sam), Emily Morgan (Mary), Charlotte Mitchell (Mrs. Tranter), Lynsey Baxter (Ernestina Freeman), Peter Vaughan (Mr. Freeman), Colin Jeavons (Vicar), Liz Smith (Mrs. Fairley), Patience Collier (Mrs. Poulteney), John Barrett (Dairyman), Leo McKern (Dr. Grogan), Edward Duke (Nathaniel Dyson), Richard Griffiths (Sir Thom Burgh), Michael Elwyn (Montague), Toni Palmer (Mrs. Endicott), David Warner (Serjeant Murphy), Alun Armstrong (Grimes), Gerard Falconetti (Davide), Penelope Wilton (Sonia), Orlando Fraser (Tom Elliott), Fredrika Morton (Girl), Alice Maschler (Second Girl), Matthew Morton (Boy), Vicky Ireland (Mrs. Tranter's Maid), Clare Travers-Deacon (Mrs. Poulteney's Maid), Jean

Faulds (Cook) Graham Fletcher-Cook (Delivery Boy), Richard Hope (Third
Assistant), Doreen Mantle (Lord on Train), Catherine Willmer (Dr. Grogan's
Housekeeper), Beverly Garland, Mary McLeod, Harriet Walter
RUNNING TIME: 124 minutes[1]
COLOR
RATING: R
VIDEO: Fox

THERE MAY BE SOME disagreement about which of Pinter's sources is the
best, but there can be no doubt that *The French Lieutenant's Woman* is his
best screenplay. In watching the other films made from his scripts, viewers
are often interested, involved, and appreciative that the movie is a good one.
In watching *The French Lieutenant's Woman,* they are fascinated from the
very beginning of the picture and aware that it is an extremely good film
verging on greatness. It is also the screenwriter's most inventive and imaginative screenplay. Indeed, it is the exemplar of Pinter's own declaration that
with screenplays, "I don't just transcribe the novel; otherwise you might as
well do the novel. In other words, these are acts of the imagination on my
part!" (Gussow, *Conversations,* 100). Seymour Chatman finds that the author is so successful in this case that *The French Lieutenant's Woman* is "the
kind of film that has a serious practical impact on film history, since it has
educated the audience to new possibilities of narrative innovation" (165).
As Ebert says, the script is "both simple and brilliant" (237).

John Fowles, whose 1969 novel of the same name served as Pinter's
source, had been "less than happy" with two previous movies made from his
novels and had spent eight or nine years trying to find the right director to
turn *The French Lieutenant's Woman* into a film. After Fred Zinnemann
failed in a two-year, "most serious attempt" with Dennis Potter as his
scriptwriter, Fowles resolved to insist on veto power over the choice of director (Fowles, "HORS D'OEUVRE," vi). In 1969, while the book was still in
proofs, the novelist and his agent, Tom Maschler, decided to approach Karel
Reisz about tackling the project. Reisz, having recently finished a difficult
period piece (*Isadora*), could not be tempted. Others considered the project:
Mike Nichols, Franklin Schaffner, Richard Lester, Michael Cascoyannis, Lindsay Anderson. Robert Bolt declined, on the basis that the novel was unfilmable.
At this point Fowles and Maschler determined that they needed to look for a
"demon barber . . . someone sufficiently skilled and independent to be able
to rethink and recast the thing from the bottom up" (viii); they also decided

Harold Pinter, John Fowles, and Karel Reisz on the set of *The French Lieutenant's Woman*. Courtesy Harold Pinter.

that Pinter was "the best man for that difficult task." By happenstance, a development deal was offered to Fowles that included Pinter, but the novelist was not interested in the others involved in the proposed project. Then, in 1978, Maschler went back to Reisz, who agreed to agree—with the proviso that Pinter had to write the script. On May 27, 1980, shooting began.

Fowles's novel is extremely popular and highly acclaimed, but the very factors that make it popular presented Pinter with an artistic challenge: how to capture the twentieth-century perspective from which the Victorian story is told, primarily through the vehicle of numerous authorial intrusions (footnotes, references, poetry quotations, opinions, philosophies, facts, descriptions) that flavor the novel.[2] The alternating plot lines in the novel have a natural cinematic equivalent in parallel editing, but it is not the essentials of plotting that preoccupied the screenwriter. In an interview with Gussow shortly after he finished the script, Pinter commented, "*The French Lieutenant's Woman*. That's been bloody, bloody hard. It's a remarkable book. The problems involved in transposing it to film are quite considerable. It pretends to be a Victorian novel, but it isn't. It's a modern novel, and it's made clear by the author that he's writing it now. The whole idea had to be retained" (*Conversations*, 53).

Although in other films he has used a voice-over narrator, the obvious choice for retaining the Fowles touch, Pinter is on record as not being fond of the device, and he wanted to avoid it here if possible. Another approach to "visualizing" the "stereoscopic vision" of the novel would be to create a persona who is both the author and a character in the Victorian story, a device used by Max Ophüls in *La Ronde,* but Fowles did not favor the technique (and he thought that only Peter Ustinov, with whom he had discussed the possibility, could have managed the role). The dual ending of the novel must have been troublesome as well. The first ending occurs in chapter 44 with a short narration of how Charles contritely accepted a loveless marriage, which he was doomed to suffer through for the rest of his life in silent accord with Victorian tradition. In the second ending (which occurs in chapter 61, more than 130 pages later), Sarah leaves. After years of searching for her, Charles, who has ended his relationship with Ernistina, finds Sarah, only to be rejected and left to rebuild his life existentially without her (or so the narrator suggests with his semihopeful references to a move to America and images of the sea—life goes on). There was also the normal dilemma of how to cut a novel-length story to fit within a typical film-length time limit, though this was a problem that the screenwriter had solved quite successfully in his earlier adaptations.

To begin, in Pinter's script there has been an enormous amount of compression. The script is equivalent to no more than about one-sixth of the length of the novel. Indeed, Pinter cut more from his source in this adaptation than in any of his others, with the exception of *The Proust Screenplay*. The entire Winsyatt inheritance subplot is eliminated, as is most of the Sam-Mary subplot (which in some ways is equivalent to the standard eighteenth-century-comedy witty couple–dull couple subplot); Mrs. Fairley's role is reduced substantially; Sam's treacherous and self-serving nondelivery of Charles's note to Sarah, which results in her leaving and Charles breaking off the engagement with Ernistina, is removed; and the Charles–prostitute/mother episode is left undeveloped—just to mention the major deletions. Like the rehearsal of Charles's American travels, most of the removals have little or no effect on the story line or the expression of the meaning of the novel—all that the cut material does is reveal a bit about Charles's nature and the Victorian world; it does not provide any elaboration on the theme.

There are, of course, additions and alterations. These range from Pinter's giving a name to the German doctor, who is simply referred to in the novel as a specialist in the kind of mental problems that Dr. Grogan assumes afflict Sarah (Pinter, 40[3]; Fowles, *The French Lieutenant's Woman*, 164), to focusing on Sarah's habit of drawing and her sketches (not dealt with in the novel but a plot device in the film), to providing a happy ending to the Victorian tale.

The addition of the name of Dr. Hartmann may be merely part of Pinter's penchant for using small details to make things appear more realistic, to touch the world outside the film that he spoke about in connection with his script for *The Caretaker*.[4] The focus on Sarah's art is more important, since it prepares for her decision to move into the Elliott household as a nanny, for the early shots of her sketching establish her desire and talent for art which will be accommodated as one of the conditions of her employment. The close-ups of the early drawings are also used to emphasize Sarah's state of mind; she is in anguish, and the expression on the face in the self-portraits is similar to that in Edvard Munch's most famous painting, *The Scream*.

Changing the home in which Sarah takes refuge from that of Dante Gabriel Rossetti, the pre-Raphaelite poet, to that of an architect named Elliott whose gender-shifted son, Tom (perhaps with a bow to one of Pinter's favorite poets, T.S. Eliot), does several things. For one, the coincidence of her ending up at the home of one of the century's better-known and more liberal characters is a little far-fetched and maybe a bit of overkill, so an architect's abode is more realistic. For another, the introduction of Rossetti's name is a tad distracting because it captures the audience's attention and threatens to shift the focus to the poet as opposed to Fowles's story; the more anonymous name in the film version keeps the focus on the story. At the same time, Tom Elliott has interesting reverberations too, since Eliot was a transitional figure; nevertheless, the name is common enough not to be overly diversionary.

Predictably, some scenes were combined and some changes were made for purely cinematic reasons, as when action is interjected effortlessly into the discussion between Charles and Mr. Freeman, Ernistina's father, by a move in locale, exchanging the static setting of the businessman's office for a walk on the wharf (Pinter, 11). Finally, Pinter's invention of a happy ending (102), the third ending to the nineteenth-century plot, is certainly more in keeping with popular Victorian models than either of the two conclusions that Fowles supplies. It is also an ingredient that is indispensable to expressing what the screenwriter is really writing about.

In a note prefacing the published version of his script, Pinter says, "The writing of this screenplay took over a year. This is the final version with which we began shooting. Inevitably a number of scenes were cut and some structural changes were made during the course of production" ([ii]). There are a great number of differences between the script and the released film. Besides the minor word changes probably introduced by the actors during the filming, there are those whole scenes that have been cut, but most of these alterations are insignificant and do not have any effect on either Fowles's or Pinter's themes.

However, Pinter's note is significant because it reveals the writer's sense of pride in his work. If it were simply a matter of publishing the script, he could have published a version taken directly from the film. The added touch of stating that it took him a year to write the screenplay, when he only infrequently comments publicly on the time that it takes him to write something, reenforces the importance that he attaches to the version of the screenplay that he considers his. It may be that he feels that once the script is tinkered with by others, it becomes collaborative to the point where it is not his product anymore or that such tinkering for practical purposes removes some of the artistic elements. He has evidenced his dissatisfaction with this kind of intrusive alteration common in Hollywood in connection with several of his film scripts.[5] Shoshana Knapp argues that Reisz was not "obligated to be faithful to Pinter's Script" (57) any more than the screenwriter was obliged to be faithful to the novel. Peter J. Conradi concludes that the film script is better than the film, that the liberties taken by Reisz resulted in too much being cut with a resultant loss of some of the subtleties and linkages of the screenplay. Whatever the case, it appears that Pinter wanted to preserve what he considers the best version.[6]

Fowles, too, has indicated his disdain for the commercial nature of filmmaking: "in a later novel, *Daniel Martin,* I did not hide the contempt I feel for many aspects of the commercial cinema—or more exactly, since cost of production and mode of recoupment make all cinema more or less commercial, of the cinema where accountants reign, where profit comes first and everything else a long way after" ("HORS D'OEUVRE," xiii). This film also proves to some extent to be an example of such a "vile ethos," of the impact of financial considerations on the cinematic art. It would appear that at least

some of the scenes cut from the screenplay were excised not for artistic reasons but because of monetary concerns at the studio. This is evidenced by
materials in box 18 in the Pinter Archives. In an "Anna, the actress who
plays Sarah" version of the script, there are seven sets of production suggestions typed on pink paper titled *"FRENCH LIEUTENANT'S WOMAN -
SAVINGS."* Page 1 contains a list of pages, scenes, what has been cut, and
the shooting time saved. The following is a sample of the cuts:

Pages	Scene	Time Saved
36	60–61 Set of INT DAIRY and Scene 60 OMITTED.[7]	1/3 day

Additional material in box 20 is further evidence of the economic side of the
project, which extends well beyond the filming.[8] The studio heads must have
been pleased to report a domestic gross of $22.6 million.[9]

Undoubtedly, the primary element of which Pinter can be proud is his
creation of a *coup de cinéma* by replacing the narrator with a twentieth-
century story line and developing a film-within-a-film structure. What is interesting about the film version of *The French Lieutenant's Woman* is not
the compression, the cuts, or the alterations of the source material; what is
interesting is what was added. The significance lies in the concept, not the
normal minutia of details or dialogue. Even though Pinter has admitted that
the idea originated with Reisz, it was the screenwriter who was responsible
for the full realization of the concept.[10] The boldness and imaginativeness of
this invention brought an appreciative acknowledgment from Fowles: "I am
convinced now, in retrospect, that the only feasible answer was the one that
Harold and Karel hit upon. We had all before been made blind to its existence by the more immediate problem of compressing an already dense and
probably over-plotted book into two hours' screen time. The idea of adding
an entirely new dimension and relationship to it would never have occurred
to us; and quite reasonably so, with almost anyone but Harold Pinter"
("HORS D'OEUVRE," xi).

Pinter deserves Fowles's approbation, for he captures the essentials of
the novelist's Victorian story, characters, and era (which is all that many
readers wanted when they went to the movie), through the utilization of the
film-within-a-film construction. He foregrounds both the dual perspective
and the underlying themes effectively. For Chatman, "where the novel's com-

The French Lieutenant's Woman (1981). Meryl Streep as Anna in her modern clothes and Jeremy Irons as Mike in his "Charles" costume. United Artists. Jerry Ohlinger Archives.

mentary explicitly conveys exposition and argument at the service of the narrative," by crosscutting,[11] "the film implies commentary through the very invention of the juxtaposed modern story" (174).

The paralleling of the two affairs as indicative of their respective societies serves to reflect the limitations of each society, the constraint of the Victorian and the license of the modern, and the film-within-a-film technique is a perfect device to demonstrate this theme by juxtaposition. For instance, the proleptic technique—Mike and Anna's sleeping together foreshadows what will happen when Charles and Sarah sleep together—is introduced easily and naturally in this format.

At the same time, the insertion of the modern plot line allows for the introduction of a sense of ambiguity. Knapp is convinced that the "casual affair" between Anna and Mike creates an "ironic perspective on the passion of Sarah and Charles" (58). Chatman believes that "each story comments on the other" too (173), but he concludes that Mike falls in love with

Sarah, a fictitious character, as part of a commentary in which modern love is found inferior to Victorian love. This ambiguity reflects the blurring of lines between reality and illusion that takes over the lives of Mike and, temporarily, Anna when they become immersed in the characters that they are playing and whose identities they incorporate into their own lives.

Audience interest in and familiarity with the art of filmmaking is evident in the popularity of movie studio shorts that were run between feature presentations in the 1940s and current television specials about filmmaking, fan magazines, and Universal Studios and Disney's MGM Studios with their "backstage" tours. This a priori interest and knowledge certainly add to the general appeal of *The French Lieutenant's Woman.*[12] And, for a contemporary audience, film provides a readily understood referential language to be used in exploring complicated abstract concepts.

Though certainly only tenuously related, there is a cinematic link with *A Double Life,* directed by George Kukor from a script by Garson Kanin, which brought Ronald Colman the 1947 Academy Award. In that movie, Colman plays a Shakespearean actor whose real life becomes intermixed with his portrayal of Othello. Ironically, this leads to his on-stage strangulation of his wife, whom he mistakenly believes guilty of Desdamona's purported sin. The sequence in which Charles, in a horse-drawn cab, tries to find Sarah in a seedy part of town is quite similar to a sequence in John Huston's *Moulin Rouge* in which Jose Ferrer as Henri de Toulouse-Lautrec searches for his red-haired prostitute/lover who has left him. Huston's film was released in 1952, seventeen years before Fowles's novel was published and twenty-nine years before Pinter's film adaptation, making the scene in the novel and later movie pictorially derivative, an homage, or a literary allusion used to comment upon the depth of the absolute self-degradation to which desperation drives these scorned men in their quests for their loves.

The components of Fowles's themes that probably attracted Pinter to this project were the manipulation of time and the exploration of the nature of reality (to some extent as related to art) that throughout his career have occupied his attention in his own writing—dramas such as *The Lover, The Collection, The Homecoming, Landscape, Night, Silence, Old Times,* and *No Man's Land*—and virtually all of his film scripts up to that time. In the script the screenwriter's interests are reflected in structure and theme alike. The challenge of the adaptation must have been irresistible.

The device of a cast party at the end of the film, which is used to bring together the characters and themes, is reminiscent of the celebratory conclusion of Lindsay Anderson's *O Lucky Man!* (1973). Perhaps surprisingly, given how dark many of Pinter's plays seem on the surface, in much of his dramatic writing, especially the major works, there is an underlying positivism and optimism. So is it with his film scripts. *The French Lieutenant's Woman* is an example of this quality. True, at the end Mike is lost in a world between reality and illusion, and he cannot distinguish one from the other, but Anna escapes into reality, divorced from her role-playing, healthy and happy in the world of her real marriage and life outside the film.

This also proves to be another rebuttal to those feminist critics who short-sightedly label Pinter a misogynist. As Billington points out, Pinter takes an almost feminist line by contrasting "Anna's growing identification with Sarah . . . with Mike's concern with the purely theatrical aspects of performance" (273). This feminist orientation is also evident in the figures about prostitutes that Anna reads aloud to Mike in the hotel room—figures that Pinter researched and added. The Pinter Archives box 17 contains the note:

Ch. 2
S 1,155,000 females
7,600,000 males
—1851.

This is the referent for the following exchange, which occurs in the film script:

ANNA (referring to the book).

Listen to this.
"In 1857 the Lancet estimated that there were eighty thousand prostitutes in the County of London. Out of every sixty houses one was a brothel."

MIKE

Mmm.

Pause.

ANNA (reading)

"We reach the surprising conclusion that at a time when the male population of London of all ages was one and a quarter million, the prostitutes were receiving clients at a rate of two million per week."

MIKE

Two million!

ANNA

You know when I say—in the graveyard scene—about
going to London? Wait.

> *She picks up her script of* The French
> Lieutenant's Woman, *flips the pages, finds the
> page. She reads aloud:*

"If I went to London I know what I should become. I
should become what some already call me in Lyme."

MIKE

Yes?

ANNA

Well, that's what she's really faced with.

> *She picks up the book.*

This man says that hundreds of the prostitutes were
nice girls like governesses who had lost their jobs. See
what I mean? You offend your boss, you lose your job.
That's it!
You're on the streets. I mean, it's real.

> MIKE *has picked up a calculator and starts
> tapping out figures.*

MIKE

The male population was a million and a quarter but
the prostitutes
had two million clients a week?

ANNA

Yes. That's what he says.

MIKE

Allow about a third off for boys and old men . . . That
means that outside
marriage—a Victorian gentleman had about two point
four fucks a week.

> *She looks at him.* (18–19)

Anna's growing identification with Sarah's character is neatly balanced by Mike's disinterested concern with numerical figures in this exchange. The irony, naturally, is that, as already indicated, in the end Anna will be able to completely distance herself from her screen persona, whereas Mike will be totally absorbed in his.

The potential blending of the characters is seen in the script:

73.   **Interior. Caravan. Present. Day.**

Anna in her caravan. A knock on the door.

ANNA

Hello!

Mike comes in.

MIKE

May I introduce myself?

ANNA

I know who you are.

They smile. He closes the door.

MIKE

So you prefer to walk alone?

ANNA

Me? Not me. Her.

MIKE

I enjoyed that.

ANNA

What?

MIKE

Our exchange. Out there.

ANNA

Did you? I never know . . .

MIKE

Know what?

> ANNA

Whether it's any good.

> MIKE

Listen. Do you find me—?

> ANNA

What?

> ANNA

What?

> MIKE

Sympathetic.

> ANNA

Mmn. Definitely.

> MIKE

I don't mean me. I mean him.

> ANNA

Definitely.

> MIKE

But you still prefer to walk alone?

> ANNA

Who? Me—or her?

> MIKE

Her. You like company.

He strokes the back of her neck.

Don't you?

> ANNA (smiling)

Not always. Sometimes I prefer to walk alone.

> MIKE

Tell me, when you said that—outside—you swished your skirt—very provocative. Did you mean it?

> ANNA

Well, it worked. Didn't it?

THIRD ASSISTANT's *face at door.*

THIRD ASSISTANT

We're going on. (25–26)

The actors have difficulty keeping straight which "me" and "you" they are talking about, and the intrusion of the Third Assistant is an abrupt reminder to the audience that there is a third reality (an idea reenforced by the character's title), that which the audience itself belongs to, which is entirely offscreen, even though as viewers in suspended disbelief they may have been caught up temporarily in the duality being experienced by the onscreen characters. An extension of this idea is found in Woody Allen's *Purple Rose of Cairo* (1985), when the Mia Farrow character's real life becomes entangled with the reel life of an actor who steps out of a movie. Her fantasy is realized when there is no distinction between the two worlds, although some confusion is created when the screen character and the actor who plays him in the movie and in the movie-within-a-movie both become her suitors. For her, as for Mike, the screen character serves as a means of escaping her everyday existence into a romantic fantasy.

An even more arresting example of Pinter's understanding of cinematic technique and his talent to use that knowledge effectively follows. It is a masterful scene created by the screenwriter that demonstrates how easily the fictional and the real sets of lives can become conjoined:

78. **Interior. Hotel. Empty billiard room. Night. Present.**

MIKE and ANNA rehearsing, holding scripts.

MIKE

Miss Woodruff!

ANNA

Just a minute, I've lost the place.

She turns pages of script.

MIKE

I suddenly see you. You've got your coat caught in brambles. I see you, then you see me. We look at each other, then I say: 'Miss Woodruff.'

ANNA

All right.

MIKE

Right. I see you. Get your coat caught in the bramble.

She mimes her coat caught in bramble.

MIKE

Right. Now I'm looking at you.
You see me. Look at me.

ANNA

I am.

MIKE

Miss Woodruff!

ANNA

I'm looking at you.

MIKE

Yes, but now you come towards me, to pass me. It's a
narrow path, muddy.

She walks towards him.

You slip in the mud.

ANNA

Whoops!

She falls.

MIKE

Beautiful. Now I have to help you up.

ANNA

Let's start over again.

She goes back to the chair.

I've got my coat caught in the brambles.
Suddenly you see me. Then I see you.

MIKE

Miss Woodruff!

*She mimes her coat caught in brambles, tugs
at it walks along carpet towards him. He steps*

aside. She moves swiftly to pass him, and
slips. She falls to her knees. He bends to help
her up. She looks up at him. He stops for a
moment, looking down, and then gently lifts
her. With his hand on her elbow, he leads her
towards the window.

I dread to think, Miss Woodruff, what would happen if
you should one day turn your ankle in a place like this.

She is silent, looking down.
He looks down at her face, her mouth.

ANNA

I must . . . go back.

MIKE

Will you permit me to say something first? I know I am
a stranger to you, but—

Sharp cut to:

79.   **Sarah turning sharply. A branch snapping.** (30–31)

In the film, the called-for match cut takes place as Anna moves to pass
Mike and slips. The slip becomes a breathtakingly seamless slide into the
Victorian story, a transition that carries the action immediately into the next
sequence and the modern couple has become the Victorians. The twin strands
of the parallel editing are spliced with this gorgeous cut, probably Pinter's
most magnificent single piece of screenwriting. It is beautifully efficacious,
welding together the past and the present, the real and the imagined. The
kicker here, of course, is that even the "real" lives are only reel lives on a
silver screen.

While the differences between Pinter's published film script for *The French
Lieutenant's Woman* and the film itself are extremely complicated and interesting, they are of a nature consonant with those explored above in relation
to many of his other screenplays. Scenes 73 and 78 in the published version,
for example, simply are brought closer together in the movie and thus more
clearly reenforce each other with the deleting of several intervening short
scenes. Still, a quick glance at the archival material reveals how hard the
screenwriter labors to achieve a desired effect, that his achievements are not
accidental.

For instance, in the archival materials there are three interrelated categories of changes that show Pinter's meticulous attention to details, the striving to get things just right.[13] These include alterations in the opening sequence, the overall structure and continuity of the scenes, and the closing sequence. On November 24, 1978, the first shot was described thus:

Clapper Board

FLW

Shooting toward shore.

Pan with figure of a woman, eventually revealing that she stands at end of stone pier staring out to sea.

On November 29, the shot becomes:

EXT. THE COBB DAY.

A clapperboard. On it is written FLW Shot 1, Take 3. It shuts and withdraws.

Revealed is the Cobb, a stone pier in the harbours of Lynne.

The camera is shooting towards the shore. It pans with the figure of a woman, moving towards the end of the Cobb. She reaches the end and stands still, staring out to sea.

By May 1, 1979 the opening scene had been altered to read:

It shuts and withdraws, leaving a close shot of Sarah. The actress is holding her hair in place against the wind.

VOICE (off).

All right. Let's go.

About a month and a half later (June 17), the fourth draft includes: "It shuts and withdraws, leaving a close shot of Sarah," and the time of day is dawn. The establishing time was day, but it was changed to dawn and back to day in the third draft. In a June 28 version, the slug line is: "*1. EXT. COBB. LYME REGIS. DAWN. 1867.*" The published wording is identical to that of the June 28 version.[14] Finally, a tan folder containing fifty-one pages of "RETYPES FROM FINAL VERSION" ("Final" meaning the version to be submitted), changes designated by the use of red ink, includes the handwritten notation, "Anna, the actress who plays Sarah." Among other things, Pinter is trying to capture and unobtrusively draw attention to the duality of the Sarah/Anna character.

The same kind of reflective consideration can be found in entries regarding the structure and continuity of the script. As important as continuity is in his other scripts, with the constant moving back and forth in time and space in *The French Lieutenant's Woman* it takes on an added significance. So, not only are there a large number of cuts, additions, and reorderings, but Pinter carefully and continually outlines the developing structure. As in *The Go-Between,* he manipulates time, but in this movie time and reality interact in new ways. Time shifts in relation to the audience's becoming absorbed in the fictive. Fowles's self-referential narrative structure, according to Peacock, "distances the plot in order to deconstruct both the art of fiction and the interpretation of the past" (194). Pinter thus creates a time in the past that momentarily becomes as real as the present of the screenplay, which is neither more nor less an artifact than the novel.

Because neither Pinter nor the British Library has made any effort to put the archival boxes or their contents into chronological order, it is difficult in many instances to determine the date of various materials.[15] Such is the case with many of the structure/continuity items. One such entry, labeled "New Continuity," is currently lodged in box 17. When I examined the contents of that box, two items several layers above this one bore the dates October 10 and December 27, while two items several layers below it were dated February 2 and December 12. This "New Continuity" item was a collection of three loose sheets containing scenes numbered 105, 106, 118, 119, 106, 120, 122, 122 (120), in that order. Farther down in the box were seven loose pages with holograph notations regarding new and old continuity.[16]

On a pad with the date May 28, there is a "New Tea Scene." On five separate pages with the date May 31, there is an outline of scene 129, "2nd Structure," followed by three pages dealing with scene 168a and later scenes. Box 16, which contains both a tan folder with "The draft I typed & my corrections & corrected pages" and a title page dated June 17, 1979, as well as material dated December 18, includes four additional pages, stapled, of an incomplete "New Continuity" and a green folder ("*Sequences*") containing eleven pages on "New Continuity" and new scenes.

The changes in the ending are even more fascinating. The first version is in box 16. The setting is "EXT. HOUSE. NIGHT" (p. 164, sc. 227 in the script). Mike calls out "Anna?" which becomes "Anna!" Then there is a holograph addition:

M runs across courtyard, up grass slope as the Merc
[Mercedes] ~~passes~~ goes out of gate. He cries out.

M - Anna!

Piano music begins.

T.O.[17]

A different version appears in box 19:

<u>New 243. EXT. HOUSE</u>

Anna's white car driving towards the gate.

<u>New 244. EXT. HOUSE WINDOW.</u>

Mike at window. He calls out:

<u>MIKE</u>

Sarah!

The published screenplay is the same as the box 19 version. In the film's
happy ending, the rowboat with Charles and Sarah in it is seen entering the
lake again.

Intriguingly, box 20 contains yet another version:

~~228~~ 240. DISSOLVE INTO INT. HOUSE. STUDIO
LONG SHOT. DAY.

In the background the piano playing. Sunlight falls across the room
through the long windows.

Charles and Sarah stand, embracing.

The camera tracks towards them and stops.

They kiss.

<u>CHARLES</u> (Softly)

Sarah.

The choice between these alternate endings is crucial. Pinter wanted to
follow Fowles's lead with multiple endings and the possibilities that they
engender, but the differences between those that the scenarist considered
create a unique meaning for his work. If Mike calls after Anna, as in the first
instance, the movie is merely the story of two actors who have an affair, one
of whom cannot admit that it has ended. If the tale ends with Charles and

Sarah together in the studio, we are back in the Victorian story, and the film no longer seems to have anything but a fictive grounding; the sense of any offscreen applicability is lost. Philosophically, the ending that Pinter chose is the most challenging, and it fits the thematic structure of the novel and the film. The addition of a repeat of the happy-ending rowboat scene in the film itself draws the audience back into the Victorian story, yet it adds a sense of romantic unrealism to it rather than being too pat like the studio ending. This dreamlike event mirrors Mike's sensitivity at the film's conclusion, for even though he has lost Anna/Sarah, it is likely that he will live in a continuing fantasy instead of coping with reality, an ending foretold in Pinter's stage play *The Lover.*

Obviously, the screenwriter fine-tuned his material constantly and over a considerable length of time in order to get what he considered the exact word or right combination or order of scenes. Sometimes he went back and forth between options several times before deciding on the final version. Just as obviously, it is not an accident that Pinter arrived successfully at the one approach that retains the essence of Fowles's masterpiece cinematically—the introduction of this new element, a modern framework within and by means of the film-within-a-film—and at the same time makes the screenplay of *The French Lieutenant's Woman* a masterpiece in its own right.

Betrayal

RELEASED: London, 1982; New York, 1982
SOURCE: *Betrayal,* Pinter's play of the same title (1978)
AWARDS: Nominated for 1983 Academy of Motion Picture Arts and Sciences
   Awards (Best Picture, Writing—Best Screenplay Based on Material from
   Another Medium)
PRODUCTION COMPANY: Horizon Pictures (GB), Ltd.; Twentieth Century–Fox
   International Classics
DIRECTOR: David Jones
EDITOR: John Bloom
PHOTOGRAPHED BY: Mike Flash
PRODUCER: Sam Spiegel
PRODUCTION DESIGNER: Eileen Diss
MUSIC: Dominic Muldowney; Mike Moran
COSTUME DESIGNERS: Jean Muir, Jane Robinson
CAST: Ben Kingsley (Robert), Jeremy Irons (Jerry), Patricia Hodge (Emma), Chloe
   Billington (Charlotte at 5), Hannah Davies (Charlotte at 9), Avril Edgar
   (Mrs. Banks), Michael Konig (Ned at 2), Ray Marioni (Waiter), Alexander
   McIntosh (Ned at 5), Caspar Norman (Sam)
RUNNING TIME: 105 minutes[1]
COLOR
RATING: R
VIDEO: CBS/Fox Video

BETRAYAL, WHICH PREMIERED as a stage play on November 15, 1978 and is
dedicated to Simon Gray, is one of Pinter's most popular dramas. This is
probably because the theme, the breakup of a love affair, is primal in human
experience and thus easily accessible to all levels of audiences. The nature of
time, the function of memory, and the concept of betrayal are intermingled
too, of course, but these are also fairly basic and straightforward elements in

the human condition. Furthermore, although the play's structure is bewildering at first, it does not take the audience long to understand that the playwright is telling a love story in reverse. Added to that is the audience's general suspicion/assumption that the drama is autobiographically based, possibly on the writer's relationship with Lady Antonia Fraser.

Rather than beginning with the meeting of the couple (Emma and Jerry) and tracing the development and then disintegration of their love, Pinter starts at the end, a couple of years after the affair has ended, and works backward in time to the beginning; he uses repetition to establish connections through the various times.[2] This structure is effective because it lends itself to dramatic irony so well, since we are aware of what the results of the characters' actions will be: we know that however heartfelt the pledges of undying love, the love will die. Even though the structure of the play slowly leads to an unfolding of the chronology being presented, given the enthusiasm and sense of wonder and innocence of the lovers, the foreknowledge that we possess before the exchanges but which they know only in retrospect imbues the play with poignancy.

In the stage version, Pinter presents the betrayal of social conventions and mores, spouses, best friends, business associates, and self, all through the metaphor of marital infidelity. The triangle involves publisher Robert (played by Daniel Massey, who is replaced in the movie by Ben Kingsley), his wife Emma (Penelope Wilton on the stage; Patricia Hodge in the film), and his best friend, Jerry (Michael Gambon on the stage; Jeremy Irons in the film), who is also the author of books that Robert has published. The drama begins in the present (1977) with Jerry and Emma meeting in a bar. Through a series of combinations and in a variety of circumstances, the three characters meet and interact as the intertwined strands of their mutual relationships are complexly woven together. Honesty and betrayal are common links (the words *honesty, betrayal,* and variations thereon appear numerous times in the play, some in expressions that hark back to James Mason as Conway in *The Pumpkin Eater*), as is the game of squash, which, particularly for Robert, comes to symbolize the masculine world, especially in terms of male bonding and the purity of friendship.[3] Husband betrays wife, wife betrays husband, best friends betray each another, business associates betray each other. Given the mutual nature of this activity, it is difficult to identify the protagonist in the tale, and there is ambiguity about all of the characters, too. Emma and Jerry are attractive in their joyful love, and the romanticism of their lost love is appealing. Yet, they are betraying Robert, who thus gains

Betrayal (1982). Jeremy Irons as Jerry, Patricia Hodge as Emma, and Ben Kingsley as Robert. Twentieth Century–Fox. Jerry Ohlinger Archives.

our sympathy—until we learn that he has been unfaithful too. Film director David Jones comments: "I found while making the film that I was constantly taking different sides. Sometimes you think how extraordinary Emma is to accommodate both men. At other times you think, 'How dare she? How could she conceivably continue the affair after her husband has discovered it?' But the story is a totally human emotional triangle about male and female insecurities. On the whole, because Harold is a man he's writing about male insecurity faced by this great enigma, this exciting enigma, this maybe destructive enigma called woman. What's so good about Harold is that he doesn't write fluffy little ladies; he's only interested in women prepared to take you on."[4]

Jones testifies that he is so in concert with the screenwriter that "What I shot in *Betrayal* was in the screenplay—exactly. What I show was exactly what was in the screenplay—well, not exactly. [The] shot of the two hands turning with their wedding rings on—this is what I saw when we filmed it and used it for the last shot. . . . [There were also some] wonderful new additions by Harold Pinter—about eight minutes. . . . the time sequence was exactly the same."[5]

The final scene takes place during a party at Robert and Emma's home nine years earlier; it is at this gathering where the two lovers first acknowledge their love for one another. Because the story is told chronologically backward in nine scenes, from a time two years after the affair between Jerry and Emma has ended back to the point at which they initiated their seven-year-long liaison, the action is filled with pathos; because the play is by Pinter, it is also filled with dramatic irony and touches of humor.

One of the strengths of *Betrayal* as a performance piece is that once the chronological disjunction is accommodated, the ideas are fairly straightforward. At the same time, there are a number of interwoven elements to fascinate those who enjoy the more subtle substance that is present as well—such as the relationship that the characters establish between squash and a definition of manhood, at least as the concept represents the separate and definable world of the male.

Questions such as "Who knew what when?" may also arise. These may parallel the sense of mystery that suffuses the fading of love or friendship or loyalty. Where did the feelings go, and when? The confusion, even among the participants in the event, about whose kitchen they were in when Jerry tossed Emma's daughter into the air, captures the nature of memory quite nicely and unobtrusively. Possibly a pivotal point in Jerry and Emma's relationship, the detail of where this act took place is lost over time and among other memories; the act itself, though, remains imbedded in their minds. It is part of the sharing that brought them together as lovers and serves as a symbol of pure happiness, lost forever.

Besides the intellectual puzzles, *Betrayal* is filled with poignant moments, as in scene 3, when the two characters meet in their apartment for what they know will be the last time. Emma gives Jerry her key to return to the landlady. Through the pain of remembrance of times past and the understanding that those times are gone forever, Emma's final words are, "I think we've made absolutely the right decision" (58). The emotional content of this scene lies in the characters' consciousness of what they have had and what they have lost. Scene 7 is powerful exactly because Jerry and Emma do not know what is going to happen, and their actions seem small and meaninglessly prosaic. The audience, however, is aware of the significance of the tablecloth that Emma has brought back from Venice to add a personal, homey touch to their rendezvous, for in scene 3 the cloth was alluded to as no longer having any value to either of the former lovers. The sadness that the audience feels in scene 7 is intensified by that foreknowledge and the dramatic irony in the realization that the couple's happiness is, in retrospect, almost illusory. The play's popularity is certainly understandable, given how this kind of seemingly innocent and insignificant touch attains significance.

The emotional impact of scene 7 also suggests the answer to the question of whether *Betrayal* would have been more effective if the author had structured the play according to regular chronology, following the lovers from the moment of their first entangling and on to the point of their meeting again several years after their affair ended. The drama certainly would have had an emotional impact. But, the impact is even greater when we see the actions of the characters and know the end results of those actions when they do not. Emma, Jerry, and Robert are a bit like W.B. Yeats's Leda—they, and we, have no idea what the consequences of any of our acts will be. By showing us the consequences first, the dramatist increases our recognition of the importance of the acts as they are occurring. As in Matthew Arnold's "Dover Beach," an awareness of the past connected to the present brings in the "eternal note of sadness." Ultimately, which character knew what when is not as important as what happens to them, and Pinter's chronology permits us to comprehend the emotional depth of that knowledge. It also effectively underscores not the chronological puzzle but rather why the game of squash is so important to Robert and how many and how intricately interwoven the levels of betrayal are.

It may seem incongruous, yet one of the impediments in many of Pinter's plays is the element of humor, which he uses effectively to underscore significant points. Simon Gray, speaking about humor in drama, notes, "One of the great hurdles that Harold has had to live with is that people, for years, have gone into the theatre straight-faced with the piety of the occasion, when actually there is nothing he likes more than to have people laughing."[6] There is a considerable amount of humor in *Betrayal,* and the cast succeeded so well in getting that humor across to the audience that several times lines were lost because the audience laughed over them. For example, upon learning that Robert has known about the affair for years yet never indicated this knowledge, Jerry incredulously notes, "But he's my best friend"—the best friend whom he had cuckolded for seven years.

Billington claims that the source for the story line in the play was not Pinter's liaison with Lady Antonia, which began in 1975, three years before the play premiered. Instead, according to Billington, the play was based on a seven-year affair between Pinter and Joan Bakewell, the "television presenter" of *Late Night Line-Up,* who was married to Michael Bakewell, a radio and television drama producer. Evidently Mr. Bakewell found out about the affair approximately two years after it started, yet said nothing about it. When Pinter, who was betraying his own wife, found out that Bakewell knew, he was indignant and apparently felt that Bakewell's silence was a form of betrayal, exacerbated by the fact that Bakewell backed Pinter at the BBC and, indeed, even helped to get some of the writer's plays produced on the air. These revelations clearly help explain some of the characters' reactions in *Betrayal* and the underlying tensions that run through the drama. And, as is often the case in Pinter's work, some of the events that occur in the play were drawn from real life: the tossing of the child into the air, for example, and Robert's intercepting one of Jerry's letters to Emma at the American Express office in Venice (according to Mrs. Bakewell, her husband found one of Pinter's letters to her in a similar incident).

In the play, Pinter explores and demonstrates the workings of the human mind and interpersonal relationships by manipulating time. The drama is related to his later memory plays—*Landscape, No Man's Land, Silence, Night*—but the film is as effective as the play because of the greater manipulation of time allowed by the cinematic medium—which becomes a prime feature in the movie. Other filmic elements are used to reenforce the intellectual effects of the manipulation of time even as they are being utilized for emotional impact. The camera's up-close focusing on the lovers' clasped hands is a case in point, for this cannot be duplicated on the stage—and it is this clasping that brings the full emotional impact of the story into focus.

Pinter began writing the script for producer Sam Spiegel (for what turned out to be the last movie that Spiegel produced) within two years of the premiere of the stage play. The writer's constant working with his script, even though it is the adaptation of his own successful drama, his attention to details, and his concern with exploring the full expression of the meaning of the work is once more evident in the variations that appear in subsequent drafts of the screenplay. The surprising thing about the *Betrayal* script is that in spite of the fact that the play had already been produced, the author was still working out the chronology of events as they originally transpired, whether for himself or for someone else involved in the filming. For example, the copy of the *First Draft,* dated "21 April 1981," is retitled with pencil additions and dated "20 December 1981" and includes blue ink holograph alterations in a "Final Draft 2 March 1982." A second version of the "Final draft" (119 pages) includes a chronology by year of the events concerning the three major characters[7] and a list of Robert and Emma's children and their ages by year.[8] Of course, these lists may have been constructed to help the actors understand vital information known by their characters that is never explicitly revealed in the film, or they may have been intended to help director Jones in some fashion. Pinter works well with Jones on stage and screen productions, and the director is careful to take full advantage of his writer's own understanding of the script, which Jones tries to reproduce as faithfully as possible.

Additional versions of the script reflect the same kind of ongoing work as evidenced in previous scripts. In the archives box there is a group of papers titled "(Words for actors shot 2)" that are typed, with holographic notes, both photocopies and carbon copies, amounting to sixty-four pages of alterations and new pages for scenes 1, 99, and others. A typescript in a large plastic bag is the same script as in the "(Words for actors shot 2)," but it is complete, including some scenes moved (46–50 become 54–57), then a different set of scenes added (46–47 to 58–61), and a conclusion. There is also a corrected earlier version of the chronology in which the dates have been moved up one year. Still another variant, from Horizon Pictures, contains new pages to be inserted.[9]

Original pages, from the Horizon Pictures set, typed, with corrections, contain a conglomeration of changes:

1 - date (1980) on screen deleted.

99 - 4 yrs. earlier to 3 yrs.

103G - inserts 38a, Int. Kilburn flat. Staircase.

104 - Adds to 38, Emma.

> But we . . .
>
> you see?
>
> ~~So we need somewhere we can rest~~
>
> ~~between appointments~~. And
>
> hotels are so expensive.

105 - Cont. of 104 changed to accommodate those changes.

109 - Adds "They kiss" is changed to "He kisses her."

> (The addition of "41a - Serpentine" is not included)

110–43 - Instead of her going into kitchen, "He goes into other room."

111 - minor change in the dialogue regarding keys and to accommodate her being in the kitchen and him in other room change in 110 (originally, he enters the kitchen) instead of her coming out.

While most of these differences are not significant, the change from "They kiss" to "He kisses her" is. There is an obvious shift in the relationship between the characters represented in this small distinction which is compounded when "He goes into the other room" rather than her going into the kitchen. The emphasis moves from the couple to Jerry, who is made more aggressive and possibly more intensely involved than his partner. These changes lead to technical adjustments as well, which is why there is a minor change in the dialogue regarding keys and the actual spatial relationship between the characters.

In the same set of papers there are documents titled "*BETRAYAL: NOTES* 19 January 1981." These five carbon pages of scenes 1 through 10 contain suggested camera movements and holographic marginalia:

- record playing at opening?

C.U. Robert (Ext. House).

. . . .

2. "Jerry walking towards pub in Kilburn.

(B) Interior pub. Play scene."

There is a difference between this opening and the filmed opening, which begins with an exterior shot of Robert and Emma's house at night. Guests are leaving a party there, and Emma is seen through the kitchen window washing the dishes.

There are pages included that are closer to the film:

KITCHEN

Emma at sink. Robert studies her.

ROBERT

How many of the men here tonight
have you fucked.

EMMA (without turning)

Go away.

ROBERT

I am. But I think I'll have a little
talk with my daughter first. Give
her a fatherly warning. I don't
want her to follow in the family tradition.

Emma goes to him, looks at him, slaps him. He slaps
her. She half falls, holds her head, sits at the table.

> ROBERT
>
> Bitch! You not only fucked my best
> friend, you're now fucking my best
> author!

Silence.

Emma moans.

Another set of nine pages of "Betrayal: Notes," on carbon paper with
penciled alterations, is dated January 14 (in a different format from the above
because the pages are smaller). Most interestingly, Pinter's refining of the
script and his continual thinking about it over a period of months is clear:

> p. 8. ~~11."Circa 1971. Jerry and Judith's kitchen."~~
>
> p. 9. [Mostly blocking directions. Carbon; pencil and black ink with
> alterations.]
>
> p. 10. Scene 9 - P. 10 - (E). [There is the suggestion regarding where to
> "play" the scene: "on terrace overlooking the lakes in Scene 2, or by the
> side of the lake or in the Water Gardens in Hyde Park." is deleted. "In
> The Serpentine" is included, as is an eight-name "ROBERT" list.]
>
> FURTHER NOTES
> This sequence, if it is worth doing at all, I think
> must go forward in time, so that the last sene [sic]
> will be (E) the announcement of her pregnancy. This
> means that (D) [Florist's shop. Florist on telephone,
> taking down message: "Congratulations and love to you
> and Ned. Judith and Jerry."] would be unworkable.
>
> One can consider other short scenes for this sequence,
> i.e., the first look at the bare flat, with the land-
> lady, or the choosing of the bed in a big store.
> The last scene in the kitchen I think can only work
> as an end credit title sequence - as an emblem, as it
> were. The actual narrative essentially ends with Jerry
> clasping Emma's arm, as in the play.

Pinter seems by this time to be paying a lot more conscious attention to
technique, how best to structure the screenplay, and similar technical questions related to the most effective explication of his work.[10]

A 125-page, unbound first draft carbon, *BETRAYAL: NOTES,*" dated "21 April 1981," with the same opening scene as in the January 19, 1981, script does not include dialogue from "(Words for actors shot 2)." Some alterations are minor (Emma's age ["38"] is deleted from the directions), but others are more significant. In this latter category is the introduction on page 21 of the manuscript of new material in the bar scene:

He goes to bar. Orders drinks.

A group of laborers burst into the pub, go to the bar. 2nd barman.

Ad libs from them:

"What is it? Jim?"

etc.

It appears that Pinter is going through the original play and looking at it as a film rather than a drama. A similar occurrence can be found on page 19: "During course of scene one or 2 other people drift in & out."

Obviously, as noted earlier, the difficulty of working with undated material is that it is not possible to determine exactly when it was written, which is necessary to determine why it might have been added, or added and then deleted, as occurs in the last set of papers contained in the archives box: thirteen loose leaves with a mixture of brief notes, pages of dialogue, a chronology, and so on. What is clear is that Pinter did not try to turn his play directly into a screenplay. And, the writing process was continual.[11]

Like Michael Crichton's novels, even the stage-play version of *Betrayal* has a cinematic quality. Indeed, in an interview with Leslie Bennetts, the playwright observed: "It was originally written for the stage in a kind of cinematic way, with a structure that possibly owes something to the films I've worked on for the last twenty years. My early plays started at the beginning and went to the end; they were linear. Then I did more and more films, and I felt that 'Betrayal'—even the stage version—comes as much out of film as it does out of the stage" (1, 23).

This comment captures the essence of the writer's accomplishment and underscores the difference between film and other artistic media. Pinter had used the short-scene structure successfully in earlier plays (especially the television plays *Tea Party* and *The Basement*), and the structural device is dramatically powerful as the audience witnesses the effects of certain past actions and then sees the actions themselves—unmediated, as they occurred, not as they are described by the actors. As Peacock notes, the screenwriter trades the subjective authorial perspectives of the novels that have been his film sources for the objective camera's viewpoint (117), an "omniscient eye" that records events as they are happening and supposedly does not intrude (although we know that there is always editing going on, whether it is in the lighting, or the camera placement, or the angles, etc.). The shifts in locales are filmic too. But, what film allows that is different from all other media is the compression or extension of time, and in this screenplay Pinter manipulates time even more effectively than he did in *The Go-Between*.

This is seen in the changes that he incorporates to take advantage of cinematic assets. There are only a very few minor changes in the dialogue, as such. The deletion of "who cares" (23) and the change from Fortnam and Mason's to Kensington Church Street (124), for instance, are insignificant and some of these changes may have occurred during shooting. There are three other alterations, however, that are tied to the screenwriter's medium. The most obvious of these is the insertion of six time-identifying titles. In addition to the clues provided by clothing, hairstyles, and makeup (the characters look increasingly younger as the drama progresses), three times the words "Two years earlier" appear on the screen leading into a scene, and three times the words "One year earlier" appear. These make the chronology easier to follow than in the stage play, in which only clothing, hairstyles, and makeup are used to indicate time changes. In the printed stage script, dates (including a "Later that year" that is not present in the movie) are given for each scene, but unless those dates are also included in the program, the audience does not know when the scenes take place.

Not as obvious are the new scenes that Pinter includes. Almost all of these involve an exterior element.[12] These additions begin with the first scene in the movie (discussed below). In what is scene 2 in the play, instead of the curtain coming up on Robert and Jerry in Jerry's apartment, we see Robert sitting in a BMW outside Jerry's apartment. The effect created by Robert's aspect is similar to that of Mick's in the opening sequence of *The Caretaker*—a sense of foreboding is created. Pinter also inserts a tension-breaker in the form of Jerry's hollering at Sam to turn down the record player (which had been prepared for when Jerry went to open the door for Robert and yelled up the stairs about his son's loud music).

The following scene, in which Emma and Jerry visit the apartment for the last time, does not begin with them already in the apartment, as it does in

the play. Rather, there is a view of Emma driving her car in Kilburn,[13] parking, and walking into the flat. During the scene, other buildings can be seen
outside through the windows, and the sound of children's voices can be heard
(perhaps a touch of "opened out" realism or a representation of the playful-
ness and innocence that is no longer attached to this relationship). At the end
of the scene in the play, Emma leaves and Jerry *"stands"* alone in the room
(58). In the movie, Jerry goes to the window and watches as she gets into her
car to leave. There is a cut to the car, and Emma is seen crying, the flat
reflected in her window.

Stage scene 4 takes place in Robert and Emma's house. In the film, Robert is seen walking through a park and Emma is seen giving Ned a bath
before Jerry arrives. Once there, Jerry and Robert visit Emma in the nursery.
None of this action is contained in the drama.

In the following sequence, Pinter has added a scene in Robert and Emma's
daughter's bedroom in Venice. When Emma and Jerry meet at the apartment
in the next segment, the writer adds a shot of Mrs. Banks peering out the
window. In this scene he also alters the dialogue. We already know that
Emma told Robert about the affair when they were in Venice because the
husband had discovered that Jerry was writing letters to her. In an addition
that parallels the letter situation, Jerry tells Emma that he was in a panic at
one point while she was in Venice because he had misplaced a letter that she
had written to him, and he was afraid that his wife would find it. In place of
a passage about Spinks, Pinter substitutes Emma's question, "What would
you have done if Judith found it?" and Jerry's answer, "I don't know what I
would have done.".

The audience is aware that Emma is asking what Jerry would have done
if he had been in the same situation that she had been in; clearly, although
she does not tell her lover that her husband knows about their infidelity, she
does feel guilty about telling Robert about the affair. This is followed in both
the play and the film with another reference to Jerry's playful tossing of
Emma's daughter in the air in his kitchen while everyone was present. The
importance not only of this moment being remembered but of any particular
moment is made clear both by the repetition of the memory in several scenes
in the play and by the context in which the repetition occurs. Memory, emotion, the moment—all are constantly brought into play.

The many layers of tension and conflict are highlighted in the restaurant
scene (scene 7), but before this happens, Pinter inserts another new scene
into the film, one of Robert at home, picking up Ned (who, he has been told,

is his child) while Emma reads. There is no dialogue. Robert's actions are in direct contrast with the words spoken in the restaurant, for no words are needed to explain his feelings when he lifts Ned (as Jerry had lifted Charlotte), and the dramatic irony present in his conversation with Jerry is enhanced by the audience's awareness of Robert's awareness of his wife and friend's illicit actions and Jerry's total lack of knowledge of what has transpired between his lover and her husband.

There are four additional new scenes. In the first, a very quiet Emma and Jerry are alone in his house while his wife and children are away. The couple is softer, younger than their more experienced selves. In the second a telephone rings upstairs, and Emma rushes up from her kitchen to find that it is Robert calling. She is obviously expecting a call and is disappointed when it is Robert on the other end of the line. As soon as she hangs up, Jerry calls. The eagerness of the couple to be together and their total involvement in one another is neatly captured in this two-scene exchange.

Another new scene follows, again involving a telephone call. And, again it is Robert who is making the unexpected call. He is in his office, and he calls Jerry, who is in his own office, and invites his friend to engage in a game of squash. Jerry, who has promised to meet Emma in the preceding scene, lies to his friend, saying that he has too much work to do and is going to meet with one of the authors whom he represents.

From this lie there is a line to other lies. In the last new scene, Jerry and Emma are seen looking at the apartment in Kilburn that they will rent. They are youthful and nervous in their transaction with the landlady, Mrs. Banks, and they lie about why they want the flat—they say that they live in Leicester and need a place in London when they have to stay over for business.[14]

A large number of lines that appeared in the original have been omitted from the screenplay in order to make accommodations for the time added by the inclusion of the extra scenes. Ranging from one line to a page in length, these cuts are interesting (often related to the writers Casey and Spinks, who are frequently mentioned to differentiate the characters of Robert and Jerry in the play but who never appear on stage), but what was excised is not necessary for an understanding of the film.[15]

Two scenes are crucial to understanding Pinter's approach to screenwriting. The differences between the stage script and the screenplay are especially evident in the opening and closing scenes in the movie, and they demonstrate again how the writer consciously uses cinematic techniques both to open out his own works and at the same time to be more intimate than is possible in a stage piece. Rather than starting with scene 1 in a pub, the movie begins with an exterior night shot—the outside of a fashionable residence—the beginning of an eight-shot sequence. As noted above, the host and hostess are cordially saying good-bye to four couples at the end of a party. Nineteen-sixties-style instrumental music is heard over, but none of the conversations can be heard. Moving from a long shot, the camera pushes in to follow Robert and Emma as he stands, drinking and watching her pick up glasses in the parlor, and then they move into the kitchen.

The first cut takes place after three minutes and forty-two seconds have passed. It is still an exterior shot, through the kitchen window. The man and wife argue; nonsynchronous sounds are heard: the barking of a dog, clock bells, a car. Clearly, the husband is upset, although he is casual in his attitude, referring to something that his wife has done. The woman slaps her husband and he slaps her back. A young boy in pajamas enters, and his mother picks him up. Later we will learn that this scene took place the evening before the second scene.

The second cut is to an automobile junkyard, establishing the kind of area in which the following action takes place. A train is passing in the background, and the camera pulls back and pans to the interior of the pub where Emma is sitting at a table by herself. The next shot is of Jerry walking down the street toward the bar. This is followed by a shot of him getting drinks from the barman and carrying them to her. Shot six is of Jerry putting down the drinks and sitting down at the table. The first word in the film (four minutes and thirty seconds in), spoken by Jerry, is "Well," as it is in the play. The alterations begin immediately, although insignificantly, as he then adds "Cheers" instead of being answered by her "How are you?" (Pinter, *Betrayal*, [11]). The camera pushes in to a two-shot as the conversation continues with alternating close-ups of each of the speakers.

By moving outside Robert and Emma's home for the opening sequence, Pinter not only connects them to an outside world, he also provides a mini–dumb show that grabs the audience's attention. Partly this is because of the contrast between the cordiality of the leave-takings and the sudden brutality of the slaps. It is likely that this action represents the early manuscript version of the movie's opening in which Robert asks "How many men here tonight have you fucked?" Because the audience does not hear the words, dramatic tension is created and some kind of resolution is demanded.

There is contrast in the subsequent sequence as well. First, the wreckage and bustle of the working-class area have been juxtaposed with the peaceful

upper-class neighborhood of the opening. Similarly, the quietness of the opening is mentally broken by the sudden physical actions of the husband and
wife, which is followed by the sedate scene in the pub, which is set in the
midst of the bustle of business. In both cases, the personal is caught within a
larger context, but it is the personal that captures our interest. Since no words
have been heard prior to Jerry's "Well," the audience must try to determine
what the relationship is between the dumb show and the meeting in the pub.

In a sense, the concluding twelve shots of the movie reverse the actions
of the opening. In the play, Emma and Jerry are in Robert and Emma's bedroom near the end of another party. For the first time, Jerry reveals his feelings for Emma, who is the wife of his best friend and at whose marriage he
acted as best man. Robert enters, there is talk about best friends and best
men. Jerry admits to telling Emma how beautiful she is, which he feels is
appropriate because "I speak as your oldest friend. Your best man" (*Betrayal*, 138). Robert replies, "You are, actually," clasps Jerry's shoulder, turns
and leaves the room. Then:

EMMA *moves towards the door.* JERRY *grasps her arm. She stops still.
They stand still, looking at each other.*

The final sequence in the film opens as the movie opened, with an exterior shot of Robert and Emma's home while a party is going on inside. The
circle has been completed. The intimacy of the last scene—and its irony—is
enhanced in the motion picture by the focusing property of the camera. The
triangular nature of the relationship is clear as Jerry delivers his "best man"
line while standing between Emma and Robert and slightly behind them.
The relationship between Robert and Jerry at that time is likewise clearly
indicated when Robert's "You are" is spoken with the two men standing
next to each other in a close-up. There is no more dialogue in the remaining
forty-seven seconds of the film. The next shot shows Robert and Jerry together, then Robert turns and goes out the bedroom doorway. In the following shot, Robert is seen coming out through the doorway, with Jerry and
Emma being revealed as he walks down the hall. The actions that follow are
basically the same as those described in the stage script, but here they are
much more communicative. As Robert moves out of the frame, Emma starts
to leave. The next shot is of Jerry grabbing her arm. In the following close-
up, Jerry's hand is seen holding her arm near the elbow. In a tight two-shot,
Emma turns to look quizzically at Jerry, as she is seen from behind him and

over his shoulder so that the two blend into a single image, her face framed by his body. This composition is duplicated in reverse angle in the next shot as Jerry looks longingly at her, as seen from behind and over Emma's shoulder. The camera is then focused on his hand moving slowly down her arm toward her hand. In another close-up, she looks longingly at him, an aspect of surrender appearing on her face. The final shot is of their hands intertwining—and their wedding bands visible. This is the shot that becomes a freeze and is held as the credits are run over and the same slightly lyrical, romantic music with an uneasy undertone that was heard at the start of the film is heard over. All of the passion and betrayals, the ironies, loss, and sadness of the story are captured emotionally in this last shot and freeze frame.

Pinter's use of a freeze-frame ending recalls Truffaut's magnificent capturing of his young protagonist's despair in *The 400 Blows* (1959) and George Roy Hill's easy way out of an unpleasant ending that still retains a sense of the legendary at the conclusion of *Butch Cassidy and the Sundance Kid* (1969). In *Betrayal* this device is an arresting and poignant *coup de cinéma,* for the shot leading up to the freeze is very sensual, and then the freeze is like Keats's Grecian urn—the lovers are frozen at the moment of perfection, at the moment when the objective is about to be realized. In a sense, the movie shows what happens when things are not frozen, as the relationship deteriorates. It is this element that links *Betrayal* to Yeats's "Leda and the Swan" in the lovers' ignorance of what the consequences of their actions will be when they initiate the affair. This may well be why there are so many references to Yeats in the play (Robert read Yeats on Torcello, for instance). It also fits with the reverse-chronology structure, which is made more touching than a straightforward telling of the story would be, again because we are aware of the dramatic irony, since we know things that the other characters do not know.

Despite the excellence of this script and the fact that there are no major thematic or structural differences between the *Betrayal* stage play and film script, to some extent writing the screenplay may have proved more difficult for Pinter because, in contrast with writing the stage play, there is less opportunity to try out a film before it is set in its "final" version. It is well documented that he uses pre-London runs to adjust the written words of his dramas to the demands of a live production. Perhaps the impossibility of achieving the same kind of tryout procedure is one of the reasons that he has not been as interested in converting his own works to the cinematic medium. The demands are different, and there is no doubt that he recognizes this and has largely been successful in adapting his writing for the screen; even so, he may find it more attractive to work with someone else's original, for he does not have to worry about reworking something that he has already worked out or to overcome his own preconceptions in doing so. To some extent, too, since he has already worked things out to his own satisfaction with his stage dramas, there is more of a challenge in approaching a new piece of material to make it fit a new medium. Nevertheless, the film version of *Betrayal* is a fine achievement.

Victory

Released: Not filmed
Source: *Victory,* by Joseph Conrad; novel (1915)

"I WROTE *VICTORY* in 1982, working with the director, Richard Lester. The finance for the film was never found," Pinter wrote in an author's note at the beginning of the published script for his adaptation of Joseph Conrad's *Victory* (*Comfort,* [166]).[1] Like *The Proust Screenplay,* however, the script is an anomaly in that it has been published even though it has never been filmed. The reason that it has not been filmed may be that a German movie was made from the novel at about the time that Pinter was trying to obtain financing for his project, and there was talk of an English-language version being planned by a production company in New Zealand as well. To top things off, the film company, Universal, rejected the script: "they simply said they didn't want to do a period film set in the Far East. It was too expensive and who cared anyway?"[2]

Some of the elements that might have attracted Pinter's interest are obvious, beginning with the intruder figures. Jones and Ricardo are parallels of *The Dumb Waiter*'s Ben and Gus. They are also representative of moral corruption and evil incarnate, forerunners of Robert in *The Comfort of Strangers* and symbolic equivalents to characters that the author would be creating in the next couple of years in Nicolas of *One for the Road* (1984) and the soldiers of *Mountain Language* (1988). The notion of detachment has occurred in Pinter's writing before, most notably in Teddy's attitude in *The Homecoming* (which also contains a battle for a female) and in the figures of Tony and Mrs. Armitage in the screenplays of *The Servant* and *The Pumpkin Eater.* The inescapability of destiny appears throughout the canon, too: Rose in *The Room,* Stanley in *The Birthday Party,* Ben and Gus in *The Dumb Waiter,* Colin and Mary in *The Comfort of Strangers.* The deaths of the hero and the heroine are ties to *The Comfort of Strangers* as well, and to *Accident, The Handmaid's Tale,* and *The Trial,* and in each case there is a strong interconnection between the concept of sex as being related to sin and death as a punishment for engaging in sex/sin. Finally, there is the challenge of translating a well-known prose work by a major writer into film.

Like *The Proust Screenplay,* the *Victory* screenplay was an adaptation of a classic novel, and as is typical of the screenwriter's cinematic versions, the adaptation is different from the source in significant ways. Published in 1915, Conrad's overly long and repetitive novel is about a Swede named Axel Heyst.[3] The story, at least some of which purportedly was told to him, is recounted by an omniscient first-person narrator who, in tone and function in his relating of a tale, is similar to the narrator who listens to Marlowe in *Heart of Darkness.* Part of Pinter's task, as in several of his other adaptations, was either to use a voice-over narrator in the film or to translate the book's narrator into cinematic images. He chose the latter. He also had to reduce the 385-page volume to approximately ninety minutes' running time.

The novel is divided into four parts. In part 1, the exposition is provided, with a narration of Heyst's background and experiences in the South China Sea (his work with Morrison and the Tropical Belt Coal Company on the island of Samburan, and his antagonistic relationship with the innkeeper Wilhelm Schomberg) that lead up to the story's actual initiating event—his rescue of the violin-playing English girl, Alma/Magdalen/Lena, from an oppressively run, touring "Italian" orchestra and the unwanted advances of Schomberg. Part 2 contains the details of Schomberg's preparation for his revenge. He convinces two murderers, Mr. Jones and his "secretary," Martin Ricardo, that Heyst has secreted a treasury of ill-gotten gains on Samburan. In part 3, Heyst and Lena arrive at Samburan and settle in to live happily together, separated from the intrusions of an unwanted outside world. In the remainder of the novel, part 4, Conrad's narrator tells what happens when the killers and their servant, Pedro, confront Heyst and Lena. The novel ends with a friendly sea captain named Davidson explaining how the woman-hating Jones shot Lena and Ricardo and then drowned, how Wang (the Chinese servant) shot Pedro with Heyst's stolen pistol, and how Heyst committed suicide by burning down his house, in which he stayed with Lena's body.

Conrad claims in a note to the first edition of *Victory* that the last word that he wrote was "the single word of the title" [vii]. What the novel is about—in other words, whose victory the title relates to—is ambiguous. In his note the novelist goes on to comment on the "Teutonic psychology" of

Schomberg, who certainly achieves a kind of victory in destroying the hated Heyst and misleading Lena. Wang, too, is victorious in that he defeats Pedro, one servant conquering the other. There is some added significance in this triumph in that Wang represents, in a minor way, a natural, primitive, moral, and non-Western civilization (he assumed, wrongfully, that Lena accepted Ricardo's advances, and he rejected Heyst because of this misconception; he allied himself with the island tribesmen, who detached themselves from the impure advances of nineteenth-century European society).

More explicit is Lena's victory over the killers; she sacrifices herself in order to procure the knife and save Heyst's life. Her victory, though, is a hollow one, for ironically it turns out to have no bearing on the outcome of the confrontation. Not only does she die, but so does Heyst, who takes his own life because he cannot live without her.

How then might Heyst be deemed victorious? He is presented as a man of detachment from the beginning of the novel, a man "disenchanted" with life who has followed his father's advice to stay out of it, to "Look on— make no sound" (Conrad, 165). First, he triumphs over his detachment under the influence of his passion for Lena. Second, in doing so he prevails in life by coming alive. Third, he rises to something intellectually greater than life by giving up life.

Perhaps there is a victory in that society defeats the antisocial, both those who choose to live outside of society (Heyst and Lena) and the outlaws (Jones, Ricardo, and Pedro). The use of Davidson at the end of the novel to relate the events to an "Excellency," an agent of social authority, supports this reading; neither of the groups who decide to ignore the established society survive, and presumably this is a moral lesson that is conveyed to the members of Davidson's society through his story.

Ultimately, though, it is probably destiny that is most victorious. Heyst and Lena find that they cannot escape their destiny, no matter where they go or what they do, no matter how sure they are that "nothing can break in on us here" (210), that "I have placed her in safety" (366), or that "she had done it! The very sting of death was in her hands; the venom of the viper in her paradise, extracted, safe in her possession" (374). Ricardo's estimate that "men will gamble as long as they have anything to put on a card. Gamble? That's nature. What's life itself? You never know what may turn up" (139) is a more accurate assessment of humankind's ability to control life.

In some ways, because the screenplay has not been filmed, it is possible to obtain a clearer view of Pinter's vision for adapting Conrad's novel than if it had been made into a movie—there has been no filtering through the director's, the editor's, or anyone else's eyes. Thus, the typescript containing 184 numbered shots has not been complicated by having been to some extent transfigured in the very process of filming. As will be demonstrated, there are some differences between the typescript and the printed script that need to be commented upon.[4]

Pinter begins by inserting a kind of dumb show such as might be found in a Renaissance drama, a series of nine shots that capture the essence of the plot, though they are not placed in chronological order and two of them (numbers five and six, the first showing armed men following barking dogs through the jungle and the second showing two men enjoying champagne on a jetty) do not seem directly related to anything that occurs in the tale. The seemingly extraneous shots may be representations of what might be imagined to have taken place off camera in two instances. This sequence takes the place of the exposition with which Conrad began the novel.

Most of the shots are mysterious and dark, and their relationships are indecipherable except in retrospect. The images of the encircling gulls (shot 1), bamboo spears and "impassive native faces" (shot 2), a door being kicked open (shot 3), the armed men (shot 5), and the long knives of the two Venezuelan Indians (shot 8) do, however, produce an overriding sense of foreboding, violence, and doom that is surely going to affect the pair of presumably innocent figures, a girl and a man, seen in shots 7 and 9. This impression is amplified by the accompanying sound effects that are specifically called for: gulls and violins "screeching" in a nice aural match cut between shots 1 and 2; "shrieking" birds (shot 4); a "hissing" gramophone (shot 7); and a "girl's stifled scream" in the concluding shot of the sequence (shot 9).

The action begins with Davidson returning to the Surabaya harbor to pick up Heyst in the year 1900, an event that takes place in part 1, chapter 5, of the novel, about 9 percent of the way into the story. By starting in medias res, Pinter has saved a great deal of time and cut out action that he considers unnecessary for his purpose.

The result of this alteration is a change in focus. Whereas in the novel Conrad wanted to establish a good portion of Heyst's character, Pinter wants to withhold or even delete this information. This is because the screenwriter is about to do what he does in his other adaptations: he is going to change the focus of the work by emphasizing an integral element from the original without trying to reproduce his source verbatim. Not only does the audience not find out about Heyst's background in general now, but when certain

1   Boat becalmed.

2   Ladies Orchestra
           —   flashes

3   Ped & Axt eating long
     fish with ~~their~~ knives.
        by bonfire.
     2 seated figures
     in   FG.

4   A slipper thrown
     out of a window.

5   ~~2 men with rifles guns~~
     Men & dogs moving
     through Jungle.

6   Cylinder gramophone
     in room. Gallieres.
                  singing.

7   2 figures suddenly
     caught in light
     in a garden at
     night.

8   A hillside.
     (high up 2 figs.
     A girl's cry.

1.   EXT. THE JAVA SEA. DAY.

Far out to sea a boat becalmed. Heat. The
mast slowly sways.

2.   LADIES' ORCHESTRA.
                    ladies orchestra.
Burst of sound. Screeching violins. Flashes of
various angles. *Bare arms.*
white dresses,
Crimson sashes.

3.   NICARAGUAN CREEK. EVENING.
Half   *Two Nicaraguan natives*
seen,   Pedro and Antonio eating fish with long knives
Through   by a fire. The backs of two *other* seated figures in
leaves,   the foreground.
hands   *Silence.*
sharpening Night sounds.
knives,

4.   A bundle thrown through a window into a
     garden at night.

                                          a
5.   Men with guns and dogs moving through jungle.

1.   A boat becalmed, far out to sea. The
     mast slowly sways. Heat haze. Red
     sun.

     Gulls encircle the boat, screeching.

2.   Screeching violins. A ladies' orchestra.
     Bare arms. White dresses. Crimson
     sashes.

3.   A wall of foliage. Bamboo spears pierce
     the foliage, quiver, stay pointed.

     Camera pans up to see, through leaves,
     impassive native faces.

4.   An island. Moonlight. Silence.

     Figures of men seen from a distance at
     the door of a low, thatched house. The
     door is kicked open. The sound
     reverberates in the night. Explosion
     of shrieking birds.

events are referred to later in the movie, they have not already been seen, so no judgment can be made as to the authenticity of the later report. The character of Morrison, for example, is removed, as, perforce, are all of the interactions between him and Heyst. In the novel, a benchmark was created through the scenes in which Heyst and Morrison meet and then interact. This benchmark was convenient as a means for elaborating on Heyst's nature and for contrast with the picture of the Swede that Schomberg later paints, a picture that is used to convince Jones and Ricardo to pursue Heyst and which also intrudes into the relationship between Heyst and Lena when she recalls hearing about how he "murdered" Morrison. Without this leavening reality, the relationship between the man and the woman is made more tentative and fragile in the film.

In addition, by withholding information, Pinter manages to create the sense of mystery that the other Europeans felt about Heyst in the novel (and coincidentally to do the same with the character of Lena), but he does so without having to tell the series of anecdotes upon which that mystery is predicated. The nicknames characterizing Heyst that were based on the uninformed observers' perceptions and misunderstanding of the protagonist's nature that grow out of those anecdotes in the novel similarly can be discarded. Furthermore, because Heyst is only referred to by name and is not even seen until scene 20, the mystery is heightened, especially since all that the audience knows up to that point is what is heard in the dialogue between Davidson, Schomberg, and Mrs. Schomberg regarding Heyst's having "run off with a whore" and "killed Morrison," being, then, the "swindler . . . ruffian . . . spy . . . impostor, [and] Schweinhund" that Schomberg portrays him to be (Pinter, 171).

At this point Pinter starts a series of flashbacks, a structure that Conrad used in the novel. First, there is a quick intercut of Pedro, Ricardo, and Jones on the banks of a Nicaraguan creek, a bit of parallel editing that links the converging plot lines (172). Next, the orchestra and Heyst are introduced. Here, however, there is also a divergence between the published script and the typescript.

In the typed manuscript there is a scene between Heyst and Morrison ("Victory," typescript, 15) in which Morrison conveys his religiously expressed appreciation for Heyst's help and declares that he will repay his savior. As in the novel (Conrad, 15), this bit of action provides one of the touchstones by which the reader is made aware of Heyst's true character. Apparently Pinter, who has shown a proclivity for such paring away in his previous writing, felt that that revelation was immaterial or at least nonessential for his purposes in the film, so the segment was excised. With it, however, also went the explanation for one of the opening dumb-show scenes—the two men drinking champagne (Pinter, 167).

One of the differences between the novel and the published screenplay is evident in the sequence that follows, in which Heyst and Lena meet and Lena is seen being mistreated by Mrs. Zangiacomo and being harassed by Schomberg. In the novel these actions are described (77); in Pinter's film script the audience actually sees the events take place (174–75). Dialogue and visual images replace the narrative. Another difference is the compression of the action so that the mistreatment of Lena and her conversations with Heyst in which she talks about her background and finds out that he lives on an island (Conrad, 82) are incorporated into the same dialogue. A third difference is in the slight changes in the actual words of that dialogue. Pinter replaces nineteenth-century phrasing and idioms with their twentieth-century equivalents. Consider Lena's protestation in Conrad:

Oh, I knew it would be all right from the first time you spoke to me! Yes, indeed, I knew directly you came up to me that evening. I knew it would be all right, if you only cared to make it so; but of course I could not tell if you meant it. . . . But you wasn't deceived. I could see you were angry with that beast of a woman. And you are clever. You spotted something at once. You saw it in my face, eh? It isn't a bad face—say? You'll never be sorry. Listen—I'm not twenty yet. It's the truth, and I can't be so bad looking, or else—I will tell you straight that I have been worried and pestered by fellows like this before. I don't know what comes to them. . . . What is it? What's the matter? . . . Is it my fault? I didn't even look at them, I tell you straight. Never! Have I looked at you? Tell me. It was you that began it. (Conrad, 80–81)

The screenwriter substitutes a shorter, simpler, more modern passage:

I saw you. I saw you. I had to come to you. . . . I knew it would be all right the first time you spoke to me. You spotted something in me, didn't you? In my face. It isn't a bad face, is it? I'm not twenty yet. All these men—they pester me all the time. . . . What is it? What's the matter? I don't lead them on. I don't look at them. Did I look at you? I did not. You began it. (Pinter, 176)

"Fellows" becomes "men," "worried and pestered" becomes "pester," "I don't know what comes to them" becomes "I don't lead them on," and so forth.

The passage also serves to change Lena's personality slightly by making her more aggressive, showing her contradicting herself in her effort to extricate herself from her unbearable condition. Additionally, Pinter excises the reference to what Lena is "called," not what her name might be—Alma or Magdalen (Conrad, 84). In the novel, the inference is that she has no name or identity sufficiently permanent to retain, and it is Heyst who gives her the name Lena (176), yet in the film script there is no suggestion that her name is anything other than Lena. This shift in characterization is an important part of Pinter's alteration and is dealt with below. As a matter of fact, it is not until nine scenes later that Lena's name is even spoken for the first time (179). For Pinter, what one is called is clearly not as important as what one does or experiences. Presumably, he does not want to take the time to present the girl as insubstantial and malleable because her change in character does not need to be so dramatic for his purposes.

Just as he cuts some of his source, so Pinter elaborates on it at times. In an inserted scene, he shows Lena's dress ripping when the hotelier tries to touch her (178), a scene that reverberates with a later scene in which her dress is ripped when she resists Heyst (189). In the novel, the later scene takes place, but there is no force involved, no ripped dress (Conrad, 203). Clearly, Pinter is drawing a parallel between the two men, and he is commenting on how Lena's presence effects them. The violence that lurks beneath the surface of many of the author's characters may be involved; it may also be that he is demonstrating that Heyst is human enough to be provoked but sufficiently strong and moral to overcome his temptations, for in the screenplay his actions lead to a "fierce embrace," whereas in the novel he sinks to the ground to kiss her.

Further elaborating on the action in the film, there are two shots, the first of the hotel garden at night, in which a bundle is thrown out of the window, and the second of a *"boat sailing away."* In the original the reader finds out about the escape when it is reported through the dialogue between Davidson and Schomberg; the actual escape is neither presented nor described. Continuing along the same line, the sceenwriter includes through action the amusing search, frantic pursuit, and farcical altercation engaged in by Schomberg and Zangiacomo that is merely described in his source. This use of humor here is a nice means of breaking the tension that has built up.

More of the crosscutting to interweave the merging plot lines occurs when Pinter inserts several silent scenes on Heyst's island (180). Heyst and Lena are seen together; Chang, who is called Wang in the novel, watches them; Lena's face is seen. This sequence is followed by an establishing shot of Surabaya Harbour and then a shot of Jones's face that provides a direct connection between Lena and Jones.[5]

Four chapters in the novel follow the arrival of Jones and Ricardo. These comprise the entire narrative that details their backgrounds and sets them at odds with Schomberg. Pinter, however, invents a scene in which Lena enters Heyst's home; he gives her his bedroom (182–83), supplying separate sleeping arrangements that are not present in the novel. The purity or nobility of Heyst's character is thus accentuated in the script. In addition, Pinter inserts two small pieces of humor as a way of further building the characters of the man and the woman, exploring their developing relationship, drawing a picture of the couple before the intrusion so that the effect of Jones and Ricardo on their lives can easily be ascertained, and holding down the tension. First, Heyst asks if Lena has said "good day" to his father, as though the father is in the room—which he is, but in the form of the portrait. Then, Heyst suggests that they listen to music on the gramophone, the music of Zangiacomo's Ladies' Orchestra.

Thereafter, the structure of the film script mirrors that of the novel, crosscutting back and forth between Heyst's island and the hotel, only at a considerably faster rate and with much shorter segments dedicated to each of the locales. There is a jarring smash cut that joins the plots together in a foreshadowing of the violent intrusion that is to come when Heyst rings a bell to call Chang to bring breakfast and the next shot is of Pedro kicking open a door to enter the hotel lobby with a tray of empty glasses. The suddenness and unexpectedness of the action, combined with Pedro's violent mannerisms, are startling, particularly in comparison to the relaxed breakfast setting with which they are juxtaposed.

Another juxtaposition occurs in the screenplay when a shot of a fully dressed Jones lying on his bed is followed by a shot of Ricardo lying on a bed naked. Since clothing is used as a social indicator, the lack of clothing symbolizes primitiveness—a contrast that in two quick visuals Pinter creates to define the nature of these two men. Conrad had drawn the distinction through numerous repeated references to Jones's gentlemanly bearing and Ricardo's beastly, feline qualities. What the novelist describes over a period of time, the screenwriter shows in a flash.

Pinter's talent for condensation is further evidenced in the sequence on Samburan when Heyst and Lena take a walk up into the mountains. Their conversation involves Heyst's relationship with Morrison and serves to replace some of the exposition that Pinter excised earlier. This segment appears in the novel, too, yet in the space of less than three pages (187–89), Pinter is able to conjure up what takes Conrad seventeen pages to describe in the novel (Conrad, 186–203)—and the adapter even uses some of the novelist's dialogue verbatim (193–94). In part the cuts are derived by removing authorial interpretations and explanations: the novelist tells; the screenwriter shows.

The divergence between the themes of the novel and the film script shows up here again, for it is in this scene that Pinter's Heyst accosts Lena and rips her dress, whereas Conrad's protagonist merely kisses her. The deviation is dramatic:

> He swerved and, stepping up to her, sank to the ground by her side. Before she could make a movement . . . he took her in his arms and kissed her lips. . . . With her hand she signed imperiously to him to leave her alone—a command which Heyst did not obey. (Conrad, 203)

> *He stands, clenched, moves away violently, and then suddenly swerves back, sits by her, takes her in his arms and kisses her. . . . He pulls her arm away. She resists. He seizes her roughly. Her dress rips. He embraces her fiercely.* (Pinter, 189)

The aftermath of this event is different in the two versions as well. In Conrad, the pair walks back down the hillside: "She felt more like herself— a poor London girl playing in an orchestra, and snatched out from the humiliations, the squalid dangers of a miserable existence, by a man like whom there was not, there could not be, another in this world. She felt this with elation, with uneasiness, with an intimate pride—and with a peculiar sinking of the heart" (204).

The emphasis in Pinter is on the man:

> *LENA walks ahead of HEYST, apart from him. As they draw nearer we see that LENA is in pain. Her dress is torn. She stumbles. HEYST is walking slowly. He stops. She continues, and then slowly stops. She stands for a moment with her back to him. He is still. She turns, looks at him. He walks to her.*
> HEYST (*Quietly*). Please . . . forgive me. (190)

There is no sharing of emotion in Pinter's picture, no coming together. Heyst is admittedly contrite for placing Lena again in the position of victim, the very condition from which he had supposedly rescued her. The action does not reflect favorably on the man. At the same time, Lena's character also is diminished by the event and her reaction to it.

When Pinter switches back to the Schomberg/Jones/Martin line (190–95), he does so in an interesting fashion. To begin, the Schomberg-Ricardo confrontation had occurred earlier in the novel (Conrad, 116–60). Now, in order to condense all of the explanatory details, the screenwriter compresses the action in such a way that repetitious and extraneous matter is omitted, and he creates a logic to the conversation between Schomberg and Ricardo by taking bits and pieces from various pages in that previous section of the novel. For instance, Ricardo's exact line, "I can make you take any card I like nine times out of ten," appears on page 117 in Conrad. The commentary "Sometimes I have a girl—you know—and I give her a nice kiss and I say to myself: 'If you only knew who's kissing you, my dear, you'd scream the place down'" is on page 122, the threat "I might get Pedro to break your neck" is moved from page 144, the revealing of the knife strapped to Ricardo's leg comes from page 129, the story about the creek in Nicaragua that begins with Jones and Ricardo appropriating the skipper's cash box starts on page 118, and the account of the treasure in the box is on page 130. Clearly, Pinter had no compunction about moving around freely in the source text.

Ricardo's narration of the tale of the two Portuguese brothers runs from page 130 to page 137 in Conrad. In Pinter, the "show, don't tell" dictum is applied, and the story is dramatized, with a few minor changes in the dialogue.[6] The suddenness of the shooting and Antonio's body sizzling when Ricardo pulls it out of the fire and kicks it into the stream are certainly intensely dramatic and vivid in the script. Moreover, the changing of Jones wiping his fingers on a plantain leaf to wiping his fingers on a silk handkerchief immediately before the shooting is a typical Pinter touch. The silk handkerchief humorously captures the stereotyped essence of the "gentleman," and it is obviously and ironically out of place in the context of the setting and of the action that follows. It is also a subtle prop that is barely noticed, in spite of these implications.

Pinter then skips forward to Schomberg's "I could put you on a track. On the track of a man," which appears on page 147 in Conrad. There is an interesting reverberation here with the cash-box description. The amount mentioned as being contained in the cash box in the novel is "one hundred twenty-seven sovereigns and some Mexican dollars" (130); in keeping with Pinter's love for specific details, in the screenplay the figures become "320 sovereigns . . . and 500 Mexican dollars" (192). The numbers are higher, and therefore more meaningful to a modern audience, and replacing "some" with "500" gives the account an added air of authenticity. Now, when Schomberg tries to convince Ricardo to pursue Heyst, he does so by holding out the promise of money that Heyst has supposedly accrued through his dirty deeds (Conrad, 149–50). For Pinter, the concept of money is transformed into "plunder" (194)—and not just any plunder, but "Minted gold" (195). This transformation makes the promised booty seem more concrete and richer, and the added detail of "Minted gold" makes Schomberg's claim seem more believable, for in identifying the nature of the plunder, he is saying that he knows specifically what Heyst has "buried or put away." Pinter's approach is far more convincing than Conrad's.

The concept of class, the "fake baron"/"hypocrite" argument on page 152 in the novel, is introduced by the screenwriter now. What he does not include, though, is Ricardo's cat-and-mouse allusion: "Have you ever seen a cat play with a mouse? It's a pretty sight." Why the cruel "pretty sight" line is not included as further evidence of Ricardo's evil nature is not clear. Perhaps Pinter felt that the qualities that mark Ricardo had been well enough established by now; perhaps it was a minor matter of time.

Having established the nature of the soon-to-be intruders, Pinter inserts an original sequence designed to reenforce the characters of Heyst and Lena and their relationship. The images of the couple sitting together, cutting the pages of a book with a kitchen knife, speaking French, in bed, Lena trimming Heyst's beard—all are calm, quiet, relaxed, and pleasantly peaceful.

The opening of the book may have an ironically symbolic significance. Lena uses a knife to cut the pages, and a knife will be the center of her attention once the intruders arrive. Furthermore, she cannot understand the book because it is in French, just as she will not really be able to understand what is happening when Jones, Ricardo, and Pedro land on the island, since their way of thinking is foreign to and in direct contrast with the civilized existence that she is enjoying with Heyst. That she wants him to "Say something to me in French" and his "Tu es très belle" (Pinter, 196) leads to lovemaking (which almost seems to be a takeoff on Charles Addams's Gomez and Morticia) is only a momentary diversion, which amusingly takes the place of Conrad's description of Heyst reading his own father's books.

It is in this section, however, that two of Conrad's most important and ironic lines are incorporated: Lena says to Heyst, "You should try to love me" (Conrad, 208; Pinter, 197), and Heyst innocently claims that "Nothing can break in on us here" (Conrad, 210). There is little doubt by now in either Conrad's or Pinter's versions of the story that Heyst loves Lena, though in Conrad, Lena's request is amplified by her saying, "It seems to me that you can never love me for myself . . . as people do love each other when it is to be for ever" (208–9); in Pinter, the "for myself" is deleted: "You should try to love me as people do love each other when it is to be for ever." The shift in emphasis is slight, but significant. By putting the onus on Heyst, the screenwriter has made the heroine a bit more independent and self-assured than she is in the novelist's portrayal.

This scene also contains another characteristic of Pinter's screenplays: according to the stage directions, the couple is listening to a gramophone recording of the singing of Rosalia Chalier. Conrad does not identify a singer, but Pinter's choice is appropriate and an accurate addition because Rosalia Chalia (1866–1961) was a famous nineteenth-century soprano who specialized in classical operatic love ballads (see page 391; "Chalier" is probably a typographical error).

This section of the script is provocative in that it reveals how and why Pinter invents and incorporates new material and moves around in his source text to create his own interpretation of a story. The novel may be his starting place, but he frequently finds thematic lines that lead in parallel yet different directions from those followed by the source's author.

That approach carries over into the next section. Conrad's depiction of the intruder's arrival (212–30) is considerably abridged in the screenplay (197–201). Pinter's presentation is more dramatic as well. Instead of having the boat jammed under the jetty, the screenwriter devises an action segment in which Heyst and Chang row out to *"The boat ricocheting against the rocks on the ocean side of the reef"* (198), and Heyst in essence takes possession of the boat in rescuing it. The law of salvage is that by virtue of tying a rope to the boat and towing it ashore, Heyst claims ownership of the boat. Thus, ironically, he is saving those who will destroy him and the only person whom he loves; the seeds of their destruction are of his own sowing. This is a theme that has run through many of the films that Pinter has scripted, beginning with *The Servant* and *Accident*. Heyst's perceived aloofness, his willingness to intrude on behalf of those in need, his falling under the control of events in spite of his desire to remain separate and uninvolved in life, all are part of the karmic puzzle that eventually destroys him. Pinter captures the substance of this in what initially seems to be a minor alteration in the plot.

The conclusion of the screenplay once more exhibits the difference between prose and film as demonstrated in Pinter's adaptations. In Conrad's novel, the narrator tells the Excellency about the burning house and Heyst holding Lena's body in the midst of the inferno. In Pinter's script, the minor points of Pedro's death (Conrad, 382) at the hands of Wang (284) and Jones's death by drowning (384) are omitted because they are moralistic rather than being central to the story, which is about Heyst and Lena. Instead, we see the conflagration, and the last shot is a long shot: the "*Camera holds on the scene*" (Pinter, 226). The impact of the ironic realization that Lena thought that she had died to save him when she had not and that he could not live without her is more powerful because it is not diminished by the extraneous moralizing, and the image of the fire remains long after the persistence of vision effect is gone.

The major difference between the typescript and the published screenplay is the cutting of some of the scenes and dialogue. This is the pattern that Pinter typically pursues in writing his film scripts—the earlier versions are fuller, more information-packed; the final version is lean, keeping only the essentials required to express his meaning. This approach is the reason that *Victory* is one of Pinter's strongest and most moving screenplays.

Turtle Diary

RELEASED: 1985

SOURCE: *Turtle Diary,* by Russell Hoban; novel (1975)

PRODUCTION COMPANY: United British Artists–Britannic, presented by the Samuel Goldwyn Company

DIRECTOR: John Irvin

EDITOR: Peter Tanner

CINEMATOGRAPHER: Peter Hannan

EXECUTIVE PRODUCER: Peter Snell

PRODUCER: Richard Johnson

PRODUCTION DESIGNER: Leo Austin

ART DIRECTORS: Diane Danklefsen and Judith Ariadne Lang

MUSIC: Geoffrey Burgon

SOUND EDITOR: Teddy Mason

COSTUME DESIGNER: Elizabeth Waller

CAST: Glenda Jackson (Neaera Duncan), Ben Kingsley (William Snow), Richard Johnson (Johnson), Michael Gambon (George Fairbairn), Rosemary Leach (Mrs. Inchcliff), Eleanor Bron (Miss Neap), Harriet Walter (Harriet Sims), Jeroen Krabbe (Sandor), Nigel Hawthorne (Publisher), Michael Aldridge (Mr. Meager), Gary Olsen (Lorry Driver), Harold Pinter (Man in Bookshop), Rom Anderson (Girl at Zoo), Tony Melody (Garage Attendant), Peter Capaldi (Assistant Keeper), Barbara Rosenblatt (American Woman), Chuck Julian (American Man), Pauline Letts (Woman in Bookshop)

RUNNING TIME: 96 minutes[1]

COLOR

VIDEO: Vestron

IN CHOOSING RUSSELL HOBAN'S novel for his source, Pinter set himself a new challenge. *Turtle Diary* is in many ways his most conventional film, a love story without the typical Pinteresque element of underlying mysterious menace. It is also probably his most "popular" motion picture, as well as the cinematic work least noticed by critics.[2]

As are several other sources for Pinter's cinematic adaptations (e.g., *The Pumpkin Eater, The Go-Between*), Hoban's novel is presented in an epistolary form as diary entries, so there is no third-person narrator. Instead, the story is told from the alternating points of view of the two protagonists, William G. and Neaera H. William, a bookstore clerk, and Neaera, the authoress of children's books, have reached a dead end in their middle-aged lives. Although not a lot is disclosed about their pasts, it is known that William is divorced and the father of grown daughters. Neaera lives alone, too, and seems to be bothered by her childhood; her father apparently had considerable influence on her life. The two are drawn together by their concern for three giant sea turtles that have been in the aquarium at the London Zoo for thirty years.

Independently, William and Neaera decide to free the turtles, to release them back into the sea. When they discover this mutual interest, they enlist the help of George Fairbairn, the turtles' keeper, and they eventually effect the animals' release. In the meantime, there is considerable individual philosophizing about themselves and about why they are involved in the escapade. In the nonturtle portion of their lives, they seek to break out of the boxes in which they are trapped. William, for instance, visits offbeat pseudotherapists who offer escape through biofeedback and "Original Therapy" (in which an American woman wrestler squeezes people between her legs). In the turtle portion of their lives, they become convinced that they are driven by fate to rescue the turtles. Mixed in are William's affair with bookstore coworker Harriett, Neaera's affair with George, William's confrontation with his childhood (which is represented by the port of Polperro), the symbolic importance of stones that the two collected in their youth, and their daily lives and work. The actual releasing of the turtles takes place about two-thirds of the way through the novel.

The events that occur in the last quarter of the book reflect how the rescue impacts on the lives of the rescuers. Like the protagonist in *Close Encounters of the Third Kind*, they have become involved in something bigger than themselves, drawn to something that they do not quite understand in order to find their own freedom. No longer are William and Neaera at the mercy of fate; they aggressively take control of their own lives. By becoming engaged in the plight of the animals, the hero and the heroine become more human. William challenges Sandor about cleaning the bathroom and the

Turtle Diary (1985). Ben Kingsley as William and Glenda Jackson as Neaera watching the turtles swim free. United British Artists–Britannic. Jerry Ohlinger Archives.

kitchen that they share in their apartment building; Neaera develops a social life with George and is freed from her writer's block. By releasing the turtles, they free themselves.

There is nothing earthshaking in the novel, but Hoban presents a picture of how easy it is for people to become trapped in apathy, living dull, meaningless lives. Through a fateful intervention, the two main characters are shaken back into being emotionally alive, not in a flamboyantly heroic, easy moon leap, but in a quietly unselfish action that is heroic nonetheless. The maiden effort of the production company UBA (United British Artists), a consortium consisting of Pinter, Glenda Jackson, Albert Finney, Maggie Smith,

John Hurt, Diana Rigg, and producer Richard Johnson, at one point *Turtle Diary* showed a domestic gross of $2,157,000. Billed as a romantic comedy, the movie is about the relationship that develops between two people dealing with environmental matters that serve as the menacing context for their antisocial yet ultimately supremely humane actions. Thus, the screenwriter must work with characters who are considerably less desperate than those who normally fill his works, and he has to transfer to the screen a story that is told in the form of diary entries written in the first person by the two protagonists, renamed William Snow and Neaera Duncan in the movie.

The result, in the words of a *Los Angeles Times* film critic, is "special and beautiful, funny, lyrical and utterly unexpected." Roger Ebert finds *Turtle Diary* "sly and immensely amusing" (676). These are not the kinds of critical reactions that Pinter's films have generally elicited. To a large extent this reaction results from the screenwriter's typical simplification of his source. In collapsing the two diaries into a third-person point of view, he reduces both the verbiage and the philosophical content drastically. All of the narrative and dialogue that compose the novel are compressed to almost nothing. Words are replaced by cinematic images. Of the dialogue that is included, some is taken nearly verbatim from the original text; an equal amount is Pinter's invention, though the flashes of wit that characterize his work are less evident than usual.

More importantly, he has changed the nature of the product by his other changes and deletions. Although the published script retains the night setting for the rescue mission, in the film the event takes place from midday to sunset—presumably to make the action more visible. Pinter also retains Polperro as the seaport from which the turtles are launched; in the film that has changed, too. In the novel William and Neaera independently assume that if the tide is in when they reach the sea, this symbolizes fate's approval of their venture. They are both pleased when they find that it is in. Pinter retains this factor in the script, but it is not included in the motion picture. The lady wrestler, the biofeedback, the incident in the café in which Neaera overhears a couple in the next booth talking and mistakenly thinks that they are William and Harriett, the stones, Sandor's attempt to reconcile with William after their second battle, the coroner's inquest—these are not incorporated in the film, though some appear in the script. This is important, for each of these elements relates to Hoban's characterization of William and Neaera. Ironically, in the movie the very matter that Pinter normally would exploit to make the artwork his own is excised. This includes all of the main characters' interior monologues, and, unlike the other cases in which he distills the substance of his source, here the elimination of the interior monologues removes some of the essence.

The reasons for some of these alterations are evident. Since the relationship between William and Harriett is not considered with all of its ramifications, owing to the absence of William's contemplations (expressed in the film only by occasional facial expressions rather than in actual thoughts, which is how it was done in the novel), the nature of that relationship changes a bit. Instead of Sandor, then, it is Harriett who visits William in his bedroom after the fight. This leaves the relationship between William and Sandor unsettled, so Sandor's gesture comes at the table after Miss Neap's suicide (he agrees with William that her funeral arrangements should be as she described in her suicide note). And, the suicide is accomplished by hanging in the novel but by an overdose in the movie, presumably because overdoses are more civilized and quiet, more in keeping with Miss Neap's character. In a sense, the Pinter-invented gesture, which obviously grows out of the shared feelings about Miss Neap's escape from her boxed-in existence, is thus more closely aligned with the theme of freedom that informs the film.

The differences between the script and the film are minimal. There is a sequence involving a policeman that is deleted;[3] Polperro becomes Devon, as does Cornwall (137); there are minor changes in dialogue, as when Sandor comments on William's carpentry (137); some details are modified to be more realistic (the height of the turtles' boxes is increased from one foot to two feet); the method of placing the turtles in the water (in the prose version, the boxes with the turtles in them are carried on a trolley and then thrown into the water) becomes more human and hands-on (William and Neaera remove the turtles from the boxes and carry them into the water, where the animals are placed gently in the wavelets) (149–50); a funny sequence in which William observes a pigeon walk onto an underground car, travel to the next stop, and then walk off, is removed (120).

In Pinter's script, the opening shot is of "GIANT TURTLES SWIMMING IN THE SEA" (103). The movie begins with a slow-motion shot of turtles swimming, but it is soon revealed that they are swimming in the tank in the aquarium. William is then seen through the glass walls of the tank, from the turtles' point of view, observing the animals. The filmed version is the more effective, especially since the final shot is of the turtles swimming in the ocean. These shots thus frame the story, and the animals' gentle, graceful gliding nicely captures the emotional uplifting that comes with their freedom. Ultimately, it is this sense of freedom that *Turtle Diary* is about. In Pinter's version, the freedom is less complicated than in Hoban's.

The dialogue is typically Pinteresque: colloquially simple, clipped, a bit unconnected, a bit fey. "I used to make things," Snow says. "What things?" asks Mrs. Inchcliff. "Oh, you know. This and that." Similarly, the screenwriter's sense of humor is present. When Pinter appears, book in hand, as the Man in the Bookshop, he asks the salesman (not William, as indicated in the script [111]), "Have you got the sequel to this?" The salesman responds, "Sequel? Is there one?" "Somebody told me there was one," answers the Man. "No, this is the sequel to the one before, you see." "The one before?" Elsewhere, when asked by Harriet whether he had "ever been married," William remembers, "I must have been. I had two daughters. They were little once. They used to sit in my lap." To Harriet's "Were you a good father?" William answers, "They thought so. But they were only children at the time" (126–27). And, in a scene changed in the film (part of the dialogue is retained in William's conversation with Fairbairn), William telephones the zoo:

MAN. Zoo here.

WILLIAM (*Voice over*). Hello, is that the Zoo?

MAN. Zoo here.

> *The following sequence is intercut between* WILLIAM *in a coin box and the receptionist.* MAN *in Zoo's reception.*

WILLIAM. I think you should be warned. I'm going to steal some of your animals.

MAN. Oh yes? What kind of animals?

WILLIAM. Big ones.

MAN. When are you going to do it?

WILLIAM. Soon.

MAN. How are you going to do it?

WILLIAM. I'm not going to tell you.

MAN. I see. Well, thanks for letting us know.

WILLIAM. Not at all. (138–39)

Billington points out that Pinter's dialogue is full of subtext that runs counter to what is being said. The biographer cites as an example the conversation between William and Neaera in which William seems to argue desperately for inaction while at the same time accepting her counters and finally ending up agreeing with her that action must be taken (300–301). The procedure has a Hamletian ring to it.

In many of Pinter's stage dramas, there is virtually no exposition. The audience observes a group of characters who are discovered in medias res, who know each other and are in the midst of a conversation the antecedents of which they are well aware but about which the audience has no clue. It is like getting on a bus and sitting behind a couple who are talking. At some point either they or we have to get off the bus, and the only information that we have is what was said during the time that we were on the bus together. We are left with what we heard and what we can infer, and if we so desire, we can try to make some sense of what we have heard. Unlike Shavian characters, Pinter's characters feel no need to explain themselves to the audience, to discuss their family backgrounds, their jobs, their salaries, their problems, their proclivities—they share that knowledge already. The characters act as we would in a similar situation. This is realism. And, Pinter views life realistically, so, as demonstrated above, occasionally vignettes are included that are tangential to the plot, although they usually shed some light on what is happening in one way or another.

In *Turtle Diary*, one of these incidents occurs in the bookshop when Pinter appears as a character and we learn that "Penrose" has died (110). Nothing further is made of this; no knowledge is relayed to the audience about who Penrose was or his relationship to the plot or characters. There is some connection with the unexpected death of Miss Neap, and the idea of the fragility of life and the ubiquitousness of death are counterpoints to the celebration of life embodied in the release of the turtles. But, again, this is what might happen in an actual bookshop, and Pinter wants his audience to be aware that while what they are watching is a work of art, at the same time it is a work of art based on a real world.

A great deal of the action in the early sequences of the film documents the simple, everyday nature of the characters' lives. They do the normal, uncomplicated things that have to do with living. In the background of one scene, an elderly man and woman are seen walking their dog. Pinter's films are filled with these little details that connect the work to life outside the theatre; they also serve to emphasize the humanity of the main characters.[4] There is the waiter who almost drops his tray while serving William and Harriet. In another scene, when William turns after talking with one of the women, the thinning hair on the back of his head has a Prufrockian resonance. Later, after receiving the telephone call from Fairbairn (played by

Michael Gambon, a veteran of several Pinter productions), in which he is told the dimensions of the boxes that he must build, William starts upstairs to go back to his room and then has to run back down to retrieve the piece of paper on which he has recorded those dimensions. This little lapse, not included in the published script, is amusing, but it is also the kind of human touch that captures an audience and helps explain why so many people are taken with this quiet film.

Some of the seemingly insignificant details have functions other than just providing a context in the aggregate. There is a large photograph of Beckett high on the bookshop wall (seen several times). Such a photograph would be appropriate for the setting, naturally, but it probably was included as an homage to Beckett as well.[5] There are many overheard partial conversations that are unconnected to the dialogue between the main characters but which bear on the meaning of the film (tidbits about the turtles' lives, for instance, delivered by recording in the aquarium, and snatches about pop music). The most important of these events occurs when Neaera sees a young woman and a young man talking in the aquarium. The couple is seen briefly in profile, backlit by one of the large tanks. "No! It's too late," the girl says. This revelation startles Neaera and leads to her dream of the shark attacking William.

For many viewers, *Turtle Diary* is a movie about the environment and animal rights. Certainly, this is an important part of the message. Naturally, there is more to it than this, or it is likely that Pinter would not have chosen to write the film script. Images of solitude—William standing outlined against the bare blue wall of his room or leaning against a curtainless window frame, Neaera asleep on her couch in an apartment devoid of life other than her water beetle—fill the opening scenes. Early on Neaera asks Fairbairn whether the turtles are happy. His answer is no. A parallel is drawn between the animals and the humans. A children's author who writes about anthropomorphic animal characters, Neaera is facing creative burnout, and she has no human connections to turn to. William has suffered through a broken marriage, he is no longer in touch with his daughters, and he has turned his back on a successful career for the low pay and minimal responsibilities of a book salesman: "I did have ambitions once. I was going to discover the Amazon. . . . I was married. I was 'in business.' Out in the big world. A long time ago. Didn't like any of it. So I thought I'd find a nice little corner, in a nice little bookshop, keep out of trouble" (126, 127). His life is as lonely as

Neaera's. Apparently this is the case with Fairbairn, too. It is also apparent that Fairbairn has considered releasing the turtles himself—he has suggested as much to his employers, and he has the drill for their release figured out in detail down to the dimensions of the wooden boxes lined with foam rubber that will be needed to transport the turtles to the sea—so a conspiracy is easily concocted between the three humans.

As they drive the turtles toward Devon, William says, "Perhaps we can ride on the back of the turtles. . . . Is that what we're doing?" Neaera responds, " I hadn't really thought." Thematically, this is a turning point in the plot. The characters, lost in their own solitary worlds, joined only by accident through the plight of the turtles, suddenly are looking beyond the turtles. Structurally, though, this is not a cinematic plot point.

The cinematic point comes with the release of the turtles into the sea and William and Neaera's joyous dance of liberation as they are silhouetted against the gorgeous sunset into which the turtles have swum. Up to this time, the tension in the movie has been generated by the questions of whether the humans can kidnap and successfully free the turtles. There is a subplot of whether the kidnappers can connect individually with other humans and escape from their own caged lives of desperate separation, maybe even in each other's company. The release of the turtles comes at about the seventy-minute mark in the film; there are another twenty-six minutes left. This is not an extended anticlimax; it is this remaining quarter of the motion picture that probably attracted Pinter.

The source of tension in the concluding segment has to do with the question of what is going to become of the characters now that they have achieved their goal. Will they be changed? At first it seems as though Pinter is going to supply a simple answer. William returns to his rooming house to find that Sandor is still leaving the bathtub and the kitchen range filthy. They have had words and scuffled over Sandor's unsavory hygiene before, and William has not managed to change his adversary's approach to cleanliness. Now, he is ready to resume his challenge. The formula is in place for a Rocky-like confrontation in which William, the embodiment of right revitalized by his turtle experience, will rise up and smite the Goliath Sandor. But, the result of the battle is that both men are brought to the ground, neither physically victorious over the other and neither managing to make his attitude prevail.

Next comes the suicide of Miss Neap. From the bright high of the turtles' deliverance into the warm currents that will carry the amphibians to Ascension Island and the location of their birth and breeding grounds, the audience is suddenly confronted with a somber death. It is out of this event that the second meaning of the motion picture arises.

What seems to be a feel-good movie about saving a trio of captive turtles is indeed that, yet those who see this as the primary theme of *Turtle Diary* underestimate the film. The first indication that there is more to the movie than this sentimental theme comes after the turtles are gone. William and Neaera repair to the van to sleep. There is a high overhead shot of the van in the middle of a virtually empty parking lot by the sea. Through time-lapse photography, the lot is seen filling up with cars and active people. Whereas William and Neaera were alone in their journey to free the turtles, now they are engulfed by society. How this differs from the previous state is revealed by Miss Neap's death. "I never knew," laments Mrs. Inchcliff. William observes, "We never asked." By changing the "I" to "We," he is sharing blame, as George did with Martha in *Who's Afraid of Virginia Woolf?* In this case, though, the blame is more societal in scope, and William's acceptance of this fact contrasts with his earlier divorcement from the rest of humanity when he refused to become engaged in the human activities of passersby.

This has been prepared for throughout the movie by the sea/water symbolism. The picture opens with the underwater shot (taken by Egil Woxholt) of the turtles swimming. The sea and water represent life and freedom to the turtles (who must be doused with a bucket-full of water every three hours on their trip to the coast). Literally and symbolically, the same meanings accrue for William and Neaera. She chooses to study a water beetle as the possible subject for her next book. Her shark dream is set in the sea—and it is another key to the meaning of the film. If she does not rescue the turtles, no one will ("No. Not mine," she shouts at the shark protectively). More importantly, she realizes that if she and William do not act, they themselves will die. The goal of the van journey is to reach the sea, and the goal is reached through cooperation (Neaera warns William when he is driving the large vehicle too close to other objects).

All of these things come together with Miss Neap's death. She and this event provide the contrast that illuminates the theme. Like William and Neaera, she has lived an isolated, solitary, depressed life. Unlike them, she seeks release in embracing death rather than in the celebration of life. William and Neaera revel in a passage from Melville's *Moby Dick:* "Ship and boat diverged; the cold damp night breeze blew between; a screaming gull flew overhead; the two hulls wildly rolled; we gave three hearty cheers and blindly plunged like fate into the lone Atlantic." They engage in a positive, life-affirming, proactive action, and it saves them. Miss Neap does not, and she dies with a copy of the *Common Book of Prayer* in her hands; it is open at "For the Burial of the Dead at Sea" (160). To a large extent, the film's music unites these meanings. The upbeat theme music is at the same time languid and gentle, yet rich and full. It duplicates the movement of the turtles in the water.

In an interesting shot, William is seen in a close-up from the side as he looks out into the night through a window. Two partial images of his face are reflected back at him in the glass pane, mirroring his fragmented state of mind. By the movie's conclusion, the three main characters have all existentially made themselves whole in terms of being able to relate to other human beings. The circle has been completed with Fairbairn's assuring Neaera that the turtles are happy now. In the prose version, there is no final conversation between William and Neaera outside the building to bring closure to this segment of their lives and to set up a future meeting. William merely delivers the bottle of champagne and then returns to work in a taxi. In the film, Neaera and Fairbairn have found each other, and Neaera and William agree to meet again in twenty years to set loose the baby turtles that will replace those already on their long journey home. They have grown immeasurably in the course of the film, and this agreed-upon appointment suggests the potential for further growth. William, who has established a relationship with Harriet, is seen walking away from the aquarium. He is alone, but the camera moves back in a high, bird's-eye crane shot revealing the zoo as a whole and then the city that surrounds it. William is striding toward the city and his reentrance into human society even as we hear zoo animal noises over.

The credits roll over a scene similar to that which opened the film: the turtles swimming. This time, though, the turtles are swimming freely in the ocean. At one point two of them come together, almost like the human characters, and nuzzle before continuing their trip back to their ancestral home.

Among the scenes in the movie that could not have been done on stage and which show the superiority of film over drama in certain instances is the filling of the car park in Devon. In the novel both of the protagonists describe the morning after the release of the turtles. William and Neaera mention almost in passing the other tourists: "Vans with curtains in the windows were parked on either side of us and people inside them were being domestic. Refreshment and souvenir stands were open at the car-park entrance" ([146]); "We slowly made our way through tourists and their children to the public lavatory" ([148]). If Hoban intends these brief comments to demonstrate the reentrance of his protagonists into the social world, the indications are very subtle.

In his script, Pinter calls for a simple shot:

EXT. CAR PARK. AFTERNOON
The car park is packed. Dozens of people, children.
Refreshments and souvenir stands at the entrance.
Bright sun. (151)

The scene could be described on stage, but it could not be realized easily. It is an important scene, though, for it does carry the idea of enveloping humanity as the two conspirators become reengaged in human society. The effectiveness of film in relaying this concept is evidenced in the stop-motion special effect that reenforces a sense of life and growth—and it does so even more effectively than Pinter's conception.

In the same vein is the scene that concludes the story, the final conversation between William and Neaera outside the aquarium. In both the novel and the film script, the entire meeting takes place inside the building. William says that he took a taxi back to work in the original; he walks toward the aquarium's exit in the screenplay. Neither of these versions carries the symbolic weight of the filmed version—the overhead shot of William in the zoo, walking toward the city—and the emotionally uplifting final sequence of the turtles swimming freely in the ocean flows much more naturally and smoothly out of the expanding image presented in the film.

Reunion

RELEASED: 1990

SOURCE: *Reunion* by Fred Uhlman, novel (1971)

AWARDS: Nominated for In Competition, Cannes Film Festival; Cannes Film Festival Best Actor nomination (Christien Anholt)

PRODUCTION COMPANY: Sovereign Pictures, Ariane Films/Burning Secret

DIRECTOR: Jerry Schatzberg

EDITOR: Martine Barraque-Currie

CINEMATOGRAPHER: Bruno de Keyzer

EXECUTIVE PRODUCER: Anne Francois

PRODUCER: Vincent Malle

ASSOCIATE PRODUCER: Henry J. Bamberger

PRODUCTION DESIGNERS: Alexander Trauner, Monty Diamond, Jurgen Kussatz

ARTISTIC DIRECTOR: Didier Naert

SOUND DESIGNER: Laurent Quaglio

MUSIC: Philippe Sarde

COSTUME DESIGNER: Dave Perry

CAST: Jason Robards (Henry Strauss), Christien Anholt (Hans Strauss), Samuel West (Konradin von Lohenburg), Francoise Fabian (Grafin von Lohenburg), Maureen Kerwin (Lisa), Jacques Brunet (Herr von Lohenburg), Barbara Jefford (Mrs. Strauss), Bert Parnaby (Herr Strauss), Alexandre Trauner (Man at Warehouse Office), Dorothea Alexander (Old Grafin), Frank Baker (The Zionist), Tim Barker (Herr Zimmerman), Imke Barnstedt (Girl in Tax Building), Gideon Boulting (Prince Hubertus), Alan Bowyer (Bollacher), Rupert Degas (Muller), Robert Dietl (Gardener), Luc-Antoine Diquero (Young Lover), Jorg Doring (Bartender), Gerd Duwner (Man at Cemetery), Gerhard Fries (Bossner), Henning Gissel (Man in Warehouse Office), James Ind (Erhard), Yang Kyu Kim (Japanese Businessman), Helmut Krauss (TV Presenter), Lee Lyford (Von Hankhofen), Nicholas Pandolfi (Reuter), Amelie Pick (Young Lover), Steven Poynter (Frank), Alf Reigel (Taxi Driver), Struan Rodger (Pompetski), Shebah Ronay (Young Gertrude Grafin), Roland

Schaefer (Judge Freisler), Peter Schiff (Elderly Man), Frederick Warder
(Muscle Max), Paula Herold, Debbie McWilliams
Running time: 110 minutes[1]
Color
Rating: PG-13
Video: HBO

In 1991, two years after *Reunion* was released, Pinter told Barry Davis
that "the Holocaust is actually the most appalling thing that has ever happened." In response to the question, "More horrific because it was the product of an advanced civilization in Germany?" he responded: "Absolutely so.
I don't think we'll ever get to the bottom of the actual guilt, of the actions of
the German people. But there's also the question of complicity." An active
opponent of capital punishment, the author also admitted in regard to the
British War Crimes Bill that "I'm on the side of the hangers in this case. . . .
I would get these boys if they are murderers"(Davis, 15). Two years later, he
essentially repeated these sentiments when he mentioned to Gussow that he
was reading about the Third Reich, which he called "the worst thing that
ever happened" (*Conversations,* 137). This opinion is one that Pinter has
held for some time.[2]

There are obvious thematic connections between *Reunion,* one of Pinter's
finest screenplays, and his scripts for *The Quiller Memorandum* and *The
Diaries of Etty Hillesum.* His concern with the politics of individual freedom
has been ongoing, at least as a subtext, since *The Room* and is clearly pronounced in his stage writing from *A Kind of Alaska* (1982) through *One for
the Road, Mountain Language,* and *Party Time* (1991) and in his screenplays *Langrishe, Go Down, The Heat of the Day,* and *The Handmaid's Tale,*
which deal with fascism. In *The Quiller Memorandum,* this is his underlying
theme; in *Reunion* he addresses the concern head on. In addition, the playwright was attracted by Uhlman's style: "My mother . . . gave me REUNION
to read about five years ago. . . . I thought it a most strong - and precise -
story, written with a great economy of style."[3]

Authors surely like some of their works better than others; *Reunion*
appears to be one of Pinter's favorites. In the long conversation that Hudgins
and I had with the writer in 1994, Pinter kept going back to the 1990 film in
his comments. It was a "very well made" and "very underrated" film, in his
opinion, and he explained why, particularly in reference to Stephen Spielberg's
blockbuster, *Schindler's List,* which had been released earlier in 1994.

The problems that Jews face in their everyday lives has long been a concern of Pinter's, going back to his own experiences as a youngster growing up in London during World War II.[4] As noted in the discussion of *The Trial*, the Jewish "question" continues to distress the writer, and the treatment of Jews in Germany during the Holocaust certainly is the ultimate symbol for this concern.

Thus, while Pinter felt that Spielberg's movie contained some excellent footage and was important because it was useful in bringing the Holocaust to the attention of the popular audience, he indicated that there were major problems in the film. The most glaring was Schindler's conversion near the end of the film. Pinter personally found the sudden change "unbelievable," and he argued that most audiences would agree with him. He contended that Schindler's sudden articulateness was equally unbelievable and therefore further undercut the credibility of the conversion.

As a counter to Schindler's sudden eloquence, the screenwriter described the scene in *Reunion* in which Hans, who is now called Henry (a psychologically suggestive change made by Pinter), has returned to Stuttgart and visits his old school. Henry tells the headmaster, Brossner, "I've had no contact with Germany at all, in fact, until now. I haven't read a German book or a German newspaper. I haven't spoken a word of the German language . . . in all that time," to which Brossner merely "*grunts*" in reply.[5] In recapping this scene, Pinter said that Brossner's reply was "Umm," a simple dismissal of Henry's statement and a refusal to comment on all that had happened in Germany during and after World War II and all that was signified by the personal statement. Jabbing his finger in the air in proud triumph, Pinter exclaimed, "I wrote that 'Umm!'" That "Umm," he felt, said everything that he wanted to say in a much more eloquent way than Schindler's oration does.

Pinter found fault with Spielberg's shower scene as well. Herding the women into a room with shower heads coming out of the ceiling that the audience knows are to be used to deliver gas, yet which are suddenly discovered to be nothing more than shower heads, he felt was "false," a conscious misleading of the audience for a "melodramatic" purpose. He claimed, in addition, that there was no reasonable purpose for giving the women a shower at that point. Furthermore, he agreed that Alain Resnais's *Night and Fog* (1955) and even Sidney Lumet's *Pawnbroker* (1964) with Rod Steiger are more devastatingly effective in their portrayal of the horror of the Holocaust. He was disappointed in the ending of *Schindler's List,* too. The anticlimactic bringing together of the survivors in the graveyard was dramatically uncalled for and ineffective, he thought.

Reunion (1990). Jason Robards as Henry at the Holocaust Museum. Sovereign Pictures/Castle Hill. Jerry Ohlinger Archives.

Speaking about his own canon, director Jerry Schatzberg has said, "Most of my films are about relationships" (Van Gelder, Jan. 22, 1988). The expression of that thought led to a minor disagreement with Pinter while *Reunion* was being filmed. From location in Germany, the director called the writer and said that the taxi-driver scene did not work because he was trying to get across the idea that there was a certain kind of personality, perhaps specifically German, but certainly a specific kind of personality that was simply not friendly. Apparently he inserted a Jewish/American slander line ("I'm tired of driving American Jews around Stuttgart") that for the director made the scene work and gave Henry the motivation for responding in German, something that the character had refused to do up to then because of his feeling that he and his family had been betrayed by their own country. Pinter's opinion is that that was not as subtle as his original, on the one hand, and that it was unbelievable, on the other. No taxi driver who is interested in a tip would say something like that, according to the screenwriter. His own vision was that the whole idea that Henry would recognize something about the self-righteous pushiness of the German character in a situation such as this was sufficient to get across a much broader and in some ways more subtle attitude toward the current generation in Germany. Perhaps Pinter felt that he had already made that point more bluntly in *Quiller,* which may be why he is so fond of the "Umm" line.

In any case, Schatzberg had high praise for his screenwriter: "I have enormous respect for Harold. I felt the combination would make a very good wedding. And it did. Including our differences and fights! But there was an openness that I liked. What Harold does is get right to the point, he doesn't flower it and decorate it. We both love the book. And it was one of the best working relationships I can remember with a writer."[6]

As he had with *The Servant,* Pinter took a novella, in this case a 101-page prose piece by a noted painter, and turned it into an excellent motion picture. Despite Arthur Koestler's claim that Fred Uhlman's original is a "minor masterpiece" (7), there is no question that Pinter's screenplay is far superior to his source.

In the novella, Hans Strauss describes his life from the time the "he," Graf von Hohenfels, called Konradin, comes into a classroom at Karl Alexander Gymnasium in Stuttgart two days after the narrator's sixteenth birthday (11). The narrator is the only child of a respected Jewish doctor who proudly fought for his country in World War I and who has an Iron Cross to show for his distinguished service. Soon Hans and Konradin become friends, and between the taunts of school bullies and the Nazi sympathizers on the school staff, the pair comes of age as they philosophize about the nature of God, sex, and the unfolding political upheaval.

The adventures are largely those that might occur in the life of a sixteen-year-old boy going to an all-boys school. Aside from the expected, however, certain themes begin to surface. Hans's next-door neighbors are the Bauers, and one day when he and Konradin are coming to his home after school, they discover that the Bauer house has burned down and the three young children are dead. This leads Hans to question the existence of God, just as the highborn Konradin's friendship with a Jew has caused Konradin to think about his family background and his mother's hatred for Jews.

As the story proceeds, the rise of the National Socialist Party intrudes on the lives of the two boys more and more. Under the tutelage of a new schoolmaster, Pompetzki, the other boys at the school turn ugly in their Jew-baiting of Hans.[7] Within a year of Konradin's first appearance, conditions in Stuttgart disintegrate rapidly, and Hans's father sends him to America to live with an uncle. In the final eight pages of the novella, Hans talks about his life in

America, where he became a successful attorney. All of the events that the mature Hans describes have been brought to his mind when he receives an appeal for a donation for a memorial to the Karl Alexander Gymnasium boys who died in the war. The lines that give the story its meaning are the final two sentences in the book: "VON HOHENFELS, Konradin, implicated in the plot to kill Hitler. *Executed*" (112).

From the first word in *Reunion*, "He," the story has really been as much about Konradin as it has been about Hans. Despite his admiration for Hitler ("as soon as one listens to him one is carried away by the sheer power of his convictions, his iron will, his demonic intensity and prophetic insight," 102–3), Konradin has learned something from Hans—"You have taught me to think" (103)—and it is this lesson that is evident in the novella's last line. Because of Hans, Konradin is able to rise above his emotions, nationalistic propaganda, and his own family's beliefs to the truth. He is willing to act on behalf of what is right (as he had on a lesser level in earlier episodes at school and in the open-air café [81]) and to suffer the consequences for his actions.

What Pinter does is to humanize the tale by focusing on Hans. The movie begins with the titles over a dark screen and the sound of slow, uneven footsteps. Soon, the image of an execution chamber appears on the screen, and a group of prisoners is being brought in. This is followed by a series of shots that turn out to be highlights in the story. There is a picture of a young girl being pushed in a swing by her father, Konradin's first entrance into the classroom, a band of Nazis marching along a lakeshore, exercises in the school gymnasium, and a scene from Josef von Sternberg's *Blue Angel,* among others. Intercut are sequences involving the adult Hans: in New York City's Central Park when he thinks that his granddaughter is being attacked by a German shepherd (and, of course, a German shepherd is featured in a later scene, when Hans's father stands up to a Nazi soldier); in his high-rise office preparing for a trip back to Germany to take care of the belongings left behind when his parents committed suicide instead of joining him in America; having lunch with his daughter.[8]

Pinter utilizes the device of a proleptic serial montage that he had developed in *The Proust Screenplay* and *Victory.* Knowles summarizes the working of this technique: "Intermittently, flashes of personal memory or public images of moment are used to supplement the narrative, endowing the image with greater significance than that of mere object or event. This technique complements the scene in the Stuttgart warehouse, in which Henry confronts the fragments of memory and history, a Germany he shut from his mind fifty-five years ago. The painful mosaic of the past is reassembled as the film progresses, the sporadic ravings of the Fascist Judge Freisler finally falling into place as he raves against the anti-Hitler conspirators" (*Understanding,* 171–72). The items that Knowles refers to in the warehouse include mustache scissors and china cups in the lot 415 packing crates that Hans examines. These are the remnants of a pleasant, antebellum life and of Hans's parents' lives, which fact is discovered in a later scene between Hans and his father when these items are seen being used by Dr. Strauss.

Essentially, what Pinter did was remake the story while at the same time staying true to Uhlman's theme. The novella itself, if filmed exactly as written, would have been too short for a film. So, Pinter expanded it. He added whole sequences, such as those related to the framing figure of Hans the elder. Hans's trip back to Stuttgart and everything that occurred there are Pinter's inventions: the visit to Konradin's old home (now a governmental tax office, where the male clerk of one version of the screenplay has become a female), the meeting with the old Grafin von Zeilarn (who is displeased with her cousin's attempted betrayal of Hitler—and, for her, Germany), Hans's return to his boyhood home, the trip to his old school. The point of these additions is to humanize Hans and his story. Simple events such as the exchange with the Japanese tourist in the bar, Hans's attempt to determine from a man on the street whether he is where the school used to be (it was destroyed by a single bomb), and the taxi ride may be considered an opening out of the novel, but more importantly they provide for insight into Hans and into the character of Germany and of differing cultures.

The delineation of national character may have been one of the reasons that Pinter included a televised discussion of the character of King Henry, as demonstrated in the acting of Laurence Olivier in Shakespeare's *Henry V* (Pinter, 59). There is a stark contrast between the heroic proclamations in the play and the out-of-control, frenzied declamations by Freisler during Konradin's trial that are intercut throughout the film (59, 91, 96, 97). After all, Henry V is considered the model not just of nationalism but also of kingship.

Hans, in trying to impress Konradin in the classroom, offers an analysis of another Shakespearean character, Hamlet, as "a classic example of schizophrenia, of split personality. On the one hand, he laments the deterioration of civilized values, the decline in standards, the breakdown of moral systems, the failure of the state—and, on the other hand, he treats people like rubbish, kills Polonius without a sign of remorse, is vicious to his mother, drives Ophelia crazy, and coldly sends Rosencrantz and Guildenstern to their deaths. The great Sigmund Freud would describe this as a classic case of schizophrenia" (66). Bollacher dismisses this interpretation because "Sigmund Freud is a Jew!" but Pinter may be drawing a parallel between Hamlet, as portrayed in Hans's analysis, and the state of Germany.

Whereas Henry V says that the glorious names of those who fight well for their nation are "freshly remember'd" in the "flowing cups" of his countrymen (58), Freisler parallels those words in a different kind of flow. In his final, and most complete, diatribe, he pulls no punches: "You stinking traitor! Your soul runs with pus! You have broken your oath not once but twice! You are a criminal hypocrite and a filthy liar! The Reich knows what to do with vermin like you!" (97). This phrasing recalls a passage in Beckett's *Waiting for Godot* when Estragon says, "Everything oozes. . . . It's never the same pus from one second to the next" (39). A devotee of Beckett's, Pinter uses similar language when Max, the father in *The Homecoming*, describes his family: "Look what I'm lumbered with. One cast-iron bunch of crap after another. One stinking flow of pus after another" (19).

Other additions may have been intended to expand the coming-of-age concept. The scene in which Hans and Konradin view *The Blue Angel* in the theatre and watch a couple in the audience kissing is followed by the bow-and-arrow episode in the Black Forest when they stumble upon a couple making love. This leads to an exchange between the two boys later in the day while they are eating lunch (a scene that contains a bit of typical Pinter humor):

KONRADIN: . . . You know . . . I don't know what we're going to do about this question of sexual desire. It's a terrible problem.

HANS: Yes. The trouble is, I just don't know any girls. How about you?

KONRADIN: Not really. Only cousins.

They sit, munching.

Delicious sandwich. What is it?

HANS: Chicken.

KONRADIN: Wonderful flavour. Honestly, I've never tasted chicken like it.

HANS: Of course, sexual desire is just an appetite like anything else. And sexual intercourse is the appetite satisfied.

KONRADIN: You mean it's like eating this sandwich?

HANS: Exactly! (75)[9]

Besides reminding us of the pheasant lines in *The Quiller Memorandum* in which two men discuss the merits of their meal in the midst of a conversation about the murder of one of their colleagues, this exchange is similar to the wonderful one in an early edition of *The Birthday Party* in which Lulu confronts Goldberg after their night together only to find that in his opinion, "One night doesn't make a harem":

LULU:. . . . You took all those liberties only to satisfy your appetite.

GOLDBERG: Now you're giving me indigestion. (*The Birthday Party*, 84)

Aside from minor changes in the chronology, Pinter made few actual changes to the basic story. One, though, is significant. In the novella, the Corinthian coin was part of Hans's collection before he met Konradin. In the film, Konradin gives him the coin, and Hans examines it on the flight back to Germany.[10] By making this change, the screenwriter lets us understand that the token has significance even before we are made aware of the close tie between the two boys.

There are some minimal differences between the published script and the film, primarily the deletion of small scenes or shots that might have been considered merely duplicative during the editing process and the rearranging of the order of a few scenes or lines of dialogue. The change from two German shepherds in the park to one, for instance, is insignificant. By and large, the film is a faithful representation of Pinter's script. Certainly part of this fidelity was a result of director Schatzberg's cordial relationship with his scenarist, and undoubtedly part was due to Pinter's calling in his script for specific shots and details such as what music would be heard and when (he retains Uhlman's *Fidelio*) and Hans's "clenched fists" when he is embarrassed by his father in front of Konradin (73) (the clenched fists occur again at the end of the film when Henry learns of his friend's fate).

One particularly effective addition gives added impact to a scene described in the novella. Uhlman's Hans tells about his trip to see the opera and how he is snubbed there by Konradin, an event that leads to Konradin's confession about his mother's attitude toward Jews. In the novella, the incident begins in the theatre with Hans already seated and the entrance of the Lohenbergs (79). In the movie, Pinter's Hans is seen in a touching scene with his mother as he gets ready for the evening. Then he arrives at the Stuttgart Opera House at the same time that a truck full of cheering Nazis drives by. There is a cut to the interior of the auditorium and the arrival of Konradin and his party. The contrast between these three scenes creates dramatic irony, for we know what the future holds and Hans does not.

The middle-class home, the noisily invaded street, and the grandeur and elegance of the Opera House reflect Hans's world, a world in which he only partly belongs and a world in transition. He ignores the boisterous, uncouth Nazis and is taken with the dignified Lohenbergs. Tension will increase dramatically from this point on, as Nazis become more and more prominent in Hans's surroundings.

Interestingly, almost all of the scenes related to Nazis are street scenes, and the groups of Nazis are on the move, marching, in trucks, bullying their way into the outdoor restaurant. Another addition, possible only in film, is a montage of summer in Germany in 1932. Hans and Konradin have bidden each other farewell for the summer with the promise that they will continue to be friends when they return to school in September (this is following Konradin's explanation about why he did not introduce Hans to his mother and father). The shots are a combination of staged actions and actual footage from the time. They demonstrate the progress of Nazism and show crucial historical developments that happened during that critical period:

A group of little girls giving the Nazi salute, beaming.

Newsreel in cinema: A parade of Hitler Youth through crowded streets.

A band playing martial music.

Hitler's arrival in Berlin. Vast crowds greeting him.

Couples dancing on an open-air terrace. The song 'I Want a Man, a Real Man.'

Newsreel in cinema: Communist demonstrations against Fascism.

Fires breaking out.

A pretty little girl in white, with flowers, giving Nazi salute.

Newsreel in cinema: Gunfire in the streets.

A Berlin fashion parade.

Newsreel in cinema: Nazi march through working-class districts.

Workers running from the police.

Panic in the streets.

Vast torchlight processions. (86)

Most of these shots, many of them stock shots, are included in the film, although the newsreel segments are merely merged with the rest of the montage and not presented as being shown in a theatre, and some shots (e.g., the little girl standing beside a baby carriage and giving the Nazi salute) are shown as part of a sequence in which Hans walks down the street after his fight with Bollacher.

All of the flashback footage has been in sepia tones. Suddenly, in a ceremony in the schoolyard following the summer montage, when the Nazi flag is raised, it is strikingly colored bright red (was *Schindler's List* influenced by this scene?). In the box 49 archival material, there is a shot described by Pinter that must have been the inspiration for this introduction of color:

16 - Back to Stuttgart.

> Blood-red posters
>
> denouncing Versailles
>
> & the Jews.
>
> Swastikas and hammer & Sickle on walls.

Some things that are part of the narration in the novella are recast in the film in dialogue, as when Dr. Strauss protests to the Zionist that he is a German Jew: "We go to synagogue on Yom Kippur and we sing 'Silent Night' at Christmas" (69). In the original, Hans describes his mother's indifferent attitude toward religion by saying, "She went to the Synagogue on the Day of Atonement, but would sing *Stille Nacht, Heilige Nacht* at Christmas" (Uhlman, 42).

Many scenes that Pinter considered including in the script were abandoned before the shooting script was completed. For instance, in box 49 there is a copy of "*Konrad's Letter,*" a seventy-four-page typed document to Hans from Conrad von Hohenfels, dated September 10, 1944. Writing from Spandau Prison, Konradin explains his actions to his friend. In box 50, there is an eighty-five-page typescript by Uhlman titled "No Coward Soul." On the cover is "The Diary of Konradin von Hohenfels, London, 1961," so this may be the original version of the novel. It is possible that Pinter was given these documents as a way of helping him explore Konradin's character.

Reunion is another "little picture." It is not an epic like *Lawrence of Arabia,* although both films are period pieces, and the focus is not on the grand sweep of things but rather on an individual or individuals. Moreover, even though it is based on history, unlike *Schindler's List* or *Saving Private*

Ryan, it is a quiet film. As usual when working with subject matter from the past, Pinter did research before writing the script. His notes refer to William L. Shirer's *Fall of the Third Reich: A History of Nazi Germany,* for instance. Some of the information that he found was used for background, and some of it is incorporated into the script.[11] One result of Pinter's research is found in the numbers in the election results reported on the radio (which elicit amusing resonances with or reflections on "Precisely," published a couple of years before he began writing *Reunion*).[12]

Pinter experimented with the chronology. Two pages clipped together are titled "Structure." This an outline of the major time-line blocks for the story:

1 March to execution

2 New York,

> Central Park
>
> ~~with Granddaughter~~

3 To Stuttgart

4 Hotel

5 ~~Selling of house~~

6 Warehouse

7 Cemetery

8 Visit to

> Gertrude

9 Present Stuttgart

10 THE PAST

[p. 2]

11 Come out of [indecipherable word]

> Past with
>
> Gertrude

12 Dream!

> The trial

13 H alone

14 Konradin's end

15 H leaving

> for New York. (box 49)

He also considered several alternative endings for the film. The published conclusion is:

> HENRY. And Lohenburg?
>
> > BROSSNER *stares at him.*
>
> BROSSNER. Lohenburg?
>
> INT. EMPTY EXECUTION ROOM. DAY
>
> *The room is bare. Two windows at the back. Winter sunshine slanting in. A rafter along the ceiling in front of the windows. Butcher's hooks hanging down.*
>
> *Over this,* BROSSNER'S *voice.*
>
> BROSSNER. (*Voice over*) You don't know? He was implicated in the plot against Hitler. Executed.
>
> *The butcher's hooks glint in the light from the window.*
> (98–99)

Box 50 contains two loose handwritten pages in which one ending is described: Henry is on the plane returning to the United States; the camera is on the coin, and the last shot is of "Germany disappearing in cloud ~~below.~~" In addition, there is an *"Alternative Ending"* included with the second draft; absent are Freisler's comments about "stinking" Jews:

> 2-97 <u>INT. PEOPLE'S COURT. BLACK AND WHITE</u>
>
> > BROSSNER
>
> Hohenfels? Oh yes—that is known, of course—Judge Freisler comes in. The court rises. He gives a Nazi salute and sits.
>
> > FREISLER
>
> Konradin von Hohenfels!
>
> 2-98 Konradin is brought forward. He is unshaven, his eyes are sunken. He stands, holding his trousers up, but erect.
>
> > FREISLER
>
> Konradin von Hohenfels—for dishonourably breaking your oath, for committing an act of treachery unparalleled in our history, for betraying our soldiers, our people, our Fuehrer and the Reich— by attempting the vile murder of our beloved

leader—thereby proving yourself a traitor to
everything we live and fight for—you are
sentenced to death.

Another alternative ending included in the same plastic holder is closer
to the ending contained in the movie (Hohenfels is changed to Lohenburg):[13]

HENRY
Hohenfels was a friend of mine.

BROSSNER
Hohenfels?

110. Int. <u>EXECUTION ROOM. EMPTY.</u>

Descript same.
Over this Brossner's voice:

BROSSNER (VO)

Oh yes. He was implicated in the plot against Hitler.
Executed. The butcher's hooks—

The history of Pinter's composition of the *Reunion* screenplay reflects
all aspects of his approach to screenwriting. It is fitting, then, that, while
Schindler's List may be the film about Nazi Germany that comes to mind for
most people, Pinter's *Reunion,* with less grandstanding, is as passionate and
affecting a film as Spielberg's.

The Handmaid's Tale

RELEASED: March 1990
SOURCE: *The Handmaid's Tale,* by Margaret Atwood; novel (1986)
AWARDS: Nominated for Berlin Film Festival In Competition
PRODUCTION COMPANY: Cinecom Entertainment Group; Warner Brothers
DIRECTOR: Volker Schlondorff
EDITOR: David Ray
CINEMATOGRAPHER: Ignor Luther
EXECUTIVE PRODUCER: Wolfgang Glattes
PRODUCER: Daniel Wilson
PRODUCTION DESIGNER: Tom Walsh
ARTISTIC DIRECTOR: Gregory Melton
SET DECORATION: Jan Pascale
SOUND MIXER: Danny Michael
MUSIC: Ryuichi Sakamoto
COSTUME DESIGNER: Coleen Atwood
CAST: Faye Dunaway (Serena Joy), Robert Duvall (Commander Fred), Miranda
    Richardson (Offred), Elizabeth McGovern (Moira), Aidan Quinn (Nick),
    Victoria Tennant (Aunt Lydia), Natasha Richardson (Kate), Blanche Baker
    (Ofglen), Traci Lind (Ofwarren/Janine), Reiner Schoene (Luke), Kathryn
    Doby (Aunt Elizabeth), David Dukes (Doctor), Lucile Dew McIntyre (Rita),
    Zoey Wilson (Aunt Helena)[1]
RUNNING TIME: 109 minutes
COLOR
RATING: R
VIDEO: HBO Video

IT IS INTERESTING THAT the two film scripts by Pinter that contain the
most violence (*The Handmaid's Tale* and *The Comfort of Strangers*) were
both released in 1990. Although there were momentary outbursts of vio-

lence in many of the earlier works (and certainly in *Victory*), there is no gratuitous violence in the writer's work for either the stage or the screen. Actually, Pinter has publicly disdained the use of such violence in the cinema. In his acceptance speech upon being awarded the David Cohen British Literature Prize in March 1995, the author dismissed the kind of film violence for which directors such as Quentin Tarantino are known. Tarantino uses violence for entertainment, Pinter claimed: "That's certainly what the Tarantino kind of film does. . . . The way violence is used is truly demeaning. It undermines the spirit and intelligence too, because it falsely represents the real thing. The real thing is appalling and this stuff on film and television is just fun. Therefore I deplore it, I find it actually disgusting" (Knowles, "1994–1995 and 1995–1996," 159). It can be argued that the violence that the writer accepts in *Victory, The Handmaid's Tale,* and *The Comfort of Strangers,* as repugnant and shocking as it is, is of a very different nature and grows out of the story. Whether the members of the audience agree with this distinction is a matter of individual determination; many argue that the violence in these film scripts by Pinter is not fully prepared for.

The source for *The Handmaid's Tale* was Margaret Atwood's novel of the same name.[2] Generally speaking, the events in the story take place in what was the United States and occur in the near future. The Republic of Gilead is a monotheocracy faced with a rapidly declining birthrate and a period of social unrest that grew out of a civil war. It is governed by an intolerant, Puritanical regime. The story is about Kate (played by Natasha Richardson), who is a Handmaid—one of the few women left who can bear children. Kate befriends Moira (Elizabeth McGovern), a "gender criminal" who has committed "gender treachery" ("I like girls," she admits) and who escapes from the prisonlike training center where the two meet. Under the strict tutelage of Aunt Lydia (Victoria Tennant), Kate learns her role as a Handmaid, to "serve God and country." She is then assigned as the Handmaid to the Commander (Robert Duvall) to bear his child, because his wife, Serena (Faye Dunaway) is infertile. There is an underground movement devoted to overthrowing the tyrannical rulership, and Nick (Aidan Quinn), a training center guard who becomes Kate's lover, is associated with this group. At the novel's end, Kate, too, is attempting to escape.

Billington says that Pinter began work on the script in 1987 at Reisz's instigation, though that date seems too early, given the dates on the scripts in the Pinter Archives. The screenwriter's willingness to work on this project might be seen as evidence of his increased interest in things political. It is an extension of the activist attitude expressed in *Turtle Diary* and of the author's increasingly pronounced public political stance during the 1980s (his 1985 trip to Turkey with Arthur Miller on behalf of PEN, his support of Vaclav Havel and other dissident writers, his connection with the June 20th Society). These public incidents resonate with his childhood experiences in World War II (flying bombs in his backyard, evacuation to the countryside), which were wedded with his Jewish background and his adventures while growing up in Hackney, facing broken-milk-bottle-wielding neofascists. The extent of his lifelong commitment to such causes was evident as early as his teens, when he took a tooth brush to court because he was sure that he would be sent to jail for being a conscientious objector. He was deeply involved in personal political activities at the time that he was writing this screenplay.

Pinter's rendition of Atwood's tale follows the plot line and examines the same themes that are presented in the novel, with a couple of major differences. Atwood's story starts with Kate already in captivity. Shot in North Carolina, in and around Durham and the Sugar Mountain Ski Resort, the film begins with Kate, her child, and her husband attempting to escape from Gilead. In an ironic opening, following the legend "Once upon a time in the recent future a country went wrong. The country was called The Republic of Gilead," there is a pan of a mountainous terrain that includes a road on which the family's SUV is seen. The car stops, and Kate, who has been driving, changes places with her husband, who has been in the passenger seat. In contrast to the ominous music that accompanies the opening shot (low strings and humming voices), the couple executes a high-five in celebration of their escape. Soon afterward they are on foot in the snow when they run into the Gilead border patrol. In the ensuing action, the husband is shot to death while trying to lead the patrol away from Kate, Kate is captured, and the daughter wanders off into the woods. It may be that this sequence was in part intended to prepare for Kate's murder of the Commander. Both the presence of violence and the motive of revenge are established immediately. This sequence also leads directly to a sequence in which Kate is processed in a setting that definitely invites comparisons with Nazi Germany. To the accompaniment of the sound of drums, military transport trucks arrive, from which crowds of men, women, and children are disgorged and then herded into areas surrounded by barbed wire fences and armed guards with attack dogs. The captives are assigned individual numbers and separated into smaller groups (according to whether they are positive or negative—i.e., can bear children), there are protestations that mistakes have been made, women are loaded into large trucks meant for hauling "Livestock" (the equivalent of the Nazis' railway cattle cars), and the number of people contained within is chalked on the sides of the trucks.

The novel does not include the murder of the Commander, and Kate's fate is left completely unresolved—the van waits in the driveway, "And so I step up, into the darkness within; or else the light" (295). The escape to Canada and the reappearance of the child and Nick are Pinter's inventions for the movie version. As shot, there is a voice-over in which Kate explains (accompanied by light symphonic music that contrasts with that of the opening scene) that she is now safe in the mountains held by the rebels. Bolstered by occasional messages from Nick, she awaits the birth of her baby while she dreams about Jill, whom she feels she is going to find eventually.

The Atwood volume ends with "Historical Notes," purportedly a scholar's commentary on the times and the tale told by Offred. Amusingly, this contrasts with the actual scholarship exhibited by Pinter in preparation for his adaptation. Archive box 63 includes an extensive clipping file of articles related to topics such as surrogate motherhood, hanging, and forced pregnancy practices. Many additional articles about similar subjects point to Pinter's interest in current reflections of the world described in Atwood's novel.[3]

All the same, the final cut of *The Handmaid's Tale* is less a product of Pinter's script than any of his other films. He contributed only part of the screenplay: reportedly he "abandoned writing the screenplay from exhaustion."[4] Although he tried to have his name removed from the credits because he was so displeased with the movie (in 1994 he told me that this was due to the great divergences from his script that occur in the movie),[5] his name remains as the screenwriter.

This is because while the film was being shot, director Volker Schlondorff called the screenwriter and asked for some changes in the script. Pinter recalls being very tired at the time, and he suggested that Schlondorff contact Atwood about the rewrites. He essentially gave the director and author carte blanche to accept whatever changes that she wanted to institute, for, as he reasoned, "I didn't think an author would want to fuck up her own work."[6] As it turned out, not only did Atwood make changes, but so did many others who were involved in the shoot. "It became," Pinter told Billington, "a hotchpotch. The whole thing fell between several stools. I worked with Karel Reisz on it for about a year. There are big public scenes in the story and Karel wanted to do them with thousands of people. The film company wouldn't sanction that so he withdrew. At which point Volker Schlondorff came into it as director. He wanted to work with me on the script, but I said I was absolutely exhausted. I more or less said, 'Do what you like. There's the script. Why not go back to the original author if you want to fiddle about?' He did go to her. And then the actors came into it. I left my name on the film because there was enough there to warrant it—just about. But it's not mine" (304).[7]

Thus, even though Pinter was not pleased with the result (and there was no way that he could determine which changes had been made by whom), he had given Schlondorff permission to make the changes, and his name remains in the credits. Unaware of these circumstances, Kauffmann calls *The Handmaid's Tale* screenplay "by far [Pinter's] worst" ("Future Tense"). When I asked whether the script would ever be published, Pinter said no—the script and the movie (for which at one point a domestic gross of $4.96 million was reported) are not the same, and he thought that there might be copyright problems under the circumstances. Because of his disregard for and refusal to take credit for the movie, and despite the reputed quality of his original, a full critical analysis is not called for.[8]

Nevertheless, it is useful to take a quick glance at the conclusions of three scripts included in the Pinter Archives that reveal Pinter's struggle over how to end the film. The earliest version of the script is dated "12 Dec. 1986." After the execution of a rebel leader at the Handmaid's gathering, and just after she has pretended admiration for the Commander, who has engineered the execution, Offred pulls a knife from her sleeve and slits his throat. He sets off an alarm as he dies, muttering "I thought you loved me," and she runs off (129).

Inside a van taking away both Nick and Offred, Nick tells some men, who are revealed as his cohorts, to hit him in the jaw, and he jumps out (131). The men take Offred to a country house. Disguised in a short leather jacket and skirt, she sees Nick on a television news program, arm in a sling. He has convinced the authorities that he was abducted by the rebels (132). We cut to the border, where Offred enters a café and drinks coffee as a woman calls her "Kate" (133–35). Then she discovers that her daughter is waiting by the phone for "Mrs. Agnew." Kate calls her daughter on the pay phone and begins to speak. The last line of this version is: "The camera pulls back. She continues speaking" (135).

A second script is dated "2 Feb. 1989."[9] The murder-of-the-Commander scene is similar, but in this version his "I thought you loved me" is cut; the Commander presses an alarm button, a more specific action than in the pre-

The Handmaid's Tale (1990). The Handmaids. Location shot at Duke University. Cinecom. Jerry Ohlinger Archives.

vious version (134). In this version, too, Nick is not in the first group of the so-called "Eyes," which captures Offred. Instead, the unit arrests Nick in the hall. In the van he tells them, "I have to stay in the field," and off he goes. The scene with him on the news program at the country house remains to let the audience know that he has convinced the authorities (135–37).

In this version, Pinter has added a new scene in "snow hills and valley" at dawn. Offred/Kate is putting on skis and rushes off as helicopters buzz in the distance (138). The script ends as we see a country street in Canada ("an ice cream wagon. Cars. Girls in short skirts. Boys riding bicycles") suggesting normalcy as Kate walks along a street and looks through a school-yard fence. The script describes children playing, and then the camera focuses on Jill, Kate's daughter, who does not see her yet. Kate looks at Jill through the wire fence: "She turns, walks along the side of the fence, and goes into the school./The laughter of children" (139).

The third version of the screenplay, undated on its cover page, includes this information: Daniel Wilson Productions, Inc., with address and phone. On its last page (147), this version is dated February 1987, and it appears to be the final draft. There is no published version of this script.

Here, as in the previous two scripts, the hanging of the "fornicator" is a simpler matter and closer to the description of the event in the novel than is the very elaborate hoisting of the victim by the Handmaids in the film version. A stool is kicked out from beneath the condemned, and "The Salvagers seize hold of the kicking feet and pull down" (126; Atwood, 276). As in Atwood's original, during the execution of the radical leader, Ofglen gives him three kicks, very fast, a merciful attempt to put him out of his misery quickly before the other women get at him (129; Atwood, 280).

This script describes a note in Offred's room telling her where the knife is hidden (131). The murder scene remains largely unchanged, but here the Commander grabs Offred as he goes down. The arrest of Nick in the hall is similar. In this case, Offred is bewildered, as are we at first, when he tells her, "Go with it" (142). The conclusion is essentially the same as in the script immediately preceding. Kate skis across the Canadian border on her own, discovers her child in the school yard, and enters the school. The last line remains "The laughter of children" (147).

Whether Pinter ran out of steam or simply could not get a handle on the essence of the novel, in the end *The Handmaid's Tale* was a bad experience for him.

The Comfort of Strangers

RELEASED: 1990

SOURCE: *The Comfort of Strangers,* by Ian McEwan; novel (1981)

PRODUCTION COMPANY: Skouras Pictures

DIRECTOR: Paul Schrader

EDITOR: Bill Pankow

DIRECTOR OF PHOTOGRAPHY: Dante Spinotti

PRODUCER: Angelo Rizzoli

PRODUCTION DESIGNERS: Gianni Quaranta, Luigi Marchione

ART DIRECTOR: Luigi Marchione

SET DECORATION: Stefano Paltrinieri

MUSIC: Angelo Badalamenti

WARDROBE: Giorgio Armani

COSTUME SUPERVISOR: Mariolina Bono

CAST: Natasha Richardson (Mary), Rupert Everett (Colin), Helen Mirren
(Caroline), Christopher Walken (Robert), Manfredi Aliquo (Concierge),
Rossana Caghiari (Hotel Maid), Fabrizio Castellani (Bar Manager), Mario
Cotone (Detective), David Ford (Waiter), Daniel Franco (Waiter), Giancarlo
Previati (First Policeman), Antonio Serrano (Second Policeman), Mary
Selway

RUNNING TIME: 105 minutes.[1]

COLOR

RATING: R

FROM THE VERY BEGINNING, the camera has been the tool of the voyeur, and the audience has sat in the voyeur's seat, whether consciously or not.[2] Among the earliest examples of a conscious exploitation of the voyeuristic nature of motion pictures are *Uncle Josh at the Moving Picture Show* and *The Story the Biograph Told,* mentioned above. In *Uncle Josh,* the naive protagonist, seeing a movie for the first time, reacts as though what he is viewing is reality, as had the Lumiere's audiences; the difference is that he tries to enter the action. In *Biograph*, a boy secretly films a man and a woman kissing in the Biograph office. Complications occur when the man and his wife later go to a movie theatre where the picture is screened.

Pinter has incorporated the voyeur concept in several of his earlier films, most notably in *The Go-Between*, but in *The Comfort of Strangers* this concept is definitely more than merely a plot device. As Andrew Ross has observed, a camera can be used to transform a subject into an object (151). In *The Comfort of Strangers*, the screenwriter is concerned with voyeurism as a symptom and as a tool of bizarre behavior that is expressed through sexuality but which is grounded in neurosis that is only partly sexually derivative. Robert's camera is the means by which his proclivity is made tangible. When he thereby objectifies his victims, he assumes an emotional and intellectual distance from them that allows him to treat them as nonhumans, things meant only to satisfy his desires and needs. This is vintage Pinter. From the beginning of his career, the author has been concerned with individual needs and the extremes to which a person is willing to go to satisfy those needs. In all of his work, he has been obsessed with dominance.[3] As he does in all of his films, harking back to *The Pumpkin Eater*, in this movie Pinter also explores social mores.

As in *The Heat of the Day*, photographs are an important element in *The Comfort of Strangers*. And, like the earlier movie, this film opens with a shot that features photography, a pan showing "*a Nikon camera with a zoom lens and strips of developed film, on a shelf*" (Pinter, 3).[4] In this case, though, there are even more sinister components to the still life: "*several cut-throat razors arranged in a fan.*" The cinematic gaze that Pinter intends to be central to *The Comfort of Strangers* is vitiated somewhat by director Paul Schrader's changes in the script. Some of the photographic images and references have been deleted from the opening shots, and Pinter's emphasis is thus diminished. Similarly, the sentimental aria sung by Beniamino Gigli that is called for by the screenwriter is replaced by the heavily foreboding music of Angelo Badalamenti.[5] In fact, many scenes, including those in which the younger couple, Mary and Colin, are lost in the maze of Venice's back alleys late at night, would not create a feeling of tension and apprehension in the viewer if it were not for the background music, which, as in a regular horror movie, quite clearly signals that they are in the presence of something sinister and dangerous.

American director Robert Zemeckis has observed that the "power of the moving image is awesome";[6] *The Comfort of Strangers* is Pinter's most powerful film. On the surface it seems to be a leisurely unfolding of a love story. Britishers Mary and Colin, who visited Venice two years earlier, have returned to try to work out their feelings about their relationship. Mary is divorced and has two young children; she and Colin have been involved for some time and profess to love one another, but they have not lived together, and they need to determine whether or not they can. Both are unsure about whether he can live with her children (the dialogue is reminiscent of the discussion between Jake and Jo's father in *The Pumpkin Eater*):

MARY. Tell me the truth. Do you like children?

COLIN. What children?

MARY. My children.

COLIN. Yes. I like your children.

MARY. No. What I meant was, do you actually like children?

COLIN. You mean all children?

MARY. Children. Do you actually like children?

COLIN. You mean as such—you mean the species—as such? (Pinter, 8)

In a preproduction interview, Schrader, the screenwriter of *Taxi Driver* and *Raging Bull* and director of *Hard Core, Cat People, Patty Hearst,* and *Mishima,* described his upcoming project as being "about a vacationing young British couple whose lives are sort of taken over by a local couple, a la something Pinter wrote years ago, 'The Servant.'" Normally, Schrader works from his own screenplays, but in this case producer Angelo Rizzoli wanted Pinter to do the writing, and the director agreed. In the interview, he went on to say that "Pinter knows his way around a word. . . . It's just beautifully written and full of innuendo and subtext. It'll be a very stylish piece. The challenge is twofold: one, to create the sort of visual world where these events can happen. Second, just to service the complexities of the writing" (Van Gelder, July 28, 1989). Elsewhere Schrader has said, "I don't think there is any better writer for the penetration of psychologies that are essentially Anglo-Saxon . . . . The only Italian element is the setting and the production. Otherwise I'd say it's a typically English tale."[7]

Adapted from Ian McEwan's 1981 novel,[8] *The Comfort of Strangers* is a horror story, not about unbelievable characters like Jason or Freddie or even Chuckie—and not filled with ghastly, bloody surprises in dark basements or cemeteries—yet it is much more sinister than the films of the genre represented by *Halloween, Scream,* and the like. The scenes in *The Comfort of Strangers* are dark but not necessarily foreboding in themselves. Much of the photography is beautiful, and indoor and outdoor shots are frequently filled with browns and other warm earth colors. The interiors were filmed in Rome; the exteriors were shot in Venice. Schrader and photographer Dante Spinotti take good advantage of the visually stunning natural set provided by one of the world's most beautiful and fascinating cities. They also take some liberties with physical reality in order to advance some thematic threads. Cemetery Island, for instance, cannot be seen from Robert's castle, as Jackson Cope points out. Importantly, though, Pinter's understanding of the concept of montage and his ability to use the concept effectively is demonstrated by the scene in which Cemetery Island supposedly is viewed as it appears in his screenplay. In *Lolita* the scene in the cave with Humbert and Annabel and the two intruding bathers is another fine example of the screenwriter's skillful use of this concept.

The opening shot of the interior of Robert's lavish apartment is typical. There is not a lot of available light present, but the heavy wooden furniture, the nineteenth-century English-style paintings of partially clothed women that line the walls and doors, the thick rugs, the wood paneling—all combine to evoke a feeling of settled, quiet, richly textured opulence. Customarily in Pinter's work, the ordinary surface action seems normal and the underlying horror is more stark because of the contrast.[9] The sense that the events could have entangled anyone is enhanced by the apparent normalcy of people and places as well. The film is very evocative of Roeg's horribly effective *Don't Look Now* in tone and even in action—the backstreet locales in Venice, the mysterious evil stranger, the unexpected, slashing murder.

Besides the fact that both take place in Venice, several literary allusions link the screenplay of *The Comfort of Strangers* with that of *Betrayal*. In Pinter's February 25, 1989, manuscript, Mary rehearses a scene about passionate love: "When you see Trigorin don't tell him anything." Trigorin is the novelist in Anton Chekhov's *Seagull,* a link to publisher Colin, perhaps, and thus, tenuously, to the literati in *Betrayal*. In scene 72 of a bound script dated March 14 of the same year that is very similar to the published version, Pinter has Mary tell Caroline, "Well, I'm out of work, but I'm doing an audition for *The Seagull* when we get back." The Chekhov reference, completely Pinter's invention, serves much the same purpose as the longer rehearsal scene with Colin in the earlier version, but this shortened version is left out of the final script, too. In the March 14 script, during his telephone call, Colin says, "I just find the bloody book exhausting, that's all. Anyway, there's too much shitting and shagging." This is followed by his criticism about making it popular: "No, no, I agree. Sure he's an artist—a crap artist." Here it is quite clear that Colin is in publishing, with all of the echoes of *Betrayal* that that brings to mind.

A manuscript on a legal pad dated January 3 includes a version of Robert's speech about his father that is almost fully developed and dialogue from a variety of scenes. Some of that dialogue is left out of the final version but is quite interesting. In the second café scene, for example, in response to Mary's question about his liking children, Colin says that he did not like himself as a child: "No. I was morbid. I was a morbid child. Nobody liked me. I was unfriendly. I used to kick people." Mary replies, "What about your mother? You never kicked your mother." These make parallels between Robert and Colin more readily apparent.

As in *The Servant*, Pinter is depicting the story of innocence under attack and ultimately being destroyed by a malevolent force. This may be a weak innocence like that displayed by Tony, vulnerable because it is not strong enough to recognize or understand the ominous depths of the corruption that is assaulting it. Still, Mary and Colin do represent innocence. It is appropriate that their names are the names of the hero and heroine whose innocent friendship/love story is recounted in Frances Hodgson Burnett's *Secret Garden* (1911). Ironically, in the children's novel the relationship strengthens the character of the individuals. Contrarily, the couple in *The Comfort of Strangers* may not be strong enough to disentangle themselves from Robert and Caroline, but, on one level at least, the reason is certainly human. It is not always easy to break off a relationship, no matter how tenuous. In the roles of these relative innocents, Natasha Richardson, who had starred in *The Handmaid's Tale,* and Rupert Everett convey a sense of naive, uncomprehending vulnerability, an aura of niceness that makes them incapable of consciously and blatantly offending anyone.

Mary and Colin are made uneasy by Robert (who is carrying a camera and wearing *"a gold imitation razor blade"* around his neck [Pinter, 13]) the first night that they meet, and they try to hide from him when they are in the palazzo restaurant; however, they do not know how to turn him down when he approaches them and invites them to his house. Even when Robert punches Colin in the stomach, Colin is embarrassed and feels socially awkward, as though he may have committed a faux pas. The lovers talk about wanting to avoid their new acquaintances, yet they do not know how to do so gracefully

The Comfort of Strangers (1990). Rupert Everett as Colin and Natasha Richardson as Mary in Venice. Skouras Pictures. Jerry Ohlinger Archives.

and thus are forced to go along for the ride. They are led deeper into the relationship because they do not know how to escape. Their exposure to Robert does not bring about the moral decay that Tony suffered as a result of his involvement with Barrett, and they may actually benefit from it at first, for it brings them closer together and helps them define their own relationship. It is ironic that, notwithstanding their renewed commitment to each because of Robert's presence, that presence brings about their destruction.

There is also a sense of inevitability present. The "accidental" meeting at night, Robert's stumbling upon Mary and Colin at the restaurant, their decision to get off the water taxi at just the wrong stop (the audience has no trouble guessing that this is what they are doing), and then the coincidence of Caroline's looking out the window and seeing them across the canal—all of these elements suggest that the events are predestined, although the dramatic irony is that the audience is aware of Robert's intrusive presence from the beginning. Furthermore, by framing the action with Robert's voice-over telling the story of his father at the beginning (the shot is of Robert's apartment) and a shot of Robert telling the same story to the police at the end, Pinter indicates that the story is Robert's, not Mary and Colin's.

"My father was a very big man. All his life he wore a black moustache. When it turned grey he used a little brush to keep it black, such as ladies use for their eyes. Mascara," Robert begins his voice-over as the film opens (Pinter, 3). Robert's relationship with his tyrannical, sadistic father was one of reverence mixed with fear (10), and he considered his father "God" (17). "Everyone was afraid of him. My mother, my four sisters. At the dining-table you could not speak unless spoken to first by my father. / But he loved me. / I was his favourite" (16), he declares. Christopher Walken's sinister and suave portrayal of Robert captures the qualities that make the character believable.[10] When the limping Caroline appears at the end of this monologue, the background elements of the tragedy have been set. The type of man that Robert's father was, Robert's relationship to him, and Caroline's physical condition indicate that something is amiss. In retrospect, it is apparent that the father created a sadistic creature out of his son, a son who needs abnormal physical stimulation as evidence of love.

Robert's story is told three times during the course of the film. The second time is when he recounts his history in its entirety at his café the night that he first forcefully moves into Mary and Colin's lives (Pinter, 15–19). The abusive, domineering, Old Testament patriarchal father's impact on his impressionable, then eleven-year-old son is obvious. Possibly there is lesbianism, voyeurism, and incest inherent in the actions of Robert's older sisters and his visits to his mother's bed:

> They took off their white socks and put on my mother's silk stockings and panties. They sauntered about the room, looking over their shoulders into mirrors. They were beautiful women. They laughed and kissed each other. They stroked each other. They giggled with each other. I was enchanted. They fed my enchantment. (Pinter, 16–17)

> My only solace was my mother. I grew so thirsty . . . at night. She brought me a glass of water every night and laid her hand upon my brow. She was so tender. When my father was away I slept in her bed. She was so warm, so tender. (18)

The innocence symbolized by the white socks that the sisters take off to assume the role of sexually mature women and the other details of Robert's remembrance imply a connection in his mind between lost innocence, sexuality, and his father's threatening macho image.

The picture that he paints of his father is that of a man of unquestioned authority who strikes out powerfully, physically, without hesitation or remorse, as when he beat the girls "with a leather belt, without mercy." "I watched this," Robert says (17). The pattern is repeated later when Robert defiles himself and his "revered," "feared," father's study as a result of overindulging his childish gluttony with "two big bottles of lemonade, a cream cake, two packets of cooking chocolate and a big box of marshmallows" and some "slightly disgusting" medicine that the girls trick him into devouring in retaliation for his having told their father about their antics. The results are predictable: "I puked and pissed and shat all over my father's carpets and walls. . . . Then he nearly killed me. And then he didn't speak to me for six months." Disapproval linked to sex and excess is expressed violently; pain and sex are equated. In an interesting parallel, while telling his story, Robert insists on plying Mary and Colin with an overabundance of wine, which causes Mary to become so ill that she vomits and the couple falls asleep in the street that night. The tale comes full circle when the two are awakened the next morning by a passing group of schoolgirls wearing Catholic uniforms—gluttony, sex, illness, youth, innocence.

Pinter's politics were close to the surface of many if not most of the plays that he wrote through the 1970s. In the 1980s, his political beliefs became central to his writing for the stage, and he spoke publicly and wrote newspaper articles articulating his positions.[11] As was the case in *Reunion,* to a British audience some of the lines in the screenplay must have sounded like warnings against the perceived authoritarianism of the Thatcherite government. When Mary states that she wants "Freedom to be free!" Robert responds, "sometimes a few rules—you know—they're not a bad thing. First and foremost society has to be protected from perverts[!]. Everybody knows that. My philosophical position is simple—put them all up against a wall and shoot them. . . . The English government is going in the right direction" (30–31). Some of his political concerns are echoed in the dinner conversation at Robert's, which is original in the film script, when Robert comments on the recent British attitude toward "freedom" as expressed in actions by the Thatcherites: "The English government is going in the right direction. In Italy we could learn a lot of lessons from the English government" (30–31).

Robert's political leanings, the opposite of Pinter's, are an expression of his identification with his father. When Colin observes to Robert, "Your father is very important to you," Robert replies, "My father and his father understood themselves clearly. They were men and they were proud of their sex. Women understood them too. Now women treat men like children, because they can't take them seriously. But men like my father and my grandfather women took very seriously. There was no uncertainty, no confusion" (29). Colin's next observation, "So this is a museum dedicated to the good old days" (30), is followed by Robert's hitting him in the stomach. No uncertainty, no confusion about someone to be taken seriously. At the dinner table Robert expresses his philosophy equally clearly in his "sometimes a few rules . . . they're not a bad thing" speech.

Robert's unsettled mind is indicated by his connection of politics and homosexuality moments later ("I respect you . . . but not if you're a communist poof. . . . Or is it 'fruit'" [31]). Despite his reservation about communist poofs, Robert apparently is not a stranger to homosexuality. In the film, the homosexual aspects of Robert's sexuality are not as obvious as they were in the novel. In fact, whereas in the novel it was Robert who kissed Colin before slashing his throat, in the movie it is Caroline who kisses him. At the same time, Schrader adds two clearly heterosexual women to the bar scene; so, as Ann Hall concludes, criticism that Robert's "violence is the result of his own conflicted homosexual tendencies misses the complexity of patriarchal relations in this film and culture."

When they meet again after the water taxi ride, Robert takes Colin back to his café and along the way speaks to several men loitering in the narrow passageways. "Did you understand what I was telling people as we walked here," he asks his guest; "I was telling them you were my lover. And that Caroline is jealous because she likes you too" (44).

Suddenly things are coming together. While Robert and Colin are gone, Caroline confides in Mary. Her revelations depict Robert, and herself, as having unhealthy tastes and tendencies: "Soon after we were married Robert started to hurt me when we made love. Not a lot, enough to make me cry out. I tried to stop him but he went on doing it. After a time I liked it. Not the pain itself—but somehow—the fact of being helpless before it, of being reduced to nothing by it—and also being punished, therefore being guilty. I felt it was right that I should be punished. And I thrilled to it. It took us over totally. It grew and grew. It seemed never ending. But there was an end to it. We both knew what it was. We knew what it had to be. We knew it. We wanted it" (43–44). What happened was, "He's terribly strong, you see. When he pulled my head backwards I blacked out with the pain—but I remember thinking: It's going to happen now. I can't go back on it now. It's going to happen—now. This is it. This is the end" (45).

Caroline's next revelation is the one that sets up the film's conclusion. She takes Mary, whom she has drugged, into the bedroom where the wall is covered with "*dozens of photographs of* COLIN." There she explains, "That was the first picture I saw of him. I'll never forget it. Robert came back so excited. Then every day he brought more and more photographs home. We became so close, incredibly close. Colin brought us together [as Robert Newton in the film *Odd Man Out* brought Deeley and Kate together in Pinter's *Old Times*]. It was my idea to put him here on the wall—so that we could see him—all the time, as we fucked" (46).

Several times during the film, the characters remark on Colin's physical attractiveness, which goes beyond handsomeness to beauty. Destruction of such beauty is the pinnacle of sexual arousal for Robert and Caroline. In the script Robert and Caroline kiss in the midst of the sacrifice:

An unfocused mating dance with three figures.
Sudden flash of razor blade.
Blood.
ROBERT *and* CAROLINE *kissing.* (48)

In the movie Robert is seen slowly drawing the blade across Colin's throat as Caroline watches; there is no splash of blood. Robert and Caroline move casually, hand in hand, to the bedroom as Colin slides down the wall into a pool of his own blood. The straight-edged razor appears to be one of the collection of icons left over from his father's daily life that Robert keeps on the side-bar shrine.

Pinter experimented with several possible endings before deciding on the one that was filmed. A manuscript dated January 17 contains a graphic version of Caroline's behavior during the murder scene. She pulls Colin's shirt from his jeans, strokes his belly, and undoes his jeans, which drop. She then undoes Robert's belt and caresses Colin.

R thrusts
R I'll show you.
    He thrusts
R Screams. Sudden Silence
    C Neck broken

The segment ends with a shot of a gondola.

In a February 7 script in the Pinter Archives box 9, the murder is by choking, though this manuscript does not include the scene directions about the broken neck; it ends with Mary in a chair. In a version dated February 19 (box 8), Robert and Caroline kiss, and then there is the phrase: "buggering a dead man" followed by "cuts wrist." Perhaps most interestingly, this manuscript includes a scene after Mary has returned to her mother's at Henley on Thames. At the cottage, her mother asks "Did Colin enjoy it?" With her kids in the background, Mary says yes. In short, in this version, we see Mary going on with her life; she doesn't even tell her mother of the events that have shaken her so. This scene changes radically several times in later versions, and finally it is omitted.

There is also an expanded version of the scene at Mary's mother's cottage in the February 25 manuscript (box 8). Kids five and seven run up to her taxi, asking for presents and telling Mary of their news. She and her mother kiss, and Mary again has a headache, as she does in the beginning of this early script version. The kids joyfully open their presents, discovering that they are the T-shirts that Colin bought them. There is a cut to a towpath by the river with Mary and her children. We hear their voices:

B I scored two goals.

G. We're going swimming tomorrow.

B I'm going to get a prize.

The murder scene changes significantly in a March 14 manuscript (box 8), including the razor to the throat. This version omits scenes with Robert and Caroline at the police station but still includes the cottage-by-the-Thames sequence, essentially unaltered from the immediately previous longer version. Here the creak of the gondolas is omitted; we see water pouring into a lock as a boat approaches: "The Sound Fades. Sound of lapping water. The voice of Gigli singing." A note in an April 9 manuscript (box 8) describes Robert's father taking a belt out of a drawer, a shot finally not used, and then another note suggests doing Robert's final speech in Italian with subtitles, followed by the English version.

In an undated manuscript in box 9, scene 130 includes the razor, though not specifically the throat slashing. The police scenes and the scene at the Thames are in this script as well. An April 24 bound typescript (box 10) includes the added scene in the morgue, where Mary combs Colin's hair with her fingers. Scene 99 is now labeled "Cottage" and includes the details of the children's response to the caricatures of them that Colin has drawn on his T-shirt gifts: "Look! It's my face! It's from Colin!" The scene ends with the water pouring in the lock and the gondolas creaking with Gigli in the background. A July 17 version (box 10), perhaps the shooting script, omits the scene at Mary's mother's cottage.

In another undated script, which appears to be late because it is nearly complete, there are modest revisions from previous versions in the murder sequence and in the scenes at the police station. This script concludes with the scene at the mother's cottage, with dialogue expanded beyond that in the earlier versions. In this version, Mary is worried that "Jack" will fall into the water and asks him to give her his hand. Her daughter asks if they can go swimming, and the camera focuses on water pouring into the lock. We then hear the creak of gondolas and "The voice of Gigli singing."

Pinter told Gale and Hudgins that these scenes of Mary back in England were not filmed primarily because of budgetary limitations and the difficulty of getting the film crew and Richardson back to a British location. In response to Hudgins's question, the screenwriter commented about the ambiguity of the concluding shots of Mary but implied that these scenes, especially one chronologically slightly later in composition, suggest a kind of courage and strength to go on, similar to that which the Julie Christie character displays in *Don't Look Now,* to which this film clearly alludes—or perhaps pays homage.

Robert's third telling of his story comes at the end of the movie. It is the shortest of the three versions, and he tells it to the police detective who is interrogating him. The detective cannot understand why he allowed himself to be caught: "You plan everything in advance—you prepare everything—you sell your bar—you sell the apartment—you buy the drug . . . but then on the other hand you leave your razor with your own fingerprints—you book tickets under your own name and you travel on your own passport—we don't get it" (50). Robert's smiling answer is to begin his story about his father. For him, and us, the story explains everything. It may even be that the voice-over at the beginning of the film is the recitation that he gives at the end, so that in essence the whole movie is a flashback.

Director Schrader's assessment of Pinter's script is, "It's quite close to the kind of thing Pinter writes for himself. Though it's an adaptation, it has the same themes and cadences of his original work, that element of dominance in relationships between men and women that is very Pinteresque" (Van Gelder, July 28, 1989). Perhaps the biggest difference between this screenplay and the author's previous works is the onscreen murder. Pinter has always included violence in his writing, and by and large it has been violence that smolders throughout most of the story before blowing up dramatically— Bert in *The Room*, Mick's frightening of Davies in *The Caretaker*, the fights in *The Basement* and *The Homecoming*, the suicide in *The Go-Between*, and so forth—but typically it has been not been of the shocking dimension of this murder. Even the death of the Commander in *The Handmaid's Tale*, as brutal and bloody as it is, does not have the impact of the casual, unnecessary dispatching of Colin.

Many of the screenwriter's film scripts end on an uplifting note (*The Caretaker, The Pumpkin Eater, Turtle Diary*); several have dark endings (*Accident, The Quiller Memorandum, Victory, The Trial*). *The Comfort of Strangers* is his bleakest work, surpassing even *The Servant* in its unfettered angst and sense of inescapable tragedy. While it is not Pinter's best film script, the last five minutes of *The Comfort of Strangers* make it his most unsettling.

As noted above, in a couple of his efforts to find an alternate ending, the screenwriter attempts to ameliorate the impact of the conclusion by showing Mary back in England with her family. This is not satisfactory, however, for he differs from his source in his focus, in essence switching from Mary to Robert as the protagonist; and the English scenes would shift his emphasis from Robert to Mary. It works better to leave these scenes out of the film, no matter what the practical reason was that they were abandoned.

McEwan prefaces his story with two quotations. The first is from Adrienne Rich: "Now we dwelt in two worlds / the daughters and the mothers / in the kingdom of the sons." The second is from Pavese: "Travelling is a brutality. It forces you to trust strangers and to lose sight of all that familiar comfort of home and friends. You are constantly off balance. Nothing is yours except the essential things—air, sleep, dreams, the sun, the sky—all things tending toward the eternal or what we imagine of it." Pinter emphasizes the first over the second. In the novel, Robert does not come into the picture until the end of chapter 2; in the movie, the opening shot is of his apartment (the description of the items on the sideboard is taken almost verbatim from page 59 in the novel) and the beginning of Robert's story is heard over. The story, which takes up almost all of chapter 3 in the novel, is stretched out in the film, broken up to reveal only bits at a time, which leads to a developing of tension. The metaphor of Mary and Colin being lost is established early in the novel, beginning in chapter 1 and repeating through most of the book as they wander through the maze of streets in Venice, look at maps, and talk about not knowing where they are, something that Pinter does with a few quick shots. That metaphor may introduce a sense of tension into the novel, but Pinter takes advantage of his medium to make the motion picture considerably more suspenseful. He does this by foregrounding Robert's photo taking.

McEwan introduces the idea of photography and the invasion of privacy with his description of the old man trying to take a picture of his wife in front of a group of beer-drinking young men (15–16). It is not until page 75 that the novelist actually describes a photograph, and it is not until page 87 that Mary realizes that the photograph that she saw in Robert's apartment was of Colin. Pinter inserts the presence of a still camera immediately when, following the opening scene, he shows Mary and Colin in their hotel room and includes a shot of "A VIEWFINDER" that contains "COLIN's *figure framed in the viewfinder*" (4). Additional shots follow that are set up to look as though they are being taken through the lens of a still camera. Pinter accomplishes two things with these additions. They introduce a more palpable sense of tension than is created in the novel because, by interjecting the mystery of who is taking the photographs and why they are being taken, especially since the action is surreptitious, the writer is drawing on a convention from spy movies and murder thrillers. And, the additions subtly place the emphasis on Robert as the main character because he is the one in control by virtue of being the picture-taker as opposed to the object in the photograph.

In the original, Robert cuts Colin's wrist and then escapes with Caroline, and the story closes with Mary leaving the hospital after combing Colin's hair with her fingers (McEwan, 123–27). In the film version, after the throat slashing, Mary combs her dead lover's hair in the police-station mortuary. She sees that Robert and Caroline have been captured, and the film ends with Robert telling the interrogating detective his story (50–51). Robert thus literally has both the first and last words in the film, and this reenforces Pinter's positioning him as the protagonist.

The screenwriter and his director seem to have had a cordial and effective working relationship. Pinter told Gale and Hudgins about Schrader ("seated on that very sofa" in the carriage house study) saying that his typical way of directing was to improvise. Pinter responded, grinning as he told the anecdote, "Well, you just go right ahead and improvise." Surprised, Schrader said "Really?" and Pinter said, "Yes, if that's the way you make a film go right ahead and improvise but be sure my name is not on the script, and not in the credits." He added that the film was made essentially as he wrote it. Pinter clearly respected Schrader's intelligence, talent, and willingness to work together.[12]

The Trial

RELEASED: 1993

SOURCE: *The Trial,* by Franz Kafka; novel (1937)

PRODUCTION COMPANY: Europanda Entertainment B.V. and BBC Films; distributed by Capitol Films

DIRECTOR: David Jones

EDITOR: John Stothart

CINEMATOGRAPHY BY: Phil Meheux

EXECUTIVE PRODUCERS: Kobi Jaeger, Reneiro Compstella, and Mark Shivas

PRODUCER: Louis Marks

PRODUCTION DESIGNER: Don Taylor

ARTISTIC DIRECTOR: Jiri Matolin

SET DECORATION: John Bush

MUSIC: Carl Davis

COSTUME DESIGNER: Anushia Nieradzik

CAST: Kyle MacLachlan (Josef K), Anthony Hopkins (Prison Chaplain), Jason Robards (Dr. Huld), Juliet Stevenson (Fraulein Burstner), Polly Walker (Leni), Alfred Molina (Titorelli), Jean Stapleton (The Landlady), Patrick Godfry (Chief Usher), Michael Kitchen (Block), Ewald Balser (Dr. Eotvos), Whit Bissell (Sam Wiltse), John Woodvine, Rafael Campos (Angel Chaves), Elisha Cook Jr. (Finn), Ernst Deutsch (Peczely Scharf), Gustav Diessl (Both), Maria Eis (M. Solymosi), Glenn Ford (David Blake), Richard Gaines (Dr. Schacter), Paul Guilfoule (Cap Grant), Anthony Haygarth (Willem), Juano Hernandez (Judge Theodore Motley), John Hodiak (John J. Armstrong), John Hoyt (Ralph Castillo), Katy Jurado (Consuela Chaves), Barry Kelley (Jim Backett), Arthur Kennedy (Barney Castle), Anna Lee (Gail Wiltse), Leon Lissed (Stairman), Dorothy McGuire (Abbe Nyle), Joseph Meinrad (Bary), Robert Middleton (A.S. "Fats" Sanders), Heinz Moog (Baron Onody), Ladislaus Morgenstern (Salomon Schwaiiz), Catherine Neilson (Washerwoman), Ivan Petrevich (Ergessy), Leopold Rudolf (Reszky), Ida

Russka (Batoti), Aglaja Schmid (Esther Solymosi), Marianne Schonauer (Julia), Eva-Maria Skala (Julca), Leo Davis, Don Henderson, John Lyons, Roger Lloyd Pack
RUNNING TIME: 120 minutes[1]
COLOR
NO MPAA RATING
VIDEO: Fox Lorber; Imagine 15 (England)

EARLY IN HIS PLAYWRITING career, Pinter acknowledged to interviewer Bensky that among his youthful literary tastes were Hemingway, Fyodor Dostoyevsky, James Joyce, Henry Miller, Beckett, and especially Kafka's novels. Although he claimed that his writing had not been influenced greatly by the authors that he had read, he did admit that "Beckett and Kafka stayed with me the most" (Bensky, 354). In another interview, the writer again admitted that Beckett and Kafka were the most influential writers in his formative years and said, "When I read them it rang a bell, that's all, within me. I thought—something's going on here which is going on in me too."[2]

In later interviews he was even more explicit about the attractions that Kafka's works held for him, particularly *The Trial* (1937). Certainly, some influence can be traced in the playwright's short prose pieces "Kullus" and "The Examination," both of which deal with solitary victims who face unspecified charges at the hands of unidentified examiners (a theme that is echoed in the inquisition scene in *The Birthday Party* and shows up in the dramatist's political plays *Mountain Language* and *One for the Road*). In both short stories, an unidentified examiner tells through first-person narration of his relationship with Kullus. As in *The Trial,* the subject of the examination is never disclosed. Perhaps some of his feeling of kinship with these victims grows out of his unpleasant experiences with neofascists and their broken bottles when he was a young, eyeglass-wearing, book-carrying Jew in Hackney after World War II.[3] In any case, his identification with Josef K was near enough to the surface of his mind that the specter of K's plight rose when he was trapped in an argument with the army over whether as a conscientious objector he was entitled to be released from his national service obligation (Billington, 23); and memories of *Boomerang!* (which is about the arrest of an innocent man) might have reverberated as well.

One of the author's own earliest characters, Stanley in *The Birthday Party* (who runs from an unknown past and is pursued by representatives of Judeo-Christian society for reasons that are never disclosed and who is eventually taken off to see "Monty"), clearly is related to the "K" of Kafka's novel. In a BBC 4 interview, Pinter acknowledged that "Kafka had an undeniable influence on me in my early life. *The Birthday Party* obviously owes a great deal to Kafka," and he told Francis Gillen that he had wanted to write the screenplay for *The Trial* since he had first read Kafka while still in his teens ("Harold Pinter on *The Trial,*" [61]).

With the aid of BBC producer Louis Marks, with whom Pinter had been a longtime collaborator on television and screenplays, the project was initiated. According to Marks, Pinter suggested the film project to him eight years before the motion picture was made. At that time, the screenwriter also intended to direct the movie. Marks, in this case also the film's producer, is of the opinion that "it is highly unlikely that . . . *The Trial* could ever have been made without the BBC."[4]

Marks recalls that he had a meeting with Pinter and his wife, Lady Antonia Fraser, during which Pinter read the script to him. Pinter indicated that he had written the screenplay in two or three weeks in what Marks described as "a great heat." Marks further said that Pinter had been very emotionally involved with the project, having felt "Jewish affinities to Kafka," and that Pinter's presence on location in Prague was quite emotional and marked by "dreamy eyes," almost as though he was in "a sort of high," especially when Vaclav Havel visited him on the set.

After several years of seeking funding and locations, together with innumerable lesser problems, filming of *The Trial* was scheduled to begin in Prague on March 15, 1992. There were some minor reschedulings, and shooting actually began on March 23. Czechoslovakia's capital is a fitting location for the film, both because it is the locale in the original and because of the milieu that the city creates and projects even today. The stellar cast includes several actors who have appeared in Pinter's works previously. Hopkins and Robards (who was featured in *Reunion*) top the list, but American audiences could have fun picking out old Hollywood actors such as Elisha Cook Jr., Glenn Ford, John Hodiak, Katy Jurado, Arthur Kennedy, Dorothy McGuire, and others.

Janet Maslin reported that "Pinter's version of Kafka's *The Trial* seems a perfect match" ("Film Review"). Some reviewers felt that the film was a failure, however, and Christopher Cornell of the Knight-Ridder News Service gave *The Trial* only two and one-half stars, complaining about Kyle "MacLachlan, acting fussy and indignant as Josef K . . . in David Jones and Harold Pinter's curiously flat adaptation of Franz Kafka's classic of paranoia."

As there had been some fits and starts at the beginning of the shooting,

so, too, were there problems with the finished film's release. Presented at the 1992 Cannes Film Festival, *The Trial* was released in both England and the United States in 1993. The world premiere had been scheduled to take place in Prague with Havel hosting on behalf of Amnesty International. The program included guest speakers, including Pinter. A disagreement between the organizers and the filmmakers led to the event's being canceled.

Advertised as "a screen interpretation written by Harold Pinter," the movie opens with a black screen over which are run the words that begin Kafka's novel, one of world literature's best-known opening lines: "Someone must have been telling lies about Josef K, for without having done anything wrong he was arrested one fine morning." This line is not included in the screenplay; but after the movie was filmed, the filmmakers decided to include it as a voice-over prior to the first photographic image.

Then comes a shot of a shopkeeper sweeping the street in front of his shop. Carl Davis's music—an accordion at the opening of the film—is quite innocent, not in the least foreboding or menacing. This shot is followed by a long series of shots of the city streets and the people on them, culminating in a long dolly shot that ends up at the apartment of Josef K.

Throughout his career, Pinter has treated the commonplace with the greatest respect. This is evident in his plays from the beginning, and it is verbally articulated in his comments on his films, as in his remarks on the "world outside" in regard to *The Caretaker,* his use of colloquial language in virtually all of his works, the death of "Penrose" in *Turtle Diary,* and so forth. When he spoke with John Russell Taylor about Resnais' direction of *Last Year at Marienbad,* he reflected that instead of surrealism, the very ordinariness of an everyday café would be "more interesting to explore" ("Accident," 183–84). It is this "very ordinariness" that is in fact explored in *The Trial.* And, from the beginning of his career Pinter has disdained abstractions. In "Writing for Myself," he declared that he "wouldn't know a symbol if I saw one," and in "Pinterview," an interview that appeared in *Newsweek,* July 23, 1962, he claimed that "you can make symbolic meat out of anything" (69), so it should be no surprise that his rendering of Kafka's story is more concrete and realistic than Welles's interpretation. In production notes for the movie, the screenwriter confesses that he has left out Kafka's analysis and K's interior monologue. Nevertheless, he admits, "Actually I believe that it is there, except that it's not expressed in the same way. It's not a novel, it's a film. The thing to do was simply to show what happens, rather than discuss it." Of course, "showing" has always been the essence of filmmaking.

The transition from the quotidian to the sinister that marks the dramatist's comedies of menace grew out of his own experiences, but undoubtedly it was influenced by his reading of Kafka as well. Pinter's interpretation of the novel suggests the chilling effect that Kafka's work has because it can be generalized to apply to anyone and everyone. It is not, he says, "about affect, effect, but about something that happens on Monday, and then on Tuesday, and then on Wednesday and then right through the week" (Gussow, *Conversations,* 89). The realization of the depth of the horror underlying the ordinariness, as contained in Kurtz's exclamation in Conrad's *Heart of Darkness,* is a constant in most of Pinter's works, from his first drama. It is this horror in the ordinary that makes the interrogation/inquisition scene in *The Birth-day Party* so terrifying. Everyone is guilty of something. No one can escape. Thus, the common street setting in the opening scenes provides a context of the everyday that will contrast so vividly with K's ordeal, an ordeal to which, like the doggy dogs and the torturer's horse in Auden's "Musée des Beaux Arts," nobody truly pays attention, or like Petey in *The Birthday Party*, people can be persuaded that it is better for them not to notice.

The dialogue of the arresters echoes *The Birthday Party*, particularly the interrogation scene in which Stanley is accused of every imaginable sin, faux pas, and crime—including some that are mutually exclusive. This ties in with the next-door neighbor's later reply to Josef's question of whether she believes that he is innocent: "Innocent? Innocent of what?" Clearly, Josef is guilty of something, as we all are. The universalizing effect is compounded by the constant sight of neighbors in the opposite building looking through their windows into Josef's apartment and watching the arrest. Many of the shots in this sequence are structured so that the voyeurs are visible in the background, and at one point Josef actually shouts at them to stop looking and mind their own business.

The crime for which Josef is arrested is never revealed, of course, to Josef or to the audience or even to those who arrest Josef, for that matter. But, then, that is probably what attracted Pinter to the novel. The idea of an unidentifiable crime is present in many of his works for both stage and film, and from the 1980s on, his concern with human rights and government abuses, and his active, public political stances focus on this kind of attack on Everyman by governmental organizations that answer to no one. And, everyone seems to be involved in some way or other, as witness the three bank clerks, the painter Titorelli, the next-door neighbor (Fraulein Burstner), the lawyer and his maid (Leni), the court clerk and his wife, the arresters, the flogger. No one is interested in Josef's side of the case—which is impossible to determine anyway, since no accusations are ever leveled at him. All he can do is protest his innocence, but then we are back to Fraulein Burstner's question, "Innocent of what?" The other characters, including the seemingly innocent bank manager and the Italian visitor, go along with what is happening, either because they do not know what is happening, because they are part of the conspiracy, or because they are afraid of what will happen to them if they do not go along. Which of these motives operates in any individual case is not always apparent, and it obviously does not matter in the long run what the motivation is. The result is the same in all cases: Josef's fate is sealed. He is like a chicken walking around with its head cut off: he is dead; he just does not know it yet.

There are some indications that the crime might be equated with sin, especially the sin of sex. The implication of sexual impropriety is clear in Josef's first meeting with Fraulein Burstner. During the session of the Court of Inquiry in the building where Josef has gone seeking the possible help of Lanz, the plumber, the sexual engagement between the court clerk's wife and her lover on the floor of the hearing room reenforces the connection, especially in view of the detached reactions of the onlookers, some of whom appear to be orthodox Jews. Later, Josef engages in several dalliances with his lawyer's attractive maid. This occurs even when it is to his disadvantage, as in their initial meeting when the important official of the court is present and his potential assistance is vital. When Josef disappears with the maid for some time, the ignored court official's aid disappears as well.

As is his wont, Pinter transported many lines from Kafka directly into the film script. Among these are the doorkeeper speech delivered by Hopkins in the cathedral and the last line—"Like a dog," uttered by Josef as he dies, pinned by the executioner's knife to the altarlike boulder in the stone quarry—a scene that reminds us of the court clerk's diatribe against the man who constantly has sex with his wife and whom he would like to pin to the stairwell wall outside the court office (and remindful, too, of lines in Eliot's "Lovesong of J. Alfred Prufrock": "The eyes that fix you in a formulated phrase, / And when I am formulated, sprawling on a pin, / When I am pinned and wriggling on the wall" [lines 56–58]). The connection between Josef's crime, his fate, and the sin of sex is thus buttressed not only by the parallel between Josef and the revenge that the court clerk wishes to extract for his wife's lover's sexual offense but also by Prufrock's tying together of sexuality and unsympathetic dismissal/punishment. In Freudian terms, then, Josef's death, with the phallically symbolic dagger plunged through his heart, is appropriate to his crime.

The place of the prison chaplain in the overall meaning of the film is understandable in the same way that the prison chaplain's role in Anthony Burgess's *Clockwork Orange* is. He represents the theoretical explanation for what is happening. In this case, Josef is told, in dialogue taken directly from chapter 9 of Kafka's novel (the "Before the Law" section), that he has failed because he has not asked the right questions, a destiny that may afflict all of modern humanity. That the answer comes from a man of the church is important, given the final scene in the film, in which an unidentifiable figure stands in the open window of a mansion with many windows, its spotlighted, white-sleeved arms upraised in benediction. Josef raises his arms to the figure in radiant supplication moments before the knife is thrust into his chest. This suggests that there is association between Josef's crime and religion. Peacock finds that the two major images in the screenplay, a figure at a window and arms outstretched, combine to imply that K's problem is not the existence of an immovable, unjust legal system but rather the burden of an existential struggle that we all carry.

The constant images of passageways, corridors, staircases, and doors take on a dual significance. Artistically, they are dramatic and impressive, but like the expressionistic sets in *The Cabinet of Dr. Caligari,* they represent a twisting journey toward truth, a journey that is filled with blind endings, blank entrances to rooms that may or may not contain answers, and endless, equally unproductive alternative routes that all lead back to the offices of the court. They are a fine symbol for the individual caught up in a contest with an overpoweringly unresponsive authority. They also are informed by a Freudian sexual symbolism. Again, Pinter has linked the thematic elements cinematically. The alleyways of Venice in the more unsettling *Comfort of Strangers* are recalled, as is the theme of that film.

Finally, Josef K's story is generalized cinematically in an interesting contrast. The film was shot in Prague during the early spring when the skies were gray and the trees still almost leafless. The whole movie has a sinisterly dark quality; even the luxurious, richly colorful embroidered clothing of several of the characters and the sumptuously decorated interior scenes in the apartments, the bank, and so forth, are muted. In the outdoor scenes the city itself is grim and gray, as in Welles's 1963 black-and-white film of the story that was influenced by the expressionist cinema of the 1930s, and in the style of the black-and-white films of eastern Europe seen in the West during the cold war. The shop names and other signs in the street scenes are in Czech, and the dress of the people is that of early-twentieth-century eastern Europe. There can be no doubt about where the tale is taking place, even if the exact country is not specified. At the same time, most of the characters (the two notable exceptions being MacLachlan and Robards) speak with distinctly British accents and language (stereotypically uttering phrases such as "Cheerio," and so on), several of them with Cockney overtones.

Peter Bogdanovich found Welles's version "uncomfortable to watch." Welles thought that the film was hilariously funny—the humor in the word play ("ovular") is Welles's—although Anthony Perkins, who played K, recounts that Welles instructed him that K was "guilty as hell . . . guilty of everything" (another tie to Stanley in *The Birthday Party*). It is noteworthy that Welles felt "no essential reverence for the original material," and in some ways his attitude is mirrored in Pinter's work, for Welles believed that as part of a collaboration, it was necessary for him to be true only to the essence of his source, which he saw as a tale of modern horror creeping up on the Austro-Hungarian Empire. He saw Kafka's novel as a modern European tale.[5] Other similarities between the Pinter and Welles scripts are the scenes of K arriving at the trial and those featuring the washerwoman and the courtroom.

Undoubtedly, the screenwriter was well aware of Welles's version of *The Trial*. In Pinter's best stage play, *Old Times*, the character Deeley says, "I wrote the film and directed it. My name is Orson Welles" (42). In two of Welles's films, the director delivers the movies' final lines in a voice-over in the same words: "I . . . wrote and directed this film. My name is Orson Welles" (*The Trial*); "I wrote the script and directed it. My name is Orson Welles" (*The Magnificent Ambersons*). Pinter found the Welles version of *The Trial* an "incoherent nightmare of spasmodic half-adjusted lines, images" (Gussow, *Conversations*, 88–89).

Pinter intended for his adaptation of the novel to be more realistic than Welles's symbol- and psychodrama-filled version, as demonstrated by the careful search for suitable shooting sites. The author told Gillen that he had envisioned a movement from "brightness, openness and optimism to darkness, suffocation, and death." The young K was to represent the belief in logic, progress, and general optimism of Europe in 1910.

Ultimately, however, while there clearly is the sense of mystery contained in the general theme of the individual trapped in something that he does not understand, there is no real sense of terror or horror present. Some critics have claimed that Josef finally comes to embrace his fate, since he accepts the fact that he must be guilty of something. If this is so, neither MacLachlan nor director Jones has made his attitude clear.[6] Josef seldom appears overly emotionally engaged in the contest at any point during the film, and at the conclusion, he seems merely to have run out his string. It is as though the movie eventually has to end, and since he cannot exonerate himself, he is dispatched. There is not a great deal of empathy for him. As in the novel, K's trial is dealing with being accused, for we never know whether the legal trial takes place. Presumably it does, since he is executed, but we do not see the court in action.

The film is interesting, but it is not gripping, not Kafkaesque enough. Kafka's sometimes dense prose, which obviously provides some of the effect, is not captured. On the one hand, possibly this is because Pinter has not successfully translated the tensions in Josef's mind from the novel to the screen. On the other hand, Kafka's prose is sometimes too heavy, and Pinter's version has lightened that effect. Unfortunately, it is the interior tensions that give the novel its impact.

Pinter's interest in the film may revolve around the figure of Josef K as a victim, though, interestingly, the screenwriter has said, "One of the captions that I would put on The Trial is simply: 'What kind of game is God playing?' That's what Josef K is really asking. And the only answer he gets is a pretty brutal one."[7] Thus, it is instructive to revisit the two Kullus pieces. The composition of these two works came at an important juncture in Pinter's development as a writer. Whereas, according to John Russell Taylor, Pinter had been interested in integrity and identity in his plays, "The Examination" represents a shift to the definition of character through social interaction and communication (*The Angry Theatre,* 13). Pinter sees "The Examination" as the point from which he developed his themes of violence, dominance, and subservience, though he admits that the themes had been present in his earlier works. He told Bensky, "I wrote a short story . . . called 'The Examination,' and my ideas of violence carried on from there. That short story dealt very explicitly with two people in one room having a battle of unspecified nature." It is in this interview that he refers to the concept of domination (362–63).

In the short story, the idea of verification that pervades the dramatist's early plays is present.[8] More important, however, is the battle between Kullus and the inquisitor, in which Kullus essentially manages to reverse their roles in terms of who is in control. By the end of the tale, "we were now in Kullus's room," he reports (Pinter, "The Examination," [87]). Hudgins is of the opinion that the character of Josef K appealed to Pinter because he did not allow the opposing forces to take control of him without opposition.[9] Kafka's view of the examiners' ultimate victory is more realistic, terrifying, and personally applicable to most readers.

In her review of the motion picture, Jeanne Connolly remarks that "The viewer of *The Trial* is restricted by the cinematic frame mainly to rooms, as in Pinter's drama. The visual text of these rooms attempts to subliminally map the film's psychological terrain" (85). Given this, why the opening sequence in which the camera sweeps through the streets of Prague? To provide a kind of establishing shot representing the time and place of the story? To elicit a sense of unease because of the subliminal associations with eastern European tyrannical governments and their secret police interrogations? To move from the exterior to the interior, whether from the street to the room or into the protagonist's mind? To stress the ordinary-looking surroundings in which the actions take place?

As Josef returns to the court after his first confusing and cantankerous appearance, he meets a seductive charwoman. The woman turns out to be the court usher's wife, and it becomes clear that she is also sexually involved with the court's chief magistrate and with a law student. The passionate relationship between the woman and the student is demonstrated when he carries her off to continue their dalliance. When Josef leaves, he meets the cuckolded husband, who complains, "If my job weren't at stake, I'd have squashed that student flat against the wall here long ago. Just beside this sign. It's a daily dream of mine. I see him squashed flat here, just a little above the floor, his arms wide, his fingers spread, his bandy legs writhing in a circle, and blood all over the floor." To this speech of frustrated anger, Pinter adds one line: "Total agony, you know what I mean?" The addition of this line works on several levels. Like Yeats's "mere anarchy" ("The Second Coming," line 4), *total* gives an added dimension to the pictorial concept of agony. Simultaneously, it is a bit over the top, it is unnecessary given the image painted, and the tag "you know what I mean" diminishes that agony by reducing it through language to the everyday, the commonplace (cf. Eliot's Prufrock).

Another of Pinter's inventions comes when K is looking for the venue of his first hearing and he pretends to be seeking a plumber named Lanz. Pinter inserts a scene:

SECOND STAIRMAN. Ah. Lanz, yes. Yes, yes there used to be a man called Lanz on the fifth floor. That's right. I remember. He was a plumber. Definitely. But I haven't been up there for years.

JOSEF K. On the Fifth floor?

SECOND STAIRMAN. I've got no reason to go up there now, you see.

JOSEF K. Thank you. (41 [1989 typescript]; 18 [1993 published screen-play])

This sounds like Mr. Kidd's discussion with Rose about how many floors there are in the apartment building in *The Room*. This simple, seemingly pointless exchange points up the absurdity of K's position, it reflects the lack of concern by public servants, and it echoes Auden's statements about the nature of suffering in "Musée des Beaux Arts."[10]

Again, this connection between suffering and the ordinary is highlighted. Connolly remarks on another twist linking the banal and the awful:

> As in the novel, an unremarkable bank closet unpredictably opens to reveal itself a flogging room. But unlike the novel, in which the victims are flogged by a brutal professional "sheathed in a sort of black leather garment," the film places the warders on all fours against an opaque glass floor lit from beneath. In effect, the choice transforms the novel's nightmare vision of sado-masochism into a metatheatrical enactment of human sacrifice. More significantly, this sacrifice is carried out in the film by a spectacled clerk in white sleeves and vest. His very ordinariness is frightening. Meaning is rewritten purely by a visual image into a Pinter "text," in which the familiar is destabilized. (85)

Connolly claims that in the episode featuring the petitioner Block in lawyer Huld's home, Pinter's distillation of the segment in the original succeeds in "condensing all the novel's themes in a single character's futile quest for justice in a style clearly his own." This observation fits with Pinter's consuming interest in political matters during the period, although director Jones says that he was attracted to the script because of its psychological content, and it goes counter to the interpretation offered by Kafka scholar Frederick R. Karl, who claims that *The Trial* is about "time and space elements removed from our usual expectations; the sense of enstiflement and suffocation; a surrealism of scene and personage; the suggestion of Hades, Lucifer, and Heaven; the sense of individual will trying to impose itself on a situation that defies change . . .; the presence of an artist figure . . .; the caged quality of the protagonist, a functionary who functions in vain" (77). Karl contends that although Pinter may be the only writer who could have translated Kafka's work for the screen, the screenwriter fails because he cannot reproduce the spaces or the time—he is too faithful to the original, and thus, while he captures Kafka, he does not capture the Kafkaesque: "Not all great twentieth-century writers translate well into visual media" (81). Pinter had worked with an unfinished novel as a source previously, *The Last Tycoon*, but Karl is also concerned with the fact that Kafka never finished this novel, so Pinter must rely on Joseph Brod's translation, which Karl feels is too linear, "orderly," and "sequenced." Only by utilizing an expressionistic approach could Pinter have succeeded, according to Karl; instead, he finds the screenwriter too "realistic" in his adaptation.

In the Pinter Archives (box 55), there are galley proofs for the single-volume edition of *The Trial,* with a cover photo of MacLachlan as Josef K. A handwritten note is attached: "This screenplay was shot in its entirety. During the editing of the film, however, a number of scenes were cut. These cuts were made with my approval." That statement is included as an "Author's note" in the published version of the screenplay over the initials H.P. The volume is dedicated to director Jones and producer Marks, suggesting that, Karl's view notwithstanding, Pinter felt that this collaborative project was a success.

Lolita

RELEASED: Not filmed
SOURCE: *Lolita,* by Vladimir Nabokov; novel (1955)

IN 1962 DIRECTOR Stanley Kubrick's film version of *Lolita* was released. Based on Vladimir Nabokov's novel (1955) and screenplay, the movie starred James Mason, Shelley Winters, Peter Sellers, and Sue Lyon.[1] Mason played the staid professor, Humbert Humbert, and Lyon was the sexually precocious Lolita. One of the finest and most fascinating novels of the twentieth century, *Lolita* was critically acclaimed, yet, although it has sold over fourteen million copies, apparently it was disparaged by the public because of its subject matter—child sexual abuse (it seemed to be, and sometimes was sold as, appealing to prurient interests).[2] The work is about the sexual abuse of a child, but it is also about cause and effect, obsession, love, and facing a moral dilemma (a particularly Shakespearean motif). Despite the nature of Nabokov's subject matter, there is no question that *Lolita* is a joy to read. The author's style is engaging, interesting philosophies are propounded, there is insight into perversion, and there is humor.

In the early 1990s, Nicholas Roeg approached Pinter with the proposal that the screenwriter create a script for a new film version that Roeg would direct.[3] Pinter was excited about the project because he had some reservations about the Kubrick movie. First and foremost, he claimed, it was about a subject—essentially the sexual abuse of a child—that was perhaps more taboo in the 1990s than it had been in the 1960s due to the prevailing atmosphere of political correctness. I believe that the pedophilia was pretty obvious in Kubrick's version, even though little actual sexual action was seen on the screen (even in the 1960s it would have been clear to the audience what was going on), but Pinter adamantly claimed that Kubrick missed the boat in not focusing more blatantly on the child-abuse element, which Pinter felt was more explicitly dealt with in his own screenplay. The more important missing element in the Kubrick film script, in my opinion, was Humbert's motivation, which is deleted with the omission of the Annabel Leigh story for which nothing else is substituted.[4]

Pinter was also bothered by the casting. He felt that Winters was simply too brash and overpowering in her portrayal of Lolita's sex-starved mother (though critics such as Leonard Maltin found her performance "outstanding")[5] and Lyon was clearly too old and mature to be playing the child's part. Most important to Pinter, however, was the fact that the movie contained "no sex!"[6] In the original film version, he notes, we hardly see the two main characters touching. Accordingly, he set out to correct these failings and spent six months hard at work on the screenplay.[7]

Before the script could be filmed, though, several things happened. As it turns out, Pinter was the second screenwriter to be offered the opportunity to write the script. Hudgins, who has written a fine explication of the screenplay,[8] says that director Adrian Lynne suggested the project to Pinter (a rewrite of James Dearden's 1991 script, which Pinter has never seen)[9] and that Pinter "knew 'Lolita' very well and loved it" (125). *Fatal Attraction* scenarist Dearden had already written a script for Carolco, an American production company, but the company was having difficulties with another film that it was trying to produce, and a decision was made to sell the rights to a French group.[10] It is not clear exactly what happened when, but according to Pinter, Carolco was still in charge of the project when he was approached with the offer.

Pinter and Roeg met for lunch to discuss the project, and during the course of the meal, Roeg exclaimed that he could hardly wait to film the scene of the two fifteen-year-old lesbians in bed. Pinter was bewildered and asked what scene it was that the director was talking about, since there is no passage in the novel about such an event. Roeg agreed but said that Pinter would write the scene, that he was the very man to do it. Pinter declined to include such a scene that was not in the book, especially when he could see no thematic reason for doing so. At this point Roeg invited Pinter to step outside so that they could settle their difference of opinion physically; Pinter reached across the table and grabbed Roeg's arm to emphasize that he would not write the scene. When the writer grasped the director's biceps, however, he realized that the arm was granite hard and remembered that Roeg had been a Special Forces paratrooper, in top physical shape from exercising and trained to kill. Pinter is not a small man, and he was still muscular in his middle sixties, but he immediately changed the grasp to a pat on the shoulder and laughed off the challenge. The scene was not written.

The script was accepted by Carolco. Regrettably, in 1994 Carolco was forced to declare bankruptcy, and the project was put on hold (Pinter was upset at the delay and uncertainty after having spent so much time on what he considered a difficult assignment, though he eventually did get paid for the work). Since Carolco was no longer in a position to produce the film, there was a great and continuous effort to sell the project to another production company, but money was a problem because those who were interested found that not only would they have to pay for the project itself but that Carolco would have to be compensated for giving it up. For months the fate of the movie was up in the air. Then in November 1994 Pinter wrote that "I've just heard that they are bringing another writer into the 'Lolita' film. It doesn't surprise me."[11] Pinter's contract contained a clause to the effect that the film company could bring in another writer, but that in such a case he could withdraw his name (which is exactly the case with *The Remains of the Day*—he had insisted on this clause since the bad experience with revisions made to his *Handmaid's Tale* script); he has never been given any reason as to why another writer was brought in.

Ironically, given the fact that he was a major influence on David Mamet's stage writing, that he directed Mamet's *Oleana* in its London premiere, and that the two men are friends, it was Mamet who was chosen to rewrite the script for director Adrian Lyne's planned remake. Mamet's script differs markedly from Pinter's in several consequential ways. Mamet deletes the voice-overs, de-emphasizes dialogue, and relies heavily on Isenstienian uninflected cuts.[12] In a double or triple irony, this screenplay was also rejected, and the project was turned over to Stephen Schiff, a *New Yorker* staff writer who had conducted a biographical interview with Pinter for *Vanity Fair* but had never sold a screenplay. This is almost like asking Shakespeare, Marlowe, and Jonson to write a play, rejecting their efforts, and settling instead on a rewrite by Ford, Massinger, or Marston—or perhaps Thomas Hariot.

Lyne began shooting on the Schiff script in North Carolina, Texas, and Louisiana in the summer of 1995 and opened at a Spanish film festival in the fall of 1997. The film starred Jeremy Irons, Melanie Griffith, and fifteen-year-old newcomer Dominique Swain.[13] Schiff pointed out that his screenplay was considerably different from Nabokov's, for "the previous movie was made at a time when the major characters couldn't even kiss on-screen."[14]

Perhaps it was fortuitous that Pinter's script was not chosen for the film, because distributors, particularly in America, proved cool to the idea of a motion picture about a pedophile. As Robert W. Butler reported, "Part of the problem is that the film industry tends to exercise a very narrow view of things. In the eyes of Hollywood, *Lolita* is simply a movie about sex with a minor." Lyne concurs: "So many studios are owned by corporate companies, who will make a phone call and say, 'No way we want to be interested in that,' and that's it."[15] It may be, then, that the project was doomed to failure, at least financially, from its inception.

Pinter is proud of his version, however, and under the circumstances, he was concerned that his original 188-page, 248-scene script dated September 26, 1994, be seen. It is this typed manuscript version of the screenplay that I analyze.[16]

The script opens in medias res as Humbert's car is seen moving slowly down a street under the caption "Coalmont Illinois 1952." Using a voice-over, Pinter immediately sets the tone and his theme of child abuse as Humbert declares, "My name is Humbert. You won't like me. I suffer from moral leprosy. I am not a nice man. I am abnormal. Don't come any further with me if you believe in moral values. I am a criminal. I am diseased. I am a monster. I am beyond redemption" (1). The scene itself is taken from much later in the novel, from chapter 29 of part 2.[17]

Interestingly, Lyne had wanted Pinter to use a great deal of voice-over to capture the complexity of Nabokov's first-person narrator, but, despite having employed this device in earlier films, the author chose to use the contrivance only a very limited number of times. Conceivably, he had come to agree with James Agee, who, in commenting on the inadequacy of voice-overs, says, "to read from the text of a novel—not to mention interior monologues—when people are performing on the screen, while it may elevate the literary tone of the production, which I doubt, certainly and inescapably plays hell with it as a movie."[18]

One of the few voice-overs that the screenwriter does include is Humbert's comment that "it was like being with the small ghost of somebody you had recently killed" (100) while he watches Lolita walk toward the car from a gas station restroom. Whereas most of the other voice-overs serve merely to advance the plot, these two instances are important because they capture Humbert's recognition of his own immorality and reflect on his character.

Following the opening voice-over, the screenwriter inserts the opening dialogue from Nabokov's work. Remaining as true as possible to his source,

Pinter retains the times and locales of the book (1952 is approximately twenty-nine years after Humbert's relationship with Lolita began in 1944). As in several of his earlier screenplays, he accommodates the first-person narrator through the device of the voice-over delivered in the approximate present, so that it is now a narrator speaking to the audience rather than writing to a reader.

Scene 5 serves as a bridge to the story of fourteen-year-old Humbert's affair with thirteen-year-old Annabel in a mimosa grove on the grounds of a Côte D'Azur hotel in 1924. The youngster's voice is heard over the close-up image of the man's face: "Darling. Darling." It is the boy talking to the girl, seen in scene 6. In part 1, chapters 3 and 4, of the novel, the narrator makes it clear that this ill-fated episode was the source for his later attraction to nymphets as he tried to recapture the burst of feelings and exploratory intimacy that he and Annabel had shared in their first adventure with love and sexuality. By use of a flashback (to twenty-four years before Humbert met Lolita), Pinter brings alive the simple narrative of the novel. He skips over the details of Humbert's family background that are presented in the novel and goes directly to the purported "source" of his protagonist's affliction. Nabokov's Humbert explicitly states that he "broke [Annabel's] spell by incarnating her in another" (Nabokov, 15)—in Lolita. Whether Pinter is trying to explain and perhaps thus to elicit sympathy for Humbert's despicable actions or whether, given the opening dialogue in which Humbert vilifies himself, this attempt on the part of the film's narrator is merely a politically correct attempt to portray himself as a victim to justify his later conduct is not clear at this time. Nevertheless, the proximity of that initial dialogue is such that it is likely that Pinter is declaring Humbert's behavior unacceptable, regardless of the cause or rationale offered for what the pedophile does. There can be no justification, no excuse.

Possibly for the same reason, or possibly because film is not a medium of words, the screenwriter skips the narrator's fascinating commentary on the nature of nymphets and how it is important to him that they "Never grow up" (Nabokov, 21), the treatment of young girls in other cultures, and so on. He omits scenes in a mental institution, too, for like Humbert's tempestuous and amusing marriage to his first wife, Valeria, which is omitted as well, these have little to do with the essence of the problem confronted in the screenplay. To the scenarist the intellectualizing is not as important as the emotional content. Nabokov explains; once again, Pinter reveals.

In the meantime, though, the screenwriter does several things that are characteristic of his style in terms of how he approaches translating work from one medium to another. To begin with, whereas the novelist provides a brief narrative summary of the children's lovemaking (12), Pinter provides the details not in summary but in action, as he creates visual images of the occurrence in scenes 6 through 13. Elsewhere, Nabokov's narrator reports that he had once had a snapshot taken by his aunt that showed Annabel and her parents at a table in a sidewalk café, where the girl was enjoying a *chocolat glacé*. In the script, Pinter *shows* the incident, complete with Annabel's father posing the group for the photograph.

Similarly, as part of the children's lovemaking segment in the novel (essentially contained in a sentence and a half), the novelist describes how "I was on my knees, and on the point of possessing my darling, when two bearded bathers, the old man of the sea and his brother, came out of the sea with exclamations of ribald encouragement, and four months later she died of typhus in Corfu" (13). Pinter is more explicit:

13. <u>CAVE ON EMPTY BEACH</u>   <u>LATE AFTERNOON</u>

    A pair of sunglasses on a rock.
    Humbert and Annabel naked in the cave.
    He moves to her and lies over her.
    Two bearded bathers suddenly come out of the sea,
    shouting and laughing.

BATHER

      That's it! Go at it! Go on!
      That's my boy!

    Annabel jumps up, skips on one foot to get into
    her shorts. Humbert tries to screen her from
    the men.

Now the physicality of lovemaking is captured in the naked bodies, which simultaneously accentuates the youth of the participants; the invasion of the bathers is abrupt and intrusive, breaking the idyllic spell of the first-time lovers; the tenderness of Humbert is demonstrated in the way in which he moves to Annabel; the raucous, ribald attitude of the bather conflicts with the gentle innocence of the lovemaking; Annabel's confusion and embarrassment in the situation are demonstrated; and the purity and intensity of Humbert's feelings for Annabel are exhibited in his effort to protect her. The scene supplies an entrance into understanding why Humbert might be tied forever to an idealized memory, as well.

Furthermore, rather than ending the account with the striking note that she died shortly thereafter, Pinter expands Nabokov's words into visuals in which he not only displays the information but also informs them with additional insight:

16.   <u>INT HOTEL ROOM</u>

        Father and Humbert.

                    FATHER
        In Corfu.
        Sound of the sea.

                    HUMBERT
            Why?
        Father looks at him.

                    HUMBERT
            Why did she die?

                    FATHER
            She died of typhus.
        Sound of the sea.

                    HUMBERT
            What is typhus?

                    FATHER
            It's a fever. There was a plague.
            In Corfu.

The sound of Pinterese is present here in the Pinteresque elements of an abrupt, unreferenced opening, short sentences, cadence and phrasing, repetition, and minimal logical connections between the speakers. The connection between Corfu and Humbert's question, "Why?" are obviously unclear to the audience when the words are uttered; it is only in retrospect that meaning can be gleaned. Moreover, the audience must determine that it was Annabel who died. The boy's further need to repeat the question with amplification, "Why did she die?" supplies part of the information needed to be processed, though it also illustrates a gulf between the father and the son in their understanding of the event—the father may think that Humbert means why in

Corfu, which would be the logical antecedent, yet for the upset young man, the concern is not where but how, or as he says, "Why?" The why has a double meaning, too, of course. Not only does it signify "in what manner," but it means "for what purpose," too. The father's answer is to the first meaning; the novel and the screenplay have to do with the abstraction of the second. Meanwhile, in the background there is the ironic sound of the sea, the symbol of life, as the father and son talk about death. Finally, Humbert's innocence and youth are illustrated by the fact that he does not know what typhus is.

Nabokov's allusion to the song from Bizet's *Carmen* (based on Propser Mérimée's tale of a manipulating woman who takes advantage of a man foolishly smitten with her, who murders her when she leaves him for another man) is replicated in Pinter's scene in which Humbert tries to keep Lolita on his lap ("Lolita," 33–37) and then is repeated by the screenwriter in an effective invented scene in the desert in which Humbert sings the song again after he has lost Lolita. During the tennis match and after Lolita's party, Pinter uses slow motion to evoke Humbert's emotional involvement.

These expansions of the material contained in the novel are representative of Pinter's attitude toward his source material when he adapts it for film: he tries to remain as true to the original as possible, given the limitations of the media, and to retain the physical elements as well as the thematic. Paradoxically, through conflation he reduces the novel to a manageable length for film, but in so doing he also accomplishes something considerably more important. In condensing the material to its essence, he simultaneously expands it by introducing supplemental considerations that reflect in greater depth and concentration the significant elements contained in his source.

Characteristically, he explores intellectual concepts through emotional expression. Thus, not only does he extract the essence, his talent lies in his ability to mold that essence in such a way that he draws more out of it than was expressed in the original, and he imprints it with his own signature, creating a new work of art in the process. He reduces and reduces the intellectual content until he distills its essence in emotionally expressed ways that reflect and supplement the intellectual content.

Characteristically, too, some of Pinter's elaborations are primarily intended to furnish an element of action, which is elemental in a motion picture, for what is fundamentally the intellectual exploration of an àbstract concept. For instance, when the narrator is driven to the Haze home in Ramsdale, New Hampshire, in a chauffeured limousine provided by a friend of the family, "we almost ran over a meddlesome suburban dog (one of those who lie in wait for cars) as we swerved into Lawn Street" (Nabokov, 36). In the script, the limousine becomes a taxi, driven by what must be someone's stereotype of the inhabitants of middle America who praise the townspeople because "They don't allow no dog shit on the streets. They go to church on Sundays. They dress nice. They're good Americans" (scene 18), as though all of these attributes are equivalent. When the dog runs across the street and barks at the car, the action is shown emphatically—"Shit! Did you see that goddamn dog?"

Pinter says that the novel has a voice the like of which had never been heard before, a very subtle and complex first-person narrative voice. Despite the director's wanting him to use a good bit of that narrative as voice-over in the film, Pinter insists that he would never use it in a description of action. It is obvious from the above how he put his opinion into practice.

Other additions are used for characterizing purposes. When Charlotte Haze first appears in both the novel and the screenplay, the descriptions are *nearly* the same:

> Presently, the lady herself—sandals, maroon slacks, yellow silk blouse, squarish face, in that order—came down the steps, her index finger still tapping upon her cigarette. (Nabokov, 37)

> Charlotte comes down the stairs. Sandals, maroon slacks, yellow silk blouse, plucked eyebrows, cigarette. (Pinter, scene 19)

The difference is subtle, yet telling. For practical purposes, screenwriters seldom include specific physical details such as "squarish face" because such a requirement would limit the actors who could play the role and thus diminish the salability of the script. The inclusion of "plucked eyebrows," however, is not a limiting factor, and in fact it provides an additional indicator of the nature of the character being portrayed. The implication that will be developed is of a lower-class woman with pretensions to sensuality, or at least romantic sexuality.

Another invented scene is inserted at the point where Humbert is about to return to the Enchanted Hunters Motel to ravish Lolita. "All we can say at this stage is that [eternity] goes on for a very very long time indeed. And even then it has hardly begun. So you can all see that it makes a lot of sense to keep on the right side of the Lord," says a cleric (86). Further on, Pinter adds dialogue between two maids who comment on Humbert and Lolita staying in bed so late when breakfast is delivered to the room: "That's some appetite" (94).

A Pinter-invented image occurs when Humbert enters Lolita's room and takes an anklet out of her chest of drawers; "he puts the anklet around two fingers and draws it tighter." Hudgins finds this to be a clear suggestion that Humbert considers "'big girls' too loose, the tight anklet becoming an image of his perverse desire for youthful flesh," in a scene that is "both horrific and titillating" (Hudgins, "*Lolita*," 137). Humbert's lustful, possessive obsession and Lolita's bemused disdain are more graphically displayed when he returns to a motel room after being sent by Lolita to get some fruit to find her dressed, with gravel on her shoes and her mouth smudged, clear evidence that she has betrayed him. "He stares at her, suddenly pushes her back onto the bed, rips her shirt off, unzips her slacks, tears them off. She does not resist. She is naked. She lies still looking up at him. She smiles at him" (Pinter, "Lolita," 146).

Among the lines that Pinter has added that reenforce the essence of Nabokov's novel is Humbert's response to Lolita's calling him a pervert: "My darling, let me tell you something. A pervert is someone who cannot love. A pervert is someone without a heart. I have a heart and it belongs to you" (108). Humbert's self-deception, the probability that he really does love her, and the triteness of the exchange are humorously demolished by Lolita's reply while she unwraps a stick of gum in cliché recognition of her age and her dismissive attitude: "Well, gee, thanks. I could really use an extra heart" (109).

Typically, Pinter's additions are based on something in Nabokov's original. The celebration of Lolita's fourteenth birthday is an example. In the novel, Humbert is enthralled by the girl's grace as she rides her "beautiful young bicycle" (171), and he mentions that "for her birthday I bought her a bicycle" (182). In the screenplay, Humbert serves Lolita an enormous breakfast, but before he lets her eat, he takes her downstairs to see her present—a new bicycle. She excitedly throws her arms around him and calls him "Dad" (127–28). Hudgins notes that a parody discussion about the nature of God and predestination, which "unobtrusively points in thematic directions" ("*Lolita*," 139), is derived from Humbert's brief mention in the novel that they engaged in such a discussion (Nabokov,182).

Hudgins believes that Pinter's decision not to begin with Humbert driving through the fog to Quilty's mansion (the Kubrick version), with Humbert's car after he has wounded Quilty (Schiff), or in a mental institution (Mamet and Dearden) is "better in that it immediately centers our interest on the crucial reunion scene and its implications of both Humbert's and Lolita's moral growth. Unlike the other scripts, it also maintains the novel's suspense about who it is that Humbert plans to kill. *And*, it avoids the caricature that flaws the tone of the Kubrick film from the start" (Hudgins, "*Lolita*," 130).

Dearden and Kubrick also omit the entire Annabel Leigh sequence, which is the key to understanding Humbert's actions. Pinter foregrounds this seminal period in Humbert's life by locating the protagonist's adolescent memory between the initial Coalmont sequence and the Ramsdale sequence so that there is a connection, through Annabel Leigh, between Coalmont and Ramsdale. He excludes most of the details contained in the novel about Humbert's detective work and the hiring of a detective to find Lolita, none of which is vital to capturing the essence of Nabokov's story or plot. Conversely, the omission of Humbert's affair with Rita might have had more of an impact because these two years in Humbert's life may demonstrate that he was moving away from the morality that governed him during his time with Lolita and thus indicate the beginnings of moral growth in the protagonist. Hudgins feels that including this subplot would distract from the central action of the film. Another Pinter omission is that of the scene in the novel in which Humbert's sexual desire for his young ward is pruriently depicted as he looks at her during her bout with a fever (Nabokov, 198). This scene is one of the more lurid examples of Humbert's unhealthy lust. By deleting it, Pinter mediates our perception of the protagonist, especially when the writer substitutes an ameliorative scene in which Humbert is seen as quite sympathetic in his compassion for the sick girl, and his outrage when he finds that she has been taken away from him (Pinter, 160–63).

The differences between the endings of the novel and the adaptation are telling. Nabokov's story concludes with Humbert seeking out Quilty in an old mansion that is the scene of continuing bacchanalian revels. In an extended and gruesome fashion, Humbert mercilessly shoots his old nemesis to death, bit by bit.[19] The narrator then draws his tale to an end by explaining that the book is his way of sharing immortality with Lolita. The Kubrick film ends with Humbert having left Lolita with her husband and then entering Quilty's disheveled house and calling out for him. This is followed by a caption in which it is explained that Humbert was convicted of Quilty's murder. Pinter's script follows the novel closely. It ends with the murder graphically depicted and Humbert's capture by the police.[20] The capture is accompanied by "a growing sound from the valley. The sound consists of a melody of children at play. It is distant. It vibrates, murmurs, sings."[21] As he is apprehended, Humbert stands still and whispers, "Lolita, light of my life, fire of my loins. My sin, my soul. Lo-lee-ta" (words taken from the opening of the novel). Two captions then appear on the screen:

HUMBERT DIED OF A CORONARY THROMBOSIS ON
NOVEMBER 16 1952

LOLITA DIED IN CHILDBIRTH ON CHRISTMAS DAY 1952 (188)

Mamet ends his screenplay with the murder, followed by a scene in which Humbert is seen in a hospital cell and then a flashback to the twelve-year-old Humbert on the beach.

The brutality of Nabokov's ending, which is somewhat diminished by Kubrick, is retained by Pinter and Mamet. Even with the caption—which clearly does not evoke the same emotional impact that the images in the Pinter and Mamet scripts do—the Kubrick-Southern cleanliness makes the end relatively soft. By retaining the original's brutality, Pinter and Mamet declare that Humbert is to be neither pitied nor admired. Pinter's caption leaves the audience with the sense of loss and irony contained in the novel; Mamet's flashback reenforces the theme of the impact of Humbert's fated tryst with Annabel on the rest of his life.

Still, Pinter somewhat ameliorates Humbert's nature by eliminating that section of Quilty's murder in which Humbert forces his victim to read a poem (Nabokov, 273–74). When the film script ends, there is no doubt that Humbert is reprehensible and that what he has done to Lolita is indefensible. The juxtapositions of innocence and perversion, of sin and soul, represented by the sounds of the children and Humbert's final words, speak to the tortured character of Humbert, who realizes the monstrosity of what he has done. At the same time, even though unforgivable, this monstrosity is tempered by the nature of a man who may be better than what he has become, at least in part through no failing of his own other than a weakness born of desperation. From the very beginning, Pinter's characters have been desperate, on the edge. People like this may not be forgiven, but perhaps they can be seen as having been pushed further in a precarious and perverse direction than most of us have, and the recognition of their humanity, however flawed, makes us realize how close we may be to a digression just as horrifying, even if in another arena. Humbert's reaction to Lolita as Lolita Schiller is indicative of his ability to change, to mature morally. This may not be sufficient to save him, though it may offer the rest of us hope for our own redemption.

Pinter's screenplay slows a bit around the midpoint, but there is no question that this is one of his best screenplays. He has added to the humor, as is his wont, creating an even more horrendous effect in exposing Humbert's corruption than would be done in a straightforward narrative because the contrast between the humor and the protagonist's actions is highlighted, emphasizing the gulf between normal human behavior and Humbert's conduct. In addition, the sex is more explicit in Pinter's script than in his source (both in quantity and in actualization), though perhaps the embodied theme of the sexual abuse of the child does not come through as powerfully as he intended—but, of course, the images that he creates in words may well be overwhelming when presented as filmic images on the large screen. Certainly, his characters would have been perceived as being vigorous.

Echoes of Pinter's own works occasionally surface, as when Lolita climbs onto Humbert's knee to ask him about his doodling. Having asked him if he can see a pimple on her chin, she jumps down and rushes off shouting that she needs some "cream" (25), a double entendre that is reminiscent of John the milkman's supposedly prurient visit in *The Lover.* A subsequent description of the girl trying to induce Humbert to allow her to act in the school play at the Beardsley School could have come from the seduction scene in *The Lover* as well, as she "dances over to him, sinking to the floor by his knees. She rests her head on his knee. She puts her hand on the inside of his knee. He continues reading. Her hand gently creeps a little way up his inner thigh" (121). As the scene progresses, he closes his eyes and she ask him to double her allowance. He says no, and she moves her hand away. Then she asks for permission to take part in the play, and her hand moves back up his thigh.

In terms of characters, Humbert is reminiscent, too, of Mosley's Stephen and his almost Lolita-like attraction to Anna and others like her that is explained in words that reverberate with *Lolita:* "I fell in love with these girls for what they were not, for the dream, the unattainable" (Mosley, 66). There is still another echo of an older man with whom Pinter deals, Leo in *The Go-Between.* Both Humbert and Leo are victims of a youthful exposure to sex that haunts them for the rest of their lives, ultimately, in fact, causing them to be stunted beyond the range of normalcy. And, finally, Pinter includes Nabokov's image of mannequins in a dress-shop window as Lolita is about to leave Humbert. In *The Comfort of Strangers,* McEwan describes Mary and Colin contemplating two mannequins lying on a bed in a store window (21), a scene that the screenwriter repeats cinematically (11–12).

Certainly, too, Pinter's depiction, his very definition of love as expressed in his plays, is not romantic or what is considered normal. As discussed in connection with *The Caretaker,* what Pinter calls love really amounts to a primary appetite. His characters require certain things from one another for their own psychological well-being, and the author considers the relationship between individuals that stems from this need to be love. Traditionally love is a relationship between individuals sustained because of an emotional attachment in which the other is intrinsically important; Pinter's lovers have an emotional dependence upon each other that is based on fulfilling their own psychological requirements. The motivations for his stage characters' actions are selfish. They are based on a necessity for emotional fulfillment, and everything that the characters do in the dramas is aimed at satisfying their personal requirements. Indeed, it is questionable whether Pinter's characters are even capable of feeling love in the customary sense, since most of the later characters share primary appetites for acceptance, affection, and emotional attachment—elements similar to those in conventional love, but essentially selfish drives. In viewing Humbert as one of those who fit the author's definition of love, the suggestion of one of the possible reasons for his being drawn to Nabokov's novel and Lynch's proposal is implicit.

In the end, the script is successful because in it the screenwriter draws upon another of his longtime interests and strengths. Nabokov plays with time in his use of flashbacks; Pinter plays with Nabokov's time. He creates a movement that is reminiscent of the intersecting currents of time in *Betrayal,* a nonlinear movement that captures the structure of the intellectual content and which synchronously becomes the structure of his expression of that content.

Bits and Pieces

IN MANY WAYS the film industry is different from any other type of business venture. For one thing, despite protestations to the contrary, and as demonstrated above, the creator of the script may have little say as to what is done with the product after it is finished.[1] After all, in filmmaking when a script is acquired, it becomes a "property." Larry Gelbart's observation on this circumstance resonates with the sarcasm born of experience: "Generally speaking, in Hollywood the first draft of a screenplay is what the author meant. Every other draft reflects executive decisions about what the writer *really* meant" (190). Jeff Arch, the writer of *Sleepless in Seattle,* proclaims, "When you cash the check, the screenplay is no longer yours" (conversation with Gale, Oct. 1994). In other words, once "they" (a director, producer, or production company) have purchased a script, it is their property, and they can do whatever they want to with it.

This custom has existed since the industry's infancy. Even in the days of silent movies, Kevin Brownlow chronicles, "A story, bought for motion-picture use, becomes an independent work" (272). Throughout time, many famous authors have found this to be true.[2] Fanny Hurst, whose short story "Humoresque" was filmed in 1920, accepts the idea: "I felt that if you sold something you made it over to those who had bought it. They should be able to do what they liked with it without interference." She also is resigned to the downside: "Very occasionally, I felt that they had improved on my concept, but only occasionally."[3] Not all writers exhibit Hurst's equanimity, but the legality of the practice was affirmed in the early 1930s when Bertolt Brecht sued German director G.W. Pabst over the adaptation of Brecht and Kurt Weill's *Threepenny Opera* and the court upheld Pabst. Brecht's comments on the decision still apply: "We have often been told (and the court expressed the same opinion) that when we sold our work to the film industry we gave up all our rights; the buyers even purchased the right to destroy what they had bought; all further claim was covered by the money. These people felt that in agreeing to deal with the film industry we put ourselves in the position of a man who lets his laundry be washed in a dirty gutter and then complains that it has been ruined. Anybody who advises us not to make use of such new apparatus just confirms the apparatus's right to do bad work. . . . At the same time he deprives us in advance of the apparatus which we need in order to produce, since this way of producing is likely more and more to supersede the present one" (47).

Certainly a novelist would hesitate to sell a novel to a publisher who might rearrange the work's structure, delete some of the chapters, and add others written by another author without prior consultation. Pinter is well aware of this industry condition. When he was honored with the Sunday Times Literary Award for Excellence at the Hay Festival in Wales on May 24, 1997, he said that he was pleased to report that of the twenty-two screenplays that he had written then, seventeen were filmed exactly as he had written them. Surely he has been fortunate in that his directors have respected both his work and his opinion. He also noted that he had never written anything directly for the screen, though he contended that he did not know why that was.

Another of the amazing things about the Hollywood system is the number of projects undertaken that are never filmed (even though the novelist or dramatist might be paid for an option and the screenwriter may receive a fee for writing a script—amounts often in the hundreds-of-thousands-of-dollars range). Pinter has been fortunate, too, that he has not suffered excessively from this syndrome. Although he is occasionally sensitive about those scripts that have not been made into movies, in comparison to other screenwriters his record is outstanding. Arch reports that he has written fifteen spec scripts (a screenplay written on speculation, not as an assignment for which one is assured payment), two of which have been optioned and made into pictures. Steven E. de Sousa, author of *Die Hard, 48 Hrs, The Flintstones, Ricochet, Commando,* and *Knock-Off* and a well-respected script doctor, wrote seven spec scripts in ten years and sold six, but only one of these has been made into a movie.[4]

Besides *The Proust Screenplay, Victory,* and *Lolita,* Pinter is known to have produced only three other scripts that have not yet been made into films. An interesting situation developed around Pinter's film script adaptation of the first of these, Kazu Ishiguro's 1989 novel *The Remains of the*

Day. For quite some time there were stories in trade journals about the screenwriter's work on the script. Indeed, in 1992 *The Hollywood Reporter* reported that the film was being shot.[5] In addition to his role as writer, Pinter was also listed as an executive producer (along with John Calley and Mike Nichols). Produced by Ismail Merchant and directed by James Ivory, the eclectic production team that was responsible for the artistically successful and critically acclaimed *A Room with a View* and *Howards End, The Remains of the Day* shooting began in London on September 21, 1992. The production company, Merchant-Ivory Productions, planned for a 1993 release to be distributed by Columbia Pictures. The picture, which was well received,[6] was photographed by Tony Pierce-Roberts and stars Anthony Hopkins, Emma Thompson, Christopher Reeve, James Fox, and Hugh Grant—Hopkins and Fox being Pinter film and stage veterans, of course.

Early in 1993, however, Pinter had his name taken off the movie, contending that "it's not my script."[7] This is not a typical occurrence, though it is certainly not unprecedented either; David Mamet worked on the cinematic version of his own *Sexual Perversity in Chicago* and then disassociated himself from the motion picture, which appeared in 1986 under the title *About Last Night* (with writing credits going to Tim Kazurinsky and others). This adds another ironic twist to Mamet's taking on the rewriting of Pinter's "Lolita" script.

According to Pinter, he read the novel *The Remains of the Day* when it was in galleys, and he liked it so much that he bought the option to the film rights. Certainly his interest in the working of time on memory must have been part of the book's appeal. When the book was published and turned out to be a big hit, a lot of people became interested in filming it, and they sought Pinter out. He did not find anyone with whom he wanted to work until director Nichols contacted him. Pinter and Nichols had wanted to work together for some time but had been unable to find a suitable project. They agreed that *The Remains of the Day* was a suitable project. A problem arose when Nichols tried to convince the production company (Columbia) that the film should be a big-money project. With the world economy staggering and film company finances reflecting that situation, the studio decided instead to assign Nichols to another film (*Wolf*), thereby removing him from consideration due to the timing of the shoot.

Merchant-Ivory Productions, a well-thought-of company that specializes in period classics, bought the script, and the two partners invited Pinter to lunch. The movie was never mentioned. Possibly they thought that a Pinter script would be too terse, not lavish enough for their audience. Subsequently, Ruth Prawer Jhabvala, the Merchant-Ivory resident screenwriter, wrote a new screenplay for the film. Parts of Pinter's script were retained, and Merchant-Ivory suggested that he be given cocredit with Jhabvala, but he declined. Indeed, based on his experience with *The Handmaid's Tale* a couple of years earlier, he insisted on a clause in his contract that permitted him to have his name removed from the film if another writer were brought in to work on the script. In fact, he even tried to have his name removed from any mention of the movie, an attempt that he was forced to continue even after shooting began, as evidenced by stories in *The Hollywood Reporter*.

Both screenplays open with a voice-over of Miss Kenton writing to her former colleague, but there are differences in what follows, some of them significant, in the divergences between the novel and Pinter's script and between Pinter's script and Jhabvala's. In the novel, for instance, Stevens has a brief, limited flash of moral and intellectual epiphany, which Pinter ignores. Edward Jones points out that Ishiguro's Stevens notes that "Lord Darlington wasn't a bad man. He wasn't a bad man at all. And at least he had the privilege of being able to say at the end of his life that he had made his own mistakes. . . . He chose a certain path in life, it proved to be a misguided one, but there, he chose it, he can say that at least. As for myself, I cannot even claim that. You see, I trusted. I trusted in his lordship's wisdom. All those years I served him, I trusted I was doing something worthwhile. I can't even say I made my own mistakes. Really—one has to ask oneself—what dignity is there in that?" (243).[8] Pinter's Stevens merely sums things up with the observation, "I think I've given all I have to give. I gave it all to him, you see" (164).

Among the minimal alterations: Pinter changed the "present" of the novel from 1956 to 1954; Jhabvala set the time as 1958. Pinter also followed Ishiguro's lead in keeping his adaptation unsentimental, in contrast to Jhabvala's emphasis on the developing (though never developed) romance between Kenton and Stevens. In another variation, Jhabvala eliminates the disclosure about Lewis that the French delegate M. Dupont makes at dinner before proposing a toast to Lord Darlington, a disclosure that is found in the novel and retained in Pinter's script. In Pinter's script the dialogue is clear:

DUPONT

But before I go on to thank our host, the most
honorable and kind Lord Darlington, there is
a small thing I wish to remove from my chest.

Some of you may say it is not good manners to
do such things at the dinner table.
Laughter.
But I have no alternative. I believe it is
imperative to openly condemn any who come here
to abuse the hospitality of the host and attempt
to sow discontent and suspicion. My only question
concerning Mr. Lewis is this—does his abominable
behavior in any way express the attitude of the
present American administration? (69)[9]

Jhabvala follows Pinter's script from this point on (beginning with Lewis's
remarks about "amateurs" rather than "professionals" in diplomacy and
Darlington's retort that "what Mr. Lewis describes as 'amateurism' I would
describe as 'honour'" [Pinter, 71]). For instance, the scene in which Miss
Kenton pursues Stevens's taste in books is a kind of apotheosis and, for the
most part, is handled in the film as Pinter wrote it in his screenplay. One
detail that seemed especially affecting in the film was the parallel of Stevens's
prying away his stricken father's hand, finger by finger, from the old man's
cart of mops and brooms and Miss Kenton's using the same gesture later.
Pinter writes in his script:

She [Miss Kenton] begins to take the book from
him, lifting his fingers one at a time from the
book. This takes place in silence, their bodies
very close. She opens the book and flicks through it.

MISS KENTON

Oh, dear, it's not scandalous at all. It's just a
sentimental old love story.

They look at each other.

STEVENS

I read these books—any books—to develop my
command and knowledge of the English language. I
read to further my education.

Pause.

MISS KENTON

Ah. I see. (103)

Finally, though, Jhabvala's ending contains symbolic overtones not found in either Ishiguro or Pinter. In the film, former Pennsylvania congressman Lewis reminds Stevens that they are in the room where he confronted Lord Darlington and his guests during the conference in 1935. Characteristically, Stevens seems otherwise engaged and displays no shock of recognition. His immediate task is to rid the room of a trapped pigeon, which, with a little encouragement, obligingly flies out an open French window in contrast to the caged Stevens, comfortably back in his butler's role, calm of mind, even his repressed passions spent.[10] An aerial shot of the Darlington Hall exterior receding into the distance ends the film, perhaps as a parallel to the withdrawal of Miss Kenton—really Mrs. Benn—back to her formerly estranged husband and now pregnant daughter.[11] Once more, she is drawn back to life, in contrast to Stevens's stagnation and passivity.

Pinter's original script is contained in the Pinter Archives (box 51).[12] It is possible, therefore, to do an in-depth comparative study with the film, and it might be interesting to see what has been retained in Jhabvala's version, as well as what has been discarded, and why Jhabvala made the changes that she did. In examining the archival materials, it is obvious that Pinter's pattern has become more systematic as he works through an outline and develops his dialogue. I have not done a comparative study for this volume, though, because of the separation between the writer and the final product.

In June 1997 it was announced that Pinter was working on an adaptation of Isak Dinesen's short story "The Dreaming Child."[13] Dinesen's *Out of Africa* (1985) had won the Academy Award for Best Picture, and the Danish adaptation of her *Babette's Feast* (1987) was the winner of an Oscar for Best Foreign Language Film.[14] Actress Julia Ormond was touted as the upcoming film's director with Indican Productions for Fox Searchlight. The script was finished in December of that year. As of summer 2002, the film was not in production, although four boxes pertaining to the script had been placed in the archives.[15] It appears in *Collected Screenplays 3*.

Dinesen's tale is about an artist, with a young boy serving as a metaphor. Pinter has changed it in some fairly significant ways. Because the tale has relatively little dialogue, the screenwriter added a considerable amount. He also changed the story, as is his practice, to reflect those things in it that most concern him. Thus, while it remains a Victorian tale, it is told from the sentimental point of view of a twentieth-century conscience. In addition, the artistic theme is sublimated, as Pinter chooses to stress sexual and social commentary. There are clearly, then, links to *The Go-Between* and *The French*

Lieutenant's Woman among his earlier film scripts and also to *Party Time, Ashes to Ashes,* and *Celebration* (2000) among his more recent stage dramas. To accommodate these elements, he created five or six new characters.

Pinter's adaptation of Shakespeare's *King Lear* was completed on March 31, 2000, and negotiations were reportedly under way to have it produced. According to actor Tim Roth, who commissioned the work with backing from Film Four (the movie division of Britain's Channel Four),[16] "This is a very hefty piece, to say the least, and I'm not interested in a bunch of people standing around a castle talking. . . . What Harold Pinter will do is rearrange, cut and then turn it from a stage piece to cinema."[17]

It is not surprising that the screenwriter eventually turned to Shakespeare as a source. He had played Macbeth and Romeo at Hackney Downs Grammar School, and his first theatre-going experience was seeing Sir Donald Wolfit play King Lear. Pinter returned five times and later acted the part of one of the king's knights in a production of *King Lear* with Wolfit. He also acted in a BBC Third Programme production of *Henry VIII* and spent eighteen months in Ireland as a member of Anew McMaster's Shakespearean tour in the early 1950s.[18] In 1953 he acted in Wolfit's classical season at King's Theatre in Hammersmith (where he met his first wife while both were acting in *As You Like It*).

King Lear (c. 1605) is always placed near the top of Shakespeare's masterpieces. The tragic story is well known: a doomed father/king decides to divide his kingdom between his three daughters in order to learn who loves him most and finds out the truth only when it is too late. Pinter's job was to capture on a cold screen the emotion that transports audiences in a live production. This had been tried before: dating back to 1909, at least eight film versions have been released.[19]

The screenwriter follows his standard procedures for working with stage plays in this adaptation. As with his own works, he is faithful to his source because the dramatic structure is already set and the time frame is well established. He does not change any of Shakespeare's words or add any of his own. Although his reason for this approach is tempered by his opinion that Shakespeare is the greatest dramatist of all time and cannot be improved upon, Pinter does concede that he "dealt with the subplot quite critically" (Gussow, "Pinter on Pinter," 31).

What he does is open the play out with action (principally exteriors) and reduce the length of the drama by removing dialogue. The first page of his script contains evidence of the pattern that he follows throughout. The film script starts with a Pinter invention: Lear leading his army away after a battle in 1100.[20] There is no dialogue. The next scene takes place ten years later and is the beginning of Shakespeare's drama, except that there are several establishing shots of the exterior and interior of a Norman castle followed by individual shots of Lear and his daughters (each daughter captured in a mirror shot) and knights arriving, in a sequence reminiscent of the beginning of *Victory*. The first couple of speeches by Kent and Gloucester that open the original are cut, and a total of forty-four lines are excised from Shakespeare's scene 1. The essence of those lines is retained—it is the glosses and amplifications that are deleted. For example, Goneril and Regan protest their love, and we see Cordelia listening, but her asides are cut during their speeches, as is the last line of her declaration of love ("To love my father all" [1.1]).

So it is through the rest of the script. For instance, shot 29 ("A VALLEY SNOW ON THE GROUND") is of *"LEAR and his KNIGHTS hunting wild boar"* (Pinter, 16), another Pinter invention, but the opening of act 2, scene 1, has eighteen lines removed from the conversation between Edmund and Curan regarding gossip about "likely wars . . . 'twixt the Dukes of Cornwall and Albany" (Pinter, 29). Twelve lines containing Edmund's lie about Edgar's planned "parricides," which the audience knows are untrue, are deleted, along with fourteen additional lines (Pinter, 30). Shot 36, *"KENT and OSWALD ride in fast. They reign their horses. KENT stares at OSWALD"* (33) replaces Shakespeare's *"Before GLOUCESTER'S castle / Enter KENT and OSWALD severally"* (2.2). In act 2, scene 3, all twenty-one lines of Edgar's speech are cut except for the concluding "Edgar I nothing am" (Pinter, 38). The dialogue is replaced by shots of Edgar running through a forest. The next scene begins with Lear riding up to Gloucester's castle. Kent's long passage in this scene is discarded, following the usual cinematic "show, don't tell" dictum. Shots of Lear, the Fool, and knights in the storm (Pinter, 48), and then Lear's horse collapsing and Lear and the Fool struggling through the rain, as the storm scene approaches its climax, are included as further Pinterian explorations. Interestingly, the scene between Goneril and Edmund (4.2) is virtually cut out in Pinter's script (67), except that the two are found in bed making love with only his concluding line, "Yours in the ranks of death," and her reply, "Oh, the difference of man and man, / To thee a woman's services are due," retained. Finally, in a series of shots harking back to *The Wild Bunch*, the act 5 battle scenes are rendered in alternating shots of Gloucester with "The sounds of battle" and silent shots of "Swords, shields etc. clashing. . . . Knights and horses collapsing. . . . Horses charging. Arrows" (79).

Pinter's eighty-eight-page film script (sixty scenes plus thirteen numbered subscenes) shows the screenwriter's appreciation for his source in the retention of the original wording. It is designed to make *King Lear* work on the screen, and it is likely that it will.

Three other projects fall into a kind of no-man's-land. *Langrishe, Go Down* and *The Heat of the Day* have been televised but were not shown in a regular theatrical release until the Pinter Festival in 2001, although *The Heat of the Day* was available on videotape; *Landscape* was filmed but not released.[21] Significantly, the screenwriter includes *Langrishe, Go Down* in his collection *The French Lieutenant's Woman and Other Screenplays*, though the program has never been released on videotape. When he finished the script in 1971, Pinter planned to direct the film, but he could not raise the capital to finance the project. It was David Jones, later the director of the American tour production of *Old Times* as well as *The Trial*, who directed and produced what Billington calls a "remarkable" television film (222) when the adaptation of Aidan Higgins's novel was telecast seven years later as the BBC-2's "Play of the Week" on September 20, 1978.[22] Starring Jeremy Irons and Judi Dench, the film features Annette Crosbie, John Molloy, Niall O'Brien, Susan Williamson, Arthur O'Sullivan, Margaret Whiting, Liam O'Callaghan, Joan O'Hara, and Michael O'Brian, with Pinter in the role of the painter, Barry Shannon.

Pinter summarizes the story as being about "three middle-aged spinsters living in a house in Ireland in the nineteen-thirties. At the lodge gate there's a cottage and a German philosophy student in his 30's working on a thesis."[23] The main action takes place in the past (1932) and the present (1937–1938, with a few events from 1900 and 1903 incorporated). The three women are the Langrishe sisters, Helen (Crosbie), who is thirty-nine in 1932, Imogen (Dench), who is forty-nine, and Lily; the Bavarian student is Otto (Irons). The title comes from the refusal of Helen to leave her bed, "I won't go down again," in the present (Pinter, *The French Lieutenant's Woman and Other Screenplays*, 122).

Beautifully photographed, the color film is quite moving as the relationships between the student and the three women develop. Otto, who is taken by Irish women because they are "remarkably pure and clean," is attracted to Imogen and Helen. In telling their story, the screenwriter takes advantage of the natural surroundings and sounds of the countryside, of the Irish villages and Dublin, and the cinematic devices of close-up and intercutting. The close-ups are used to emphasize specific points, but it is the intercutting of images of the actions of the two women in the past and the present that is especially effective in presenting the contrast between their life of passion and a life of dry withdrawal. In a note in the published version of the script, Pinter says that the camera directions are "particularly detailed" because of his intention of directing it himself, and although Jones "did not observe every direction. . . . The structure of the film . . . remained the structure as written" ([107]).

There are a couple of elements in the film that are standard in Pinter's scripts. Recordings of Galli-Curci singing are heard (echoes of *Victory* and *The Comfort of Strangers*), and humorous dialogue that reflects the author's position that nothing can be taken for granted. For example, Imogen and Otto talk about stars and planets:

IMOGEN

I thought that they were the same.

OTTO

The same? The same as what? (123)

The Heat of the Day, which was telecast on the BBC in Britain in December 1989 and in the United States on PBS's Masterpiece Theatre on September 30, 1990 (the videotape is distributed by Anchor Bay), is also contained in *Collected Screenplays 3*. The copyright date for the tape is 1991. The two-hour program, telecast in America on PBS (WGBH, Boston), was introduced by Alistair Cooke and included an interview, "Harold Pinter on Adapting *The Heat of the Day*." The actual running time for the taped version is 106 minutes, not the 120 minutes indicated on the cover of the tape box, and does not include either the introduction or the interview. It, too, was shown during the Lincoln Center festival. Based on the novel by Elizabeth Bowen, the film was directed for Granada Television by Christopher Morahan, produced by June Wyndham-Davies, and starred Patricia Hodge (who appeared in *Betrayal*), Michael York, and Michael Gambon (who was in *Turtle Diary* and the stage version of *Betrayal*) in the lead roles, with Peggy Ashcroft (who had performed in *Landscape*) and Anna Carteret. *The Heat of the Day* was compared to Graham Greene's *Third Man* by Masterpiece Theatre host Alistair Cooke, who called Bowen's novel "the greatest book ever written about war time

London." Wyndham-Davies, who had already produced a television version of another Bowen novel, *The Death of the Heart,* asked Pinter to write the script. While not one of his best screenplays, it is superior to his source.

World War II is a subject that Pinter might have been expected to deal with earlier in his career, given his experiences during the war. He was a youngster when he saw the first flying bomb, he saw his garden in flames, and he was evacuated to the country (taking only his favorite cricket bat with him) to escape the Blitz.[24] Still, although the story is supposed to be about the war, it is really about subjects examined within the context of a war, not the war itself, which might also be expected with a Pinter screenplay. The story is from a different perspective than that of a John Wayne movie or even that of *Reunion.* We hear the sound of bombing over in the opening scene and again at the film's conclusion, and war is talked about, but it really is never seen.

In the script Pinter is faithful to the varying forms of betrayal found in the novel, and he incorporates a good amount of Bowen's dialogue, much of which is Pinteresque in nature. As to be expected, there are the anticipated alterations demanded by the translation to the cinematic medium. For instance, Louie's role is considerably diminished, Roderick's part is reduced, Connie is dropped altogether, and a portion of the novel detailing Stella's actions between Robert's death and the reappearance of Harrison is tremendously compacted.

However, the screenwriter signals a major departure from the original in the opening sequence. In the novel Harrison experiences a strong physical desire for Stella. Pinter inserts a romantic element into that desire when the movie opens with Harrison, his back to the audience, looking at his surveillance photographs of Robert and Stella. The foreboding music lightens, and Harrison takes a photograph of Stella alone and pins it to the wall while the music changes to a decidedly romantic tone. Pinter has inserted a romantic motive for a character who in his source was an antiromantic pragmatist. Harrison reveals this aspect of his character when he tells Stella, "The first time I saw you . . . you were lying quite like this . . . on the grass in Regent's Park. Your eyes were closed. Then you opened your eyes and you looked up at the sky. You didn't know I was watching every move you made. . . . And then it got worse. . . . and now it's hell." The words recall Beth's languidly romantic imagery in Pinter's *Landscape* (1968) when she "remembers" her lover standing over her at the beach.[25] In the final scene, Harrison says that he will leave when the air raid is over, implying that the relationship is more complicated than his merely trying to blackmail her into saving her fiancé by becoming his lover and her being willing to make that sacrifice; the movie ends with the two of them still sitting after the all-clear sounds.

In addition, the particular photograph that Harrison chooses is one of Stella reclining in a park deck chair, a position that recurs in the film. As Knowles declares, "Photographs are literal and symbolic in the screenplay, both part of Harrison's work and icons of his obsession" (*Understanding*, 172–73). The photographs reverberate with *The Comfort of Strangers*—they are taken and viewed by Harrison throughout, and other pictures are re-marked upon in Robert's childhood bedroom at the inherited estate (where his sister straightens one, as Stella later straightens a depiction of the sinking of the *Titanic*). Other links to *The Comfort of Strangers* are found in the dialogue, especially in the Thatcherite echoes in Bowen's Robert's lines "there must be law" (302) and "It bred my father out of me" (307; changed to "drove my father out of me" in the film) and Pinter's summarizing "Strength over freedom" and "I want order . . . shape . . . discipline."

Advertised as a spy story (but not one like *The Quiller Memorandum*), what begins as an engaging mystery about national betrayal soon becomes something else in Pinter's hands. The intriguing treason quickly metamor-phoses into a tale about a sinister intruder (*The Room, The Birthday Party,* and so forth) and personal fidelity (*Betrayal*). It also contains elements that are familiar: Harrison's trouble breathing recalls Goldberg in *The Birthday Party;* there is black humor (the estate's owner dies owing a cab driver ten bob, which the cab driver—who does not know that his fare has died—cannot collect, he is told, because the man took it with him; the woman in the park and bar who bothers Harrison is like the intrusive woman at the hairdresser's in *The Pumpkin Eater;* a servant informs Stella that "We killed a little chicken for your supper," to which she replies, "how nice."[26] Linguis-tic miscommunications appear: Robert seems to misunderstand Stella's ref-erence to the picture of the *Titanic* as "that" when he says "Talking of that, why don't we marry?" (Bowen, 218). There is even a bit of somewhat styl-ized screenplay writing that is reminiscent of other Pinter scripts: several "My God"s and other Pinteresque phrasings and rhythm (Harrison: "So far the best thing has been touching your coat. I know where I am with your coat") and the suggestion when Robert and Stella meet his mother that the couple take a "stroll before tea," which is immediately followed by a dialogueless shot of them walking and laughing.

Landscape (broadcast on the BBC Third Programme, April 28, 1968, and first staged on July 2, 1969) was filmed and reportedly had a theatrical release in 1996. According to producer Rex Pyke, "The film was made on 35mm at Pinewood Studios, in association with the Royal Shakespeare Company. We tried to keep as close to the original Aldwich [Theatre] production as possible, with Sir Peter Hall directing and Dame Peggy Ashcroft and David Waller staring [sic]."[27] At first, the thirty-six-minute film version of one of the author's finest and most intriguing plays was seen only at festivals, but it is now available on video.[28]

There have also been reports about projects that Pinter was supposed to have been involved in but which never materialized. In 1992 Claudia Eller reported in *Variety* that Columbia Pictures had been interested in a script by Pinter of Wilde's *The Picture of Dorian Gray*. The company turned down this remake of MGM's 1945 melodrama because of "creative differences." Pinter, who was supposed to have asked for four hundred thousand dollars and creative autonomy, says that it was not a matter of money. Fox, too, appeared interested in the movie at one time, and Eller announced that Sandollar was going to shoot the film. Nothing has materialized.

In 1993 Pinter was reported to be working on an adaptation of *An Interrupted Life: The Diaries of Etty Hillesum 1941–1943,* a Holocaust narrative.[29] Esther (Etty) Hillesum recorded the events of her life in Amsterdam during the Nazi occupation in this diary and wrote letters on her way to Auschwitz (where she died in 1943). The intimate details of her transformation from a worldly, pleasure-loving, twenty-seven-year-old Dutch Jew to a person who directly confronts the stark realities of the occupation and the Holocaust and addresses the moral questions brought about by the horrors that surrounded her fits into Pinter's interest in the Jewish perspective and experiences during that time period.

In *Fragile Geometry: The Films, Philosophy, and Misadventures of Nicolas Roeg,* Joseph Lanza quotes screenwriter Allan Scott as saying that Roeg was going to direct *Julia* from a Pinter screenplay based on the Lillian Hellman story *Pentimento* (122), and he includes "*Julia* (Screenplay by Harold Pinter)" in a list of Roeg's "Miscellaneous Unfilmed Projects" (168). In our 1994 meeting, Pinter said that he had never written the script. This tentative association with Hellman's autobiographical tale drawn from her involvement with the European resistance movement in the 1930s would have set up reverberations similar to those in *The Diaries of Etty Hillesum.* Parenthetically, the writer's interest in these two strong, moral women appears to be another of the many instances in his work that are inconsistent with the term *misogynist* that feminist critics sometimes use to label him. Peter Hall purportedly recommended Pinter to an American film company that approached Hall to direct the film, but the project did not go forward, because Pinter declined the offer.

Given Pinter's statements about violence, even more interesting is the case of American director Sam Peckinpah's *Straw Dogs* (1971). A series of four letters in the Peckinpah Collection (file no. 46) in the Margaret Herrick Library at the Academy of Motion Picture Arts and Sciences is revealing. The first letter is a two-page handwritten note to Peckinpah from Pinter dated May 10, [1970]:

> *Dear Sam*
> It was great to meet / and talk with you—but I can't write / the film. It remains / something in itself—that I don't / feel 100% for—and I think that's / what you've got to feel. I'm sorry. . . . But I'll see the film—and you, I hope. It was most good—as the Peruvians don't say. And all the best
> Yours
> Harold

The "it" being referred to is Peckinpah's adaptation of Gordon Williams's novel *Siege at Trencher's Farm* (1969), which was the original title for the motion picture as well. The story is about a pacifistic American mathematician (portrayed in the film by Dustin Hoffman) who moves with his British wife (Susan George) to an isolated village in England. There the couple is terrorized by a group of local hooligans. The movie was one of the most controversial films of the time because of the violence depicted.

On December 4, 1970, Peckinpah wrote to Pinter at the author's agent's address in Cadogan Lane:

> Dear Harold Pinter:
> You got me into this, the least you can do is give me your comments or give a smashing performance of Scutt.
> Take your pick your [*sic*] have no options.
> Kindest regards,
> Sam Peckinpah

In a typed letter from his home on Hanover Terrace five days later, Pinter replied:

Dear Sam Peckinpah,

I enjoyed our meeting very much a while ago, but I'm sorry you've asked me for my comments on the script. I have to tell you that I detest it with unqualified detestation. It seems to me totally unreal, obscene not only in its unequivocal delight in rape and violence but in its absolute lack of connection with anything that is recognizable or that is saying anything "important" about human beings.

How you can associate yourself with it is beyond me. However that's your business. I can only say I consider it an abomination.

Yours sincerely,
Harold Pinter

Peckinpah responded from his J.S.P. Productions studio in Middlesex on December 16:

Dear Harold Pinter:

Of course . . . . !

Your comments on "THE SIEGE OF TRENCHER'S FARM" are absolutely correct.

But that's the point isn't it? If it wasn't the joke would be too monstrous to behold.

Gracias.

Sam Peckinpah

There is a last, predictable, irony, given the nature of movie audiences: in 1973 a report on the American Broadcasting Company's first thirty-six theatrical films showed a loss on thirty of the motion pictures (including *The Birthday Party*); *Straw Dogs* was one of the six that was in the black. After two years the movie had the company's third highest return with a profit of $1.425 million.

One additional project deserves some attention: *Butley*. Given that Pinter directed this film taken from Simon Gray's play of the same name,[30] and because it is often instructive to approach things from different points of view, it is germane to consider his taking the director's chair and his subsequent screenwriting.

The stage version of *Butley,* which premiered at the Oxford Playhouse on July 7, 1971,[31] was one of Pinter's many successful efforts as a theatre director, and in 1973 he directed the adaptation.[32] A part of the American Film Theatre program, like the film version of *The Homecoming, Butley* was released in 1974. The 130-minute movie was adapted for the screen by Gray. The film script is essentially the drama itself with the simple addition of a few nondialogue scenes outside Butley's office, in his flat, on the underground, and in a pub.

There are several reasons for Pinter's having chosen *Butley* as his first film to direct. Thematically it is related to his own writing.[33] In an interview on the Shepperton Studios set of *Butley,* Pinter talked with Langely about one of his major concerns. "Threat is part of it," he said, "but it's much more than that. It's to do with the sinews of human nature. The complacency of so many people is really quite remarkable. It is . . . pathetic." Pinter's description of Gray's tragicomedy is close to his descriptions of his own plays, notably *The Caretaker* and *The Homecoming,* for he sees that "it is on the face of it a comedy, but ultimately there's no laughter."[34]

Moreover, Pinter clearly has enjoyed stage directing—though he prefers to direct someone else's material because he thinks that actors are inhibited by his presence when they work on one of his plays. He states that he is afraid that they do not believe that he is objective (he insists that he is), but Pleasence proclaims Pinter to be "the most truly honest and indeed best director" with whom he has worked in the theatre.[35] Harwood, for whom he directed *Taking Sides,* says, "He's a wonderful director . . . because he lets nothing go by. Also, he's a minimalist as a director. When actors get up and start to move, Harold says, 'Why are you moving there?' And they say, 'Well, I just thought . . . I've been sitting here for so long.' 'No. There's no need to move.' And the actors go back and sit. And, what you get from a Pinter production is such a concentration on the text."[36] The writer's acting career created an understanding of an actor's needs and inner processes that makes him an extremely effective director. Finally, Pinter has found film exciting from his first exposure to cinematic techniques, as evidenced in his comments to Langley about deleting dialogue and altering rhythm. He also understands the dangers of film directing: "Film directors have got to be very careful not to get a glib and facile effect. The use of music, the ready tears. Cliché comes more swiftly in films than any other medium, if one isn't careful," he told Langley. "All the component parts, including dialogue, however spare or prolix, have to be treated with considerable discipline and lack of indulgence. Making a film demands clearsightedness and respect" ("From 'Caretaker' to 'Servant'").

Given Pinter's interest in directing and his excitement about film, it is not surprising that he has combined the two successfully. In spite of the author's claim that "I'm still a beginner. Everyone remains a beginner in films for a hell of a long time," Alan Bates found that there was "no sense of an outsider struggling with a new medium" in his directing. Bates also agrees with Pleasence about Pinter's ability as a director: "Harold is known for a sense of economy, precision and subtlety, all of which are very filmic things. At any rate he seems a totally natural director."[37] *Time* critic Jay Cocks concurred: "it is greatly to Pinter's credit that he makes the physical constriction of the play work for the movie. Butley seems all the more locked in. . . . As might be expected of Pinter, the pace of the piece is finely measured and orchestrated with musical precision. The actors . . . have been admirably tutored in the parlor arts of undertone, implicit insult and glancing innuendo" ("A Touch of Class," 77).

To some extent, Pinter's attitude about directing the film may have helped make that task easier, for the constitution of the original material made his directing a natural exercise. "The play Butley was written for the stage," he says, "The film *Butley* was conceived for the screen. I was concerned with expressing the work in terms of film and I was dealing with a work which in fact dictated itself in terms of how you look at it."[38] Happily, Pinter emerged from his first experience with film-directing enthusiastically, as demonstrated by his 1973 statement in the *Daily Telegraph Magazine* that in spite of the difficulties involved, he would like to direct more films.[39]

Besides Bates, whose tour-de-force stage portrayals of the main character in both London and New York won him best actor awards, the film's cast also includes Richard O'Callaghan (Joey) and Michael Byrne (Reg) from the original London production, along with Jessica Tandy (Edna), Susan Engel (Anne), Georgina Hale (Miss Heasman), and Simon Rouse (Gardner).

The story is a day in the life of Ben Butley, an English lecturer at a college of London University. In some ways Butley has taken the license to act as most people would like to act at times; he has assumed the freedom to act toward individuals who disturb him much as James Thurber's Walter Mitty (filmed in 1947) or the Tom Courtney character in John Schlesinger's 1963 film *Billy Liar* (based on Keith Waterhouse's novel and play) do only in their fantasies. Throughout the drama the protagonist wittily baits his wife, from whom he is estranged, his homosexual roommate, who is a former student

Butley (1974). Alan Bates as Butley. American Film Theater. Jerry Ohlinger Archives.

of his, the roommate's new lover, and other members of the faculty; he avoids students and occasionally relies on the bottle for reenforcement. The game has become meaningless for him, though, and at the final curtain he has been unable to muster enough desire to initiate another relationship with a new student, although by now he knows the pattern so well that it has become a ritual. Ultimately, he remains isolated from the world of social relationships, from which he has knowingly separated himself. On stage all of the action in the two-act play takes place in Butley's office.

From the outset it is clear what kind of person Butley is, for even the office set reflects the nature of his mind. His desk, for example, "*is a chaos of papers, books, detritus,*"[40] in contrast to Joey Keyston's neat, almost bare desk. Similarly reflecting the unsettled state of his mind, Butley's bookcase is "*chaotic with old essays and mimeographed sheets scattered among the books.*" Butley's attitude toward his profession is evident in the photograph of T.S. Eliot that is taped to the wall beside his desk, an indication of the kind of literature that interests Butley (and, incidentally, a visual reference to the source of some of the literary allusions that embellish Butley's conversations). The soiled, curled corner of the photograph establishes the fact that things that once were important to Butley have ceased to hold his attention. The desk lamp that will not work is further evidence of the lack of connections in his life, the way that things no longer work for him (in the film this incident is deleted). Butley's egocentrism and the tactics that he uses to isolate himself from other people and from his professional responsibilities are demonstrated in his opening dialogue.

The comic touch of Butley's taking a squashed banana from his pocket and throwing the peel on Joey's desk momentarily seems to lighten the seriousness of Butley's lying, but it soon becomes evident that this action is merely another indication of the character's sloppy habits, his lack of consideration for others, and his deliberate attempts to belittle everyone. The piece of cotton wool stuck to his chin to stop the blood from a cut sustained while he was shaving (we actually see him cut himself in the film) is a parallel to the banana. Obviously, Butley does not demonstrate much respect for himself, and he shows even less for others.

The two major categories of differences between the original and the cinematic version that typically occur in a literal adaptation of a stage play, alterations in the dialogue and an opening out of the action, are both present in the film. Most of the changes in dialogue are minimal and inconsequential, the insertion of dozens of "Nows," "wells," and so forth that probably simply sounded natural to the cast during the filming. A few words are changed, too, with no major effect on the text.[41] The word "question" becomes "point," for example, in Butley's line, "He's too dull to be anything else; the question is, why has he stopped being busy with me?" (Gray, 20). Other minor changes may have been incorporated to make the dialogue more accessible to a film audience. References to the "Senate House" incident and the "Vellum Aristotle" become the "university library" incident and the "Aristotle collection," for instance, and perhaps in consideration of a potential American audience the term "char" is removed in favor of "cleaning woman" and Reg's university is changed from Hull to York.[42] Along the same lines, many of the literary allusions that appear in the play are deleted from the motion picture. The implied assumption is that a movie audience is not as sophisticated and well read as a theatre audience and does not share a common culture to the same extent that the viewers of a live production do.

The most obvious difference between the stage play and the film script, of course, is the utilization of a camera to record the action. One of the major things that this can accomplish is that it allows the writer and director to use the camera's eye to follow the action and to direct the audience to what they want seen (and to hide what they do not want seen). Gray, Pinter, and Director of Photography Fisher utilize camera movement and focusing effectively. It is interesting that most of the shots in the conversational segments are medium shots, but through close-ups and reaction shots the action is kept flowing smoothly. The movement of the camera back and forth between the characters' faces during their discussions for all intents and purposes takes the place of physical movement on stage. In the conversation between Butley and Joey about Reg's father's butcher shop early in act 1, for instance, in the play Joey walks away from his office mate (21). In the film a close-up of Joey's face is substituted for the character's physical movement. Not only is this more economical, but it also conveys Joey's feelings more clearly than was possible on the stage, because his emotions are seen reflected on his face rather than inferred from his movements.

The employment of two-shots allows the audience to observe the relative positions of the characters. In the conversation sections, the inclusion of both men in the frame emphasizes their relationship and gives a closed feeling to the action. They are involved in a discussion between themselves, set off from the world outside their relationship, and their proximity is underscored. Coincidentally, in the first half of the film, Butley is normally situated in the frame either on a level with Joey or, more typically, above him. Frequently Joey's head will be seen from the back, in profile, or in a three-quarter-turn shot in the lower foreground while Butley's figure is seen full-front, looming above him in the center of the frame. This composition reflects the older partner's dominance over the younger man. In the second half of the movie, once Joey's independence from Butley has been posited, the positions within the frame are more often reversed (now it is Butley who mostly sits while Joey stands), making the men's psychological status visible and inviting a comparison with the situation that existed at the beginning of the film. In between these two extremes is the segment featuring Reg's appearance, throughout much of which three-shots show Butley and Reg standing on either side of Joey, all three men at the same level and evenly spaced within the frame, clearly denoting the conflict for Joey's affections; Butley and Reg actually talk across Joey.

Elsewhere a complementary commentary on the action is successfully produced with camera angles and shot composition, as when Butley shuts the door to his office after Joey leaves, and he stands huddled between a bookcase and the doorjamb (56). His despair and alienation is manifest purely from the combination of cinematic devices exploited—including the composition within the frame, the camera angle and distance from the figure, and the narrowing of the viewer's breadth of vision to focus on the character.

Two examples illustrate how opening out and showing that there is a real world outside the stage-set walls affects what goes on inside the proscenium arch, reenforces the themes, and incorporates humor into the expression of those themes. First, the stage play contains cinematic elements (this may well be true of most drama written after the emergence of film as an art form), and the adaptation goes beyond the physical limitations imposed by the stage in developing the protagonist's character, limitations that naturally lead to a reliance on words. It is important to note that Butley's use of literary allusions as weapons provides insight into his nature in much the same manner that Robert Browning's speakers reveal themselves through their dramatic monologues. His allusions epitomize his hollowness. Perhaps one of the reasons that some of these literary allusions are omitted from the film is the employment of the camera itself—which allows for the visual equivalent of the allusions by demonstrating aspects of Butley's personality that even he may be unaware of, through a sort of combination of "a picture is worth a thousand words" and "actions speak louder than words." From the very beginning, what we see in the film that was not present on stage speaks wordlessly yet eloquently and invests the movie with the quality of a dramatic monologue.

Second, the movie begins with a four-minute, thirty-second sequence that was not part of the stage play. For sixteen seconds the titles are run over an amorphous design. As the titles end, there is a nonsynchronous cough, and nineteen seconds into the film, an out-of-focus image begins coalescing into Butley's face reflected as he peers at himself in a steam-fogged mirror. Why does the motion picture open with a scene in Butley's home? Might it be to show the similarities between his disorderly home life and his office? To introduce the idea that he is having a bad day from the beginning? These may, indeed, be reasons for making such a choice, but there are much more important implications inherent in the situation and in its presentation.

In this first view of the protagonist it appears that he is trying to see who he is. It is likely that Pinter had an influence on this scene. His own experience with writing screenplays for films directed by Losey (*The Servant,* in particular) exposed him to the masterful symbolic use of mirrors. Perhaps even more importantly, in talking about the concepts of verification and identity, he has commented that it is impossible to determine who someone else is, for when he looks in the mirror in the morning while he is shaving, he is not even sure who he is seeing. This thought, connected with images in mirrors, is contained in several of his plays—most notably in *The Dwarfs,* but elsewhere as well.[43] As the scene progresses, considerably more is revealed about Butley's character. His practice of squirting shaving cream directly from the can onto his face is not the normal approach to using shaving cream and thus suggests a quirkiness in his nature. That he is out of shaving cream suggests that he is not practical and that he does not pay attention to details. He makes do with a bar of soap to lather his face, but this is instrumental in his cutting himself with the dirty razor, which elicits the first dialogue in the film, the expletive "Shit!" The entire shaving scene takes two minutes and eight seconds.

There is a jump cut to Butley standing on an underground platform waiting for the train. When he moves to board the subway, a sign visible in the background indicates that he is at Kilburn Park station, which is in a fairly far out, unfashionable suburb of London.[44] With no additional dialogue, this quick and simple sequence brings the outside world into the action and simultaneously comments on Butley's economic and social status.

We next observe Butley on board the underground train, where his actions are unsociable and insensitive. He pushes through the crowd to take a seat that a fellow passenger is about to claim. Immediately, he lights a cigarette and blows the smoke carelessly upward so that it annoys the man whose seat he has just taken (we see the man's reaction of disgust with this inconsiderate and egocentric act in an intercut close-up). Then Butley takes out a copy of a children's book and reads it. During the one-minute, twenty-four-second duration of this sequence, he has shown himself to be childish in his attitude toward society, an attitude that is mirrored in his choice of reading matter.

A twelve-second section shows him walking along the street to the entrance of the university. This is followed by a thirty-second sequence in which he walks through the college halls, into the departmental office, and thence into his own office. In the departmental office, where he has gone to collect his mail, he overhears Edna trying to get information on "Gardner, J.K." from the secretary. In the shot Butley is seen in close-up, with Edna visible and talking to the offscreen secretary behind him. Butley is looking into the camera, and from his facial reaction to the name of the student and his quick movement back out of the room, it is evident not only that he attaches some significance to the name but that he does not want Edna to see him, especially with that name still hanging in the air.

Butley's actions throughout the opening sequence serve as foreshadowing, preparing us for what is to come, not because of the actions themselves but because of the character of the man that is defined by those actions. This might have been accomplished in the stage version, although not as efficiently as on the screen, because the cinematic visuals reenforce the thematic content. Over the course of the entire sequence Butley is seen alone or isolated in the middle of crowds on the subway, on the street, and in university passageways. The overall image of the protagonist established by this vision is more effective in conveying the inner man than is his antisocial exhibition of purposeful irritation and his combative obnoxiousness. All of this is provided in material added to the film and takes place before the play begins so that the audience is aware and sensitized to what is likely to occur. In a sense, these literal pictures correspond to the dramatic technique of having characters discuss someone before his or her first appearance on stage, as in the opening scene of *Hamlet*.

A final sequence demonstrating the use of the camera to open up Gray's play merits attention. What in the play would be seen as continuous action is in the film portrayed in seven distinct shots. This occurs when Miss Heasman returns for her second visit, interrupting Butley as he is about to ask Joey whether Reg's mother and father know that Joey and Reg "have it off together" (24). The first shot shows Butley at his desk talking to Joey when footsteps are heard approaching the door. The camera follows Butley as he jumps to the his feet and hurries to the door, where he greets Miss Heasman and pretends that he must hasten off to attend to some administrative "tangle." Teacher and student move into the hall, the camera tracking them, and Butley continues walking around the corner and out of sight. Miss Heasman turns and looks back into the office. There is a cut to Joey watching her; he looks a bit embarrassed as he gets up and collects his briefcase and then pushes the door closed. A third shot is of Miss Heasman in the hallway, moving to look after Butley. The fourth shot is of the empty hall down which Butley has disappeared. Miss Heasman walks into the frame past the camera. The camera tracks her as she walks down the hall—in the barren hall and growing smaller as she moves farther from the camera, she looks quite vulnerable. There is a pan to pick up Butley coming out of the infirmary and thanking the nurse who is seen in the background (in dialogue added to cover what is happening: "Thank you very much, indeed, nurse") and then walking down the hall to peer around the corner. There is a cut to the retreating Miss Heasman at the far end of the hall in the fifth shot. The sixth shot cuts back to Butley, watching her, and then pans to follow Butley back into his office; the seventh shot is of Joey in the office and Butley rushing in through the doorway to finish his question.

The lengths to which Butley will go to avoid dealing with his students and his disregard for other people are evident in this sequence to a greater extent than they are in the play because of the shots that have been introduced of Miss Heasman, lonely, lost, and confused in the empty hall, and the inclusion of the nurse's office incident. Furthermore, the break in Butley's question, "do they know—[with Joey's "Know what?" inserted] . . . that you and Reg have it off together?" is more abrupt, prolonged, and amusing because of the expansion of the interruption when he continues as though there has been no interruption.

Butley is not stunningly innovative, but it is competent and well crafted. The movie is an accurate adaptation that captures the essence of its original admirably and even enhances it by adding dimensions that could not be attained on stage. As such, it shows that Pinter is aware of what he is doing cinematically—he knows how to take advantage of specific filmic devices and when to use them—which must make his subsequent screenwriting easier. It is a shame this is the only film that Pinter has directed, because he did such a fine job with it.[45]

The Creative/Collaborative Process

THAT IT WAS SIMON GRAY and not Pinter who wrote the screenplay for *Butley* reveals something about Pinter. In a biographical sketch, Gray recounts that it was not until four of his dramas already had been produced that his education in the theatre "properly began": "It wasn't . . . until I met up with Harold Pinter for our first play together, *Butley*, that I was encouraged to discover that my responsibilities as a playwright didn't consist solely of handing over the script and refraining from comment. He demanded, in fact, that I become a kind of codirector, speaking freely at rehearsals and consulting at length with him at the end of the day" ("Simon Gray," 113). Pinter's attitude about collaboration in the theatre certainly carries over into his work in film.

Screenwriter Alvin Sargent says, "As a screenwriter, you work with others."[1] Donald Chase is of the opinion that there are screenwriters "who would fault Sargent on his choice of preposition, and suggest that 'for,' 'around,' and 'on' be substituted for 'with'" (47). In fact, the screenwriter's role is an ambiguous one. Leonard Spigalglass points out that "The advent of the film changed the whole relationship between the creator of the work of art, of the drama, and the implementer of the work of art, of the drama. Up until the motion picture, there was really no such thing as a director. A director was a man who directed traffic on the stage. . . . There was never the signature of the director on a play."[2]

The shift in emphasis from the writer as creator to the director as creator is historically fascinating. In the silent era, films were made by directors who worked without a script; starting with nothing more than an idea, they "winged it" on the set, making up the script as they went. Sometimes they hired people to write the captions to be displayed on the screen, usually after the fact. Amazingly, D.W. Griffith shot *Intolerance* without a script. When scenarios were used, they were not the equivalent of a shooting script; they were simply the sequence of scenes, "the story told in visual terms."[3] Later, "scenario" departments were established, usually a small group of women who were responsible for turning literary sources into those visual sequences. One of the first and best known of the early scenario writers who actually created original scripts was Anita Loos, of *Gentlemen Prefer Blondes* fame. Loos was hired by Griffith when she was quite young, and by the time she was fifteen she was writing three scripts a week for him. It was not until the 1920s that writers were publicly credited for their work on a film: "photo-dramatist" H.H. Van Loan's name appeared on San Francisco's Strand Theatre marquee in November 1920, and in 1929 Ralph Spence was singled out in the same manner for his titles for a silent movie.

Even today there is considerable ambiguity about the writer's role, as evidenced in William Goldman's commentary:

> Since I'm there first, I know the most about a movie at the earliest
> point, and then gradually there is that time when I must hand over and
> be severed, because the technicians . . . and when I say director, I meant
> technicians . . . I meant all the technicians: the actors, the cinematogra-
> phers, the sound people, the production designers, the directors. They're
> all crucial. . . . There is undeniably an adversary relationship between
> writers and directors in movies. . . . Nobody messes with the composer
> because not everybody can write songs. Nobody messes with the
> cinematographer because nobody knows how to light things. Even
> producers know letters, an alphabet. And directors . . . everybody likes
> to fiddle, it makes them feel creative. One of the reasons there are no
> happy screenwriters is because you have all those people who think they
> can write better than you can . . . and things get altered. There is this
> lunatic myth . . . that the movie is the director's, and that's about as
> much sense as the Flat Earth Society. . . . I have been involved with too
> many world class directors who have called me from all across the world
> saying, What do I shoot tomorrow?[4]

Reinforcing Goldman's sentiment is the ascendancy of the "pitch." A pitch is a presentation, typically oral, of the essence of the plot of a proposed film.[5] In Hollywood, the pitch is sometimes more important than the product. In film schools and institutes, students are taught how to write and present pitches, because, as often as not, if the pitch is not successful, the script will not get read—and just getting the script read is frequently the most difficult part of the whole process for a screenwriter. One of the favorite devices used in the pitch is the "meets" trope, as in "*The Maltese Falcon meets The Sound of Music.*" More than one film has been made based on nothing more than a catchy phrase, a mere sound bite intended as a "hook," with the quality of the script being of secondary concern (for many reasons, perhaps, some of them even legitimate, since the purchaser of the property expects that rewrites will be in order).

There is disagreement about how the adapter works at his or her job, too, even among adapters, as is evident in the discussion of the art of adaptation in the introduction. Nunnally Johnson believes that "When a man writes the script, he directs it at the same time."[6] Sargent agrees, saying that he writes "a lot of detail, a lot of direction, basically for myself,"[7] as does W.D. Richter, who writes a screenplay that is "very readable, and in that sense, it's directed, because it's a story, it's not just a blueprint for somebody to step into and provide the imagination. I direct the movie in my own mind when I write it because I see it."[8] Leigh Brackett disagrees: "No director worth his salt wants some writer telling him where to put his camera."[9]

During the course of this study, certain conclusions have become obvious. I have talked about the kinds of things that Pinter does in writing a screenplay in terms of his preparation, alterations, and discussions with others during the creation of individual scripts, but there are three strategies in particular that I would like to stress: his research, his constant rewriting, and his acceptance of the collaborative nature of filmmaking. There are four main points that can be demonstrated in a discussion of these elements. First, he does not write completely spontaneously, or as he would say, "naturally." Second, although he may, as he claims, write without much conscious intellectual consideration of the mechanics of his writing, he is, nevertheless, a careful craftsman who rewrites and rewrites. Third, due to the collaborative nature of the filmmaking process, once the screenplay is written and accepted, to some extent he loses control of what the final product will be. Fourth, tracing these elements through the entire process provides for some insight into how the author creates—what artistic decisions he makes at what points and why he makes those decisions.

To begin with the obvious, Pinter reads the novels that he is going to adapt before he begins the adaptation. More often than not, some discussion with the potential director precedes this point in the process, for many of the books are recommended to him by someone who would like to film them. Once he has read the novel, and usually before he begins the actual writing, he has further discussions with the director in very general terms about what is to be done and how they will effectively translate the novel to the screen. Then, while it appears that occasionally he starts out by writing the first scene or two (which frequently are retained pretty much intact in the filmed version), oftentimes he begins with a standard outline approach; that is, he simply writes down a brief notation of the chronology of the scenes as he anticipates they might be arranged. This outline may be changed any number of times before the script itself is begun, as well as during the composition of the script and sometimes even during the filming.

In the Pinter Archives there are innumerable examples of the preparatory segment of Pinter's writing. For instance, his naming of the female singer whose recording is played on the island in *Victory* is no accident. An undated letter from Irene Thomas of London is evidence that she was asked for information on female opera singers of the period in question. Thomas reports that a Mr. Hughes of the British Institute of Recorded Sound informed her that "it would not have been very likely that records of opera-singers would have been available before about 1898 onwards" and that the recordings would have been on cylinders. Thomas goes on to describe some of the singers who were recorded at the time, even providing the titles of some of the works recorded and suggesting that Rosalia Chalia, among others, would seem to suit Pinter's purposes (box 59).

There is an indication of Pinter's research and his careful concern with details in a note in an early typed version of *Victory*. Shot 13, "THE QUAYSIDE," is part of the dumb-show sequence with which he opens the film. The shot is of Davidson stepping out of a sampan and hailing a dogcart. Among those visible on the quayside are "Malays, Chinese, Negroes, Arabs, Javanese, some Europeans. Native carriers with bamboo poles over their shoulders, baskets hanging front and back." This scene is retained in the printed version (*Comfort,* 168), though the note is not, perhaps because the note has to do with the film as a film, whereas the published text does not. The note reads:

> The Arabs wear traditional dress—long white garments.
>
> Chinese—linen jackets and trousers, pigtails.
>
> Javanese natives—sarong and kabaja (a loose jacket).
>
> Europeans in white suits.

Similarly, there are ample illustrations of his rewriting. In addition to the rewriting done in consideration of how to make a novel come alive as a motion picture, however, there is also a plethora of evidence that he is concerned with style as he polishes and repolishes his scripts continually throughout the process, at times changing merely a word or two. Many of these instances grow out of a realization that something does not work or that he might add something that, for one reason or another, will work even better than what he has already written. In a majority of the archive boxes, there are numerous legal pads on which he has rewritten, by hand, the entire script, sometimes up to a half-dozen times. Each of these pads is different from its predecessor as he expands or conflates or alters the order of his scenes.

In trying to assess the amount of Pinter's responsibility in creating the final cut of his films, it should be remembered that none of his directors fits the French auteur profile. In Britain and in America particularly, filmmaking has been considered a collaborative process, and it is clear that this has been the case in transforming Pinter's written pages into celluloid images. As a dramatist, he has always been intimately involved in the translation of his words into action. In interviews, stage directors Peter Hall and David Jones, as well as set designer Bury, have commented on his contributions in production discussions. It is indisputable that this practice has carried over into the cinema, as witness Losey's comments below.

Besides the cases already cited in which the screenwriter confers with his director and others as part of the collaborative feature of filmmaking, there is confirmation of his directors' respect for his writing and a reliance on his judgment. Losey describes their partnership thus: "we had various discussions over a period of years. . . . Since [working on *The Servant*] we've never had any difficulty at all. With Harold now, it's a question of detailed discussion of intent; then he usually writes a first draft, which I comment on, and which he then rewrites; and there may or may not be small rewrites during the course of shooting—more often than not there aren't. I may ask for additions, there may be tiny things within a scene—he's very often around during shooting."[10] *Accident* provides an example of Losey's attitude in action: "The only line changed in *Accident* was changed by Pinter's wife, Vivien Merchant, with his consent and my approval—a very slight change. I *believe* in the writer's contribution and I foster it."[11]

Pinter, commenting about his relationship with Losey, says that it is "one of the high points of my life" (Gussow, "Pinter on Pinter," 26); "[W]e knew each other's mind . . . one image . . . would spark another—engender another." This kind of synergy carries over to his work with other directors.

There are additional archival materials that reveal how well Pinter works in a collaborative context with his directors. Ultimately, it is clear that he is primarily interested in producing the best artistic product that he can. He recognizes both that he has to collaborate in filmmaking because that is the way the business is run and that those with whom he works may well be able to make valuable contributions because their perspective is different from his (and he chooses his colleagues carefully, often working with the same people on numerous projects—it is amazing how many interconnections there are between writers, directors, actors, and films). In one extreme example, involving the filming of *Reunion,* he stayed in London while the movie was being shot in Germany, and he and director Schatzberg conferred by telephone when problems required the writer to rewrite to accommodate the needs imposed by the new reality that developed during the location shooting. While he insists that he seldom rewrites once shooting begins, because it is "just too difficult," occasionally he has no choice.[12]

Two two-page letters written by Pinter and addressed to Lester in connection with the script for *Victory* are illustrative of the screenwriter's attitude toward his coworkers. Dated Oxford, May 15, [1982], the first letter contains a clear indication that the conversation between the two men has been ongoing:

Dear Richard,

Here are the results of my latest explorations. I had to make decisions and act on them, even if they were the wrong ones, or I'd be sitting here till Xmas. It's obvious to me and will be obvious to you that some of it is too thin, some of it too fat, some of it too fast, some of it too slow. But if you think the ingredients are there I feel we're in business.

How much information do we need, of various kinds?

So much more detail to investigate.

Naturally the big scenes (Heyst/Lena, Ricardo/Schomberg) are open to any amount of discussion. But at least we have something to discuss.

I wrote the speech on P. 41 about Father before I decided to incorporate scene 74, so the speech could be superfluous. But I've left it for your perusal. Or you may not like 74. (I must say I do).

Ricardo goes on a bit but I couldn't resist him. I didn't think voice over worked in 69–71.

What I'm very pleased about is that we still have Jones more or less up our sleeve.

I look forward to our next meeting.

P.S. One thing I thought about but did not pursue was an intercut sequence with Heyst and Lena on island and the boat setting [out], approaching etc., Heyst and Lena unaware of its approach. I take it such would be the classic construction and perhaps you'd like me to try it. The reason I didn't is because, as things now stand, we don't *know* that Jones and Ricardo will take the bait. I also felt that scene 74 suspends time, so that the arrival of the boat in the next scene, apart from being (I hope) a sudden shock, would not be questioned in terms of time.

But I could be wrong.

In the second letter (addressed to Lester at Twickenham Studios, dated "14 June 1982," a bit more of what Pinter and Lester are trying to do and how Pinter thinks it can (or cannot) be done is disclosed:

Dear Richard,

Here it is. At least something is now mapped out. And now that it is mapped out I know we'll have a good deal to say about the whole damn thing.

Various matters to discuss obviously include the introduction of Morrison's name earlier; the establishing of Heyst as a Swede, the question of having him as a Baron; the question of Wang's wife.

If we hold to the principle of the opening sequences, I think it does mean that we have to bring Davidson back later. Perhaps there is a way of bringing him in at the end of the film convincingly. I think there may be.

I have omitted the sequence of Jones' boat crashing against the reef for three reasons:

a) I like the fact of the mast being taken off the boat and therefore Heyst unable to escape in the boat.

b) If they don't bring their bags off the boat we lose what I think is a marvelous image in Scene 142—Jones in blue silk dressing gown, with two candles burning.

c) I prefer the discovery of the boat under the jetty anyway.

However, we can easily insert a reef sequence should you think it necessary.

The Heyst/Lena shaving scene raises problems: if he possesses a cut-throat razor he can't really complain about having only blunt knives.

I don't think this is the most brilliant scene I've ever written anyway and I know that the whole section needs looking at.

I suspect that Heyst explains himself too much in the central sequence.

Looking forward to Wednesday.

Correspondence between Pinter and Fowles shows the same kind of relationship. In a letter dated "4 March 1981," the screenwriter comments on *The French Lieutenant's Woman:*

Dear John.

I have kept quite closely in touch with the editing of FRENCH LIEUTENANT'S WOMAN, and a couple of weeks ago saw what was more or less the final cut. It is undoubtedly very exciting.

However I have had a running discussion with Karel for some time about his desire to cut one scene: the last scene between Charles and Grogan, before Charles returns to Exeter. I consider this scene to be very important, as it announces the idea of "freedom." It therefore, in my view, was essential in its relation to the exchange about freedom in the last scene between Charles and Sarah. Karel agreed with all this, but felt that he had directed the scene badly and that Jeremy had failed in it. He re-cut the scene a number of times, and I know has done everything he can to make it work from his point of view. But he now feels that it cannot work and so the scene is cut.

I thought I must tell you that I regret this, but I understand Karel's position and that's that. I am not, by the way, talking, as it were, behind his back.

That's show business.

Aside from Pinter's ironically humorous observation about show business, the business side intrudes in other ways too. Commenting about *The Servant,* Losey recalls that although he made the ultimate decision, extraneous concerns led to questions: there was a "strange" scene "in the dining room which was removed and which I now regret. The film was originally about twenty minutes longer. Everyone was terrified of it from the distribution angle, and I thought maybe it's difficult, maybe it's too long, maybe it shouldn't run over two hours—so I cut twenty minutes out of it. I learned long ago—and should have known then—that you never shorten a film or increase its pace by cutting, if it has been shot a certain way."[13]

The intrusion of finances can occur even before shooting begins. There are those lists in *The French Lieutenant's Woman* archive box of how time may be saved in the filming of the script. Who determined what would be cut and why, other than to save time, which is money, is not indicated, though the pages were generated by the film company. It may be that suggestions that these cuts be made came from Reisz or Pinter, or both, and that a cost-effectiveness study was done to determine what the savings would be; or, it may be that the process was the other way around (the most likely scenario).[14]

Despite the negative intrusion of financial considerations, it is clear that collaboration can result in a fine product. The creation of both the film script of *The French Lieutenant's Woman* and the film itself are excellent examples of the collaborative process in action on several levels. Pinter told Garis that he "very much indeed" derived pleasure from working on someone else's material, because "the technical demands are, to use a cliché, a great challenge to solve." And, he continued, "it's entering into another man's mind which is very interesting . . . to try to find the true mind." The screenwriter recognizes a certain freedom in working in the cinematic medium, yet "I always work—and certainly in the case of 'The French Lieutenant's Woman'—from a substantial respect of the work itself. The excitement exists in finding out how it can properly live in film. So it was a question of how to keep faith with Fowles' complexity without being tortuous in film terms" (54).

And, Fowles was pleased with Pinter's script from the beginning. The reason was "the brilliant compression."[15] As part of the process, of course, Fowles had a hand in writing the script as well. In addition to the input recorded in the chapter on the movie above, it was the novelist who suggested that the last line in the movie be "Sarah."

Collaboration can be seen in other areas, too. For instance, production designer Assheton Gorton created sixty-two settings with roughly one hundred different areas for filming during the twenty-two-week schedule. The attention to detail by the production team shows up in the use of the earliest working steamboat extant for Charles's trip across Lake Windermere and the shooting of the sequences in Charles's town club that were filmed at the historic Garrick Club in London (electric lights were replaced by crystal candelabras and real candles).

Costume designer Tom Rand used old photographs for ideas in fashioning some of the characters' clothing, some of the clothing was rented from theatrical costumers, some came from antique markets in London (Charles's elegant black evening cloak), and some was modeled on items purchased at antique stores (the delicate silk bodice for Sarah's dress at Aunt Tranter's tea party was fabricated after the design of a piece that also provided the fancy braiding and was bought in Camden Passage for about eight dollars). Streep, who studied period costume design in college and was well informed on the subject, was delighted to be involved as well.

As was the case with *The Go-Between,* the weather duplicated that of the time being depicted. It was reported in the London *Times* that the summer of 1980 was the wettest in 113 years. In other words, conditions were the same as they had been in 1867, the year in which the story is set. Still, shooting might have been stopped by the weather except for the utilization of a newly invented photographic system called Lightflex. Lightflex operates by means of an illuminated glass that is placed over the camera lens and controls the exposure and speed of the film. On another level, Reisz and Director of Photography Freddie Francis had agreed on a low-key visual style to reflect the twilight Victorian mood, and since Lightflex has the effect of "slightly coloring the film and can be used to bring out nuances of the drama by producing expressive tints," the system was perfect to fulfill their needs (*United Artists Pressbook,* 3).

Finally, though, Pinter's screenplay for *The French Lieutenant's Woman* is another example of his writing being strong enough to overcome a director's apparent failure to fully understand the nature of the material on which he is working. Reisz told Harlan Kennedy that "The use of the clapperboard is the only place in the film where we use an illusion-and-reality contrast. The intercutting device isn't about film and life or illusion and reality. It's simply a way of showing two parallel love stories" (28).

The respect that Pinter has for his coworkers is further evident in his relating of how decisions were made in the composition of *Remembrance of Things Past.* He and Losey talked about "whether it was possible to have Marcel as the subjective camera," but the writer felt that "it becomes a device, it becomes a burden in itself," and that approach was abandoned. On another technical question, there was more discussion. Shot 14 (of 455) reads: "*Continue* MARCEL'S *progress into the drawing room. Voices. Faces. The wigs and makeup, combined with the extreme age of those who with difficulty stand, sit, gesture, laugh, give the impression of grotesque fancy dress.*"[16] Pinter and Losey pondered over how this scene would be shot: "It's a question of images of very old age and decrepitude. The manufactured faces . . . they *look* as if they're made up. Proust describes it so vividly and remorselessly that it seemed to us that we should employ all means available on film to make it as vivid and remorseless. The intention there . . . was not to veer away from it, not to hide from it."[17] Their solution was to shoot the scene on color stock but in black-and-white, so that, in Menick's words, there would be the "impression [of] a sudden draining of life from the screen; the spectral hues, the dim metallic greens and purples that you get from the use of color stock, would lend an even greater depth to the contrast" (47).

In his screenwriting, Pinter's work loosely parallels his stage writing in terms of the themes, concepts, and even techniques that interest him during different periods in his career. Thus, in the early stages, in *The Room* and *The Servant*, for example, his concerns are with intruders, menace, and the question of dominance. In later works, *Old Times* and *The Go-Between*, memory and the working of the mind capture his attention. In more recent years, political matters are foregrounded in oeuvres such as *One for the Road* and *The Trial*. Obviously, there are overlappings, and in some cases the subject matter from one period fits perfectly well in another period, although the emphasis may differ.

Nevertheless, the author does not seem to have gone through the drastic thematic and related stylistic changes that are so evident in his dramatic writing—the differences between *The Homecoming* and *Landscape* are startling; there is no correlative in his screenwriting. To some extent, the very nature of screenwriting precludes such an analog. The film script is considerably less a representation of the final product than a stage script is. On the surface it would seem as though there is virtually no difference between the two kinds of scripts, both of them consisting basically of dialogue. A stage play may be seen as a blueprint, but because of the camera, the screenplay is only a sketch of the interior to which the director and the cinematographer add the exterior. In spite of the negatives associated with collaboration, Pinter has functioned well within the system. That the staircase in *The Servant* can become such an important image/symbol for Losey shows how the process works both ways. Pinter has been lucky—or perceptive and insistent enough—that his vision and that of his directors have generally meshed well.

In *Butter's Going Up: A Critical Analysis of Harold Pinter's Work,* I talk about the author's ability to create stage plays that are demonstrably his, no matter who the directors or designers or actors are. As a dramatist, he created dialogue and approaches to his themes that quickly established him as a major force in twentieth-century theatre. His emergence as a master of the cinematic medium is based on the same kind of performance, at least in part because he works so well within the framework of the collaborative process.

One of the marks of Pinter's genius as a screenwriter is that he elicits from a very disparate group of directors, photographers, editors, and artistic and musical directors an outstanding and characteristic body of work that surpasses the work that they have done for any other screenwriter. That this is so is a tribute to the guidance provided in his film scripts, for it is his words on paper that have the power to conjure up the images and symbols that others put on celluloid.

Conclusions

IN *BUTTER'S GOING UP*, I concluded that at that point in his writing career, Pinter's screenplays, except for *The Servant, The Caretaker, The Birthday Party,* and *The Homecoming,* had not been his most successful artistic efforts. The movies certainly are not bad, I said, they just have not always lived up to what might be expected from such a talented author (or the promotional claims, for that matter).

Although they are full of mood and occasionally contain sparkling bits of Pinteresque dialogue, often the films are slow-moving. Some reviewers find them disappointing. For instance, Kael claims that Pinter's weaknesses as a scenarist are "organization, purpose, dramatic clarity" ("The Comedy of Depravity," in *Kiss Kiss Bang Bang,* 130)—the basics of good writing. She also faults the screenwriter for an "inability to achieve a dramatic climax," an obvious result of his other failings. Sounding like Max in his assessment of Joey's boxing prowess in *The Homecoming,* she goes so far as to say that "in movies Pinter doesn't avoid exposition—he's just no good at it" (133). What on stage becomes cumulatively meaningful turns into two hours of pictures on the screen—a tranquilizing process, since the true poetry is lost—yet the presentation of mood is one of his cinematic strong points.

In the immediacy of the playhouse, audience members (or as the French say, the participants) are much more involved with what is taking place on stage than the corresponding moviegoer-screen relationship allows, partly because a film is primarily composed of grouped visual images, the montage. Consequently, film depends more on action and movement (even if it is only a cut to a different shooting angle), and the intense, psychological, emotional shared experience of the play becomes watered down because it takes too much time to express through a building series of cryptic exchanges. With the magnifying and focusing power of the camera, dialogue that is

Steven H. Gale and Harold Pinter in London, 2000. Courtesy Kathy Johnson Gale.

perfectly acceptable spoken across the footlights becomes stilted and drawn out on the screen. As a result, a film drags if the screenwriter tries to transfer plot and conversation to celluloid using stage techniques and conceptual parameters. Pinter is too intense and subtle to move directly into the medium of film with the same artistic success that marks his drama, making his achievements, especially in translating his own plays to the screen, all the more praiseworthy. With *The Go-Between* and *The French Lieutenant's Woman,* however, he emerged as a major force in the modern cinema, as well as in contemporary drama. Indeed, as he continues to concentrate on his filmwriting, it is safe to assume that a writer of Pinter's enormous talent and energy will improve and produce screenplays of even greater quality than those he has already written.

Over twenty years have passed since I reached these conclusions about Pinter's screenwriting. In retrospect and given the advantage of quite a few additional screenplays, my qualms have disappeared. One of the interesting phenomena shared by many Pinter scholars and fans is that whenever he writes a new major play, the first reaction tends to be one of disappointment.

It takes time to adjust to where he is going. The theatre in general was faced with this dilemma early in his career because his work was judged against a preconceived notion of what plays are, what they are supposed to do, and how they are supposed to accomplish that goal. It took the critics and the theatre-going public alike some time to realize that Pinter's dramas had to be accepted on their own terms—and audiences that refused to go to the first run of *The Birthday Party* in 1958 (it failed miserably, closing in London after one week) flocked to the revival in 1964. In the meantime, *The Caretaker* premiered and was cited as the best play of 1960 in London and New York.

As in his writing for the stage, Pinter does not recreate the same work over and over. While there are similarities among and groupings of his films, there is not a clear-cut thematic development from one film script to the next, as there is in much of his theatrical writing. Stylistically, he started out strong, and he has continued to develop, although there has been no sea change in his style as there was between his dramatic works *The Homecoming* and *Landscape*, a stylistic adjustment made to accommodate a new set of themes. *The French Lieutenant's Woman* stands out as a major shift in his cinematic style, but it is hard to sustain a singular style when working from other people's originals. Still, as it was with his stage plays, the more careful attention paid to what he is doing and how he does it, a broader critical stance, and a maturation in the ability to accept the works on their own ground have led to a better appreciation of his cinematic achievements.

Pinter's primary achievement as a screenwriter lies in his ability to adapt other writers' work to film. He manages to distill the essence of a novel in appropriate cinematic images that capture the original's most important elements (and he manages sometimes to show that the elements upon which he focuses are, indeed, the most important). Frequently, the images are introduced by Pinter, although they are certainly in keeping with the spirit of his source. The windmill in *Accident,* the ball game on the staircase in *The Servant,* and the film-within-a-film in *The French Lieutenant's Woman* are prime examples of this ability. The result is a work of art that is unique. It is related to its source, but it is different, for the source has been transformed into something that is new, almost at times independent; it is Pinter's own vision rendered as a cinematic artwork.

Pinter writes interesting, provocative, and entertaining screenplays. But, how are his screenplays distinctive? That is, how do they differ from the majority of other film scripts in ways that make them worthy of study? The most fundamental difference is that Pinter concentrates on character rather than on plot.

Perhaps typical of the best European filmmakers of the 1960s (Bergman, Fellini, Truffaut), Pinter frequently is less concerned with the kind of storytelling models that are predominant in American films—the narrative conventions of classical cinema followed by Frank Capra, John Ford, Howard Hawks, and others. Instead, following the lines of the French New Wave, often he favors character delineation through mood at the expense of action. Basically, his works for the live theatre are more idea-oriented than plot-oriented, and his scenarios are in much the same vein. Theme and the atmospherics used to express and bolster the theme are not subordinated to the story line. Movement and action are primarily internalized, within the characters' minds. How they think is more important than what they do.

Categorically speaking, Pinter's movies would be labeled realistic as opposed to formalistic. It is probably at least in part because of his pattern of eschewing broad physical action that critics such as Kael find his film work tedious and ambiguous. In culinary terms, Pinter's films are to be savored, like nouvelle cuisine, instead of being devoured, like fast food. The elegance of a Fred Astaire dance step may give the viewer the sense that it is simple when in fact is far more complex than the robust, gymnastic movements of a Gene Kelly dance step. Connoisseurs appreciate Astaire.

Besides the question of dominance and subservience, Pinter has indicated throughout his writing career that he is interested in "the terror of the loneliness of the human situation," people on the "extreme edge of living, where they are living pretty much alone." These elements are abundantly evident throughout both his dramas and his film scripts. It is not surprising, therefore, that he began writing films at a high level of competence. At the same time, he has stated that one of the things that drew him to *The Trial* was Joseph K's resistance, the idea that it is people who battle to the end who are worthy of attention. It is fitting, then, that several of his films, no matter how dark they may be in the interim, end on an upbeat note (e.g., *The Caretaker, The Homecoming, The Pumpkin Eater, Turtle Diary, The Handmaid's Tale*) and that others, which end pessimistically, still chronicle actions that can be defined as heroic (*The Birthday Party, The Trial*). It would appear, though, that there are fewer upbeat endings in the later films than there were in the earlier ones. Perhaps this is partly because the films become noticeably more violent as he progresses—the blood-spattered corpses of *The Handmaid's*

Tale, The Comfort of Strangers, and *The Trial* have no real counterparts in the preceding movies.

Interestingly, too, it is apparent from looking at the script collection in the British Library that the screenwriter pays more and more attention to the technical details of filmmaking as he matures. In the first films, he was most concerned with telling a story and expressing its meaning, much as these were his primary concerns in the plays, and he paid little attention to cinematic techniques in the scripts. In the later films, he calls for specific shots and combinations of shots, and his attention to cinematic devices and approaches to storytelling is manifestly evident as he develops the scripts from his first thoughts through the final drafts. Recall his comment about writing *The Go-Between,* how he had to "see" it as shots. In his restructuring and other revisions, he takes into account how the story will be told on film as opposed to how it might have been told in a dramatic narrative. He does not deny that he makes these changes—as evidenced by Adam Hall's reaction to *The Quiller Memorandum* script—but he indicates that he does not do this consciously, preferring instead to claim that the process is a "natural" one. For Pinter, the definition of natural in this sense seems to be "aesthetically intuitive," a distinction that he repeated several times in our October 1994 conversation, emphasizing the importance that he apparently attaches to not being overly conscious of his art. Elsewhere, he has also admitted that he works hard at his craft. Speaking of his play writing, he says, "I do all the donkey work . . . I pay meticulous attention to the shape of things, from the shape of a sentence to the overall structure of the play" (*Various Voices,* 19). There can be no doubt that he applies this approach, this careful and considered attention to details, to his screenwriting. That the application of his aesthetic intuition and his craftsman's concern with the minute fundamentals is not contradictory is evident throughout his cinematic canon.

Although the source of the process is probably not important, by way of a conclusion, several general statements can be made about Pinter's screenwriting. To begin with, he is truly an international screenwriter. The list of his sources, directors, and actors is indicative of this aspect of his writing, as even a quick glance will verify. His audiences and his acclaim, too, are international. There have been Pinter film festivals in Britain, the United States, France, and Italy, and it has been amply documented that his films have done well in such disparate venues as Ireland, Germany, the Netherlands, and Japan as well. The answer to why the movies travel well is contained in the conclusions drawn about what it is that he does with a script that makes it uniquely his.

The beginnings of Pinter's screenplays appear to come to him fairly easily. This is evident from documents such as the two loose pages in the Pinter Archives (box 52), the first eight scenes of *The Servant* handwritten in black ink on the front and back of 4 by 8 pad paper. Pinter's earliest attempt to put his thoughts on paper differs very little from the shooting script. For instance, scene 1 is on the main road in Condon, and scene 6 is set in the garden where Tony is seen in lying in the grass. Although in the published script it is in Knightsbridge where we first see Barrett standing on the sidewalk, and Tony is lying on a deck chair in the conservatory (*Five Screenplays*, [3]), the main ideas are the same.

This is not the case with the screenplays' endings. Based on the variations between the conclusions found in different versions of the scripts, the writer seems to have more trouble with ending his tales than with beginning them. This is probably because in trying to capture the essence of his source rather than aiming for word-for-word fidelity, he changes things, not only thematically but in turning the originals technically into cinematic presentations (this is obvious in the insertion of the film-company element in *The French Lieutenant's Woman* and the trip back to Germany in *Reunion*, for instance). So, he has to bring his vision and the original vision together, which is why scripts for *The Comfort of Strangers* and *The Handmaid's Tale* presented problems for him. In a sense, that this is the reason for his difficulty in finding an appropriate conclusion is substantiated by the fact that the problem is not so pronounced in the case of his own stage plays and *Butley*—the essence is already distilled, and the presentation of the dramas is already visually oriented.

In classical cutting the shots are psychologically connected rather than being separated by real time and space, and the process thereby creates mental and emotional drama rather than a literal representation. For Bazin the technique is intrusive and distorts or destroys the unity of space. This kind of cutting, he feels, is more nuanced than real, for it forces the audience to analyze the components themselves and to focus on a series of details. In contrast, Soviet formalist theorists such as Pudovkin believe that the "foundation of film art is editing." Pudovkin favors "constructive editing" because he feels that every individual shot should make a point and that it is through the juxtaposition of shots that meaning is created. As Hitchcock says, "Cinema is form."[1] Lev Kuleshov, in a protodeconstructionist state-ment, insists that filmmakers assemble the material, but it is the viewer who creates meaning out of that material.[2]

Pudovkin fancies cutting as opposed to extended long shots because cut-ting allows for the creation of the linkages necessary to give movies true realism as opposed to theatrical realism. Thus, instead of replicating sur-faces, cinema can capture essences. With the emergence of the New Wave in the 1950s, the idea that the meaning of a film is determined by how that meaning is expressed became a theoretical rationale for choosing a particu-lar approach to making individual films. Bazin, whose realist aesthetic led to the auteur theory, agrees, and it is for this very reason that he dismisses classical editing. He feels that the classical approach to editing results in a product composed of shots that represent what the filmmaker considers im-portant (i.e., nonrelevant elements, which may be present in nature, are re-moved), not what the audience might consider important. But, this is the nature of art and the role of the artist—to present his or her view of reality. It is clear from Pinter's deliberate calling for shots that are juxtaposed in a way that emphasizes the psychological instead of the linear time-space con-tinuum that he believes that the manipulation of the material is the best way to recreate reality.

In the theoretical debate over whether film is enhanced or degraded drama or a separate and different medium, critics such as Ernest Lindgren consider film a medium that is defined as independent of drama only when the direc-tor imposes a creative vision on the material. Otherwise, such a person "will fall back on glib, superficial, and essentially non-filmic methods, such as relying on . . . actors and using cinematography simply to record their per-formance" (167). Current film theorists adopt the literary paradigm in their discussions, especially the model of the novel. Metz talks about "texts," which are "units of discourse" (*Language and Cinema*, 21). James Monaco's termi-nology revolves around the definition of movie viewers as readers. Suzanne Langer finds cinematic structure closer to narrative than to drama. Armes points out that there is even a discrepancy in the fact that *diegesis* (the re-counting of an action or the verbal statement of a case) is used instead of *mimesis* (the imitation of an action) to describe film (11–12).

Other theoretical considerations include the fact that the reader is guided through a novel by the author (Willis and D'Arienzo, 183), whereas in drama, which is an outgrowth of oral literature, the storyteller/actor employs ac-tion, tone of voice, the audience, and a number of other elements to convey meaning and emotion, and some scholars contend that in film the camera takes the place of the implied author.[3] Furthermore, prose is fixed (words printed on a page), while each performance of a play is unique. Where, then, does film fit into this pattern?

For Pinter, the problem does not seem to be so much about how to define the media, whether film opens out drama or how motion pictures are theoretically dissimilar from novels; it is a matter of how to adapt the source material in the most effective way possible. This is where his sense of aesthetic intuition comes into play. His stage works exemplify Raymond Williams's recognition that playwrights compose a drama "in such a manner that it can be directly performed" (150). Likewise, Pinter's screenplays are written for filming; that is, they are designed to be executed through cinematic techniques. The mobility of the camera, the close-up, and montage have been designated by Peter Szondi as definitive of film since because of these developments the motion picture "ceases to be filmed theatre and becomes an independent pictorial narrative" (Szondi, 68), and Pinter's film scripts evidence the writer's competence in incorporating these elements into his storytelling. As Jean-Claude Carriere says, "a scenario is already the film" (12).[4]

Ironically, at least for those critics who are so involved with these questions, in film the images and auxiliary elements are ultimately more important than the dialogue; action is preeminent over words. Robert Scholes has suggested that the active participation of the audience is important because the operation of film images and recorded sounds make film "closest to actuality, to undifferentiated experience," in that the photographic image does not name what it shows. Therefore, the distance and generalization experienced by the novel reader are diminished for the motion picture viewer, who, rather than needing to create mental images, is forced to follow "a more categorical and abstract narrativity" that will lead to "some level of reflection, of conceptualization" (67). Certainly, too, to some extent the distinction between the media can be determined by how time is used. In drama real time is the key—what we see happening on stage happens in the same amount of time as it happens in the real world. It is not under the control of the reader, as in prose, nor is it manipulated, as in the stop motion, slow motion, fast motion, and intercutting that can be utilized in film.

Some critics contend that the primary problem involved in adaptation is the handling of space and time. As Giannetti has observed, compared to drama, in which "the meaning of the language is determined by the fact that the characters are on the same stage at the same time, reacting to the same words," in film "time and space are fragmented by the individual shots."[5] At the same time, however, it must be recognized that correlating words with visual images that capture the essence of those words is a prime concern of the adapter.

While in conversations and interviews Pinter includes references indicating that he is familiar with such theoretical musings, these are considerations that he has apparently intuited. He knows, as Benjamin Bennett has said, that in *Hamlet,* "for the reader . . . Hamlet is in effect simply *not* there until, in due course, his name and the first words he speaks are arrived at" (66). Pinter is aware also, as illustrated in *Old Times* (in which a character appears on stage before she becomes an active part of the drama), that on stage or film this is not the case. Moreover, the audience is simultaneously cognizant of the reactions of one character to another. An extension of this recognized characteristic is found in Robbe-Grillet's contention that one of the strengths of film is "the possibility of playing on two senses at the same time, the eye and the ear" (146).

Perhaps an important key to understanding what Pinter does as a screenwriter is seeing how well he applies a principle that Bennett mentions in his discussion of modern drama: "Since the performance generates meanings that belong to the work but *are not there for the reader* . . . we are compelled to recognize that true understanding occurs *only* via performances, whereas the situation of the reader makes available, at best, a defective, verbally conditioned *selection of* meanings" (76). As demonstrated repeatedly in the film analyses in this volume, Pinter understands what Armes calls "the proper status of the camera in the creation of meaning that is crucial to the understanding of dramatic structure in cinema" (42). Dramatic structure is dependent upon the relationship of text and subtext and is, according to Esslin, "analogous to musical structure, depends on the interaction, in sequence, and contrapuntally, at any given moment, of melodic and rhythmic elements that are established, varied, juxtaposed, combined and recombined" (*Field of Drama,* 119).

Another element that is apparent in Pinter's screenplays is his awareness that the theatre-going experience, whether dramatic or cinematic, is incorporated into the audience's perception of the product being offered, yet at the same time the audience is also capable of accepting the image of reality being reflected from the screen. Metz describes this condition when he says that the "total unreality of the filmic means" allows "the fictional context of the film to assume reality" (*Film Language,* 194).

Possibly the single most critical element in Pinter's success as a screen-writer is his understanding of and ability to express his story in the *here-and-now* of the movie theatre. Metz has asserted that movement in film is reproduced each time the film is shown and that each time the movement takes place in the present (*Language and Cinema,* 9). John Peter observes that a play is experienced as "a unique kind of narrative because it is a story which tells itself *by taking place*"; the same contention can certainly be made about film. "It is important to realize too that the relation of simultaneity between spectator and performer, which exists phenomenologically in stage drama and which is convincingly reproduced in the cinema, is only part of the organization of time in a dramatic performance," according to Armes (59). "The unfolding of action that offers no pause for reflection," he goes on to say, is common to both stage and screen drama (60). Thus, he concludes, "Participation as a spectator in a dramatic action is quite the opposite of being duped by an illusion. It is, potentially at least, a profound and all-involving experience." It is the eliciting of this experience with such power that characterizes Pinter's work in film.

He does this by accepting a challenge and conquering the problems which that challenge presents. In adapting a novel to the screen, for instance, he knows that his source is realistic in tone, that the original is based on a one-on-one relationship between the author and the reader, that time is treated differently on the page than on the screen, and that in the role of a reader the audience's interrelation with time is different from what it is when the role is that of a viewer. The novel reader chooses the pace at which the work of art is ingested, and this allows for absorption of and reflection on the meaning of the work over time. A film must be designed for immediate comprehension, and reflection on the meaning comes after the fact.

As an author, Pinter forces the approach to his text from the leisure of reading to the rapidity of viewing, with possibly a corresponding increased acceptance of the reality presented on film. Essentially, he determines what is missing from the novel when he writes a performance script, and he adds those elements. He creates photographic images that do not name what they show. He takes into account the components of performance—aural and visual signs—that are part of the *here-and-now* presentation in film but which are absent in the novel, and he incorporates them into the action that tells the story. At the same time, sound, which normally is used to intensify realism, to magnify emotional ingredients, is an aspect of the filmic art that is not so prevalent in Pinter's scripts (though it is inlaid in some of his films by the directors). Perhaps he does not use as much sound as others do because of his stage background, in which sound effects and mood music are not widespread; more likely, he is attempting to retain a more realistic flavor than that of his compeers. When he calls for specific sounds, they are a natural part of the scene (Laine singing in *The Servant* and the operatic music in *Victory* and *The Comfort of Strangers,* for instance). In many ways, then, he "realizes" the story, in the way that the French understand "realize" when applied in cinematic terms. The result is a more realistic, immediate way of telling the story than was available in his source material. Dramas he opens out when he translates them cinematically; novels he transforms.

Film is frozen in a way that drama and prose fiction are not. Nonetheless, because of the richness of details supplied by camera angles, sets, composition within a frame, acting nuances, and the like, and the fact that the movie is continuous motion, subsequent viewings of the film can lead to an enhanced understanding. Indeed, the audience's first reaction may carry the substantially emotional reaction typically associated with live drama, whereas the intellectual component more commonly associated with prose may be a later and ongoing augmentation.

There is a difference between what is lifelike (the automatons at Disneyland, for example) and what is live. This is especially pertinent in distinguishing between what can be done in prose fiction and what can be done in film. A novel, like a painting or a photograph, can be lifelike, realistic, but we know that it is not real. The characters are inextricably tied to the page. This does not mean that the words cannot cause us to laugh or cry, but we have to mentally picture what the characters are doing. With film we can *see* the characters act, react, think, and feel, and what we see seems real because of the movement and sound.

Paradoxically, the cinematic image is both real and not real. I can explain this paradox with a personal anecdote. On the day that my wife and I arrived in Monrovia, the capital city of Liberia, we left the house unattended for half an hour; thieves broke in and stole a number of valuables. As a result, I spent many hours sitting in the local police station waiting to talk to the detectives. The small room was furnished with a wooden bench (on which I sat), several desks across from the bench, and a couple of file cabinets behind them. On one visit I noticed a young boy of about six or seven sitting in the far corner of the room. On the floor midway between him and the file cabinets, which were in the opposite corner, was a "country devil." A country devil is a grass costume used in religious rituals and dances. It covers the performer's body and is topped with a wooden mask (in this case the mask was missing). During the ceremonies, the people of the tribe know on some level that the being who sways in their midst is a relative and friend. On another level, they do not recognize the man but accept the symbol, which to them is in actuality a spirit. Thus, the figure becomes more than a symbol, it becomes the thing itself.

While I waited, I overheard the detectives conversing about the boy. Apparently, he had stolen the country devil costume—no one knew why. The detectives, all of whom were sufficiently educated to be able to speak, read, and write English as well as their native dialects, were having great fun at the youngster's expense. They laughed and talked about his foolishness, and they reveled in the superstitious implications of what he had done. Still, I noticed that whenever they had to walk past that pile of dried grass clothing on their way to the file cabinets, they quietly and carefully gave the costume wide berth.

When I attended the movies in Monrovia, the audience members had a similar relationship with the images in the film. The people kept up a running dialogue with one another, making sure that everyone knew exactly what was transpiring on the screen. Frequently they reacted as Partridge did in Henry Fielding's *Tom Jones*: they called out to the figures on the screen. "Don't trust her," they warned Sean Connery's James Bond; "Look out James, she's got a gun," they screamed to him in another scene. For the people in that audience, the actors were as human as their sons and daughters were when they watched performances of the University Players productions that I directed on the University of Liberia campus later that year, and in both cases the characters were real to them.

Pinter's audiences are much more experienced with film and considerably more sophisticated than those just described, yet he has the ability to make his characters come alive and the action seem real in ways that utilize the film medium more effectively than is done by most other screenwriters. He takes the scripts that he creates beyond their sources. The result is a new work of art of amazing vitality and depth.

In the final analysis, Pinter consistently does two things that set his work off from that of other screenwriters. First, he has the ability to identify, isolate, and extract the essence of his source material. In *The Servant*, this means that he focuses on Tony's weaknesses. That may seem a simple exercise, but it means that the writer discards those elements of the novel that do not have a direct bearing on the meaning, and he emphasizes and sometimes adds elements that reenforce that meaning. Second, in translating his source cinematically, he chooses techniques that are cinematic in nature. In other words, he recognizes the essential differences between the media. For instance, a narrator is perfectly appropriate in the prose version of *Lolita* (and perhaps the best way to express Humbert's personality through his convoluted, philosophical meanderings). Most screenwriters would automatically turn to the obvious technique of a voice-over to capture Nabakov's message and to remain faithful their source (i.e., to retain as much of the book as possible). But, time is different in prose than it is in film. The reader ponders Humbert's interesting musings leisurely, thinks with the protagonist as he thinks, tastes the words as they are read and reread. The viewer is moved quickly, is assaulted by the impact of visual images that are compounded as they bombard her or him one at a time and in a montage. Pinter's genius is his understanding that a voice-over is not as effective in this film as more cinematic methods for exposing Humbert's thoughts. Moreover, to express them, he does not share them as thoughts but shows them as actions.

Likewise, the authorial asides in Fowles's *The French Lieutenant's Woman* carry much of the meaning of the novel, and they give it the special flavor that so many of Fowles's readers enjoy and appreciate. Pinter eschews these elements. They are too time-consuming, too massive. He is forced by the comparative length of a film to omit these intrusions or to reduce pages of them to a single line of dialogue or image. And, in this film, Pinter invents an entirely new parallel plot, ironically in order to bring together all of the strands of Fowles's 366-page novel encapsulated in a relatively compact two-hour-and-three-minute movie. The end product of Pinter's adaptation process is a new work of art, one that is cinematic and which has grown out of another work of art, one that is always as good as the original and often better.

Film is a highly visually saturated medium. Each shot is densely packed with informational details, and shots are edited together so that the cinema audience is not required to interpret these details; a theatrical audience must determine which visual elements to focus upon. One of the characteristics of Pinter's film scripts is an extension of his playwriting: even with the presence of visual detail supplied by the camera, he manages to withhold enough information so that the meaning of the details is obscured until the moment that he wants to reveal it. In essence, Pinter is going against the nature of film in doing this. Whether he is considered a superb artist who can transcend the normal restrictions of his medium or a failure who does not adequately utilize the basic elements of that medium probably depends on the viewer's taste.

On the one hand, by negating the medium's natural effect, Pinter may be exposing his own failings. On the other hand, he may be demonstrating that he is an artist rather than a craftsman. His ability to force film to produce his desired effects, to maintain a sense of confinement, even when this is contrary to the nature of the medium, may ultimately prove that he is a true artist. The reversal might also explain why his films seem to move so slowly upon first viewing. His effects are so subtle that subsequent viewings are required for the audience to appreciate what he is actually doing. Like his stage scripts, Pinter's film scripts tend to be understated. But, that is what film is all about anyway—creating visual equivalents to communicate logical meaning and emotional content.

There can be no doubt that heretofore Pinter's contribution to screenwriting has been undervalued because many literary scholars do not consider it as equivalent to the level of his contributions to the stage, perhaps the most important of which was to force audiences to come to the theatre with an open mind. Nevertheless, he has accomplished a great deal, particularly in bringing opened-out versions of his stage dramas to the screen. He has also created the screenplays for at least a half-dozen significant motion pictures, some of the most interesting, imaginative, and important film scripts of the past forty years. There also can be no doubt that he has made important contributions to the cinema, not the least of which has to do with the primary characteristics of his screenplays—in almost every case he has produced a script that was superior to his source. More importantly, in virtually every instance, that script is a work of art in its own right, one that stands by itself and is worthy of the highest praise. This is an admirable accomplishment.

Appendixes

Appendix A: Quick Reference

TITLE	DATE	PRODUCTION COMPANY	DIRECTOR	SOURCE
Accident	1967	London Independent Producers	Joseph Losey	Accident: Nicholas Mosley, 1965
The Basement	1967	BBC-2 Television	Charles Jarrott	The Basement: Pinter, 1963
Betrayal	1982	Horizon Pictures (GB) Limited; Twentieth Century-Fox International	David Jones	Betrayal: Pinter, 1978
The Birthday Party	1968	Palomar Pictures/Continental	William Friedkin	The Birthday Party: Pinter, 1960
Butley	1974	American Express Films	Harold Pinter	Butley: Simon Gray, 1971
The Caretaker	1964	BL; Janus	Clive Donner	The Caretaker: Pinter, 1960
The Comfort of Strangers	1990	Skouras Pictures	Paul Schrader	The Comfort of Strangers: Ian Mcwan, 1981
The Diaries of Etty Hillesum		Not scripted		An Interrupted Life. The Diaries of Etty Hillesum 1941–1943: Esther Hillesum, 1983
The Dreaming Child		Not filmed		"The Dreaming Child": Isak Dinesen, 1995
The French Lieutenant's Woman	1981	Parlon Productions; United Artists	Karl Reisz	The French Lieutenant's Woman: John Fowles, 1969
The Go-Between	1971	Columbia/World Film Services	Joseph Losey	The Go-Between: L.P. Hartley, 1953
The Handmaid's Tale	1990	Cinecom Entertainment Group; Warner Brothers	Volker Schlondorff	The Handmaid's Tale: Margaret Atwood, 1986
The Homecoming	1973	American Film Theatre	Peter Hall	The Homecoming: Pinter, 1965
The Last Tycoon	1976	Paramount	Elia Kazan	The Last Tycoon: F. Scott Fitzgerald, 1941

Appendix A: Quick Reference

TITLE	DATE	PRODUCTION COMPANY	DIRECTOR	SOURCE
Julia		Not scripted		Pentimento: Lillian Hellman, 1973
King Lear	2000	Not filmed		The Tragedy of King Lear: William Shakespeare
Lolita		Film based on another's screenplay		Lolita: Vladimir Nabokov, 1955
The Portrait of Dorian Gray		Not scripted		The Portrait of Dorian Gray: Oscar Wilde, 1891
The Proust Screenplay		Not filmed		À la recherché du temps perdu (Remembrance of Things Past): Marcel Proust, 1913–1927
The Pumpkin Eater	1964	Royal International-Columbia Pictures	Jack Clayton	The Pumpkin Eater: Penelope Mortimer, 1962
The Quiller Memorandum	1966	Twentieth Century-Fox; Paramount; National General Corporation; The Rank Organization	Michael Anderson	The Berlin Memorandum: Adam Hall, 1965
The Remains of the Day		Film based on from another's screenplay		The Remains of the Day: Kazuo Ishiguro, 1989
Reunion	1990	Soverign Pictures; Ariane Films	Jerry Schatzberg	Reunion: Fred Uhlman, 1971
The Servant	1963	Landau/Springbok-Elstree; Warner-Pathe	Joseph Losey	The Servant: Robin Maugham, 1948
Straw Dogs		Not scripted		The Seige at Trencher's Farm: Gordon Williams, 1969

Appendix A: Quick Reference

TITLE	DATE	PRODUCTION COMPANY	DIRECTOR	SOURCE
The Trial	1993	Europanda Entertainment B../ BBC Films; Capitol	David Jones	*The Trial*: Franz Kafka, 1937
Turtle Diary	1985	United British Artists-Britannic	John Irvin	*Turtle Diary*: Russell Hoban, 1975
Victory		Not filmed		*Victory*: Joseph Conrad, 1915

Appendix B: Honors and Awards for Screenwriting

Accident: Cannes Film Festival Special Jury Prize; Movie Critics of the Foreign Language Association Award, Best British Film; UNICRIT Prize, 1967; Premio de Selezione di Sorrento Award, 1967; Grand Prix de l'Union de la Critique de Cinema (Belgium), 1967; National Board of Review Award, one of the ten best films of the year

Betrayal: Nominated for Academy of Motion Picture Arts and Sciences Awards (Best Picture, Best Screenplay Based on Material from Another Medium)

The Caretaker: Berlin Film Festival Silver Bear; Edinburgh Festival Certificate of Merit

The French Lieutenant's Woman: Nominated for Academy of Motion Picture Arts and Sciences Awards (Best Picture, Best Screenplay Based on Material from Another Medium); nominated for a Golden Globe (Best Screenplay–Motion Picture); 1982 Donatello Award (Italy) for Best Foreign Screenplay

The Go-Between: British Film Academy Award (Best Screenplay); Cannes Film Festival Palme d'Or Award; Society of Film and Television Arts, Best Screenplay; INTER Film Award

The Last Tycoon: National Board of Review Best English-Language Film Award; Ennio Flaiano Award for Screenwriting; Donatello Prize (Italy)

The Lover: Guild of British Television Producers and Directors Award; Prix Italia (Naples) for Television Drama

The Pumpkin Eater: British Film Academy Award for Best Screenplay

The Servant: British Screenwriters Guild Award; Los Angeles Film Critics; New York Film Critics Best Writing Award; New York Times listing, one of the ten best films of the year

Appendix C: Film and Television Directing

Butley (1974)

The Rear Column (Simon Gray, April 13, 1979, BBC1)

The Hothouse (1982, BBC)

Mountain Language (December 11, 1988, BBC2)

Party Time (1992, Channel 4)

Landscape (October 21, 1995, BBC2)

Ashes to Ashes (1998, RAI TV, Italy)

Appendix D: Movie and Television Roles Acted by Pinter

A Night Out (ABC-TV, March 1960): Seeley

The Basement (BBC-TV, February 1967): Stott

Pinter People (NBC-TV, 1969): Voices of Mr. Fibbs in "Trouble in the Works" and Barman in "Last to Go"

The Caretaker: Man in the Street

The Servant: Society Man

Accident: Bell

No Exit (BBC-TV, 1965): García

Rogue Male (1976): Saul Abrahams

Langrishe, Go Down (BBC 2-TV, September 20, 1978): Barry Shannon

The Birthday Party (BBC-TV, 1986): Goldberg

Turtle Diary: Man in Bookstore

The Rise and Rise of Michael Rimmer: Steven Hench

Breaking the Code (TV—BBC 1, February 5, 1996; PBS, 1996): John Smith

Mojo: Sam Ross

Mansfield Park: Sir Thomas Bertram

Wit (HBO, March 24, 2001): Father

Catastrophe: Director

Notes

Preface

1. Quoted in Sinyard, *Filming Literature*, 157.

Introduction

1. A shorter Vitagraph version of *Oliver Twist* had appeared in America in 1910 as well; *The Life and Death of King Richard III* is the oldest known surviving American feature film.

2. This was primarily a function of the kind of equipment then in use—large, heavy cameras and stationary microphones.

3. Among his many honors, he has been knighted (C.B.E. in 1996), named a Companion of Honour (2002), and nominated for the Nobel Prize in literature.

4. See my *Butter's Going Up*.

5. Higson, *Waving the Flag*, 4.

6. See Walker's *Hollywood UK* for a detailed discussion of this subject.

7. Louis Giannetti turns to *The Pumpkin Eater* and *The Caretaker* to exemplify the use of dolly or traveling shots: in *The Pumpkin Eater*, "a distraught wife . . . returns to an ex-husband's house where she has an adulterous liaison with him. As the two lie in bed, she asks him if he had been upset over their divorce and whether or not he missed her. He assures her that he wasn't upset, but while their voices continue on the soundtrack, the camera belies his words by slowly dollying through his living room, revealing pictures and mementos of the ex-wife"; "the dialogue [in *The Caretaker*] . . . is evasive and not very helpful in providing an understanding of the characters. . . . Each brother has a crucial speech in which the camera slowly tracks from a long range to a close-up. Neither of the speeches is really very informative, at least not on a literal level. It is with the juxtaposition of the dialogue with the implications of the dolly shot that the audience feels it has finally 'arrived' at an understanding of each character" (*Understanding Movies*, 26–36).

8. See Bensky, "Harold Pinter: An Interview"; all quotations from Bensky come from the reprint, "Harold Pinter," in *Writers at Work: The Paris Review Interviews*,

Third Series, 360–61. For a graphic dramatic expression of this approach, see Len's speech in Pinter's *The Dwarfs,* in *Three Plays* (New York: Grove, 1962), 103. In recent years he has become more politically engaged in his writing.

9. *Montage* is a French word meaning "mounting" and is generally used to refer to the assemblage of a film by editing or the art of editing. I use it here for the arrangement of individual shots that create a whole. Giannetti also defines the word as "transitional sequences of rapidly edited images, used to suggest the lapse of time or the passing of events" (515), which is sometimes called American or Hollywood montage. Other types of montage are "accelerated" (the use of editing to increase the speed of action), "attraction" (two separate images are related because of visual or contextual similarities), "narrative" (the editing together of shots and scenes arranged in chronological order), "rhythmic" (the length of shots is used to enhance an effect or emphasize a thematic element), and "Russian" (a collective term referring to the theoretical and practical approaches advocated by Sergi Eisenstein, Lev Kuleshov, Vsevolod I. Pudovkin, and Dziga Vertov, which are discussed below). See also Beaver, *Dictionary of Film Terms,* 200–208.

10. Pinter selected eleven films (including *Langrishe, Go Down,* which is still not available on video) to be shown in the fall of 1996 at the National Film Theatre as part of this retrospective on his films. Michael Billington, Pinter's biographer (*Life and Work of Harold Pinter*), wrote the introductory notes for the program (*National Film Theatre Programme,* Oct.–Nov. 1996, 4–8). In its second Pinter Festival, the Gate Theatre in Dublin included television screenings and viewings of some of his works at the Irish Film Centre. Further recognizing and validating Pinter's importance as a screenwriter, in 2000 Faber and Faber published a three-volume set containing sixteen of his screenplays (see Works Cited for a complete listing of these film scripts), and in 2001 eight of his films were shown in conjunction with the Pinter Festival in New York City, sponsored by the Lincoln Center for the Performing Arts.

11. In the last couple of years, a trend seems to have been developing in which the importance of the screenwriter has been recognized more publicly (with some consequent diminishing of the accentuation of the director), in terms of placing the writer's name in the credits (following instead of preceding the producer) and in payment for services.

12. Quoted in Caute, *Joseph Losey,* 206.

13. *Night School* was the first of Pinter's plays written specifically for television; he reportedly was not happy with it. According to J.L. Styan, *A Night Out* was the highest-rated television program during the week that it was televised. See Styan, "Television Drama," 203. *The Lover* won the Prix Italia (Naples) for Television Drama and the Guild of British Television Producers and Directors Award. *Tea Party* was broadcast by the European Broadcasting Union to all sixteen member nations, a huge audience.

14. Some filmographies include *Two by Pinter,* a video available from Films for the Humanities, but this is merely a videotape of stage production of *Landscape* and *Party Time.*

15. Pinter, in a letter dated Jan. 5, 1991, in response to my letter to him of Oct. 22, 1990, in which I asked, "When you approach a script for television, such as *The Heat of the Day,* how do you view the project differently than when you are working on something that will be seen on a theatrical screen? In other words, are there techniques that you use differently for television and the movies? And, do you make a conscious distinction between television and the cinema in terms of how artistic, effective, valuable, important, or prestigious they are?"

16. Pinter, quoted in Langley, "From 'Caretaker' to 'Servant.'"

17. See Gale, "The Use of a Cinematic Device in Harold Pinter's *Old Times,*" 11–12; Gale, "The Significance of Orson Welles in Pinter's *Old Times,*" 11; and Hudgins, "Inside Out," for discussions of these techniques.

18. One method for avoiding the cropping is "letterboxing," which retains the original ratio by blacking out the screen and placing the film within an elongated box on the screen. Most audiences do not like this format, because it reduces the size of the picture even further, though there is some evidence that this attitude is changing now that elongated and flat-screen televisions are in the marketplace.

19. Once high-definition television becomes commonplace, with its 1,125 lines compared to the current format of 525 or 625 lines, this is likely to be considerably less true.

20. Some critics claim that it was the films that Losey made from Pinter's scripts that brought the director international recognition, especially in France.

21. Quoted in Leahy, *Cinema of Joseph Losey,* 126.

22. Further discussion of this topic will be found below, and this subject is dealt with in too many books and articles for me to list them all here, but many of these sources are listed in Works Cited and the Selected Bibliography. Film is a legitimate genre of literature, one in which the artist can do things that cannot be done in other genres and one in which the artist cannot do things that can be done in another genre. This means that film has certain advantages and certain limitations when compared with other literary genres, but it does not mean that film is either superior or inferior to the other genres; it is merely different, a conclusion with which not all of the above-mentioned scholars seem to agree.

23. Quoted in Packard, *The Art of Screenwriting,* 44.

24. Ray Bradbury, in Chase, *Filmmaking,* 35. Chase's chapter "The Screenwriter" contains the insights of many authors into the role of the writer in filmmaking.

25. Nunnally Johnson, quoted in ibid., 34.

26. Ibid., 36.

27. William Goldman, in Sanders and Mock, *Word into Image,* 30. Among the films that Goldman scripted are *Butch Cassidy and the Sundance Kid* (Academy Award for Original Screenplay), *Marathon Man, Harper,* and *All the President's Men* (Academy Award for Screenwriting).

28. Field, *Screenplay,* 204–5.

29. Esslin, in discussions at the International Pinter Festival, Ohio State University, Apr. 20, 1991.

30. Quoted in Bensky, "Harold Pinter," 365.

31. Typescript provided by Pinter to Gale, Apr. 26, 1990.

32. *The Way Ahead,* he told Mel Gussow, was "a great British war film, with David Niven, Carol Reed directed it, and Peter Ustinov wrote the script." "Vivien [Merchant] was in it. She was nine. She played Stanley Holloway's daughter" (Gussow, *Conversations,* 138).

33. Other genre films of the period that are part of the background context out of which Pinter's interest in film developed include Michael Powell's *Contraband* (1940) and Alberto Cavalcanti's *They Made Me a Fugitive* (1947), along with two of Alfred Hitchcock's movies, which Pinter would have been too young to see in their first run, *The Thirty-Nine Steps* (1935) and *The Lady Vanishes* (1938). In an interesting connection, Cavalcanti's cinematographer, Otto Heller, was the cameraman for *Alfie,* which starred Vivien Merchant, Pinter's wife at the time.

34. Despite Pinter's avowal that he was not influenced by his reading, his novel *The Dwarfs* has a Beckettian flavor; also, his early television plays *The Basement* and *Tea Party* are not as avant-garde as *Un Chien andalou,* but there are reverberations of the experimental, expressionistic essence of the Buñuel/Salvador Dali script in them.

35. Among Pinter's film roles have been parts in *The Servant* (Society Man), *The Caretaker* (Man in the Street), *Accident* (Bell), *Rogue Male* (Saul Abrahams), *Turtle Diary* (Man in Bookstore), *The Rise and Rise of Michael Rimmer* (Steven Hench), *Mojo* (Sam Ross), his highly praised portrayal of Sir Thomas Bertram in *Mansfield Park, Catastrophe* (Director), and the wonderful Uncle Benny (with a Goldbergian idiom and a tailor's costume remindful of his own father's trade) in *The Tailor of Panama.*

His television roles have included an appearance in the "NBC Experiment in Television: *Pinter People*" (1969), in which he was the voice for characters in the cartoon versions of his revue sketches "Trouble in the Works" (as Mr. Fibbs) and "Last to Go" (the Barman), along with Seeley in his *Night Out* (BBC Third Programme, Mar. 1, 1960, and ABC-TV, Apr. 24, 1960), Garcia in Jean-Paul Sartre's *No Exit* (BBC Television, Nov. 15, 1965), Stott in *The Basement* (BBC Television, Feb. 28, 1967), Barry Shannon in *Langrishe, Go Down* (BBC-2 Television, Sept. 20, 1978), Goldberg in *The Birthday Party* (BBC, June 21, 1986), John Smith in *Breaking the Code* (PBS, 1996), and Father in *Wit* (HBO, Mar. 24, 2001).

Presumably it is because of this acting background that, whether on stage or screen, Pinter, who started out as a repertory actor, has the actors' perspective in mind when he writes. This may help account for the amazing number of best actor and actress nominations that have come out of his films. His directing experience includes the television versions of *A Night Out, Butley* (which he had directed on the stage), *Landscape* (1968), and *The Hothouse* (1983).

36. Quoted in "Genius—A Change in Direction."

37. Again, see Gale, "Use of a Cinematic Device in Harold Pinter's *Old Times.*"

38. Mamet's opinions regarding filmmaking are of special interest because of his connections with Pinter—including Pinter's influence on the language in Mamet's

plays, his directing of the London run of *Oleana,* and his acting in the film version of Samuel Beckett's *Catastrophe* (2000), which Mamet directed.

39. George Bernard Shaw, *Metropolitan Magazine,* cited in Lindsay, *Art of the Moving Picture* (1970 ed.).

40. Pinter, quoted in Caute, *Joseph Losey,* 260.

41. In *Film Form,* Eisenstein does distinguish between different kinds, or uses, of montage (as distinct from Pudovkin's theorizing in *Film Technique*), but the basic definition is a constant.

42. See the discussion of this element and Pinter's reaction to it, especially in the *Caretaker* chapter.

43. Among the modern textual scholars who have tried to define the copy-text (that is, the authoritative published text) are W.W. Greg, T.H. Howard-Hill, Fredson Bowers, James Thorpe, Philip Gaskell, G. Thomas Tanselle, and Jerome J. McGann.

44. Pinter in a letter to Gale dated Jan. 5, 1991.

45. Mamet, however, who admits to being influenced by Pinter, hates the collaborative element of filmmaking, as he makes clear in *On Directing* and in "Producers," which is included in *Jafsie and John Henry.* Insights into writing for the movies are also found in his *Some Freaks* and *Writing in Restaurants,* in which he calls the screenwriter a "laborer" (75).

46. Interviews with Hall, Bury, and actors John Normington and Paul Rogers, attesting to the dramatist's involvement, can be found in Lahr, *Casebook on Harold Pinter's The Homecoming,* for instance. There are ample additional examples as well, some of which are cited in Gale, *Butter's Going Up.*

47. For example, four seconds of the copulation scene in *The Go-Between* were cut out of the prints for KABC-TV and American Airlines showings. Another complication is the insertion of commercials when a film is shown on television because such an interruption can unquestionably have a great effect on the impact of the film, breaking up a train of thought or action, releasing tension, disturbing the timing, and so forth. As an aside, the choice of commercials for inclusion in itself provides for a study in popular culture and in advertising.

48. *Langrishe, Go Down; The Heat of the Day;* and *The Dreaming Child* are included in the three-volume *Collected Screenplays.*

49. This is obvious in Mamet's career. Although he laments in "A First-Time Film Director," in *Some Freaks,* 119–20, that he was "completely ignorant" about the "visual" area of directing films and relied on Eisenstein's theories while preparing for his directorial debut (*House of Games,* 1987), the opening sequence of *The Verdict* demonstrates that he is able to create a successful montage of "uninflected" shots. Given Mamet's work in the theatre, where the word is predominant, his plea of ignorance is understandable and sympathy-eliciting. In "Encased by Technology" (also in *Some Freaks*), Mamet notes that "movies are the first art to link the plastic and the temporal. They take place both tangibly, in the image, and continually, in the juxtaposition of those images" (160). Obviously he is attracted to the essence of film as "art" and its suggestive nature—which is the creation of an image "not on the

screen, but in the mind of the beholder." Later, he elaborates when he states that "Lumiere et al" were "juxtaposing pictures *to create an idea in the mind* of the audience" (161, emphasis mine).

50. Quoted in Taylor, "Accident," 184.

51. Cherrapunji averages more than an inch of rainfall a day, and Mount Waialeale records an average annual rainfall of 460 inches, but in areas of the Sahara there are entire years when no measurable rainfall occurs.

52. See Gale, *Butter's Going Up,* for a discussion of this technique.

53. Quoted in Philip Gaskell, "*Night and Day:* Development of a Play Text" in *Textual Criticism and Literary Interpretation,* ed. Jerome J. McGann (Chicago: Univ. of Chicago Press, 1985), 176.

54. See Gussow, "A Conversation."

55. Lahr interview with Normington, in the galley proof of *A Casebook on Harold Pinter's The Homecoming* but not included in the published version.

56. Steven H. Gale, "Observations on Two Productions of Harold Pinter's *Old Times," Pinter Review* 1, no. 1 (1987): 40–43.

The Servant

1. It is possible that there were two cuts released, since I timed it at 115 minutes on a stopwatch, yet in one source the running time is listed as 112 minutes. This differential may be a result of the method of timing, etc., and may not be important, yet two or three minutes in a film can be significant, and thus I note throughout when a difference in timing occurs.

2. Losey—an American director forced abroad to find work—found it ironic that he was voted the best *foreign* director of the year for *Accident* by the Independent Distributors of the United States.

3. "How impressed and moved I was. . . . It has an intensity and inner truth both horrifying and purgative. There are few things, if any, I have seen on British TV that can compare with it." Quoted in Caute, "Golden Triangle."

4. Bogarde, in the role that made him an international star, is certainly playing against type in this film, for in the 1950s he had been a matinee idol in England ("our first home-grown film star," according to Glenda Jackson in an Associate Press report in the *Lexington* (Ky.) *Herald-Leader,* "English Movie Idol Dirk Bogarde Dies," May 9, 1999, B2). Losey also suggested that Ralph Richardson might play Barrett, and he recommended that Maurice Oliver (as Fox called himself then) be given the part of Tony. The girl outside the telephone box was played by Dorothy Bromiley, Losey's estranged wife.

5. See Maugham, *Servant,* 20, 21, 31, e.g., for evidence of the homosexual undertones found in the novel.

6. Quoted from a BBC *New Comment* transcript in Hinchliffe, *Harold Pinter,* 128.

7. In the 1961 version that Pinter had written for Anderson, e.g., there is the following exchange:

SALLY: Does he give you breakfast in bed?

TONY (*laughing*): No. I draw the line at that.

In the 1963 version, Losey changes Tony's response to "Of course." As Caute points out (*Joseph Losey*, chap. 1), it is clear that the screenwriter and the director freely worked together on script revisions.

8. Pinter, *Five Screenplays*, 25. All subsequent citations of the film script refer to this source.

9. See also Gilliatt's review in the *Observer*, Nov. 17, 1963, for a similar observation.

10. Although Maugham's stage-play version of *The Servant* existed when Pinter wrote the screenplay, according to a note in the table of contents of *Five Screenplays*, the movie version was based "solely" on the novel. In the *Corel All-Movie Guide 2*, the reviewer notes that "many of the incidents in *The Servant* can be traced back to the curiously similar *Early to Bed*, a 1928 Laurel and Hardy 2-reeler!"

11. In technique, length, and use to set the theme, this is reminiscent of the more-than-three-minute-long crane shot that opens Welles's *Touch of Evil* (1958).

12. Losey quoted in Walker, *Hollywood UK*, 210. Some critics have said that Losey's *King and Country*, released a year after *The Servant*, was a rewrite of *The Servant* set in wartime. An interesting approach, if true, and clearly Losey's exploration of the theme of class differences is the same (and the movie does star Bogarde); but in fact, Evan Jones's screenplay was an adaptation of the play by John Wilson, which was in turn based on a story by James Lansdale Hodson.

13. The reactions of the curious people in the background indicate that this location shot is being observed by regular passersby who are not connected with the filmmaking.

14. There is a subgenre of films dealing with intruders who are welcomed into a home (the gang members in Stanley Kubrick's 1971 film *A Clockwork Orange*, adapted from Anthony Burgess's novel, actually invades a place called Home and are psychically related to the characters in director Richard Brooks's adaptation of Truman Capote's *In Cold Blood*) and then, in some way or other, overstay their welcome—sometimes with villainy and viciousness. See, e.g., *Kind Lady*, a 1936 film (directed by George B. Seita) adapted from Edward Chodrov's play, which was based on a Hugh Walpole story, sometimes with humorous effect, and the George S. Kaufman–Moss Hart play *The Man Who Came to Dinner* (filmed in 1941, directed by William Keighley).

15. The most famous shot in the picture is that of Bogarde and the round mirror, which is very similar to a shot of Orson Welles in Welles's version of *Othello*.

16. Taylor, *Anger and After*, rev. ed., 325.

17. The term *magic bunny* refers to a continuity mistake—a character wears a red tie in one shot and a blue tie in the next one, for instance.

18. See, e.g., Petrie, *Creativity and Constraint*. Referring to *The Servant* in *Hollywood UK*, Alexander Walker asserts that "Losey had never before had to work so

tightly within the disciplining limits of another man's 'frame'" (215). He further suggests that Pinter curbed Losey's tendencies to baroque romanticism while Losey amplified Pinter's economy with visual suggestiveness.

19. Pinter's familiarity with and use of stock comic characters in his dramas has been commented upon by Elin Diamond in her study *Pinter's Comic Play* (Lewisburg, Pa.: Bucknell Univ. Press, 1985).

20. His "I'm not your servant" sounds like Davies in *The Caretaker* when Davies says it's not his job to clean up.

21. It is interesting that the singer is not identified in the script, other than as "GIRL SINGING ON RECORD" (12), whereas in later screenplays, such as *Victory*, Pinter actually names the songstress.

22. For instance, a second set of loose papers, five 8 x 10 pages, contain the handwritten outlines for scenes 6 through 32, although 6 through 8 are different from the original notes and occur later in the script. Scene 1 is of a "hand swinging by body" on the "Main road—Condon." Scene 6 is "Garden. Tony's body in grass. From grass see feet approach" (in the film, Tony is sprawled in an old deck chair in the conservatory). In a later set of notes covering 131 scenes (on thirty-two pages of loose paper titled "*The Servant*"), the screenplay begins on Sloane Street in Knightsbridge.

In terms of content, there are a couple of segments that reveal Pinter mentally working his way through various possibilities for handling certain incidents. In the second set of papers, Vera is introduced in scene 23, and in scene 31 the writer has her in the bath, with a comment to himself, "Possible dinner party?" In the thirty-two pages titled "*The Servant*," she is not introduced until scene 56, and in scene 69 Pinter has "Vera in towel." In the published screenplay, Vera's voice is heard over the telephone in scene 38 and she is first seen in scene 40. The bath scene does not occur until scenes 57 and 58.

Another set of loose pages titled "*The Servant*" is a six-page typescript of forty-five scenes in which the action is outlined. The hint of one of Pinter's funniest exchanges is contained in these pages. Set in Chelsea, there is a series of scenes that eventually leads to the Mountsets: scene 10, "Lunch in house for three male friends" (cut from later versions); 31, "Tony at Dorchester. Sally with escort. Sally caustic. See Vera shopping with B. Dinner. Lady DuckMuck. Tony doesn't eat, drinks. Snaps at Sally. Her escort calls him outside. Rude to her, to your hosts. What was the matter with dinner? You stupid bastard, what do you know about life? Fight?" (Pinter actually uses the name Lady Duck Muck in *Mountain Language*, 37.)

Following this is a group of thirty-four loose pages detailing 131 scenes, beginning with the Knightsbridge (Sloane Street) opening. Scene 70 (on pages numbered 117 and 118) is the "Ponchos" dialogue, set in "Lady Mountsets house."

The final item in the box is a typescript, "*THE SERVANT/HAROLD PINTER/* Adapted from the novel by Robin Maugham." The eighty-two pages, with holographic alterations, still have Tony in the grass; Vera appears in scene 61 (on page

31); scene 75 takes place on "*Lord & Lady Mountsets' houseboat on the river near Datchet*" (p. 37), which is where the "Ponchos" dialogue now occurs (p. 38).

The Caretaker

1. By 2001 prints of the movie were judged to be so dark that Pinter announced that there were plans to digitally enhance the master.

2. Donner's film *Rogue Male,* in which Pinter appeared three years after *The Caretaker* was filmed, is not nearly as good a motion picture as *The Caretaker.* This is early proof that it is Pinter's scripts that determine the quality of the product and that his directors do their best work from those scripts.

3. The 1980 National Theatre production, directed by Kenneth Ives and starring Jonathan Pryce, Warren Mitchell, and Kenneth Cranham, was transferred to television in 1981.

4. Quoted from a BBC *New Comment* transcript in Hinchliffe, *Harold Pinter,* 99.

5. See Gale, *Butter's Going Up,* 81–95.

6. Quoted in Popkin, *Modern British Drama,* 24.

7. A valuable introduction to cinematic kinesthesia can be found in chapter 3 of Giannetti's *Understanding Movies.*

8. See Gale, *Butter's Going Up,* for an extended discussion of the mechanics involved in this signature thematic cluster and its application throughout Pinter's canon.

9. Quoted in Hinchliffe, *Harold Pinter,* [8].

10. See Wardle, "A Director's Approach."

11. Pinter has said a great deal about the meaning of this play, though at times one is reminded of Davies, who replies to Mick's query, "Are you Welsh?" by saying "Well, I been around you know." For instance, the action in the drama is sometimes funny. An example of this is the obviously intended humor of Mick and Aston passing Davies's bag back and forth. It is the comic shtick of the English music hall and Yiddish comedy, like that done by Laurel and Hardy, Abbott and Costello, and the Three Stooges in movies, or even in Beckett's *Waiting for Godot.* But, in answering criticism in the London *Sunday Times* that the audience laughed at *The Caretaker* as if it were a farce, Pinter said: "Certainly I laughed myself while writing 'The Caretaker' but not all the time, not 'indiscriminately.' An element of the absurd is, I think, one of the features of the play, but at the same time I did not intend it to be merely a laughable farce. If there hadn't been other issues at stake the play would not have been written. . . . As far as I'm concerned, 'The Caretaker' is funny, up to a point. Beyond that point it ceases to be funny, and it was because of that point that I wrote it" (Letter to the editor). This sounds like Pinter's definition of tragedy as given in an interview with Hallam Tennyson: "Everything is funny; the greatest earnestness is funny. Even tragedy is funny. And I think what I try to do in my plays is to get to this recognizable reality of the absurdity of what we do and how we behave and how we

speak. The point about tragedy is that it is *no longer funny*. It is funny, and then it becomes no longer funny."

12. See Gale, *Butter's Going Up,* for a discussion of this element in the thematic development of the author's plays.

13. See discussions of this technique in ibid., 256–75, and in Esslin's *Pinter: A Study of His Plays,* 210–41, expanded edition.

14. Regarding the subject of realistic language, *The Caretaker* figured in an amusing instance of censorship. When first presented at the Duchess Theatre in 1960, the phrase "piss off" was not allowed by the Lord Chamberlain's office. Esslin reports that the objectionable phrase was "she does fuck-all," for which "buggar-all" was suggested as a substitute. Pinter refused to accept the change on the grounds that the two syllable word would destroy the rhythm of the text (see Gillen and Gale, *Pinter Review: Collected Essays, 1997–98,* 142), a fine example of the author's sense of craftsmanship. In 1965 the managers of the Nottingham Playhouse requested special permission to use the phrase in their production of the play, on the grounds that the British Board of Film Censors had allowed it in the film version, which had been publicly released the previous year.

15. The earliest *dated* material related to the film is that in the *Caretaker* box (box 6) in the British Museum. The October 15, 1962 "DRAFT SCREENPLAY FROM THE PLAY" is eighty-four typed pages long (with an additional twelve pages of blue-ink alterations inserted) and contains eighty-seven scenes. Bates, Shaw, and Pleasence are listed as the actors. A later version ("14th June 1963") is labeled "THE CARE-TAKER/DOMESTIC VERSION/EXPORT SCRIPT." This thirteen-page mimeo-graphed document contains forty-three scenes. It is a breakdown of the scenes by length, including line-by-line numbered dialogue, and so on, with Pinter's penciled alterations. The subtitle "Domestic Version, Export Script" is further evidence of the existence of variations. As in another manuscript in the box, "THE CARETAKER/ a play in three acts," the changes in these scripts do not reveal a great deal; rather, they amount to fine-tuning: Davies is described in the "final draft" of the play version as being dressed in a "pullover," which is changed to a "waistcoat," and "live like nits" becomes "live like pigs," and so forth. The most provocative of the contents of the box is a sheaf of ten loose sheets on which are written scenes 1 through 36, along with several other scenes. On one of the pages there is a reference to "p. 22 French," evidence that the author was using the Samuel French acting edition of the play as his text. More intriguing is the incompletely rendered "roundabout" addition. As mentioned above, this scene is one of the first examples of Pinter's attempts to "open out" his dramas when transferring them to the screen. Unfortunately, it is impossible to determine exactly when he contemplated adding this scene, for the pages are un-dated, which is too bad since it would be interesting to know how far into the process of thinking about or actually writing the screenplay this occurred. In the later film scripts, it is clear that the writer thinks about the cinematic viewpoint at the very beginning of the process, almost certainly even while he is reading the novel to be

adapted. Presumably, these ten pages are an indication that he was thinking along the same lines at an early stage in the modification of this script too.

16. Due to a complicated printing history, pagination and the text itself vary slightly from edition to edition. The extensive nature of Pinter's revisions and their effect on the meaning of the text are outlined in Gale, *Butter's Going Up,* 258–63.

The Pumpkin Eater

1. There is a second verse to the rhyme cited in Opie and Opie, *The Oxford Dictionary of Nursery Rhymes*: "Had another, and didn't love her; Peter learned to read and spell, / and then he loved her very well" (346–47). Kathy Johnson Gale believes that Jake's affair is reflected in the "had another" and that "learned to read and spell" indicates that he comes to understand what he has done and that he still loves and wants his wife.

2. Bancroft had to fight for the part. The Academy Award for *The Miracle Worker* the year before had created an image of her that the director did not think worked—she had to go to him and ask to be considered.

3. Unfortunately, Pinter has not been able to find any of his *Pumpkin Eater* material, so it is not included in the British Library Archives.

4. Conway says in the novel, "I call myself a tradesman because that's the only thing I've any respect for—a man's trade. Take these head-shrinkers now, you can't call that decent work, man's work, no, not in my honest opinion. In my opinion the whole bunch of them are a lot of frauds" (Mortimer, *Pumpkin Eater,* 117); and Mr. Armitage asks Jake, "Do you . . . like children? . . . Have you *known* many children?" (18).

5. Knowles is of the opinion that the objects in Harrod's represent "comfortable and gracious middle-class life" and are contrasted by the shots of Jo isolated in the "empty new house as she removes a hat and earrings by a window," the empty house reflecting her empty and meaningless life (*Understanding,* 96).

6. One of the most striking images in the movie, the matchsticks in the water bowl, is left over from the novel and the sex/sin theme; it might be bewildering to someone who has not read the novel.

7. An appointment with the psychiatrist opens the novel, and several additional meetings with him occur during the course of the action; in the film the doctor does not appear until after Mrs. Armitage's breakdown in Harrod's (the department store is not identified in Mortimer's book [47–48]).

The Quiller Memorandum

1. There are a very few, very minimal and basically stylistic, differences between the British publication (*The Berlin Memorandum*) and the American edition (*The Quiller Memorandum*): in *Quiller,* for example, a sentence ("The paper he was holding almost fluttered") has been added to the first paragraph of chapter 18 (com-

pare *Berlin,* 186, and *Quiller,* 165), and a word has been changed ("quivering" in *Berlin* [186] becomes "fluttering" in *Quiller* [165]).

2. In a telephone conversation with me, Oct. 12, 1990, Dukore called *The Quiller Memorandum* one of the best films of its genre.

3. Jacket note for the American paperback edition.

4. Pinter praised Segal highly in our conversation on Oct. 26, 1994.

5. Producer Robert Wise's protests at this incident caused Fox, which had distribution rights for the film only in the United States, Japan, and Latin America, to revise its German representation system.

6. See the discussion of *Lolita,* below, for Pinter's opinion of the current politically correct climate in the United States.

7. Joseph Morgenstern, "Breaking the Bond," *Newsweek,* Dec. 26, 1966, 72.

8. Rich, *"The Quiller Memorandum.*

9. Quoted in Bensky, "Harold Pinter: An Interview," 363.

10. As a sidebar that allows some insights into the moviemaking business, the filming of *The Quiller Memorandum* brought two noteworthy firsts to British filmmaking. For the first time ever, Berlin's Frei Universität allowed a "motion picture production company to shoot within its halls and on its campus" ("'Quiller' Crashes Gates"), and for the first time since the reign of Charles I in the seventeenth century, the British customs service allowed the importation of foreign beer bottles without the payment of any duty. British law provides that an excise tax must be paid on imported bottles, even if they are empty, but director Anderson insisted on importing 192 bottles of Berliner Kindl, a West Berlin beer, for a bar scene with Segal and Guinness. Her Majesty's Excise Department allowed the shipment (although by parliamentary law the bottles had to be destroyed after the scene was shot).

The Basement

1. Begun as a novel around 1950, *The Dwarfs* was turned into a play in 1960 and then revised and published in novel form in 1990 (chapter 10 appeared in *Pinter Review,* 2 [1988]: 5–7; the novel was published by Faber and Faber in London and Grove Weidenfeld in New York). Very underrated, the play is about a group of friends (based on Pinter and his youthful chums), one of whom is going mad, and has to do with the nature of reality.

2. A full explication of this play is contained in Gale, *Butter's Going Up,* 156–64. Among other things, I point out that *The Basement* is a beautiful example of the elements from the sacred-tree-of-Diana myth, a somewhat esoteric interpretation that should not be overemphasized. While valid, it is not central to the impact on the audience as part of the dramatic experience. For that matter, "Request Stop" effectively portrays a cyclical ritual that is entirely divorced from pagan mythology.

3. In *Time,* Nov. 10, 1961, Pinter discusses the actual event in some detail. While attending a party in London, he saw two men in a small room. The smaller of the two, a little barefooted man, was "carrying on a lively and rather literate conversa-

tion, and at the table next to him sat an enormous lorry driver. He had his cap on and never spoke a word. And all the while, as he talked, the little man was feeding the big man—cutting his bread, buttering it, and so on. Well, this image would never leave me." The image had to be expressed: "I went into a room one day and saw a couple of people in it. This stuck with me for some time afterwards, and I felt that the only way I could give it expression and get it off my mind was dramatically. I started off with this picture of two people and let them carry on from there."

4. At Hackney Downs Grammar School, not only did Pinter engage in debate and act the parts of Macbeth and Romeo, but he also played football and cricket and ran the one-hundred-yard dash in ten point two, a school record at the time. For many years he played cricket on a regular basis on a team that included Stoppard.

5. Since there are no scene divisions, the actual number of scenes cannot be determined with certainty, and it is possible that if the acts had been divided, there might be as many as twelve scenes.

6. Until the inclusion of a beach, backyard, and bar in this play, the dramatist's setting had generally been either a house or a flat, the only exceptions being a phone booth (*The Collection*), a nightclub (*Night School*), and the locales of *A Night Out*, *The Dwarfs*, and the revue sketches, all of which remain stably decorated.

7. The uses of setting (furnishings) and nature are ambitious in *The Basement*, and a dual effect is achieved as the different settings mirror the personalities of those involved (allowing a contrast between them), and the seasonal revolutions reflect the attitude of constant change (Jane is commonly with Stott in the winter and with Law in the summer, for instance). Replicating this format on stage would be extremely taxing, although a stage version of *The Basement* premiered as a companion piece to the stage version of *Tea Party* on Oct. 10, 1968, at the Eastside Playhouse in New York City, and it was done again in September 1971 with Pleasence taking the part of Law.

Accident

1. It is possible that there were two cuts released, since in one source the running time is given as 100 minutes and in another source it is 105 minutes.

2. In the novel Stephen's family name is given—Jervis. In the film it is never revealed. This may be partly because Pinter is trying to increase his audience's intimacy with the main character and partly as a result of his cutting most of the situations in which the last name was used, which he did because he was narrowing his focus.

3. Losey's biographer, Caute, calls *Accident* "Losey's best film" (*Joseph Losey*, [182]). Caute's chapter on *Accident* is filled with fascinating details about the actual incident that was the inspiration for Mosley's story, commentary on the differences between the novel and the film, and events and costs connected with the movie's production.

4. Taylor, "*Accident*," 183.

5. William is seen only in flashbacks, since he died in the opening sequence—like Shelley's Grecian urn figures, William is frozen in time, eternally young and full of promise.

6. The importance attached to Seyrig's participation in the film is articulated by Losey, who recalled that she "was enormously busy and expensive and I got her to play the role on the basis of spending two days shooting in England. She came over on a Friday, we read and rehearsed, we shot the restaurant on Sunday, and the scene in the flat on Monday. . . . she was gone before we saw the rushes on Tuesday" (Milne, *Losey on Losey,* 115, 117).

7. Some reviewers conclude that because of Stephen's lack of reaction to the second accident, it did not actually happen except as an echo in his mind, where it exists so forcefully that by this time it has become so much a part of him that he hears what is not there. That the audience sees the dog and hears the sound of the crash, however, would seem to negate that reading of the movie's conclusion.

8. Ironically, Douglas Slocombe, not Fisher, was Losey's first choice for director of photography (Milne, *Losey on Losey,* 159).

9. Quoted by Taylor, "Accident," 184. In a 1967 London interview with Rex Reed (reprinted in Reed's *Conversations in the Raw,* 116–20), director Losey makes much the same point when he praises the terseness of Pinter's script: "It's 100 pages long and only about 60 pages of that is talk, so there's room for the visual things" (118).

10. Quotation on the back cover of the Dalkey Archive Press edition.

11. Pinter's desire to have a cordial relationship with Mosley is evident in their having lunch together so that he could explain that he wanted "the screenplay to stick as close to the book as possible." Additionally, Pinter asked a couple of questions—"Was the girl, Anna, a victim or a bitch? And we agreed—Both" (Mosley, *Efforts at Truth,* 164).

12. Consider, for example, in his comments in "Writing for the Theatre," in which he discusses the impossibility of distinguishing between what is real and what is not real, the difficulty, if not impossibility, of verifying the past, and the ambiguity of words: "The desire for verification . . . is understandable, but cannot always be satisfied. . . . there can be no hard distinctions between what is real and what is unreal, nor between what is true and what is false. A thing is not necessarily either true or false; it can be both true and false" (*Complete Works: One,* 11). Or, as Goldberg contends in *The Birthday Party,* "Of course it's true. It's more than true. It's a fact" (ibid., 38). These concepts are at the heart of many of Pinter's plays from *The Room* on, and many critics have discussed his exploration of them (see, e.g., the analysis of *The Dwarfs* in Gale, *Butter's Going Up*).

13. Aristotle's definition is spelled out explicitly in the *Metaphysica,* book delta (5), chap. 30, and is amplified in the *Physica,* 2.4–5, and in the *Posterior Analytics,* 1.75a. I appreciate the help given me by my Kentucky State University colleague Professor of Philosophy George Shields in this section. Professor Shields suggests that those interested in a deeper understanding of Aristotle's concept of accident consult Boethius's glosses in *The Consolation of Philosophy* (5.1) and Porphyry's commentaries.

14. After reworking *The Dwarfs* in 1989, Pinter finally published the book in 1990.

15. Pinter, in a letter to Gale dated Jan. 5, 1991.

16. In the printed script, p. 237, "Slaughtered" is used instead of killed. Possibly the original word was considered too loaded, suggesting a conscious, ritualistic sacrifice rather than simply a death with no emotional context appended.

17. I have seen a 16mm version of *Accident* in which this triangle shot does not appear; also missing are a few other less critical shots, such as one showing Stephen's feet as he runs across the grass toward the accident in the opening sequence. It may be that the excisions were a result of the condition of the old and often-projected celluloid—presumably it had broken and been spliced—or this may be another example of purposefully made alterations, though for what purpose is a mystery.

18. Lurcy Professor in the Department of Art History and Archeology at Columbia University, Middleton gives a brief tour of Syon House in the "Age of Reason, Age of Passion" segment of the 1989 PBS *Art of the Western World* series.

19. Pinter was athletic in his youth; reference his track record in school, for instance. His affection for cricket has been noted many times—he reports trying to save nothing but his favorite cricket bat when flying bombs fell in his backyard during World War II; he has collected cricket bats, and he played cricket (see Gale, *Butter's Going Up,* for other examples). Besides the tennis and cricket matches portrayed in this film, sporting games figure in *The Go-Between, Tea Party,* and *The Basement,* there is the stairwell game in *The Servant* and references to boxing (*The Homecoming*), squash (*Betrayal*), and cricket (the character's names in *No Man's Land*), to mention just a few examples of how this interest is revealed in his writing.

20. Janson, *History of Art,* 117.

21. In Mosley's description of Anna's room, the placement of "a lot of picture-postcards on the mantelpiece" is included (178). These are missing in the film, because they are not needed as a characterizing device.

22. Dillon, a professionally trained architect, created functional designs for the sets. The house interior set, for instance, was so meticulously matched with the exterior that there was virtually no "cheating"—there may have been an extra foot in the hall in order to get the camera in. Dillon is quoted in Taylor, "Accident," 182.

23. Quoted in Mosley's autobiography, *Efforts at Truth,* 164–65. Pinter sent the letter to Mosley, along with a copy of the screenplay, with the request that the letter be read only after the novelist had read the script.

24. The movie was filmed on location at Cobham, London, and Syon House (and at Twickenham Studios) from July through September.

The Birthday Party

1. As might be anticipated, there must be more than one version of the film available. The first time that I saw the film, soon after it was released, McCann's first-act gargle was included (it was in the earliest published version of the play, too,

but cut from a later edition), yet when I viewed the movie some years later, the gargle had been edited out.

2. For the dramatist, as he explained in the interview with Hallam Tennyson in 1960, "Everything is funny. . . . It is funny, and then it becomes no longer funny."

Further discussing with Tennyson the effect of recognizing the absurdities and uncertainties in life, Pinter says, "the fact that it [life] is verging on the unknown leads us to the next step, which seems to occur in my plays. There is a kind of horror about and I think this horror and absurdity go together."

3. See Gale, *Butter's Going Up,* for a discussion of how this pattern is developed. *The Room* and *The Dumb Waiter,* directed by Robert Altman, were telecast on ABC in 1987.

4. Pinter, quoted in Bensky, "Harold Pinter: An Interview," 352.

5. After seeing Pinter's review sketches, Peter Willes had asked to read *The Birthday Party* and then to meet with the author: "At this meeting he immediately accused me of causing him at least four sleepless nights from his reading of 'The Birthday Party' and then said he would produce it on television immediately" (quoted in Merritt, "Pinter Playing Pinter," 81). Willes was the producer for that first television production. In 1995, while playing the role of Roote in *The Hothouse* on the stage, Pinter wore a subtly striped, brown three-piece wool suit, which he got from Carlo Manzi Rentals when he recognized it as having belonged to Willes, who had died four years earlier. A BBC "Theatre Night" series production was also televised, on June 21, 1987. The director was Kenneth Ives, and the cast was composed of Kenneth Cranham (Stanley), Pinter (Goldberg), Colin Blakely (McCann), Joan Plowright (Meg), Robert Lang (Petey), and Julia Walters (Lulu).

6. Harold Pinter, *Complete Works: One* (New York: Grove, 1977), 34. Subsequent quotations from the play come from this edition.

7. Goldberg and McCann may also represent another form of conventionality—organized religion. Their names, the foods mentioned by Goldberg and his Jewish phrasing of "sacred clichés," their ritualistic approach, and the reference to McCann's recent leaving the cloth ("He's only been unfrocked six months" [91]) have been seen by Ruby Cohn ("World of Harold Pinter") and Bernard Dukore ("Theater of Harold Pinter") as evidence of this limiting force that is brought to bear on the artist by the Judeo-Christian tradition. The two men also convey a feeling of inevitability, an aspect of most religions. As Goldberg tells Meg when she professes happiness that the two men arrived when they did, "If we hadn't come today, we'd have come tomorrow" (35). Other critics agree that Goldberg stands for family, school, and social relationships and McCann serves the interests of politics and religion. In view of one of the most characteristic elements in Pinter's craftsmanship, his attention to details, it is interesting to note throughout the play, and in particular during the inquisition and party scenes, McCann's accusations and references, which are clear evidence of his preoccupation with politics (especially Irish independence) and religion (primarily Catholicism). The probability that Pinter intended for McCann to be seen as a

representative, with Goldberg, of the repressive aspects of the Judeo-Christian tradition that is the basis of Western society is enhanced by the extent to which the dramatist expresses the Irishman's allegiances. See Gale, *Butter's Going Up*, for a full catalogue of these allusions.

8. The foreign rentals (moneys remitted by exhibitors to the distributor—that is, the distributor's share of box-office grosses—on all theatrical engagements other than U.S. and Canadian) were seven times those of domestic rentals; the total revenues were $400,000. The costs associated with the film's distribution included $120,000 in distribution fees, $275,000 for prints and advertising (print manufacture, ad-pub campaign preparation, local advertising, and miscellaneous distribution expenses), $40,000 in negative cost (the total budget outlay for production, inclusive of a 10% overhead charge), and $90,000 for bank loan interest related to the financing of the production. Other debits are not identified, but the total cost for the picture was listed as $1,125,000, and the film lost $725,000. See Beaupre, "ABC Films Results."

9. For those interested in doing a close analysis of the film script, besides the material in box 5 in the Pinter Archives, the William Friedkin Collection in the Margaret Herrick Library at the Academy of Motion Picture Arts and Sciences Center for Motion Picture Study, Beverly Hills, Calif., contains two fascinating *Birthday Party* files: (1) a copy of the Samuel French (British) acting edition of *The Birthday Party* with Friedkin's handwritten (mostly in pencil, with some black ink) alterations, camera shots, and stage directions needed for the film adaptation; and (2) an orange Boots Ringplan Note Book (9 x 7 inches) with notes, mostly in pencil, for shooting the film version. These notes include numbered shots and blocking diagrams.

The Go-Between

1. My timing. Internet Movie Data Base lists the running time as 118 minutes.

2. See Canby, *New York Times*, July 30, 1971, 21; Crist, "Passport to the Past"; and George Melly, *Observer*, Sept. 26, 1971. In a deliciously ironic move, MGM lost faith in the film and sold it to Columbia just before the Cannes Festival.

3. Caute's chapter "The Palme d'Or" in *Joseph Losey* is filled with interesting information about the background negotiating for the film rights, financing, the choice of actors, details of the filming (including trouble with the lighting because of the weather), and problems with distributors.

4. Truly a minor masterpiece in British literature, Hartley's book was called "An almost perfect novel" by a reviewer for the *New Yorker*.

5. Quoted by Grenier in "Americans Sweep Prizes."

6. Losey claims that Pinter conceived *Old Times* while a houseguest at the director's Marsh Barn. See Losey, "Norfolk Jackets," 7. The location was so important to the moviemakers that they rented fields to be used for the harvesting sequence a year before shooting began and sowed them so that the right crops would be avail-

able for that segment—and then hoped that the weather would make the crops harvestable when the narrow window for shooting was open.

7. Pinter quoted in Taylor, "The Go-Between."

8. Hartley, *The Go-Between*, 11; Pinter, *The Go-Between*, in *Five Screen-plays*, [287].

9. "You flew too near sun. . . . This cindery creature is what you made me."— "You were vanquished, Colston . . . and so was your precious century that you hoped so much for" (20); "chiaroscuro, patches of light and dark" (32); "at dinner, pink glow of candles, shine of silver" (34); "Atropa belladonna" (38); "sense of well being . . . like wind filling a glass—impression of wings and flashes as of air displaced by the flight of a bird" (47); "I yearned to travel far [into the heat] . . . there was a heart of the heat I should attain to" (50); "resplendent beings, golden with sovereigns" (51); "Dear Mother—not enjoying myself" (178); "Delenda est belladonna—2 voices" (240); "not really losing it, you know, but not quite remembering what happened yesterday/ Why did Ted shoot himself? Wasn't he a good shot?" (276); "isn't it dull for you to live here alone . . . Alone? . . . I'm quite a place of pilgrimage" (277); "Does he remind you of anyone—His grandfather" (278).

10. As a very rough gauge, typically one page of script is equivalent to about one minute of film.

11. He is given a green suit and a green bicycle; Marcus taunts him by calling him green: "you are green yourself. It's your true colour" (Hartley, 209; Pinter, 343).

12. In the script, Leo goes down a flight of steps before looking through the banister; in the movie, he looks through it before descending, a change that saves time and footage.

13. Pinter adheres to his model in the smoking-room scene when he incorporates Leo's discomfort at seeing the paintings by David Teniers, but he omits Teniers's name from the dialogue (see Hartley, 226).

14. Among them the introduction of the sides and Trimmingham's ironic suggestion, "you should make him run errands for you, Burgess" (Hartley, 137).

15. Among the many instances that can be used to exemplify Pinter's condensing and combining of scenes and dialogue is the smoking-room scene (Hartley, 224 ff.). In addition, Marcus's besting of Leo in the use of French is missing from the film. This is a relatively important item in the novel, for it emphasizes the class differences even between the two boys, yet it is not needed to advance Pinter's thematic concern, and the lines delivered in French would be incomprehensible to many moviegoers.

16. There is a date visible in Leo's diary, but it is from the past (April 21)—when he created the spell that he cast upon the two bullies at school—and the dates of his birthday and the ball are mentioned, but no year is declared for either the past or the present sequences.

17. See, e.g., Pinter, 311, 315, 316, 320, 336–37, 340, 341–43, 349–50, 351, 354, 358.

18. See the discussion of *Old Times* and the other memory plays in Gale, *Butter's Going Up*.

The Homecoming

1. Enoch Brater records the running time as 116 minutes; the televised version shown on WOR-TV, Secaucus, N.J., was 113 minutes.

2. American Express Films, in collaboration with the Ely Landau Organization, presented the American Film Theatre productions, filmed versions of eight major modern dramas. These motion pictures were screened at more than five hundred theatres across the United States at a price that was then considered "not-so-bargain": $3.75. The first in the series was Eugene O'Neill's *The Iceman Cometh*. *The Homecoming* was the second film in the series, which included Pinter's directorial debut in motion pictures with his filmed version of Simon Gray's *Butley*. Other plays filmed for the series included Edward Albee's *Delicate Balance*, Ionesco's *Rhinoceros*, and Anton Chekhov's *Three Sisters*.

3. One of the few differences between the stage script and the film script is that the six years becomes nine years in the movie, possibly to make the age of Teddy and Ruth's sons older and thereby increase the plausibility of her being willing to forgo returning to them. It is then easier to accept the couple's actions as tragic rather than as depraved.

4. Lenny's refusal to take advantage of the girl's offer (and she had been "searching for [him] for days") tenuously links him with character types such as Davies in *The Caretaker* and James in Pinter's *The Collection* (1961), for although the tale is probably fantasy, it can be seen as symbolic of his subconscious rejection of women and, more importantly, his willingness to make up stories if doing so might improve his lot in life. Related to this is the tale of Joey's conquest of the girl in the Scrubs (83) and Lenny's description of a hat that he bought for a girl ("It had a bunch of daffodils on it, tied with a black satin bow, and then it was covered with a cloche with black veiling" [73])—they are without a doubt flights of fancy and no more based on reality than Mick's description of the kitchen with "teal-blue, copper and parchment linoleum squares" in *The Caretaker* (69).

5. "I would want at least three rooms and a bathroom. . . . A personal maid . . . . You would have to regard your original outlay simply as a capital investment . . . . I would naturally want to draw up an inventory of everything I would need, which would require your signatures in the presence of witnesses. . . . All aspects of the agreement and conditions of employment would have to be clarified to our mutual satisfaction before we finalized the contract" (76–78).

6. Pinter, in Hewes, "Probing Pinter's Play," 57.

7. Quoted in Boulton, "Harold Pinter," 132.

8. Hewes, "Probing Pinter's Play," 56.

9. Pinter, in Halton, "Pinter," 239.

10. Ibid.

11. For a full, detailed analysis of the play, see Gale, *Butter's Going Up*, 136–56. To trace the evolution of the film script in detail and to see how the dramatic themes are realized in the film, the materials in the Pinter Archive, box 24, may be used for reference.

12. "Harold Pinter, Director," 8.

13. An exception to this is the change in the tableau at the end. In the movie we see the chair with Ruth in it from the rear, Sam's head is visible as he lies in front of her, and neither Max nor Joey is seen in full. Lenny stands in front of her, facing her, instead of behind her chair. There does not seem to be a good reason for this change, and it diminishes the traditional family-portrait effect, unless that is what was desired, to show the dysfunctional family broken into semiconnected portions radiating out from the chair like the blocks of humanity in a Picasso painting.

The Proust Screenplay

1. Material on *The Proust Screenplay* is contained in boxes 45–47 in the Pinter Archives at the British Library.

2. Letters to me dated Dec. 17, 1971, and Mar. 28, 1972.

3. Losey quoted in Ciment, *Conversations with Losey*, 242.

4. Pinter, quoted in Menick, "Remembrance of Things Future," 47.

5. Eder, "Losey to Film 'Remembrance.'"

6. The presence of a copy of the film script dated Oct. 25, 1972, in the Gregory Peck Collection, Margaret Herrick Library, Academy of Motion Picture Arts and Sciences, Beverly Hills, Calif., suggests that Peck was considered for one of the roles in the film.

7. In 1999 Chilean director Raoul Ruiz did release his own adaptation of *Le temps retrouvé.*

8. "I was lying on the sofa . . . reading the paper and something flashed in my mind. It wasn't anything to do with the paper. . . . The sofa perhaps. . . . I rushed upstairs to my room. . . . I think [the thought] was the first couple of lines of the play. I don't know if they were actually the first lines. . . . Two people talking about someone else. . . . then I really went at it." Quoted in Gussow, *Conversations*, 26–27.

9. Peacock cites as an example Beth's lines in *Landscape:* "Two women looked at me, turned and stared. No. I was walking, they were still. I turned" (Peacock, *Harold Pinter*, 39).

10. A full discussion of the deletions from the massive masterpiece would take a book in itself.

11. Pinter, quoted in Menick, "Remembrance of Things Future," 46.

The Last Tycoon

1. It is possible that multiple cuts were released, since in one source the running time is given as 122 minutes by IMBD, 123 minutes is given in another source, and in a third source it is listed as 125 minutes.

2. Quoted in Cole and Plimpton, "The Art of Fiction," in *Writers at Work*, 252. In a letter to Gale (17 Dec. 1971) Pinter admitted hs admiration of Perelman (and the Marx Brothers).

3. Cole and Plimpton, 253.

4. Both Kazan and Spiegel were already well established, of course. Kazan's film directoral credits included *A Tree Grows in Brooklyn* (1945), *Gentlemen's Agreement* (1947, Academy Award), *A Streetcar Named Desire* (1951), *Viva Zapata!* (1952), *On the Waterfront* (1954, Academy Award), and *East of Eden* (1955); Spiegel's credits included *The African Queen* (1951), *On the Waterfront*, *The Bridge on the River Kwai* (1957), and *Lawrence of Arabia* (1962).

5. This and all subsequent quotations from the screenplay are taken from Pinter, *The Last Tycoon*, in *The French Lieutenant's Woman and Other Screenplays*, 191–277.

6. The camera remains on the empty open door of the sound stage for one minute and forty seconds while the credits roll. For another thirty-five seconds, the screen remains black, with the music playing over. This allows the audience to retain the mood of the end of the picture, which they would lose if they jumped up and left the theatre immediately.

7. Pinter's first draft was dated Jan. 1, 1974. In November he was still working on the script. The screenwriter's struggle with the ending is mirrored in the materials in the Pinter Archive box 31. The typed first draft, no. 1, with handwritten alterations, reads:

> Flash GARBO IN CAMILLE. [handwritten]
> KATHLEEN AT MALIBU.
> Lying on Floor. [handwritten]
>
> MINA ON DEATHBED.
> STAHR INTO CAMERA.
> STAHR (smiling)
> I don't want to lose you.
> He smiles [handwritten]

The Mar. 5, 1974, ending:

> 145. <u>MINA ON HER DEATH BED.</u>
> Over these last two shots, BOXLEY'S voice
> running down:
> BOXLEY
> And . . . here's . . . the . . .
> nickel . . .
> 146. STAHR INTO CAMERA Etc.

The May 31 ending:

> 135. <u>EXT. BACK LOT. STUDIO DAY</u>
> The back lot is deserted.
> The camera tracks through the back lot.

136. STAHR INTO CAMERA.
   STAHR
   I don't want to lose you.

"THE LAST TYCOON NOTES," dated Nov. 1974, include "*End - moviola - at pace - starting and stopping - allowing sections of film to be repeated then quickening - finally broken film.*"

8. The best-known early film about filmmaking is probably *Man with a Movie Camera* (1928) by Russian writer-director Dziga Vertov.

The French Lieutenant's Woman

1. My time. IMDB lists the running time as 127 minutes. Unfortunately, those familiar with the film only in the commercial television version may react to this with confusion. Thirty minutes of what the network called "extraneous" material was omitted, to the detriment of plot, structure, and theme.

2. Among other things, *The French Lieutenant's Woman* was a Book-of-the-Month Club selection, and between 1970 and 1981 the Signet paperback edition went through twenty-seven printings. The cover of the paperback edition that followed the release of the film showed how some American publishers take liberties with everything: there is a picture of Meryl Streep as Sarah in the opening sequence when she is on the stone breakwater wearing her hooded cloak, looking back; there is also an artist's rendering of Sarah and Charles standing on the breakwater and kissing, an improbable invention by the book's cover artist.

3. All quotations from the screenplay come from *The French Lieutenant's Woman: A Screenplay.*

4. Pinter's reference (and Fowles's—the "clever German doctor") is probably to Eduard von Hartmann, a metaphysical philosopher who wrote about the melancholy career of the unconscious. Hartmann's best-known work was *Die Philosophie des Unbewussten* (The philosophy of the unconscious), published in 1870. Although the time of the film is identified as 1867—and Pinter is very careful about historical facts—the period is the same, and it is likely that someone like Dr. Grogan could have read some of Hartmann's papers before the three-volume tome was published. That Pinter would know—or, more likely, find out—such a detail speaks to the seriousness with which he approaches his art.

5. See discussions in this volume of *The Last Tycoon, The Handmaid's Tale,* and *The Remains of the Day.* Pinter now makes sure that his contracts provide that he has final say on the shooting script.

6. Additional discussion of the effect of collaboration on *The French Lieutenant's Woman* is contained in "The Creative/Collaborative Process," below.

7. See "The Creative/Collaborative Process" for further examples.

8. I include a list of these contents, which reveal informative and amusing aspects of filmmaking, in "Harold Pinter's *The French Lieutenant's Woman*: A Masterpiece of Cinematic Adaptation," in Gale, *Films of Harold Pinter,* 84–85.

9. According to a report in the *Hollywood Reporter* ("Box Office Samplings"), in the first five months after its October 15 release, the film garnered grosses totaling $8,861,000 in eleven foreign markets. The top five were Britain, $5,400,000 (315 dates); Spain, $863,000 (twenty-six houses, eight weeks); Denmark, $178,000 (five weeks); Israel, $214,000 (fifteen weeks).

10. Billington, *Life and Work of Harold Pinter,* 272.

11. Reisz is the author of *The Technique of Film Editing.*

12. Besides Pinter's own *Last Tycoon,* there are numerous films in which film-making is a subject, Fellini's *8 1/2* and Truffaut's *Day for Night* being among the most famous.

13. He even composed a list of the names of selected authors of the epigraphs that appear in the novel: chapter 9, Matthew Arnold; chapter 17, Thomas Hardy; chapter 35, Charles Darwin; chapter 41, Alfred, Lord Tennyson; chapter 55, Lewis Carroll; and so on.

14. The published version is

1. Exterior. The Cobb. Lyme Regis. Dawn. 1867.

> *A clapperboard. On it is written:* THE FRENCH LIEUTENANT'S WOMAN. SCENE 1. TAKE 3.
> *It shuts and withdraws, leaving a close shot of* ANNA, *the actress who plays* SARAH. *She is holding her hair in place against the wind.*

VOICE (*off screen*)

All right. Let's go.

> *The actress nods, releases her hair. The wind catches it.*

VOICE (*off screen*)

Action.

> SARAH *starts to walk along the Cobb, a stone pier in the Harbour of Lyme. It is dawn. Windy. Deserted. She is dressed in black. She reaches the end of the Cobb and stands still, staring out to sea.* (1)

15. Sometimes one can deduce different dates of composition within the same document because part of the entry is holograph and part typed or because different colors of ink are used.

16. *New Continuity*

 1 The Cobb S
 2 Carriage C & S
 3 Proposal (3A Present)
 4 Cobb. Meeting with S
 5 E & C. Tea. FLW. (Haberdashery Dept.? Winsyatt? How big?)
 6 Freeman. Emporium.
 7 London. Mrs. P interviews Sarah.
 8 Present

9 Winsyatt.

10 Millie seg.

11 Hotel. Lynne. C. Shaving

Take flowers–will be calling in one hour.

12 Flowers

13 M & Ern.

14 C. gives news, kiss

Happy future.

15 Present

16 Undercliff.

Old Continuity

1 The Cobb

2 Carriage

3 News from London

Engagement

8 _____

9 - 11 Present

12 - 15 The Cobb

16 Meeting with Sarah. Tea - discussion of Sarah.

17 - 18 S interview with Mrs. P. Gets job.

19 Present.

20 Grogan Street

21 - 22 Winsyatt.

23 Millie scene

24 Sam with flowers

25 - 26 E & Mary - flowers

27 Fossil shop

28 . . . Undercliff

Note that the script includes Pinter's own questions about details (often even down to minuscule things such as "<u>NOTE</u> Mike takes boots off - where?").

17. T.O. stands for titles over.

Betrayal

1. It is possible that there were two cuts released; the video runs 95 minutes, yet in another source the running time is listed as 105 minutes.

2. In the mid-1970s David Hare complained, in a conversation with me in Gainesville, Florida, that Pinter had copied the structure of *Plenty*, which Hare had finished at about the same time that Pinter was working on *Betrayal*. Some critics have mentioned a resemblance to Gray's *Otherwise Engaged* (1975) as well. There is an interesting parallel with the creation of *The Lover* and Edward Albee's *Who's Afraid of Virginia Woolf?* which, unbeknownst to either dramatist, were being written within five months of each other, and which deal with the same themes—the

destruction of an illusion that has held together a marriage—although neither playwright was aware of the other's work and they came to different conclusions regarding whether the illusion was necessary. Pinter claims that he was unaware of Hare's play during the composition of *Betrayal.*

3. The word *honesty* appears on pages 34, 66, 68, 69, 80, and 87; the word *betrayal* appears on pages 25, 42, and 78; the word *squash* appears on pages 39, 43, 67, 68, 69, 70, and 71. See Pinter, *Betrayal.*

4. Quoted in Billington, *Life and Work of Harold Pinter,* 267.

5. Jones, at the "Directors on Pinter" symposium at the Lincoln Center, July 21, 2001. Jones also remarks that Pinter is "marvelous with non-appearing characters—Judith [is an] excruciatingly boring character." He reveals, too, that the film actors had to get used to the idea that their characters are "wordy."

6. Quoted in Raymond, "Q and A with Simon Gray," 25.

7. Pinter's chronology includes

> R and J meet at U 1962
> J and J marry 65
> R and E marry 66

8. The list of children and their ages:

> 67 - Sam born
> 68 - Charlotte born
> 71 - Sarah born
> 76 - Ned born

> 72 Sam is 5. Ch is 4. Sarah is 1.
> 73 Sam is 6. Ch is 5. Sarah is 2.
> 75 Sam is 8. Ch is 7. Sarah is 4.
> 77 Sam is 10. Ch is 9. Sarah is 6.
> 78 Sam is 11. Ch is 10. Sarah is 7. Ned is 2.
> 79 Sam is 12. Ch is 11. Sarah is 8. Ned is 3.
> 81 Sam is 14. Ch is 13. Sarah is 10. Ned is 5.

9. 1, 99, 103G, 104, 105, 110, 111, 118.

10. Interestingly, the archives box also contains one sheet of carbon paper with the title "*ROBERT*" on which there is a typed list of actors' names: Peter Egan, Robin Ellis, Jon Finch, James Fox, Alan Howard, Ian McKellen, Michael Pennington, Simon Ward; John Hurst is added in black ink at the end.

11. Among these papers is still another outline, with Pinter still questioning:

> 1977 Pub
> 77 Jerry's house
> 75 Kilburn
> 74 E's house

> 73 Venice
> 73 Kilburn
> 73 Soho restaurant
> 71 Kilburn
> 68 E's house
> 77(a) Charlotte in kitchen
>   (b) Ext. pub. Emma arriving.
> 77(2) J waiting for R. Sam upstairs?
> 75 E and J arriving
> 74 Ned in bath? Call from below.
> 73(a) Venice canal
>   (a) E dropping cat school
>   (b) E racing upstairs
>   (c) R alone in restaurant. J parking car?
> 1971(9)? E with stew[?] J in behind her.
> Play scene in kitchen?
> 1968 Charlotte in bed? E into her - out and into bedroom.
>   (a) E station wagon - kids
>   (b) E in bath
>   (c) E crawling around with Ned in restaurant.

12. There is a mistaken rumor that the garden of Pinter's London home was used as a location; in a communication with me in 2001, the writer said that none of the film was shot in his garden.

13. Kilburn is the unfashionable suburb visited by Butley.

14. Many of the additions, especially those like the boisterous entrance of several men in the bar scene, are part of Pinter's cinematic opening out; other than providing the sense of reality that the writer seeks in moving from stage to screen, they have little or no impact on the story or the meaning of the work.

15. Pages in the published stage play version on which at least one line is deleted are 26, 28, [33]–34, 38–39, 44–45, [61], 92, 93, 94, 97–98, 100, 105–6, 106–8, 110, 111–12, [121]–23, 125, 134.

Victory

1. All screenplay citations are to this source unless otherwise indicated.

2. Pinter, quoted in Billington, *Life and Work of Harold Pinter,* 289. This long-lasting prejudice against period pieces is endemic among the Hollywood motion picture community, despite evidence of its foolishness—in 1999 four of the five nominees for best picture Oscar (and big grossers as well) were period pieces: *Saving Private Ryan, Elizabeth, Shakespeare in Love,* and the award-winning *Life Is Beautiful.* Furthermore, in 1998 Miramax released its version of *Victory,* written and directed by Mark Peploe, produced by Jeremy Thomas, starring Willem Dafoe as Heyst, Irene Jacog as Alma, and Sam Neill as Jones, and filmed in Indonesia.

3. Conrad gave his protagonist the name of the title character in Villiers de L'Isle's play *Axel*.

4. The typed manuscript that was given to me by Pinter is not dated, though it preexisted the publication of the *The Comfort of Strangers and Other Screenplays* volume. There are 181 shots in the printed version.

5. Another example of the kind of minor change in dialogue that Pinter makes is found here. Conrad's "There must be a boarding-house somewhere near the port— some grog-shop where they could let him have a mat to sleep on" (95) becomes "Pedro needs a mat to sleep on. Any grog-shop will do" in Pinter's script (181). The effect of the shortness of the sentences, the exclusion of the mention of the boarding-house possibility, and the statement that, like an animal, Pedro only needs a mat to sleep on is both to dehumanize Pedro and to illustrate Jones's attitude toward his servant, whom he treats like an animal.

6. See Conrad, 135, and Pinter, 193, for example.

Turtle Diary

1. It is possible that there were two cuts released, as I timed the running time at ninety-six minutes and in another source it is listed at ninety minutes.

2. Maltin does give the movie three stars.

3. Pinter, *Turtle Diary*, in *The Comfort of Strangers and Other Screenplays,* 143. Page citations in this chapter are to this edition of the film script unless otherwise indicated.

4. The fascination with details, especially as expressed in numbers, harks back to Pinter's early dramas. William sets the conditions for the van rental: "[£]15.99p a day, 7p a mile, [£]80 deposit" (133). Later Neaera recites the route to the sea: "We stay on the M4 until after Swindon. Then we go through Chippenham, Trowbridge, Frome, Shepton Mallet, Glastonbury, Taunton, Exeter, Plymouth, across the Tamar, go through Looe, and there's Polperro" (143). When Polperro was changed to Devon, there were corresponding changes in her recital.

5. Pinter has openly talked about his relationship with Beckett, without whose plays he says his own could never have been written.

Reunion

1. It is possible that there were at least three cuts released: I timed the video at 110 minutes, in another source the running time is listed at 120 minutes, and the version telecast on HBO runs 150 minutes, despite the excision of several scenes (the older Hans examining the Corinthian coin on the plane and the Japanese businessman [59–60 in the film script] among them). In addition, Pinter's friend and colleague Eric Kahane, who worked on French adaptations of his plays, was responsible for a French adaptation of this film.

2. It is interesting that in his stage play *Ashes to Ashes*, which premiered in 1996, Pinter implies that the Holocaust has become ingrained as a sort of racial or

Jungian consciousness in contemporary society. The heroine of that drama remembers her lover snatching babies from their mothers' arms at a railway station, a fate that she claims to have suffered even though she is clearly too young to have witnessed such events firsthand—she is in her forties and the play is set in the present.

3. Quoted in an untitled and unattributed photocopy in the *Reunion* file at the Margaret Herrick Library, Beverly Hills, Calif.; it appears to be taken from a studio promotion packet.

4. See Gale, *Butter's Going Up;* Esslin, *Peopled Wound;* and Billington, *Life and Work of Harold Pinter,* for discussions of this background.

5. Pinter, *Reunion,* in *The Comfort of Strangers and Other Screenplays,* 98. All subsequent screenplay quotations are taken from this edition unless otherwise stated.

6. Quoted in an untitled and unattributed photocopy in the Margaret Herrick Library *Reunion* file; the photocopy appears to be taken from a studio promotion packet. A letter in the Pinter Archives to Pinter from Schatzberg, dated Sept. 7, 1988, illustrates how well the screenwriter and the director worked together. Signed "As always, Jerry," the letter contains various suggestions:

> 1. *The End.* Suggestion that the "coin makes a wonderful reunion. He could be on a bench, in a plane, in Central Park, just about anywhere. What do you think?"
>
> 2. Notation from Anne about documentary footage - "stay away from it" - "All Freisler material can be done theatrically, this gives you more freedom if you want to tailor the dialog. The montage can be discussed. I always felt it was going to be a created montage. I think in doing it, part can be documentary, part theatrical. The documentary part could appear in the film as being news-reel footage."
>
> 3. The museum - "as we discussed on the telephone, could start with close-ups of selected painting with contemporary dialogue off screen - dinner, gossip - politics in the US, China or South Africa, Nicaragua, subjects that are near and dear to all of us."
>
> 4. Reinforce family's assimilation: "Day of Atonement" and "Silent Night" in book - "injected into the scene after the Zionist, or the scene with his mother before the Opera, or in a scene with Konradin when they talk about religion or God."
>
> 5. "*Scene #80,* I would like to discuss with you. I love the fact that they have a difficult time finding something to talk about, and I think it would reinforce how important this friendship is, if Konradin would make one more effort to gain forgiveness from Hans. In the book Konradin says, "you expect too much from simple mortal, so do try to understand and forgive me, and *let's go on being friends.*" I think this allows some hope for the friendship. (box 50)

7. For a British audience, some of the screenwriter's additions may have resonated with actions by Prime Minister Margaret Thatcher's government. In Pinter's

mind, his countrymen might have been reminded of the perceived threat of authoritarianism at the time by the right-wing sentiment intrinsic in the words of Pompetski: "We will have order in this country and I shall have order in this school" (88).

8. Handwritten notes dated June 20 show that Pinter considered additional contemporary scenes for this sequence: "Scene in New York at ballgame? - or Bloomingdales" (typical American/Manhattan scenes), and "Central Park - Carousel. Granddaughter - 4. Balloon" (carefree innocence), all for contrast with Germany and the past.

9. There was no "Peeping Tom" scene in the first draft, dated Sept. 2, 1987 (confusingly, there is also a partial draft with the notation "Corrected Sept. 1, 1987"); Pinter added it when he expanded the Black Forest sequence in the second draft, which is dated Oct. 13, 1987.

10. This change was made in a black-ink alteration to the first draft when the coin is inserted on page 68, shot 71 - K's room.

11. There are three pages of German history typed on white paper. Among the events listed are "March 13, 1932 - result of German presidential election. Hitler becomes Chancellor on January 30, 1933." Other examples from the archive holdings include a repeat, "Hitler made Chancellor in 1933, Jan. 30," and "Burning of books - May 13, 33." Related is the notation found elsewhere to be used for background, "Peter Shertz–Photos of Stuttgart"; photographs are seen when Henry visits a gallery.

12. "The National Socialist Party has received 13,750,000 votes. Their seats in Parliament have increased by 123 - from 107 to 230" (Pinter, *Comfort*, 82). These numbers were taken from Shirer. Archive notes: "received 13,745,000 votes - seats in Parliament have increased by 127 [possibly a handwriting misread], from 107 to 230 seats." Other numbers vary in the different manuscript versions.

13. There are two bits of material contained in the archives that give some insight into the nature of filmmaking. A typed memorandum in box 50 from "Production" to "Directors Department/Art Department, re Aristocratic names" consists of a list of "Names not mentioned in GOTHA. Should nevertheless not be used." Alternatives are provided: von Hankhofen instead of Baron von Waldeslut, von Zeilarn for Baron von Klumpf, Von Henkel "is mentioned in GOTHA. Therefore should not be used," but von Lohenburg can be substituted for Von Hohenfels and Petershagen Wildenheim can become Hubestus Price von Schleim-Gleim Liechtenstein.

The Handmaid's Tale

1. It was reported in *Cinefile* on Sept. 4, 1988, that Sigourney Weaver was to act in the film.

2. The tale may be a variation on the biblical story of Jacob's wives, sisters Rachel and Leah (Genesis 29), in which the two women become barren and compete by having their maids bear their husbands' children in their place.

3. Included are an article on the spread of the practice of surrogate motherhood

(*New York Times,* Oct. 6, 1986); an article on new Islamic law allowing "temporary" marriages, often with prisoners (*Times* [London], Jan. 2, 1986); two articles on Christian right-wing anti-Semitism in the United States; an article on the rise of sexism and resentment of women's dress as promoting rape; an article on the Pakistani custom of bartering off daughters for marriage; two articles on abortion clinic bombings in the United States; an article on President Reagan's support for burial services for aborted fetuses; an article on Argentina and the abduction of politically errant women and their children; an article on the Nazi practice of allowing the elite to father children with volunteers—the children resulting from such unions were called "lebensborn," and SS married men without children were especially encouraged to find additional partners; an article on the Ku Klux Klan and racial violence; an article on the torture of women prisoners in Iran, including the viewing of hanged men, with a special emphasis on requiring women to torture or execute others to demonstrate repentance; an article on the high U.S. death rate for black infants; an article on Romanian women forced to give birth to expand the labor force; an article on fundamentalist Catholic opposition to federal funding of abortion in the U.S.; an article on Pat Robertson (a right-wing Christian fundamentalist) seeking the American presidency.

4. Pinter, quoted in Peacock, *Harold Pinter,* 195.

5. Peacock claims that the reason for the divergences was that the script was completed by the actors under the guidance of the director during filming (ibid., 198 n. 24).

6. Pinter, in a conversation with Gale, Oct. 26, 1994.

7. Losey had suffered through a similarly trying circumstance while *The Go-Between* was in production. In order to sell Losey's *Secret Ceremony* to television, Universal Studios had cut part of the picture and then added scenes and characters; the director managed to have his name removed from the altered version.

8. The novel itself is one of those most often referred to in Atwood's canon, and in 1999 Atwood was named one of the one hundred outstanding writers of the twentieth century by *Writer's Digest.*

9. There is a script in box 63 labeled "Second Draft, Nov. 17, 1986," so there is some confusion regarding the dating of the various scripts.

The Comfort of Strangers

1. Multiple cuts may have been released, as in one source the running time is given as 102 minutes, in another source it is 107, and in a third it is 105 minutes.

2. Early film historians, theorists, and social commentators such as Charles Horton Cooley (*Social Organizations* [New York: Scribner's, 1909]) recognized this, and it has been commented upon more recently by Bazin (*What Is Cinema?*), Comolli ("Technique and Ideology"), and others. In the late twentieth century, the concept merged with Jacques Lacan's differentiation between "look" and "gaze" and gained notori-

ety because it was adopted by feminist critics who see film as a vehicle that men use to observe and control women. See, for example, two studies by Mayne: *Private Novels, Public Films* and *Women at the Keyhole.*

3. See Bensky, "Harold Pinter: An Interview," 363.

4. This and all subsequent quotations from the screenplay are taken from Harold Pinter, *The Comfort of Strangers and Other Screenplays* (London: Faber and Faber, 1990).

5. Beniamino Gigli, 1890–1957, the grand Italian tenor; perhaps suggestive for our vision of Robert, one of Gigli's most well-known roles was as Faust in Arrigo Boito's *Mefistofele.*

6. In a graduation address at the University of Southern California, June 1995.

7. Schrader, quoted in an untitled and unattributed photocopy in the *Reunion* file of the Margaret Herrick Library, Beverly Hills, Calif. This page appears to be taken from a studio promotion packet.

8. McEwan's own cinematic adaptation of another of his novels, *The Innocent,* was released in 1993.

9. The sense of the existence of something terrifying and dangerous lurking below the seemingly benign everyday surfaces of life can be traced back to Pinter's earliest writing—it is evident in his poetry and in the room imagery that characterizes his comedies of menace, for example—and may be an outgrowth of his childhood experiences in London during the Blitz and after the war when he faced those East End thugs in back alleys. See again Bensky, "Harold Pinter: An Interview"; Pinter's "Talk of the Town" interview in the *New Yorker,* Feb. 25, 1967; Esslin, *Peopled Wound;* Billington, *Life and Work of Harold Pinter;* and Gale, *Butter's Going Up,* 8–9, [17]–18, 20 ff.

10. Robert De Niro, who had been fine in *The Last Tycoon,* was considered for the part of Robert, but Pinter agrees with Hudgins that he would not have worked well in that role. Al Pacino was in the running as well; in a July 6, 1989, letter to Pinter, Schrader asks for a fresh copy of the script when revisions are completed, noting that he is "having a read through of the script tonight with Pacino, Helen Mirren and two other actors. If Al doesn't come on board tomorrow we'll make an offer to Walken." This decision must have pleased Walken, for in a 1996 interview on Bravo's "Inside the Actor's Theatre," he said that seeing Sir Ralph Richardson and Sir John Gielgud in Pinter's *No Man's Land* (1973) had been one of the three or four most important theatrical moments in his life.

11. While a young man, Pinter was tried twice for being a conscientious objector and anticipated going to jail for his principles. His bitter political diatribes continued into 2001 (e.g., in February 1997 he published "America the Hun" in *Z Magazine,* one of his many pieces taking America to task for a variety of human-rights and ecological violations, and as late as September 10, 2001, he was attacking U.S. politics in speeches, though following September 11, 2001, he issued statements supporting the American people. Other examples can be found in Pinter's *Various Voices).*

12. Correspondence contained in box 10 reflects the kindred spirit of the writer

and the director. In a faxed letter from Schrader to Pinter dated July 6, 1989, Schrader thanks Pinter for a letter and an article that Pinter had sent him: "It's disconcerting that others take you as seriously as you take yourself." In regard to the screenplay, there is a letter of July 7, 1989, from Schrader to Pinter: "Perhaps we can retain [the restaurant scene] and reinduce the sexual claustrophobia by deleting scene 51 and placing scene 52–53 inside the hotel room. I want a chance to lock these two in their own world, wreaking visual havoc upon them." This refers to eliminating the shot of Mary on the balcony while Colin is on the phone about the "bloody book." In addition, Schrader thanks Pinter for his patience in the face of "uninformed opinionatedness," praises the script, and praises Pinter for holding back and letting actors fill in the blanks. Furthermore, the director admits, "I've done an 180 degree turn on the matter of thematic explicitness." He concludes by asking Pinter for a signed collection of his plays, a nice compliment.

Schrader wrote to Pinter on July 13, 1989, asking for a few introductory lines to Caroline's revelation speech to Mary to "build emotion," and finally agrees that "Robert's monologue will remain at full length. Rehearsals will tell." This had clearly been a bone of some contention, and Pinter emphasized to Gale and Hudgins, in a conversation in London, Oct. 26, 1994, that the speech was shot as he had written it and much to his pleasure. Schrader also asks if Pinter would like to be kept appraised of any changes made to accommodate logistics of sets and locations, another nice compliment.

The Trial

1. It is likely that there were multiple cuts released, as I timed the movie at 120 minutes, in another source it is listed at 108 minutes, and the British videotape is 116 minutes long.

2. Quoted in John Sherwood, "The Rising Generation," 7. Citation in Knowles, *Understanding*, 178.

3. See Bensky, "Harold Pinter: An Interview," 363.

4. Letter to Gale dated Dec. 1, 1997. In a Dec. 20, 1996, telephone conversation with me, Marks also stated that Billington's account of the obtaining of the rights to film the novel in which he talks about a Hungarian director is factually incorrect.

5. See Welles and Bogdanovich, *This Is Orson Welles*.

6. Jeanne Connolly claims that Jones refused to "assert an aggressive point of view, to force meaning on the viewer" and that this neutrality leaves the film "incomplete." See "*The Trial*," 87.

7. *The Trial, Production Notes*.

8. See Gale, *Butter's Going Up*, for an extended discussion of this thematic element in Pinter's canon.

9. Conversation with Gale, Oct. 26, 1994.

10. Additional alterations are found in box 56 of the Pinter Archives, which

contains a complete script bound in plastic, with a light yellow cover page on which is written, "The sending of this script does not constitute an offer of a contract for any part of it," under a BBC Films heading and the lines "Shooting Script, Jan. 1992." Demonstrating that, as usual, Pinter's rewriting continued during the entire course of the process, even this late version of the script includes some corrections. For example, scene 30, the beer hall scene, is scratched through where K sings "slightly less boisterously than the others." The script also contains some typical Pinter elements: the comment about the "nice nightshirt" is reminiscent of lines from *The Dwarfs,* "What a suit, what a piece of cloth," and Meg's cornflakes panegyric in *The Birthday Party,* for instance.

Lolita

1. Sellers was then relatively unknown among the fans of popular movies in the United States, and Kubrick planned for the part of Quilty to total only about five minutes. Seller's ability to ad lib with two or three cameras rolling led to an expansion of his part and to a large degree built the black humor of the film to the point where he dominated the picture—much to Mason's chagrin (especially since Mason's role had been offered to David Niven, Rex Harrision, and Noel Coward, all of whom refused it). Amusingly, producer James B. Harris told Nabokov that his script was "the best screenplay ever written in Holywood," yet he later confided that it was so long "You couldn't make it. You couldn't *lift* it" (Richard Corliss, *Lolita* [London: British Film Institute, 1994], 16, 19).

2. In 1998 *Lolita* was ranked number four on the Modern Library list of one hundred best English-language novels of the twentieth century.

3. Roeg's respect for Pinter's talent is revealed in *Bad Timing* (1980), when the character Milena reads a German edition of *No Man's Land.*

4. It is interesting that the director of the version finally filmed, Adrian Lynne, had drafted a thirty-five-page outline titled "Preparatory Notes on Nabokov's novel," in which he indicated his primary concern that the audience would not know what to make of antihero Humbert. "The movie should start in prison," he wrote, "because . . . if the audience understands that Humbert is paying his dues, it may help our case."

5. Maltin, *TV Movies and Video Guide,* 675.

6. Pinter, in a conversation with Gale and Hudgins, Oct. 26, 1994.

7. In his talk with Gale and Hudgins, he admitted to being a bit leery about the prospects of making a "Hollywood" film, because of the budget considerations and because of the current emphasis in the United States on family values, particularly as evidenced in a push for a broad audience, and especially for a young audience.

8. Hudgins, "Harold Pinter's *Lolita.*"

9. James Albee had also written a screen adaptation of the novel, but Pinter has not seen that script either.

10. See Flemming, "Carolco's Fire Sale" and Farrell, "Charguers gets Lolita Rights."

11. Letter to Gale dated Nov. 11, 1994, enclosed with manuscript copy of *Lolita*.

12. This analysis is based on an unpublished photocopied typescript of Mamet's screenplay dated Mar. 10, 1995.

13. Pinter once told a director, "If you want an actor who isn't afraid of looking bad, get Jeremy Irons."

14. Quoted in Walter Scott, "Personality Parade," *Parade*, Dec. 24, 1995, 2. As Pinter predicted, even once the film was in the can, there was considerable difficulty in getting it distributed, especially in the United States. Its American debut eventually came as an Aug. 2, 1998, telecast on the Showtime cable/satellite channel, and theatrical release followed, one year after the film first appeared on screens in Britain.

15. Quoted in Butler, "New 'Lolita' Isn't a Hit," 15. Lynne tried to attract an American audience by showing the film on cable and pay-per-view direct satellite telecasts.

16. Although the manuscript that I analyzed was a copy provided by Pinter, a copy exists in the Pinter Archives in the British Library: boxes 65 and 66 contain *Lolita* material.

17. Nabokov, *Lolita*.

18. Agee, "Agee on Film."

19. "A burst of royal purple where his ear had been. . . . 'Get out, get out of here,' he said coughing and spitting; and in a nightmare of wonder, I saw this blood-spattered but still buoyant person get into his bed and wrap himself up in the chaotic bedclothes. I hit him at very close range through the blankets, and then he lay back, and a big pink bubble with juvenile connotations formed on his lips, grew to the size of a toy balloon, and vanished. . . . a quarter of his face [was] gone" (Nabokov, *Lolita* [1989], 304).

20. "Quilty gets into his bed and wraps himself in the sheets. Humbert fires again./A big pink bubble forms in Quilty's mouth and suddenly vanishes" (Pinter, "Lolita" [typescript], 185). Hudgins calls Dearden's version truncated and Schiff's less concise (Hudgins, "Harold Pinter's *Lolita*," 142).

21. Pinter, "Lolita" [typescript], 188.

Bits and Pieces

1. Kevin Spacey on *Larry King Live*, CNN, June 28, 2001, claimed that the primary responsibility of an actor is to serve the "writer" of a script.

2. Among those who have shared this Hollywood experience are Somerset Maugham, Maurice Maeterlinck, Gertrude Atherton, Hemingway, Fitzgerald, and William Faulkner.

3. Quoted in Brownlow, *The Parade's Gone By*, 272.

4. Interviews by Gale at the Maui Writers Conference, Sept. 6, 1998.

5. The *Hollywood Reporter* published these details in its weekly "Films in Preparation" and then "Films in Production" sections from September through November 1992.

6. It received Academy Award nominations for best picture (also nominated for a British Academy Award), best director (also nominated for a British Academy Award), best actor (Anthony Hopkins, who was also nominated for a British Academy Award and a New York Film Critics Circle Award), best actress (Emma Thompson, also nominated for a British Academy Award), best adapted screenplay (Ruth Prawer Jhabvala, also nominated for a British Academy Award), best costume design, and best score.

7. Letter to Gale dated Mar. 8, 1993.

8. See Jones, "On *The Remains of the Day.*"

9. Pinter has always cast a jaundiced eye on American politics.

10. In *Instinct* (1999) Hopkins says of a gorilla that has been in captivity for thirty years that it will not leave its cage when the door is open because it has lost its sense of freedom—his character in *The Remains of the Day* is caught in the same trap and has the same expression on his face.

11. This is the opposite of the effect in *Turtle Diary.*

12. The screenplay has not been published, as is the case with the scripts of his adaptations of his own stage plays.

13. See "Pinter to Pen Child" and "*The Dreaming Child.*"

14. "The Angelic Avengers" was reportedly under development at Universal Pictures as well.

15. Box 70 contains "The Dreaming Child Research Notes," and boxes 71–73 contain "The Dreaming Child Screenplay" material.

16. In a February 13, 2002, E-mail, Pinter's agent, Judy Daish, said that they hoped that shooting would begin in the near future.

17. The *Independent on Sunday,* Feb. 6, 2000, 10, quoted in Knowles, "Harold Pinter 1998–2000," 189.

18. In *Mac* he recalls this adventure of playing Horatio, Bassanio, and Cassio fondly. It was on this tour that he met Alun Owen, Patrick Magee, and Barry Foster. See also Billington's biography for more information on this period in the writer's life.

19. The first was directed by J. Stuart Blackton and William V. Ranous, with Ranous playing Lear. Eugene Mullin and others received writing credit. Frederick Warde took the role of Lear in Ernest C. Warde's 1916 version; Philip Lonergan and others were credited with the adaptation. In 1971 Peter Brook directed Paul Scofield as Lear along with Cyril Cusack and Patrick Magee in a movie version, and in 1987 Jean-Luc Godard directed Peter Sellers and a bizarre cast in a release that was panned (Norman Mailer joined Godard in the writing). Less familiar avatars were *The Yiddish King Lear* (directed by Harry Thomashefsky and written by Abraham Armband, 1934), *Korol Lir* (Soviet Union, written and directed by Grigori Kozintsev, starring Jüri Järvet as Lear, 1961), a British production directed by Steve Rumbelow (1976), and a production from Ernst Kaufmann's script in 2000. At least seven television movies were made from Shakespeare's drama between 1948 and 1997. One of the more interesting uses of the play is in Ronald Harwood's stage drama *The Dresser* (filmed in 1983 from Harwood's screenplay), in which Tom Courtenay works backstage for Albert Finney, who is appearing in a stage production of *Lear.*

20. Pinter, typed manuscript copy of *The Tragedy of King Lear* by William Shakespeare, March 31, 2000, 1 (Gale collection).

21. There is material in box 29 in the Pinter Archives at the British Library related to *Langrishe, Go Down,* and boxes 22 and 23 contain material on *The Heat of the Day.*

22. The BBC in London has a copy of the program in its files that can be viewed on the premises for a rather steep price. My recollection is that I paid over £135 (worth US$220 at the time) to watch the film in a private screening room in 1987 (and I was the only one who could be in the room at the time; there would have been an additional charge per person beyond myself). It was screened publicly as part of the Lincoln Center festival in 2001 and then given a regular theatrical release date of July 17, 2002.

23. Quoted in Gussow, *Conversations,* 37.

24. The impact of evacuation on him has been demonstrated in numerous interviews, particularly in "Evacuees," an interview by B.S. Johnson that Pinter allowed to be published in *Pinter Review: Annual Essays 1994,* [8]–13.

25. See Gale, *Butter's Going Up,* for a discussion of the significance of this scene and dialogue.

26. In the original: "For the supper, . . . we killed a little chicken" (183).

27. Rex Pyke, letter to Gale dated July 10, 1997.

28. See Gale, *Butter's Going Up,* 176–81, for an analysis of the drama.

29. Cited in "The Peterborough Column" in the Jan. 14, 1993, *Daily Telegraph* (London). See also Knowles, "Harold Pinter 1993–1994," 117. *The Diaries of Etty Hillesum* was published by Jonathan Cape (London) in 1983. Originally titled *Het Verstoorde leven: Dagoek van Etty Hillesum, 1941–1943,* the volume was translated from the Dutch by Arno Pomerans.

30. *Butley* is Gray's most successful work, both artistically and financially. This may well be because two important elements in his playwriting career evolved directly from his educational background. Not only was he exposed to literary and dramatic traditions in his course work, but his postgraduate life has been spent in academia too. The drama is dedicated to "the staff and students, past, present and future, of the English Department, Queen Mary College, London." Gray's statement that he "went to university when [he] was seventeen and [he] never left" is true metaphorically as well as literally—after teaching at Trinity College, Cambridge, from 1965 through 1966, Gray joined the faculty at Queen Mary College in 1966 and has maintained that affiliation since.

31. The play moved to the Criterion Theatre in London exactly one week later and subsequently began an American tour at the Morosco Theatre in New York City on Oct. 31, 1972. Interestingly, Pinter has been involved in Gray's theatrical life on several occasions, and Gray's admiration for his fellow dramatist is evidenced by his choosing Pinter to direct several of his plays and by his comments in numerous interviews. In a mutual joke, at one time Pinter and Gray pretended that Gray was the president of a British Harold Pinter Society. There are other connections as well:

Bates appears in several of Pinter's dramas and films, most distinctively earlier in both versions of *The Caretaker*; Engel, then a student at the Old Vic School, acted the part of Rose in the premiere of *The Room*.

32. Released 1974; source: *Butley* by Simon Gray (play, 1970); production company, American Express Films and Ely Landau Organization for American Film Theater; director, Harold Pinter; screenwriter, Simon Gray; editor, Malcolm Cooke; photographed by Gerry Fisher; executive producer, Otto Plaschkes; producer, Ely Landau; artistic director, Carmen Dillon; costume consultant, Robin Fraer Paye; cast: Alan Bates (Ben Butley), Richard O'Callaghan (Joey Keystone), Michael Byrne (Reg Nuttal), Jessica Tandy (Edna Shaft), Susan Engel (Anne Butley), Georgina Hale (Carol Heasman), Simon Rouse (Gardner), Oliver Maguire (Man in the Tube), Colin Haigh (First Student), Darien Angadi (Second Student), John Savident (James), Susan Wooldridge (Student), Lindsay Ingram, Patti Love; running time, 130 minutes; color; rating R.

33. In his interview with Raymond, Gray admitted that he decided to write for the stage after seeing *The Homecoming*: "It made me laugh. I also found its individuality very attractive. The thought that the theater should be able to accommodate many different voices was very liberating. This was not the case in contemporary British theater before *The Homecoming*. Well, actually, before *The Caretaker*, but I didn't see that first, so I went expecting to hate every minute of *The Homecoming* and found myself laughing continuously. I also liked the way it managed it [*sic*] draw you through the actors into a world" ("Q and A with Simon Gray," 25).

34. See his quoted comments in the introduction to this book and in Langley, "Genius—A Change in Direction."

35. In a letter to Gale dated Nov. 9, 1973.

36. Harwood in a public interview in London, June 17, 2000.

37. The Alan Bates Archive, http://www.tiac.net/users/claret/bates.html.

38. "Harold Pinter, Director," 8.

39. See his quoted comments in the introduction and in Langley, "Genius—A Change in Direction."

40. Gray, *Butley* (1972), [7]. All subsequent quotations from the play come from this edition.

41. Since there is no published script of the film available, I have relied on a frame-by-frame viewing of the movie for my analysis, and the quotations and other observations included in this study are drawn from that screening.

42. Gray, *Butley,* 28, 33, 63.

43. See, for instance, *The Dwarfs* (New York: Dramatists Play Service, 1965), 13–14. Other examples in Pinter's dramaturgy include the significant presence of mirrors and reflections in *The Collection* and *The Lover.*

44. Kilburn is the locale of the lover's flat in *Betrayal.*

45. Displaying his typical sense of humor when asked by Gussow whether he would ever again direct a film, Pinter joked, no, he "couldn't get up so early in the morning" ("Pinter on Pinter," 31).

The Creative/Collaborative Process

1. Alvin Sargent (author of screenplays for *Gambit, The Sterile Cuckoo, The Effect of Gamma Rays on Man-in-the-Moon Marigolds,* and *Paper Moon,* among others), quoted in Chase, *Filmmaking,* 47.

2. Leonard Spigalglass (former president of the Writers Guild and author of scripts for *All through the Night, I Was a Male War Bride, A Majority of One,* and of the adaptation of his own stage play, *Gypsy*), quoted in ibid., 29.

3. Brownlow, *The Parade's Gone By,* [270]. Brownlow's depiction of the motion picture industry during this early period is absorbing.

4. Goldman, quoted in Sanders and Mock, *Word into Image,* 33–34.

5. The pitch should be deliverable in as little as fifteen to thirty seconds (recommendations are that it be no more than five lines in length if written out), although a three-minute telephone pitch or up to fifteen minutes in a face-to-face personal pitch are acceptable. Andy Cohen of Grade A Productions says that the pitch should represent a formula that contains only essential information: the genre (comedy, action, etc.), tone, who the two or three main characters are, and a brief, three-act plot summary, all delivered in the requisite time.

6. Johnson (author of scripts for *Jesse James, The Grapes of Wrath, Roxie Hart, The Desert Fox, How to Marry a Millionaire, The Three Faces of Eve, The Man in the Gray Flannel Suit,* and many more), quoted in Chase, *Filmmaking,* 43.

7. Sargent, quoted in ibid.

8. Richter, quoted in ibid., 44.

9. Brackett (author of *The Big Sleep, Rio Bravo, Hatari!, The Long Goodbye,* and others), quoted in ibid.

10. Losey quoted in Milne, *Losey on Losey,* 152–53.

11. Losey quoted in ibid., 149.

12. Pinter in a conversation with Gale, Oct. 1994.

13. Losey quoted in Milne, *Losey on Losey,* 137.

14. In addition to the cuts mentioned in the chapter on the film, the following is typical:

FRENCH LIEUTENANT'S WOMAN - SAVINGS

Pages	Scene		Time Saved
3	6	Dialogue cuts.	
6–10	12–22	Dialogue cuts.	
		Two sets cut: GARDEN ROOM	
		and LIVING ROOM become one.	
		MRS TRANTER'S ROOM (17,21)	
		Cut.	
17/20, 21	32	Dialogue cuts.	Bits
31, 32	43	Dialogue changes	
36	60–61	Set of INTERIOR DAIRY and	
		Scene 60 OMITTED.	1/3 DAY

Pages	Scene		Time Saved
47–50	70–74	Two pages cut.	
		Two very simple shots (New 71 & New 72) replace whole sequence 71–74	
		Two sets cut: LANDING OF MRS PULTNEY'S	
		MILLIE'S ROOM.	2/3 DAY
53	78	Dialogue cuts.	
74/75	115	OMITTED	A bit
76–77	120–126	120–121–122 NIGHT	
		EXTERIORS OMITTED	1/2 DAY
100–101	155–160	156–157–158–159 OMITTED	
		Set Cut: SALON THE BROTHEL	1 3/4 DAYS
		156–157 London Night	
		Exterior Cut	1/2 DAY
102–etc	161–167	DROP TWO SETS IN CHARLES' HOUSE:	
		LIVING ROOM	
		BEDROOM	Bits
114, 115,			
116	180–187	OMITTED: 180, 181, 182, 183, 187	
		Set Cut: HOTEL ROOM, EXETER	
		180	1/4 DAY
		181, 182, 183	1/3 DAY
120	190	Rearrangement.	
123	194	Dialogue change	

SAVINGS SUMMARY

Sets Omitted:	STUDIO	BROTHEL/EXHIBITION
		MRS TRANTER'S GARDEN ROOM
		MRS TRANTER'S BEDROOM
		MRS PULTNEY LANDING AND STAIRS
		MRS PULTNEY: MILLIE'S ROOM
		CHARLES' LONDON LIVING ROOM
		CHARLES' LONDON BEDROOM
		HOTEL INTERIOR - EXETER
	LOCATION	DAIRY INTERIOR

Days saved from previous schedule–4 1/3 day and bits

15. Fowles, quoted in Combs, "In Search of *The French Lieutenant's Woman*," 39.

16. Harold Pinter, *The Proust Screenplay: À la recherche du temps perdu* (New York: Grove Press, 1977), 4.

17. Pinter quoted in Menick, "Remembrance of Things Future," 47.

Conclusions

1. See Giannetti, *Understanding Movies*, 137–38, 150, 151.

2. In a famous experiment designed to demonstrate this statement, Lev Kuleshov created three combinations of shots that included the same closeup of an actor with a neutral expression on his face. In the first combination he juxtaposed the man's face with a bowl of soup, in the second combination the photo was juxtaposed with a coffin that contained a female corpse, and in the third he juxtaposed the shot with a picture of a little girl playing. When audiences saw these combinations, they were amazed at the actor's ability to portray the emotions of hunger, sorrow, and paternal pride.

3. See Pfister, *Theory and Analysis of Drama*, 24–25.

4. Along the same lines, Benjamin Bennett claims that film and theatre share a fundamental paradox, that performance "contributes to constituting the very object (the work) of which it is an interpretation" (*Theater as Problem*, 67), and Terry Eagleton insists that "a dramatic production does not 'express,' 'reflect' or 'reproduce' the text on which it is based; it 'produces' the text, transforming it into a unique and irreducible entity" (Eagleton, 64).

5. Giannetti comments on the function of time in film throughout *Understanding Movies*, fourth edition (Englewood Cliffs, N.J.: Prentice-Hall, 1987), and specifically in relation to adaptations of stage plays (300–301).

Bibliography

Works Cited

Screenplays and Sources for the Screenplays

Atwood, Margaret. *The Handmaid's Tale*. Boston: Houghton Mifflin, 1986.

Bowen, Elizabeth. *The Heat of the Day*. London: Jonathan Cape, 1949. Reprint, New York: Alfred A. Knopf, 1949.

Conrad, Joseph. *Victory*. London: Collins, 1915. Reprint, New York: Doubleday, 1957. Reprint, New York: Random House/Modern Library, n.d.

Dinesen, Isak. "The Dreaming Child." In *The Dreaming Child and Other Stories*, 153–87. New York: Random House, 1942. Reprint, London: Penguin, 1995. Page citations are to the 1942 edition.

Fitzgerald, F. Scott. *The Last Tycoon*. Foreword by Edmund Wilson. New York: Scribner's, 1941. Reprint, Scribner Classic/Collier Edition, 1986.

Fowles, John. *The French Lieutenant's Woman*. Boston: Little, Brown, 1969.

Gray, Simon. *Butley*. London: Methuen, 1971. Reprint, New York: Viking, 1972.

Hall, Adam. *The Berlin Memorandum*. London: Collins, 1965. Reprinted as *The Quiller Memorandum* (New York: Simon and Schuster, 1965; New York: Pyramid Books, 1966). Page citations are to the 1966 edition.

Hartley, L[eslie] P[oles]. *The Go-Between*. London: Hamish and Hamilton, 1953; New York: Avon, 1971. Page citations are to the 1971 edition.

Higgins, Aidan. *Langrishe, Go Down*. London: John Calder, 1966.

Hoban, Russell. *Turtle Diary*. New York: Random, 1976. Reprint, New York: Pocket Books, 1986.

Ishiguro, Kazuo. *The Remains of the Day*. London: Faber and Faber; New York: Knopf, 1989. Reprint, New York: Vintage/Random House, 1990.

Kafka, Franz. *The Trial*. 1937. Reprint, New York: Alfred A. Knopf, 1937.

Maugham, Robin (Sir Robert). *The Servant*. London: Falcon, 1948; New York: Harcourt, Brace, 1949. Page citations are to the 1949 edition.

McEwan, Ian. *The Comfort of Strangers*. London: Jonathan Cape, 1981; New York: Simon and Schuster, 1981; New York: Vintage, 1994. Page citations are to the 1994 edition.

Mortimer, Penelope. *The Pumpkin Eater*. London: Hutchison, 1962; New York: McGraw-Hill, 1962. Page citations are to the McGraw-Hill edition.

Mosley, Nicholas. *Accident*. London: Hodder and Stoughton, 1965. Reprint, Elmwood Park, Ill.: Dalkey Archive Press, 1985. Page citations are to the 1985 edition.

Nabokov, Vladimir. *Lolita*. New York: Random House, 1955. Reprint, New York: Vintage, 1989. Page citations are to the 1989 edition.

Pinter, Harold. *Accident*. In Pinter, *Five Screenplays*.

———. *The Basement*. In *The Lover, Tea Party, The Basement*. New York: Grove, 1963.

———. *Betrayal*. London: Methuen, 1978. Reprint, New York: Grove, 1979. Page citations are to the 1978 edition.

———. *The Birthday Party*. London: Methuen, 1960. Reprinted in *The Birthday Party and The Room: Two Plays by Harold Pinter* (New York: Grove, 1961). Reprinted in *Complete Works: One* (New York: Grove, 1978).

———. *The Caretaker*. London: Methuen, 1960. Reprinted in *The Caretaker and The Dumb Waiter* (New York: Grove, 1960). Reprinted in *Complete Works: Two*, by Harold Pinter (New York: Grove, 1978). Page citations are to the 1960 Grove edition.

———. *The Comfort of Strangers and Other Screenplays*. New York: Grove Wiedenfield; London: Faber and Faber, 1990. Includes *The Comfort of Strangers, Reunion, Turtle Diary,* and *Victory*.

———. *The Compartment*. See Pinter, *The Basement*.

———. *The Dumb Waiter*. London: Methuen, 1962. Also in *The Caretaker and The Dumb Waiter* (New York: Grove, 1960).

———. *The Dwarfs* (novel). London: Faber and Faber, 1990. Reprint, New York: Grove Weidenfield, 1990.

———. *The Dwarfs* (play). In *The Dwarfs and Eight Revue Sketches*. New York: Dramatists Play Service, 1965.

———. "The Examination." In *The Collection and The Lover*. London: Methuen, 1970.

———. *Five Screenplays*. London: Methuen, 1971. Reprint, New York: Grove, 1973. Includes *The Servant, The Pumpkin Eater, The Quiller Memorandum, Accident,* and *The Go-Between*.

———. *The French Lieutenant's Woman: A Screenplay*. Foreword by John Fowles. Boston: Little, Brown, 1981.

———. *The French Lieutenant's Woman and Other Screenplays*. London: Methuen, 1982. Includes *The French Lieutenant's Woman, The Last Tycoon,* and *Langrishe, Go Down*.

———. "From *The Dwarfs* (Chapter Ten)." *Pinter Review* 2 (1988): 5–7.

———. *The Go-Between*. In Pinter, *Five Screenplays*.

———. "The Handmaid's Tale." Several unpublished typescripts and holograph scripts, with various dates, are housed in the Pinter Archives, British Library, London.

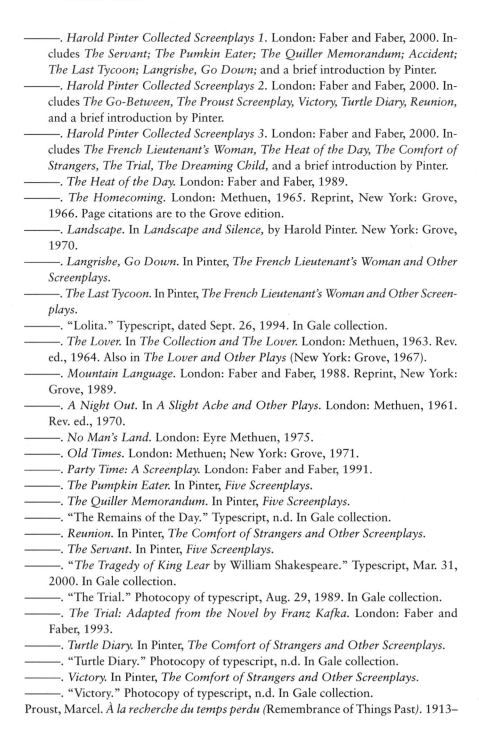

———. *Harold Pinter Collected Screenplays 1*. London: Faber and Faber, 2000. Includes *The Servant; The Pumkin Eater; The Quiller Memorandum; Accident; The Last Tycoon; Langrishe, Go Down;* and a brief introduction by Pinter.

———. *Harold Pinter Collected Screenplays 2*. London: Faber and Faber, 2000. Includes *The Go-Between, The Proust Screenplay, Victory, Turtle Diary, Reunion,* and a brief introduction by Pinter.

———. *Harold Pinter Collected Screenplays 3*. London: Faber and Faber, 2000. Includes *The French Lieutenant's Woman, The Heat of the Day, The Comfort of Strangers, The Trial, The Dreaming Child,* and a brief introduction by Pinter.

———. *The Heat of the Day*. London: Faber and Faber, 1989.

———. *The Homecoming*. London: Methuen, 1965. Reprint, New York: Grove, 1966. Page citations are to the Grove edition.

———. *Landscape*. In *Landscape and Silence,* by Harold Pinter. New York: Grove, 1970.

———. *Langrishe, Go Down*. In Pinter, *The French Lieutenant's Woman and Other Screenplays.*

———. *The Last Tycoon*. In Pinter, *The French Lieutenant's Woman and Other Screenplays.*

———. "Lolita." Typescript, dated Sept. 26, 1994. In Gale collection.

———. *The Lover*. In *The Collection and The Lover*. London: Methuen, 1963. Rev. ed., 1964. Also in *The Lover and Other Plays* (New York: Grove, 1967).

———. *Mountain Language*. London: Faber and Faber, 1988. Reprint, New York: Grove, 1989.

———. *A Night Out*. In *A Slight Ache and Other Plays*. London: Methuen, 1961. Rev. ed., 1970.

———. *No Man's Land*. London: Eyre Methuen, 1975.

———. *Old Times*. London: Methuen; New York: Grove, 1971.

———. *Party Time: A Screenplay*. London: Faber and Faber, 1991.

———. *The Pumpkin Eater*. In Pinter, *Five Screenplays.*

———. *The Quiller Memorandum*. In Pinter, *Five Screenplays.*

———. "The Remains of the Day." Typescript, n.d. In Gale collection.

———. *Reunion*. In Pinter, *The Comfort of Strangers and Other Screenplays.*

———. *The Servant*. In Pinter, *Five Screenplays.*

———. "*The Tragedy of King Lear* by William Shakespeare." Typescript, Mar. 31, 2000. In Gale collection.

———. "The Trial." Photocopy of typescript, Aug. 29, 1989. In Gale collection.

———. *The Trial: Adapted from the Novel by Franz Kafka*. London: Faber and Faber, 1993.

———. *Turtle Diary*. In Pinter, *The Comfort of Strangers and Other Screenplays.*

———. "Turtle Diary." Photocopy of typescript, n.d. In Gale collection.

———. *Victory*. In Pinter, *The Comfort of Strangers and Other Screenplays.*

———. "Victory." Photocopy of typescript, n.d. In Gale collection.

Proust, Marcel. *À la recherche du temps perdu (*Remembrance of Things Past*)*. 1913–

1927. Trans. C.K. Scott Moncrieff. London: Chatto and Windus, 1922–1931. Reprint, New York: Modern Library. Page citations are to the Modern Library edition.

Shakespeare, William. *The Tragedie of King Lear.* London, c. 1605.

Uhlman, Fred. *Reunion.* London: Adam Books, 1971. Reprint, London: Collins and Harvill Press, 1977. Reprint, Harmondsworth, Eng.: Penguin, 1978. Reprint, London: Fontana, 1985. Page citations are to the Collins and Harvill edition.

Critical Studies, Reviews, and Miscellanea

Adams, Michael. "Gatsby, Tycoon, Islands, and the Film Critics." In *Fitzgerald/ Hemingway Annual: 1978,* ed. Matthew J. Bruccoli and Richard Laymen, 297– 306. Detroit: Gale, 1979.

Adler, Thomas P. "Pinter/Proust/Pinter." In *Harold Pinter: Critical Approaches,* ed. Steven H. Gale, 128–38. Madison, N.J.: Fairleigh Dickinson Univ. Press, 1986.

Agee, James. "Agee on Film." *Nation,* Mar. 10, 1945.

Alpert, Hollis. "The Losey Situation." *Saturday Review,* Aug. 14, 1971, 42–43.

———. "The Sour Smell of Failure." *Saturday Review,* Nov. 21, 1964, 34.

———. "Where It's Happening," *Saturday Review,* Apr. 4, 1967, 47. Reprinted in Boyun and Scott, *Film as Film,* 27.

Andrew, Dudley. *Concepts in Film Theory.* New York: Oxford Univ. Press, 1984.

Arden, John. "The Caretaker." *New Theatre Magazine,* no. 4 (July 1960): 29–30.

Armes, Roy. *Action and Image: Dramatic Structure in Cinema.* Manchester, Eng.: Manchester Univ. Press; New York: St. Martin's Press, 1994.

"Bag of Tricks." *Newsweek,* Nov. 16, 1964, 102.

Bazin, André. *What Is Cinema?* Ed. Hugh Gray. Berkeley: Univ. of California Press, 1971, 1994.

Beaupre, Lee. "ABC Films Results: 30 of 36 in Red: Total Loss $47 Mil." *Variety,* May 31, 1973, 3.

Beaver, Frank. *Dictionary of Film Terms.* New York: McGraw-Hill, 1983.

Beckett, Samuel. *Waiting for Godot: A Tragicomedy in Two Acts.* New York: Grove, 1954.

Bednerik, Marya. "The Ecology of *The Go-Between* with a Peek into Harold Pinter's Own Garden." In Gale, *The Films of Harold Pinter,* 38–53.

Bennett, Benjamin. *Theater as Problem: Modern Drama and Its Place in Literature.* Ithaca, N.Y.: Cornell Univ. Press, 1990.

Bennetts, Leslie. "On Film: Pinter's *Betrayal* Displays New Subtleties." *New York Times,* Feb. 27, 1993, sec. H, 1, 23.

Bensky, Lawrence M. "Harold Pinter: An Interview." *Paris Review* 10, no. 20 (fall 1966): 12–37. Reprinted as "Harold Pinter" in *Writers at Work: The Paris Review Interviews, Third Series,* ed. George Plimpton, 347–68 (New York: Viking, 1967). Page citations are to the reprint.

Bergman, Ingmar. "Each Film Is My Last." *Tulane Drama Review* 33 (fall 1966): 94–101.

———. "Introduction: Bergman Discusses Film-Making." In *Four Screenplays of Ingmar Bergman,* trans. Lars Malmstrom and David Kushner. New York: Clarion, 1960.

Billington, Michael. *The Life and Work of Harold Pinter.* London: Faber and Faber, 1996.

Bogarde, Dirk. *Snakes and Ladders.* New York: Henry Holt, 1979.

Boulton, James T. "Harold Pinter: *The Caretaker* and Other Plays." *Modern Drama* 6, no. 2 (Sept. 1963): 131–40.

"Box Office Samplings." *Hollywood Reporter,* Mar. 12, 1982.

Boyum, Joy Gould, and Adrienne Scott. *Film as Film: Critical Responses to Film Art.* Boston: Allyn and Bacon, 1971.

Brater, Enoch. "Pinter's Homecoming on Celluloid." *Modern Drama* 18, no. 4 (Dec. 1974): 443–48.

Brecht, Bertolt. "The Film, the Novel, and Epic Theatre." In *Brecht on Theatre,* ed. John Willett, 47–51. New York: Hill and Wang, 1964.

Brent, Peter. *How to Tell Your Fortune.* London: Marshall Cavendish, 1975.

Brown, Geoff. "'Sister of the Stage': British Film and British Theatre." In *All Our Yesterdays,* ed. Charles Barr. London: British Film Institute/Rutledge & Kegan Paul, 1986.

Brownlow, Kevin. *The Parade's Gone By . . .* New York: Alfred A. Knopf, 1969.

Bryden, Mary. "The Proust Screenplay on BBC Radio." In Gillen and Gale, *Pinter Review: Annual Essays 1995–1996,* 186–88.

Burkman, Katherine, and John Kundert-Gibbs. *Pinter at Sixty.* Bloomington: Indiana Univ. Press, 1993.

Burkman, Katherine, and Mijeong Kim. "The Tragedy of Illusion: Harold Pinter in *The Last Tycoon.*" In Gale, *Films of Harold Pinter,* 54–67.

Butler, Robert W. "New 'Lolita' Isn't a Hit with U.S. Film Distributors." *Lexington (Ky.) Herald-Leader,* Apr. 4, 1998, "Home and Garden," 15.

Callahan, John F. "The Unfinished Business of The Last Tycoon." *Literature/Film Quarterly* 6 (summer 1978): 204–13.

Canby, Vincent. *New York Times,* July 30, 1971, 21.

Carriere, Jean-Claude, and Pascal Bonitzer. *Exercice du scenario.* Paris: Femis, 1990.

Caute, David. "Golden Triangle." *Independent on Sunday* (London), Nov. 7, 1993, "Sunday Review," 24.

———. *Joseph Losey, A Revenge on Life.* New York: Oxford Univ. Press, 1994.

Chase, Donald. *Filmmaking: The Collaborative Art.* New York: Little, Brown, 1975.

Chatman, Seymour. *Coming to Terms: The Rhetoric of Narrative in Fiction and Film.* Ithaca, N.Y.: Cornell Univ. Press, 1990.

Ciment, Michel. *Le Livre de Losey.* Paris: n.p., 1979. Rev. and trans. as *Conversations with Losey* (London: Methuen, 1985).

Clurman, Harold. "Films." *Nation,* Jan. 6, 1969, 29–30.

Cocks, Jay. "Fire and Ice." *Time,* Dec. 17, 1973, 70.

———. "A Touch of Class." *Time,* Apr. 29, 1974, 76–77.

Cohn, Ruby. "The World of Harold Pinter." *Tulane Drama Revue* 6 (Mar. 1962): 55–68.

Cole, William, and George Plimpton. "The Art of Fiction: S. J. Perelman." *Paris Review* 8, no. 30 (fall 1963). Reprinted in *Writers at Work: The Paris Review Interviews, Second Series,* 241–56 (New York: Compass Books, 1965).

Combs, Richard. "In Search of *The French Lieutenant's Woman.*" *Sight and Sound* 50 (1980–1981): 34–39.

Comolli, Jean-Louis. "Technique and Ideology: Camera, Perspective, and Depth of Field." In *Movies and Methods,* vol. 2, ed. Bill Nichols, 41–57. Berkeley: Univ. of California Press, 1985. Published as "Technique et Ideologie" in *Cahiers du Cinema,* May–June 1971.

Connolly, Jeanne. "*The Trial.*" In Gillen and Gale, *Pinter Review: Annual Essays 1994,* [84]–88.

Conradi, Peter J. "*The French Lieutenant's Woman*: Novel, Screenplay, Film." *Critical Quarterly* 24, no. 1 (1982): 41–57.

Cook, David A. *A History of the Narrative Film.* New York: W.W. Norton, 1981.

Corel All-Movie Guide 2. B&N Software, 1996.

Cornell, Christopher. "Videos." *Lexington (Ky.) Herald-Leader,* July 1, 1994, "Weekender," 7.

Crist, Judith. "The Agony beneath the Skin Revealed with Surgical Skill," *New York World Journal Tribune,* Apr. 18, 1967. Reprinted in Boyum and Scott, *Film as Film,* 29.

———. "Passport to the Past." *New York Magazine,* July 26, 1971, 50.

"Cut Radical Right (Neo Nazi) Terrorists out of 'Quiller' in West German Playoff." *Variety Weekly,* Mar. 1, 1967, 18.

Davidson, David. "Pinter in No Man's Land: *The Proust Screenplay.*" *Comparative Literature* 34, no. 2 (spring 1982): 157–70.

Davis, Barry. "The 22 from Hackney to Chelsea: A Conversation with Harold Pinter." *Jewish Quarterly* 38, no. 4 (winter 1991–1992): 9–17.

Deer, Harriet, and Irving Deer. "Pinter's *The Birthday Party*: The Film and the Play." *South Atlantic Bulletin* 45, no. 2 (1980): 26–30.

Dixon, Wheeler Winston. "The Eternal Summer of Losey and Pinter's *Accident.*" In Gale, *Films of Harold Pinter,* 27–37.

"*The Dreaming Child* Heads for Fox Searchlight." *Entertainment Today,* June 27, 1997.

Dukore, Bernard F. "Pinter's Spy Movie." In *The Pinter Review: Annual Essays 1991,* ed. Francis X. Gillen and Steven H. Gale, 10–16. Tampa, Fla.: Univ. of Tampa Press, 1991. Revised paper originally presented at the International Pinter Festival, Columbus, Ohio, Apr. 19, 1991.

————. "The Theater of Harold Pinter." *Tulane Drama Review* 6, no. 3 (Mar. 1962): 43–54.

Eagleton, Terry. *Literary Theory.* Minneapolis: Univ. of Minnesota Press, 1996.

Ebert, Roger. *Roger Ebert's Movie Home Companion 1989 Edition.* Kansas City, Mo.: Andrews and McMeel, 1988.

Eder, Richard. "Losey to Film 'Remembrance.'" *New York Times,* Feb. 14, 1973, 24.

Eisenstein, Sergi. *Film Form.* Trans. Jay Leda. New York: Harcourt, 1949.

Eliot, T.S. "Burnt Norton." In *Collected Poems,* by T.S. Eliot. London, 1936.

Eller, Claudia. "Dish." *Variety,* July 14, 1992.

Elsaesser, Thomas. "Screen Violence: Emotional Structure and Ideological Function in 'A Clockwork Orange.'" In *Approaches to Popular Culture,* ed. C.W.E. Bigsby, 171–200. Bowling Green, Ohio: Bowling Green Univ. Popular Press, 1976.

Emerson, Ralph Waldo. "Nature." *Essays, Second Series.* 1844

"English Movie Idol Dirk Bogarde Dies." *Lexington (Ky.) Herald-Leader,* May 9, 1999, B2.

Esslin, Martin. *The Field of Drama.* London: Methuen, 1987.

————. *The Peopled Wound: The Work of Harold Pinter.* New York: Doubleday/Anchor, 1970. Revised and expanded as *Pinter: A Study of His Plays* (New York: Norton, 1973).

————. *The Theatre of the Absurd.* New York: Doubleday/Anchor, 1961. Rev. ed., 1969.

Farrell, Pia. "Charguers gets Lolita Rights." *Hollywood Reporter,* Dec. 5, 1994, 20.

Field, Syd. *Screenplay: The Foundations of Screenwriting.* New York: Dell, 1994.

Flemming, Michael. "Carolco's Fire Sale." *Variety,* Oct. 27, 1994, sec. 1, 35.

Forster, E.M. *Aspects of the Novel.* New York: Harcourt, Brace, 1927.

Fowles, John. "HORS D'OEUVRE." Photocopy of typescript dated July 1980, in box 18, Pinter Archives, British Library, London. Published as the foreword to Pinter, *The French Lieutenant's Woman: A Screenplay.* Page citations are to the published version.

Freed, Donald. "Harold Pinter and the 'Unfashionable Theatre': An Interview with Ronald Harwood." In Gillen and Gale, *The Pinter Review: Collected Essays 2001–2002,* 1-13.

Gale, Steven H. *Butter's Going Up: A Critical Analysis of Harold Pinter's Work.* Durham, N.C.: Duke Univ. Press, 1977.

————. "Harold Pinter." In *Encyclopedia of British Humor,* ed. Steven H. Gale, 2:847–62. New York: Garland, 1996.

————. *Harold Pinter: An Annotated Bibliography.* Boston: G.K. Hall, 1978.

————. "The Significance of Orson Welles in Harold Pinter's *Old Times.*" *Notes on Contemporary Literature* 13, no. 12 (Mar. 1983): 11–12.

————. "The Use of a Cinematic Device in Harold Pinter's *Old Times.*" *Notes on Contemporary Literature* 10, no. 1 (Jan. 1980): 11.

————, ed. *Critical Essays on Harold Pinter.* Boston: G.K. Hall, 1990.

————, ed. *The Films of Harold Pinter.* Albany: State Univ. of New York Press, 2001.

————, ed. *Harold Pinter: Critical Approaches.* Cranberry, N.J.: Fairleigh Dickinson Univ. Press, 1986.

Gale, Steven H., and Christopher C. Hudgins. "The Harold Pinter Archives II: A Description of the Filmscript Materials in the Archive in the British Library." In Gillen and Gale, *Pinter Review: Annual Essays, 1995–96,* 101–42.

Garis, Leslie. "Translating Fowles into Film." *New York Times Magazine,* Aug. 30, 1981.

Gelbart, Larry. *Laughing Matters.* New York: Random House, 1998.

Giannetti, Louis. *Understanding Movies.* 8th ed. Englewood Cliffs, N.J.: Prentice-Hall, 1999.

Giannetti, Louis, and Scott Eyman. *Flashback, a Brief History of Film.* 3d ed. Englewood Cliffs, N.J.: Prentice-Hall, 1996.

Gibson, Walter B. *The Complete Illustrated Book of Divination and Prophecy.* New York: Doubleday, 1973.

Gill, Brendan. "Inside the Redoubt," *New Yorker,* April 15, 1967. Reprinted in Boyum and Scott, *Film as Film,* 36–37.

Gillen, Francis. "From Novel to Film: Harold Pinter's Adaptation of *The Trial.*" In *Pinter at Sixty,* ed. Katherine H. Burkman and John L. Kundert-Gibbs, 137–48. Bloomington: Indiana Univ. Press, 1993.

————. "Harold Pinter on *The Trial.*" In Gillen and Gale, *Pinter Review: Annual Essays 1992–1993,* 61–62.

Gillen, Francis X., and Steven H. Gale, eds. *The Pinter Review: Annual Essays 1992–1993.* Tampa, Fla.: Univ. of Tampa Press, 1993.

————. *The Pinter Review: Annual Essays 1994.* Tampa, Fla.: Univ. of Tampa Press, 1994.

————. *The Pinter Review: Annual Essays 1995–1996.* Tampa, Fla.: Univ. of Tampa Press, 1997.

————. *The Pinter Review: Annual Essays 1997–1998.* Tampa, Fla.: Univ. of Tampa Press, 1999.

————. *The Pinter Review: Collected Essays 1999 and 2000.* Tampa, Fla.: Univ. of Tampa Press, 2000.

————. *The Pinter Review: Collected Essays 2001–2002.* Tampa, Fla.: Univ. of Tampa Press, 2002.

Gilliat, Penelope. "The Conversion of a Tramp." *Observer* (London), Mar. 15, 1964, 24.

Goodman, Paul. "The Proustian Camera Eye." *Trend,* Jan.–Feb. 1935. Reprinted in Kauffmann and Henstell, *American Film Criticism,* 311–14.

Gordon, Lois. *Harold Pinter: A Casebook.* New York: Garland, 1990.

Graham, Mark. "The Proust Screenplay: *Temps perdu* for Harold Pinter?" *Literature/Film Quarterly* 10, no. 1 (1982): 38–53.

Gray, Simon. "Simon Gray." In *Contemporary Authors Autobiography Series,* ed. Adele Sarkissian, 3:101–15. Detroit: Gale Research, 1986.

Grenier, Cynthia. "Americans Sweep Prizes at Cannes Festival." *New York Times,* May 28, 1971, 20.

Gussow, Mel. "A Conversation (Pause) with Harold Pinter," *New York Times Magazine,* Dec. 5, 1971, 42 ff.

———. *Conversations with Pinter.* London: Nick Hern Books, 1994.

———. "Pinter on Pinter: The Lincoln Center Interview." In Gillen and Gale, *Pinter Review: Collected Essays 2001–2002,* 14–37.

Hall, Ann. "Daddy Dearest: Harold Pinter's *The Comfort of Strangers.*" Paper read at the Modern Language Association Convention, Toronto, Dec. 1997.

Halliwell, Leslie. *The Filmgoer's Companion.* 3d ed. New York: Avon (Equinox), 1971.

Halton, Kathleen. "Pinter." *Vogue,* Oct. 1, 1967.

Hamlett, Christina. "Film, Stage, or Novel?" *Screen Writes* (winter 1999–2000).

"Harold Pinter, Director." *Cinebill* 1, no. 7 (January 1974): 7–8.

Hartung, Philip T. "The Screen: Had a Wife." *Commonweal,* Nov. 27, 1964, 332.

———. "The Screen: A Successful Accident." *Commonweal,* April 28, 1967.

Hawthorne, Nathaniel. "The Birth-Mark." 1843.

———. "Drowne's Wooden Image." 1844.

Hewes, Henry. "Probing Pinter's Play." *Saturday Review,* Apr. 8, 1967, 56-58.

Higson, Andrew. *Waving the Flag: Constructing a National Cinema in Britain.* Oxford: Clarendon Press, 1995.

Hillesum, Etty [Esther]. *An Interrupted Life: The Diaries of Etty Hillesum 1941–1943.* Trans. Arnold J. Pomerans. London: Jonathan Cape, 1983. Reprint, New York: Pantheon, 1984.

Hinchliffe, Arnold P. *Harold Pinter.* Boston: Twayne, 1967. Rev. ed., 1981. Page citations are to the 1967 edition.

Hirsch, Foster. *Joseph Losey.* Boston: Twayne, 1980.

Houston, Beverle, and Marsha Kinder. "The Losey-Pinter Collaboration," *Film Quarterly* 32 (1978): 17–30. Reprinted in Gale, *Critical Essays on Harold Pinter,* 191–208.

Hudgins, Christopher C. "Harold Pinter's *Lolita:* 'My Sin, My Soul.'" In Gale, *Films of Harold Pinter,* 123–46.

———. "Harold Pinter's *The Comfort of Strangers:* Fathers and Sons and Other Victims." In Gillen and Gale, *Pinter Review: Annual Essays 1995–1996,* 101–42.

———. "Inside Out: Filmic Technique and the Theatrical Depiction of a Consciousness in Harold Pinter's *Old Times.*" *Genre* 13 (fall 1980): 355–76.

Jackson, Glenda. "English Movie Idol Dirk Bogarde Dies." *Lexington (Ky.) Herald Leader,* May 9, 1999, B2.

Janson, H.W. *History of Art: A Survey of the Major Visual Arts from the Dawn of History to the Present Day.* New York: Harry N. Abrams, [1962].

Johnstone, Iain. "Special K." *Sunday Times* (London), June 20, 1993, sec. 9, 10.

Jones, Edward T. "On *The Remains of the Day:* Pinter Remaindered." In Gale, *Films of Harold Pinter,* 99–107.

Kael, Pauline. "The Cinema." *New Yorker,* Nov. 29, 1976.

———. "The Comedy of Depravity: *Accident.*" *New Republic,* June 3, 1967, 338–41. Reprinted in *Kiss Kiss Bang Bang* (New York: Little, Brown, 1968); reprint, New York: Bantam, 1969, 131–32.

———. "Frightening the Horses." *New Yorker,* Dec. 21, 1968, 90–91. Reprinted in *Going Steady,* ed. Pauline Kael, 260–61 (New York: Bantam, 1971).

Karl, Frederick R. "Comments on Harold Pinter's Adaptation of Franz Kafka's *The Trial.*" In Gillen and Gale, *Pinter Review: Annual Essays 1994,* 76–83.

Kauffmann, Stanley. "The Birthday Party." *New Republic,* Jan. 4, 1969, 34.

———. "Future Tense." *New Republic,* Mar. 19, 1990, 267.

———. "The Guest." *New Republic,* Jan. 25, 1964. Reprinted in *World on Film: Criticism and Comment,* ed. Stanley Kauffmann, 213–15 (New York: Dell/Delta, 1969).

———. "The Homecoming." *New Republic,* Dec. 8, 1973.

———. "The Proust Screenplay." *New Republic,* Dec. 24–31, 1977, 22–23.

———. "Stanley Kauffmann on Films: The Last Tycoon." *New Republic,* Dec. 4, 1976, pp. 20–21.

Kauffmann, Stanley, and Bruce Henstell, eds. *American Film Criticism.* New York: Liveright, 1972.

Kennedy, Harlan. "The Czech Director's Woman." *Film Comment* 17 (Sept.–Oct. 1981).

Kershaw, John. Interview with Harold Pinter, ITV, 1964.

———. *The Present Stage.* London: Collins, 1966.

Klein, Joanne. *Making Pictures: The Pinter Screenplays.* Columbus: Ohio State Univ. Press, 1985.

Knapp, Shoshona. "The Transformation of a Pinter Screenplay: Freedom and Calculators in *The French Lieutenant's Woman.*" *Modern Drama* 28, no. 1 (1985): 55–70.

Knowles, Ronald. "From London: *Harold Pinter 1991.*" In *The Pinter Review: Annual Essays 1991,* ed. Francis X. Gillen and Steven H. Gale, 64–73. Tampa, Fla.: Univ. of Tampa Press, 1991.

———. "From London: Harold Pinter 1993–1994." In Gillen and Gale, *Pinter Review: Annual Essays 1994,* 115–29.

———. "From London: Harold Pinter 1994–1995 and 1995–1996." In Gillen and Gale, *Pinter Review: Annual Essays 1995–1996,* [152]–67.

———. "London Report: Harold Pinter 1998–2000." In *The Pinter Review: Collected Essays 1999 and 2000,* ed. Francis X. Gillen and Steven H. Gale, [168]–90. Tampa, Fla.: Univ. of Tampa Press, 2000.

———. *Understanding Harold Pinter.* Columbia: Univ. of South Carolina Press, 1995.

Koestler, Arthur. Introduction to *Reunion,* by Fred Uhlman. London: Collins and Harvill Press, 1977.

Kroll, Jack. "Breath by Breath." *Newsweek,* April 24, 1967, 96–97.

Lahr, John, ed. *A Casebook on Harold Pinter's The Homecoming.* New York: Grove, 1971.

Langer, Susanne K. *Feeling and Form.* New York: Scribners, 1953.

Langley, Lee. "From 'Caretaker' to 'Servant.'" *New York Herald Tribune,* Mar. 1, 1964, 24.

———. "Genius—A Change in Direction." *Daily Telegraph Magazine* (London), Nov. 23, 1973, 30–36.

Lanza, Joseph. *Fragile Geometry: The Films, Philosophy, and Misadventures of Nicolas Roeg.* New York: PAJ Publications, 1989.

Leahy, James. *The Cinema of Joseph Losey.* International Film Guide Series. London: A. Zwemmer; New York: A.S. Barnes, 1967.

Leech, Clifford. "Two Romantics: Arnold Wesker and Harold Pinter." In *The Contemporary Theatre,* ed. Allan Lewis, 11–31. New York: Crown, 1971.

Lindgren, Ernest. *The Art of the Film.* 2d ed. London: George Allen and Unwin, 1963.

Lindsay, Vachel. *The Art of the Moving Picture.* New York: Liveright, 1915. Rev. ed., New York: Macmillan, 1922; Liveright, 1970.

Lodge, David. "Last to Go: A Structuralist Reading." In Gordon, *Harold Pinter,* 61–79.

Losey, Joseph. "Norfolk Jackets: The Making of *The Go-Between.*" In *Writers of East Anglia,* ed. Angus Wilson, 3–8. London: Secker and Warburg, 1977.

Maltin, Leonard. *TV Movies and Video Guide.* New York: New American Library, 1991.

Mamet, David. *Jafsie and John Henry: Essays.* New York: Free Press, 1999.

———. *Lolita.* Unpublished photocopy of typescript screenplay, dated Mar. 10, 1995. In Christopher C. Hudgins's collection.

———. *On Directing Film.* New York: Penguin, 1991.

———. *Some Freaks.* New York: Viking, 1989.

———. *Writing in Restaurants.* New York: Penguin, 1986.

Marks, Louis. "Producing Pinter." In *Pinter at Sixty,* ed. Katherine H. Burkman and John L. Kundert-Gibbs, 18–26. Bloomington: Indiana Univ. Press, 1993.

Marowitz, Charles. "Theatre Abroad." *Village Voice,* Sept. 1, 1960.

Maslin, Janet. "Film Review: Janet Maslin Reports NY at 6." WQXR, New York, Nov. 25, 1993, 6:30 P.M., ET, IND, FM Radio, local.

Mayne, Judith, *Private Novels, Public Films.* Athens: Univ. of Georgia Press, 1988.

———. *The Women at the Keyhole: Feminism and Women's Cinema.* Bloomington: Indiana Univ. Press, 1990.

Megahey, Leslie. *With Orson Welles: Stories from a Life in Film.* Filmed interview, 1989.

Melly, George. *Observer* (London), Sept. 26, 1971.

Melville, Herman. *Moby-Dick.* 1851.

Menick, Stephen. "Remembrance of Things Future." *Village Voice,* Dec. 12, 1977, 45–47.

Merritt, Susan Hollis. "Pinter Playing Pinter: *The Hothouse.*" In Gillen and Gale, *Pinter Review: Annual Essays 1995–1996, 73–84.*

Metz, Christian. *Film Language: A Semiotics of the Cinema.* Trans. Michael Taylor. New York: Oxford Univ. Press, 1974.

———. *Language and Cinema.* Trans. Donna Jean Umiker-Sebeok. The Hague: Mouton, 1974.

Miller, Henry. *Tropic of Cancer.* Paris, 1934.

———. *Tropic of Capricorn.* Paris, 1939.

Miller, Walter James, and Bonnie E. Nelson. *Samuel Beckett's Waiting for Godot and Other Works.* New York: Monarch, 1971.

Milne, Tom. *Losey on Losey.* London: Secker and Warburg (in association with the British Film Institute), 1967. Reprint, Garden City, N.Y.: Doubleday, 1968. Page citations are to the reprint edition.

———. "Two Films (1): 'Accident.'" *Sight and Sound* 36 (1967): 57–59.

Monaco, James. *How to Read a Film.* New York: Oxford Univ. Press, 1977.

M[orgenstern], J[oseph]. "Stalking Stanley." *Newsweek,* Dec. 23, 1968, 89–90.

Mosley, Nicholas. *Efforts at Truth.* London: Secker and Warburg, 1994. Reprint, Normal, Ill.: Dalkey Archive Press, 1996. Page citations are to the 1994 edition.

Murch, Fiona. Interview with Harold Pinter. *Channel Four News Report,* BBC 4, London, May 22, 1922.

Murphy, Robert. *Sixties British Cinema.* London: British Film Institute, 1992.

Nelson, Gerald. "Harold Pinter Goes to the Movies." *Chicago Review* 17, no. 1 (summer 1966): 33–43.

Opie, Iona, and Peter Opie. *The Oxford Dictionary of Nursery Rhymes.* Oxford: Clarendon, 1951.

Packard, William. *The Art of Screenwriting.* New York: Paragon, 1987.

Peacock, D. Keith. *Harold Pinter and the New British Theatre.* Westport, Conn.: Greenwood, 1997.

Petley, Julian. "The Lost Continent." In *All Our Yesterdays,* ed. Charles Barr. London: British Film Institute/Rutledge & Kegan Paul, 1986.

Petrie, Duncan J. *Creativity and Constraint in the British Film Industry.* New York: St. Martin's Press, 1991.

Pfister, Manfred. *The Theory and Analysis of Drama.* Cambridge: Cambridge Univ. Press, 1988.

Pinter, Harold. "Between the Lines." *Sunday Times* (London), Mar. 4, 1962, p. 25.

———. *The Dwarfs.* London: Faber and Faber, 1990.

———. "Evacuees." In Gillen and Gale, *Pinter Review: Annual Essays 1994,* [8]–13.

———. "Kullus." In *Poems,* collected by Alan Clodd. London: Enitharmon, 1968.

———. Letter to the editor. *Sunday Times* (London), Aug. 14, 1960, 21.

———. *Mac.* London: Emanuel Wax for Pendragon, 1968.

———. *No Man's Land.* London: Eyre Methuen, 1975. Reprint, New York: Grove, 1975.

———. "Oh, Superman." BBC Channel 4, May 31, 1990.

———. "Precisely." In *Harold Pinter: Plays 40.* London: Faber and Faber, 1993, 215–20.

———. "Speech: Hamburg 1970." *Theatre Quarterly* 1, no. 3 (July–September 1971): 3–4. Reprinted as "Pinter on Pinter," *Cinebill* 1, no. 2 (Oct. 1973): 7.

———. "Speech: Realism and Post-Realism in the French Cinema." *Hackney Downs School Magazine,* autumn 1947, 13.

———. "Speech: Supporting the Motion That 'In View of Its Progress in the Last Decade, the Film Is More Promising in Its Future as an Art than the Theatre.'" *Hackney Downs School Magazine,* spring 1948, 12.

———. *Various Voices: Prose, Poetry, Politics, 1948–1998.* New York: Grove/Atlantic, 2001.

———. "Writing for Myself." *Twentieth Century,* Feb. 1961, 172–75. Reprinted in Harold Pinter, *Complete Works: Two,* 9–12 (New York: Grove, 1978).

———. "Writing for the Theatre." *Evergreen Review* 8 (Aug.–Sept. 1964). Reprinted in Harold Pinter, *Complete Works: One,* 9–16 (New York: Grove, 1978). Page citations are to the reprint.

Pinter, Harold, and Clive Donner. "Filming 'The Caretaker.'" *Transatlantic Review,* no. 13 (summer 1963): 17–26. Reprinted in *Behind the Scenes: Theatre and Film Interviews from the Transatlantic Review,* ed. Joseph F. McCrindle (New York: Holt, Rinehart, and Winston, 1971). Page citations are to the original.

"Pinter to Pen Child for Fox/Ormond to Produce Child." *Variety,* June 6, 1997.

"Pinterview." *Newsweek,* July 23, 1962, 69.

Popkin, Henry. *Modern British Drama.* New York: Grove, 1969.

Pratley, Gerald. *The Cinema of Otto Preminger.* New York: Castle Books, 1971.

Preminger, Otto. *Preminger, An Autobiography.* New York: Doubleday, 1977.

Pudovkin, V.I. *Film Techniques and Film Acting.* London: Vision Pres, 1959; New York: Grove Press, 1960.

"'Quiller' Crashes Gates." *Hollywood Reporter,* June 5, 1966.

Rafferty, Terrence. "The Current Cinema: Yes, But." *New Yorker,* May 4, 1992, 74–76.

Raymond, Gerard. "Letter from London." *TheaterWeek,* Mar. 25–31, 1991, 38–39.

———. "Q and A with Simon Gray." *TheatreWeek,* Oct. 12–18, 1992, 21–25.

Reames, Wilbur H., Jr. "Harold Pinter: An Introduction to the Literature of His Screenplays." Ph.D. diss., Univ. of Georgia, 1978.

Reed, Rex. *Conversations in the Raw.* New York: Signet, 1970.

Reisz, Karel. *The Technique of Film Editing.* London: Butterworth, 1981.

Rich [Richard Gold]. "*The Quiller Memorandum,*" *Variety,* Nov. 16, 1966. Reprinted in *Variety Film Reviews,* 41 (New York: Garland, 1983).

Robbe-Grillet, Alain. *Snapshots and Towards a New Novel.* London: Marion Boyars, 1965.

Robinson, David. "The Improved Pumpkin Eater." *Financial Times* (London), July 17, 1964, 24.

Ross, Andrew. "The Everyday Life of Lou Andreas-Salome: Marking Video History." In *Feminism and Psychoanalysis,* ed. Richard Feldstein and Judith Roof, 142–63. Ithaca: Cornell Univ. Press, 1989.

Sanders, Terry, and Freida Lee Mock, comps. *Word into Image: Writers on Screenwriting.* Santa Monica, Calif.: American Film Foundation, 1981.

Sarris, Andrew. "Accident." *Village Voice,* May 18, 1967. Reprinted in Boyum and Scott, *Film as Film,* 31.

———. *The American Cinema: Directors and Directions 1929–1968.* New York: E. P. Dutton; Toronto: Clarke, Irwin, 1968.

Schlesinger, Arthur, Jr. "*The Go-Between.*" *Vogue,* Sept. 15, 1971.

Schaefer, Stephen. "Back to the World of Seduction and Sleekness." *Los Angeles Times,* Feb. 18, 1990.

Schiff, Stephen. "Pinter's Passions." *Vanity Fair,* July 1999.

Scholes, Robert. *Semiotics and Interpretation.* New Haven, Conn.: Yale Univ. Press, 1982.

Sherwood, John. "The Rising Generation—A Playwright—Harold Pinter." BBC transcript, Mar. 3, 1960.

Shirer, William L. *The Fall of the Third Reich: A History of Nazi Germany.* New York: Simon and Schuster, 1988.

Sinyard, Neil. *Filming Literature: The Art of Screen Adaptation.* New York: St. Martin's Press, 1986.

Styan, J.L. "Television Drama." In *Contemporary Theatre,* ed. John Russell Brown and Bernard Harris, 185–204. London: Edward Arnold, 1962.

Szondi, Peter. *Theory of the Modern Drama.* Cambridge: Polity Press, 1987.

"Talk of the Town: Two People in a Room." *New Yorker,* Feb. 25, 1967, 34–36.

Taylor, John Russell. "Accident." *Sight and Sound 35,* no. 4 (autumn 1966): 179-84.

———. *Anger and After: A Guide to New British Drama.* Rev. ed. London: Methuen, 1969. Reprinted as *The Angry Theatre,* rev. ed. (New York: Hill and Wang, 1969). Page citations are to *The Angry Theatre.*

———. "The Go-Between." *Sight and Sound* 39 (autumn 1970): 203.

———. "The Guest." *Sight and Sound* 33, no. 1 (winter 1963–1964): 38–39.

———. *Harold Pinter.* London: Longmans Green, 1969.

Tennyson, Hallam. Interview with Pinter on the BBC General Overseas Service, broadcast Aug. 7, 1960. Cited in Esslin, *Peopled Wound,* 257.

Tucker, Stephanie. "Cinematic Proust Manifested by Pinter." *Theatre Annual* 41 (1986): 37–47.

Tynan, Kenneth. Interview broadcast on the BBC Home Service, Oct. 28, 1960. Duplicated manuscript exists.

United Artists Pressbook: The French Lieutenant's Woman. 1981.

Van Gelder, Lawrence. "At the Movies." *New York Times,* Jan. 22, 1988, C6.

———. "At the Movies." *New York Times,* July 28, 1989, C8.

Walker, Alexander. *Hollywood UK: The British Film Industries in the Sixties.* New York: Stein and Day, 1974.

Wardle, Irving. "A Director's Approach." In Lahr, *Casebook on Harold Pinter's The Homecoming,* 9–25.

Weisenburger, Steven. "An Afterword." In *Accident,* by Nicholas Moseley, 193–98. Elmwood Park, Ill.: Dalkey Archive Press, 1985.

Welles, Orson, and Peter Bogdanovich. *This Is Orson Welles.* New York: Da Capo Press, 1998.

Westerbeck, Colin L., Jr. "The Screen." *Commonweal,* January 21, 1977, 51–52.

Wilde, Oscar. *The Picture of Dorian Gray.* 1891.

Williams, Gordon M. *The Siege at Trencher's Farm.* New York: Morrow, 1969.

Williams, Raymond. *Drama in Performance.* Philadelphia: Open Univ. Press, 1991.

Willis, E.E., and C. D'Arienzo. *Writing Scripts for Television, Radio, and Film.* New York: Holt, Rinehart, and Winston, 1981.

Wilson, Edmund. Foreword to *The Last Tycoon,* by F. Scott Fitzgerald. New York: Scribner's, 1941. Reprint, Scribner Classic/Collier Edition, 1986. Page citations are to the reprint edition.

Wright, Ian. "New Films in London." *Guardian* (Manchester), July 17, 1964, 7.

Zimmerman, Paul D. "Theater in the Camera." *Newsweek,* Dec. 3, 1973.

Selected Bibliography

This selected bibliography is primarily a list of critical works dealing with Pinter's films and reviews of those films that are not included in Works Cited but which contain information that scholars of this subject may find valuable. Also included are publications that are useful for ascertaining the context in which Pinter works and in the field of film studies. It should be noted, too, that a considerable collection of Pinter material (seventy-four boxes of manuscripts, etc., including various versions of the film scripts) is held in the Pinter Archives, British Library, London. A description of that material may be found in *The Pinter Review: Annual Essays 1994,* ed. Francis X. Gillen and Steven H. Gale (Tampa, Fla.: Univ. of Tampa Press, 1994); and *The Pinter Review: Annual Essays, 1995–1996,* ed. Francis X. Gillen and Steven H. Gale (Tampa, Fla.: Univ. of Tampa Press, 1997).

For additional information on Pinter's films, the annual bibliography in Gillen and Gale, *The Pinter Review: Collected Essays* is normally the most comprehensive and most up-to-date source. Other sources that might be consulted include

Abstracts of English Studies
American Humanities Index
Annual Bibliography of English Language and Literature
Arts and Humanities Citation Index
British Humanities Index
Dissertation Abstracts International
English Studies
Film Literature Index
Film Quarterly
Film Research in Progress
Humanities Index

Index to Theses (Great Britain)
International Bibliography of Theatre
Literature and Essay Index
Literature/Film Quarterly
MLA International Bibliography
The New York Times Index
Reader's Guide to Periodical Literature
The Times Index (London)
Twentieth Century Literature
The Year's Work in English Studies

Variety and *The Hollywood Reporter* are also sources for information about the films, particularly for following the progress of an individual film from the earliest stages of production through its performance at the box office. In odd-numbered years *Variety's Film Reviews,* which contains the magazine's reviews published during the preceeding two years, is published by R.R. Bowker (New Providence, N.J.).

Web sites that carry information on Pinter's films include

The Alan Bates Archive, http://www.tiac.net/users/claret/bates.html
Cinema Connection, http://socialchange.net.au/TCC/index.html
The Harold Pinter Society Message Board, http://www.odc.edu/academic/
  pinter
Internet Movie Database, http://us.imdb.com/

There are also a number of software programs that contain useful information. Among these are B&N Software's Corel All-Movie Guide 2 (1996); Blockbuster Video Guide to Movies and Videos; Microsoft's Cinemedia; and the Facets Guide to Films. All of these have their limitations, and they may include erroneous material.

Armes, Roy. *Film and Reality: An Historical Survey.* Harmondsworth, Eng.: Penguin, 1974.
Armstrong, Raymond. *Kafka and Pinter: Shadow-Boxing.* London: Macmillan, 1999.
Arnheim, Rudolf. *Film as Art.* London: Faber and Faber, 1958.
Atkins, Irene Kahn. "Hollywood Revisited: A Sad Homecoming." *Literature/Film Quarterly* 5 (1977): 105–11.
Auburn, Mark. "Pinter, Quiller, and the Violence of Film." Paper presented at the International Pinter Festival, Columbus, Ohio, Apr. 19, 1991.
Aumont, Jacques, and Michel Marie. *L'analyse des films.* Paris: Nathan, 1989.

Autry, Martyan, and Nick Roddick, eds. *British Cinema Now.* London: British Film Insitute, 1985.

Ayock, Wendell, and Michael Schoenecke, eds. *Film and Literature: A Comparative Approach to Adaptation.* Lubbock: Texas Tech Univ. Press, 1988.

Balázs, Béla. *Theory of Film: Character and Growth of a New Art.* Trans. Edith Bone. New York: Dover, 1970.

Barr, Charles, ed. *All Our Yesterdays: 90 Years of British Cinema.* London: British Film Institute, 1986.

Barricelli, Jean-Pierre, and Joseph Gibaldi. *Interrelations of Literature.* New York: Modern Language Association, 1982.

Battistin, Martin C. "Osborne's *Tom Jones:* Adapting a Classic." In *Man and the Movies,* ed. W.R. Robinson, 31–45. Baton Rouge: Louisiana State Univ. Press, 1967. Reprint, Baltimore: Penguin, 1969.

Beja, Morris. *Film and Literature.* New York: Longman, 1979.

Bluestone, George. *Novels into Film.* Baltimore: Johns Hopkins Univ. Press, 1957. Reprint, Berkeley: Univ. of California Press, 1966.

Bordwell, David. *Making Meaning: Inference and Rhetoric in Interpretation of Cinema.* Cambridge, Mass.: Harvard Univ. Press, 1989.

———. *Narration in the Fiction Film.* Madison: Univ. of Wisconsin Press, 1985.

Boyum, Joy Gould. *Double Exposure: Fiction into Film.* New York: Universe Books, 1985.

Brater, Enoch. "Cinematic Fidelity and Forms of Pinter's Betrayal." *Modern Drama* 24, no. 4 (Dec. 1981): 503–13. Reprinted in *Essays from Modern Drama,* ed. Hersh Zeifman, 28–40 (Toronto: Univ. of Toronto Press, 1993).

———. "Time and Memory in Pinter's Proust Screenplay. *Comparative Drama* 13, no. 2 (summer 1979): 121–26.

Braudy, Leo. "Art at the Movies." *Michigan Quarterly Review* 22, no. 1 (winter 1983): 9–29.

Brookeer-Bowers, Nancy. *The Hollywood Novel and Other Novels about Film: An Annotated Bibliography.* New York: Garland, 1985.

Buckland, Warren, ed. *The Film Spectator: From Sign to Mind.* Ann Arbor: Univ. of Michigan Press, 1995.

Burch, Nöel. *Theory of Film Practice.* Trans. Helen Lane. Princeton, N.J.: Princeton Univ. Press, 1981.

Burkman, Katherine H. "Harold Pinter's Death in Venice: The Comfort of Strangers." In *The Pinter Review: Annual Essays 1992–1993,* ed. Francis X. Gillen and Steven H. Gale, 38–45. Tampa, Fla.: Univ. of Tampa Press, 1993.

Campbell, Bob. "Films in Focus: New Versions of 'The Trial' Lacks Nuances of Original." *Newark (N.J.) Star-Ledger,* Nov. 26, 1993, "ART 37," G10.

Campbell-Johnston, Rachel. "Kafka's Matinee Metamorphosis." *Times* (London), Aug. 2, 1995, "Features."

Canby, Vincent. "Review/Film: Remains of the Day: Blind Dignity: A Butler's Story." *New York Times,* Nov. 5, 1993, "Weekend," C1.

Carroll, Noel. *Mystifying Movies: Fads and Fallacies in Contemporary Film Theory.* New York: Columbia Univ. Press, 1988.

———. *Philosophical Problems of Classical Film Theory.* Princeton, N.J.: Princeton Univ. Press, 1988.

Casetti, Francesco. *D'un regard l'autre: Le film et son spectateur.* Lyon, France: Presses Universitaires de Lyon, 1990.

Casetti, Francesco, and Federico di Chio. *Analisi del film.* Milan: Bompiani, 1990.

Cavell, Stanley. *The World Viewed: Reflections on the Ontology of Film.* New York: Viking, 1971. 2d ed. New York: Viking, 1979.

Chatman, Seymour. *Story and Discourse: Narrative Structure in Fiction and Film.* Ithaca, N.Y.: Cornell Univ. Press, 1978.

Chung, Moonyoung. "The Deterritorialized Space in Pinter's Screenplay *The French Lieutenant's Woman.*" Paper presented at the Pinter in London Conference, London, June 16, 2000.

Cima, Gay G. "Acting on the Cutting Edge: Pinter and the Syntax of Cinema." *Theatre* 36 (Mar. 1984): 43–56.

Cima, Gay Gibson. *Performing Women: Female Characters, Male Playwrights and the Modern Stage.* Ithaca, N.Y.: Cornell Univ. Press, 1993.

Ciment, Michel. "Expatriate." *Film Comment,* May 1989, 16–19.

———. "Visually Speaking: Harold Pinter Interviewed by Michel Ciment." *Film Comment,* May 1989, 20–23.

Cocks, Jay. "Two by Losey." *Time,* Aug. 9, 1971, 63.

Coe, Marguerite. "His and Hers: A Feminist Critique of Harold Pinter's Screenplay and Margaret Atwood's Novel, *The Handmaid's Tale.*" Paper presented at the International Pinter Festival, Columbus, Ohio, Apr. 19, 1991.

Cohen, Keith. *Film and Fiction: The Dynamics of Exchange.* New Haven, Conn.: Yale Univ. Press, 1979.

Cohen-Seat, Gilbert. *Essai sur les principes d'une philosophie du cinéma.* Paris: PUF, 1946.

Combs, Richard. "In Search of *The French Lieutenant's Woman.*" *Sight and Sound* 50 (1980–1981): 34–39.

———. "Last Word: Hilarious Kafka." *Guardian* (London), "Features," July 15, 1993, 6.

Cori, Elisabetta. "The Proust Screenplay: Pinter alla ricerca del tempo transcodificato." *Strumenti Critici* 9 (Jan. 1994): 99–116.

Corliss, Richard. "When Acting Becomes Alchemy." *Time,* Dec. 7, 1981, 48–50.

Corrigan, Timothy. *Film and Literature: An Introduction and Reader.* Upper Saddle River, N.J.: Prentice-Hall, 1998.

Crist, Judith. "Movie Dims Stage's Magic." *New York Herald Tribune,* Jan. 21, 1964, 12.

Crowther, Bosley. "The Pumpkin Eater." *New York Times,* Nov. 10, 1964, 58.

Curtis, Quentin. "Cinema: A Masterly Servant." *Independent* (London), June 20, 1993, "Arts," 19.

———. "Film: Without a Leg to Stand On." *Independent* (London), June 18, 1993, "Arts," 19.

Cycnos. Special issue on Pinter, vol. 14, no. 1 (1977).

Dauvergne, Eve-Marie. "Pinter as Screenwriter." Paper presented at the Pinter in London Conference, London, June 16, 2000.

Deer, Harriet A. "Melodramatic Problematics in Pinter's Film of *Betrayal.*" In *The Pinter Review: Annual Essays, 1990,* ed. Francis X. Gillen and Steven H. Gale, 61–70. Tampa, Fla.: Univ. of Tampa Press, 1990.

De Nitto, Dennis, and William Herman. *Film and the Critical Eye.* Riverside, N.J.: Macmillan, 1975. Includes reviews of the films *The Servant* and *The Caretaker.*

Dent, Alan. "A Case of Non-Involvement." *Illustrated London News,* Aug. 1, 1964, 170.

Denzin, Norman K. *The Cinematic Society: The Voyeur's Gaze.* London: Sage, 1995.

Desy, Jeanne. "Refracted Light in Pinter's Film Adaptations." Paper presented at the International Pinter Festival, Columbus, Ohio, Apr. 19, 1991.

Dukore, Bernard. *Dramatic Theory and Criticism.* New York: Holt, 1974.

Durgnat, Raymond. "Losey: Puritan Maids." *Films and Filming,* Apr. 1966, 28–33.

———. *Sexual Alienation in the Cinema.* London: Studio Vista, 1972.

Egerton, Gary R., ed. *Film and the Arts in Symbiosis: A Research Guide.* New York: Greenwood Press, 1988.

Eisenstein, Sergi. *The Film Sense.* Trans. Jay Leda. New York: Harcourt, 1947.

Ellis, John. "The Literary Adaptation: An Introduction." *Screen* 23, no. 1 (1982): 3–4.

———. *Visible Fictions.* London: Routledge, 1982.

Epstein, Grace. "Nothing to Fight For: Repression of the Romance Plot in Harold Pinter's Screenplay of *The Handmaid's Tale.*" In *The Pinter Review: Annual Essays 1992–1993,* ed. Francis X. Gillen and Steven H. Gale, 54–60. Tampa, Fla.: Univ. of Tampa Press, 1994. Paper originally presented at the International Pinter Festival, Columbus, Ohio, Apr. 19, 1991.

Eyre, Richard. *Harold Pinter: A Celebration.* London: Faber and Faber, 2000.

Feineman, Neil. *Nicolas Roeg.* Boston: Twayne, 1978.

Feldstein, Elayne. "From Novel to Film. The Impact of Harold Pinter on Robert Maugham's *The Servant.*" *Studies in the Humanities* 5, no. 2 (1976): 9–14.

Fell, John L. *Film and the Narrative Tradition.* Berkeley: Univ. of California Press, 1974.

Findlater, Richard. *The Unholy Trade.* London: Gollancz, 1952.

Fine, Marshall. "'The Trial' Proves Kafka Difficult to Capture on Film." Gannett News Service, Nov. 24, 1993.

Fleishman, Avrom. *Narrated Films: Storytelling Situations in Cinema History.* Baltimore: Johns Hopkins Univ. Press, 1992.

Fowler, Alastair. *Kinds of Literature.* Cambridge, Mass.: Harvard, 1982.

Gale, Steven H. "Butley (Gray)." In *The International Dictionary of the Theatre,* vol. 1, *Plays,* ed. Mark Hawkins-Dady, 95–96. London: St. James, 1991.

———. "Film and Drama: The Opening Sequence of the Filmed Version of Harold Pinter's *The Caretaker (The Guest).*" In *Harold Pinter: A Casebook,* ed. Lois Gordon, 119–28. New York: Garland, 1990.

———. "Harold Pinter." In *The International Dictionary of the Theatre,* vol. 2, *Playwrights,* ed. Mark Hawkins-Dady, 748–52. London: St. James, 1991.

———. *Harold Pinter: An Annotated Bibliography.* Boston: G.K. Hall, 1978.

———. "Harold Pinter Materials in the Margaret Herrick Library at The Academy of Motion Picture Arts and Sciences Center for Motion Picture Study." In *The Pinter Review: Annual Essays 2001 and 2002,* ed. Francis X. Gillen and Steven H. Gale, 213-19. Tampa, Fla.: Univ. of Tampa Press, 2002.

———. "Harold Pinter: The Screenplays." In *Cambridge Companion to Pinter,* ed. Peter Raby. Cambridge: Cambridge Univ. Press, 2001.

———. "Harold Pinter's Film Version of The Servant: Adapting Robin Maugham's Novel for the Screen." In *The Pinter Review: Annual Essays 1990,* ed. Francis X. Gillen and Steven H. Gale, 4–20. Tampa, Fla.: Univ. of Tampa Press, 1990.

———. "Harold Pinter's Screenplays: The Creative/Collaborative Process." In *The Pinter Review: Collected Essays 1999 and 2000,* ed. Francis X. Gillen and Steven H. Gale, 85-91. Tampa, Fla.: Univ. of Tampa Press, 2000.

———. "Harold Pinter's Screenplays: The Creative/Collaborative Process." Paper presented at the Pinter in London Conference, London, June 17, 2000.

———. "'Opening Out': Harold Pinter's The Caretaker from Stage to Screen." *Cycnos* 14, no. 1 (1997): [113]–24.

———. "Simon Gray." In *Critical Survey of Drama,* ed. Frank Magill, 2:804–13. Englewood Cliffs, N.J.: Salem Press, 1985.

———. "Simon Gray's *Butley*: From Stage to Screen." In *Simon Gray: A Casebook,* ed. Katharine H. Burkman, 85–99. New York: Garland, 1992.

———. "The Use of Art Objects as Metaphors in Harold Pinter's Films." Paper presented at the International Pinter Festival, Columbus, Ohio, Apr. 19, 1991.

———. "A Woman's Place: Changing Perceptions of the Female Role—Individualism and the Community in Harold Pinter's Film Version of *The Pump-*

kin Eater." Paper presented at the National Conference on Film, Individualism and Community, Baltimore, Mar. 1992.

Gallagher, Brian. "Film Imagery, Literary Imagery: Some Distinctions." *College Literature* 5 (1978): 157–73.

Gauthier, Tim. "The Externalization of Self in Harold Pinter's Screenplay of *Turtle Diary.*" Paper presented at the Pinter in London Conference, London, June 16, 2000.

Geduld, Harry M., ed. *Authors on Film.* Bloomington: Indiana Univ. Press, 1972.

Giddings, Robert, Keith Selby, and Chris Wensley. *Screening the Novel: The Theory and Practice of Literary Dramatisation.* London: Macmillan, 1987.

Gill, David, and Kevin Brownlow. *Hollywood: A Celebration of the American Silent Film.* A thirteen-episode series. Thames Television, broadcast on TCM, Sept. 7, 1997.

Gillen, Francis X. "'My Dark House': Harold Pinter's Political Vision in His Screen Adaptation of Karen Blixen's 'The Dreaming Child." In *The Pinter Review: Annual Essays, 1999 and 2000,* ed. Francis X. Gillen and Steven H. Gale, [110]–22. Tampa, Fla.: Univ. of Tampa Press, 2000.

Gillen, Francis, and Anne Blake Cummings. "'The Dark Is in My Mouth': *Reunion, The Comfort of Strangers,* and *Party Time.*" *Text & Performance: The Journal of the Comparative Drama Conference,* 8 (1992): 25–30.

Gillen, Francis X., and Lawrence E. Letourneau. "*The Trial:* From the Novel to Pinter's Screenplay." Paper presented at the International Pinter Festival, Columbus, Ohio, Apr. 19, 1991.

Goodwin, James. "Literature and Film: A Review of Criticism." *Quarterly Review of Film Studies* 4, no. 2 (1979): 227–46.

Gordon, Lois. "*The Go-Between*—Hartley by Pinter." *Kansas Quarterly* 4, no. 2 (1972): 81–92.

———. "Harold Pinter in New York." *Pinter Review* (1989): 48–52.

Gray, Simon. "Co-Directing: The Pitfalls of a Common Pursuit." *New York Times,* May 10, 1987, sec. 5, 32.

Gray, W. Russel. "The Time of Our Minds: The Presence of the Past in *The Go-Between.*" Paper presented at the Pinter in London Conference, London, June 16, 2000.

Gross, Miriam. "Pinter on Pinter." *Sunday Observer Review* (London), Oct. 5, 1980, 25.

Guarino, Ann. "Few Happy Returns in Enigmatic 'Party.'" *New York Daily News,* Dec. 10, 1968. Review of the film version of *The Birthday Party.*

Hall, Ann C. "Lost in the Funhouse: Pinter's *The Trial.*" Paper presented at the Pinter in London Conference, London, June 17, 2000.

Harrington, John, ed. *Film and/as Literature.* Englewood Cliffs, N.J.: Prentice-Hall, 1977.

Heath, Stephen. *Questions of Cinema.* Bloomington: Indiana Univ. Press, 1981. Reprint, London: Jonathan Cape, 1983. Reprint, New York: Pantheon, 1984.

Homan, Sidney, et al. *Pinter's Odd Man Out: Staging and Filming Old Times.* Lewisburg, Pa.: Bucknell Univ. Press, 1993.

Houston, Penelope. *The Contemporary Cinema 1945–1963.* Harmondsworth, Eng.: Penguin, 1963.

Hudgins, Christopher C. "Harold Pinter's *The French Lieutenant's Woman* and the Pinter Archive." Paper presented at the Modern Language Association Convention, San Francisco, Dec. 28, 1998.

———. "Harold Pinter's *The Go-Between:* The Courage to Be." *Cycnos* 14, no. 1 (1997): [125]–44.

———. "Harold Pinter's *The Servant* and Audience Response: Structural Images, Heroic Women, and Faint-Hearted Men." Paper presented at the Pinter in London Conference, London, June 17, 2000.

———. "Lolita 1996: The Four Film Scripts." *Film/Literature Quarterly* (Jan. 1997).

———. "Victory: A Pinter Screenplay Based on the Conrad Novel." In *The Pinter Review: Annual Essays 1991,* ed. Francis X. Gillen and Steven H. Gale, 23–32. Tampa: Univ. of Tampa Press, 1991. Revised version of "Victory: An Unpublished Pinter Script of the Conrad Novel and the Film in the Can," paper presented at the International Pinter Festival, Columbus, Ohio, Apr. 19, 1991.

Izod, John. *Reading the Screen.* Harlow, Eng.: Longman, 1984.

Japa. "The Birthday Party." *Variety,* Dec. 18, 1968, 26. Review of the film version of *The Birthday Party.*

Jarvie, Ian. *Philosophy of the Film.* New York: Routledge, 1987.

Jones, Edward T. "Harold Pinter: A Conversation." *Literature/Film Quarterly* 21, no. 1 (1993): 2–10.

———. "Re-Viewing the Losey-Pinter Go-Between." In *Re-Viewing British Cinema, 1900–1992: Essays and Interviews,* ed. Wheeler Winston Dixon, 211–20. Albany: State Univ. of New York Press, 1994.

Kane, Leslie. "Peopling the Wound: Harold Pinter's Screenplay for Kafka's *The Trial.*" *Cycnos* 14, no. 1 (1997): [145]–59.

Kauffmann, Stanley. "An Imaginary Past." *New Republic,* Sept. 23, 1981, 22–24.

Kawin, Bruce. "Authorial and Systemic Self-Consciouness in Literature and Film." *Literature/Film Quarterly* 10, no. 1 (1982): 3–11.

Kendzora, Kathryn Louise. "Going between Novel and Film: Harold Pinter's Adaptation of *The Go-Between.*" Ph.D. diss., Univ. of California, Irvine, 1986.

Kerr, Walter. "It's Mating Season at the Theatre." *New York Times*, May 17, 1987, sec. 2, 41–43.

King, Kimball. "Satire on Television: *The Basement* and *The Tea Party.*" In *The Pinter Review: Annual Essays 1991*, ed. Francis X. Gillen and Steven H. Gale, 42–45. Tampa, Fla.: Univ. of Tampa Press, 1991.

King, Noel. "Pinter's Screenplays: The Menace of the Past." *Southern Review* 14, no. 1 (1981): 78–90.

Kirtz, Mary K. "Teaching Literature through Film: An Interdisciplinary Approach to *Surfacing* and *The Handmaid's Tale.*" In *Approaches to Teaching Atwood's The Handmaid's Tale and Other Works*, ed. Sharon R. Wilson, Thoms B. Friedman, and Shannon Hengen, [140]–45. New York: Modern Language Association, 1996.

Kittredge, William, and Steven M. Krauzner, eds. *Stories into Film*. New York: Harper Colophon Books, 1979.

Korte, Barbara. "Die Kunst des Adapteurs: Zue Situationsverknupfung in den Drehbuchern Harold Pinters." *Zeitschrift fur Anglistik und Amerikanistik* 39, no. 2 (1991): 113–23.

Knowles, Ronald. *Text and Performance: The Birthday Party and The Caretaker*. London: Macmillan Education, 1988.

Kracauer, Siegfried. *Theory of Film: The Redemption of Physical Reality*. Oxford: Oxford Univ. Press, 1960.

Lawson, John H. *Film: The Creative Process*. New York: Hill and Wang, 1967.

Lehman, Peter. *Defining Cinema*. London: Athlone, 1997.

Lindgren, Ernest. *The Art of Film*. 2d ed. London: George Allen & Unwin, 1963.

Lorch, Susan E. "Pinter Fails Fowles: Narration in *The French Lieutenant's Woman.*" *Literature/Film Quarterly* 16 (1988): 144–52.

Lorman, Jurij. *Semiotics of Cinema*. Ann Arbor: Univ. of Michigan Press, 1976.

Losey, Joseph. *Coming to Terms with Hollywood*. London: British Film Institute, 1981.

Lynes, Jeanette. "On *The Handmaid's Tale.*" Paper presented at the International Pinter Festival, Columbus, Ohio, Apr. 19, 1991.

MácCann, Richard Dyer, ed. *Film: A Montage of Theories*. New York: Dutton, 1966.

MacDonald, Dwight. *On Movies*. Englewood Cliffs, N.J.: Prentice-Hall, 1969.

Mann, Bruce. "*The Handmaid's Tale*: From Novel to Film." Paper presented at the International Pinter Festival, Columbus, Ohio, Apr. 19, 1991.

Marcus, Fred. *Film and Literature: Contrasts in Media*. Scranton, Pa.: Chandler, 1971.

———. "Review/Film: Kafka's Sinister World by Way of Pinter." *New York Times*, Nov. 24, 1993, C16.

Mast, Gerald. "Literature and Film." In *Interrelations of Literature,* ed. Jeann-Pierre Barricelli and Joseph Gibaldi, [278]–306. New York: Modern Language Association, 1982.

Mast, Gerald, and Marshall Cohen, eds. *Film Theory and Criticism.* New York: Oxford Univ. Press, 1979. 3d ed., New York: Oxford Univ. Press, 1992.

McConnell, Frank. *Storytelling and Mythmaking: Images from Film and Literature.* New York: Oxford Univ. Press, 1970.

McDougal, Stuart Y. *Made into Movies: From Literature to Film.* Niles, Ill.: Holt, Rinehart, and Winston, 1985.

McGarry, Mary. "The Adaptation Process As Seen through Selected Plays and Screenplays of Harold Pinter." Ph.D. diss., Northwestern Univ., 1976.

Michaels, I. Lloyd. "Auteurism, Creativity and Entropy in *The Last Tycoon.*" *Literature/Film Quarterly* 10, no. 1 (1982): 110–20.

Miles, Peter, and Malcolm Smith. *Cinema, Literature, and Society: Elite and Mass Culture in Interwar Britain.* London: Croom Helm, 1987.

Miller, Gabriel. *Screening the Novel: Rediscovered American Fiction in Film.* New York: Ungar, 1980.

Milne, Tom. "Accident." *Sight and Sound* (spring 1967): 57–59. Reprinted in *Film as Film: Critical Responses to Film Art,* ed. Joy Gould Boyum and Adrienne Scott, 38–44. Boston: Allyn and Bacon, 1971.

Moore, Gene M. *Conrad on Film.* Cambridge: Cambridge Univ. Press, 1998.

Morrissette, Bruce. *Novel and Film: Essays in Two Genres.* Chicago: Univ. of Chicago Press, 1985.

Morse, Magaret. "Paradoxes of Realism: The Rise of Film in the Train of the Novel." In *Explorations in Film Theory: Selected Essays from Cine-Tracts,* ed. Ron Burnett. Bloomington: Indiana Univ. Press, 1991.

Mulvey, Laura. "Visual Pleasure and Narrative Cinema." *Screen* 16, no. 3 (autumn 1975): 6–18. Reprinted in *Visual and Other Pleasures,* ed. Laura Mulvey, 14–26 (Bloomington: Indiana Univ. Press, 1989).

Munsterberg, Hugo. *The Film: A Psychological Study.* 1916. Reprint, New York: Dover, 1970.

Murray, Edward. *The Cinematic Imagination: Writer and the Motion Pictures.* New York: Ungar, 1972.

"News." Production Notes: "The Go-Between." Hollywood: Columbia Pictures, n.d.

Nicoll, Allardyce. *Film and Theatre.* New York: Crowell, 1936. Reprint, New York: Arno, 1972.

Ong, Hee Yah. "The General Problem of Textuality in the Films of Harold Pinter." Master's thesis, National Univ. of Singapore, 1993.

Orr, John. *Tragicomedy and Contemporary Culture: Play and Performance from Beckett to Shepard.* Ann Arbor: Univ. of Michigan Press, 1991.

Palmer, James, and Michael Riley. *The Films of Joseph Losey.* Cambridge: Cambridge Univ. Press, 1993.

Palmer, Jerry. *The Logic of the Absurd on Film and Television Comedy.* London: BFI Publishing, 1987.

Pasquale-Maguire, Therese. "Narrative Voices and Past Tenses in Novel and Film: Proust's *À la recherche du temps perdu* and the Pinter Screenplay." Ph.D. diss., Univ. of Massachausetts, 1982.

Pellow, Kenneth. *Films as Critiques of Novels: Transformational Criticism.* Lewiston, N.Y.: Mellen Press, 1995.

Phillips, Gene. *Conrad and Cinema.* New York: Lang, 1995.

Prentice, Penelope. "Madness in Harold Pinter's Plays and Filmscripts: The Public Consequences of Private Madness." *Cithara* 37, no. 1 (Nov. 1987): 31–37.

Price, Steven T. "Whydunnit?: Pinter's Revival of *Twelve Angry Men.*" *Cycnos* 14, no. 1 (1997): [161]–68.

Pritchard, R.E. "L. P. Hartley's *The Go-Between.*" *Critical Quarterly* 22, no. 1 (1980): 45–55.

Raby, Peter, ed. *Cambridge Companion to Pinter.* Cambridge: Cambridge Univ. Press, 2001.

Randall, Phyllis. "Pinter and Bowen: *The Heat of the Day.*" In Burkman and Kundert-Gibbs, 173–84.

Rapf, Joanna E. "*The Last Tycoon,* or 'A Nickel for the Movies.'" *Literature/Film Quarterly* 16, no. 2 (1988): 76–82.

Reames, Wilbur, Jr. "Harold Pinter: An Introduction to the Literature of His Screenplays." Ph.D. diss., Univ. of Georgia, 1978.

Renton, Linda. "'A Figure Glimpsed, Moving through Trees': Vision and Desire in the Opening Sequence of Harold Pinter's Screenplay of *The Handmaid's Tale.*" Paper presented at the Pinter in London Conference, London, June 16, 2000.

———. "From Real to Real: Pinter and the Object of Desire in *Party Time* and *The Remains of the Day.*" In *The Pinter Review: Annual Essays 1999 and 2000,* ed. Francis X. Gillen and Steven H. Gale, [97]–109. Tampa, Fla.: Univ. of Tampa Press, 2000.

———. "Pinter and the Object of Desire: A Study of the Pinter Screenplays in Relation to Lacan's object petita." Ph.D. diss., Univ. of the West of England, Bristol, 1999.

Richards, Jeffrey, and Anthony Aldgate. *Best of British: Cinema and Society from 1930 to Present.* London: I.B. Tauris, 1999.

Richardson, Robert. *Literature and Film.* Bloomington: Indiana Univ. Press, 1969.

Robinson, W[illiam] R. *Man and the Movies.* Baton Rouge: Louisiana State Univ. Press, 1967. Reprint, Baltimore: Penguin, 1969.

Ropars-Wuillemier, Marie-Claire. *De la littérature au cinéma: Genèse d'un écriture*. Paris: Collin, 1970.

Ross, Harris. *Film as Literature: Literature as Film*. New York: Greenwood, 1987.

Rothman, William. *The "I" of the Camera: Essays in Film Criticism, History, and Aesthetics*. New York: Cambridge Univ. Press, 1988.

Ruchti, Unrich, and Sybil Taylor. *Story into Film*. New York: Dell, 1978.

Russell, William. "Mad about the Feel-Good Factor." *Herald* (Glasgow), July 10, 1993, 24.

Ryan, Desmond. "Silences Speak Volumes in Pinter's 'Betrayal.'" *Philadelphia Inquirer*, Dec. 4, 1992, "Features Weekend," 8.

Sarris, Andrew. *Confessions of a Cultist: On the Cinema, 1955–1969*. New York: Simon and Schuster, 1970. Includes "The Birthday Party," 409–14.

———. "Second Thoughts about *Accident*." *Village Voice*, June 8, 1967. Reprinted in *Film as Film: Critical Responses to Film Art*, ed. Joy Gould Boyum and Adrienne Scott, 34–35 (Boston: Allyn and Bacon, 1971).

Shattuck, Roger. "Fact in Film and Literature." *Partisan Review* 44 (1977): 539–50.

Simmons, Kenith L. "*The French Lieutenant's Woman* as Metaphor: Karel Reisz's Non-Plot Centered Editing." *New Orleans Review* 11, no. 2 (summer 1989): 17–22.

Simon, John. *Movies into Film: Film Criticism, 1967–70*. New York: Delta Books, 1971.

Sinyard, Neil. "Pinter's *Go-Between*." *Critical Quarterly* 22, no. 3 (1980): 21–33.

Sitney, P. Adams, ed. *Film Culture Reader*. New York: Praeger, 1970.

Sontag, Susan. "Film and Theatre." In *Film Theory and Criticism: Introductory Readings*, ed. Gerald Mast and Marshall Cohen, 359–77. 2d ed. New York: Oxford Univ. Press, 1979.

Souriau, Etienne, ed. *L'univers filmique*. Paris: Flammarion, 1953.

Spiegel, Alan. *Fiction and the Camera Eye: Visual Consciousness in the Film and the Modern Novel*. Charlottesville: Univ. of Virginia Press, 1976.

Stam, Robert. *Reflexivity in Film and Literature: From Don Quixote in Jean-Luc Godard*. New York: Columbia Univ. Press, 1992.

Stein, Karen F. "*The French Lieutenant's Woman* and the Screenwriter's Woman: Two Pinter Screenplays." Paper presented at the International Pinter Festival, Columbus, Ohio, Apr. 19, 1991.

Stephenson, Ralph, and J.R. Debrix. *The Cinema as Art*. Harmondsworth, Eng.: Penguin, 1965.

Talbot, Daniel, ed. *Film: An Anthology*. New York: Simon and Schuster, 1967.

"Tales from the Script." *Time Out,* Nov. 28, 1990, 19.

Taylor, John Russell. "*The Servant* and *The Caretaker.*" *Sight and Sound* 33 (winter 1963–1964): 39.

Thiher, Allen. *The Cinematic Muse.* Columbia: Univ. of Missouri Press, 1979.

Thomson, David. *America in the Dark.* London: Hutchinson, 1978.

Toles, George E., ed. *Film/Literature.* Winnipeg: Univ. of Manitoba Press, 1983.

Tomme, Joy. "Adapting Kafka: A Conversation with David Jones—Director of *The Trial.*" *Anglika Filmbill,* Nov.–Dec. 1993.

Tucker, Stephanie. "Cold Comfort: Harold Pinter's *The Comfort of Strangers.*" In *The Pinter Review: Annual Essays, 1992–1993,* ed. Francis X. Gillen and Steven H. Gale, 46–53. Tampa, Fla.: Univ. of Tampa Press, 1994.

———. "Despair Not, Neither to Presume: *The French Lieutenant's Woman:* A Screenplay." *Literature-Film Quarterly* 24, no. 1 (1994): 210–11.

———. "Spies, Scofflaws, and Scoundrels: Pinter's Political Screenplays." Paper presented at the International Pinter Festival, Columbus, Ohio, Apr. 19, 1991.

Turim, Maureen. *Flashbacks in Film: Memory and History.* New York: Routledge, 1989.

Updike, John. "Pinter's Unproduced Proust Printed." *New Yorker,* Feb. 20, 1978, 135.

Vardac, A. Nicholas. *Stage to Screen: Theatrical Method from Garrick to Griffith.* Cambridge, Mass.: Harvard Univ. Press, 1949.

Variety Weekly, August 10, 1966.

Vertov, Dziga. *Provisional Instructions to Kino-Eye Groups.* 1926. Reprinted as *Kino-Eye: The Writings of Dziga Vertov.* Edited and with an introduction by Annette Michelson. Translated by Kevin O'Brien. Berkeley: Univ. of California Press, 1995.

Wagner, Geoffrey. *The Novel and Cinema.* Rutherford, N.J.: Fairleigh Dickinson Univ. Press, 1975.

Walker, Alexander. "Lethal Kind of Love." *Evening Standard* (London), June 17, 1993, 32.

Waller, Gregory. *The Stage/Screen Debate: A Study in Popular Aesthetics.* New York: Garland, 1983.

Welch, Geoffrey Egan. *Literature and Film: An Annotated Bibliography, 1909–1977.* London: Garland, 1981.

Welsh, James. "Joseph Losey, with (and without) Pinter: *The Films of Joseph Losey,* by James Palmer and Michael Riley." *Literature-Film Quarterly* 22, no. 3 (1994): 210–11.

Wicks, Ulrich. "Literature/Film: A Bibliography." *Literature/Film Quarterly* 6 (1978): 135–43.

Wilkins, Caroline. "Back to the Drawing Room: Reisz's, Pinter's, and Fowles's

Critiques of Convention in *The French Lieutenant's Woman.*" Paper presented at the Pinter in London Conference, London, June 16, 2000.

Williams, Hugo. "After Pilkington." *New Statesman,* Jan. 30, 1987, 26.

Williams, Linda. *Viewing Positions: Ways of Seeing Film.* London: Athlone, 1995.

Winston, Douglas Garrett. *The Screenplay as Literature.* Rutherford, N.J.: Fairleigh Dickinson Univ. Press; London: Tantivy Press, 1973.

Wollen, Peter. *Signs and Meaning in the Cinema.* Rev. 3d ed. Bloomington: Indiana Univ. Press, 1972.

Film Reviews

Accident

Alpert, Hollis. "Where It's Happening." *Saturday Review,* Apr. 29, 1967, 47.

Fisher, Gerry. "The Current Cinema, 'Inside the Redoubt.'" *The New Yorker,* Apr. 22, 1967, 150–51.

Kotlowitz, Robert. "Four Films from Europe." *Harper's Magazine,* June 1967, 110–11.

New York Times, Apr. 18, 1967, 33; Apr. 30, 1967, sec. 2, 1; May 7, 1967, sec. 2, 1.

Life, Apr. 21, 1967, 12.

Time, Apr. 21, 1967, 101.

Nation, May 15, 1967, 638.

Esquire, June 1967, 110–11.

Vogue, June 1967, 77.

Christian Century, June 7, 1967, 754–55.

À la Recherche du Temps Perdu

Kauffmann, Stanley. "A la Recherche du Temps Perdu." *The New Republic,* Dec. 31, 1977, 22–23.

The Birthday Party

Alpert, Hollis. "The Birthday Party." *Saturday Review,* Dec. 7, 1968, 68.

Hartung, Philip T. "The Screen." *Commonweal,* Feb. 7, 1969, 591.

New Republic, Jan. 4, 1967, 34.

New York Times, Dec. 10, 1968, 54.

New Yorker, Dec. 21, 1968, 90–91; Feb. 13, 1971, 52.

Newsweek, Dec. 23, 1968, 89–90.

Vogue, Jan. 1, 1969, 66.

Nation, Jan. 6, 1969, 29–30.

Holiday, Mar. 1969, 30.

Time, Feb. 22, 1971, 52.

Butley

Zimmerman, Paul D. "Angry Old Chap." *Newsweek*, May 20, 1974, 106.

The Caretaker (The Guest)

Coleman, John. "The Road to Sidcup." *New Statesman*, March 13, 1964, 423.
Knight, Arthur. "The Mechanics of Laughter." *Saturday Review*, Feb. 15, 1964, 33.
Winsten, Archer. "Reviewing Stand." *New York Post*, Jan. 21, 1964, 44.
Town, Dec. 1963.
Films and Filming, Jan. 4, 1964, 24–25.
New York Times, Jan. 21, 1964, 25.
Newsweek, Feb. 10, 1964, 84.
Observer (London), Mar. 15, 1964, 24.
"Rheum at the Top." *Time*, Jan. 24, 1964, 52.
Sunday Times (London), Mar. 15, 1964, 33.
Spectator, Mar. 20, 1964, 381.

The Comfort of Strangers

Auld, Deborah. "From the Terrace." *Village Voice*, Dec. 12, 1989, 106.
Rafferty, Terrence. "The Comfort of Strangers." *The New Yorker*, Apr. 8, 1999, 84.

The Dumb Waiter

Rissik, Andrew. "Word Perfect." *New Statesman*, Aug. 2, 1985, 31–32.

The French Lieutenant's Woman

Ansen, David. "The Woman on the Quay." *Newsweek*, Sept. 21, 1981, 96–98.
Whall, Tony. "Karel Reisz's *The French Lieutenant's Woman*: Only the Name Remains the Same." *Literature/Film Quarterly* 10, no. 1 (1982): 75–82.

The Go-Between

Cooper, Arthur. "Sunburn." *Newsweek*, Aug. 16, 1971, 86.
Gilliatt, Penelope. "The Current Cinema." *The New Yorker*, July 31, 1971, 55–57.
Hale, Wanda. "'The Go-Between' Is Movie to Remember." *New York Daily News*, July 30, 1971, 54.
Hartung, Philip T. "The Screen." *Commonweal*, Sept. 17, 1971, 480–81.
Hatch, Robert. "The Go-Between." *Nation*, Oct. 4, 1971, 316–17.
Kauffmann, Stanley. "The Go-Between." *The New Republic*, Sept. 11, 1971, 26, 33–34.
Kohn, Steven. "Cinematically Speaking." *The Gramercy Herald*, July 23, 1971, 7.
Rossell, Deac. "Pinter and Losey's The Go-Between." *Boston after Dark*, Aug. 17, 1971, 12.

Winsten, Archer. "'The Go-Between' Arrives at 68th St. Playhouse." *New York Post,* July 30, 1971, 21.

New York Times, July 30, 1971, 21; Aug. 11, 1971, 44; Sept. 12, 1971; Sept. 19, 1971.

Reader's Digest, Oct. 1971, G-13.

Film Quarterly 25 (spring 1972): 37–41.

The Homecoming

Kael, Pauline. "Harold Pinter's 'The Homecoming.'" *The New Yorker,* Nov. 26, 1973, 185–86.

The Last Tycoon

Atkins, Irene. "Hollywood Revisited: A Sad Homecoming." *Literature/Film Quarterly,* 5, no. 2 (1977): 105–11.

Cocks, Jay. "Babylon Revisited." *Time,* Dec. 6, 1976, 87–88.

Hatch, Robert. "Films, The Last Tycoon." *Nation,* Dec. 11, 1976, 637.

Kauffmann, Stanley. "The Last Tycoon." *The New Republic,* Dec. 4, 1976, 20–21.

Koch, Stephen. "Humiliation in Hollywood, 'A Review of The Last Tycoon.'" *Harper's,* March 1977, 102–4.

Kroll, Jack. "Falling Stahr." *Newsweek,* Nov. 22, 1976, 107–8.

Saturday Review, Dec. 11, 1976, 77–78.

Pinter People

Christian Science Monitor, Apr. 4, 1969, 6.

New York Times, Apr. 7, 1969, 86.

The Proust Screenplay

Turk, Edward Baron. "The Proust Screenplay, Harold Pinter." *Yale Daily News Magazine,* March 30, 1978, 16.

The Pumpkin Eater

Sight and Sound (summer 1964): 168.

Life, Nov. 13, 1964, 15.

Time, Nov. 13, 1964, 125.

New Yorker, Nov. 14, 1964, 148.

New York Times, Nov. 15, 1964, sec. 2, 1.

Newsweek, Nov. 16, 1964, 102.

Saturday Review, Nov. 21, 1964, 332.

Commonweal, Nov. 27, 1964, 332.

New Republic, Dec. 19, 1964, 28–29.
Vogue, Jan. 1, 1965, 66.

The Quiller Memorandum

Hartung, Philip T. "The Quiller Memorandum." *Commonweal,* Feb. 3, 1967, 489.
Kauffmann, Stanley "The Quiller Memorandum." *The New Republic,* Jan. 14, 1967, 42–44.
Luft, Friedrich. "Where Have All New Nazis Gone?" *Variety Weekly,* March 8, 1967.
Morgenstern, Joseph. "Breaking the Bond." *Newsweek,* Dec. 26, 1966, 72.
New York Times, Dec. 16, 1966, sec. 16, 59.
Time, Dec. 23, 1966, 75.
Life, Jan. 27, 1967, 15.
America, Feb. 4, 1967, 194.

Reunion

Maslin, Janet. "Memories Both Painful and Pretty in 'Reunion.'" *New York Times,* Mar. 15, 1991, 16.
New York Times, Jan. 22, 1988, C6.

The Servant

Alpert, Hollis. "Knock, Knock. What's There?" *Saturday Review,* March 14, 1964, 17.
Caute, David. "Golden Triangle." *Independent on Sunday* (London), July 11, 1993, 24, 26.
Gill, Brendon. "The Current Cinema: Sinister and Sunny." *The New Yorker,* March 21, 1964, 172.
Hatch, Robert. "The Servant: Yesterday, Today and Tomorrow." *Nation,* Apr. 6, 1964, 354–55.
Kauffmann, Stanley. "High Life Below Stairs." *The New Republic,* March 21, 1964, 27–28.
Observer (London), Nov. 17, 1963.
New Yorker, Nov. 30, 1963, 207.
Sight and Sound (winter 1963–1964): 38–39.
New York Times, Mar. 17, 1964, 30; Mar. 29, 1964, sec. 2, 1.
Commonweal, Mar. 20, 1964, 751.
Time, Mar. 20, 1964, 94–95.
Newsweek, Mar. 23, 1964, 95–96.

The Trial

Andrews, Nigel. "Narcissistic Trip through Hell—Cinema." *Financial Times* (London), June 17, 1993, "Arts," 19.

Armstrong, John. "Straight from Oz, the Return of Yahoo You Can't Be Serious." *Vancouver Sun,* Sept. 9, 1994, "Entertainment: Video," C1.

"The Arts: Putting a Gloss on Kafka's Black Farce." *Daily Telegraph* (London), June 18, 1993, 18.

"The Arts: Sex and the Single Policewoman." *Daily Telegraph* (London), Dec. 20, 1993, 17.

Birnie, Peter. "Trial True to Kafka's Angst." *Vancouver Sun,* Aug. 6, 1994, "Entertainment," C9.

Blowen, Michael. "A Split Verdict on 'The Trial.'" *Boston Globe,* June 10, 1994, city ed., "Living," 56.

Brownstein, Bill. "Harrowing Film Brings Kafka's The Trial Back to Trouble Us." *Gazette* (Montreal) Apr. 16, 1994, "Entertainment: Show," C10.

Burley, Leo. "Film: The Jury Is Still Out on Joseph K." *Independent* (London), Apr. 23, 1993, "Arts," 17.

Carr, Jay. "'The Trial' Doesn't Quite Do Justice to Kafka." *Boston Globe,* city ed., Mar. 25, 1994, "Arts & Film," 51.

Curtis, Quentin. "Film: Without a Leg to Stand On." *Independent* (London), June 20, 1993, "Arts," 19.

Ebert, Roger. "'Trial' Can't Match Kafka Novel." *Lexington (Ky.) Herald- Leader,* May 13, 1994, "Weekender," 9.

———. "'Trial' Verdict: Kafka's Terror Tamed, but So Is Impact." *Chicago Sun-Times,* final ed., Apr. 8, 1994, "Weekend Plus, Movies," 37.

Haeseker, Fred. "BBC Tackles Kafka's The Trial." *Calgary Herald,* Aug. 26, 1994, "Entertainment," F10.

Hartl, John. "'Silver Stallion' Heads from Festival to Videotape." *Seattle Times,* June 9, 1994, "Arts, Entertainment, Video Watch," 1.

Hutchinson, Tom. "Melanie Goes to Washington: Films: *The Trial.*" *Mail on Sunday* (London), June 20, 1993, 39.

Johnson, Brian D. "Trial and Tribulation." *Maclean's,* Apr. 25, 1994, 63.

Johnston, Sheila. "Film: One of Those Nights." *Independent* (London), June 18, 1993, "Arts," 18.

Johnstone, Iain. "Special K." *Sunday Times* (London), June 20, 1993, sec. 9, 10.

Josipovici, Gabriel. "Showy but Not Telling: *The Trial* with Screenplay Written by Harold Pinter Based on a Work by Franz Kafka." *TLS: The Times Literary Supplement* (London), July 9, 1993, 19.

LaSalle, Mick. "'The Trial' Nightmare in the Mundane." *San Francisco Chronicle,* final ed., Apr. 29, 1994, "Daily Datebook," C3.

Meany, Helen. "'The Trial,' IFC, Dublin, Members and Guests Only." *Irish Times* (Dublin), city ed., Aug. 6, 1993, "Sound & Vision: Cinema," 9.

McCarthy, Todd. "The Trial." *Variety,* Feb. 1, 1993, 99.

"Movie Takes." *Financial Post* (London), Apr. 30, 1994, "Spectrum: Arts & Leisure," ST, sec. 4 (reprinted from *Toronto Sun*).

"New Releases: *The Trial.*" *Calgary Herald,* Sept. 8, 1994, "Entertainment, New Releases," A20.

Paterson, Peter. "Suspect Past Its Prime." *Daily Mail* (London), Dec. 20, 1993, 27.

Robinson, David. "Living and Dying by Desire." *Times* (London), June 17, 1993, "Features."

Rosenberg, Scott. "'Trial' and Terror, Kafka Comes Alive: Film Adaptation Captures Nightmare of a 'Guilty' Man." *San Francisco Examiner,* Apr. 29, 1994, "Weekend," B6.

Salem, Rob. "Kafkaesque and Well Acted." *Toronto Star,* final ed., Apr. 22, 1994, "Entertainment," C9

Stone, Jay. "Powerful Tale Is Told in The Trial." *Ottawa Citizen,* Apr. 22, 1994, "Movies," B3.

Terry, Clifford. "'The Trial' Examines Facelessness of Evil." *Chicago Tribune,* final ed., Apr. 8, 1994, "Friday's Guide to Movies & Music: Movie Review," 1.

Thomas, Kevin. "Movie Review: Adaptation of Kafka's 'Trial' Better Suited to the Stage." *Los Angeles Times,* Apr. 22, 1994, "Calendar, Part F," 8.

"The Trial." *Cineman Video Reviews,* July 4, 1994, Home Video Report.

Whitty, Stephen. "A Funny Thing about Kafka: 'The Trial' Shows What's Been Lost in Generalities." *San Jose (Calif.) Mercury News,* morning final ed., Apr. 29, 1994, "Eye," 5.

Index

Note: H.P. denotes Harold Pinter; n within a page number indicates a note; p after a page number indicates a photograph

DATE DUE